Fodor's

New EDITION

SO-ATV-548

Portugal

"When it comes to information on regional history, what to see and do, and shopping, these guides are exhaustive."

—*USAir Magazine*

"Usable, sophisticated restaurant coverage, with an emphasis on good value."

—Andy Birsh, *Gourmet Magazine* columnist

"Valuable because of their comprehensiveness."

—*Minneapolis Star-Tribune*

"Fodor's always delivers high quality...thoughtfully presented...thorough."

—*Houston Post*

"An excellent choice for those who want everything under one cover."

—*Washington Post*

Fodor's Travel Publications, Inc.
New York • Toronto • London • Sydney • Auckland
http://www.fodors.com/

Fodor's Portugal

Editors: Andrea E. Lehman, Chelsea S. Mauldin, Rebecca Miller, Kristen D. Perrault

Editorial Contributors: Robert Andrews, Robert Blake, David Brown, Jules Brown, Audra Epstein, Janet Foley, Dennis Jaffe, Heidi Sarna, Helayne Schiff, Mary Ellen Schultz, M. T. Schwartzman (Gold Guide editor), Dinah Spritzer

Creative Director: Fabrizio La Rocca

Associate Art Director: Guido Caroti

Photo Researcher: Jolie Novak

Cartographers: David Lindroth, Inc.; Mapping Specialists

Cover Photograph: Bob Krist

Text Design: Between the Covers

Copyright

Special Sales

Fodor's Travel Publications are available at special discounts for bulk purchases for sales promotions or premiums. Special editions, including personalized covers, excerpts of existing guides, and corporate imprints, can be created in large quantities for special needs. For more information, contact your local bookseller or write to Special Markets, Fodor's Travel Publications, 201 East 50th Street, New York, NY 10022. Inquiries from Canada should be directed to your local Canadian bookseller or sent to Random House of Canada, Ltd., Marketing Department, 1265 Aerowood Drive, Mississauga, Ontario L4W 1B9. Inquiries from the United Kingdom should be sent to Fodor's Travel Publications, 20 Vauxhall Bridge Road, London SW1V 2SA, England.

PRINTED IN THE UNITED STATES OF AMERICA

10 9 8 7 6 5 4 3 2 1

CONTENTS

Maps

ON THE ROAD WITH FODOR'S

WE'RE ALWAYS THRILLED to get letters from readers, and it's a special treat when they're like this one:

It took us an hour to decide what book to buy and we now know we picked the best one. Your book was wonderful, easy to follow, very accurate, and good on pointing out eating places, informal as well as formal. When we saw other people using your book, we would look at each other and smile.

Our editors and writers are deeply committed to making every Fodor's guide "the best one"— not only accurate but always charming, brimming with sound recommendations and solid ideas, right on the mark in describing restaurants and hotels, and full of fascinating facts that make you view what you've traveled to see in a rich new light.

About Our Writers

Our success in achieving our goals—and in helping to make your trip the best of all possible vacations—is a credit to the hard work of our extraordinary writers.

Jules Brown was born in Africa and hasn't stopped traveling since. An editor and freelance writer based in London, he has covered the world, from the Utah desert and England's Lake District to Hong Kong by way of the Bahamas.

An American who has lived in Europe since 1975, **Dennis Jaffe** now spends at least part of every year in the Algarve. He has written extensively about Portugal, Turkey, Germany, and Switzerland and, with his wife, Tina, is the author of *Biking Through Europe* and the *Camper's Companions to Northern and Southern Europe*.

New York–based writer and translator **Mary Ellen Schultz** has been exploring Portugal since her first visit as a child. Convinced that she spent a previous life painting azulejos by day and singing fado by night, this Lusophile says she'd move to Lisbon in a heartbeat. And probably will.

We'd also like to thank the people who have assisted in preparing this guide: Licinia Rangel of the Tourist Office in Porto, Anabela Avila and Saul Ferreira of the Portuguese National Tourist Office in New York, and Maria Jose and Louis Pinto, freelance tour guides in Lisbon.

New This Year

This year we've reformatted our guides to make them easier to use. Each chapter of *Fodor's Portugal* begins with brand-new recommended itineraries to help you decide what to see in the time you have; a section called When to Tour points out the optimal time of day, day of the week, and season for your journey. You may also notice our fresh graphics, new in 1996. More readable and more helpful than ever? We think so—and we hope you do, too.

On the Web

Check out Fodor's Web site (http://www.fodors.com/), where you'll find travel information on major destinations around the world and an ever-changing array of travel-savvy interactive features.

How to Use This Book

Organization

Up front is the **Gold Guide**. Its first section, **Important Contacts A to Z,** gives addresses and telephone numbers of organizations and companies that offer destination-related services and detailed information. **Smart Travel Tips A to Z,** the Gold Guide's second section, gives specific information on how to accomplish what you need to in Portugal as well as tips on savvy traveling. Both sections are in alphabetical order by topic.

Destination chapters in *Fodor's Portugal* are arranged starting with Lisbon, the first destination of most visitors, and flow south through central Portugal to the sunny Algarve. The final chapters cover northern Portugal and the island of Madeira, the country's more unspoiled and remote corners. In the Lisbon chapter, sights are arranged by neighborhood and then listed in alphabetical order; some neighborhoods include recommended walking tours. Each regional chapter is divided by geographical area; within each area, towns are covered in logical geographical order, and attractive stretches of road and minor points of interest between them are indicated by the designation *En Route*.

To help you decide what to visit in the time you have, chapters begin with recommended itineraries; you can mix and match those from several chapters to create a complete vacation. The A to Z section, which ends all chapters, covers getting there, getting around, and helpful contacts and resources.

Icons and Symbols

★	Our special recommendations
✕	Restaurant
🏠	Lodging establishment
✕🏠	Lodging establishment whose restaurant warrants a detour
🐤	Good for kids (rubber duckie)
☞	Sends you to another section of the guide for more information
✉	Address
☎	Telephone number
⏰	Opening times
💰	Admission prices (those we give apply only to adults; substantially reduced fees are almost always available for children, students, and senior citizens)

Numbers in white and black circles that appear on the maps, in the margins, and within the tours correspond to one another.

Dining and Lodging Prices

The restaurants and lodgings we list are the cream of the crop in each price range. Dollar-sign ratings are based on the following categories:

Dining

CATEGORY	COST*
$$$$	over 5,500$00
$$$	3,500$00–5,500$00
$$	2,000$00–3,500$00
$	under 2,000$00

for a three-course dinner, including tax and service, but not drinks

Lodging

CATEGORY	COST*
$$$$	over 40,000$00
$$$	20,000$00–40,000$00
$$	15,000$00–20,000$00
$	8,000$00–15,000$00
¢	under 8,000$00

for a standard double room, including tax, in high season (off-season rates may be lower)

Hotel Facilities

We always list the facilities that are available—but we don't specify whether they cost extra: When pricing accommodations, always ask what's included. All rooms have private bathrooms unless we note otherwise.

Restaurant Reservations and Dress Codes

Reservations are always a good idea; we note only when they're essential or when they are not accepted. Book as far ahead as you can and reconfirm when you get to town. Unless otherwise noted, the restaurants listed are open daily for lunch and dinner. We mention dress only when men are required to wear a jacket or a jacket and tie.

Credit Cards

The following abbreviations are used: **AE,** American Express; **DC,** Diners Club; **MC,** MasterCard; and **V,** Visa.

Please Write to Us

You can use this book in the confidence that all prices and opening times are based on information supplied to us at press time; Fodor's cannot accept responsibility for any errors. Time inevitably brings changes, so always confirm information when it matters—especially if you're making a detour to visit a specific place. In addition, when making reservations be sure to mention if you have a disability or are traveling with children, if you prefer a private bath or a certain type of bed, or if you have specific dietary needs or any other concerns.

Were the restaurants we recommended as described? Did our hotel picks exceed your expectations? Did you find a museum we recommended a waste of time? If you have complaints, we'll look into them and revise our entries when the facts warrant it. If you've discovered a special place that we haven't included, we'll pass the information along to our correspondents and have them check it out. So send your feedback, positive *and* negative, to the Portugal editor at 201 East 50th Street, New York, New York 10022—and have a wonderful trip!

Karen Cure

Karen Cure
Editorial Director

Portugal

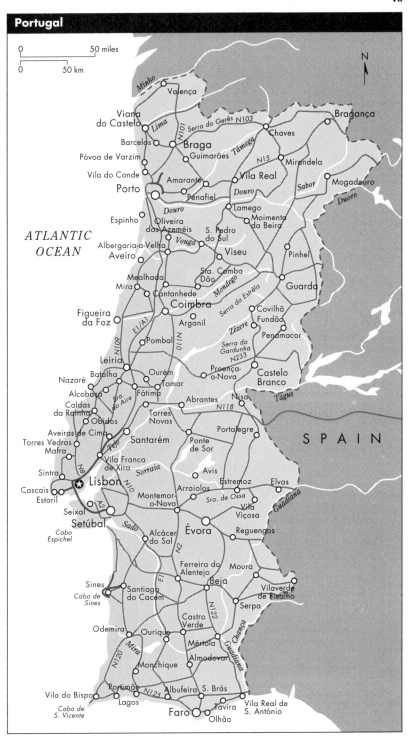

0   50 miles
0   50 km

N

Minho

Valença

Viana
do Castelo

Lima

Serra do Gerês N103

Chaves

Bragança

Barcelos

Braga

Tâmega

Póvoa de Varzim

Guimarães

N15

Mirandela

Vila do Conde

Amarante

Vila Real

Sabor

Mogadouro

Porto

Penafiel

Douro

Lamego

Moimenta
da Beira

Douro

Espinho

Douro

Oliveira
dos Azeméis

S. Pedro
do Sul

ATLANTIC
OCEAN

Albergaria-a-Velha

Vouga

Viseu

Pinhel

Aveiro

Mealhada

Sta. Comba
Dão

Mondego

Guarda

Mira

Cantanhede

Coimbra

Serra da Estrela

Covilhã

Figueira
da Foz

E1/A1

Arganil

Zézere

Fundão

Penamacor

N110

Pombal

Serra da
Gardunha

N233

N109

Leiria

Proença-
a-Nova

Castelo
Branco

Batalha

Ourém

Nazaré

*Sra.
do Aire*

Tomar

Abrantes

Nisa

Tagus

Alcobaça

Fátima

N118

Caldas
da Rainha

Torres
Novas

Óbidos

Aveiras de Cima

Tejo

Santarém

Portalegre

Torres Vedras

Ponte
de Sor

Mafra

Vila Franca
de Xira

Avis

Sintra

Sorraia

Estremoz

Elvas

Cascais

Lisbon

N10

Arraiolos

Sra. de Ossa

Estoril

Montemor-
o-Novo

Vila
Viçosa

Seixal

A2

Guadiana

Setúbal

*Cabo
Espichel*

Sado

Alcácer
do Sal

Évora

Reguengos

N2

Ferreira do
Alentejo

Moura

Sines

E1

Beja

Vilaverde
de Ficalho

*Cabo de
Sines*

Santiago
do Cacém

Serpa

Castro
Verde

N122

Chança

Odemira

Ourique

Mértola

Mira

Almodôvar

Guadiana

N120

Monchique

N125

Portimão

Albufeira

S. Brás

Vila do Bispo

Lagos

Faro

Tavira

Vila Real de
S. António

*Cabo de
S. Vicente*

Olhão

S P A I N

Europe

ICELAND
Reykjavík

NORWAY
Bergen

SCOTLAND
NORTHERN
IRELAND
Edinburgh

*North
Sea*

Skagerrak

Belfast
IRELAND
*Irish
Sea*
DENMARK

Dublin
UNITED
KINGDOM
WALES
ENGLAND
NETHERLANDS
Hamburg

Cardiff
London
The Hague
Amsterdam
Rotterdam

GERM

*ATLANTIC
OCEAN*

English Channel
Brussels
BELGIUM
Bonn

Paris
LUXEMBOURG
Frankfurt

F R A N C E
Zürich
Munich

Bern
SWITZERLAND

Lyon
LIECHTENSTEIN

Milan
Venic

PORTUGAL

Madrid
ANDORRA
Marseille
Nice
Monte
Carlo
MONACO
Florence

Lisbon

Barcelona
Corsica

S P A I N

Seville
Granada
Sardinia

*Balearic
Islands*
Tyrrhenia

Gibraltar
Mediterranean Sea

MOROCCO
ALGERIA

0 ____ 400 miles

0 ____ 600 km
TUNISIA

x

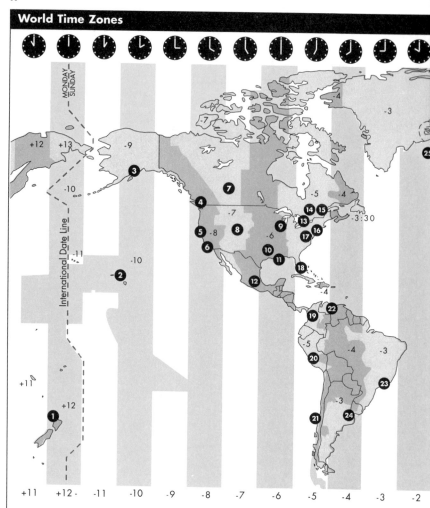

Numbers below vertical bands relate each zone to Greenwich Mean Time (0 hrs.).
Local times frequently differ from these general indications,
as indicated by light-face numbers on map.

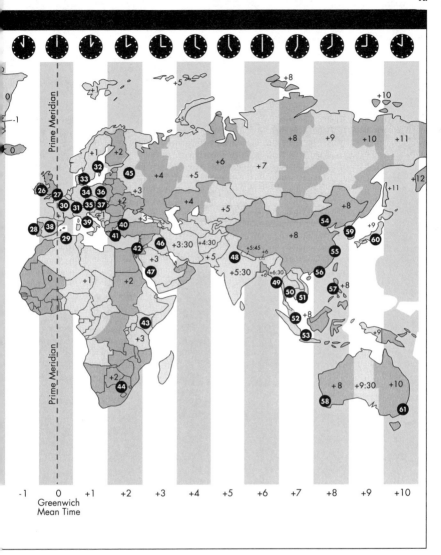

-1   0   +1   +2   +3   +4   +5   +6   +7   +8   +9   +10

Greenwich
Mean Time

Mecca, **47**
Mexico City, **12**
Miami, **18**
Montréal, **15**
Moscow, **45**
Nairobi, **43**
New Orleans, **11**
New York City, **16**

Ottawa, **14**
Paris, **30**
Perth, **58**
Reykjavík, **25**
Rio de Janeiro, **23**
Rome, **39**
Saigon (Ho Chi Minh City), **51**

San Francisco, **5**
Santiago, **21**
Seoul, **59**
Shanghai, **55**
Singapore, **52**
Stockholm, **32**
Sydney, **61**
Tokyo, **60**

Toronto, **13**
Vancouver, **4**
Vienna, **35**
Warsaw, **36**
Washington, D.C., **17**
Yangon, **49**
Zürich, **31**

IMPORTANT CONTACTS A TO Z

An Alphabetical Listing of Publications, Organizations, and Companies That Will Help You Before, During, and After Your Trip

A

AIR TRAVEL

The major gateway to Portugal is Lisbon's **Portela Airport** (☎ 01/840–2060), approximately 5 miles from the center of the city.

FLYING TIME

Flying time to Lisbon is 6½ hours from New York, 9 hours from Chicago, and 15 hours from Los Angeles.

CARRIERS

Carriers serving Portugal from the United States include **TAP Air Portugal** (☎ 800/221–7370); **TWA** (☎ 800/892–4141); and **Delta** (☎ 800/241–4141). There is no nonstop scheduled service to Portugal from Canada; connections have to made through New York or London. For nonstop charter flights from Canada, contact **Lawson Tours** (✉ 2 Carlton St., Suite 620, Toronto, Ontario M5B 1J2, ☎ 416/977–3000 or 800/268–9162 in Canada only).

FROM THE U.K.

For flights from the United Kingdom, contact **British Airways** (☎ 0181/897–4000 or 0345/222–111 outside London) or **Portuguese Airlines** (✉ Gillingham House, 38–44 Gillingham St., London SW1V 1JW, ☎ 0171/630–9223).

COMPLAINTS

To register complaints about charter and scheduled airlines, contact the U.S. Department of Transportation's **Aviation Consumer Protection Division** (✉ C–75, Washington, DC 20590, ☎ 202/366–2220). Complaints about lost baggage or ticketing problems and safety concerns may also be logged with the **Federal Aviation Administration (FAA) Consumer Hotline** (☎ 800/322–7873).

CONSOLIDATORS

For the names of reputable air-ticket consolidators, contact the **United States Air Consolidators Association** (925 L St., Suite 220, Sacramento, CA 95814, ☎ 916/441–4166, ℻ 916/441–3520). For discount air-ticketing agencies, *see* Discounts & Deals, *below*.

PUBLICATIONS

For general information about charter carriers, ask for the Department of Transportation's free brochure **"Plane Talk: Public Charter Flights"** (✉ Aviation Consumer Protection Division, C–75, Washington, DC 20590, ☎ 202/366–2220). The Department of Transportation also publishes a 58-page booklet, **"Fly Rights,"** available from the Consumer Information Center (✉ Supt. of Documents, Dept. 136C, Pueblo, CO 81009; $1.75).

For other tips and hints, consult the Consumers Union's monthly **"Consumer Reports Travel Letter"** (✉ Box 53629, Boulder, CO 80322, ☎ 800/234–1970; $39 1st yr).

WITHIN PORTUGAL

TAP Air Portugal (Lisbon, ☎ 01/841–6990, or toll-free throughout the country, ☎ 0500–5555) is the main domestic airline in Portugal, with flights from Lisbon to all major cities and many interregional flights, including to Madeira and the Azores. **Portugalia** (☎ 01/847–0570) flies between Lisbon and Oporto and offers charter service to Funchal in Madeira. Travel in Portugal can be time consuming; trains are slow and roads can be bad, so flying is sometimes the best option.

B

BETTER BUSINESS BUREAU

For local contacts in the hometown of a tour operator you may be considering, consult the **Council of Better Business Bureaus** (✉ 4200 Wilson Blvd., Suite 800, Arlington, VA 22203, ☎ 703/276–0100, ℻ 703/525–8277).

BICYCLING

Ask the tourist office for a brochure or contact the **Direção-Geral de Desportos** (Av. Infante Santo 74–4, 1300 Lisbon, ☎ 01/647–0095 or 01/674–1181).

BUS TRAVEL

For information and reservations on bus service from the U.K., contact **National Express/Eurolines** (✉ Coach Travel Center, 13 Regent St., London SW1Y 4LR, ☎ 0171/730–0202), **Campus Travel** (✉ 52 Grosvenor Gardens, London SW1W 0AU, ☎ 0171/730–8235), or any **National Express**–appointed agent.

WITHIN PORTUGAL

Rodoviaria Nacional (✉ Av. Columbano Bordalo Pinheiro 86, 1000 Lisbon, ☎ 01/726–7123; ✉ Av. Casal Ribeiro 18, ☎ 01/454–5439), the national bus company, has regular service throughout Portugal.

C

CAR RENTAL

The major car-rental companies represented in Portugal are **Avis** (☎ 800/331–1084; in Canada, 800/879–2847), **Budget** (☎ 800/527–0700; in the U.K., 0800/181181), **Dollar** (☎ 800/800–4000; in the U.K., 0990/565656, where it is known as Eurodollar), **Hertz** (☎ 800/654–3001; in Canada, 800/263–0600; in the U.K., 0345/555888), and **National InterRent** (sometimes known as Europcar InterRent outside North America; ☎ 800/227–3876; in the U.K., 01345/222–525). Shop around because rates can vary, and special rates are sometimes in effect if you book before leaving the States. Rates in Lisbon begin at $24 a day and $114 a week for an economy car with unlimited mileage. This does not include tax on car rentals, which is 17%.

RENTAL WHOLESALERS

Contact **Auto Europe** (☎ 207/828–2525 or 800/223–5555), **Europe by Car** (☎ 800/223–1516; in CA, 800/252–9401), and the **Kemwel Group** (☎ 914/835–5555 or 800/678–0678).

CHILDREN & TRAVEL

FLYING

Look into **"Flying with Baby"** (✉ Third Street Press, Box 261250, Littleton, CO 80163, ☎ 303/595–5959; $4.95 includes shipping), cowritten by a flight attendant. **"Kids and Teens in Flight,"** free from the U.S. Department of Transportation's Aviation Consumer Protection Division (✉ C–75, Washington, DC 20590, ☎ 202/366–2220), offers tips on children flying alone. Every two years the February issue of *Family Travel Times* (☞ Know-How, *below*) details children's services on three dozen airlines. **"Flying Alone, Handy Advice for Kids Traveling Solo"** is available free from the American Automobile Association (AAA) (send stamped, self-addressed, legal-size envelope: ✉ Flying Alone, Mail Stop 800, 1000 AAA Dr., Heathrow, FL 32746).

KNOW-HOW

Family Travel Times, published quarterly by Travel with Your Children (✉ TWYCH, 40 5th Ave., New York, NY 10011, ☎ 212/477–5524; $40 per yr), covers destinations, types of vacations, and modes of travel.

CUSTOMS

IN THE U.S.

The **U.S. Customs Service** (✉ Box 7407, Washington, DC 20044, ☎ 202/927–6724) can answer questions on duty-free limits and publishes a helpful brochure, **"Know Before You Go."** For information on registering foreign-made articles, call 202/927–0540 or write the U.S. Customs Service, Resource Management, 1301 Constitution Ave. NW, Washington DC, 20229.

COMPLAINTS➤ Note the inspector's badge number and write to the commissioner's office (✉ 1301 Constitution Ave. NW, Washington, DC 20229).

CANADIANS

Contact **Revenue Canada** (✉ 2265 St. Laurent Blvd. S, Ottawa, Ontario K1G 4K3, ☎ 613/993–0534) for a copy of the free brochure **"I Declare/Je Déclare"** and for details on duty-free limits. For recorded information (within Canada only), call 800/461–9999.

THE GOLD GUIDE / IMPORTANT CONTACTS

U.K. CITIZENS

HM Customs and Excise (⊠ Dorset House, Stamford St., London SE1 9NG, ☎ 0171/202–4227) can answer questions about U.K. customs regulations and publishes a free pamphlet, **"A Guide for Travellers,"** detailing standard procedures and import rules.

D

DISABILITIES & ACCESSIBILITY

COMPLAINTS

To register complaints under the provisions of the Americans with Disabilities Act, contact the U.S. Department of Justice's **Disability Rights Section** (⊠ Box 66738, Washington, DC 20035, ☎ 202/514–0301 or 800/514–0301, FAX 202/307–1198, TTY 202/514–0383 or 800/514–0383). For airline-related problems, contact the U.S. Department of Transportation's **Aviation Consumer Protection Division** (☞ Air Travel, *above*). For complaints about surface transportation, contact the Department of Transportation's **Civil Rights Office** (⊠ 400 7th St. SW, Room 10215, Washington DC, 20590 ☎ 202/366–4648).

ORGANIZATIONS

TRAVELERS WITH HEARING IMPAIRMENTS➤ The **American Academy of Otolaryngology** (⊠ 1 Prince St., Alexandria, VA 22314, ☎ 703/836–4444, FAX 703/683–5100, TTY 703/519–1585) publishes a brochure, **"Travel Tips for Hearing Impaired People."**

TRAVELERS WITH MOBILITY PROBLEMS➤ Contact the **Information Center for Individuals with Disabilities** (⊠ Box 256, Boston, MA 02117, ☎ 617/450–9888; in MA, 800/462–5015; TTY 617/424–6855); **Mobility International USA** (⊠ Box 10767, Eugene, OR 97440, ☎ and TTY 541/343–1284, FAX 541/343–6812), the U.S. branch of a Belgium-based organization (☞ *below*) with affiliates in 30 countries; **MossRehab Hospital Travel Information Service** (☎ 215/456–9600, TTY 215/456–9602), a telephone information resource for travelers with physical disabilities; the **Society for the Advancement of Travel for the Handicapped** (⊠ 347 5th Ave., Suite 610, New York, NY 10016, ☎ 212/447–7284, FAX 212/725–8253; membership $45); and **Travelin' Talk** (⊠ Box 3534, Clarksville, TN 37043, ☎ 615/552–6670, FAX 615/552–1182), which provides local contacts worldwide for travelers with disabilities.

TRAVELERS WITH VISION IMPAIRMENTS➤ Contact the **American Council of the Blind** (⊠ 1155 15th St. NW, Suite 720, Washington, DC 20005, ☎ 202/467–5081, FAX 202/467–5085) for a list of travelers' resources or the **American Foundation for the Blind** (⊠ 11 Penn Plaza, Suite 300, New York, NY 10001, ☎ 212/502–7600 or 800/232–5463, TTY 212/502–7662), which

provides general advice and publishes "Access to Art" ($19.95), a directory of museums that accommodate travelers with vision impairments.

IN THE U.K.

Contact the **Royal Association for Disability and Rehabilitation** (⊠ RADAR, 12 City Forum, 250 City Rd., London EC1V 8AF, ☎ 0171/250–3222) or **Mobility International** (⊠ Rue de Manchester 25, B-1080 Brussels, Belgium, ☎ 00–322–410–6297, FAX 00–322–410–6874), an international travel-information clearinghouse for people with disabilities.

PUBLICATIONS

Several publications for travelers with disabilities are available from the **Consumer Information Center** (⊠ Box 100, Pueblo, CO 81009, ☎ 719/948–3334). Call or write for its free catalog of current titles. The Society for the Advancement of Travel for the Handicapped (☞ Organizations, *above*) publishes the quarterly magazine **"Access to Travel"** ($13 for 1-yr subscription).

The 500-page **Travelin' Talk Directory** (⊠ Box 3534, Clarksville, TN 37043, ☎ 615/552–6670, FAX 615/552–1182; $35) lists people and organizations who help travelers with disabilities. For travel agents worldwide, consult the **Directory of Travel Agencies for the Disabled** (⊠ Twin Peaks Press, Box 129, Vancouver, WA 98666, ☎ 360/694–2462 or 800/

637–2256, FAX 360/696–3210; $19.95 plus $3 shipping).

TRAVEL AGENCIES & TOUR OPERATORS

The Americans with Disabilities Act requires that all travel firms serve the needs of all travelers. That said, you should note that some agencies and operators specialize in making travel arrangements for individuals and groups with disabilities, among them **Access Adventures** (✉ 206 Chestnut Ridge Rd., Rochester, NY 14624, ☎ 716/889–9096), run by a former physical-rehabilitation counselor.

TRAVELERS WITH MOBILITY PROBLEMS➤ Contact **Hinsdale Travel Service** (✉ 201 E. Ogden Ave., Suite 100, Hinsdale, IL 60521, ☎ 708/325–1335), a travel agency that benefits from the advice of wheelchair traveler Janice Perkins; and **Wheelchair Journeys** (✉ 16979 Redmond Way, Redmond, WA 98052, ☎ 206/885–2210 or 800/313–4751), which can handle arrangements worldwide.

TRAVELERS WITH DEVELOPMENTAL DISABILITIES➤ Contact the nonprofit **New Directions** (✉ 5276 Hollister Ave., Suite 207, Santa Barbara, CA 93111, ☎ 805/967–2841).

TRAVEL GEAR

The **Magellan's** catalog (☎ 800/962–4943, FAX 805/568–5406) includes a section devoted to products designed for travelers with disabilities.

AIRFARES

For the lowest airfares to Portugal, call 800/FLY–4–LESS.

CLUBS

Contact **Entertainment Travel Editions** (✉ Box 1068, Trumbull, CT 06611, ☎ 800/445–4137; $28–$53, depending on destination), **Great American Traveler** (✉ Box 27965, Salt Lake City, UT 84127, ☎ 800/548–2812; $49.95 per yr), **Moment's Notice Discount Travel Club** (✉ 7301 New Utrecht Ave., Brooklyn, NY 11204, ☎ 718/234–6295; $25 per yr, single or family), **Privilege Card** (✉ 3391 Peachtree Rd. NE, Suite 110, Atlanta, GA 30326, ☎ 404/262–0222 or 800/236–9732; $74.95 per yr), **Travelers Advantage** (✉ CUC Travel Service, 49 Music Sq. W, Nashville, TN 37203, ☎ 800/548–1116 or 800/648–4037; $49 per yr, single or family), or **Worldwide Discount Travel Club** (✉ 1674 Meridian Ave., Miami Beach, FL 33139, ☎ 305/534–2082; $50 per yr for family, $40 single).

HOTEL ROOMS

For hotel room rates guaranteed in U.S. dollars, call **Steigenberger Reservation Service** (☎ 800/223–5652).

PASSES

☞ Train Travel, *below.*

STUDENTS

Members of Hostelling International–American Youth Hostels (☞ Students, *below*) are eligible for discounts on car rentals, admissions to attractions, and other selected travel expenses.

PUBLICATIONS

Consult **The Frugal Globetrotter,** by Bruce Northam (✉ Fulcrum Publishing, 350 Indiana St., Suite 350, Golden, CO 80401, ☎ 800/992–2908; $16.95 plus $4 shipping). For publications that tell how to find the lowest prices on plane tickets, *see* Air Travel, *above.*

Also see **Fodor's Affordable Europe** (available in bookstores, or ☎ 800/533–6478; $18.50).

AUTO CLUBS

The large car-rental companies, Hertz and Avis, have 24-hour breakdown service. If you are a member of an automobile club (AAA, CAA, or AA), you can get assistance from the **Portuguese Automobile Club** (ACP/Automovel Clube de Portugal, ✉ Rua Rosa Araujo 24, 1200 Lisbon, ☎ 01/387–1880; ✉ Rua Gonçalo Cristovão 2–6, 4000 Oporto, ☎ 02/316732).

To become a member of the AAA, call 800/564–6222. In the United Kingdom, contact the Automobile Association (AA) or the Royal Automobile Club (RAC).

ORGANIZATIONS

The **International Gay Travel Association** (✉ Box 4974, Key West,

FL 33041, ☎ 800/448–8550, FAX 305/296–6633), a consortium of more than 1,000 travel companies, can supply names of gay-friendly travel agents, tour operators, and accommodations.

PUBLICATIONS

The premier international travel magazine for gays and lesbians is **Our World** (⊠ 1104 N. Nova Rd., Suite 251, Daytona Beach, FL 32117, ☎ 904/441–5367, FAX 904/441–5604; $35 for 10 issues). The 16-page monthly **"Out & About"** (☎ 212/645–6922 or 800/929–2268, FAX 800/929–2215; $49 for 10 issues and quarterly calendar) covers gay-friendly resorts, hotels, cruise lines, and airlines.

TOUR OPERATORS

Toto Tours (⊠ 1326 W. Albion Ave., Suite 3W, Chicago, IL 60626, ☎ 312/274–8686 or 800/565–1241, FAX 312/274–8695) offers group tours to worldwide destinations. **IMTC** (3390 Peachtree Rd. NE, Lenox Towers, Suite 538, Atlanta GA 30326, ☎ 404/240–0949), with a tour operator in Portugal, offers "Paths Less Taken" tours, including a sophisticated, gay-exclusive wine-and-cheese route through Lusitania.

TRAVEL AGENCIES

The largest agencies serving gay travelers are **Advance Travel** (⊠ 10700 Northwest Fwy., Suite 160, Houston, TX 77092, ☎ 713/682–2002 or 800/292–0500),

Islanders/Kennedy Travel (⊠ 183 W. 10th St., New York, NY 10014, ☎ 212/242–3222 or 800/988–1181), **Now Voyager** (⊠ 4406 18th St., San Francisco, CA 94114, ☎ 415/626–1169 or 800/255–6951), and **Yellowbrick Road** (⊠ 1500 W. Balmoral Ave., Chicago, IL 60640, ☎ 312/561–1800 or 800/642–2488). **Skylink Women's Travel** (⊠ 2460 W. 3rd St., Suite 215, Santa Rosa, CA 95401, ☎ 707/570–0105 or 800/225–5759) serves lesbian travelers.

H

HEALTH

FINDING A DOCTOR

For its members, the **International Association for Medical Assistance to Travellers** (IAMAT, membership free; ⊠ 17 Center St., Lewiston, NY 14092, ☎ 716/754–4883; ⊠ 40 Regal Rd., Guelph, Ontario N1K 1B5, ☎ 519/836–0102; ⊠ 1287 St. Clair Ave. W, Toronto, Ontario M6E 1B8, ☎ 416/652–0137; ⊠ 57 Voirets, 1212 Grand-Lancy, Geneva, Switzerland, no phone) publishes a worldwide directory of English-speaking physicians meeting IAMAT standards.

MEDICAL ASSISTANCE COMPANIES

The following companies are concerned primarily with emergency medical assistance, although they may provide some insurance as part of their coverage. For a list of full-service travel insurance companies, *see* Insurance, *below*.

Contact **International SOS Assistance** (⊠ Box 11568, Philadelphia, PA 19116, ☎ 215/244–1500 or 800/523–8930; ⊠ 1C1, ☎ 514/874–7674 or 800/363–0263; ⊠ 7 Old Lodge Pl., St. Margarets, Twickenham TW1 1RQ, England, ☎ 0181/744–0033), **Medex Assistance Corporation** (⊠ Box 5375, Timonium, MD 21094-5375, ☎ 410/453–6300 or 800/537–2029), **Traveler's Emergency Network** (⊠ 3100 Tower Blvd., Suite 3100A, Durham, NC 27702, ☎ 919/490–6065 or 800/275–4836, FAX 919/493–8262), **TravMed** (⊠ Box 5375, Timonium, MD 21094, ☎ 410/453–6380 or 800/732–5309), or **Worldwide Assistance Services** (⊠ 1133 15th St. NW, Suite 400, Washington, DC 20005, ☎ 202/331–1609 or 800/821–2828, FAX 202/828–5896).

I

INSURANCE

IN CANADA

Contact **Mutual of Omaha** (⊠ Travel Division, 500 University Ave., Toronto, Ontario M5G 1V8, ☎ 800/465–0267 (in Canada) or 416/598-4083).

IN THE U.S.

Travel insurance covering baggage, health, and trip cancellations or interruptions is available from **Access America** (⊠ 6600 W. Broad

St., Richmond, VA 23230, ☎ 804/285–3300 or 800/334–7525), **Carefree Travel Insurance** (✉ Box 9366, 100 Garden City Plaza, Garden City, NY 11530, ☎ 516/294–0220 or 800/323–3149), **Near Travel Services** (✉ Box 1339, Calumet City, IL 60409, ☎ 708/868–6700 or 800/654–6700), **Tele-Trip** (✉ Mutual of Omaha Plaza, Box 31716, Omaha, NE 68131, ☎ 800/228–9792), **Travel Guard International** (✉ 1145 Clark St., Stevens Point, WI 54481, ☎ 715/345–0505 or 800/826–1300), **Travel Insured International** (✉ Box 280568, East Hartford, CT 06128, ☎ 203/528–7663 or 800/243–3174), and **Wallach & Company** (✉ 107 W. Federal St., Box 480, Middleburg, VA 22117, ☎ 540/687–3166 or 800/237–6615).

IN THE U.K.

The **Association of British Insurers** (✉ 51 Gresham St., London EC2V 7HQ, ☎ 0171/600–3333) gives advice by phone and publishes the free pamphlet **"Holiday Insurance and Motoring Abroad,"** which sets out typical policy provisions and costs.

L

LODGING

For information on hotel consolidators, *see* Discounts & Deals, *above.*

APARTMENT & VILLA RENTAL

Among the companies to contact are **At Home Abroad** (✉ 405 E. 56th St., Suite 6H, New York, NY 10022, ☎ 212/421–9165, ℻ 212/752–1591), **Europa-Let** (✉ 92 N. Main St., Ashland, OR 97520, ☎ 541/482–5806 or 800/462–4486, ℻ 541/482–0660), **Hometours International** (✉ Box 11503, Knoxville, TN 37939, ☎ 423/588–8722 or 800/367–4668), **Property Rentals International** (✉ 1008 Mansfield Crossing Rd., Richmond, VA 23236, ☎ 804/378–6054 or 800/220–3332, ℻ 804/379–2073), **Rental Directories International** (✉ 2044 Rittenhouse Sq., Philadelphia, PA 19103, ☎ 215/985–4001, ℻ 215/985–0323), **Rent-a-Home International** (✉ 7200 34th Ave. NW, Seattle, WA 98117, ☎ 206/789–9377 or 800/488–7368, ℻ 206/789–9379, rentahome-international@msn.com), **Vacation Home Rentals Worldwide** (✉ 235 Kensington Ave., Norwood, NJ 07648, ☎ 201/767–9393 or 800/633–3284, ℻ 201/767–5510), **Villas and Apartments Abroad** (✉ 420 Madison Ave., Suite 1003, New York, NY 10017, ☎ 212/759–1025 or 800/433–3020, ℻ 212/755–8316), and **Villas International** (✉ 605 Market St., Suite 510, San Francisco, CA 94105, ☎ 415/281–0910 or 800/221–2260, ℻ 415/281–0919). Members of the travel club **Hideaways International** (✉ 767 Islington St., Portsmouth, NH 03801, ☎ 603/430–4433 or 800/843–4433, ℻ 603/430–4444, info@hideaways.com; $99 per yr) receive two annual guides plus quarterly newsletters and arrange rentals among themselves.

CAMPING

For a list of campgrounds, contact the **Turismo** offices or the **Federação Portuguesa de Campismo e Caravanismo** (Portuguese Camping and Caravanning Federation, ✉ Av. 5 de Outubro 15–3, 1000 Lisbon, ☎ 01/315–2715 or 01/522–3308).

COUNTRY HOUSES

For details about country-house stays, contact your tourism office, or **Promoçõese Idéias Turísticas** (PIT; ✉ Alto da Pampilheira, Torre D-2-8A, 2750 Cascais, ☎ 01/486–7958) or **ANTER** (✉ Rua 24 de Julho 1, 7000 Évora, ☎ 066/744–555) for homes in the center and south; or **Direção-Geral do Turismo, Divisão do Turismo no Espaço Rural** (✉ Av. António Augusto de Aguiar 86, 1099 Lisbon, ☎ 01/286–7958), **Privetur** (✉ Largo das Pereiras, 4990 Ponte de Lima, ☎ 058/741–493), and **Turihab** (✉ Praça da República, 4990 Ponte de Lima, ☎ 058/942–729 or 058/741–672), for accommodations in more rural areas in the north of the country.

HOME EXCHANGE

Some of the principal clearinghouses are **HomeLink International/Vacation Exchange Club** (✉ Box 650, Key West, FL 33041, ☎ 305/294–1448 or 800/638–

THE GOLD GUIDE / IMPORTANT CONTACTS

3841, FAX 305/294–1148; $78 per yr), which sends members five annual directories, with a listing in one, plus updates; **Intervac International** (⊠ Box 590504, San Francisco, CA 94159, ☎ 415/435–3497, FAX 415/435–7440; $65 per yr), which publishes four annual directories.

HOTELS

Contact the Portuguese National Tourist Office (⊠ 590 5th Ave., New York, NY 10036, ☎ 212/354–4403 or 212/354–4404, FAX 212/764–6137) for their basic hotel directory, in addition to the list of **Hotels de Charme,** a newly associated group of 16 small hotels and *pousadas* throughout the country.

POUSADAS

For information on pousadas, contact the tourist office or **ENATUR** (⊠ Av. Sta. Joana a Princesa 10-A, 1700 Lisbon, ☎ 01/848–1221, FAX 01/847–8525); in the United States, **Marketing Ahead** (⊠ 433 5th Ave., New York, NY 10016, ☎ 212/686–9213 or 800/223–1356, FAX 212/686–0271); in the United Kingdom, **Keytel International** (⊠ 402 Edgeware Rd., London W2 1ED, ☎ 0171/402–8182).

SPAS

For complete listings and reservations information, contact the Portuguese tourism office nearest you, **Marketing Ahead** (☞ *above*), or the **Associ-ação Nacional dos Industriais de Aguas Minero-Medicinais de**

Mesa (⊠ Av. Miguel Bombarda 110–2, 1050 Lisbon, ☎ 01/794–0574).

M
MONEY

ATMS

For specific foreign **Cirrus** locations, call 800/424–7787; for foreign **Plus** locations, consult the Plus directory at your local bank.

CURRENCY EXCHANGE

If your bank doesn't exchange currency, contact **Thomas Cook Currency Services** (☎ 800/287–7362 for locations). **Ruesch International** (☎ 800/424–2923 for locations) can also provide you with foreign banknotes before you leave home and publishes a number of useful brochures, including a "Foreign Currency Guide" and "Foreign Exchange Tips."

WIRING FUNDS

Funds can be wired via **MoneyGram℠** (for locations and information in the United States and Canada, ☎ 800/926–9400) or **Western Union** (for agent locations or to send money using MasterCard or Visa, ☎ 800/325–6000; in Canada, 800/321–2923; in the U.K., 0800/833833; or visit the Western Union office at the nearest major post office).

P
PACKING

For strategies on packing light, get a copy of *The Packing Book,* by Judith Gilford (⊠ Ten

Speed Press, Box 7123, Berkeley, CA 94707, ☎ 510/559–1600 or 800/841–2665, FAX 510/524–4588; $7.95 plus $3.50 shipping).

PASSPORTS & VISAS

IN THE U.S.

For fees, documentation requirements, and other information, call the State Department's **Office of Passport Services** information line (☎ 202/647–0518).

CANADIANS

For fees, documentation requirements, and other information, call the Ministry of Foreign Affairs and International Trade's **Passport Office** (☎ 819/994–3500 or 800/567–6868).

U.K. CITIZENS

For fees, documentation requirements, and to request an emergency passport, call the **London Passport Office** (☎ 0990/210410).

PHOTO HELP

The **Kodak Information Center** (☎ 800/242–2424) answers consumer questions about film and photography. The *Kodak Guide to Shooting Great Travel Pictures* (available in bookstores, or contact Fodor's Travel Publications, ☎ 800/533–6478; $16.50 plus $4 shipping) explains how to take expert travel photographs.

S
SAFETY

"Trouble-Free Travel," from AAA, is a booklet of tips for protecting yourself and your belongings when away from home. Send a stamped, self-addressed, legal-size envelope to Trouble-Free Travel (✉ Mail Stop 75, 1000 AAA Dr., Heathrow, FL 32746).

EDUCATIONAL TRAVEL

The nonprofit **Elderhostel** (✉ 75 Federal St., 3rd Floor, Boston, MA 02110, ☎ 617/426–7788), for people 55 and older, has offered inexpensive study programs since 1975. Courses cover everything from marine science to Greek mythology and cowboy poetry. Costs for two- to three-week international trips—including room, board, and transportation from the United States—range from $1,800 to $4,500.

Interhostel (✉ University of New Hampshire, 6 Garrison Ave., Durham, NH 03824, ☎ 603/862–1147 or 800/733–9753), for travelers 50 and older, has two- to three-week trips; most last two weeks and cost $2,000–$3,500, including airfare.

ORGANIZATIONS

Contact the **American Association of Retired Persons** (✉ AARP, 601 E St. NW, Washington, DC 20049, ☎ 202/434–2277; annual

dues $8 per person or couple). Its Purchase Privilege Program secures discounts for members on lodging, car rentals, and sightseeing.

Additional sources for discounts on lodgings, car rentals, and other travel expenses, as well as helpful magazines and newsletters, are the **National Council of Senior Citizens** (✉ 1331 F St. NW, Washington, DC 20004, ☎ 202/347–8800; annual membership $12) and Sears's **Mature Outlook** (✉ Box 10448, Des Moines, IA 50306, ☎ 800/336–6330; annual membership $14.95).

GOLF

Contact the tourism office for detailed descriptions of courses and a list of greens fees or the **Federação Portuguesa de Golf** (Portuguese Golf Federation, ✉ 9 Rua Almeida Brandão 39, 1200 Lisbon, ☎ 01/867–4658) or the **Clube de Campo de Portugal** (✉ Herdade de Aroeira, Fonte da Telha, 2825 Monte de Caparica, Aoeira, ☎ 065/226–1802, FAX 065/297–1358).

FISHING

The **Clube dos Amadores de Pesca de Lisboa** (✉ Travessa do Adro 12–1, 1100 Lisbon, ☎ 01/356–

1375) and the **Clube dos Amadores de Pesca da Costa do Sol** (✉ Rua dos Fontainhos 16, 2750 Cascais, ☎ 01/284–1691) are for fishermen in the Lisbon area, or contact the tourist office for a booklet on fishing throughout the country.

HORSEBACK RIDING

For information on **horseback riding** in Portugal, contact the **Federação Equestre Portuguesa** (Portuguese Equestrian Federation, ✉ Av. Duque d'Avila 9–4, 1000 Lisbon, ☎ 01/352–5676) or the **Centro Equestre e Desportivo Costa Azul** (the Sporting & Equestrian Center of the Costa Azul, ✉ Sobreda da Caparica, ☎ 01/295–5581).

TENNIS

Tennis pros offer classes almost all year long in the resorts; contact the tourism office for a list of courts in the resort areas. For further information, contact the **Federação Portuguesa de Tenis** (Portuguese Tennis Federation, ✉ Estadio Nacional, Caxias, 2480 Oeiras, ☎ 01/419–5244 or 01/419–8472).

WATER SPORTS

For further information contact the **Federação Portuguesa de Vela** (Portuguese Sailing Federation, ✉ Doca de

Belem, 1300 Lisbon, ☎ 01/364–7324 or 362–3925), the **Associação Naval de Lisboa** (✉ Doca de Belem, ☎ 01/363–5861), or **Federação Portuguesa de Atividades Sub-aquáticas** (Portuguese Underwater Sports Federation, ✉ Rua Almeida Brandão 39, 1200 Lisbon, ☎ 01/396–4322); **Federação Portuguesa de Canoagem** (Portuguese Canoeing Federation, ✉ Rua António Pinto Machado 60, 4100 Porto, ☎ 02/697350). For surfing, head to Cascais (rent a board there at **Windsurf Portugal,** ☎ 01/486–1883) and continue on to the awesome beach at Guincho, where shooting a curl is popular even in the mild winters. Water-skiers should contact the **Clube Naval de Cascais** (the Cascais Navy Club, ✉ Esplanada Pricipe D. Luis Filipe, 2750 Cascais, ☎ 01/483–0125).

HOSTELING

In the United States, contact **Hostelling International–American Youth Hostels** (✉ 733 15th St. NW, Suite 840, Washington, DC 20005, ☎ 202/783–6161, FAX 202/783–6171); in Canada, **Hostelling International–Canada** (✉ 205 Catherine St., Suite 400, Ottawa, Ontario K2P 1C3, ☎ 613/237–7884); and in the United Kingdom, the **Youth Hostel Association of England and Wales** (✉ Trevelyan House, 8 St. Stephen's Hill, St. Albans, Hertfordshire AL1 2DY, ☎ 01727/

855215 or 01727/845047). Membership (in the U.S., $25; in Canada, C$26.75; in the U.K., £9.30) gives you access to 5,000 hostels in 77 countries that charge $5–$40 per person per night.

ORGANIZATIONS

A major contact is the **Council on International Educational Exchange** (mail orders only: ✉ CIEE, 205 E. 42nd St., 16th Floor, New York, NY 10017, ☎ 212/661–1450, info@ciee.org). The **Educational Travel Centre** (✉ 438 N. Frances St., Madison, WI 53703, ☎ 608/256–5551 or 800/747–5551, FAX 608/256–2042) offers rail passes and low-cost airline tickets, mostly for flights that depart from Chicago.

In Canada, also contact **Travel Cuts** (✉ 187 College St., Toronto, Ontario M5T 1P7, ☎ 416/979–2406 or 800/667–2887).

PUBLICATIONS

Check out the *Berkeley Guide to Europe* (available in bookstores; or contact Fodor's Travel Publications, ☎ 800/533–6478; $18.95 plus $4 shipping).

T

The country code for Portugal is 351. For local access numbers abroad, contact **AT&T** USADirect (☎ 800/874–4000), **MCI** Call USA (☎ 800/444–4444), or **Sprint** Express (☎ 800/793–1153).

The national upgrading of the **telephone system**

is still causing havoc for tourists and locals alike. Numbers throughout the country are changing in a rolling program, and official publications have been slow to catch up; always double-check.

Among the companies that sell tours and packages to Portugal, the following are nationally known, have a proven reputation, and offer plenty of options.

GROUP TOURS

SUPER-DELUXE➤ **Abercrombie & Kent** (✉ 1520 Kensington Rd., Oak Brook, IL 60521-2141, ☎ 708/954–2944 or 800/323–7308, FAX 708/954–3324) and **Travcoa** (✉ Box 2630, 2350 S.E. Bristol St., Newport Beach, CA 92660, ☎ 714/476–2800 or 800/992–2003, FAX 714/476–2538).

DELUXE➤ **Globus** (✉ 5301 S. Federal Circle, Littleton, CO 80123-2980, ☎ 303/797–2800 or 800/221–0090, FAX 303/795–0962), **Maupintour** (✉ Box 807, 1515 St. Andrews Dr., Lawrence, KS 66047, ☎ 913/843–1211 or 800/255–4266, FAX 913/843–8351), and **Tauck Tours** (✉ Box 5027, 276 Post Rd. W, Westport, CT 06881, ☎ 203/226–6911 or 800/468–2825, FAX 203/221–6828).

FIRST CLASS➤ **Abreu Tours** (✉ 25 W. 45th St., #1309, New York, NY 10036-4902, ☎ 212/869–1840 or 800/223–1580, FAX 212/354–1840), **Brendan Tours** (✉ 15137 Califa

St., Van Nuys, CA 91411, ☎ 818/785–9696 or 800/421–8446, ⨳ 818/902–9876), **Caravan Tours** (⊠ 401 N. Michigan Ave., Chicago, IL 60611, ☎ 312/321–9800 or 800/227–2826), **Collette Tours** (⊠ 162 Middle St., Pawtucket, RI 02860, ☎ 401/728–3805 or 800/832–4656, ⨳ 401/728–1380), **Insight International Tours** (⊠ 745 Atlantic Ave., #720, Boston, MA 02111, ☎ 617/482-2000 or 800/582–8380, ⨳ 617/482–2884 or 800/622–5015), **Odysseys Adventures** (⊠ Box 305, 537 Chestnut St., Cedarhurst, NY 11516-2223, ☎ 516/569–2812 or 800/344–0013, ⨳ 516/569–2998), **Sun Holidays** (⊠ 7280 W. Palmetto Park Rd., Boca Raton, FL 33433, ☎ 407/367–0105 or 800/422–8000, ⨳ 407/393–3870), **Trafalgar Tours** (⊠ 11 E. 26th St., New York, NY 10010, ☎ 212/689–8977 or 800/854–0103, ⨳ 800/457–6644), and **Viajes Corte Ingles** (⊠ 500 5th Ave., #1044, New York, NY 10110, ☎ 212/944–9400 or 800/333–2469).

Budget➤ **Cosmos** (☞ Globus, *above*) and **Trafalgar Tours** (☞ *above*).

PACKAGES

Just about every airline that flies to Portugal sells packages that include round-trip airfare and hotel accommodations. Among U.S. carriers, contact **Delta Dream Vacations** (☎ 800/872–7786). Other leading packagers

include: **DER Tours** (⊠ 11933 Wilshire Blvd., Los Angeles, CA 90025, ☎ 310/479–4140 or 800/937–1235), **4th Dimension Tours** (⊠ 7101 S.W. 99th Ave., #105, Miami, FL 33173, ☎ 305/279–0014 or 800/877–1525, ⨳ 305/273–9777, http://www.4thdimension.com), **Jet Vacations** (⊠ 1775 Broadway, New York, NY 10019, ☎ 212/474–8740 or 800/538–2762), and **Spain Tours and Beyond** (⊠ 261 W. 70th St., New York, NY 10023, ☎ 212/595–2400, ⨳ 212/580–8935). **Gogo Tours,** based in Ramsey, New Jersey, sells packages only through travel agents.

FROM THE U.K.

Contact the **Abreo Travel Agency** (⊠ 109 Westbourne Grove, London W2 4UL, ☎ 0171/22–9905), **Mundi Color** (⊠ 276 Vauxhall Bridge Rd., London SW1V 1BE, ☎ 0171/828–6021), or **Magic of Portugal** (⊠ 227 Shepherds Bush Rd., London W6 7AS, ☎ 0181/741–1181).

THEME TRIPS

Art and Architecture➤ Contact **Esplanade Tours** (⊠ 581 Boylston St., Boston, MA 02116, ☎ 617/266–7465 or 800/426–5492, ⨳ 617/262–9829) for expedition cruise tours along the Portuguese coast.

Bicycling➤ Bike tours are available from **Backroads** (⊠ 1516 5th St., Berkeley, CA 94710-1740, ☎ 510/577–1555 or 800/462–2848, ⨳ 510/527–

1444, goactive@Backroads.com), **Butterfield & Robinson** (⊠ 70 Bond St., Toronto, Ontario M5B 1X3, ☎ 416/864–1354 or 800/678–1147, ⨳ 416/864–0541, info@butterfield.com), **Euro-Bike Tours** (⊠ Box 990, De Kalb, IL 60115, ☎ 800/321–6060, ⨳ 815/758–8851), **Progressive Travels** (⊠ 224 W. Galer Ave., #C, Seattle, WA 98119, ☎ 206/285–1987 or 800/245–2229, ⨳ 206/285–1988), and **Uniquely Europe** (⊠ 2819 1st Ave., #280, Seattle, WA 98121-1113, ☎ 206/441–8682 or 800/426–3615, ⨳ 206/441–8862).

Food and Wine➤ **Odysseys Adventures** (☞ Group Tours, *above*) organizes wine-tasting tours coupled with meals in fine restaurants around the country.

Gardens➤ **Coopersmith's England** (⊠ Box 900, Inverness, CA 94937, ☎ 415/669–1914, ⨳ 510/339–7135) explores the gardens, art, and architecture of Lisbon and Madeira.

Golf➤ For golf packages try **Golf International** (⊠ 275 Madison Ave., New York, NY 10016, ☎ 212/986–9176 or 800/833–1389, ⨳ 212/986–3720), **ITC Golf Tours** (⊠ 4134 Atlantic Ave., #205, Long Beach, CA 90807, ☎ 310/595–6905 or 800/257–4981) and **Odysseys Adventures** (☞ Group Tours, *above*).

HIKING/WALKING➤ Meander through Portugal with the **Adventure Center** (✉ 1311 63rd St., #200, Emeryville, CA 94608, ☎ 510/654–1879 or 800/227–8747, FAX 510/654–4200) and **Progressive Travels** (☞ Bicycling, *above*).

HORSEBACK RIDING➤ **FITS Equestrian** (✉ 685 Lateen Rd., Solvang, CA 93463, ☎ 805/688–9494 or 800/666–3487, FAX 805/688–2943) has year-round departures and tours for every level of rider.

JEWISH HERITAGE➤ **Abreu Tours** (☞ Group Tours, *above*) and **Odysseys Adventures** (☞ Group Tours, *above*) visit synagogues and historic Jewish sites throughout Portugal.

KAYAKING➤ **Mountain Travel-Sobek** (✉ 6420 Fairmount Ave., El Cerrito, CA 94530, ☎ 510/527–8100 or 800/227–2384, FAX 510/525–7710, Info@MTSobek.com, http://www.MTSobek.com) leads kayakers through Portugal's Douro River valley.

LEARNING➤ Contact **Smithsonian Study Tours and Seminars** (✉ 1100 Jefferson Dr. SW, Room 3045, MRC 702, Washington, DC 20560, ☎ 202/357–4700, FAX 202/633–9250).

VILLA RENTALS➤ Contact **Eurovillas** (✉ 1398 55th St., Emeryville, CA 94608, ☎ FAX 707/648–0266) and **Villas International** (✉ 605 Market St., San Francisco, CA 94105, ☎ 415/281–0910 or 800/281–0919).

YACHT CHARTERS➤ **Lynn Jachney Charters** (✉ Box 302 Marblehead, MA 01945, ☎ 617/639–0787 or 800/223–2050, FAX 617/639–0216).

ORGANIZATIONS

The **National Tour Association** (✉ NTA, 546 E. Main St., Lexington, KY 40508, ☎ 606/226–4444 or 800/755–8687) and the **United States Tour Operators Association** (✉ USTOA, 211 E. 51st St., Suite 12B, New York, NY 10022, ☎ 212/750–7371) can provide lists of members and information on booking tours.

PUBLICATIONS

Contact the USTOA (☞ Organizations, *above*) for its **"Smart Traveler's Planning Kit."** Pamphlets in the kit include the "Worldwide Tour and Vacation Package Finder," "How to Select a Tour or Vacation Package," and information on the organization's consumer protection plan. Also get a copy of the Better Business Bureau's **"Tips on Travel Packages"** (✉ Publication 24-195, 4200 Wilson Blvd., Arlington, VA 22203; $2).

If Spain is your only destination in Europe, **consider purchasing a Portuguese Rail Pass.** The cost is $99 for four days of first-class train travel in a 15-day period.

DISCOUNT PASSES

Portuguese rail passes are sold by travel agents as well as **Rail Europe** (✉ 226–230 Westches-ter Ave., White Plains, NY 10604, ☎ 914/682–5172 or 800/438–7245; ✉ 2087 Dundas E, Suite 105, Mississauga, Ontario L4X 1M2, ☎ 416/602–4195).

Eurail and EuroPasses are available through travel agents and **Rail Europe** (✉ 226-230 Westchester Ave., White Plains, NY 10604, ☎ 914/682–5172 or 800/438–7245; ✉ 2087 Dundas E, Suite 105, Mississauga, Ontario L4X 1M2, ☎ 416/602–4195, **DER Tours** (✉ Box 1606, Des Plaines, IL 60017, ☎ 800/782–2424, FAX 800/282–7474), or **CIT Tours Corp.** (✉ 342 Madison Ave., Suite 207, New York, NY 10173, ☎ 212/697–2100 or 800/248–8687 or 800/248–7245 in western U.S.).

FROM THE U.K.

Campus Travel (✉ 52 Grosvenor Gardens, London SW1W OAG, ☎ 0171/730–3402) and **Transalpino** (✉ 71–75 Buckingham Palace Rd., London SW1W ORE, ☎ 0171/834–9656) both offer excellent deals for those under 26. Otherwise book through **British Rail International** (☎ 0171/834–2345) or **French Railways SNCF** (✉ 179 Piccadilly, London W1V OBA, ☎ 0171/409–3518).

For names of reputable agencies in your area, contact the **American Society of Travel Agents** (✉ ASTA, 1101 King St., Suite 200, Alexandria, VA 22314, ☎ 703/739–2782), the

Association of Canadian Travel Agents (✉ Suite 201, 1729 Bank St., Ottawa, Ontario K1V 7Z5, ☎ 613/521–0474, FAX 613/521–0805), or the **Association of British Travel Agents** (✉ 55-57 Newman St., London W1P 4AH, ☎ 0171/637–2444, FAX 0171/637–0713).

TRAVEL GEAR

For travel apparel, appliances, personal-care items, and other travel necessities, get a free catalog from **Magellan's** (☎ 800/962–4943, FAX 805/568–5406), **Orvis Travel** (☎ 800/541–3541, FAX 703/343–7053), or **Travel-Smith** (☎ 800/950–1600, FAX 415/455–0554).

ELECTRICAL CONVERTERS

Send a self-addressed, stamped envelope to the **Franzus Company** (✉ Customer Service, Dept. B50, Murtha Industrial Park, Box 142, Beacon Falls, CT 06403, ☎ 203/723–6664) for a copy of the free brochure "Foreign Electricity Is No Deep, Dark Secret."

U

U.S. GOVERNMENT TRAVEL BRIEFINGS

The U.S. Department of State's American Citizens Services office (✉ Room 4811, Washington, DC 20520; enclose SASE) issues **Consular Information Sheets** on all foreign countries. These cover issues such as crime, security, political climate, and health risks as well as listing embassy locations, entry requirements, currency regulations, and providing other useful information. For the latest information, stop in at any U.S. passport office, consulate, or embassy; call the interactive hot line (☎ 202/647–5225, FAX 202/647–3000); or with your PC's modem, tap into the department's computer bulletin board (☎ 202/647–9225).

V

VISITOR INFORMATION

Contact the **Portuguese National Tourist Office** (✉ 590 5th Ave., 4th Floor, New York, NY 10036, ☎ 212/354–4403, FAX 212/764–

6137. In Canada: ✉ 60 Bloor St. W, Suite 1005, Toronto, Ontario M4W 3BS, ☎ 416/921–7376, FAX 416/921–1353. In the United Kingdom: 2✉ 2–25A Sackville St., London W1X 1DE, ☎ 0171/494–1441.

FROM THE U.K.

Portuguese Tourist Office (✉ 22–25A Sackville St., London W1X 1DE, ☎ 0171/494–1441, FAX 0171/494–1868).

W

WEATHER

For current conditions and forecasts, plus the local time and helpful travel tips, call the **Weather Channel Connection** (☎ 900/932–8437; 95¢ per minute) from a Touch-Tone phone.

The *International Traveler's Weather Guide* (✉ Weather Press, Box 660606, Sacramento, CA 95866, ☎ 916/974–0201 or 800/972–0201; $10.95 includes shipping), written by two meteorologists, provides month-by-month information on temperature, humidity, and precipitation in more than 175 cities worldwide.

THE GOLD GUIDE / IMPORTANT CONTACTS

SMART TRAVEL TIPS A TO Z

Basic Information on Traveling in Portugal and Savvy Tips to Make Your Trip a Breeze

A

AIR TRAVEL

If time is an issue, **always look for nonstop flights,** which require no change of plane. If possible, **avoid connecting flights,** which stop at least once and can involve a change of plane, even though the flight number remains the same; if the first leg is late, the second waits.

For better service, **fly smaller or regional carriers,** which often have higher passenger satisfaction ratings. Sometimes they have such in-flight amenities as leather seats or greater legroom and they often have better food.

CUTTING COSTS

The Sunday travel section of most newspapers is a good place to look for deals.

MAJOR AIRLINES➤ The least expensive airfares from the major airlines are priced for round-trip travel and are subject to restrictions. Usually, you must **book in advance and buy the ticket within 24 hours** to get cheaper fares, and you may have to **stay over a Saturday night.** The lowest fare is subject to availability, and only a small percentage of the plane's total seats is sold at that price. It's smart to **call a number of airlines, and when you are quoted a good price, book it on**

the spot—the same fare may not be available on the same flight the next day. Airlines generally allow you to change your return date for a $25 to $50 fee. If you don't use your ticket, you can apply the cost toward the purchase of a new ticket, again for a small charge. However, most low-fare tickets are nonrefundable. To get the lowest airfare, **check different routings.** If your destination has more than one gateway, **compare prices to different airports.**

FROM THE U.K.➤ To save money on flights, **look into an APEX or Super-Pex ticket.** APEX tickets must be booked in advance and have certain restrictions. Super-Pex tickets can be purchased right at the airport.

CONSOLIDATORS➤ Consolidators buy tickets for scheduled flights at reduced rates from the airlines, then sell them at prices below the lowest available from the airlines directly—usually without advance restrictions. Sometimes you can even get your money back if you need to return the ticket. Carefully read the fine print detailing penalties for changes and cancellations. If you doubt the reliability of a consolidator, **confirm your reservation with the airline.**

ALOFT

AIRLINE FOOD➤ If you hate airline food, **ask for special meals when booking.** These can be vegetarian, low cholesterol, or kosher, for example; commonly prepared to order in smaller quantities than standard fare, they can be tastier.

JET LAG➤ To avoid this syndrome, which occurs when travel disrupts your body's natural cycles, try to maintain a normal routine. At night, **get some sleep.** By day, move about the cabin to **stretch your legs, eat light meals, and drink water—not alcohol.**

SMOKING➤ Smoking is not allowed on flights of six hours or less within the continental United States. Smoking is also prohibited on flights within Canada. For U.S. flights longer than six hours or international flights, **contact your carrier regarding their smoking policy.** Some carriers have prohibited smoking throughout their system; others allow smoking only on certain routes or even certain departures of that route.

B

BICYCLING

Portugal is one of Europe's more mountainous countries. Although country roads can sometimes be crowded with speeding trucks, bicycle trips can take you along some unforgettably scenic routes.

FROM THE U.K.

The Eurolines/National Express consortium runs regular bus service to Lisbon (twice weekly), Faro and Lagos in the Algarve on the south coast (twice weekly), and weekly to Coimbra. Buses leave London's Victoria Coach Station and reach Coimbra, Lisbon, and Faro on the third day.

BANKS

Banks are generally open weekdays 8:30–3. Money exchanges at airports and train stations are usually open all day (24 hours at Portela Airport in Lisbon), and some hotels will be able to accommodate you, although at a slightly lower rate than at a bank.

MUSEUMS

Most museums open at 10, close for lunch between 12:30 and 2, and close at 5 (a few big ones stay open at midday—check beforehand). They are closed on Monday and holidays; palaces close on Tuesday and holidays.

SHOPS

One of the most inconvenient things about shopping in Portugal is the midday closing of most shops for approximately two hours. Store hours are weekdays 9– 1 and 3–7, Saturday 9–

1. In December Saturday hours are the same as weekdays. Shops are closed on Sunday, although some *hipermercados* (supermarkets) and shopping centers are open seven days a week, 10 AM–midnight.

C

IN TRANSIT

Always **keep your film, tape, or disks out of the sun;** never put these on the dashboard of a car. Carry an extra supply of batteries and **be prepared to turn on your camera, camcorder, or laptop computer for security personnel** to prove that it's real.

X RAYS

Always **ask for hand inspection at security.** Such requests are virtually always honored at U.S. airports and are usually accommodated abroad. Photographic film becomes clouded after successive exposure to airport X-ray machines. Videotapes and computer disks are not harmed by X rays, but **keep your tapes and disks away from metal detectors.**

CUSTOMS

Before departing, **register your foreign-made camera or laptop with U.S. Customs.** If your equipment is U.S.-made, call the consulate of the country you'll be visiting to find out whether it should be registered with local customs upon arrival.

CUTTING COSTS

To get the best deal, **book through a travel agent who is willing to shop around.** Ask your agent to **look for fly-drive packages,** which also save you money, and **ask if local taxes are included** in the rental or fly-drive price. These can be as high as 20% in some destinations. Don't forget to find out about required deposits, cancellation penalties, drop-off charges, and the cost of any required insurance coverage.

Also **ask your travel agent about a company's customer-service record.** How has it responded to late plane arrivals and vehicle mishaps? Are there often lines at the rental counter and—if you're traveling during a holiday period—does a confirmed reservation guarantee you a car?

Always **find out what equipment is standard** at your destination before specifying what you want; automatic transmission and air-conditioning are usually optional—and very expensive.

Be sure to **look into wholesalers**—companies that do not own their own fleets but rent in bulk from those that do and ften offer better rates than traditional car-rental operations. Prices are best during off-peak periods; rentals booked through wholesales must be paid for by you leave the United States.

INSURANCE

When driving a rented car, you are generally

responsible for any damage to or loss of the rental vehicle. Before you rent, **see what coverage you already have** under the terms of your personal auto-insurance policy and credit cards.

If you do not have auto insurance or an umbrella insurance policy that covers damage to third parties, purchasing CDW or LDW is highly recommended.

Collision policies sold by car-rental companies for European rentals typically do not cover stolen vehicles. Before you buy additional coverage for theft, find out if your credit card or personal auto insurance will cover the loss.

LICENSE REQUIREMENTS

In Portugal your own driver's license is acceptable. An International Driver's Permit is a good idea; it's available from the American or Canadian automobile associations, or, in the United Kingdom, from the AA or RAC.

SURCHARGES

Before you pick up a car in one city and leave it in another, **ask about drop-off charges or one-way service fees,** which can be substantial. Note, too, that some rental agencies charge extra if you return the car before the time specified on your contract. To avoid a hefty refueling fee, **fill the tank just before you turn in the car**—but be aware that gas stations near the rental outlet may overcharge.

CHILDREN & TRAVEL

The Portuguese are very family-oriented and love children, so don't hesitate to take them along on your trip. You'll see children of all ages accompanying their parents everywhere, including bars and restaurants. Shopkeepers will smile and offer your child a *bom-bom* (candy), and even the coldest waiters tend to be friendlier when you have a child with you. Kitchens are usually willing to fix something special for children, but you won't find children's menus anywhere. On the road, even the smallest *tasca* (town restaurant/bar) will be able to make a *sandes de queijo* (cheese sandwich), and roast chicken (*frango assado*) is on most menus. Museum admissions, buses, and metro rides are generally free for children under five and half-price for children under 12.

When traveling with children, **plan ahead** and **involve your youngsters** as you outline your trip. When packing, **include a supply of things to keep them busy** en route (☞ Children & Travel *in* Important Contacts A to Z, *above*). On sightseeing days, try to **schedule activities of special interest to your children,** like a trip to a zoo or a playground. If you **plan your itinerary around seasonal festivals,** you'll never lack for things to do. In addition, **check local newspapers for special events** mounted by public libraries, museums, and parks.

BABY-SITTING

For recommended local sitters, **check with your hotel desk.**

DRIVING

If you are renting a car, don't forget to **arrange for a car seat when you reserve.** Sometimes they're free.

FLYING

As a general rule, infants under two not occupying a seat fly at greatly reduced fares and occasionally for free. If your children are two or older, **ask about special children's fares.** Age limits for these fares vary among carriers. Rules also vary regarding unaccompanied minors, so again, check with your airline.

BAGGAGE➤ In general, the adult baggage allowance applies to children paying half or more of the adult fare. If you are traveling with an infant, **ask about carry-on allowances** before departure. In general, for infants charged 10% of the adult fare, you are allowed one carry-on bag and a collapsible stroller, which may have to be checked; you may be limited to less if the flight is full.

SAFETY SEATS➤ According to the FAA, it's a good idea to **use safety seats aloft** for children weighing less than 40 pounds. Airline policies vary. U.S. carriers allow FAA-approved models but usually require that you buy a ticket, even if your child would otherwise ride free, since the seats must be strapped into regular seats. However, some U.S. and foreign-flag airlines may require you to hold your baby during takeoff and landing—defeating the seat's purpose. Other foreign carriers may not allow infant seats at all or may charge a child rather than an infant fare for their use.

FACILITIES➣ When making your reservation, **request children's meals or freestanding bassinets** if you need them; the latter are available only to those seated at the bulkhead, where there's enough legroom. If you don't need a bassinet, **think twice before requesting bulkhead seats**—the only storage space for in-flight necessities is in inconveniently distant overhead bins.

GAMES

Milton Bradley and Parker Brothers have travel versions of some of their most popular games, including Yahtzee, Trouble, Sorry, and Monopoly. Prices run $5 to $8. Look for them in the travel section of your local toy store.

LODGING

Most hotels allow children under a certain age to stay in their parents' room at no extra charge; others charge children as additional adults. Be sure to **ask about the cutoff age.**

CUSTOMS & DUTIES

To speed your clearance through customs, **keep receipts for all your purchases abroad** and **be ready to show the inspector what you've bought.** If you feel that you've been incorrectly or unfairly charged a duty, you can **appeal assessments in dispute.** First ask to see a supervisor. If you are still unsatisfied, **write to the port director** at your point of entry, sending your customs receipt and any other appropriate documentation. The address will be listed on your receipt. If you still don't get satisfaction, you can take your case to customs headquarters in Washington.

IN PORTUGAL

Visitors age 15 and over are permitted to bring in 200 cigarettes, or 100 cigarillos, or 50 cigars, or 250 grams of loose tobacco. Those 17 years of age and older may bring in one liter of liquor over 22 proof and two liters of wine. Perfume is limited to 50 grams, eau de cologne to ¼ liter. Dogs and cats are admitted, providing they have up-to-date vaccination records from the home country.

It is a good idea to carry along sales receipts for expensive personal belongings to avoid paying export duties when you leave.

All visitors to Madeira over one year old who are traveling from an infected area need a certificate of vaccination against yellow fever.

IN THE U.S.

You may bring home $400 worth of foreign goods duty-free if you've been out of the country for at least 48 hours and haven't already used the $400 allowance, or any part of it, in the past 30 days.

Travelers 21 or older may bring back one liter of alcohol duty-free, provided the beverage laws of the state through which they reenter the United States allow it. In addition, regardless of their age, they are allowed 100 non-Cuban cigars and 200 cigarettes. Antiques, which the U.S. Customs Service defines as objects more than 100 years old, are duty-free. Original works of art done entirely by hand are also duty-free. These include, but are not limited to, paintings, drawings, and sculptures.

Duty-free, travelers may mail packages valued at up to $200 to themselves and up to $100 to others, with a limit of one parcel per addressee per day (and no alcohol or tobacco products or perfume valued at more than $5); on the outside, the package must be labeled as being either for personal use or as an unsolicited gift, and a list of its contents and their retail value must be attached. Mailed items do not affect your duty-free allowance on your return.

IN CANADA

If you've been out of Canada for at least seven days, you may bring in C$500 worth of goods duty-free. If you've been away fewer than seven days but for more than 48 hours, the duty-free allowance drops to C$200.If your trip lasts between 24 and 48 hours, the allowance is C$50. You cannot pool allowances with family members. Goods claimed under the C$500 exemption may follow you by mail; those claimed under the lesser exemptions must accompany you.

Alcohol and tobacco products may be included in the seven-day and 48-hour exemptions but not in the 24-hour exemption. If you meet the age requirements of the province or territory through which you reenter Canada, you may bring in, duty-free, 1.14 liters (40 imperial ounces) of wine or liquor or 24 12-ounce cans or bottles of beer or ale. If you are 16 or older, you may bring in, duty-free, 200 cigarettes, 50 cigars or cigarillos, and 400 tobacco sticks or 400 grams of manufactured tobacco. Alcohol and tobacco must accompany you on your return.

An unlimited number of gifts with a value of up to C$60 each may be mailed to Canada duty-free. These do not affect your duty-free allowance on your return. Label the package "Unsolicited Gift—Value Under $60." Alcohol and tobacco are excluded.

IN THE U.K.

If your journey was wholly within European Union (EU) countries, you no longer need to pass through customs when you return to the United Kingdom. If you plan to bring back large quantities of alcohol or tobacco, check in advance on EU limits.

D

DINING

Breakfast is the lightest meal; lunch, the main meal of the day, is served between noon and 2:30, although nowadays, office workers in cities often grab a quick sandwich in a bar instead of stopping for a big lunch. About 5 there's an afternoon break for coffee or tea and a pastry, and dinner is eaten around 7.

As in many European countries, Portuguese restaurants use an *ementa (or prato) do dia,* or set menu. This can be a real bargain—usually 80% of the cost of three courses ordered separately.

DISABILITIES & ACCESSIBILITY

Portugal is not one of the easiest countries for travelers with disabilities, although efforts are slowly being made to accommodate those voyagers for whom the word "travel" all too often means travail. Many of the smaller towns and out-of-the-way hilltop castles are difficult terrain for any visitor. Things are beginning to change, however, and buildings constructed here within the last five years should be accessible, as are some of the larger museums and other tourist sites. It's best to check either the tourist office or directly with the hotel, or with your travel agent before booking a reservation or heading off to a museum or other attraction.

When discussing accessibility with an operator or reservationist, **ask hard questions.** Are there any stairs, inside *or* out? Are there grab bars next to the toilet *and* in the shower/tub? How wide is the doorway to the room? To the bathroom? For the most extensive facilities meeting the latest legal specifications, **opt for newer accommodations,** which more often have been designed with access in mind. Older properties or ships must usually be retrofitted and may offer more limited facilities as a result. Be sure to **discuss your needs before booking.**

DISCOUNTS & DEALS

You shouldn't have to pay for a discount. In fact, you may already be eligible for all kinds of savings. Here are some time-honored strategies for getting the best deal.

LOOK IN YOUR WALLET

When you **use your credit card to make travel purchases,** you may get free travel-accident insurance, collision damage insurance, medical or legal assistance, depending on the card and bank that issued it. Visa and MasterCard provide one or more of these services, so **get a copy of your card's travel benefits.** If you are a member of the AAA or an oil-company-sponsored road-assistance plan, always **ask hotel or car-rental reserva-**

tionists for auto-club discounts. Some clubs offer additional discounts on tours, cruises, or admission to attractions. And don't forget that auto-club membership entitles you to free maps and trip-planning services.

SENIORS CITIZENS & STUDENTS

As a senior-citizen traveler, you may be eligible for special rates, but you should mention your senior-citizen status up front. If you're a student or under 26, you can also get discounts, especially if you have an official ID card (☞ Senior-Citizen Discounts *and* Students on the Road, *below*).

DIAL FOR DOLLARS

To save money, **look into "1-800" discount reservations services,** which often have lower rates. These services use their buying power to get a better price on hotels, airline tickets, and sometimes even car rentals. When booking a room, always **call the hotel's local toll-free number** (if one is available) rather than the central reservations number—you'll often get a better price. Ask the reservationist about special packages or corporate rates, which are usually available even if you're not traveling on business.

JOIN A CLUB?

Discount clubs can be a legitimate source of savings, but you must use the participating hotels and visit the participating attractions in order to realize any benefits. Remember,

too, that you have to pay a fee to join, so **determine if you'll save enough to warrant your membership fee.** Before booking with a club, **make sure the hotel or other supplier isn't offering a better deal.**

GET A GUARANTEE

When shopping for the best deal on hotels and car rentals, **look for guaranteed exchange rates,** which protect you against a falling dollar. With your rate locked in, you won't pay more, even if the price goes up in the local currency.

DRIVING

DRIVING

Major work is being done on Portugal's highway system; a new superhighway runs between Lisbon and Oporto, and *autoestradas* (four-lane toll roads) circumvent many of the more congested areas of these cities. Most highway driving, however, is still on two-lane roads, with the risk of backups behind heavy trucks, but even so, it is the best way to see the rural areas and get off the beaten track.

In the north, the IP5 has improved the drive from Aveiro to the Spanish border at Guarda, so you're unlikely to get stuck in a line behind a truck. You can pick up the IP2 just southwest of Bragança and continue to Ourique in the Alentejo, where it connects to the IP1 straight down to Albufeira on the southern coast. This same IP1 is now an autoestrada from Albufeira east along the Algarve coast

to Ayamonte on the Spanish border. In the north, the IP4 crosses east from Porto through Vila Real, opening up the way to Bragança. Heading southeast from Lisbon through the southern part of the Alentejo, the new E52 highway connects Beija to Vilaverde de Ficalho, near the Spanish frontier town of Rosal de la Frontera. In the south, a new Algarve highway from Albufeira to Vila Real de Santo António runs inland from the coastal routes, defusing many frustrating delays.

Tolls seem steep in Portugal, but time saved by traveling the autoestradas usually makes them worthwhile.

RULES OF THE ROAD

Residents of EU countries can use their national driver's license in Portugal. Others should have an International Driver's Permit, although your national license and passport will usually suffice. Driving is on the right, and a red warning-triangle must be carried to place on the road behind your car in case of a breakdown. Seat belts are obligatory, and children under 12 must ride in the back seat. Horns are banned in built-up areas (but that doesn't seem to stop the Portuguese). The city speed limit is 60 kilometers (37 miles) per hour; on the autoestrada the limit is 120 kph (74 mph); on the *nacional* (national two-lane highway) the limit is 100 kph (62 mph), and on other roads it is 90 kph (56 mph) unless otherwise signposted.

Billboards warning you not to drink and drive dot the countryside, and punishable alcohol levels are low. Portuguese drivers are notoriously rash, and the country has one of the highest traffic-fatality rates in Europe, so driving defensively is strongly recommended.

GAS

Gas stations are plentiful throughout Portugal. Prices are controlled by the government and are the same everywhere. At press time gasoline cost 160$00 a liter (approximately ¼ gallon) for normal (92 octane) and 162$00 a liter for super (97 octane). Unleaded gas is now available for 165$00.

Credit cards are frequently accepted, especially along main roads.

FROM THE U.K.

The least expensive route to Portugal by car, though not necessarily the fastest, is by cross-channel ferry to France. The drawbacks are that the shortest and cheapest ferry crossing (Dover–Calais) leaves you with the greatest amount of driving; this can be tiring and expensive if you take toll roads through France and spend many nights en route. It is some 2,121 kilometers (1,318 miles) from Calais to Lisbon. For a distance such as this, unless time is short, consider going as far as possible by ferry, or using Motorail for part of the journey, to reduce the tiring

drive to a minimum. Brittany Ferries (✉ Millbay Docks, Plymouth, PL1 3EW, ☎ 01752/221–321) offers a range of vacation motor tours to Portugal via the Plymouth–Santander (northern Spain) ferry route, with lodging in hotels, private houses, or pousadas.

H
HEALTH

Sunburn and sunstroke are common problems in summer in mainland Portugal and virtually year-round in Madeira. On a hot, sunny day, even people not normally bothered by a strong sun should cover up with a long-sleeve shirt, a hat, and slacks or a beach wrap. Carry sunscreen for nose, ears, and other sensitive areas; be sure to drink enough liquids; and above all, limit your sun exposure for the first few days until you become accustomed to the heat.

No special shots are required before visiting Portugal (except for yellow-fever shots if you want to visit Madeira and have come from an infected area).

I
INSURANCE

Travel insurance can protect your monetary investment, replace your luggage and its contents, or provide for medical coverage should you fall ill during your trip. Most tour operators, travel agents, and insurance agents sell specialized health-and-accident, flight, trip-cancellation,

and luggage insurance as well as comprehensive policies with some or all of these coverages. Comprehensive policies may also reimburse you for delays due to weather—an important consideration if you're traveling during the winter months. Some health-insurance policies do not cover preexisting conditions, but waivers may be available in specific cases. Coverage is sold by the companies listed under Insurance in Important Contacts A to Z; these companies act as the policy's administrators. The actual insurance is usually underwritten by a well-known name, such as The Travelers or Continental Insurance.

Before you make any purchase, **review your existing health and home-owner's policies** to find out whether they cover expenses incurred while traveling.

BAGGAGE

Airline liability for baggage is limited to $1,250 per person on domestic flights. On international flights, it amounts to $9.07 per pound or $20 per kilogram for checked baggage (roughly $640 per 70-pound bag) and $400 per passenger for unchecked baggage. Insurance for losses exceeding the terms of your airline ticket can be bought directly from the airline at check-in for about $10 per $1,000 of coverage; note that it excludes a rather extensive list of items, as shown on your airline ticket.

COMPREHENSIVE

Comprehensive insurance policies include all the coverages described above plus some that may not be available in more specific policies. If you have purchased an expensive vacation, especially one that involves travel abroad, comprehensive insurance is a must; **look for policies that include trip-delay insurance,** which will protect you in the event that weather problems cause you to miss your flight, tour, or cruise. A few insurers will also sell you a waiver for preexisting medical conditions. Some of the companies that offer both these features are Access America, Carefree Travel, Travel Insured International, and Travel Guard (☞ Insurance *in* Important Contacts A to Z, *above*).

FLIGHT

You should **think twice before buying flight insurance.** Often purchased as a last-minute impulse at the airport, it pays a lump sum when a plane crashes, either to a beneficiary if the insured dies or sometimes to a surviving passenger who loses his or her eyesight or a limb. Supplementing the airlines' coverage described in the limits-of-liability paragraphs on your ticket, it's expensive and basically unnecessary. Charging an airline ticket to a major credit card often automatically provides you with coverage that may also extend to travel by bus, train, and ship.

HEALTH

Neither Medicare nor many privately issued policies generally covers health-care costs outside the United States. If your own health-insurance policy does not cover you outside the United States, **consider buying supplemental medical coverage.** It can reimburse you for $1,000–$150,000 worth of medical and/or dental expenses incurred as a result of an accident or illness during a trip. These policies also may include a personal-accident or death-and-dismemberment provision, which pays a lump sum ranging from $15,000 to $500,000 to your beneficiaries if you die or to you if you lose one or more limbs or your eyesight, and a medical-assistance provision, which may either reimburse you for the cost of referrals, evacuation, or repatriation and other services or automatically enroll you as a member of a particular medical-assistance company. (☞ Health *in* Important Contacts A to Z, *above*.)

U.K. TRAVELERS

You can buy an annual travel-insurance policy valid for most vacations during the year in which it's purchased. If you are pregnant or have a preexisting medical condition, make sure you're covered before buying such a policy.

TRIP

Without insurance, you will lose all or most of your money if you cancel your trip, regardless of the reason. Especially if your airline ticket, cruise, or package tour is nonrefundable and cannot be changed, it's essential that you **buy trip-cancellation-and-interruption insurance.** When considering how much coverage you need, look for a policy that will cover the cost of your trip plus the nondiscounted price of a one-way airline ticket should you need to return home early. Read the fine print carefully, especially sections that define "family member" and "preexisting medical conditions." Also **consider default or bankruptcy insurance,** which protects you against a supplier's failure to deliver. Be aware, however, that if you buy such a policy from a travel agency, tour operator, airline, or cruise line, it may not cover default by the firm in question.

L

LANGUAGE

Despite its Slavic-sounding inflections and nasal intonations, Portuguese is essentially a romance language, of Latin origin, and is now the seventh most widely spoken language in the world. Roughly half the people a tourist comes in contact with (at least in the larger cities) will speak some English. Any attempt by visitors to speak Portuguese will be warmly appreciated. Written Portuguese resembles Spanish, although pronunciation can be markedly different (*see* Vocabulary at the end of this guide).

THE GOLD GUIDE / SMART TRAVEL TIPS

THE GOLD GUIDE / SMART TRAVEL TIPS

Portugal offers accommodations to suit every taste and budget, from palaces to pensions, from mansions to ultramodern hotels. Many visitors design their itineraries around pousadas (☞ *below*). Luxurious resorts provide self-contained surroundings that can tempt guests not to leave.

There are new high-rise hotels in cities, *residências* (in what were once private homes—the term *residencial* is also often used), and *aparto* hotel-style pensions (with suites or one-bedroom units and kitchenettes) in the smallest of towns.

APARTMENT & VILLA RENTAL

If you want a home base that's roomy enough for a family and comes with cooking facilities, **consider taking a furnished rental.** This can also save you money, but not always—some rentals are luxury properties (economical only when your party is large). Home-exchange directories list rentals—often second homes owned by prospective house swappers—and some services search for a house or apartment for you (even a castle, if that's your fancy) and handle the paperwork. Some send an illustrated catalog; others send photographs only of specific properties, sometimes at a charge; up-front registration fees may apply.

CAMPING

More than 100 good campgrounds are available in Portugal, where camping has been on the upswing over the past few years. One of the largest is the *Monsanto Parque Florestal,* along the Estoril autostrada not far from the city center, with tennis, a swimming pool, a bank, a restaurant, cafés, a chapel, a library, a game room, and a minimarket. Another very pleasant site is five minutes from Guincho Beach, Cascais; it's operated by **Orbitur** (⊠ Rua Diogo Couto 1–8F, Lisbon 1100, ☎ 01/815–4871), which also has several other well-equipped camps, some with four-person chalets to rent.

COUNTRY HOUSES

Manors, farm estates, and country houses have been modified to receive small numbers of guests, in a fairly new venture called *Turismo de Habitação* (Country House Tourism), mostly operating in the north of the country. These guest houses, which offer an alternative kind of comfort, are in bucolic settings removed from the cities, near parks or monuments, and in historic villages. Breakfast is always included in the price.

HOME EXCHANGE

If you would like to find a house, an apartment, or some other type of vacation property to exchange for your own while on holiday, **become a member of a home-exchange organization,** which will send you its updated listings of available exchanges for a year and will include your own listing in at least one of them. Arrangements for the actual exchange are made by the two parties involved, not by the organization.

HOTELS

High season means not only the summer months, but also Easter week and anytime a town is holding a festival. However, in the off-season (November through March) many hotels' rates are as much as 20% lower. In Portugal, a Continental breakfast is usually included in the price of the room.

POUSADAS

The term **pousada** is derived from the Portuguese verb *pousar* (to rest). Portugal has an easily accessible network of more than 40 of these state-run hotels, which are in wonderfully restored castles, palaces, monasteries, convents, and other charming historic buildings. Each pousada is set in a particularly scenic and tranquil part of the country and is tastefully furnished with traditional regional crafts, antiques, and artwork. All have restaurants that present regional specialties; you may stop for a meal or a drink at a pousada without spending the night. Rates are reasonable, considering that most pousadas are four- and five-star hotels and a stay in a pousada can be the highlight of your visit. However, they are extremely popular with foreigners and Portuguese alike, so make reservations in advance, especially during summer months, since some have 10 or fewer rooms.

SPAS

Portugal has been favored with a profusion of thermal springs, whose waters reputedly can cure whatever ails you. In the smaller spas, hotels are rather simple; in the more famous ones, they are first-class. Most are open from May through October.

M

MAIL

Airmail letters to the United States and Canada cost 145$00 up to 15 grams, postcards are also 145$00. Letters to the United Kingdom and other countries in the European Union cost 90$00 up to 20 grams. Letters within Portugal are 65$00. Postcards are charged the same rate as letters. Stamps (*selos*) can be bought at post offices and government-run tobacco shops.

RECEIVING MAIL

Because mail delivery can often be slow and unreliable, it is best to have your mail sent to American Express (☎ 800/543–4080); call for lists of offices in Portugal. An alternative is to have mail held at a Portuguese post office; have it addressed to *lista de correios* (general delivery) in a town you will be visiting. Postal addresses should include the name of the province and district—for example, Figueira da Foz (Coimbra).

MEDICAL ASSISTANCE

No one plans to get sick while traveling, but it happens, so **consider signing up with a medical assistance company.** These outfits provide referrals, emergency evacuation or repatriation, 24-hour telephone hot lines for medical consultation, cash for emergencies, and other personal and legal assistance. They also dispatch medical personnel and arrange for the relay of medical records.

MONEY

Portugal's currency unit is the escudo, which is divided into 100 centavos. The number of escudos is written to the left of the $ sign and the centavos to the right; thus, 2 escudos and 50 centavos is written 2$50. Coins are issued for 200$00, 100$00, 50$00, 20$00, 10$00, 5$00, 2$50, and 1$00. Bills in circulation are for 10,000$00, 5,000$00, 2,000$00, 1,000$00, and 500$00. Units of 1,000$00 are often referred to as *contos*. At press time (summer 1996), the exchange rate was about 151$00 to the U.S. dollar, 115$00 per Canadian dollar, and 262$00 to the pound sterling.

ATMS

CASH ADVANCES➤ Before leaving home, **make sure that your credit cards have been programmed for ATM use** in Portugal. Note that Discover is accepted mostly in the United States. Local bank cards often do not work overseas either; **ask your bank about a MasterCard/Cirrus or Visa debit card,** which works like a bank card but can be used at any ATM displaying a MasterCard/Cirrus or Visa logo.

TRANSACTION FEES➤ Although fees charged for ATM transactions may be higher abroad than at home, Cirrus and Plus exchange rates are excellent because they are based on wholesale rates offered only by major banks.

COSTS

As Portugal moves to catch up with the rest of Europe, prices keep climbing; annual inflation runs around 8%. The weakening U.S. dollar has lost about 15% of its value against the escudo in recent years. Lisbon is still not as expensive as other international capitals, but it is not the extraordinary bargain it used to be. The coastal resort areas from Cascais and Estoril down to the Algarve can also be expensive, but lower-price hotels and restaurants catering mainly to the package-tour trade are certainly popular. The traveler who heads off the beaten track will find substantially cheaper food and lodging.

Transportation is still cheap in Portugal when compared with the rest of Europe. Gas prices are controlled by the government, and train and bus travel are inexpensive. Highway tolls are steep but may be worth the cost if you want to bypass the small towns and villages. Flights within the country on the state-owned TAP airlines are costly.

Some sample prices—Coffee in a bar: 80$00 (standing), 150$00 (seated). Draft beer in a bar: 100$00 (standing), 175$00 (seated); bottle of beer, 150$00. Small glass of wine in a bar: 80$00; glass of port: 175$00–2,000$00, depending on brand and vintage. Bottle of ordinary table wine (*vinho da casa*): 350$00; half bottle, 200$00. Coca-Cola: 100$00. Ham-and-cheese sandwich: 200$00. One-mile taxi ride: 250$00 (but the meter keeps ticking in traffic jams). Local bus ride: 150$00 if purchased from driver. Subway ride: 75$00. Ferry ride in Lisbon: 150$00–600$00 round-trip. Opera or theater seat: about 4,000$00–6,000$00, depending on location. Nightclub cover charge: 3,000$00–5,000$00. Fado performance: 2,500$00 cover charge or 5,000$00–6,000$000 for dinner. Movie ticket: 450$00–800$00 (depending which night of the week you go; Mondays are traditionally the lower-price ticket nights). Foreign newspaper: 250$00–300$00.

EXCHANGING CURRENCY

For the most favorable rates, **change money at banks.** You won't do as well at exchange booths in airports or rail and bus stations, in hotels, in restaurants, or in stores, although you may find their hours

more convenient. To avoid lines at airport exchange booths, **get a small amount of the local currency before you leave home.**

TAXES

HOTEL➤ Value-added tax (IVA) is 8% for hotels. By law prices must be posted at the reception desk and should indicate whether tax is included.

RESTAURANTS➤ Restaurant menus generally state at the bottom whether tax is included (*IVA incluido*) or not (*mas 8% IVA*). Higher-end restaurants are required to charge 8% IVA. When in doubt about whether tax is included in a price, ask: *Está incluido o IVA* (ee-vah)?

VAT➤ A number of shops, particularly large stores and shops in holiday resorts, offer a refund of the 12% IVA sales tax on large purchases (the purchase must be a single item worth more than 11,700$00, about $85). Be sure to ask for your tax-free check; you show your passport, fill out a form, and the store mails you the refund at home. Or for a cash refund before you leave the country, simply present the signed form and the merchandise at the tax-free counter at the airport or at the border crossing into Spain. If there is no tax-free refund counter when you leave the country, mail your forms back to the address listed on them, and the amount will either be transferred to your credit-card account or sent to

you as an international check.

TRAVELER'S CHECKS

Whether or not to buy traveler's checks depends on where you are headed: **Take cash to rural areas and small towns; traveler's checks to cities.** The most widely recognized checks are issued by American Express, Citicorp, Thomas Cook, and Visa. These are sold by major commercial banks, which will charge you 1%–3% of the checks' face value—it pays to **shop around.** Both American Express and Thomas Cook issue checks that can be countersigned and used by either you or your traveling companion. So you won't be left with excess foreign currency, **buy a few checks in small denominations** to cash toward the end of your trip. Before leaving home, **contact your issuer for information on where to cash your checks** without a incurring a transaction fee. Record the serial numbers of all your checks and keep this listing in a separate place, crossing off the numbers of checks you have cashed.

WIRING MONEY

For a fee of 3%–10%, depending on the amount of the transaction, you can have money sent to you from home through Money-Gram^SM or Western Union (☞ Money *in* Important Contacts A to Z, *above*). The transferred funds and the service fee can be charged to a Master-Card or Visa account.

P

PACKING FOR PORTUGAL

The Portuguese, like the Spanish, tend to dress up more than do Americans or the British. Summer can be brutally hot; spring and fall, mild to chilly; and winter, cold and rainy. Sightseeing calls for casual, comfortable clothing (well-broken-in low-heel shoes, for example), but in the cities, dressier outfits are needed for restaurants and nightclubs. American tourists can be spotted easily in Portugal because they wear sneakers; if you want to blend in, wear leather shoes instead. Jeans are another story: nowadays they blend in anywhere. For the most part, there is no dress code, but people still frown on shorts in churches, and bathing suits on the street or in restaurants and shops are not considered good taste.

Sunscreen and sunglasses are a good idea any time of the year, since the sun in Portugal is particularly bright. Bring an extra pair of eyeglasses or contact lenses in your carry-on luggage, and if you have a health problem, **pack enough medication** to last the trip or have your doctor write you a prescription using the drug's generic name, because brand names vary from country to country (you'll then need a duplicate prescription from a local doctor). It's important that you **don't put prescription drugs** or valuables in luggage to be checked, for it could go astray. To avoid problems with customs officials, carry medications in the original packaging. Also, remember to take addresses of offices that handle refunds of lost traveler's checks.

ELECTRICITY

To use your U.S.-purchased electric-powered equipment, **bring a converter and an adapter.** The electrical current in Portugal is 220 volts, 50 cycles alternating current (AC); wall outlets take plugs with two round prongs.

If your appliances are dual-voltage, you'll need only an adapter. Hotels sometimes have 110-volt outlets for low-wattage appliances near the sink. They are marked FOR SHAVERS ONLY; don't use them for high-wattage appliances like blow-dryers. If your laptop computer is older, carry a converter; new laptops operate equally well on 110 and 220 volts, so you only need an adapter.

LUGGAGE

Airline baggage allowances depend on the airline, the route, and the class of your ticket; ask in advance. In general, on domestic flights and on international flights between the United States and foreign destinations, you are entitled to check two bags. A third piece may be brought on board, but it must fit easily under the seat in front of you or in the overhead compartment. In the United States, the FAA gives airlines broad latitude regarding carry-on allowances, and they tend to tailor them to different aircraft and operational conditions. Charges for excess, oversize, or overweight pieces vary.

If you are flying between two foreign destinations, note that baggage allowances may be determined not by piece but by weight—generally 88 pounds (40 kilograms) in first class, 66 pounds (30 kilograms) in business class, and 44 pounds (20 kilograms) in economy. If your flight between two cities abroad *connects* with your transatlantic or transpacific flight, the piece method still applies.

SAFEGUARDING YOUR LUGGAGE➤ Before leaving home, **itemize your bags' contents** and their worth and label them with your name, address, and phone number. (If you use your home address, cover it so that potential thieves can't see it readily.) Inside each bag, **pack a copy of your itinerary.** At check-in, **make sure that each bag is correctly tagged** with the destination airport's three-letter code. If your bags arrive damaged—or fail to arrive at all—file a written report with the airline before leaving the airport.

PASSPORTS & VISAS

If you don't already have one, **get a passport.** It is advisable that you **leave one photo-copy of your passport's data page** with some-one at home and keep another with you, separated from your passport, while travel-ing. If you lose your passport, promptly call the nearest embassy or consulate and the local police; having the data page information can speed replacement.

IN THE U.S.

All U.S. citizens, even infants, need a valid passport to enter Portu-gal for stays of up to 60 days; no visa is re-quired. Application forms for both first-time and renewal pass-ports are available at any of the 13 U.S. Passport Agency offices and at some post offices and courthouses. Pass-ports are usually mailed within four weeks; allow five weeks or more in spring and summer.

CANADIANS

You only need a valid passport to enter Portu-gal for stays of up to 60 days. Passport applica-tion forms are available at 28 regional passport offices, as well as post offices and travel agen-cies. Whether for a first or a renewal passport, you must apply in person. Children under 16 may be included on a parent's passport but must have their own to travel alone. Passports are valid for five years and are usually mailed within two to three weeks of application.

U.K. CITIZENS

Citizens of the United Kingdom need only a valid passport to enter Portugal for stays of up to 60 days. Applica-tions for new and renewal passports are available from main post offices and at the passport offices in Belfast, Glasgow, Liver-pool, London, New-port, and Peterborough. You may apply in person at all passport offices or by mail to all except the London office. Children under 16 may travel on an accompanying parent's passport. All passports are valid for 10 years. Allow a month for processing.

S

SENIOR-CITIZEN DISCOUNTS

To qualify for age-related discounts, **mention your senior-citizen status up front** when booking hotel reservations, not when checking out, and before you're seated in restaurants, not when paying the bill. Note that discounts may be limited to certain menus, days, or hours. When renting a car, **ask about promotional car-rental discounts**—they can net even lower costs than your senior-citizen discount.

STUDENTS ON THE ROAD

To save money, **look into deals available through student-ori-ented travel agencies.** To qualify, you'll need to have a bona fide student ID card. Mem-bers of international student groups are also eligible (☞ Students *in* Important Contacts A to Z, *above*).

T

TELEPHONES

Public phones can be frustrating, and phone numbers in Portugal are being changed to a seven-digit system (often without notice), so you might have trouble getting through. Ask either at your hotel or at a local phone office for help. The easiest way to make a local call is to go into a café or bar and ask the bartender if you may use the phone. Bar phones are metered, and the bartender will charge you after you've finished.

At a pay phone, insert coins and wait for a dial tone. The minimum cost for a local call is 10$00, 50$00 to call another province, for which you must dial the area code. On the old pay phones, you line up the coins in a groove on top of the dial, and they drop down as needed. The new CrediFone or T-Sete phone booths take phone debit cards, which can be purchased at post offices for either 800$00 or 1,800$00. These phones have digital readouts, so you can see your time tick-ing away, and they are uncomplicated to use—the booths have instruc-tions in several languages, including English. The phones accept Visa and Master-Card, and a country-wide "freephone" information line can be reached at 145311, 145883, or 145662.

To make calls to other areas within Portugal, precede the provincial code with 0 (most phone booths have a chart inside listing the various province codes). The 0 is unnecessary when dialing from outside Portugal.

LONG-DISTANCE

Calling abroad is awkward from public pay phones and can be expensive from hotels, which often add a considerable surcharge. The best way to make an international call is to go to the local telephone office and have someone place it for you. Every town has an office, and big cities have several. When the call is connected, you will be sent to a quiet cubicle and charged according to the meter. If the price is 500$00 or more, you may pay with Visa or Master-Card or use the Credi-Fone card (☞ *above*). In Lisbon the main telephone office is in the Praça dos Restauradores, right off the Rossio.

To make an international call yourself, dial 00 and wait for a tone. Then dial the country code (1 for the United States; 44 for the United Kingdom), followed by the area code and number.

The long-distance services of AT&T, MCI, and Sprint make calling home relatively convenient, but in many hotels you may find it impossible to dial the access number. The hotel operator may also refuse to make the connection. Instead, the hotel will charge you a premium rate—as much as 400% more than a calling card—for calls placed from your hotel room. To avoid such price gouging, travel with more than one company's long-distance calling card—a hotel may block Sprint but not MCI. If the hotel operator claims that you cannot use any phone card, ask to be connected to an international operator, who will help you to access your phone card. You can also dial the international operator yourself. If none of this works, try calling your phone company collect in the United States. If collect calls are also blocked, call from a pay phone in the hotel lobby.

Dial 05017–1–288, and you'll be connected with an **AT&T** operator in the States. For an **MCI** operator, dial 05017–1–234, and to access **Sprint,** dial 05017–1–877. You can then make a collect or calling-card call.

OPERATORS AND INFORMATION

The national number for emergencies is 115; for general information dial, 118; the international information and assistance operator is 098. These are good numbers to keep handy, since Portugal is in the process of changing numbers and adding digits.

TIPPING

Service is included in café, restaurant, and hotel bills, but waiters and other service people are poorly paid, and you can be sure your contribution will be appreciated. However, if you received bad service, never feel obligated (or intimidated) to leave a tip. An acceptable tip is 10%–15% of the total bill, and if you have a sandwich or *petiscos* (appetizers) at a bar, leave less, just enough to round out the bill to the nearest 100. Cocktail waiters get 50$00–75$00 a drink, depending on the bar.

Taxi drivers get about 10% of the meter, but more for long rides or extra help with luggage, and there is an official surcharge for airport runs and baggage.

Hotel porters are tipped 100$00 a bag; 100$00 also goes for room service or a doorman who calls you a taxi. If you stay in a hotel for more than two nights, tip the maid about 100$00 per night. The concierge should be tipped for any additional help he or she gives you.

Tour guides should be tipped about 200$00–500$00; ushers in theaters or bullfights, 100$00; barbers, at least 100$00; hairdressers, at least 200$00 for a wash and set. Washroom attendants are tipped 100$00.

TOUR OPERATORS

A package or tour to Portugal can make your vacation less expensive and more hassle-free. Firms that sell tours and packages reserve airline seats, hotel rooms, and rental cars in bulk and pass some of the savings on to you. In addition, the best operators have local representatives available to help you at your destination.

THE GOLD GUIDE / SMART TRAVEL TIPS

A GOOD DEAL?

The more your package or tour includes, the better you can predict the ultimate cost of your vacation. Make sure you know exactly what is covered and **beware of hidden costs.** Are taxes, tips, and service charges included? Transfers and baggage handling? Entertainment and excursions? These can add up.

Most packages and tours are rated deluxe, first-class superior, first class, tourist, or budget. The key difference is usually accommodations. If the package or tour you are considering is priced lower than in your wildest dreams, **be skeptical.** Also, **make sure your travel agent knows the accommodations** and other services. Ask about the hotel's location, room size, beds, and whether it has a pool, room service, or programs for children, if you care about these. Has your agent been there in person or sent others you can contact?

BUYER BEWARE

Each year a number of consumers are stranded or lose their money when operators—even very large ones with excellent reputations—go out of business. To avoid becoming one of them, take the time to **check out the operator**—find out how long the company has been in business and ask several agents about its reputation. Next, **don't book unless the firm has a consumer-protection program.** Members of the

USTOA and the NTA are required to set aside funds for the sole purpose of covering your payments and travel arrangements in case of default. Nonmember operators may instead carry insurance; look for the details in the operator's brochure—and for the name of an underwriter with a solid reputation. Note: When it comes to tour operators, **don't trust escrow accounts.** Although there are laws governing those of charter-flight operators, no governmental body prevents tour operators from raiding the till.

Next, **contact your local Better Business Bureau and the attorney general's office** in both your own state and the operator's; have any complaints been filed? Finally, **pay with a major credit card.** Then you can cancel payment, provided that you can document your complaint. Always **consider trip-cancellation insurance** (☞ Insurance, *above*).

BIG VS. SMALL➤ Operators that handle several hundred thousand travelers per year can use their purchasing power to give you a good price. Their high volume may also indicate financial stability. But some small companies provide more personalized service; because they tend to specialize, they may also be more knowledgeable about a given area.

USING AN AGENT

Travel agents are excellent resources. In fact, large operators accept

bookings made only through travel agents. But it's good to **collect brochures from several agencies** because some agents' suggestions may be skewed by promotional relationships with tour and package firms that reward them for volume sales. If you have a special interest, **find an agent with expertise in that area;** ASTA can provide leads in the United States. (Don't rely solely on your agent, though; agents may be unaware of small-niche operators, and some special-interest travel companies only sell direct.)

SINGLE TRAVELERS

Prices are usually quoted per person, based on two sharing a room. If traveling solo, you may be required to pay the full double-occupancy rate. Some operators eliminate this surcharge if you agree to be matched up with a roommate of the same sex, even if one is not found by departure time.

TRAIN TRAVEL

Portugal is one of 17 countries in which you can **use EurailPasses,** which provide unlimited first-class rail travel in all of the participating countries for the duration of the pass. If you plan to rack up the miles, get a standard pass. These are available for 15 days ($522), 21 days ($678), one month ($838), two months ($1,148), and three months ($1,468).

In addition to standard EurailPasses, **ask about special rail-pass plans.**

Among these are the Eurail Youthpass (for those under age 26), the Eurail Saverpass (which gives a discount for two or more people traveling together), a Eurail Flexipass (which allows a certain number of travel days within a set period), the Euraildrive Pass, and the Europass Drive (which combines travel by train and rental car).

Whichever pass you choose, remember that you must **purchase your pass before you leave** for Europe.

Many travelers assume that rail passes guarantee them seats on the trains they wish to ride. Not so. You need to **book seats ahead even if you are using a rail pass**; seat reservations are required on some European trains, particularly high-speed trains, and are a good idea on trains that may be crowded—particularly in summer on popular routes. You will also need a reservation if you purchase sleeping accommodations.

SMOKING

CP provides no-smoking cars on all long-distance trips and most short runs; be sure to specify if you want a no-smoking seat or bunk, because many Portuguese will contentedly smoke all night long.

FROM THE U.K.

Train services to Portugal are not as frequent, fast, or inexpensive as plane travel. Getting to Lisbon by rail takes 2–2½ days; the fastest connection to Paris is the **Hoverspeed City**

Link rail–hovercraft–rail service from London's Victoria Station, with up to four daily departures to choose from. From Paris the luxurious overnight Paris–Madrid TALGO or the Puerta del Sol leave the Gare d'Austerlitz, transfer in Madrid to the Lisboa Express, and reach Lisbon in about nine hours. Advance reservations are obligatory in both trains; book well in advance to guarantee a place.

TRAVEL GEAR

Travel catalogs specialize in useful items that can **save space when packing** and make life on the road more convenient. Compact alarm clocks, travel irons, travel wallets, and personal-care kits are among the most common items you'll find. They also carry dual-voltage appliances, currency converters and foreign-language phrase books. Some catalogs even carry miniature coffeemakers and water purifiers.

U

U.S.
GOVERNMENT

The U.S. government can be an excellent source of travel information. Some is free and some available for a nominal charge. When planning your trip, **find out what government materials are available.** For just a couple of dollars, you can get a variety of publications from the Consumer Information Center in Pueblo, Colorado. Free consumer

information also is available from individual government agencies, such as the Department of Transportation or the U.S. Customs Service. For specific titles, *see* the appropriate publications entry *in* Important Contacts A to Z, *above.*

W

WHEN TO GO

The tourist season begins in spring and lasts through the autumn. In midsummer it is never unbearably hot (except in parts of the Algarve and on the mainland plains), and it is especially pleasant along the coast, where a cool breeze springs up in the evening. Winter is mild and frequently rainy, except in Madeira, where winter has long been popular; off-season travelers throughout the country have the advantage of reduced hotel rates. In the Algarve, springtime begins in February with a marvelous range of wildflowers. Late September and early October herald Indian summer, which ensures warm sunshine through November.

PUBLIC HOLIDAYS

January 1 (New Year's Day), February 11 (Mardi Gras—a holiday in Lisbon and other towns), March 28 (Good Friday), April 25 (Liberty Day), May 1 (Labor Day), June 10 (Portugal's and Camões Day; also Corpus Christi), June 13 (St. Anthony's Day—Lisbon), August 15 (Assumption), October 5 (Republic Day), November 1 (All Saints'

Day), December 1 (Independence Day), December 8 (the Feast of the Immaculate Conception), December 24 (Christmas Eve), and December 25 (Christmas Day).

If a national holiday falls on a Tuesday or Thursday, many businesses also close on the Monday or Friday in between, for a long weekend called a *ponte* (bridge).

CLIMATE

The following are average daily maximum and minimum temperatures for major cities in Portugal.

FARO

Jan.	59F	15C	May	72F	22C	Sept.	79F	26C
	48	9		57	14		66	19
Feb.	61F	16C	June	77F	25C	Oct.	72F	22C
	50	10		64	18		61	16
Mar.	64F	18C	July	82F	28C	Nov.	66F	19C
	52	11		68	20		55	13
Apr.	68F	20C	Aug.	82F	28C	Dec.	61F	16C
	55	13		68	20		60	10

LISBON

Jan.	57F	14C	May	71F	21C	Sept.	79F	26C
	46	8		55	13		62	17
Feb.	59F	15C	June	77F	25C	Oct.	72F	22C
	47	8		60	15		58	14
Mar.	63F	17C	July	81F	27C	Nov.	63F	17C
	50	10		63	17		52	11
Apr.	67F	20C	Aug.	82F	28C	Dec.	58F	15C
	53	12		63	17		47	9

PORTO

Jan.	55F	13C	May	68F	20C	Sept.	75F	24C
	41	5		52	11		57	14
Feb.	57F	14C	June	73F	23C	Oct.	70F	21C
	41	5		55	13		52	11
Mar.	61F	16C	July	77F	25C	Nov.	63F	17C
	46	8		59	15		46	8
Apr.	64F	18C	Aug.	77F	25C	Dec.	57F	14C
	48	9		59	15		41	5

1 Destination: Portugal

WHERE EUROPE AND THE ATLANTIC MEET

WEST ACROSS THE Iberian Peninsula from Spain's arid plains and burning sun, Portugal springs perhaps Europe's greatest surprise on the unwary traveler. Its landscape unfolds in astonishing variety to reveal a mountainous, green interior and a sweeping coastline. Portugal provides many things you might expect if you're familiar with Spain, including fine food and wine, spectacularly sited castles, medieval hilltop villages, and excellent beaches. But the similarities are far outweighed by the myriad differences, by the country's delightful distinctions. Portugal seems to revel in its often contrary identity. Despite its proximity, the language is a world apart from Spanish; and though, like Spain, Portugal has a Mediterranean air, it is firmly Atlantic facing. Even the people seem undecided as to their origins, looking markedly Celtic in the north and rather Moorish in the south. But most important for the visitor, Portugal sees far less tourism than Spain, and it's still possible to travel into the heart of the provinces and be among few, if any, visitors.

High economic growth (in excess of that of most of its European partners) and heavy foreign investment have benefited large sectors of the population. Many people are employed in the tourism industry, which now accounts for about 10% of the country's gross national product. Accordingly, the resort areas and cities are now anything but undiscovered: The Algarve coast, for example, is one of Europe's most visited regions. Lisbon, too, has rapidly acquired the trappings of a forward-looking commercial capital. Many of its turn-of-the-century buildings are being replaced by skyscrapers, and renovation and modernization have touched every part of the capital. Much of the architecture and culture that once made Portugal unique now stand side by side with contemporary styles and lifestyles, an all-too-familiar development in late-20th-century Europe. Away from Lisbon and the busy Algarve, however, there are still country villages, isolated beaches, crumbling historic towns, and hidden valleys that have barely changed over the past few hundred years.

The Romans and the Moors

Blessed with a salubrious climate and abundant game and fish, this part of the Iberian Peninsula once supported a flourishing prehistoric population. Few traces of the culture remain, however, save the sculpted-stone boar fertility symbols found in Trás-os-Montes and the huge Colossus of Pedralva, a mysterious seated figure in granite, on display in the Museu Martins Sarmento in Guimarães. The later arrival of Celtic peoples in northern Portugal (700 BC–600 BC) is recorded in a series of *citânias* (fortified hill settlements), which appear throughout the Minho; the most impressive example is at Briteiros, between Braga and Guimarães. Phoenicians traded at the site of present-day Lisbon, and the Carthaginians and Greeks set up trading posts on Portugal's southern shore, but it wasn't until the Roman annexation of the peninsula after the Second Punic War (218–202 BC) that the region came under any kind of unified control.

There was resistance to the Roman advance, particularly in central Portugal, where the heroic chieftain Viriatus of the Lusitani tribe held the legions at bay for several decades, until his eventual defeat in 139 BC. Despite the subsequent colonization of much of the country, little of the Roman period survives in modern Portugal. Roads, aqueducts, and elegant bridges (like those at Chaves and Ponte de Lima) were built, and cities founded, though the only substantial remains are at Évora, where there's a fine temple from the 2nd century, and at the preserved Roman town of Conimbriga, near Coimbra. A less obvious Roman relic is the system of vast agricultural estates—latifundia—established in the Alentejo. Here the Romans introduced the crops that are now mainstays of the Portuguese economy: wheat, barley, olives, and grapes.

The Moorish invasion of the Iberian Peninsula in 711 had a lasting effect on the country, particularly in the south, where place-names and people's features still reflect those times. The Moors established a capital at Silves in the Algarve (derived from the Moorish, *al-Gharb,* meaning "west of the land beyond"), planted great orchards on irrigated land, and spread a Moorish Arab culture of great significance, although they allowed freedom of worship.

Arab rule stood firm until the 12th century, when Christian forces under Dom (King) Afonso Henriques moved south from their stronghold at Guimarães in the Minho to take successive Moorish towns and castles at Leiria, Santarém, and Sintra. The ramparts and battlements of these fortresses are all visible today, a reminder of both the Moorish genius for siting defenses and of the Christian effort involved in overcoming them. The most significant victory was at Lisbon in 1147, with the storming of the Moorish fortress on the site of the present-day Castelo de São Jorge. A Burgundian by descent, Afonso Henriques was by then being called the first king of all Portugal, and he ordered the building of Lisbon's proud Sé (cathedral) in celebration of the victory. Many other churches in Portugal mark the path of the reconquest (as the Moors were pushed south), particularly the numerous Romanesque chapels that cover the landscape between the Rio Minho and Rio Douro.

Southern Alentejo and the Algarve remained in Arab hands until the mid-13th century, by which time the fledgling kingdom of Portugal extended to its current borders. The country reached its final shape in 1260, when Afonso III—who retook Faro and the western Algarve from the Moors—moved the capital from Coimbra to Lisbon.

An Empire on the Atlantic

The early kings of Portugal, from the dynastic House of Burgundy, moved quickly to establish their independent country. Recognition was gained from the neighboring Castilian rulers, although fortresses were built along the Spanish frontier as a precaution. Those at Beja and Estremoz are evocative examples. A *Cortes* (parliament) was assembled, and a university founded, initially in Lisbon in 1290 but transferred to Coimbra in 1308. (The grand university buildings that you see in Coimbra today date from the 16th century, when the scholastic foundation was declared permanent, but the evident sense of pride in the city goes back to the university's origins; it remained the only university in Portugal until this century.)

The House of Burgundy was succeeded by the House of Aviz, whose first king, Dom João I, roundly defeated the Castilian army at the Battle of Aljubarrota (1385) to end any lingering Castilian thoughts of dominion over Portugal. It was a significant victory, which secured the independence of Portugal for nearly two centuries and allowed Portuguese kings to turn their attention to the maritime ventures that were to guarantee them fabulous colonial wealth. João I marked the victory by building the extraordinarily beautiful abbey of Santa Maria da Vitoria at Batalha in Estremadura, not far from the battlefield. Triumphant in tone, the abbey celebrates not only the Portuguese release from Castilian interference, but also an important historic link with England. The Treaty of Windsor, signed a year after the battle, confirmed the Anglo-Portuguese alliance, and in 1387 João I married Philippa of Lancaster, daughter of John of Gaunt. Philippa and João are buried side by side in the abbey's chapel, as are their children, one of whom was Prince Henry the Navigator, the man who did the most to influence Portugal's rapid 15th-century expansion.

Based at Sagres, on the western tip of the Algarve, Prince Henry surrounded himself with seamen, mapmakers, and astrologers. Under the protection of the mighty *fortaleza* (fortress), which still stands, these men were the first to establish the principles of navigation on the high seas. The caravelle, a ship capable of navigating in a crosswind, was developed, and famous maritime discoveries were soon under way: Madeira and the Azores were discovered in 1419 and 1427, respectively, and by 1460 (when Henry died) the west coast of Africa was known to Portuguese seamen. There were no limits to the inquisitiveness or to the bravery of the Portuguese sailors. Bartolomeu Dias rounded the southern tip of Africa in 1487, naming it the Cape of Good Hope; just 10 years later, Vasco da Gama reached India; and in 1500 Pedro Alvares Cabral sailed to Brazil. By the mid-16th century, the Portuguese empire had spread over four continents, with trading posts in the Far East and a Portuguese monopoly in force throughout the Indian Ocean.

The wealth gained from this aggressive expansionism knew no bounds. Portugal was at the height of her influence, with Lisbon the richest city in Europe, and under Dom Manuel I (1495–1521), the Crown intervened to take a fifth of the maritime trading profits. With the proceeds, Manuel began to adorn Portugal with buildings and monuments worthy of an imperial power, and the late-Gothic architecture that evolved has since come to be called Manueline style. If there's any doubt about the brimming confidence of that era, one look at the Manueline buildings of Portugal will dispel it immediately. The interior decoration of the Igreja de Jesus (Church of Jesus), begun in 1494 in Setúbal, near Lisbon, is generally considered to be the earliest appearance of the Manueline style in Portugal. It was soon overshadowed by exuberant works in the capital itself, at Belém, where the Mosteiro dos Jerónimos (Jerónimos Monastery) and the Torre de Belém (Belém Tower) are two of the most visited surviving examples in the country. The abbey of Batalha was transformed by its Manueline renovations, in particular the portal of the Capelas Imperfeitas (Unfinished Chapels), which is among the most impressive of all Manueline works. A tour of any of these buildings is a requisite to understanding the untrammeled power and influence of 16th-century Portugal, but also perhaps to recognizing the strong national identity that the Portuguese retain today. The pride in these buildings, which goes beyond mere architectural prowess, is most evident in Tomar's Convento de Cristo, whose supreme Manueline ornamentation (windows of the Chapter House) stands as the most eloquent reminder of the Portuguese age of discovery.

The buildings have survived, but the glories of the Portuguese empire were relatively short-lived. Arts and literature flourished for a while with the emergence of the 16th-century dramatist Gil Vicente and the publication in 1572 of the great poet Luís de Camões's epic *Lusiads,* which told of the proud era of discovery. But the disastrous crusade in Morocco by the young Dom Sebastião in 1578, where the king perished alongside most of the country's nobility, allowed Phillip II of Spain to renew his claim to Portugal. Camões

died in the same year Portugal fell to Spain, and it's said his last words were, "I am dying at the same time as my country."

Portugal's Dark Ages

Spanish rule lasted 60 years (1580–1640), during which time many of Portugal's overseas possessions were lost, but in 1640 the Portuguese took back their throne when a nobleman from the powerful Portuguese House of Bragança was installed as Dom João IV. The Bragança dynasty was to last until the first years of the 20th century, but for the most part there was a hollow ring to its pretensions as a power. Fueled by the gold and diamonds extracted from Brazil, there was extravagant spending on irrationally grand projects, like the massive monastery at Mafra (which employed 50,000 workmen), the university library at Coimbra, and the excessive decoration of the Capela de São João Baptista (Chapel of St. John the Baptist) in Lisbon. However, with the domestic economy still weak, and society strictly feudal, it took the appalling devastation of the 1755 earthquake, which destroyed Lisbon, to breathe new life into commerce and industry.

The king's chief minister at the time, the Marquês de Pombal, ordered that the capital's dead be buried and the living fed. He then immediately set about creating a new, planned Lisbon that took heed of the most advanced architectural and social ideas of the age, resulting in an elegant but restrained style of building later known as Pombaline. To walk through downtown Lisbon today is to walk through shades of the 18th century, starting in the elegant, colonnaded riverside square, the Praça do Comércio, and through the gridded Baixa (Lower) District, expressly designed by Pombal to house the trades and commercial concerns he was keen to promote. Lisbon's glory is its 18th-century buildings and its sense of measured space, an early example of town planning that's repeated elsewhere in Portugal, most notably in the gridded streets of Vila Real de Santo António, the easternmost town of the Algarve.

These developments proved to be mere diversions from the economic, social, and moral poverty of the Portuguese crown. Napoléon's invasions during the Peninsular War left the country devastated, and the monarchy was finally overthrown in 1910. A republic was proclaimed, but the rot of instability had set in, and during the next 16 years 44 different governments attempted to rescue Portugal from its malaise. A coup d'état followed in 1926, and from 1928 onward the country was governed by the right-wing dictatorship of António Salazar, who—first as minister of finance, then as prime minister—was strongly influenced by the contemporary Italian and Spanish fascist movements led by Mussolini and Franco, respectively. The dictatorship was to last until 1974.

Contemporary Politics, Culture, and Economy

In the 20th century, industrialization passed Portugal by, the economy remained agricultural, the political system was unreformed, and the lot of the people did not improve. The country preserved its age-old traditions and customs within an almost feudal social structure, causing it to fall behind developing nations. Portugal was ready for change. In 1968 its government appointed Dr. Marcelo Caetano to replace then-dictator António de Oliveira Salazar, who had just suffered a severe stroke. Long-brewing discontent in the African colonies of Angola and Mozambique led to the revolution that occurred six years later, on April 25, 1974, in which Caetano was ousted in a virtually bloodless coup (fewer than 20 people were killed) led by General António de Spinola. It was the move that the Portuguese people had long awaited, and huge demonstrations in support of the left-wing, officer-led Movimento das Forças Armadas (Armed Forces Movement) left no doubt that Portugal had entered a new era. The remaining colonies were granted independence. Initially it was a relatively peaceful operation in Mozambique and Guinea-Bissau, but in Angola and East Timor it was fraught with conflict. Land on the huge estates of the Alentejo was redistributed, and in the name of democracy, free elections produced a popular Socialist government.

Today Portugal is a stable country, its people keen to share in the prosperity offered by the developments within the European Union, of which it held the presidency in 1992. In 1994 the capital came of age when Lisbon was selected as European City of Culture. The government has shifted steadily to the right since the heady days of revolution; the Social Democrats have been the largest party in government since 1985. Visitors may find the obvious stability surprising, given the relatively short time since the revolution, and indeed it speaks well for the inherent qualities of the Portuguese people. Moreover, since 1975 more than 700,000 refugees from former Portuguese colonies in Africa and Indonesia have been absorbed into the country—a remarkable integration in that short period, given that the refugees now represent more than 7% of the total population.

The refugees have bestowed a welcome new face on Portugal; in Lisbon, for example, African music and dance is extremely popular, and dozens of places serve authentic Brazilian, Mozambican, Angolan, and Goan food. And in the final chapter of Portugal's colonial adventures, because the country has agreed to take in as many citizens of Macau as wish to leave before the handover of that territory to China in 1999, there are sure to be more Chinese and Macanese restaurants opening up. There's a buoyancy in other cultural matters, too, with Lisbon, Porto, Coimbra, and other major towns providing visitors with plenty of opportunity to see the best in contemporary Portuguese art, music, and dance. Excellent modern-art museums in both Porto and Lisbon are high on many itineraries: the painter Maria-Helena Vieira da Silva is the most famous name Portugal has produced this century, though others have also been influential, including pioneer modernist Almada Negreiros, and Amadeu de Sousa Cardoso (who has a separate gallery for his works in Amarante). Contemporary writers whose works are translated into English include José Cardoso Pires, António Lobo Antunes, and José Saramago, and architects strive to recreate that imperial Portuguese sense of confidence in their buildings—Lisbon's vast, colorful Amoreiras shopping and residential complex and the new Cultural Center in Belém are as bold as such projects come.

Political stability and artistic confidence couldn't have been maintained without improvements in the economy, and there have been great strides forward since 1974. Membership in the European Union has undoubtedly helped in reviving the economy, with grants and subsidies paying for the modernization of agriculture; massive aid and loans from the United States have also played a part. One effect of this regeneration is that Portugal has become more expensive over the last few years, though you're unlikely to find costs prohibitive. The government, of course, faces its own problems, not least a marked disparity in economic development between the north and south of the country. In addition, there are relatively high illiteracy and infant mortality rates; inflation causes concern; and agriculture is stubbornly inefficient, despite modernization.

The challenges to the government and people of Portugal during the remainder of the 1990s are clear, and there are few countries in Europe better equipped to deal with them, since a young democracy often has an uncommon will to succeed. But there's a challenge to the visitor, too. Take time to get off the beaten track, and you'll be rewarded—more than anywhere else in western Europe—with glimpses of a traditional life and culture that has been shaped by the memories of empire and tempered by the experience of revolution.

WHAT'S WHERE

The major surprise for most visitors to Portugal is its topography: It's a far greener land than Spain, with a riot of flowers, trees, and shrubs that provide color and shade throughout the country. There's also an enormous variety of landscapes in this relatively small European nation. A long rectangle slightly larger than the state of Indiana, it's just 560 kilometers (350 miles) from north to south and 220 kilometers (138 miles) at its widest east–west point. It's bordered on the north and east by Spain and on the south and west by the Atlantic Ocean and is temperate year-round, especially along the coasts. Portugal rarely suffers the extreme heat of other southern European countries.

Lisbon

With a total population of about 1 million, Lisbon is one of Europe's smallest capital cities, and to many visitors, it immediately becomes one of the most likeable. In parts of the city, the centuries seem to collide: Out of 17th-century buildings trip designer-clad youths; the fish market at Cais do Sodré resonates with traditional sights and smells; and just a few minutes' walk from Lisbon's 18th-century aqueduct sits Portugal's modernistic Amoreiras Shopping Center.

Lisbon's Environs

The palaces, gardens, and luxury *quintas* (country manor houses) of Sintra are justly celebrated. At Cascais and Estoril life revolves around the sea, and visitors can take part in time-honored pastimes: a stroll along the shore, a seafood meal, a game of tennis, a flutter at the casino. To the north, around Guincho's rocky promontory and the Praia das Maças coast, the Atlantic Ocean is often windswept and rough, but there's good sailboarding and surfing, as well as excellent views for coastal drives.

The best of the sand beaches lie to the south of the Rio Tejo, on the Setúbal Peninsula, a scenic area known for its rural traditions, festivals, and agriculture. Visitors can laze around at Sesimbra Beach, sample some of the county's best wines, explore the attractive, dramatic mountain scenery of the Serra da Arrábida (Arrábida Mountains), and indulge themselves by lodging in one of two ancient castles, now converted into *pousadas* (luxury inns). One is in the large port of Setúbal, where architectural history was made in the late-15th century with the building of the first church in the Manueline style.

The Estremadura and the Ribatejo

The provinces of the Estremadura and the Ribatejo extend north and east of Lisbon, following a line drawn by the wide valley of the Rio Tejo (River Tagus). The populous Estremadura's rolling hills and glorious coastline contain some of the country's most famous towns and monuments. Summers are long, hot, and bright, particularly in the seaside resorts, which stretch south as far as the Estoril Coast, west of Lisbon. There's a unique microclimate at work here, which ensures that the winters are milder than in the capital; in summer, the resorts of Estoril and Cascais enjoy a permanent breeze that offsets the high temperatures that plague Lisbon itself. Out of the capital, and across the Rio Tejo, you're soon in the Ribatejo (literally translated as the "banks of the

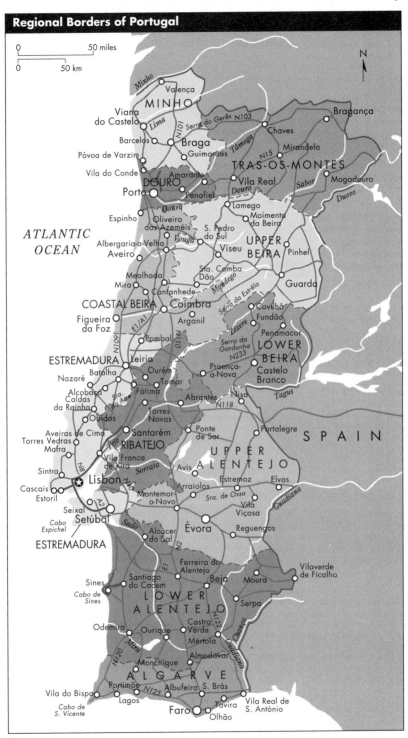

Regional Borders of Portugal

0   50 miles
0   50 km

N

ATLANTIC OCEAN

MINHO

Valença

Viana do Castelo

Barcelos

Póvoa de Varzim

Vila do Conde

Braga

Guimarães

DOURO

Porto

Espinho

Amarante

Penafiel

Oliveira dos Azeméis

Albergaria-a-Velha

Aveiro

Serra do Gerês   N103

Chaves

Mirandela

TRAS-OS-MONTES

Bragança

Vila Real

Mogadouro

Sabor

Lamego

Moimenta da Beira

S. Pedro do Sul

Viseu

UPPER BEIRA

Pinhel

Mealhada

Mira

Cantanhede

Sta. Comba Dão

COASTAL BEIRA

Coimbra

Guarda

Figueira da Foz

Arganil

Serra da Estrêla

Covilhã

Fundão

Pombal

ESTREMADURA

Leiria

Ourém

Nazaré

Batalha

Fátima

Tomar

Alcobaça

Caldas da Rainha

Óbidos

Torres Novas

Abrantes

Nisa

Serra da Gardunha   N233

Proença-a-Nova

LOWER BEIRA

Penamacor

Castelo Branco

Tagus

Aveiras de Cima

Torres Vedras

Mafra

Sintra

Cascais

Estoril

Santarém

RIBATEJO

Vila Franca de Xira

Ponte de Sor

Portalegre

S P A I N

UPPER ALENTEJO

Avis

Arraiolos

Estremoz

Elvas

Cabo Espichel

Lisbon

Seixal

Setúbal

Montemor-o-Novo

Sra. de Ossa

Vila Viçosa

Reguengos

Guadiana

ESTREMADURA

Alcácer do Sal

Évora

Ferreira do Alentejo

Sines

Cabo de Sines

Santiago do Cacém

Beja

Moura

Vilaverde de Ficalho

Serpa

Odemira

Ourique

Castro Verde

Mértola

LOWER ALENTEJO

Chança

Almodôvar

Monchique

ALGARVE

Portimão

Vila do Bispo

Lagos

Cabo de S. Vicente

Albufeira

S. Brás

Faro

Tavira

Olhão

Vila Real de S. António

River Tagus"), famous as a bull-breeding district, whose mainly flat lands fade into the vast plains of the southern Alentejo region.

Évora and the Alentejo

Once known as the granary of Portugal, the Alentejo is a thinly populated, largely agricultural region of grain fields, cork, and olive trees and is as remote in its way as Trás-os-Montes (☞ Porto and the North, *below*), though with none of the compensating grandeur. That said, there are some impressive Atlantic beaches (whipped year-round by a strong wind), and a pretty eastern section, where the Rio Guadiana forms the frontier with Spain. In the Alentejo summer starts early (March), and there's little shade from the sun. There's also very little rainfall, except perhaps in early spring and autumn.

The Algarve

Dividing the Alentejo from Portugal's southernmost coastal province, the Algarve, is a continuous range of mountains—the Serra de Monchique (Monchique Mountains) and the Serra de Caldeirão (Caldeirão Mountains). The Algarve boasts some 3,000 hours of sunshine annually, and its low-lying plains, rocky coastline (in the west), sand-bar islands (in the east), and sweeping beaches make up Portugal's busiest tourist region. In August, when the sun is hottest, this is probably the Portuguese province where the midday heat is most unbearable, though it's easy to cool off in a pool or in the sea. The Algarve is also the only real year-round destination in Portugal, despite the general clemency of the climate elsewhere. The region feels semitropical: Coastal winter days are warm and bright, the wildflowers strung across the low hills start to bloom early in February, and temperatures stay high until late October.

Coimbra and the Beiras

The central Beira region contains Portugal's highest mountains, the Serra da Estrela (Estrela Mountains), which reach a height of 6,530 feet and offer the country's best hiking and skiing. In the Beira Alta (Upper Beira)—between Viseu, Guarda, and Covilha—the winter frost is fierce, and the wind whistles through a string of hill towns that, while little known to foreigners, are at the heart of Portugal's history. As in the very north of the country, there's a distinct geographical and climatic shift as you move west toward the coast, leaving the mountains behind for the fertile expanses of the Beira Litoral (Coastal Beira) plain. It's a temperate, low-lying country, threatened by flooding from the mountains, though at Aveiro in the north of the region the water has been tamed by an extensive network of canals and drainage channels. The coast itself, the pine-forested Costa da Prata, is one of the finest sandy stretches in the country, and inland from its main resort of Figuera da Foz, the famous university town of Coimbra stands on the banks of the Rio Mondego.

Porto and the North

The mountainous northeast provides the greatest contrast for travelers who have just left the central plains of Spain. This seldom-visited region with the Shangri-la name of Trás-os-Montes (Beyond the Mountains) is an unspoiled area of rugged beauty, with tumbling rivers, expansive forests, hilltop castles, and sparsely populated villages. Extremes of temperature dictate custom and the local economy: the northern part of the region often has long, harsh, winters, but June, July, and August are dry and hot, turning the land tawny. In the milder, more fertile, southern part lie the vineyards of the Upper Douro Valley. Grapes from this area contribute to the country's most famous export, port wine. The vineyards, like all the land of Trás-os-Montes, depend upon the Rio Douro (river Douro), whose tributaries (the Tamega, Corgo, and Tua) lace the area.

To the west, beyond Vila Real, lies the region known as the Minho. Touching the Atlantic and stretching from the northern border south to Porto (the country's second-largest city), the Minho displays a gentler character. It contains the lush hinterland of the Rio Minho, the Lima, and the Douro. In this mass of predominantly green landscape are the Costa Verde (Green Coast), the beautiful pine-tree-lined coast north of Porto, and the inland hills and valleys where the slightly sparkling *vinho verde* (green wine) is produced. Winters are mild here, with plenty of rain, and the Minho is heavily cultivated. Summers are short and temperate—a climate akin to that of Galicia, in northwest Spain, which the Minho resembles at several points.

Madeira

Off the coast of Morocco, about 375 miles due west of Casablanca, lies the Madeiran archipelago, an autonomous possession of Portugal. The archipelago consists of Madeira (the largest island of the group), nearby Porto Santo, and Ilhas Desertas and Ilhas Selvagens, a tiny number of uninhabited islets that make up two other island groups within the archipelago. (The Azores, whose remote location and relative poverty keep them somewhat unvisited, are Portugal's other autonomous possession; they are not covered in this book.)

A mountain range, volcanic in origin, dominates the center of Madeira, creating spectacular summits that overlook the sea. Pico Ruivo, the island's highest peak, reaches an altitude of 6,104 feet. On the lush northern coast, high cliffs pierce the sea, while to the west, the Paúl da Serra plateau is much more arid. Moving south along the coast, the landscape becomes gentler—and much more populated. Funchal, the capital, lies close to the southeastern corner of the island. Some 30 miles (48 kilometers) northeast of Madeira, the 6½-mile long island of Porto Santo has no mountains or ravines, but lots of sandy beaches and a desertlike climate.

PLEASURES AND PASTIMES

Azulejos

Aside from the baroque and rococo work in buildings and churches all over the country, one of the most notable images of Portugal that visitors take away is the abundance of *azulejos* (painted ceramic tiles), originally introduced by the Moors. Throughout the country, in nearly every town and village—adorning churches, palaces, fountains, public buildings, and private homes—you can see a veritable open-air art display of the tiles, reflecting the Portuguese love of decoration and ostentation. The tiles feature geometrical designs and come in a wide variety of colors; the Paço Real (Royal Palace) in Sintra is one of the most remarkable examples of their decorative effect.

By the 17th century the early styles were being replaced by whole panels depicting religious or secular motifs, often based on engravings and colored blue and white. These are the most enduring of all Portugal's azulejos, with fine examples throughout the country, especially at the Fronteira palace on the outskirts of Lisbon.

Anyone particularly interested in the development of the tile work should visit at least one of the museums that exhibit well-preserved examples: Lisbon's Museu do Azulejo and Museu de Arte Antiga and Coimbra's Museu Machado de Castro. Also, Portugal's baroque country residences (called *quintas* or *solares*) often display the most delightful combinations: for instance, an elegant pastel-color house whose outside walls and landscaped gardens are lavishly adorned with grandiose panels of azulejos. The most interesting examples are found in the Minho region in the north, though there are also attractive quintas on the Setúbal Peninsula.

Beaches

Despite the tourist boom that has almost completely developed large stretches of the Algarve and the Costa de Prata, you can commune with the sea and the sky in relative solitude along the Costa Azul and the beaches of the Minho and Costa Verde. Decide whether you want the excitement and glamour of a world-class resort, complete with casino and 24-hour nightlife, or whether your spirit would be more refreshed by amber cliffs and yellow sand leading into an indigo sea down south in the Algarve, or lush green mountains and oyster sand meeting the blue-gray ocean, as in the north.

Dining

Although it is a small country, Portugal has a large, rich, and varied gastronomy. The Portuguese introduced coriander, pepper, ginger, curry, saffron, and paprika to Europe as a result of their explorations and establishment of trade routes with the East. They brought back tea from the Orient—it was the 11th-century Portuguese princess Catherine of Bragança, wife of England's King Charles II, who popularized the aromatic beverage in England—coffee and peanuts from Africa, and pineapples, tomatoes, and potatoes from the New World.

...vers and its proximity to the ...sh- and seafood-oriented gas-...my. Be sure to try the *caldeirada* (national seafood stew) and fresh *sardinhas assadas* (grilled sardines). *Lulas recheadas*, squid stuffed with sausage and rice, is a unique combination of texture and flavor. Chicken and pork are good everywhere, and the mention of golden and crunchy *leitão da Bairrada* (roast suckling pig) in the north is enough to give anyone an appetite. Sautéed or grilled *bife à português* (steak), often cooked in a port-wine sauce, is served throughout the country. *Bacalhau* (codfish) can be served 365 different ways (or so legend has it). Soups of all kinds are popular, and most restaurants serve *caldo verde*, a filling blend of shredded cabbage and potatoes. The famous pork-and-clam dish called *porco à Alentejana* is made with diced marinated pork and clams and served with potatoes or rice. Desserts tend to be sweet and egg-based, with *pudim flan,* a caramel custard, almost a national passion. The country also produces a wide range of delicious wines (☞ Wine, *below*).

Fado Music

There is one perennial art form, best encountered in cities, that is the essence of Portugal and the Portuguese. In bars and clubs, especially in Lisbon and Coimbra, you can hear fado—"fate" music—a mournful, soulful singing tradition thought to have originated in African slave songs and imported from the colonies by way of the slave trade. There are two distinct strands of fado: in Lisbon, emotive feeling is the dominant force in the lyrics, while Coimbra's fado (said to date to the age of the troubadours) has a more intellectual edge. But both are timeless—the lament of the past, the acceptance of the future.

Literature

In literature, there was a long, barren period after the time of Camões, only briefly illuminated in the 18th century by the lyric poet, Bocage. Revival came in the 19th century with the Romantic Movement, whose most brilliant exponent was Almeida Garrett, a novelist, dramatist, and poet, who died in 1854. Garrett influenced a whole generation of remarkable writers, including novelists Camilo Castelo Branco and Julio Dinis; the historians Alexandre Herculano and Oliveira Martins; and the poets Antero de Quental and António de Castilho. The latter half of the 19th century almost exactly covered the life of the great Portuguese novelist Eça de Queiroz, an early realist, while the first half of the 20th century only produced one outstanding figure, the poet Fernando Pessoa, who died in 1935.

Manueline and Rococo Architecture

Under Dom Manuel I (1495–1521), Portugal became a great imperial power, and fabulously ornamented buildings, funded by the nation's rich overseas acquisitions, began to be constructed. The elaborate decoration that is the hallmark of Manueline architecture is at once both inspiring in its sheer novelty and instructive in that it could only have been the outpouring of a great maritime nation. Buildings and monuments are supported by twisted stone columns and covered with sculpted emblems of Portugal's conquests on the high seas and in distant lands. Representations of anchors, seaweed, and rigging mingle with exotic animals and strange, occasionally pagan, symbols—a fusion of diverse cultures and civilizations brought together under the umbrella of a Christian Portuguese empire.

The Manueline style is perhaps the most obvious manifestation of the Portuguese national character, but other developments proved to be of similar significance. Following the discovery of gold in Brazil at the end of the 17th century, buildings—churches, in particular—began to be embellished in an extraordinary rococo style, which employed *talha dourada* (polychrome and gilded carved wood) to stupendous pictorial effect. Sadly, the great golden interior of the Cistercian Abbey at Alcobaça was removed at the beginning of this century, leaving its structure evocative but bare. Nevertheless, there are superb surviving examples at the churches of São Francisco in Porto and Santo António in Lagos, and at the Convento de Jesus at Aveiro. In contrast, to see rococo at its most restrained, you must visit the lovely royal palace at Queluz, near Lisbon.

Nature Reserves

A result of Portugal's varied geography and climate has been that the country has become a fascinating spot for nature lovers.

Many regions have been turned into nature reserves, which are excellent places to see the country's flora and fauna. The oldest reserve is Peneda-Gerês, in the extreme north of the country, reaching up to the Spanish border, where wild boar and horses roam the mountains. Lesser northern reserves are those of Alvão, near Vila Real, and the Serra da Malcata on the Spanish frontier, east of the peaks of the Serra da Estrela. Interesting wildlife areas farther south include the mountainous regions around Sintra, near Lisbon, and the Serra da Arrábida (Arrábida Mountains), near Setúbal, while water-based reserves include the estuary of the Rio Sado, south of Lisbon, and the Algarve Coast, from Faro east to Vila Real de Santo António. This last region is a stopover for waders and seabirds on their migration south.

Painting and Sculpture

Sculpting and painting styles in Portugal were inspired first by the excitement of the newly emerging Portuguese nation and subsequently by the baroque experimentation allowed by the wealth available from the colonies. The earlier, rarer works still speak volumes about the confidence of those caught up in the imperial age. A Portuguese tradition in sculpture found its first outlet in grand royal and noble funerary monuments, as witnessed by the realism on display on the Gothic tombs in the cathedrals of Lisbon, Guarda, and Braga. These were precursors of the masterpiece of their kind: the 14th-century tombs of Pedro and Inês at Alcobaça; similarly eloquent are the hand-clasped figures of Dom João I and his queen, Philippa, in the chapel at Batalha. Portuguese painting came into its own in the 15th century with the completion of Nuno Gonçalves's Flemish-inspired polyptych of São Vicente (St. Vincent), which portrayed the princes and knights, monks and fishermen, court figures and ordinary people of imperial Portugal in six remarkable painted panels. It's on display in Lisbon's Museu de Arte Antiga. The next great Portuguese painter, the 16th-century Vasco Fernandes (known as *Grão Vasco,* "the Great Vasco"), was also influenced by the Flemish tradition, but his work has an expressive, realistic vigor. Grão Vasco's masterpieces are on show in Viseu, at the Museu Grão Vasco.

In contrast, the later baroque styles in art and sculpture said less about the country and more about the indiscriminate use of wealth. There were flamboyant creations, to be sure—including the unsurpassed granite-and-plaster staircases, pilgrimage shrines, and sculptures at Bom Jesus and Lamego, in the Minho—but these were built at a time when the monarchy had lost the vision and moral will that had sustained it during earlier, greater periods. Nevertheless, there were always sculptors and artists ready to work in styles that drew on the strengths of the Portuguese character and not the weaknesses. The 18th century saw the emergence of the sculptor Machado de Castro, who produced perhaps the greatest equestrian statue of his time, that of Dom José I in Lisbon's Praça do Comércio. Domingos António Sequeira (1768–1837) painted historic and religious subjects of international renown, while portrait and landscape painting became popular in the 19th century; the works of José Malhôa and Miguel Angelo Lupi can be seen in the Museu de José Malhôa in Caldas da Rainha. Other museums throughout the country display the works of talented contemporaries. The Museu Soares dos Reis in Porto—named after the 19th-century sculptor António Soares dos Reis (1847–1889)—was the first national museum in the country. His pupil was António Teixeira Lopes (1866–1942), who achieved great popular success, and who also has a museum named after him in Porto, in the suburb of Vila Nova de Gaia.

Shopping

Superbly woven baskets found in markets and gift shops make lightweight and practical gifts. Beautifully hand-embroidered table linens don't weigh much, nor do the embroidered organdy blouses or initialed handkerchiefs that are the specialty of Madeira. Traditional embroidered silk bedspreads are still made in Castelo Branco, and exquisite handmade lace can be found in Vila do Conde near Porto.

The country's lovely glazed tiles can be found in either single patterns or pictorial panels that can be shipped home by freight. Porcelain and pottery are also very attractive and sometimes irresistible; Vista Alegre is the oldest and most famous porcelain, with works near Aveiro.

Pottery differs from place to place. The brightly colored roosters (symbol of Portugal) are made in Barcelos, black pottery in Vila Real, polychrome in Aveiro, blue and white in Coimbra and Alcobaça. Caldas da Rainha is famous for green glazed plates and dishes made in the form of leaves, vegetables, fruit, and animals. In the Alentejo, particularly in Estremoz, you will find early Etruscan and Roman shapes reproduced in unglazed red clay pots and jars. There is also a large range of glazed cooking pots in all shapes and sizes, and colored figurines.

Marinha Grande is the center for glassware of every kind, and Atlantis Crystal is particularly worth seeking out; its local factory is renowned.

The Alantejo is the home of natural cork; here you'll find picture frames, lidded buckets (*tarros*) in which food can be kept hot or cold, and other lightweight gifts. Carved wooden spoons and boxes and lambskin and goatskin slippers are also from this part of the country. Attractive lanterns, fire screens, and outdoor furniture are made from tin, brass, copper, and other metals in the Algarve and Trás-os-Montes. Primitive as well as sophisticated musical instruments (such as guitars, horns, flutes, and bells) are made in the Minho, Trás-os-Montes, and the Beiras. Coimbra is famous for guitars, and clay whistles are made in Estremoz.

Fine leather shoes, handbags, and belts can be bought all over the country, as can textiles such as cotton and wool blankets in cheerfully colored stripes. Needlepoint and embroidered carpets and rugs are the specialty of Arraiolas in the Alentejo, and Portalegre has the finest tapestry shops in Portugal.

Portuguese jewelry is also lovely: The gold is 19.25 carats here, and you can find modern brooches and earrings, as well as many exquisite pieces based on ancient designs. Fine-leather bookbinding is another specialty, along with other leather products, such as clothing, wallets, luggage, belts, and gloves. For children's gifts stop in at any stationery shop, where you'll find a wide selection of unusual pen-and-pencil boxes, notebooks, erasers, and other items not seen in the United States.

Wine

With the exception of those classic kings of wines, port and Madeira, the wines that Portugal produces are mainly honest and straightforward, unaccompanied by the snobbish mystique that shrouds French vintages. This is a country where the ordinary visitor who likes wine can enjoy an endless procession of delicious experiments for little more than the cost of a good beer. It is also possible to find wines of some age that in other countries would be very expensive, but can be enjoyed here at a very moderate cost.

But don't draw the conclusion that the history of wine in Portugal is shorter or less distinguished than the history of wine in other Continental countries: It stretches back beyond the Romans to the Phoenicians, flourished still under the teetotaling Muslims, and went through a checkered time after the Moors were expelled. One of the mainstays of the wine trade's prosperity in Portugal—especially where port was concerned—was the firm link with Britain. The trade between the two countries predates the 1386 Treaty of Windsor possibly by two centuries. After a long period of generally spasmodic development, with some regions flourishing while others, such as the Algarve, almost ceased production, the situation was taken in hand by Pombal—one of the many facets of Portuguese life he tried to improve by diktat. In 1756 he put into operation a national plan for "demarcated" regions, geographically delineating growing areas and controlling their output and marketing, with the port-making region the first to be demarcated.

Demarcation, and the attendant control of quality, really took off in the first years of this century, and there are now 10 regions officially demarcated—the Algarve, Moscatel de Setúbal, Bucelas, Carcavelos, Colares, Bairrada, Dão, Douro, Vinho Verde, and the island of Madeira. Several areas that are still undemarcated (such as those around Évora) also produce excellent wines.

The official body that looks after wine production is the Junta Nacional do Vinho (J.N.V.), based in Lisbon. It controls all the facets of viniculture and of marketing, runs competitions, promotes cooperatives (important in the new political climate of the country), and empowers growers to use a seal of approval (*selo de origem*). Rather like the French *appelation d'origine*, the seal acts as a guarantee and protection for the public.

It is still too early to judge how the EU's convoluted regulations on wine will affect Spain and Portugal, recent recruits to the organization. But as both countries represent a threat to the entrenched interests of the older members, especially France, it is certain that they will have a considerable impact in the long run.

The Algarve and the Alentejo

Starting in the south, and working our way up-country, we will begin with a quick look at the wines produced in the southernmost demarcated region, the Algarve. The vast proportion of tourism to Portugal is down here, among the almond blossoms, concrete hotels, and wide sandy beaches. Most of the Algarve's wine is produced in a comparatively narrow strip of land stretching between the mountains and the sea. Algarve wine is largely red, with a tiny proportion of white, and is often not unlike a good table wine, a carafe type. Among the better makes are *Lagoa* and *Tavira*.

Higher up-country lies the Alentejo, usually known to visitors—at least in its southern reaches—simply as a wide tract of land to get across as quickly as possible when heading for the Algarve beaches. But this view isn't really fair to the province, which can be quite lovely at certain times of year, especially in spring. The Alentejo vineyards, not yet demarcated, are almost all in the top part of the province, around Évora and over toward the Spanish border. The wines they produce even have a Spanish look and taste to them—*Redondo*, *Borba* (with its lovely dark color and slightly metallic flavor), *Reguengos de Monsaraz*, and *Vidigueira*. They are all worth seeking out—the reds rich in color, the whites tending to be pale with a distinct tang. All are very high in alcohol content, so drink carefully.

Moscatel de Setúbal

The Setúbal Peninsula lies below Lisbon, across the Tagus, and is now easily reached by a through highway. It is worth exploring for many reasons, not least to discover the peace of the wooded and rocky Serra d'Arrábida. The wines produced here are well known abroad, mainly through the 150-year efforts of the House of Fonseca, based in Azeitão in the heart of the peninsula. The Moscatel that Fonseca produces, together with the small vine growers who make up the local co-operative in Palmela—a few miles east of Azeitão and boasting a superb pousada—is best known as a fortified dessert wine, aged and with a mouthwatering taste of honey. If you manage to find some that is, say, 25 years old, then you will discover it has developed a licorice color; enjoy its sweet scent and taste. Fonseca and the co-operative produce many other wines besides the Moscatel—fine reds (notably one called Periquita, or "little parrot"); rosés, of which Lancers and Faisca are much exported; and a few ordinary whites, as distinct from the dessert ones.

Although Fonseca has a very old winery in Azeitão itself, there is a fascinating modern installation on the eastern edge of the little town. It is a series of great white tanks, looking for all the world like a collection of half-buried flying saucers.

Bucelas

The Bucelas region is situated around 30 kilometers (19 miles) north of the capital, in the valley of the River Trancão. Though wine from here has a considerable history and was very popular with the British soldiers under Wellington in the Peninsular War, this is quite a small demarcated region, and all the wine it produces appears under the Caves Velhas label. The Bucelas wine is usually straw colored, with a distinctively full nose and a fruity taste, which can sometimes verge on the citrusy. It makes an extremely good companion for veal and poultry and is especially appropriate with fish.

Carcavelos

Carcavelos consists of just one smallish vineyard, the Quinta do Barão, sandwiched between Lisbon and Estoril along a stretch of overdeveloped and popular coastline. This is not an easy wine to find—the yearly output is quite small—but if you are interested in wines with a history, it would be worth searching out for your collection. Carcavelos is another fortified dessert wine, topaz colored, with a nutty aroma and a slightly almond taste, mostly drunk as an aperitif.

Colares

The last of the four demarcated regions around Lisbon is Colares, on the westernmost tip of Portugal, beyond Sintra. It is a fairly hostile place for vine growing, with sandy soil and exposure to the Atlantic winds. Like Carcavelos, the spread of Lisbon's commuter belt has squeezed this region, which is a pity, as it has a long and distinguished history of wine production and still yields some very individual vintages, especially its red. A wine that improves with age, the red has a full ruby color, an aromatic nose, and an aftertaste likened to black currants. It can be a little astringent when young, so it is always wise to try to find one of the older years. One label to seek out might be Colares Chita. The Colares whites are straw colored, slightly nutty in taste, and—like the reds—improve with age. They should be drunk well chilled.

Bairrada and Dão

Higher up the Atlantic coast, and not far south of Porto, is the region of Bairrada. Although it was not that long ago—1979—that Bairrada was demarcated, the quality of its output suggests that it probably should have received that status long before. This is a region made up mainly of small holdings, gathered into six cooperatives. Taken all together, they turn out a fairly large quantity of wine. The reds are of an intense color, with a delicious nose and a fruity, rich, and lasting taste. They mellow with age and go very well with stronger dishes, such as game, roasts, and the more pungent cheeses. There are not too many whites in this region, and most of them are slightly sparkling (es-pumantes), often made by the champagne method, though of course they cannot be called that, as the French champagne area has fought several legal battles to protect the name. The whites mirror the reds in their slightly darkish straw color, with a heavy, rather spicy nose. They go well with fish, pasta, and pâtés. One of the biggest names in the region, and one which has been largely exported, is Aliança, though several others such as São Domingos, and Frei João are worth tracking down. The hotel at Buçaco has its own wines in an extensive cellar, and they add a delicious dimension to a visit to that exceptional place.

The demarcated region known as Dão—pronounced something like "down" with an adenoidal twang—is also a name quite well known outside Portugal. This region is just south of the Douro in the mountainous heart of northern Portugal, crossed

by the valleys of the rivers Dão, Mondego, and Alva. Because of its terrain, the climate is very capricious here—cold, wet winters, scorchingly hot summers. Unlike the sandy or clay soils to the south, the terrain is made up of granite and schist, a rock that shatters easily, with the resultant changes in the kind of grapes that are cultivated. A very high proportion of wine here is red, matured—they are known as vinhos maduros—in oak casks for at least 18 months before being bottled. When they are fully mature, they have an attractively dark reddish-brown color, almost the hue of garnets, a "complex" nose, and a lasting velvety taste. They are best drunk at room temperature after being allowed to breathe well and go excellently with the favorite roasts of Portugal, lamb and pork. Some of the best names to look for are São Domingos, Terras Altas, and Porta dos Cavaleiros, or any of the labels where the word Dão precedes the name of the supplier—Dão Aliança, Dão Caves Velhas, Dão Serra, or Dão Fundação. The Dão whites are less common. They spend shorter times maturing in casks, though still 10 months or more, have the color of light straw, a full nose, and a dry, earthy flavor. The white Grão Vasco is certainly one to try, or Meia Encosta.

Douro and Port

The secret of port is found first of all in the nature of the arid, volcanic soil and the hothouse temperature of the Douro Valley. Some 800 years ago, when the father of Afonso Henriques took possession of his new domain between Douro and Minho, he planted a stock brought from Burgundy. The vine, like Count Henri, adjusted itself to the alien soil. "Eating lava and drinking sunshine," the Burgundy vines stretched, little by little, to the river's edge. They fought a bitter fight, strangling in ravines, wandering in fits and starts, to force their roots through schistous soil. Nothing but the vine could survive in this torrid pass. With tireless obstinacy, the men of the Douro broke up slate, built terraces with stone retaining walls, struggled against drought and phylloxera, and made the lost valley the most prosperous in Portugal.

It comes alive during the grape gathering, which lasts for several weeks, since the grapes ripen according to exposure and altitude. In the vineyards sited at lower levels, the gathering is often finished long before the higher plantations are ripe, for cold winds blow down from the Serra do Marão. The region, usually drowsy—the population is scattered because of water shortage—suddenly springs into activity at the time of picking. Workers hurry in from neighboring provinces. From dawn until dusk women are busy filling baskets, which the men carry on their backs, supporting as much as 150 pounds with the aid of a leather band looped over their foreheads. They descend in long files toward the *lagares* at the foot of the slopes, pile the fruit in these enormous vessels, ready for treading. Over 40 varieties of grape go into the making of port, creating the wide diversity of taste that the finished wines can have. The harvesters gather about the vats before the *must* has begun to ferment; the atmosphere is steamy, the feverish excitement of new wine induces singing and dancing. In the spring the young wine goes down by road to the lodges in Vila Nova de Gaia. Since the building of a dam across the river the age-old transportation of the wine by *rabelos,* those strange boats of Douro that look somewhat like ancient Phoenician craft, has ceased.

Port, born as it is of a soil rich in lava, is divided into two great families—vintage and blended. When a year is outstanding—as in 1945, '47, '48, '55, '58, '63, '70, '75, '77, '80, '83, and '85—the wine is unblended and, after reinforcement and bottling, left to mature. These are the vintage wines, which will take upwards of 20 years to mature; the old bottles, dusty with cobwebs, are brought up from the cellar for weddings and christenings and must be decanted before drinking.

By far the greater quantity of port, though, even of good quality, is made of a carefully studied blend of new wine with old vintages, thereby obtaining a wide range of taste. For a long time, when England was the biggest market for port, the first choice was given to full-bodied tawnies; these were served at the end of dinner, with cheese or an apple and walnuts. However, there is a lot to be said for the white ports, either sweet, as an after-dinner drink, or dry, as an aperitif with ice and a twist of lemon.

The visitor to Porto should definitely visit one of the lodges to learn more about port, taste it, and maybe, buy a bottle of one of the vintages that takes your fancy. It is quite an experience for anyone interested in wine to see these huge old cellars and find out some of the long, fascinating history that port has gathered, like the cobwebs, over the centuries. Language will be no problem, as there has been an alliance for more than 200 years between the English and Portuguese in the port trade, and many of the families are totally bilingual.

Of course, not all the wine produced in the Douro demarcated region is port. The reds here are of a deep ruby color, extremely fruity, and with a rounded taste. They go well with richer foods, a variety of meats, casseroles, and stews—anything that tends to be well flavored with herbs. The whites are dry, by and large, a pleasant pale-yellow color, with a full nose. They go well with salads, hors d'oeuvres, and chicken dishes. Look for Mesão Frio, San Marco, Quinta da Cotto, and Santa Marta.

Vinho Verde

This is the largest demarcated region in the country, divided into six subregions: Monção, Lima, Amarante, Basto, Braga, and Penafiel. The area lies inland from the Atlantic coast, threaded by a sequence of westward-flowing rivers, and enjoys a fairly mild climate, with Portugal's highest rainfall.

Like retsina in Greece, vinho verde has come to represent all Portuguese wine to many people. The name, which translates as "green wine," refers not to the wine's color but to the fact that it is not aged. For anyone who enjoys wine purely as a refreshing, mildly intoxicating beverage, a kind of celestial 7-Up, vinho verde is unquestionably *the* drink—gently sparkling (what the experts call *pétillant*), with a delicate fruity flavor, it embodies the coolness and fragrance of summer gardens. Vinho verde goes especially well with fish or any kind of seafood. The reds are important to the region, but will mostly be found on their home ground; they don't travel much. They also are refreshingly thirst quenching, sharp rather than heavy, with a vermilion-to-purple color. Naturally, they go ideally with almost any meat dish. Try for Alvarinho and Quinta de São Claudio.

The vineyards are particularly noticeable in the Vinho Verde District, as this is an area where they are frequently terraced, climbing up the hillsides away from the rivers like agricultural fortifications. Also, in places they actually arch over the roads and often march alongside as you drive, the vines held high on colonnaded rows of pillars, reaching up to the sun. The grapes hang so high they ripen in direct sunlight without any rising heat from the ground.

Madeira

Like port, Madeira—our last demarcated region—deserves a chapter all to itself. This is a volcanic island, rising up to the misty retreat of Curral das Freiras, huddled in an old crater. The soil is clearly volcanic, and the beaches, such as they are, are black. The temperate climate here, which can be humid in summer, provides exactly the conditions in which vines can thrive—although they seldom grow below 300 feet above sea level; that warmer zone is taken up by bananas and sugarcane production.

The history of viniculture on Madeira is almost as long as the history of humans on the island, and that started in 1419. Like port, Madeira—the wine and its preparation—is a way of life, and a way of life in which Portuguese and British families are bound together. When Charles II married Catherine of Bragança in 1662 he, perhaps foolishly, declined to accept the island, which was offered as part of her dowry.

Again like port, the modern wine has changed a great deal from the traditional drink much favored by George Washington, among many other famous people. The modern, light, dry versions have become popular as the public's tastes have altered. Madeira is a fortified wine, and most often blended, too. The main styles are: *Boal* and *Malmsey* or *Malvasia*, the sweeter, heavier ones, which make excellent dessert wines; *Verdelho*, not so sweet and useful as a light between-times drink, perhaps as an alternative to sherry; and *Sercial*, dry and light, which makes an excellent aperitif. None of these, of course, is the kind of wine you are likely to drink as accompaniment to the main course of a meal, but they are all attractive occasional wines, and when they are really aged, as they often are, can provide the dedicated drinker with a rare experience.

The labels to look for—and they date back in some cases for a couple of centuries—include Blandy, Cossart Gordon, Rutherford and Miles, Leacock, and Miles and Luis Gomes (you see what we mean about British and Portuguese families). A visit to a wine lodge in Funchal is an educational and delectable way of passing a couple of hours during your vacation.

Portuguese Wine Words

Adamado	Medium sweet
Adega	Wine vault
Adega Cooperativa	Wine cooperative
Aguardente	Brandy
Branco	White
Bruto	Extra dry (for sparkling wines)
Caves	Wine cellars
Colheita	Grape harvest (thus a vintage, e.g., Colh. 1980)
Doce	Sweet
Espumante	Sparkling wine
Garrafeira (or *Reserva*)	Fine and mature wine, or special vintage
Generoso	A sweet dessert wine, highly alcoholic
Meio Seco	Medium dry
Região Demarcada	Demarcated region
Rosado	Rosé
Seco	Dry
Tinto	Red
Velho	Old
Vinho da Mesa	Table wine
Vinho da Casa	House wine

FODOR'S CHOICE

No two people will agree on what makes a perfect vacation, but it can be fun and helpful to know what others think. We hope you'll have a chance to experience some of Fodor's choices yourself while visiting Portugal. For detailed information about individual entries, see the relevant sections of this guidebook.

Castles and Palaces

★**Castelo de Bragança, Bragança.** It would be hard to find a better place that this imposing castle and walled village, overlooking a medieval town in the remote Tras-os Montes, to meditate on how really good it must have been to be king. (☞ Chapter 8)

★ **Castelo de São Jorge, Lisbon.** This imposing castle, set on one of the highest hills the city's Moorish Alfama District, is a grand place to get your bearings and take in supreme views over the whole of Lisbon. (☞ Chapter 2)

★ **Fortaleza de Sagres, Sagres.** Characterized by an enormous run of defensive walls that sit high in a spectacular location above the crashing ocean, the fortress contains buildings often claimed to be Prince Henry's house and school. (☞ Chapter 6)

★ **Palácio dos Biscainhos, Braga.** Elegant silver and porcelain are displayed in this 17-century palace below exquisitely carved wooden ceilings; the flagstoned ground floor was designed to allow carriages to pass through the interior on the way to the stables. (☞ Chapter 8)

★ **Palácio Nacional de Pena, Sintra.** A splendid park surrounds this drawbridged palace, whose turrets, ramparts, and domes comprise styles from Arabian to Victorian; furnished with a rich, sometimes vulgar, and often bizarre collection of Edwardian and Victorian furniture, ornaments, and paintings, the interior is equally eclectic. (☞ Chapter 3)

★ **Palácio Nacional de Queluz, Queluz.** Inspired in part by the palace at Versailles, this salmon-pink rococo edifice took 40 years to complete. The building is surrounded by formal grounds—with ponds, a canal, statues, fountains, hedges—in a carefully executed baroque plan. (☞ Chapter 3)

Towns and Villages

★ **Batalha.** This town is home to the imposing monastery church of Santa Maria da Vitoria (St. Mary of Victory), built to commemorate a decisive Portuguese victory over the Spanish, which contains the elaborately carved tomb of Henry the Navigator. (☞ Chapter 4)

★ **Câmara de Lobos.** Date palms climb the hillsides, and pastel-color cottages dot the landscape of this tranquil, coastal village, which Sir Winston Churchill, a frequent visitor to Madeira, painted several times. (☞ Chapter 9)

★ **Cascais.** Now a tourist resort, this former fishing village has retained some small-town feel, best seen around the harbor, with its fishing boats and yachts, and in old squares where you'll find lace shops, cafés, and restaurants galore. (☞ Chapter 3)

★ **Coimbra.** An attractive town on the banks of the Mondego, Coimbra was the first capital of Portugal and is best known for its ancient university. (☞ Chapter 7)

★ **Évora.** The flourishing capital of the rich agricultural Alentejo province, Évora is a university center and one of the world's great architectural treasures (so classified by UNESCO in 1986). (☞ Chapter 5)

★ **Guimarães.** Feel the centuries slip away as you wander the narrow, cobbled streets of the old town, where small bars open onto the sidewalk and pastel-color houses with flowers blooming on windowsills overhang little squares. (☞ Chapter 8)

★ **Óbidos.** With its narrow streets, massive castle, and impressive walls and battlements, Óbidos represents a bit of medieval Portugal, preserved and transported into the 20th century. (☞ Chapter 4)

★ **Porto.** Clinging to a steep hillside above the Rio Douro is the second-largest city in Portugal, a curious combination of late-20th-century industrial capitalism, fin-de-siècle grandeur, and run-down, medieval-feeling neighborhoods. (☞ Chapter 8)

★ **Santana.** Inland off the northeast coast of Madeira, this true storybook town has thatched-roof cottages lining cobblestone streets. (☞ Chapter 9)

★ **Silves.** Crowned by a mighty fortress, Silves, once the Moorish capital of the Algarve, is one of the region's most intriguing inland towns. (☞ Chapter 6)

★ **Sintra.** The palaces, gardens, wooded paths, and viewpoints of Sintra are scintillating, while horse-drawn carriages and elegant old hotels in the vicinity add to its agreeable 19th-century air. (☞ Chapter 3)

★ **Viana do Castelo.** Northern Portugal's folkloric heart beats in this lovely city on an estuary of the Rio Lima. Be prepared to yield the road to oxcarts calmly plodding alongside men with weatherbeaten faces or enviably straight-postured women carrying baskets on their heads piled with turnip greens for caldo verde. (☞ Chapter 8)

★**Vila do Conde.** This Costa Verde town, with sandy beaches and a formidable fleet of sardine fishermen, celebrates its lace makers during June's Feast of St. John. The handiwork of these artistic women is sold in shops and at makeshift roadside stands. (☞ Chapter 8)

Churches and Monasteries

★**Basilica de Santa Luzia, Viana do Castelo.** This white, domed basilica looks over the town from its wooded heights, providing extraordinarily beautiful coastal views. (☞ Chapter 8)

★**Convento de São Gonçalo, Amarante.** A very popular likeness of St. Gonçalo is housed in this imposing 16th-century convent, his face worn smooth by the hands of the many who believe that touching him guarantees marriage. (☞ Chapter 8)

★**Igreja de Sao Domingos, Guimarães.** The cloister and surrounding buildings of this church contain one of the town's finest museums, the Museu Martins Sarmento, with richly evocative finds from the nearby 300 BC Celtic settlement at Citânia de Briteiros. (☞ Chapter 8)

★**Igreja de São Roque, Lisbon.** Don't be fooled by the plain facade: Inside, the side chapels of this Renaissance church are superbly decorated with rare stones and mosaics that resemble oil paintings. (☞ Chapter 2)

★**Mosteiro de Alcobaça, Alcobaça.** One of Portugal's most impressive religious monuments, the Church and Monastery of St. Mary of Alcobaça was built by a 12th century king in gratitude for a decisive battle won. (☞ Chapter 4)

★**Mosteiro-Palácio Nacional de Mafra, Mafra.** An enormous 18th-century religious complex containing a Franciscan monastery, an imposing basilica, and a grandiose royal palace, the Mosteiro was built to celebrate a royal birth. (☞ Chapter 4)

★**Mosteiro dos Jerónimos, Lisbon.** The enormous bulk of Belém's famous monastery is a supreme example of the Manueline style of building; a grand vision of great individuality, much of the design is characterized by elaborate sculptural details. (☞ Chapter 2)

★**Sé Velha, Coimbra.** The imposing Old Cathedral, designed and constructed in the 12th century, is made of massive granite blocks and crowned by a ring of battlements that make it look more like a fortress than a house of worship. (☞ Chapter 7)

★**Templo Romano, Évora.** This well-preserved temple, built during the second and third centuries, is considered one of the finest Roman ruins on the Iberian Peninsula. (☞ Chapter 5)

Museums

★**Museu Calouste Gulbenkian, Lisbon.** Portugal's finest museum is relatively small, but the quality of the pieces on display is magnificent. View astounding Egyptian artifacts, Greek and Roman coins and statuary, Chinese porcelain, Japanese prints, and a set of rich 16th- and 17th-century Persian tapestries. The European art section has pieces representing all major schools from the 15th through the 20th centuries. (☞ Chapter 2)

★**Museu de Arte Antiga, Lisbon.** A 17th-century palace is home to a beautifully displayed collection of Portuguese art (mainly from the 15th to 19th centuries), pieces by Flemish painters who influenced the Portuguese, and extensive collections of French silver, Portuguese furniture and tapestries, and Asian ceramics. (☞ Chapter 2)

★**Museu de Grão Vasco, Viseu.** On display here are works by the great 16th-century Portuguese painter Vasco Fernandes (Grão Vasco) and his Viseu School. (☞ Chapter 7)

★**Museu de Machado de Castro, Coimbra.** The museum, housed in a wonderful 12th-century palace, contains one of Portugal's finest collections of sculpture. (☞ Chapter 7)

★**Museu do Convento de Jesus, Aveiro.** It's the spectacular baroque interior—with elaborately gilded wood carvings, ornate ceiling, and azulejo panels—that is worth seeing here. (☞ Chapter 7)

★**Museu Municipal de Viana, Viana do Castelo.** The outstanding collection of 17th-century ceramics and ornate period furniture housed in this carefully preserved 18th-century mansion makes for an eye-popping visit. (☞ Chapter 8)

★**Ruinas de Conímbriga, Conímbriga.** In a bucolic setting southwest of Coimbra, these ruins and an adjacent museum constitute one of the Iberian Peninsula's most important archaeological sites. (☞ Chapter 7)

Squares, Parks, and Gardens

★**Jardim do Antigo Paço Episcopal, Castelo Branco.** These 18th-century gardens, planted with rows of hedges cut in all sorts of bizarre shapes, contain a most unusual assemblage of sculpture, which includes granite statues of the Apostles, the Evangelists, and the kings of Portugal. (☞ Chapter 7)

★**Parque Nacional de Peneda-Gerês.** Nearly 173,000 acres were set aside in 1970 to protect the diverse flora and fauna of this region. Wild stretches of land, mountain, lakes, and woods combine with towns and remote hilltop villages to provide soul-soothing beauty. Bring your binoculars. (☞ Chapter 8)

★**Praça da República, Viana do Castelo.** This triangular plaza is faced by the striking Miseracórdia, a 16th-century almshouse unusually decorated with tall caryatids (carved, draped, beautifully nubile female figures). A splashing stone fountain sits at the center, just waiting for you to toss in a coin and make a wish. (☞ Chapter 8)

★**Praça de Dom Duarte, Viseu.** Just the right combination of rough stone pavement, splendid old houses, wrought-iron balconies, and views of an ancient cathedral come together here to produce a magical effect. (☞ Chapter 7)

★**Praça do Giraldo, Évora.** The bustling, arcade-lined square in the center of the old town, named after the city's liberator, Gerald the Fearless, was once a Roman forum. (☞ Chapter 5)

★**Rossio, Lisbon.** The capital's main square since the Middle Ages is now a grand space sporting ornate French fountains and renowned sidewalk cafés. (☞ Chapter 2)

Restaurants

★**Aviz, Lisbon.** This exclusive restaurant, hidden on a side street, has rich but subtle belle-epoque decor and a classy French and international menu. $$$$ (☞ Chapter 2)

★**Palace Hotel Buçaco, Buçaco.** It's worth ordering a meal in the dining room just to sit at the finely laid table and take in the ornate, carved-wood ceiling, inlaid hardwood floors, and massive, arched Manueline windows. $$$$ (☞ Chapter 7)

★**Tavares Rico, Lisbon.** Superb French-inspired food, an excellent wine list, and a splendid Edwardian dining room have made this restaurant—founded as a café in the 18th century—one of the city's most famous. $$$$ (☞ Chapter 2)

★**Cidade Velha, Faro.** In an 18th-century house beside the cathedral and within the walls of the old town, this small, intimate restaurant is easy to reach and serves excellent international cuisine. $$$ (☞ Chapter 6)

★**Restaurante de Cozinha Velha, Queluz.** Formerly the kitchen of the great Queluz Palace, this magnificent restaurant takes full advantage of its heritage: Certain dishes are inspired by 18th-century recipes, and the imposing open fireplace, vast oak table, and fine reproduction antiques catch the eye. $$$ (☞ Chapter 3)

★**A Ruina, Albufeira.** This big, multilevel rustic restaurant on the beach is the place to go for charcoal-grilled seafood, especially the fresh sardines or tuna steak (the day's catch comes from the nearby fish market). $$–$$$ (☞ Chapter 6)

★**A Veranda da Sé, Viseu.** A cozy Portuguese bistro has been created in an ancient stone building that was once a warehouse. $$–$$$ (☞ Chapter 7)

★**Os Tres Potes, Viana do Castelo.** On a quiet side street off the Praça da República, you can enjoy delicious regional cooking in an engagingly rustic setting, with local singers and folk dancers to entertain you on the weekends. $$ (☞ Chapter 8)

★**Pedro dos Letões, Curia.** Of the several restaurants clustered on the N1 from Coimbra to Porto that specialize in suckling pig, Suckling Pig Pete is the most popular. A meal here is one of those traditional things that you do when visiting Portugal. $$ (☞ Chapter 7)

★**Bomjardim, Lisbon.** Known locally as *Rei dos Frangos* (the King of Chickens), Bomjardim specializes in superbly cooked spit-roasted chicken, best eaten with fries and a salad; watching the frenzied waiters is entertainment in itself. $ (☞ Chapter 2)

⭐**O Peleiro, Figueira da Foz.** An excellent traditional restaurant in an old tannery, it's in the heart of a quiet village 10 kilometers (6 miles) from Figueira. $ (☞ Chapter 7)

Hotels

⭐**Palace Hotel Buçaco, Buçaco.** A former royal hunting lodge set in a historic 250-acre forest, the hotel is a delightful hodge-podge of architectural styles, ranging from Gothic to neo-Manueline to early Walt Disney. $$$$ (☞ Chapter 7)

⭐**Pousada da Ria, Aveiro.** Built on the edge of a scenic lagoon, this light and airy two-story inn is filled with and surrounded by plants and flowers. $$$$ (☞ Chapter 7)

⭐**Pousada dos Lóios, Évora.** The pousada, in the historic 15th-century monastery opposite the Roman Temple of Diana, rates among the most luxurious in the chain. $$$$ (☞ Chapter 5)

⭐**Reids, Funchal.** Long popular as a getaway for aristocrats and British tycoons, this decadently luxurious property is often described as one of the most gracious hotels in the world. $$$$ (☞ Chapter 9)

⭐**Ritz Lisboa, Lisbon.** Excellent service is the trademark of the Ritz, one of the finest hotels in Europe. Guest rooms have luxurious bathrooms, private terraces, and elegant furniture, while the public rooms feature tapestries, antique reproductions, and fine paintings. $$$$ (☞ Chapter 2)

⭐**Grão Vasco, Viseu.** For many years the Grão Vasco has been Viseu's leading hotel, and recently remodeled, it still retains that distinction. Its location in a wooded park just a few steps from the main square is ideal, offering the convenience of the city and the quiet of the countryside. $$$ (☞ Chapter 7)

⭐**Hotel Palácio, Estoril.** During World War II, exiled European courts lived in this luxurious 1930s hotel. The attractive and elegant rooms can be your home away from home, too—that is, when you're not at the beach, two minutes away; on the championship golf course; or dining in the nationally known Four Seasons Grill. $$$ (☞ Chapter 3)

⭐**Pousada de Santa Marinha, Guimarães.** Vast stretches of tiled walls depicting Portuguese life in the 18th century decorate this most impressive mountaintop structure, which began life as a monastery in the 12th century. Now that it's a luxury pousada, you can spend a very comfortable night in what used to be a monk's cell. $$$ (☞ Chapter 8)

⭐**Pousada de São Felipe, Setúbal.** Perched atop a hill where it overlooks the town and the Rio Sado, this 16th-century castle is now a picture-book pousada. The historic location, the splendid views from the rooms and ramparts, and the interior awash with azulejo tiling make for a magnificent overnight stop. $$$ (☞ Chapter 3)

⭐**Pousada de São Pedro, Tomar.** Originally built in 1946 to house engineers building the dam on the Rio Zezere, this pousada, which sits on a wooded hill and overlooks the man-made lake, has recently undergone extensive remodeling. $$$ (☞ Chapter 4)

⭐**Quinta das Sequóias, Sintra.** This 19th-century manor house, set in 40 acres of wooded grounds, has been transformed into a lovely small hotel; the half-dozen rooms have charming furniture and modern bathrooms. $$–$$$ (☞ Chapter 3)

⭐**Albergaria Senhora do Monte, Lisbon.** This small, unpretentious hotel in the oldest part of town, near Castelo de São Jorge, offers some of the best views of Lisbon. $$ (☞ Chapter 2)

⭐**Arcada, Aveiro.** The location of this comfortable, family-owned Portuguese classic, at the foot of the bridge over the central canal, couldn't be more convenient. $$ (☞ Chapter 7)

⭐**Dona Inês, Coimbra.** The best of several recently constructed three-star facilities, this modern glass-and-marble hotel, conveniently located on the banks of the Mondego, is just a few minutes' walk from Coimbra's main commercial district. $$ (☞ Chapter 7)

⭐**Grande Hotel do Porto, Porto.** For luxury on a budget, this turn-of-the-century beauty has wonderfully ornate public rooms and cheerfully cross-century guest quarters that combine chandeliers with satellite-cable TV. $$ (☞ Chapter 8)

★**Hotel Praia, Nazeré.** This comfortable and clean hotel is set near the beach and was recently remodeled. *$$* (☞ Chapter 4)

★**Pousada do Arieiro, Madeira.** At this quaint hotel in the mountains, at an altitude of 5,963 feet, you'll feel as if you're in heaven when you step out on your terrace and look *down* onto the clouds. *$$* (☞ Chapter 9)

★**Casa de Lumena, Faro.** This graceful 150-year-old mansion has been tastefully converted into a small hotel. *$* (☞ Chapter 6)

FESTIVALS AND SEASONAL EVENTS

It is said that there is a different market day or festival every day of the year in Portugal. **Religious festivals** called *romarias* are held throughout the year. Some of the leading annual festivals, fairs, and folk pilgrimages are listed below. Verify the dates with the Portuguese tourism office, which can also send you its complete listing of the numerous events, plus advice on when to book hotel reservations (well in advance).

Market days, whether in big cities or small towns, are an irresistible attraction. **In Lisbon:** the Thieves Market, Tuesday and Saturday, behind the Church of São Vicente de Fora.

Near Lisbon: every Wednesday and Saturday in Cascais; the second and fourth Sunday of the month in São Pedro de Sintra (known for antiques and handicrafts); every Thursday at Malveira, near Mafra, and at Carcavelos, on the Cascais train line; and every first Sunday at Azeitão, south of the Rio Tejo (Tagus).

In the north: every second Monday at Ponte de Lima; every Thursday at Barcelos; Monday through Friday and Saturday morning in Porto (look for *palmitos,* sprays of flowers made of golden foil paper), at the Bolhão Market on Rua Sá da Bandeira.

In the Algarve: every third Sunday at Albufeira; every first Saturday at Lagos; every first Monday at Portimão; every third Monday at Silves; every third Mon-

day at Tavira; and every Saturday at Loule and at São Braz de Alportel.

SPRING

EARLY MARCH➤ **Festivities of Carnival (Mardi Gras),** the final festival before Lent, are held throughout the country, with processions of masked participants, parades of vehicles decked out with satirical motifs, and exuberant flowers.

MID-APRIL➤ **Holy Week Festivities** are held in Braga, Ovar, Póvoa de Varzim, and other major cities, with the most important events taking place on Monday, Thursday, and Good Friday, when the faithful march in parades.

LATE APRIL➤ The **Flower Festival,** in the last week of April, brightens downtown Funchal with a carpet of flowers, a parade, and lots of music.

EARLY MAY➤ The **Festival of the Crosses** (Festas das Cruzes) in Barcelos includes a large fair with handicrafts, concerts, an affecting Procession of the Holy Cross, and a spectacular display of fireworks on the Rio Cavado.

EARLY–MID-MAY➤ **First Annual Pilgrimage to Fátima.** Hundreds of thousands from all over the world travel to Fátima for the commemoration of the first apparition of the Virgin to the little shepherd children on May 13, 1917.

MAY–JUNE➤ The **Algarve Music Festival,** in the larger towns of the Algarve, features more than 40 concerts by leading Portuguese and foreign artists.

SUMMER

EARLY JUNE➤ The **National Fair of Agriculture** in Santarém is the most important agricultural fair in Portugal, with a colorful program of bullfighting, folk songs and dancing, and typical fair amusements.

LATE JUNE➤ **Festivities in honor of St. Anthony** in Lisbon honor the city's patron saint with an impressive show of *marchas* (walking groups of singers and musicians) parading along the Avenida da Liberdade, while the various city districts carry on their own music, dances, and bonfires. **Festivities in honor of St. John** are held in many towns, but the festivities in Porto are the most colorful. Every corner has its own *cascatas* (arrangements of religious motifs), bonfires, and all-night groups of singing and dancing merrymakers.

EARLY JULY➤ The **Red Waistcoat** Festival (Coletes Encarnado) in Vila Franca de Xira honors the *campinos,* Portuguese cowboys who guard the brave bulls in the pasturelands of the Ribatejo.

JULY–AUGUST➤ The **Estoril Music Festival** features

leading Portuguese and foreign artists in Estoril, Cascais, and other towns of the Estoril Coast.

EARLY AUGUST➤ **St. Walter's Festival** (Festas Gualterianas) in Guimarães is a fascinating show of music bands, folk dance groups, and the spectacular Procession of St. Walter.

MID-AUGUST➤ The **Festival of Nossa Senhora do Monte,** the patron saint of Madeira, attracts pilgrims from all corners of the island. The village of Machico celebrates the **Santissimo Sacramento** festival, one of the more unusual feast days on Madeira, with a sunset bonfire of pine-tree logs, branches, and cones in the center of town under a specially constructed, flower-bedecked ceremonial arch.

MID–LATE AUGUST➤ **Our Lady of Agony Festivities** in Viana do Castelo are extremely colorful, with the Lady paraded throughout the town over lush carpets of flowers, and spectacular fireworks.

LATE AUGUST–LATE SEPTEMBER➤ **St. Matthew's Fair** in Viseu is an important agricultural and livestock fair with folk dancing and singing, held since the Middle Ages.

FALL

EARLY SEPTEMBER➤ The **Wine Harvest Festival** in Palmela has a colorful parade of harvesters, wine tastings, the election of the Queen of the Wine, and a spectacular fireworks display.

EARLY–MID-SEPTEMBER➤ **Our Lady of Nazaré Festivities** has bullfights, folk dancing and singing, and three festive processions of Nazaré fishermen carrying the Lady's image on their shoulders.

MID-SEPTEMBER➤ In the annual **Folk Music and Dance Festival,** singing and dancing in all the Algarve's larger towns culminate at Praia da Rocha with performances by groups from all over the country. **Our Lady of Good Voyage Festivities** takes place in the ancient town of Moita (near Setúbal), bathed by the waters of the Rio Tejo, and center on the blessing of the fishing boats.

LATE SEPTEMBER➤ The **Wine Harvest Festival,** which involves plenty of singing, dancing, and wine tasting, is celebrated in both Funchal and nearby Estreito da Câmara de Lobos, the center of Madeira's wine-growing region.

EARLY OCTOBER➤ **October Fair** in Vila Franca de Xira, a short distance from Lisbon, has farming and agricultural activities, handicraft displays, bullfights, and the traditional running of bulls in the streets.

OCTOBER 12–13➤ The **Last Pilgrimage to Fátima** brings thousands of pilgrims from all over the world to Fátima to honor the last apparition of the Virgin on October 12, 1917.

LATE OCTOBER–EARLY NOVEMBER➤ The **National Gastronomy Festival** in Santerém presents traditional regional dishes, cooking contests, and lectures.

EARLY NOVEMBER➤ **St. Martin's Fair** and the **National Horse Show** in Golega combine parades of saddle horses and bullfight horses with riding competitions, handicrafts exhibitions, and wine tasting.

WINTER

DECEMBER 31➤ **St. Sylvester's Festival,** on New Year's Eve, transforms Funchal, Madeira, into a vast fairground, with bands of strolling dancers and singers, thousands of lights, and a breathtaking fireworks display over the city's beautiful bay.

MID-JANUARY➤ **St. Gonçalo** and **St. Cristovão Festivities** in Vila Nova de Gaia, Porto; **St. Gonçalinho Festivities** in Aveiro.

MID–LATE JANUARY➤ **St. Sebastião or Fogaceiras Festivities** in Santa Maria da Feira in Aveiro.

EARLY FEBRUARY➤ **Our Lady of Candeias Festivities,** Mourão (in Évora).

2 Lisbon

With a total population of about 1 million, Lisbon is one of Europe's smallest capital cities, and to many visitors it immediately becomes one of the most likeable. In parts of the city, the centuries seem to collide: Out of 17th-century buildings trip designer-clad youths; the fish market at Cais do Sodré resonates with traditional sights and smells; and just a few minutes' walk from Lisbon's 18th-century aqueduct sits Portugal's modernistic Amoreiras shopping center.

LYING NORTH OF THE RIO TEJO (River Tagus) estuary and spread over a string of seven hills, Lisbon offers a variety of faces to anyone with the energy to nego-

By Jules Brown   tiate its switchback streets. In the oldest parts of the city, tiny, stepped alleys are lined with pastel-color houses, across which drying laundry is strung; here and there you come across a *miradouro,* a natural van- tage point with spectacular views of the city and river. In the grand 18th-century center, wide boulevards are bordered by black-and-white mosaic cobblestone sidewalks. There's a legacy of fine art-nouveau build- ings, too, and everywhere—on church walls, around fountains, and in restaurants and bars—you'll see the striking blue-and-white *azulejos* (painted and glazed ceramic tiles) for which the country is famous.

Lisbon's earliest history is a little unclear, but historians believe the city was probably founded by the Phoenicians. It was not until 205 BC, how- ever, when the Romans linked it by road to the great Spanish cities of the Iberian Peninsula, that Lisbon prospered. The Visigoths followed in the 5th century and built the earliest fortifications on the site of the Castelo de São Jorge, but it was with the arrival of the Moors in the 8th century that Lisbon came into its own. The city became a flour- ishing trading center during the 300 years of Moorish rule, and the Alfama—the oldest district of Lisbon—retains its intricate Arab-in- fluenced layout. In 1147 the Moorish period ended when the Chris- tian army, led by Dom Afonso Henriques, took the city after a siege that lasted 17 weeks. To give thanks for the end of Moorish rule, Hen- riques planned a great cathedral, and the building was dedicated three years later. Just over a century later, the rise of Lisbon was complete when the royal seat of power was transferred here from Coimbra, and Lisbon was declared capital of Portugal.

The next great period in the city's history—"the Discoveries"—came in the 16th century, after the voyages of discovery led by the great Por- tuguese navigators to India, Africa, and Brazil. The wealth realized by these expeditions was phenomenal: Gold, jewels, ivory, porcelain, and spices helped finance grand new buildings and impressive commercial activity. Late–Portuguese Gothic architecture—called Manueline (after the king Dom Manuel I)—assumed a rich, individualistic style, char- acterized by elaborate sculptural details, often with a maritime motif. Torre de Belém and the Mosteiro dos Jerónimos (Belém's tower and monastery) are supreme examples of this period.

With independence from Spain in 1640 and assumption of the throne by successive dukes of the House of Bragança, Lisbon became ever more prosperous, only to suffer calamity on November 1, 1755, when the city was hit by the last of a series of earthquakes. Two-thirds of Lis- bon was destroyed, and tremors were felt as far north as Scotland; 40,000 people in Lisbon died, and entire sections of the city were swept away by a tidal wave.

Under the direction of the prime minister, the Marquês de Pombal, Lis- bon was rebuilt quickly and ruthlessly. The old medieval quarters were leveled and replaced with broad boulevards; the city's commercial center, the Baixa, was laid out in a grid; and the great Praça do Comér- cio, the riverfront square, was planned. Essentially this is how down- town Lisbon appears to visitors today. Its 18th-century character largely consists of an elegant layout that remains as pleasing and effi- cient in modern times as it was intended to be 250 years ago.

Of course, there are parts of Lisbon that lack charm, particularly the modern city that extends beyond the center in a series of often dreary suburbs. Even some of the elegant downtown sections are losing their appeal, as restorations and renovations replace turn-of-the-century art-nouveau buildings with shiny new office blocks. But the beauty of much of the city should compensate.

Despite the traditional sights and experiences, in recent years all talk in Lisbon has been of development and progress. Money has poured in from the European Union, which has financed many new projects in the city. Moreover, for the first time in many years, Lisbon has moved into the international limelight following its stint as European City of Culture in 1994. Since it was announced that the city would host the 1998 World Exposition (the last this century), much of the capital has been subject to intense redevelopment. There will be gleaming new museums and public buildings, an Expo site, improved transportation links (including an extension to the metro) and landmark projects, like the completion of a new bridge across the Rio Tejo.

Pleasures and Pastimes

Dining

Although only a few of Lisbon's restaurants can compare with the best establishments in other European capitals, there's no doubt that dining here is taken seriously. Fresh ingredients—especially fish and shellfish—are used everywhere, and you can find excellent meals all over the city, often in seemingly modest places. Sometimes the dining experience is boosted by the setting: Many restaurants are housed in historic buildings, some have city and river views, and others offer outdoor dining in summer.

With the exception of some very expensive restaurants, many featuring French-influenced fare, a large number of places serve Portuguese cuisine, characterized by grilled sardines, simple steaks and cutlets, fresh seafood (always ask the price before ordering), and salads. Local specialties include *açorda* (a thick bread-and-shellfish stew) and different varieties of *bacalhau* (cod). In addition, the capital manages to attract the best of the country's regional foods and specialties, too—you'll be able to enjoy game, lampreys from the Minho, and other seasonal delights (though often at a higher price than in their respective Portuguese regions). If you want more variety, however, try restaurants that specialize in colonial Portuguese food—principally Brazilian, but also Mozambican and Goan (Indian) cuisine.

Wine is excellent and reasonably priced everywhere, especially the *vinho da casa* (house wine), which—in cheaper and more expensive restaurants alike—is carefully selected for its quality. Don't forget to finish your meal with a glass of port—if you stop by the renowned Instituto do Vinho do Porto (☞ Exploring Lisbon, *below*) during your visit, you can taste different varieties and pick your favorite.

Museums

Lisbon has some splendid museums, all of which are very reasonably priced. In particular, no visitor would want to miss the Museu Calouste Gulbenkian and the Museu de Arte Antiga, which have the finest collections of art and artifacts in the country. Just as entertaining are a number of specialist museums that each emphasize a particular enthusiasm—from puppets to model ships to folk costumes.

EXPLORING LISBON

Although there's no doubt that Lisbon is now a thoroughly modern city, it's the traditional means of getting around that still appeal. Because the center city is small enough to cover on foot, you can quickly get a feel for the different historical areas. Nevertheless, visitors are often surprised to find that because of the hills, places appearing close to one another on a map are on different levels and actually quite far apart. But the local transportation system, an entertainment in itself, will complement your walking tours. It consists of marvelous old trams, buses, and a subway system, plus turn-of-the-century funicular railways and elevators to take you up the steep hills. And whatever your vantage point, the river is never far away: Chances are either you'll be looking over it or walking alongside it, close to the fishing boats, container ships, and passenger ferries that make up its traffic.

The center of Lisbon stretches north from the spacious Praça do Comércio—one of the largest riverside squares in Europe—to the Rossío, a smaller square lined with shops and sidewalk cafés. The district in between is known as the Baixa (Lower Town), an attractive grid of parallel streets built after the 1755 earthquake and tidal wave destroyed much of the city.

The Alfama, the old Moorish quarter that survived the earthquake, lies east of the Baixa. In this part of town are the Sé (the city's cathedral) and, on the hill above, the Castelo de São Jorge (St. George's Castle). West of the Baixa, sprawled across another of Lisbon's hills, is the Bairro Alto (Upper Town), a fascinating area of intricate 17th-century streets, peeling houses, and churches. Five kilometers (3 miles) farther west is Belém, site of the famous Jerónimos Monastery, as well as several royal palaces and museums.

The modern city begins at Praça dos Restauradores, adjacent to the Rossío. From here the main Avenida da Liberdade stretches northwest to the landmark Praça de Marquês de Pombal, headed by the green expanse of the Parque Eduardo VII beyond.

Great Itineraries

You could spend a week in Lisbon, exploring neighborhoods, museums, and parks at your leisure; some of Lisbon's greatest attractions and pleasures are to be found in the "hidden" squares and streets and in some of the agreeable café-bars for which the city is known. But it's easy to get a feel for the city in even a couple of days, partly because Lisbon is nicely divided into a series of self-contained neighborhoods. By using taxis and public transportation, you can combine multiple neighborhoods in a single day of sightseeing—the Alfama and the Baixa fit together particularly well, and the Chiado and the Bairro Alto make a good unit. Four days, then, is a reasonable compromise, allowing you time to see every major sight in the city and quite a few of the minor ones, too.

IF YOU HAVE 2 DAYS

To view all of Lisbon's major attractions in two days, you'll have to get up early. Starting in the **Rossío,** the main downtown square, stroll through the Baixa, pausing to window-shop or take a coffee in one of the sidewalk cafés. You can then wander into the Alfama quarter by way of the city's cathedral, the **Sé,** following the winding roads past lookout points and churches as far as the **Castelo de São Jorge,** on the top of one of Lisbon's hills. From here the views are magnificent, and there are plenty of cafés and restaurants in the nearby streets when it's time for lunch. A tram ride takes you back down to the Baixa, where in the riverside **Praça do Comércio** you pick up a second tram for the rattling ride west through the suburbs to Belém to see the magnificent **Mosteiro dos Jerónimos,** as well as the other acclaimed monuments—the **Torre de Belém** and the **Monumento dos Descobrimentos.** On the way back in to the center, you can stop off at the **Museu de Arte Antiga** for a brief look at the country's finest art museum.

Your second day can be less hectic, starting with a walk through the Chiado shopping area, followed by the ride up to the Bairro Alto using the **Elevador de Santa Justa.** The Bairro Alto can easily take up the rest of the morning: browsing in the galleries and stores, visiting the marvelous **Igreja de São Roque** and its small museum, and popping into the **Instituto do Vinho do Porto** for a glass of port. Lunch is best taken at one of the small taverns or smarter restaurants. In the afternoon, you can return to the lower town by the second of the elevadors—the **Elevador da Glória**—and then take the metro uptown to the Fundação Calouste Gulbenkian. Here, you can profitably spend three or four hours viewing the amazing collections in the **Museu Calouste Gulbenkian** and the adjacent **Centro de Arte Moderna.**

IF YOU HAVE 4 DAYS
On the first day, spend the morning in the Baixa, where the shops and cafés are most inviting. At the riverside Praça do Comércio, you can even take a ferry across the river and back for fine views of the city. Have lunch in the suburb of Cacilhas, where the ferry docks, or return to **Praça dos Restauradores,** just north of the Rossío, where a side street just off the square—Rua das Portas de Santo Antão—is lined with well-known fish restaurants. The afternoon can then be spent in the Alfama, taking in the Sé, the Castelo de São Jorge, and the applied arts on display in the **Museu das Artes Decorativas.**

On your second day, catch a tram out toward Belém. Spend half the day exploring the monastery and monuments; you'll also have time for at least one of the specialized museums—**Museu da Marinha, Museu Nacional de Coches,** and **Museu de Arte Popular**—devoted to maritime history, ornate coaches, and folk art, respectively. On your way to or from Belém, stop for a morning or afternoon at the Museu de Arte Antiga.

Your two remaining days can be split between old and modern Lisbon. One full day should involve seeing the Chiado shopping area and exploring the Bairro Alto. Devoting a full day, rather than half as above, to these areas means that you can pop into the **Convento do Carmo** archaeological museum and make a side trip to the **Estrêla Gardens.**

On the final day, walk the length of the boulevardlike Avenida da Liberdade to the city's main park, **Parque Eduardo VII,** where the greenhouses are a rare treat. From here, it's a simple metro ride to the Museu Calouste Gulbenkian and the adjacent Centro de Arte Moderna. Some visitors have been known to spend a full day just in these two galleries, but if you crave a change and have a little extra time, you could use the metro to take you farther north into the modern city: the **Jardim Zoológico** and the **Palácio dos Marqueses da Fronteira** are easily accessible.

When to Tour Lisbon
It's best not to visit at the height of summer, when the city positively steams and lodgings are at their most expensive—and most crowded. Winters are generally mild and usually accompanied by bright blue skies, but for optimum Lisbon weather, visit on either side of summer, in May or late September through October.

The Alfama

The Moors, who imposed their rule on most of the southern Iberian peninsula during the 8th century, left their mark on much of Lisbon but nowhere so evidently as in the Alfama district. Here narrow, twisting streets and soaring flights of steps wind up to an imposing castle set on one of the city's highest hills. This is a grand place to get your bearings and take in supreme views over the whole of Lisbon. Because its foundation is dense bedrock, the district—a jumble of whitewashed houses with flower-laden balconies and red-tile roofs—has managed to survive the wear and tear of the ages, including the great earthquake of 1755. The timeless alleys and little squares enjoy a notoriously confusing layout, but the Alfama is relatively compact, and you'll keep circling back to the same buildings and streets. It's clear that time has taken its toll, and what in the Moorish period was the most exclusive part of the city—replete with summer palaces—is now a somewhat rundown neighborhood. However, smart bars and restaurants are slowly moving into the neighborhood, while its down-to-earth charm is most apparent in June, during the festivals of the *santos populares* (popular saints), when the entire quarter turns out to eat, drink, and be merry.

Numbers in the text correspond to numbers in the margin and on the Exploring Lisbon map.

A Good Walk

The Alfama's streets and alleys are very steep, and its levels are connected by flights of stone steps, which means it is easier to tour the area from the top down. Take a taxi up to the castle or approach it by tram (No. 28 from Rua Conceição in the Baixa) or bus (No. 37 from Rossío).

From the Moorish **Castelo de São Jorge** ①, follow the castle walls around, and you'll emerge close to the **Museu da Marioneta** ②, with its unique collection of Portuguese and foreign puppets. From the puppet museum, it's a 10-minute walk down Rua de Santa Marinha and Rua São Vicente to the **Mosteiro de São Vicente** ③, where you can examine the tombs of the Bragança dynasty. Tram 28 from outside the church (or a 10-minute walk) leads to the Alfama's prettiest square, **Largo das Portas do Sol,** whose terrace offers glorious views of the streets below, dotted with drying laundry draped across the stepped alleys. Just off the square you'll find the **Museu das Artes Decorativas** ④, with its splendid decorative-art collections, while down the hill about 100 meters is the **Igreja de Santa Luzia** ⑤ and its adjacent view-laden miradouro (terrace). Head southwest from the miradouro along Rua do Limoeiro, which eventually becomes Rua Augusto Rosa. This route takes you past the **Sé** ⑥—Lisbon's cathedral—and to complete your tour of this district, you can then walk around and below the cathedral to the **Casa dos Bicos** ⑦, a mansion that survived the 1755 earthquake. From here it's an easy walk to the adjacent Baixa district, or retrace your steps to the cathedral, outside which Tram 28 stops before heading to the Baixa.

TIMING

Allow two to three hours to walk the route, perhaps more on a hot day when you'll want to rest in the castle grounds or stop for drinks in one of the pleasant cafés. A visit to the Museu das Artes Decorativas will occupy at least an hour, though other museums and churches require much less attention. Note that museums are closed on Mondays, and that churches generally close for a couple of hours in the middle of the day.

Exploring Lisbon

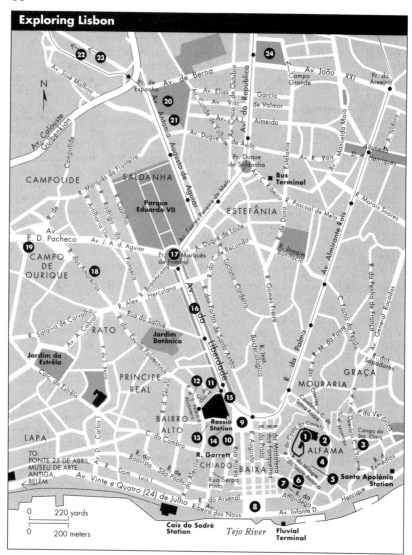

Sights to See

❼ Casa dos Bicos. For a view of a Lisbon town house that survived the 1755 earthquake, take a look at the Casa dos Bicos, whose striking facade is studded with pointed white-stone diamonds. The interior is similarly impressive, although it's not usually open to the public except when it hosts occasional special exhibitions—check with the tourist office for upcoming events. ⊠ *Rua dos Bacalhoeiros, no phone.*

★ ❶ Castelo de São Jorge. Although the Castelo de São Jorge (St. George's Castle) was constructed by the Moors, the site on which it stands dates to the 5th century, when the Visigoths first raised a fortification here. At the castle's main entrance is a statue of Dom Afonso Henriques, who in 1147 besieged the castle and ultimately drove the Moors out of Lisbon. Within the preserved Moorish walls and the castle's ramparts and towers (restored to their former glory in 1938) are the scant remnants of a palace that was the residence of the kings of Portugal until the 16th century. The well-kept grounds are home to swans, turkeys, ducks, ravens, and other birds, while the outer walls encompass the (restored) medieval church of Santa Cruz, a few simple houses, and more restaurants and souvenir shops. Panoramic views of Lisbon can be seen from the walls, but visitors should take care because the footing is uneven and slippery. There are entrances to the castle from Largo do Chão da Feira or Largo do Menino de Deus. ⊠ *Castelo de São Jorge, no phone.* ◻ *Free.* ☉ *Apr.–Sept., daily 9–9; Oct.–Mar., daily 9–7.*

❺ Igreja de Santa Luzia. One of the most attractive of churches in the Alfama is the Igreja de Santa Luzia (Church of Santa Luzia), whose fine exterior azulejos tell the story of the siege of the castle and the conquest of Lisbon from the Moors. The church is usually locked, so you can't view the interior, but the adjacent terrace, the **Miradouro Santa Luzia,** offers another sweeping view of the Alfama and the river. ⊠ *Largo da Santa Luzia, no phone.*

❸ Mosteiro de São Vicente. The bright Italianate facade of twin-towered Mosteiro de São Vicente (St. Vincent's Monastery) heralds an airy church with a barrel-vault ceiling. Although there's nothing left of the original 12th-century monastery, the present church (completed in 1704) features a superbly tiled cloister depicting the fall of Lisbon to the Moors, while the former monastery refectory is the pantheon of the Bragança dynasty, who were the first rulers of an independent Portugal. In the pantheon, among the great, solid tombs and weighty inscriptions, lies Catherine of Bragança, who married Charles II of England in 1661. ⊠ *Largo de São Vicente, no phone.* ◻ *Church free; cloister 200$00 plus tip for guide.* ☉ *Daily 10–1 and 2:30–5.*

❹ Museu das Artes Decorativas. The Museu das Artes Decorativas (Museum and School of Decorative Arts) is housed in the beautifully restored 17th-century Azurara Palace. Its furnishings, dating from the 15th to 19th centuries, have been lovingly restored and maintained and include *arraiolos* (traditional, hand-embroidered Portuguese carpets) that are brightly colored and based on imported Arabic designs; other exhibits range from silver work and ceramics to paintings and jewelry. With so many rich items to preserve, the museum has developed into a major center for restoration: Specialized crafts like bookbinding, carving, and cabinetmaking are all undertaken here by highly trained staff, and the restoration work can be viewed by appointment. ⊠ *Largo das Portas do Sol 2,* ☎ *01/886–2184.* ◻ *500$00.* ☉ *Wed. and Fri.–Sun. 10–5, Tues. and Thurs. 10–6.*

NEED A
BREAK?
At Largo das Portas do Sol, you'll find a number of small café-bars with outside seats from which you can watch the ships' activities on the Rio Tejo. **Cerca Moura** (⊠ Largo das Portas do Sol 4, ☎ 01/887-4859)—named after the Moorish walls that surround the district—is one of the best, with a full menu of drinks and snacks from which to choose.[/r]

🕐 ❷ **Museu da Marioneta.** The intricate workmanship that went into the creation of the puppets on display in the Museu da Marioneta (Puppet Museum) is remarkable. The collection encompasses both Portuguese and foreign puppets; occasionally the museum staff performs a traditional puppet show, but schedules are not regular so you should inquire at the museum or tourist office about upcoming events. ⊠ *Largo Rodrigues de Freitas 19,* ☎ *01/888-2841.* ⊡ *300$00.* ☉ *Tues.–Sun. 10–1 and 2–6.*

❻ **Sé.** Lisbon's cathedral—or Sé—was founded in 1150 to commemorate the defeat of the Moors; to rub salt in the wound, the conquerors built the sanctuary on the site where Moorish Lisbon's main mosque once stood. Aside from the austere Romanesque interior and a fine rose window, there's little to detain you, save a splendid 13th-century **cloister** and the treasure-filled **sacristy**, which among other things contains the relics of the martyr St. Vincent. According to legend, the relics were carried from the Algarve to Lisbon in a ship piloted by ravens. ⊠ *Largo da Sé, no phone.* ⊡ *Cathedral free, cloister 100$00, sacristy 300$00.* ☉ *Cathedral daily 9–noon and 2–6, sacristy daily 10–1 and 2–6.*

OFF THE
BEATEN PATH
MUSEU DO AZULEJO – To fully understand the craftsmanship that goes into making the ubiquitous azulejos, visit the engaging Museu do Azulejo (Azulejo Museum) at the 16th-century Madre de Deus convent and cloister. Some of the ceramics on display date to the 1700s, with representative examples from each century to the present. A highlight of the display is the 118-foot, 18th-century *Panorama of Lisbon*, a beautifully detailed study of the city and waterfront and reputedly the country's longest azulejo work. While you're here, you may want to take a look at the richly furnished convent-church, too, since it contains some noteworthy gilt baroque decoration. To reach the museum, take Tram 3 or 16 from Praça do Comércio to the eastern suburb of Xabregas (20 minutes away). ⊠ *Rua Madre de Deus 4,* ☎ *01/814-7747.* ⊡ *200$00.* ☉ *Tues.–Sun. 10–1 and 2–5.*

The Baixa

The earthquake of 1755, a massive tidal wave, and subsequent fires killed thousands of people and reduced proud 18th-century Lisbon to rubble. But within 10 years, frantic rebuilding under the direction of the king's minister, the Marquês de Pombal, had given the city a new look: a neoclassical grid design. This can be seen perfectly today in the impressive Baixa (Lower Town), Lisbon's main shopping and banking district, which stretches from the riverfront to the square known as the Rossío. Pombal intended the various streets to house certain trades and crafts, something that is still reflected in the street names: Rua dos Sapateiros (Cobblers' Street), Rua da Prata (Silversmiths' Street), and Rua do Ouro (now the Rua Aurea: Goldsmiths' Street). The central street—Rua Augusta—and some of the cross streets have been closed to cars, making window-shopping easy.

Numbers in the margin correspond to points of interest on the Exploring Lisbon map.

Sights to See

★ ⓾ **Elevador de Santa Justa.** The Elevador de Santa Justa, a street elevator built in 1902 by Raul Mésnier, is one of Lisbon's more extraordinary structures. Sitting inside its own Gothic-style tower, the lift whisks
passengers from the Baixa up to Largo do Carmo in the Bairro Alto
in less than a minute, saving you a very steep walk. ⊠ *Junction of Rua
Aurea and Rua de Santa Justa, no phone.* ☜ *150$00; free with tourist
pass.* ☉ *Daily 7 AM–midnight.*

❽ **Praça do Comércio.** When the Marquês de Pombal completed his neoclassical plan for Lisbon, he offset the gridded streets with the enormous riverfront Praça do Comércio. Known also as the Terreiro do
Paço, after the royal palace (Paço) that once stood here, it is indeed a
regal square, lined with serene, arcaded 18th-century buildings. The
equestrian statue is of Dom José, who was king at the time of the earthquake and during subsequent rebuilding. Steps—once used by occu-
pants of the royal barges that docked here—lead up from the water
onto the square. The square itself is a hub for public transportation
(trams to Belém leave from here), and at times it may look like nothing
more than a parking lot. Indeed, the best views of the square are from
any of the ferries that regularly cross the Tejo at this point. It's also
worth coming down to the square on Sunday mornings, when a market of old coins and banknotes takes place under the arches of the arcade.

NEED A
BREAK?

One of the original buildings on Praça do Comércio houses the elegant
Café Martinho da Arcada (⊠ Praça do Comércio 3, ☎ 01/887-9259),
situated, as its name suggests, in the 18th-century arcade. A literary
haunt since 1782, the main rooms now contain an expensive restaurant
full of old-style atmosphere; adjacent to it there's a more modest café-
bar.

★ ❾ **Rossío.** Lisbon's main square since the Middle Ages is popularly known
as the Rossío, though its official name is Praça Dom Pedro IV (whom
the central statue commemorates). It's a grand space—though rather
overwhelmed by circling traffic these days—sporting ornate French fountains and on its northern edge, the mid-19th-century **Teatro Nacional**
(National Theater), built on the site of the earlier Palace of the Inquisition. Public executions were once carried out in the Rossío; slightly
less dramatic performances these days are on show in the theater (productions are in Portuguese). However, most visitors will probably do
what the locals do when they come to the Rossío: pick up a newspaper
at a newspaper stand and sit at one of the renowned sidewalk cafés
lining the east and west sides of the square. These are good places to
have your shoes shined by one of the roaming shoe shiners who solicit
their trade in the square. Before you agree to take their services, though,
make sure you establish the price.

The Bairro Alto and Chiado

Lisbon's most chic shopping district, known as the Chiado, forms the
western side of the Baixa grid, its streets leading uphill to the Bairro
Alto. In 1988 this area suffered great damage from a calamitous fire
that destroyed many of the older shops in the vicinity of Rua Garrett.
Today, though, an ambitious rebuilding program is under way and despite the damage—some of which you can see from Rua do Carmo—
the Chiado remains a fashionable place to shop. Scattered throughout
the Chiado you'll find some of the best shoe shops in Europe; glitter-

ing jewelry stores; and a host of cafés and delicatessens selling wines, cheeses, and pastries.

Lisbon's Bairro Alto (Upper Town) extends west of the Baixa and, like the latter, is laid out in a grid. Unlike the Baixa, however, the streets of the Bairro Alto are narrow and cobbled, following the contours of the hills, which can make getting around the district fairly confusing. This is one neighborhood that you'll have to see on foot, though that is no bad thing since there's plenty here to delay you. Apart from the specific attractions, the back streets are lively with the sounds of daily life: Children scuffle amid the drying laundry, women carry huge bundles from shop to shop, and old men clog the doorways of neighborhood barrooms.

Although the settlement of the Bairro Alto dates back to the 17th century, most of the buildings are from the 18th and 19th centuries and comprise an appealing mixture of small churches, warehouses, antiques and art galleries, artisans' shops, and town houses with wrought-iron balconies. Historically, the *bairro* was considered rather rough-and-ready, and there are still a thriving red-light district and back alleys down which it would be unwise to venture after dark. On the whole, however, it's never less than safe to walk around here; indeed, the Bairro Alto is Lisbon's premier nightlife center, and with the opening of smart boutiques and trendy eateries, some gentrification has come. There are more bars, restaurants, fado clubs, and discos tucked into these streets than anywhere else in the city.

Numbers in the text correspond to numbers in the margin and on the Exploring Lisbon map.

A Good Walk

As the Bairro Alto is spread across steep hills, the least taxing way to explore is from the top down. From Praça dos Restauradores, you can catch the **Elevador da Glória** ⑪, a creaking funicular railway that deposits you immediately across the street from the wonderful **Instituto do Vinho do Porto** ⑫. After sampling the institute's collection of port wines, turn right and walk down Rua São Pedro de Alcântara. At Largo Trindade Coelho, on your left, is the **Igreja de São Roque** ⑬, with its associated museum. From the southeast corner of the church's square, follow Rua Nova da Trindade downhill and take a left at the second corner, Rua da Trindade. This small street leads toward Largo do Carmo, a pretty square on which stands the **Convento do Carmo** ⑭, a charming ruin housing an interesting archaeological museum.

If you want to browse among the shops of the Chiado before exploring the Bairro Alto, then you can follow the above tour in reverse: For a comfortable ascent to the Bairro Alto, take Rua do Carmo north from the eastern end of Rua Garrett, the Chiado's main street, over to the lower terminus of the Elevador de Santa Justa (☞ The Baixa, *above*). The upper station of the elevador is down a narrow alley behind the Convento do Carmo, from which you can proceed in backwards order to São Roque Church and the Port Wine Institute. Or hike up the steep hill from Rua Garrett to Largo do Carmo; Calle do Sacramento will take you straight there, or head up Rua Serpa Pinto and jog east on Travessa do Carmo.

The Bairro Alto is the also best starting point for side trips to two interesting gardens. From the Elevador de Santa Justa, you can make the lengthy trip across the quarter (by tram if you prefer) to the **Jardim da Estrêla** on the western edge of the district. From the Elevador da Glória, it's a 20-minute walk north to the **Jardim Botânico,** which is also the site of the **Museu de História Natural.**

TIMING

The Bairro Alto is remarkably compact, and it actually takes very little time to walk from one end to the other; an hour would cover it. But once you start diving off into the side streets and lingering in the shops, galleries, and bars, you'll find you can quite happily spend a morning or afternoon here. Neither the Igreja de São Roque or the Convento do Carmo will occupy you for more than half an hour or so. If you don't like crowds, avoid the Bairro Alto late at night, especially on weekends, when seemingly the whole of Lisbon comes here to eat, drink, and party.

Sights to See

🔴 **Convento do Carmo.** The partially ruined Convento do Carmo (Carmo Convent)—once Lisbon's largest convent—was severely damaged in the 1755 earthquake, but open-air summer orchestral concerts are held beneath its majestic archways. Its sacristy houses the **Museu Arqueológico do Carmo** (Archaeological Museum), a small but worthy collection of ceramic tiles, medieval tombs, ancient coins, and other city finds. ⊠ *Largo do Carmo,* ☎ *01/346–0473.* ☜ *300$00.* ⊙ *Apr.–Sept., Mon.–Sat. 10–6; Oct.–Mar., Mon.–Sat. 10–1 and 2–5.*

🔴 **Elevador da Glória.** One of the finest approaches to the Bairro Alto is via the Elevador da Glória, a funicular railway on the western side of Avenida da Liberdade, near Praça dos Restauradores. The *elevador* runs up the steep hill and takes only about a minute to reach the São Pedro de Alcântara Miradouro, a viewing point that looks out over the castle and the Alfama. ⊠ *Calçada da Glória, no phone.* ☜ *150$00; free with tourist pass.* ⊙ *Daily 7 AM–midnight.*

★ 🔴 **Igreja de São Roque.** The same architect who designed São Vicente on the outskirts of the Alfama was also responsible for the Renaissance Igreja de São Roque (Church of St. Roque). Curb your impatience with its plain facade and venture inside. Its side chapels are superbly decorated. The last chapel on the left before the altar, the 18th-century **Capela de São João Baptista** (Chapel of St. John the Baptist) is extraordinary: Designed and built in Rome, with rare stones and mosaics that resemble oil paintings, the chapel was taken apart, shipped to Lisbon, and installed in 1747. You may find a guide who will escort you around the church and switch on the appropriate lights so the beauty of the chapels are revealed. Adjoining the church, the **Museu de Arte Sacra** (Museum of Sacred Art) displays a collection of 16th- to 18th-century paintings and a series of Italian clerical vestments and liturgical objects. ⊠ *Largo Trinidade Coelho,* ☎ *01/346–0361.* ⊙ *Church daily 8:30–6, museum Tues.–Sun. 10–1 and 2–5.* ☜ *Church free; museum 150$00, free Sun.*

★ 🔴 **Instituto do Vinho do Porto.** In the cozy, clublike lounge of the Instituto do Vinho do Porto (the Port Wine Institute), visitors can sample more than 300 types and vintages of port, from extra-dry white varieties to red vintages. Service can be a bit slow, but eventually someone will bring you a wine list, and you may order by the glass or bottle. ⊠ *Rua de São Pedro de Alcântara 45,* ☎ *01/342–3307.* ☜ *Free; prices of tastings vary, starting at 200$00.* ⊙ *Mon.–Sat. 10–10.*

Jardim Botânico and Museu de História Natural. Lisbon's main botanical gardens, the hillside Jardim Botânico, were first laid out in 1874. Hidden between back streets to the north of the Bairro Alto, they make an attractive stop, with 10 acres of garden containing paths, park benches, and nearly 15,000 species of subtropical plants; there's also a 19th-century meteorological observatory. Moreover, the gardens form part of the **Museu de História Natural** (Natural History Museum), whose buildings present mineral and geological displays and zoological and anthropological exhibits. The gardens are about a mile north of the Bairro Alto, beyond the Port Wine Institute. ⊠ *Rua da Escola Politécnica 58,* ☎ *01/396–1521.* 🎟 *Gardens 200$00, museums free.* ☉ *Mineral/geological and zoological/anthropological sections weekdays 9–noon and 2–5, Sat. 3–6. Botanical gardens May–Oct., daily 9–8; Nov.–Apr., weekdays 9–6; guided tours yr-round Sat. at 11. Reservations required for tours.*

Jardim da Estrêla. Inside the attractively laid out Jardim da Estrêla (Estrêla Gardens), old men sit at tables playing card games. Watch them awhile, stroll the shaded paths, and then pull up a chair at the outdoor garden café for a drink or a snack. Towering over the southwestern side is the 18th-century **Basilica da Estrêla** (Estrêla Basilica), which is open 7:30–1 and 3–7. This spacious baroque church has an unusually restrained interior and offers views of the city from its *zimborio* (dome). The gardens lie on the western edge of the Bairro Alto. You can walk there, though it's more pleasant to catch Tram 28, which runs from Rua do Loreto, near Praça Luis de Camões, just west of Largo do Carmo.

Rua Garrett. The Chiado's principal street is lined with old department stores and a series of comfortable, turn-of-the-century, wood-paneled coffee shops that attract locals and tourists alike. The most famous of the Chiado's coffee shops is **A Brasileira** (⊠ Rua Garrett 120, ☎ 01/346–9541), which features a life-size statue of Portugal's national poet, Fernando Pessoa, seated at a table.

The Modern City

Modern (i.e., post-18th-century) Lisbon is the least uniform in character of the city's districts. It's easy enough to chart where it begins—at the large square called Praça dos Restauradores, north of Rossío—but its attractions are then so diverse (and so widespread) it defies any attempt to see it as a whole. Nonetheless, the modern city's southern reaches do at least echo the rather grand surroundings of the Baixa, and many visitors find time to walk up the impressive Avenida da Liberdade as far as the city's main park, Parque Eduardo VII. North of here, the modern city stretches into residential suburbs, with only the occasional stop to tempt the tourist. What particular attractions there are—namely Portugal's finest museum and a clutch of other minor diversions—can all be reached by public transportation.

Numbers in the margin correspond to points of interest on the Exploring Lisbon map.

Sights to See

⑲ Amoreiras. Lisbon's most ambitious post-modern building is the gigantic pink-and-blue Amoreiras, a commercial-and-residential complex. Designed by Tomás Taveira and visible from just about everywhere in the city, Amoreiras houses a huge shopping center, a 10-screen movie theater, a "food street" of restaurants and bars, and information boards at every turn. On weekends it seems all of Lisbon turns out to parade the corridors. ⊠ *Av. Eng. Duarte Pacheco (metro: Rotunda),* ☎ *01/383–2558.* ☉ *Shops and restaurants daily 9 AM–11 PM.*

⑱ Aqueduto das Aguas Livres. Lisbon was formerly provided with clean drinking water by means of the Aqueduto das Aguas Livres, an 18th-century aqueduct supported by 14 arches. Nineteenth-century lore tells of one character who had a penchant for hurling his victims the 200 feet to the ground below. ⊠ *Largo das Amoreiras (metro: Rotunda). For organized visits to the aqueduct,* ☎ *01/813–5522 or ask at the tourist information office.*

⑯ Avenida da Liberdade. The city's main avenue—Avenida da Liberdade—is 1½ kilometers (1 mile) long and about 325 feet wide in places. Sadly, the thoroughfare that was laid out in 1879 isn't as grand as it once was: Many turn-of-the-century mansions and art-deco buildings that graced the route have been demolished; others are covered in scaffolding as "renovation" work—the practice of turning historic buildings into soulless office blocks—continues. Nevertheless, you should take a leisurely stroll up the avenue from Praça dos Restauradores to the Parque Eduardo VII. Among the many cafés serving coffee and cool drinks is an open-air *esplanada* (garden café), in a central, tree-shaded location at the south end.

㉔ Campo Pequeno. This site—impossible to overlook—is the city's circular, redbrick, Moorish-style bullring, which sports small cupolas atop its four main towers. The bullring holds about 9,000 people who crowd in to watch the weekly bullfights, held every Thursday between June and September. ⊠ *Praça de Touros do Campo Pequeno, Avda. da República (metro: Campo Pequeno),* ☎ *01/793–2093.*

㉑ Centro de Arte Moderna. In the gardens outside the Fundação Calouste Gulbenkian, sculptures hide in every recess. You may want to spend a little time here before following signs through the garden to the foundation's Centro de Arte Moderna, where modern and contemporary Portuguese and foreign art are displayed on two floors. There's also a special section set aside for drawings and prints. Although the range of exhibits here is more limited than that of the Gulbenkian Museum itself, modern-art fans will appreciate this venue for the finest collection of its sort in Portugal. Naturally, Portuguese artists are best represented: Look for pieces by Amadeo de Sousa Cardoso, whose painting style varied greatly in his short life; abstract works by Viera da Silva; and the childhood themes explored in the paintings of Paula Rego. ⊠ *Rua Dr. N. Bettencourt (metro: Palhavã),* ☎ *01/795–0241.* 🎟 *200$00, free Sun.* ⊙ *June–Sept., Tues., Thurs.–Fri., and Sun. 10–5; Wed. and Sat. 2–7:30; Oct.–May, Tues.–Sun. 10–5.*

㉒ Jardim Zoológico. With a menagerie of 2,000 animals from over 370 species, the city zoo is always a popular spot. In addition to the usual exhibits there is a children's zoo, with miniature houses and small animals; a dolphin show, presented at 11 and 3; and even a cemetery for dogs. There are snack bars and restaurants on site, or you can pack a lunch for a picnic. ⊠ *Estrada de Benfica 158 (metro: Sete Ríos),* ☎ *01/726–8041 or 01/726–8017.* 🎟 *Zoo 550$00, dolphin show 800$00.* ⊙ *Daily 9–8.*

★ ⑳ Museu Calouste Gulbenkian. Set on its own lush grounds, the museum of the celebrated Fundação Calouste Gulbenkian, a cultural-trust foundation, houses treasures collected by Armenian oil magnate Calouste Gulbenkian (1869–1955) and donated to the people of Portugal in return for tax concessions. The Museu Calouste Gulbenkian is the main part of the foundation's buildings and is easily Portugal's finest museum. The collection it houses is split in two: One part is devoted to Egyptian, Greek, Roman, Islamic, and Asian art and the other to European acquisitions. Both holdings are relatively small, but the quality of the pieces on display is magnificent, and you should aim to spend at least two hours here or even the better part of a day. English-language notes are available throughout the museum.

You might first visit the astounding Egyptian Room, highlighted by a haunting gold mummy mask. Greek and Roman coins and statuary, Chinese porcelain, Japanese prints, and a set of rich 16th- and 17th-century Persian tapestries follow. No less comprehensive is the European art section, with pieces representing all major schools from the 15th through the 20th centuries. A room of vivid 18th-century Venetian scenes by Francesco Guardi and paintings by Rembrandt, Rubens, Monet, and Renoir stimulate the senses, as do the Italian and Spanish ceramics, gleaming French furniture, textiles, and art-nouveau jewelry. In short, this collection rates as one of the most satisfying and complete holdings of artistic brilliance in the world.

If it's all too much to take in at one time, break up your visit with a stop in the pleasant café-restaurant in the basement. There's an exhibition room here, too, featuring temporary displays of art. As you leave the museum, you can purchase superb (and inexpensive) posters and postcards at the main desk. The foundation also houses two concert halls, where music and ballet festivals are held in winter and spring. Thanks to the Gulbenkian Foundation, modestly priced tickets are available at the box office. ⊠ *Av. de Berna 45 (metro: Palhavã),* ☎ *01/795–0236.* ☏ *200$00, free Sun.* ☉ *June–Sept., Tues., Thurs.–Fri., and Sun. 10–5; Wed. and Sat. 2–7:30; Oct.–May, Tues.–Sun. 10–5.*

㉓ Palácio dos Marqueses da Fronteira. Built in the late 17th century, the Palácio dos Marqueses da Fronteira remains one of the most beautiful private houses in the capital, containing splendid reception rooms with 17th- and 18th-century decorative tiles, contemporary furniture, and paintings. The grounds, which harbor a terraced walk, a topiary garden, and statuary and fountains, are stunning. The palace is northwest of the city, in the suburb of São Domingo de Benfica (near the zoo). ⊠ *Largo de São Domingo de Benfica 1 (metro: Sete Ríos),* ☎ *01/778–2023.* ☏ *Weekdays, gardens 300$00, palace and gardens 1,000$00; Sat., gardens 500$00, palace and gardens 1,500$00.* ☉ *June–Sept., Mon.–Sat. for guided tours 4 times daily; arrive between 10:30 and noon. Oct.–May, Mon.–Sat., 2 tours daily, at 11 AM and noon.*

Parque Eduardo VII. Established at the beginning of this century, the city's main park, the Parque Eduardo VII, was named in honor of King Edward VII of England, who visited Lisbon in 1903. Bordering the park, particularly on the western side, are several of Lisbon's luxury hotels, including the Ritz and the Lisboa Meridien. (Many of the hotels have private terraces that guarantee you a room with a view.) The park is best known for its two **estufas**: the *estufa fria* (cold greenhouse) and *estufa quente* (hot greenhouse), which contain rare flowers, trees, and shrubs from tropical and subtropical climes. The estufa fria is also one of the city's most bizarre concert venues, used on occasion by orchestras and soloists. ⊠ *Parque Eduardo VII (Metro: Rotunda),* ☎ *01/388–2278.* ☏ *Estufas 75$00.* ☉ *Apr.–Sept., daily 9–6; Oct.–Mar., daily 9–5.*

⑰ Praça Marquês de Pombal. As a pointed reminder of who was responsible for the layout of the city before you, dominating the Praça Marquês de Pombal is a central statue of the Marquês himself, designer of the new Lisbon that emerged from the ruins of the 1755 earthquake. The square is effectively a large roundabout—and a useful orientation point, since it stands at the northern end of the main Avenida da Liberdade, with the city's main park, Parque Eduardo VII, just behind. It's also known as the Rotunda, which is the name of the metro station.

⑮ Praça dos Restauradores. The square adjacent to Rossío metro station—Praça dos Restauradores—marks the beginning of modern Lisbon. The name commemorates the uprising in 1640 against Spanish rule, which ushered in the era of Portuguese independence. Here the broad, tree-lined Avenida da Liberdade starts its northwesterly ascent, and there's also a metro station where trains will take you to points of interest in the modern city. There's little of interest in the square itself, save the 18th-century **Palácio Foz,** on the west side, which houses the main tourist office.

Rua das Portas de Santo Antão. If you want to eat seafood in the center of Lisbon, you come to Rua das Portas de Santo Antão, a largely pedestrian-only street of fish restaurants, with waiters lurking at every door. There's a varied range of eating places—cafés to high-class restaurants—but most display great tanks of lobsters and fish on ice slabs; choose your meal and then sit outside on the cobblestones to enjoy it. The street is on the eastern side of Praça dos Restauradores, a block east from the square and running parallel to it.

Belém and the Museu de Arte Antiga

To see the best examples of the uniquely Portuguese late-Gothic architecture known as Manueline, you should head for Belém, at the far southwestern edge of Lisbon. If you are traveling in a group of three or four, taxis are the cheapest means of transportation. Otherwise, for a more scenic—if bumpier—20- to 30-minute journey, take Tram 15, 16, or 17 from Praça do Comércio, which stop close to your destination. The route passes through the wealthy district of Lapa, with its Museu de Arte Antiga (Ancient Art Museum), and at about the halfway point you'll pass under the magnificent Ponte 25 de Abril, spanning the Rio Tejo. Standing 230 feet above the water and stretching almost 2½ kilometers (1½ miles), this suspension bridge was completed in 1966 but later renamed to commemorate the 1974 revolution. It's worth noting that almost all the sights in Belém, including the Museu de Arte Antiga, are closed Mondays; conversely, Sunday sees free or reduced admission at many attractions.

Numbers in the margin correspond to points of interest on the Exploring Belém map.

Sights to See

㉛ Centro Cultural de Belém. Built of pink granite and marble, the contentious design of the Centro Cultural de Belém (Belém Cultural Center) has few friends, though all of Lisbon appreciates the cultural activities on offer. It contains exhibition space, a restaurant, and a concert hall, and it has fine views of the monastery and the river from its attractive roof gardens and terrace bar. Stop by reception to pick up an events brochure. ⊠ *Avda. da India,* ☎ *01/301–9606.* ⊙ *Exhibition hall and café daily 11–8, terrace bar weekdays 3–9.*

㉞ Jardim Botânico da Ajuda. To see the oldest botanical garden in Portugal, you need to visit the Jardim Botânico da Ajuda (Ajuda Botanical Gardens). Laid out in 1768, it remains an enjoyable place to spend a half hour or so, especially on a summer's afternoon, when you can stroll up here from the river at Belém. The many species of flora, labeled in Latin, are contained in several greenhouses covering 10 acres. ⊠ *Calçada da Ajuda, no phone.* ▧ *50$00.* ⊙ *June–Sept., Tues.–Sun. 10–7; Oct.–May, Tues.–Sun. 10–6.*

㉙ Monumento dos Descobrimentos. Built in 1960, the tall, white Monumento dos Descobrimentos (Monument of the Discoveries) was designed as a modern tribute to the country's seafaring explorers. Fittingly, it was erected to commemorate the 500th anniversary of the death of mariner-king Prince Henry the Navigator and was built on what was the departure point for many voyages of discovery, including those of Vasco de Gama. At the prow is Henry the Navigator, facing the water; lined up behind him are the Portuguese explorers of Brazil and Asia, as well as other national heroes, including Camões the poet, who can

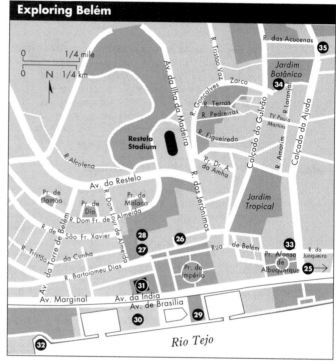

Exploring Belém

be recognized by the book in his hand. On the ground adjacent to the monument, an inlaid map shows the extent of the explorations undertaken by the 15th- and 16th-century Portuguese sailors. Walk inside and take the elevator to the top for river views. ✉ *Avda. de Brasília, no phone.* 🎟 *300$00.* ☉ *Tues.–Sun. 9:30–7.*

★ ❷❻ **Mosteiro dos Jerónimos.** Conceived and commissioned by Dom Manuel I, the enormous bulk of Belém's famous Mosteiro dos Jerónimos (Jerónimos Monastery) was financed largely by treasures brought back from the so-called *descobrimentos*—the Portuguese "discoveries" of Africa, Asia, and South America. Construction began in 1502 under the supervision of Diogo de Boitaca (architect of the pioneering Igreja de Jesus at Setúbal) and his successor João de Castilho, a Spaniard.

It's a supreme example of the Manueline style of building (named after King Dom Manuel I), which represented a marked departure from the prevailing Gothic. A grand vision of great individuality, much of the design is characterized by elaborate sculptural details, often with a maritime motif. João de Castilho was responsible for the superb southern portal, which forms the main entrance to the church: The figure on the central pillar is Henry the Navigator, and the canopy shows a hierarchy of statues contained within niches. Inside, the remarkably spacious interior contrasts with the riot of decorative detail on the six nave columns, which disappear into a complex latticework ceiling.

Don't leave the monastery without visiting the Gothic- and Renaissance-style **double cloister,** the lower level of which was also designed to stunning effect by Castilho. The arches and pillars are heavily sculpted with marine motifs. ✉ *Praça do Império,* 🕿 *01/362–0034.* 🎟 *Church free;*

cloister 400$00 June–Sept., 250$00 Oct.–May, free Sun. ☉ *June–Sept.,*
Tues.–Sun. 10–6:30; Oct.–May, Tues.–Sun. 10–1 and 2:30–5.

NEED A
BREAK?
For a real taste of Lisbon, stop at the impressive **Fabrica dos Pasteis de
Belém** (✉ Rua de Belém 86–88, ☎ 01/363-7423), a pastry shop and
café that serves delicious, hot custard pastries sprinkled with cinnamon
and powdered sugar. Although you can buy these treats throughout Lisbon, they're made best here.

★ ㉕ **Museu de Arte Antiga.** The only museum in Lisbon to approach the
status of the Gulbenkian is the Museu de Arte Antiga (Ancient Art Museum). Housed in a 17th-century palace, the museum features a beautifully displayed collection of Portuguese art mainly from the 15th
through 19th centuries, which superbly complements the Gulbenkian's
general collection. Indeed, Gulbenkian himself donated several pieces
to this museum, which opened in 1883.

Of all the holdings, the religious works of the Portuguese School of
artists (characterized by fine portraiture with a distinct Flemish influence) stand out, especially the acknowledged masterpiece of Nuno
Gonçalves, the *St. Vincent Altarpiece.* Painted between 1467 and 1470
for St. Vincent Chapel in Lisbon's cathedral, the altarpiece has six panels showing the patron saint of Lisbon receiving the homage of king,
court, and citizens. Sixty different figures can be identified, including
Henry the Navigator, the archbishop of Lisbon, and sundry dukes,
monks, fishermen, knights, and religious figures. In the top left corner
of the two central panels is a figure purported to be that of Gonçalves
himself.

Besides the Portuguese works, there are pieces by Flemish painters who
influenced the Portuguese. There are also extensive collections of
French silver, Portuguese furniture and tapestries, Asian ceramics, and
other works from former Portuguese colonies.

Tram 19 from Rua do Arsenal, near Praça do Comércio, stops outside
the museum. Coming from Belém, Buses 27 and 49 run from Rua de
Belém across from the monastery and stop near the museum on their
way back to downtown Lisbon. ✉ *Rua das Janelas Verdes,* ☎ *01/397–
6001.* ⊟ *500$00, free Sun. 10–1.* ☉ *Tues.–Sun. 10–1 and 2–5.*

㉚ **Museu de Arte Popular.** Housed in the squat building of the Museu de
Arte Popular (Popular Art Museum) are examples of the country's folk
art. It's a rather shabby structure these days—although perhaps future
renovation will rescue it—but persevere since inside you'll find a fascinating collection of ceramics, costumes, furniture, domestic and farm
implements, and other ethnographic pieces. Displays are organized according to the province from which the objects came. ✉ *Avda. Brasília,*
☎ *01/301–1282.* ⊟ *300$00, free Sun.* ☉ *Tues.–Sun. 10–12:30 and
2–5.*

㉗ **Museu da Marinha.** There are two museums in the complex of buildings adjoining the Mosteiro dos Jerónimos, but the Museu da Marinha is the most inviting to the layperson. Inside the large, well-laid-out
Maritime Museum, you get a real grasp of the importance of the seafaring tradition in Portugal. There's something for everyone, including early maps and maritime codes, navigational equipment, real and
model ships (some displaying an inordinate amount of detail), uniforms,
and weapons. ✉ *Praça do Império,* ☎ *01/362–0010.* ⊟ *250$00, free
Sun.* ☉ *Tues.–Sun. 10–5.*

33 **Museu Nacional de Coches.** This museum houses one of the largest collections of coaches in the world in buildings that once accommodated a riding school. The oldest vehicle on display was made for Phillip II of Spain in the late 16th century, and among the most stunning exhibits are three gold coaches created in Rome for King John V in 1716. This collection of gloriously painted, gilded baroque coaches is dazzling, and it's one of the most popular collections in Lisbon. ⊠ *Praça Afonso de Albuquerque,* ☎ *01/363–8022.* ▨ *June–Sept. 450$00, Oct.–May 250$00; free Sun.* ⊙ *June–Sept., Tues.–Sun. 10–1 and 2:30–6:30; Oct.–May, Tues.–Sun. 10–1 and 2:30–5:30.*

35 **Palácio da Ajuda.** In 1802 construction began on the Palácio da Ajuda (Ajuda Palace), which was intended as a royal residence; its last royal occupant died here in 1911. Today the overblown, fussily designed building is home to a museum of 18th- and 19th-century paintings, furniture, and tapestries, but unless you're especially interested in such works, this attraction is not an essential sight. It's a 20-minute walk north along Calçada da Ajuda from the coach museum, but Bus 14 runs this way, too. ⊠ *Largo da Ajuda,* ☎ *01/363–7095.* ▨ *500$00, free Sun. 10–2. Guided tours arranged on request.* ⊙ *Thurs.–Tues. 10–5.*

28 **Planetário Calouste Gulbenkian.** In Belém, behind the Maritime Museum, the Planetário Calouste Gulbenkian (Planetarium) presents interesting astronomical shows and displays several times a week. A bulletin posted in the window announces the current program, or you can get updates from the Palácio da Foz tourist office. ⊠ *Praça do Imperio,* ☎ *01/362–0002.* ▨ *300$00.* ⊙ *Schedules vary, so check in advance.*

★ **32** **Torre de Belém.** The openwork balconies and domed turrets of the fanciful Torre de Belém (Belém Tower) make this perhaps the purest Manueline structure in the country. Although it was built in the early 16th century on an island in the middle of the Rio Tejo, today the chalk-white tower stands near what has become the north bank—evidence of the changing course of the river. Built to defend the entrance to the port, the tower served as a prison from the late 16th through the 19th centuries; its inmates were incarcerated in the dungeons. Cross the wood gangway and walk inside, not necessarily to see the rather plain interior but to clamber up the steep stone steps to the very top. From this vantage point you'll have a bird's-eye view of the Tejo and central Lisbon. ⊠ *Av. da India,* ☎ *01/301–6892.* ▨ *400$00 June–Sept., 250$00 Oct.–May.* ⊙ *June–Sept., Tues.–Sun. 10–6:30; Oct.–May, Tues.–Sun. 10–1 and 2:30–5.*

DINING

Almost all restaurants offer an *ementa turistica* (tourist menu), a set-price meal, most often served at lunchtime. Meals vary in quality but generally include three courses, a drink, and coffee, all for about 2,000$00–3,000$00. The selections are nearly always of good value but can be limited in scope. At all restaurants, be wary of eating anything brought as an appetizer that you haven't specifically ordered. You'll be charged extra, even if you eat just one olive, and it's surprising how much this can add to the cost of a meal. Lisbon's restaurants usually serve lunch from noon until 3 and dinner from 7:30 until 11; many establishments are closed Sunday.

Unless otherwise noted below, restaurants don't accept reservations; this is especially true of inexpensive places. In the traditional *cervejarias* (beer hall/restaurants), which frequently have huge dining rooms, you'll probably have to wait for a table, but usually not more than 15 or 20 minutes. In the Bairro Alto, many of the reasonably priced *tascas* (taverns) are on the small side: If you can't reserve a table, either wait in line or move on to the next place. Throughout Lisbon, dress for meals is usually casual, but exceptions are noted below.

$$$$ ✗ **António Clara.** This classic French restaurant, named for its owner, is housed in an attractive art-nouveau building in the north of Lisbon, in the modern part of the city. In addition to French fare, international dishes with a flourish are served in an elegant room that has a decorated ceiling, oil paintings, heavy draperies, and a huge chandelier. The menu is seasonal (fish is always well presented), the service extremely attentive, and there's a fine wine list. A private dining club for businesspeople and the piano bar attract an upmarket clientele. ⊠ *Av. da República 38,* ☎ *01/796–6380. Reservations essential. Jacket and tie. AE, DC, MC, V. Closed Sun.*

$$$$ ✗ **Aviz.** One of the best and classiest restaurants in Lisbon, Aviz has
★ a rich but subtle belle-epoque decor, which includes turn-of-the-century furnishings, fine wood paneling, leather chairs, and crisp linen tablecloths. This exclusive restaurant is hidden on a side street off the Baixa's Rua Garrett. The mainly French and international menu is enhanced by Portuguese elements such as *bacalhau* (cod), virtually the Portuguese national dish, and complemented by a superior wine list. Afternoon tea is served, too, which makes a more economical way to eat in the grand interior. ⊠ *Rua Serpa Pinto 12–13,* ☎ *01/342–8391. Reservations essential. Jacket and tie. AE, DC, MC, V. Closed Sun. No lunch Sat.*

$$$$ ✗ **Gambrinus.** One of Lisbon's older and smarter restaurants, Gambrinus is renowned for its fish and shellfish. On a busy street that bulges with fish restaurants, this establishment is understated—a quality that only adds to its appeal. Once inside the front door you'll find many small dining rooms. Your waiter will regale you with a list of the day's seafood specials, which vary enormously in price; prawns, lobster, and crab are always available and always excellent. (There are meat dishes, too.) For a less formal but satisfying meal, you can eat at the wood-paneled bar during lunchtime. ⊠ *Rua Portas de S. Antão 23–25,* ☎ *01/346–8974 or 01/342–1466. AE, DC, MC, V.*

$$$$ ✗ **Tagide.** Delicious Portuguese food and wine are served in this fine old house that looks out over the Baixa and Rio Tejo. Renovations have created an elegant dining room lined with 17th-century tiles—a lovely backdrop for sampling the impressive list of Portuguese regional dishes, including the famous *presunto* (smoked ham) from Chaves. Also offered is a smaller but no less succulent selection of French-influenced international dishes. For the best effect, try to sit at a table by the window. ⊠ *Largo Academia das Belas Artes 18–20,* ☎ *01/346–0570. Reservations essential. AE, DC, MC, V. Closed weekends.*

$$$$ ✗ **Tavares Rico.** Superb food, an excellent wine list, and a handsome
★ Edwardian dining room have made this one of Lisbon's most famous and formal restaurants. Tavares Rico—founded as a café in the 18th century—pleases customers with the splendor of its furnishings, the quality of its service, and its French-inspired menu, which features seasonal ingredients. A wise choice for an entrée is the sole cooked in champagne sauce. ⊠ *Rua Misericórdia 35–37,* ☎ *01/342–1112. Reservations essential. AE, DC, MC, V. No lunch weekends.*

$$$ ✗ **Alcântara Café.** This large bar-restaurant has a glorious modern design that impressively and effectively combines wood, leather, velvet, and steel to re-create something of the 1920s in Lisbon. Locals bring visitors here when they want to impress them, and it rarely fails. Old Portuguese specialties highlight the menu, and fish is always a good choice. There's a large wine list, too, and a splendid bar if you want

44

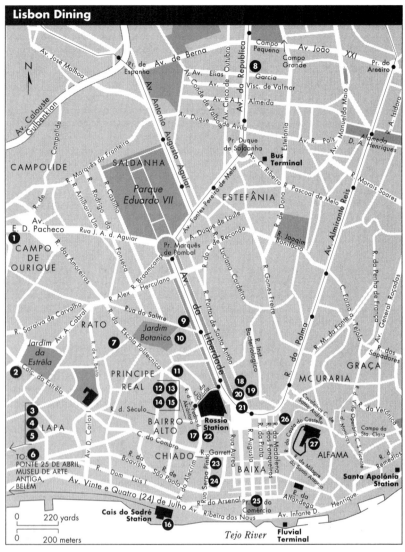

Adega do
Ribatejo, **14**
Alcântara Café, **3**
Andorra, **18**
António Clara, **8**
Aviz, **23**
Bota Alta, **15**
Bonjardim, **20**
Café Martinho da
Arcada, **25**
Cais da Ribeira, **16**
Casa Faz Frio, **11**

Cervejaria
Trindade, **22**
Comida de Santo, **7**
Farah's Tandoori, **2**
Gambrinus, **21**
Já Sei, **4**
O Cantinho
do Aziz, **26**
O Madeirense, **1**
O Manel, **10**
Michel, **27**
Ribadouro, **9**

São Jerónimo, **5**
Sinal Vermelho, **12**
Solmar, **19**
Sua Excêlencia, **6**
Tagide, **24**
Tavares Rico, **17**
Vá e Volte, **13**

to sip an aperitif before dinner or stay on afterward—the bar serves drinks until 3 AM. The restaurant is outside the city center, near Ponte 25 de Abril, and the kitchen stays open until 1 AM. ⊠ *Rua Maria Luísa Holstein 15, near Rua Coz. Económica,* ☎ *01/363–7176. AE, DC, MC, V. No lunch.*

$$$ ✕ **Café Martinho da Arcada.** This famous café-restaurant, founded in 1782 beneath the arcades of Praça do Comércio in Baixa, was once frequented by the Portuguese poet Fernando Pessoa and other literary stars. These days the lunchtime crowd in its wood-paneled dining room is mainly businesspeople from the surrounding shops and offices. The menu offers regional Portuguese cuisine, some of which reveals a French influence. Try a *cataplana* (clam stew) from the Algarve, especially if you won't be heading south on this trip. ⊠ *Praça do Comércio 3,* ☎ *01/887–9259. MC, V. Closed Sun.*

$$$ ✕ **Cais da Ribeira.** Converted from an old fisherman's warehouse, this small restaurant, perched on the waterfront behind Cais do Sodré station, specializes in fish grilled over charcoal, as well as a filling *caldeirada* (fish stew). The pretty, split-level wooden interior makes good use of the old warehouse shell. Whatever you order, the views over the river will complement your meal nicely. Remember that this is not the most desirable area for walking late at night: You can get a taxi just around the corner, in front of the train station. ⊠ *Cais do Sodré,* ☎ *01/342–3611 or 01/347–6653. AE, DC, MC, V. Closed Sun. No lunch Sat.*

$$$ ✕ **Já Sei.** Because of its prime location above the river at Belém, this is a fine lunchtime stop, especially in summer, when you can sit on the attractive outdoor terrace. Smooth service and impressive meals—*arroz de marisco* (seafood rice) for two, for example—make this a memorable choice. ⊠ *Avda. Brasília 202, Belém,* ☎ *01/301–5969. Reservations essential. AE, DC, MC, V. Closed Sun. No dinner Mon.*

$$$ ✕ **Michel.** Innovative French cooking with Portuguese flourishes is
★ served in this intimate and attractive green-painted restaurant just outside the walls of St. George's Castle. Curtains—which add to the dignified ambience—shut out the sun beaming in from the dusty square outside. Choose from such dishes as bass fillet with champagne sauce and *porco a alentejana* (pork with clams), a Portuguese classic. ⊠ *Largo S. Cruz do Castelo 5,* ☎ *01/886–4338. AE, DC, MC, V. Closed Sun. No lunch Sat.*

$$$ ✕ **O Madeirense.** Even though it's set inside the Amoreiras Shopping Center, Lisbon's only Madeiran restaurant goes overboard making patrons feel they're on the island itself: Rural scenes adorn the walls, the wait staff is in traditional costume, and the place is filled with wood, rattan, and rubber plants. But this is no mere theme restaurant; the cooking is assured, and the consistent quality of the food and service appeals to the mainly business clientele. Start with a glass of Madeira wine while you ponder the menu: the *espedata* is traditional—a skewer of steak fillet, rubbed with salt and spices, is hung above the table from a stand so you can serve yourself at will. Tuna and swordfish make an appearance on the menu, too, and you might try the fried corn-cube appetizer. ⊠ *Loja 3027, Amoreiras Shopping Center, Av. Eng. Duarte Pacheco,* ☎ *01/383–0827. Reservations essential for Sun. lunch. AE, DC, MC, V.*

$$$ ✕ **O Manel.** Tucked away in a strange little enclave of theaters and restaurants behind the Lisboa Plaza Hotel, O Manel is a fish and shellfish house that attracts the capital's politicians and media types. You have to know it's here to find it, but once you've made your way, you're greeted by a roaring fire, two small dining rooms, and great food—the açorda with prawns is immensely filling; other fish (and meat) are grilled to perfection. There's a wine list, but the house wine is very drinkable; the staff is short on English but happy to help. To get here, walk through the gates on Travessa do Salitre into the theater complex—it looks like an amusement park, and you may have to pay a nominal entrance fee, but it's the right place—bear left into the parking lot, and then turn right. Anyone can direct you if you get lost. ⊠ *Parque Mayer, Avda. de Liberdade,* ☎ *01/346–3167. DC, MC, V.*

$$$ ✕ **São Jerónimo.** Contemporary decor and classy presentation of Portuguese food attract Lisbon's elite to São Jerónimo. Favorites include grilled shrimp and other fresh seafood dishes, and there are regional specialties, too, which change daily. This quiet restaurant beside the monastery in Belém offers discreet, stylish dining. ⊠ *Rua dos Jerónimos 12, Belém,* ☎ *01/364–8797. Reservations essential. AE, DC, MC, V. Closed Sun.*

$$$ ✕ **Solmar.** Best known for its fish and shellfish (and the excellent seafood soup), Solmar's menu may surprise some with its occasional offering of boar or venison (when in season). Competent waiters move briskly about the two-floor dining area. A central fountain is the focus, and a huge mosaic of an underwater scene carries out Solmar's oceanic theme. Some have complained that Solmar is resting on its laurels, but the cooking remains more hit than miss, and it's an ideal lunch stop for sightseers. ⊠ *Rua Portas de S. Antão 108,* ☎ *01/342–3371. AE, DC, MC, V.*

$$$ ✕ **Sua Excêlencia.** In this cozy little pink town-house restaurant, the
★ English-speaking owner will personally talk you through the outstanding Portuguese dishes on the menu. Specialties include smoked swordfish (an Algarve favorite), baked bacalhau, and Angolan-style chicken. And a good-value tourist menu costs less than 4,000$00. This is a handy place for those staying at York House or at As Janelas Verdes (☞ *Lodging, below*), and it provides an intimate dining experience after a hectic day's sightseeing. ⊠ *Rua do Conde 42,* ☎ *01/603614. MC, V. Closed Wed. and Sept. No lunch weekends.*

$$ ✕ **Adega do Ribatejo.** There are plenty of fado clubs in the Bairro Alto, but none so accessible as this thoroughly enjoyable, tiled *adega* (tavern). Primarily it's a restaurant, and the food is reasonably good, though not outstanding by local standards. Dishes like steaks, bacalhau, veal, and fried fish are often on the changing menu. What makes it a real treat, however, is the nightly fado-singing session, when professional musicians serenade diners with ear-splitting renditions of traditional songs. The manager works the tables and sings himself on occasion; even the cooks sometimes get in on the act. Note that there's a minimum charge of 2000$00 and that you'll probably have to wait in line unless you arrive before 8 PM. ⊠ *Rua Diário de Noticias 23,* ☎ *01/346–8343. MC, V. Closed Sun.*

$$ ✕ **Bota Alta.** This tiny, wood-paneled tavern in the heart of the Bairro Alto is one of the neighborhood's oldest and most favored eating places. There's very little space between the tables, but this only enhances the buzz: lines form outside the door by 8 PM. Once you've secured a table, choose from a menu strong on traditional Portuguese dishes—perhaps bacalhau cooked in cream, homemade sausages, steaks in wine sauce, or grilled fish. The house wine comes in ceramic jugs and is very good. ⊠ *Trav. da Queimada 37,* ☎ *01/342–7959. No credit cards. Closed Sun. No lunch Sat.*

$$ ✕ **Cervejaria Trindade.** Relatively inexpensive and hearty Portuguese
★ cuisine, including açorda and grilled seafood, makes the short wait for a table here worthwhile. The walls inside this 19th-century Bairro Alto beer hall–restaurant are adorned with colorful tiles, and high vaulted ceilings and frenetic service create a lively, spacious feel. The garden is an enjoyable spot for dining in summer. ⊠ *Rua Nova da Trindade 20,* ☎ *01/342–3506. AE, DC, MC, V.*

$$ ✕ **Comida de Santo.** Excellent Brazilian food served in an attractive, brightly painted dining room and lively Brazilian music ensure a steady clientele and keep this place packed until closing time, at 1 AM. Come early and enjoy classic dishes, such as *fejoada* (meat-and-bean stew) or *vatapa* (a spicy shrimp dish). Order a *caipirinha* (rum cocktail) while you're waiting—they're lethal. ⊠ *Calçada Engenheiro Miguel Pais 39,* ☎ *01/396–3339. AE, DC, MC, V.*

$$ ✕ **Farah's Tandoori.** A small, simple place on two floors, Farah's is known as one of the best and friendliest Indian restaurants in Lisbon. All the curries, served with Indian bread if you choose, are sure bets for a good meal. Specialties include coconut prawns, *birianis* (mixed rice dishes) and a good tandoori chicken, while there's also plenty of choice for vegetarians. Take a taxi—it's in an anonymous side street off Rua Buenos Aires and is a bit tricky to find at night. ⊠ *Rua de Sant'Ana à Lapa 73,* ☎ *01/609219. MC, V. Closed Tues.*

$$ ✕ **Ribadouro.** Go to this bustling basement restaurant on the main avenue for the finely prepared seafood, including crab and crayfish. The surroundings are functional, not fancy, but the layout allows you to watch the delectable crustaceans being prepared at the counter. Try to arrive before 8, although even on the busiest nights you shouldn't have to wait too long to be seated. If you eat at the bar, prices are even more reasonable. ⊠ *Avda. da Liberdade 155,* ☎ *01/354–9411. AE, DC, MC, V.*

$$ ✕ **Sinal Vermelho.** This restaurant in the heart of the Bairro Alto up-
★ dates the traditional Lisbon adega. The split-level dining room is traditionally tiled, and the food is thoroughly Portuguese, but the prints on the wall are modern, the clientele firmly professional (and in-the-know tourist), and the wine list wide-ranging (if completely Portuguese). Start perhaps with a plate of clams drenched in oil and parsley and follow with the fresh fish and seafood, which is rarely disappointing; the meat dishes are less inspiring, though if you're feeling adventurous, you might try the tripe or the kidneys. ⊠ *Rua das Gáveas 89,* ☎ *01/346–1252. Reservations essential on weekends. MC, V. Closed Sun.*

$ ✕ **Andorra.** On the renowned Baixa street of fish restaurants sits the Andorra. It's a perfect place for a simple lunch, with an outdoor terrace where you can watch the lively street scenes and smell the charcoal-grilled sardines. The friendly staff serves up plates of well-cooked Portuguese favorites, and you can choose from a short wine list that caters for most tastes. If it's a dull day, you can sit at tables in the functional but pleasant dining room. ⊠ *Rua Portas de S. Antão 82,* ☎ *01/342–6047. MC, V. Closed Sun.*

$ ✕ **Bonjardim.** Set in an alley between Praça dos Restauradores and Rua
★ Portas de Santo Antão and known locally as *Rei dos Frangos* (the King of Chickens), Bonjardim specializes in superbly cooked spit-roasted chicken, best eaten with fries and a salad. The restaurant is crowded at peak times (8 PM–10 PM), but you shouldn't have to wait long and watching the frenzied waiters is entertainment in itself. ⊠ *Travessa de S. Antão 11,* ☎ *01/342–7424. AE, DC, MC, V.*

$ ✕ **Casa Faz Frio.** Here is an *adega tipica* (traditional wine cellar) on the edge of the Bairro Alto, complete with wood beams, blue tiling, and bunches of garlic suspended from the ceiling. The list of Portuguese dishes changes daily, and although there's not a large choice, there's usually bacalhau, rissoles, grilled pork, and quail. Surroundings are simple but convivial, and you'd be hard pushed to spend more than 2,000$00, including drinks and coffee. ⊠ *Rua de Dom Pedro V 96–98,* ☎ *01/346–1860. No credit cards.*

$ ✕ **O Cantinho do Aziz.** Hidden in the ring of tiny streets below the castle, this small, family-run Mozambican restaurant offers *comida Indio-Africana*—plenty of rich curried meat and fish dishes accompanied by coconut-flavored rice. The surroundings are rudimentary and the TV occasionally deafening, but the tasty food comes with a smile. Climb the flight of steps from Poco do Borratem, near Praça da Figueira, and turn left when you reach the white wall at the top. ⊠ *Rua de S. Lourenço 3–5,* ☎ *01/887–6472. No credit cards. Closed Sun.*

$ ✕ **Vá e Volte.** For one-plate budget Bairro Alto fare, look no farther. In a restaurant that's little more than a bar with a couple of small dining rooms, the owner, his wife, the cook, and the small staff keep the meals coming with speed and good humor. Fried or grilled fish or meat dishes are served with enough salad, potatoes, and vegetables to keep the wolf from the door, and the *arroz doce* (rice pudding) is homemade. The house wine is fine, but even if you choose a regional specialty from the wine list, the price won't break the bank. ⊠ *Rua do Diario de Noticias 100,* ☎ *01/342–7888. MC, V.*

Café-Bars and Pastelarias

Lisbon has some glorious old cafés, and you should make every effort to visit at least a few. Most are wonderfully decorated and have rich interiors of burnished and carved wood, mirrors, and traditional tiling. Also, many cafés have outdoor seating, so you can order a coffee, beer, or snack and watch the city pass by. *Pastelarias* are perhaps the city's greatest contribution to the gastronomic arts: Be sure to sample some pastries and cakes at one of the places listed below, all of which serve drinks, too.

✕ **Café a Brasileira.** Less exclusive than it once was, this coffeehouse in the heart of the shopping district is still the most famous of Lisbon's old haunts. For a feel of bygone days it's best to come before dark, because at night every table (and the long bar) is taken over by beer-drinking young people. ⊠ *Rua Garrett 120.*

✕ **Café Martinho da Arcada.** A stand-up café under the arches, next to the famous restaurant of the same name (☞ *above*), this is a welcome stop for a coffee and specialty *pasteís de nata* (cream cake) before catching your tram to Belém. Tradition oozes from the tiled walls, and the waiters rush to and fro, while the hard-working cooks fry scrumptious rissoles and pastries behind the bar. ⊠ *Praça do Comércio 3. Closed Sun.*

✕ **Café Nicola.** With its grand interior and suitably aloof waiters, this "in" café is one of the prime and priciest spots for sitting down and taking in downtown Lisbon. ⊠ *Rossío, west side.*

✕ **Casa Chineza.** Join the locals for a midmorning stand-up snack and coffee at this traditional Baixa pastelaria. Enjoy the pastry, admire the fine decor, and then on with the shopping! ⊠ *Rua Aurea 274–278.*

✕ **Leiteria a Camponeza.** This is an old-fashioned Baixa *leiteria* (specializing in milk products and pastries), whose blue-tiled walls display bucolic scenes. The coffee, cakes, and sandwiches are all good. ⊠ *Rua dos Sapateiros 155–157. Closed Sun.*

✕ **Pastelaria Suiça.** This huge café-pastelaria stretches all the way back to the adjacent Praça da Figueira. The renowned cakes draw such crowds that it may be easier to go to the inside counter and order pastries to go. Outdoor tables are at a premium, especially on nice days. ⊠ *Rossío 96, east side.*

✕ **Versailles.** In the modern part of the city, the Versailles (founded in 1929) has retained its grand furnishings. Homemade cakes and hot chocolate are house specialties. ⊠ *Av. de República 15 (metro: Saldanha).*

LODGING

A spate of new hotels has gone up in Lisbon in recent years, and old favorites have been modernized, so guests of the city can now choose from a range of accommodations. However, hotels in Lisbon are not, by and large, the bargain restaurants are, and staying in the top-rated hotels may cost as much here as in any European capital.

Nevertheless, it's still possible to find reasonably priced rooms among the city's dozens of modest *pensões* (guest houses), many of which cost less than 8,000$00 a night. If you plan to stay in a pensão, be aware that the toilet may be down the hall, and you may have to share a shower room with other guests. The quality varies greatly from one guest house to another, but the best are spotless and friendly, and many are concentrated downtown around the Rossío and the Praça dos Restauradores and in the Bairro Alto. In summer it's often difficult to find a pensão with vacancies, so you may have to go door to door looking for a suitable place. The tourist office can make reservations for you, but they usually don't recommend the very cheap places, and you won't be able to see your room first.

There is no real tourist season in Lisbon because the capital is host to trade fairs and conventions year-round, so it's best to secure a room in advance of your trip. Particularly busy periods are Easter–June and September–November; at the budget end of the scale, pensões are very busy over the high summer months. If you've arrived without accommodations, stop by the hotel-reservations desk at the airport or at the main downtown tourist-information office (Palácio Foz, Praça dos Restauradores, ☎ 01/346–3314; ☉ Mon.–Sat. 9–8, Sun. 10–6). The staff at both locations speaks English, and there's no fee for their services.

Despite the high year-round occupancy, substantial discounts abound from November through February, sometimes as much as 30%–40%. Even pensões drop their prices by a couple of thousand escudos at this time. So it's always worth asking.

All lodgings listed below include private baths in rooms unless otherwise noted. Breakfast is usually included, but not always at hotels in the $$ and $ categories; particularly good deals are noted below.

$$$$ 🏨 **Lisboa Sheraton and Towers.** Typical of Sheraton properties, this 30-floor hotel has a huge reception area with a comfortable bar, but less impressive—although still eminently likable—guest quarters. A separate desk in the lobby and a private lounge accommodate visitors staying in the more deluxe Towers section; guest rooms in the Towers are about the same size as the others, but their appointments are luxurious and the views better. The range of facilities available to all guests is extensive. The only drawback is location—you're not far from Parque Eduardo VII, but for other sights, your days will start and end with a taxi ride. ✉ *Rua Latino Coelho 1, 1000 Lisboa,* ☎ *01/357–5757,* FAX *01/354–7164. 384 rooms. Restaurant, bar, grill, pool, massage, sauna, health club, laundry service, business services. AE, DC, MC, V.*

$$$$ 🏨 **Meridien Lisboa.** The stepped facade and decorative metal canopy above the entrance are just two of the details that make this mid-'80s accommodation one of the most distinctive modern luxury hotels in Lisbon. Most rooms are fairly small, but they're bright, soundproof, and attractively decorated; ask for one in front with a view of the Parque Eduardo VII. The impressive public areas and good facilities more than enhance a stay; in addition, there is diverse entertainment, from

50

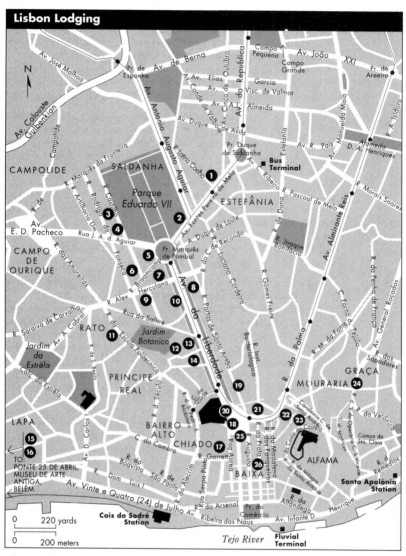

live music nightly in the bar to special buffets in the restaurants. ⊠ *Rua Castilho 149, 1000 Lisboa,* ☎ *01/383–0400,* FAX *01/383–3231. 330 rooms. 2 restaurants, bar, coffee shop, no-smoking floors, beauty salon, sauna, shops, baby-sitting, laundry service, business services. AE, DC, MC, V.*

$$$$ 🏨 **Ritz Lisboa.** One of the finest hotels in Europe, this member of the
★ Inter-Continental chain is renowned for its excellent service and comfortable surroundings. You know you're in good hands from the minute you step into the spacious marble reception area and discover a glittering array of jewelry stores and a bar with a summer terrace overlooking the park. There's more space in the Ritz's corridors than in most hotels' guest rooms, and the accommodations, including the suites, live up to the public areas. Large, light, and airy, they have luxurious bathrooms, private terraces, and elegant furniture. In a similar vein, the public rooms feature tapestries, antique reproductions, and fine paintings. Rooms in the back looking over the park are the best choice; on a clear day you can see the castle and the river from the upper floors. There's a lunchtime buffet at the Veranda restaurant, which, like the bar and lounge, has a wonderful summer terrace. The famous Ritz Grill is currently closed for renovations. ⊠ *Rua Rodrigo da Fonseca 88, 1200 Lisboa,* ☎ *01/383–2020,* FAX *01/383–1783. 304 rooms. Restaurant, bar, snack bar, no-smoking floor, room service, exercise room, shops, baby-sitting, laundry service. AE, DC, MC, V.*

$$$$ 🏨 **Tivoli Lisboa.** On Lisbon's main avenue, this well-run property has
★ a large public area and bar furnished with inviting armchairs and sofas. A pianist plays here nightly. Fresh decor, reasonable rates, and pleasant, well-equipped—although modestly sized—guest quarters make the Tivoli a popular choice. Rooms in the rear are most quiet, though double glazing throughout keeps out traffic noise. In warmer months the outdoor pool and garden offer respite from the bustling city; the grill on the top floor presents wonderful views of the city and the Tejo. There's also a good restaurant off the lobby, where a filling morning buffet is presented. ⊠ *Av. da Liberdade 185, 1250 Lisboa,* ☎ *01/353–0181,* FAX *01/357–9461. 327 rooms. Restaurant, 2 bars, coffee shop, grill, room service, pool, tennis courts, shops, baby-sitting, laundry service. AE, DC, MC, V.*

$$$ 🏨 **Altis.** A member of the Best Western group of hotels, this large, modern lodging has a broad range of facilities, including an indoor pool and an art gallery. The mezzanine bar and lounge, above the lobby, is a relaxing spot. Rooms are welcoming, if unexceptional; those on higher floors have some fine views of Parque Eduardo VII, as does the restaurant, the Don Fernando Grill, on the top floor. ⊠ *Rua Castilho 11, 1200 Lisboa,* ☎ *01/314–2496,* FAX *01/354–8696. 307 rooms. 2 restaurants, 4 bars, room service, pool, sauna, exercise room, shops, laundry service. AE, DC, MC, V.*

$$$ 🏨 **As Janelas Verdes.** Owned and managed by the capable family
★ firms that founded the Tivoli Lisboa and the Lisboa Plaza, As Janelas Verdes joins the capital's select band of historic buildings now converted into fine hotels. The late-18th-century mansion is on the same street as the Museum of Ancient Art; and it was once the home of famous Portuguese novelist Eça de Queirós. Its 17 guest rooms have been marvelously restored and are individually furnished to a high standard—bathrooms are particularly pleasing, and some rooms have direct access to the garden by an exterior staircase. Fittings, furnishings, paintings, and tilework throughout are in keeping with the building's historic character; and in the lovely ivy-covered patio garden you can eat breakfast and imagine yourself in a different age. The hotel isn't particularly central, though you are halfway to Belém (the tram stops

nearby) and close to the Sua Excêlencia restaurant. Reservations are vital at this hotel, since it's as popular as it is small; rates in winter are slightly reduced. ⊠ *Rua das Janelas Verdes 47, 1200 Lisboa,* ☎ *01/396–8143,* 𝕱𝕬𝕏 *01/396–8144. 17 rooms. Dining room. AE, DC, MC, V.*

$$$ 🏨 **Avenida Palace.** Between the Rossío and Praça dos Restauradores, right next to the Rossío Station building, this is Lisbon's most central big hotel. Furnishings and decor throughout are turn-of-the-century, and the grand public areas—lobby, central staircase, and corridors—are all suitably overwhelming in scale. Rooms are not of the same dimensions (and single travelers may occasionally find themselves rather poorly served), but all have high ceilings, individual furnishings, and smart (if small) bathrooms lined with marble. Street noise can be a problem, but the hotel's proximity to the best downtown restaurants and bars may be compensation enough. ⊠ *Rua 1 de Dezembro 123, 1200 Lisboa,* ☎ *01/346–0151,* 𝕱𝕬𝕏 *01/342–2884. 92 rooms. Restaurant, bar, room service. AE, DC, MC, V.*

$$$ 🏨 **Britania.** The gleaming lobby is typical of the decor in this fine restored town-house hotel, occupying one of the few buildings from the 1940s near the Avenida da Liberdade to have survived unscathed. There are art-deco touches throughout, and you will also find other appealing features: fair-sized guest rooms (with off-season discounts), dried flowers, good bathrooms, and helpful staff. The atmospheric bar is a reminder of yesteryear; while good restaurants are within walking distance, since you're just 160 feet from the main avenue. ⊠ *Rua Rodrigues Sampaio 17, 1100 Lisboa,* ☎ *01/315–5016,* 𝕱𝕬𝕏 *01/315–5021. 30 rooms. Bar. AE, DC, MC, V.*

$$$ 🏨 **Eduardo VII.** This reasonably priced hotel is well situated near the park of the same name, although you'll have to rely on public transportation to see the rest of the city. Its anonymous 1930s exterior opens up to reveal 10 floors of shipshape rooms that are short on space, but smart and comfortable. The hotel is at the bottom of this price category, unless you reserve one of the few suites—the only quarters with a real sense of space. The hotel's singular attraction is the superb view of the Libson skyline from the top-floor Varanda restaurant and Lanterna bar—a fine treat. ⊠ *Av. Fontes Pereira de Melo 5, 1000 Lisboa,* ☎ *01/353–0141,* 𝕱𝕬𝕏 *01/353–3879. 140 rooms. Restaurant, bar. AE, DC, MC, V.*

$$$ 🏨 **Lisboa Plaza.** This family-owned hotel behind Avenida da Liberdade
★ is a most comfortable and welcoming lodging. It's been in business for more than 40 years, and the experience shines through every aspect of its operation. Service is friendly and helpful, and an ongoing renovation program has smartened up the air-conditioned guest rooms and public areas without detracting from their character. Pastel colors, prints on the walls, attractive ornaments, dried-flower arrangements, and smart, well-stocked marble bathrooms all add to the charm. The best rooms are at the back, looking up to the botanical gardens; those at the front are closer to the main road and don't have the views, but double glazing keeps everything nice and quiet. The bar is a particularly pleasant place to unwind after sightseeing, and an excellent buffet breakfast is included in the room rate. ⊠ *Travessa do Salitre 7, 1200 Lisboa,* ☎ *01/346–3922,* 𝕱𝕬𝕏 *01/347–1630. 106 rooms. Restaurant, bar, no-smoking rooms, room service, laundry service, business services. AE, DC, MC, V.*

$$$ 🏨 **Principe Real.** This small hotel close to the botanical gardens has a large repeat clientele, which enjoys the friendly atmosphere and excellent central location. Each of the comfortable rooms is decorated in a different style with harmonious color schemes and features a neat bathroom. There's a restaurant, with good views of the city, serving a

complimentary buffet breakfast, and while there are few other facilities that you might find in the larger hotels, this is more than made up for by fine personal service and a distinct, individual charm. ⊠ *Rua da Alegria 53, 1200 Lisboa,* ☎ *01/346–0116,* FAX *01/342–2104. 24 rooms. Restaurant, bar. AE, DC, MC, V.*

$$$ ⌂ **Sofitel Lisboa.** One of the latest additions to the Avenida da Liberdade, the Sofitel is a handsome, modern hotel with a high-tech edge to its design. Business travelers especially seem happy to have discovered such up-to-the-minute lodgings in so central a location. Rooms are pleasingly contemporary in style, decorated in attractive colors, and comfortably appointed. The intimate piano bar makes a good stop after a day's downtown touring, while the Cais da Avenida restaurant, with an entrance on the avenue, can seat diners by the window for sidewalk views of the attractive central artery. ⊠ *Av. da Liberdade 123–125, 1200 Lisboa,* ☎ *01/342–9202,* FAX *01/342–9222. 170 rooms. Restaurant, bar, room service, laundry service, business services. AE, DC, MC, V.*

$$$
★ ⌂ **York House.** A convent in the 17th century, this attractive inn is near the Museum of Ancient Art and has its own shady courtyard garden, where drinks are served. Despite its somewhat inconvenient location, west of the center, the York House has a loyal following (especially among English visitors), and you'll need to book well in advance. The reason is obvious—from the vine-covered staircase that climbs to the garden from the street to the wonderfully individual rooms with original features and good reproduction furniture, the whole inn is a delight. Rooms have four-poster beds and lovely rugs, and corridors, too, are tiled and spread with rugs—surely an improvement on the austerity of convent days here. ⊠ *Rua das Janelas Verdes 32, 1200 Lisboa,* ☎ *01/396–2435,* FAX *01/397–2793. 36 rooms with bath. Restaurant, bar. AE, DC, MC, V.*

$$
★ ⌂ **Albergaria Senhora do Monte.** This small, unpretentious hotel in the oldest part of town, near St. George's Castle, offers some of the best views of Lisbon, especially at night, when the castle is softly illuminated. When you book a room, request one of the four with a terrace, so you can take advantage of the scenery (these rooms fall in the $$$ category). The top-floor grill has a picture window, the neighborhood is quiet, and parking is available. Without a car, you'll face a steep walk every time you return to the Albergaria; Tram 28 runs nearby. ⊠ *Calçada do Monte 39, 1100 Lisboa,* ☎ *01/886–6002,* FAX *01/887–7783. 28 rooms. Bar, grill. AE, DC, MC, V.*

$$ ⌂ **Fénix.** At the top of Avenida da Liberdade, on Praça Marquês de Pombal, this hotel has marble trappings in its bright, air-conditioned public rooms, its large guest rooms, and its pleasant first-floor bar. Rooms at the front have good views over the Rotunda and its swirling traffic (double glazing keeps out the noise); all rooms have plenty of closet space, comfortable armchairs, gleaming bathrooms, TVs, and phones. The basement restaurant, O Bodegon, serves good Spanish and Portuguese food in rustic surroundings. ⊠ *Praça Marquês de Pombal 8, 1200 Lisboa,* ☎ *01/386–2121,* FAX *01/386–0131. 119 rooms. Restaurant, bar, room service, laundry service. AE, DC, MC, V.*

$$ ⌂ **Flamingo.** This comfortable old city-center hotel has perhaps seen better days but still offers good-value lodgings popular with tourists. It's a small place near the top of the Avenida da Liberdade, with friendly staff and cheerful guest rooms, which are a bit on the small side but pleasant nonetheless. Those in front tend to be noisy. Amenities include a Portuguese-Continental restaurant; a comfortable, relaxing bar; and a pay parking lot next door (guests receive a 20% discount), a bonus in this busy area. ⊠ *Rua Castilho 41, 1250 Lisboa,* ☎ *01/386–*

2191, ℻ 01/386–1216. 39 rooms. Restaurant, bar, baby-sitting. AE, DC, MC, V.

$$ 🏨 **Flórida.** Set back from the main avenue and thus a good bit quieter than some other hotels in the locality, the Flórida is an unassuming place in a fair location, near the Parque Eduardo VII. Public areas are smart, if somewhat stuck in the 1970s; the guest rooms are comfortable—although not big—and have decent marble bathrooms. Breakfast is the only meal available, but there is a bar that stays open late. ⊠ *Rua Duque de Palmela 32, 1200 Lisboa,* ☏ *01/357–6145,* ℻ *01/354–3584. 112 rooms. Bar. AE, DC, MC, V.*

$$ 🏨 **Métropole.** The mere existence of a turn-of-the century hotel right on the glorious Rossío plaza has been known to bring a Cheshire Cat grin to the faces of some regular Lisbon visitors. The elegant, light-filled rooms have antique furnishings and an inviting atmosphere, and those in front overlook the square, with its flower sellers and cascading fountain, the Alfama and St. George's Castle in the background; other quarters provide constantly changing tableaux of life in the Baixa. A substantial breakfast buffet is included in the room price; try the hazelnut yogurt. ⊠ *Rossío 30, 1100 Lisboa,* ☏ *01/346–9164,* ℻ *01/346–9166. 36 rooms. Bar, breakfast room, meeting room. AE, DC, MC, V.*

$$ 🏨 **Mundial.** A few steps away from both the Rossío and Restauradores squares, this large and bustling property manages to combine the efficiency of a modern hotel with the friendly attentiveness of a cozy inn. Completely renovated in 1995, the comfortable rooms are an interesting hybrid of '50s furnishings—think International-style curved-wood furniture—and sleek '90s appointments. Breakfast (included in the room rate) is served in the rooftop restaurant, Varanda de Lisboa, which has spectacular panoramic views and is a popular spot for power lunches and family dinners. ⊠ *Rua Duarte 4, 1100 Lisboa,* ☏ *01/886–3101,* ℻ *01/887–9129. 147 rooms, 6 suites. Restaurant, bar, coffee shop, meeting room. AE, DC, MC, V.*

$ 🏨 **Arco Bandeira.** The plain rooms in this friendly fourth-floor pen-
★ são are reasonably quiet, given its location at the bottom of the Rossío (under the arch at the top of Rua dos Sapateiros). Common areas, including the shared bathrooms, are spotless; some rooms have excellent views of Praça da Figueira. The staff is very friendly and used to tourists (though they don't speak much English). You'll pay under 6,000$00 per room most of the year, making this pensão a bargain budget choice. ⊠ *Rua dos Sapateiros 226, 1100 Lisboa,* ☏ *01/342–3478. 8 rooms. No credit cards.*

$ 🏨 **Beira-Minho.** The best rooms in this second-floor pensão have sweeping views of one of Lisbon's busiest squares, and prices begin at about 5,000$00. Make sure you ask to see a range of rooms, though, since some singles and doubles are fairly poor. The Beira-Minho's location makes this a good base for city-center sightseeing, and it's just across from the Pastelaria Suiça, an excellent place for breakfast. You can expect a fair amount of street noise throughout the night. ⊠ *Praça da Figueira 6, 1100 Lisboa,* ☏ *01/346–1846. 19 rooms, 12 with bath. No credit cards.*

$ 🏨 **Borges.** Set in the heart of the Chiado District, this dependable hotel, much favored by European tour groups and characterized by old-fashioned charm and good, modern service, is convenient for guests who plan to shop till they drop. It's more expensive than all the surrounding pensões, but the quality here is generally higher, and you'll have no trouble finding staff who can speak English. The Borges offers decent-size rooms and an option for breakfast, but taking a coffee and pastry at the famous Café Brasileira (just steps away) is a better bet.

⊠ *Rua Garrett 108–110, 1200 Lisboa,* ☎ *01/346–1951,* ⅎ𝔸𝕏 *01/342–6617. 99 rooms. Bar, breakfast room. MC, V.*

$ ⊡ **Casa de São Mamede.** Behind the botanical gardens and halfway between the main avenue, Avenida da Liberdade, and the Amoreiras Shopping Center, this attractive, friendly, old-fashioned residência (originally built as a private home) is a fine value. There's a real charm to the public areas—which still reflect the history of the building—and if some of the guest rooms appear frayed at the edges, then so be it: This is historic Europe at budget prices. ⊠ *Rua da Escola Politécnica 159, 1200 Lisboa,* ☎ *01/396–3166,* ⅎ𝔸𝕏 *01/395–1896. 30 rooms. MC, V.*

$ ⊡ **Duas Nações.** What you're really paying for in this fairly basic, sometimes noisy pensão is its superb location, in the heart of the Baixa grid. Here, you're within walking distance of all the downtown sights, shops, and restaurants. Duas Nações is comfortable enough but has few amenities, although the dining room, retaining its original large dimensions and decor, raises eyebrows in surprise. Guest rooms are functional, plain, and without individual spark—but that's hardly a unique complaint in Portugal. The quieter rooms face the back. ⊠ *Rua da Vitória 41, 1100 Lisboa,* ☎ *01/346–0710. 66 rooms, 42 with bath. Bar, dining room. No credit cards.*

$ ⊡ **Florescente.** One block from Praça dos Restauradores, on a street well-known to seafood lovers because of its many restaurants, this residencia is in a prime position. Rooms are spread across four floors—there's no elevator—and the best are airy and freshly painted, with their own small bathrooms and TVs. There is a great variety of rooms, however, and you may not be too impressed with the cheaper choices on the upper floors, where you share bathrooms, so ask to see a selection, if necessary. You won't do better for inexpensive, central lodgings, and although not even breakfast is served, you couldn't be better placed for downtown cafés and restaurants. ⊠ *Rua Portas de Santo Antão 99, 1100 Lisboa,* ☎ *01/342–6609,* ⅎ𝔸𝕏 *01/342–7733. 100 rooms, 50 with bath or shower. MC, V.*

$ ⊡ **Ninho das Aguias.** Perched below the castle, within walking distance of the Alfama, this budget-price pensão is a good find, although it's a bit far from the center of Lisbon. Rooms are simply furnished, though most have high ceilings and freshly painted walls; the main attraction is the garden terrace, which has a superb view of the city center. It's essential to call ahead: It's a long way to come just to find there's no room. ⊠ *Costa do Castelo 74, 1100 Lisboa,* ☎ *01/886–7008. 16 rooms, 6 with shower. No credit cards.*

NIGHTLIFE AND THE ARTS

Lisbon has an extensive arts-and-nightlife scene, and you'll find listings of music, theater, film, and other entertainment in the monthly *Agenda Cultural* booklet, available from the tourist office. Also the Friday editions of both the *Diario de Noticias* and *O Independente* newspapers have separate magazines with entertainment listings. Although written in Portuguese, listings are fairly easy to decipher, or you can ask the tourist-information office or someone at your hotel reception desk to interpret.

Tickets to musical and theatrical performances are best purchased at the box offices, but you can also get them at special booths around the city: There's one in Praça dos Restauradores, near the main post office, called **ABEP** (☎ 01/347–5823).

Nightlife

Lisbon has an extremely active nightlife, revolving mostly around the bars and discos of the Bairro Alto and those along Avenida 24 de Julho, northwest of Cais do Sodré, where a 20- to 30-year-old crowd hangs out. In both districts, you'll find dozens of places to eat, drink, and dance the night away. On weekends the mobs are shoulder to shoulder in the street, as each passing hour heralds a move to the next trendy spot. For a less boisterous evening out, visit one of the *adegas tipicas* (taverns with food and music) in the Bairro Alto to hear fado. Still other venues host a variety of live events, from rock and roll to African music.

Bars

For late-night partying, there are two main areas. The **Bairro Alto,** long the principal center of Lisbon's nightlife, is still best if you don't want to walk too far between drinks. Most bars here stay open until 3 AM or so. Recently, though, many new designer bars have opened along and around **Avenida 24 de Julho.** Because this isn't a residential area (as the Bairro Alto still is), bars here can stay open until 5 or 6 AM. Whichever district you choose, note that not all bars have signs outside, so to discover the latest hot spots it may be necessary to follow the crowds or try a half-open door. Don't expect to have a quiet drink: The company is generally young and excitable.

Without question the best place to start off your evening is the refined **Instituto do Vinho do Porto** (⊠ Rua de São Pedro de Alcântara 45, Bairro Alto, ☏ 01/347–5707; closed Sun.), a formidable old building in which you can sink into an armchair and sample a selection of port. **Harry's Bar** (⊠ Rua de São Pedro de Alcântara 57, Bairro Alto, ☏ 01/346–0760; closed Sun.) is a famous old location that attracts a mixed tourist and local clientele. For a more bizarre experience, visit the **Pavilhão Chinês** (⊠ Rua Dom Pedro V 89, Bairro Alto, ☏ 01/342–4729), a comfortable bar that is decorated with extraordinary bric-a-brac from around the world—statues, tankards, ceramics, baubles, and toys.

The well-heeled young crowd packs the loud and fashionable **Cena de Copos** (⊠ Rua da Barroca 103–105, Bairro Alto, ☏ 01/347–3372). **Apollo XIII** (⊠ Trav. da Cara 8, Bairro Alto, ☏ 01/342–4952) attracts a mainly student crowd into its tiny drinking den. **Pintaí** (⊠ Largo Trindade Coelho 22, Bairro Alto, ☏ 01/343–4802; closed Mon.) serves up mighty Brazilian cocktails and features good South American music. **A Tasca** (⊠ Trav. de Quiemada 13–15, Bairro Alto, ☏ 01/342–4910) is a bright bar with tequila as its specialty drink.

Café Central (⊠ Av. 24 de Julho 112, ☏ 01/395–6111), with its designer style and rock videos, is typical of the new places opening up along Avenida 24 de Julho. At **Trifásica** (⊠ Av. 24 de Julho 66, ☏ 01/395–7576) the music—loud though it is—takes second place to the snooker tables.

If you prefer a quieter drink in an older part of town, seek out **Cerca Moura** (⊠ Largo das Portas do Sol 4, ☏ 01/887–4859), in the Alfama, which has outdoor seating and views of the river.

Discos and Clubs

Again, discos and clubs are split between two areas: the Bairro Alto and the Avenida 24 de Julho district, with a smattering of cool, up-market places in the suburbs of Santos and Alcântara (note that new discos open and close frequently in Lisbon). Most charge about 1,500$00–2,000$00 (more on weekends), which usually includes one drink. Some clubs have strict door policies, and bouncers may scrutinize you and your clothes—it's best to ask around first about the age of the patrons. Clubs are open from about 11 PM until 4 or 5 AM, although few get going until well after midnight.

Fragil (⊠ Rua da Atalaia 126, Bairro Alto, ☎ 01/346–9578; closed Sun.) is a longstanding favorite that attracts a partly gay crowd. For a mixture of rap, soul, and house music, **Keops** (⊠ Rua da Rosa 157–159, Bairro Alto, no phone) is a funky place, with Egyptian decor. **Kapital** (⊠ Av. 24 de Julho 68, ☎ 01/395–5963) is typical of the new high-fashion, high-price venues down on the *avenida*; its terrace is its nicest feature. **Kremlin** (⊠ Escadinhas da Praia 5, ☎ 01/608768; closed Sun., Mon., and Wed.) continues to attract the trendiest Lisboetas, though no one turns up much before 2 AM (it stays open until 7 AM).

Clubs in Alcântara tend to be more exclusive than most in the city; it's also a ways out, and you'll need to come back by taxi. The ritzy **Alcântara Mar** (⊠ Rua da Cozinha Económica 11, ☎ 01/363–6432; closed Mon.–Tues.) is one of the most enjoyable of the discos, with over-the-top decor and a boisterous clientele.

Fado

One of Lisbon's most famous nighttime diversions is going to an adega tipica to hear fado, a haunting blues-style music rooted in African slave songs. During colonial times fado was exported to Portugal; later, Lisbon's Alfama was recognized as the birthplace of the style; and today most performances occur in the Bairro Alto. In the adegas tipicas food and wine are served, and fado plays late into the night: The singing starts at 10 or 11, and the adegas often stay open until 3 AM. Unfortunately, it's becoming increasingly difficult to find an authentic adega tipica, since tourism has encouraged proprietors to charge admission fees and dilute real fado with other, more "accessible" forms of music. It's always best to ask around for a personal recommendation of an adega tipica.

Senhor Vinho (⊠ Rua do Meio á Lapa 18, ☎ 01/397–2681; closed Sun.) is an institution in the Bairro Alto and attracts some of the most accomplished fado singers in the country. **Lisboa a Noite** (⊠ Rua das Gaveas 69, ☎ 01/346–8557; closed Sun.) is more touristy (and more expensive) than most, but visitors always enjoy the flamboyant shows. One of the oldest fado clubs is **Adega do Machado** (⊠ Rua do Norte 91, ☎ 01/342–8713; closed Mon.), a typical, bustling place. For fado at budget prices, consider a meal in the **Adega do Ribatejo** (⊠ Rua Diario de Noticias 23, ☎ 01/346–8343), a popular local haunt, where there is live entertainment every night. Best place in the Alfama is **Parreirinha d'Alfama** (⊠ Beco do Espírito Santo 1, ☎ 01/886–8209), a little club with highly rated singers. **Timpanas** (⊠ Rua Gilberto Rola 24, ☎ 01/397–2431; closed Mon.), is farther out of the center than all the others but is considered one of the most authentic.

Gay and Lesbian Clubs

Lisbon has a well-established gay and lesbian scene, mostly concentrated in and around the Bairro Alto. **Trumps** (⊠ Rua Imprensa Nacional 104b, ☎ 01/397–1059; closed Mon.) is the city's biggest gay disco. **Memorial** (⊠ Rua Gustavo Sequeira 42, ☎ 01/396–8891; closed Mon.) is popular with both gay and lesbian visitors and can get packed on the weekends. **Tatoo** (⊠ Rua de Sao Marcal 15, ☎ 01/393–2726; closed Sun.) is a boisterous club and bar with a certain amount of sophistication. **Fragil** (☞ Discos and Clubs, *above*), while not exclusively gay, does attract a good, mixed crowd of people.

Live Music

For a change from fado, there are plenty of places offering live rock, pop, and jazz. Big-name American and British bands, as well as the superstar Brazilian singers so beloved in Portugal, often play in Lisbon's large concert halls and stadiums. Local newspapers have details of upcoming performances, and keep an eye out for advertising posters around the city. Advance tickets may be bought at the venue or at the ticket booth in Praça dos Restauradores.

African music is immensely popular in Lisbon, with touring groups from Cabo Verde and Angola playing regularly alongside homegrown talent. The **Ritz** (⊠ Rua da Glória 55, ☏ 01/346–5898) is Lisbon's biggest African club. It's on the edge of the Bairro Alto, in a rather seedy area, but is renowned as a friendly place where you can dance to live music. In the Alfama, **Pê Sujo** (⊠ Largo de São Martinho 6, ☏ 01/886–5269; closed Mon.) specializes in live Brazilian music, aided and abetted by superb *caipirinhas* (Brazil's lethal national cocktail).

The Arts

The prime mover behind Lisbon's artistic-and-cultural scene is the **Fundação Calouste Gulbenkian** (⊠ Av. de Berna 45, ☏ 01/793–5131), which not only presents exhibitions and concerts in its buildings but also sponsors events throughout the city. The foundation publishes a frequently updated schedule of activities, which you can pick up at the reception desk. The tourist-information office can also assist with queries about upcoming events. The **Centro Cultural de Belém** (⊠ Av. da India, ☏ 01/301–9606) puts on a full range of reasonably priced concerts and exhibitions, featuring national and international artists and musicians. Its monthly program of events is available at the reception desk inside the center.

Art Galleries

The Centro Cultural de Belém (☞ *above*) has an ever-changing program of art exhibitions, while Lisbon's major art museums often put on temporary exhibitions alongside their permanent collections; you'll find details in the local press. Other galleries of interest include: **Galeria de Arte Cervejaria Trindade** (⊠ Rua Nova da Trindade 20, ☏ 01/342–3506), **Galeria de São Bento** (⊠ Rua do Machadinho 1, ☏ 01/397–4325), **Galeria Valentim de Carvalho** (⊠ Palácio Alcáçovas, Rua Cruz dos Poiais 111, ☏ 01/608619), and **Movimento Arte Contemporânea** (⊠ Rua do Sol ao Rato 9, ☏ 01/385–0789).

Concerts

Classical-music concerts are staged from about October through June by the **Fundação Calouste Gulbenkian,** which has three concert halls. Of particular interest is the annual **Early Music and Baroque Festival,** held in churches and museums around Lisbon every spring. You may also be in town during a performance of the **Nova Filarmonica,** one of Portugal's national orchestras, which gives concerts around the country throughout the year. Consult local newspapers for details.

Other venues where regular concerts take place include the **Centro Cultural de Belém** (☞ *above*), the **Teatro Nacional de São Carlos** (☞ Theater, *below*), the **Sé** (☞ The Alfama, *above*), the **Igreja do Carmo** (⊠ Largo do Carmo, for summer outdoor concerts), and the **Basilica da Estrêla** (☞ Jardim da Estrêla *under* Bairro Alto, *above*).

Film

Surprisingly, all films shown in Lisbon appear in their original language accompanied by Portuguese subtitles, and you can usually find the latest Hollywood releases playing around town. Ticket prices are low (around 600$00) and even cheaper on Monday; it's best to get to the movie theater early on any day to be assured a seat. Some of the theaters are in preserved art-deco buildings and are attractions in their own right.

There are dozens of movie houses throughout the city, including a selection on and around Praça dos Restauradores and Avenida da Liberdade. A modern cinema complex, in the **Amoreiras Shopping Center** (⊠ Av. Eng. Duarte Pacheco, ☎ 01/383–1275), has 10 screens. Portugal's national film theater, the **Instituto da Cinemateca Portuguesa** (⊠ Rua Barata Salgueiro 39, ☎ 01/353–3180), has regular daily screenings: This is the place to catch contemporary Portuguese films and art-house reruns.

Theater

Plays are performed in Portuguese at the **Teatro Nacional de Dona Maria II** (⊠ Praça Dom Pedro V, ☎ 01/347–2246), Lisbon's principal theater. Performances are given August–June, and there's the occasional foreign-language production, too. The **Teatro Nacional de São Carlos** (⊠ Rua Serpa Pinto 9, ☎ 01/346–5914) hosts an opera season September–June.

If you're traveling with children, it's worth inquiring about productions at the **Teatro Infantil de Lisboa** (⊠ Rua Leão de Oliveira 1, ☎ 01/363–9974), a children's theater that stages productions in Portuguese but uses mime and other media that can be understood by children of all nationalities.

OUTDOOR ACTIVITIES AND SPORTS

Participant Sports

There are few sports facilities in Lisbon itself; for most outdoor activities—scuba diving, fishing, horseback riding, water sports—you'll have to go outside the city (☞ Outdoor Activities and Sports *in* Chapter 3).

Golf

There are a half dozen golf courses in Lisbon's environs, most of which are concentrated along the Estoril Coast. Indeed, if you're planning to play golf, it's best to arrange to stay at one of the hotels outside Lisbon that offer special golf packages (☞ Chapter 3). The nearest 18-hole golf course to the city is at **Lisboa Sport Club** (⊠ Casal da Carregueira, near Belas, ☎ 01/432–1474), about 20 minutes by car from the city.

Swimming

If your hotel doesn't have a pool, you can visit one of the city's municipal pools: **Piscina do Areeiro** (⊠ Av. de Roma, ☎ 01/848–6794), **Piscina do Campo Grande** (⊠ Campo Grande, ☎ 01/796–6305), or **Piscina dos Olivais** (⊠ Av. Dr. Francisco Luís Gomes, 5 km/3 mi northeast of town, ☎ 01/851–4630). The **Lisboa Sport Club** (☞ *above*) also has a swimming pool.

Another option is the **Aquaparque de Lisboa** (⊠ Av. das Descobertas, ☎ 01/301–5017, ☉ Daily 9:30–8), a complex of pools, slides, waterfalls, cafés, and restaurants in Restelo Park, near Belém.

Tennis

There are public tennis courts at **Campo Grande** (⊠ Estádio 1 de Maio at Alvalade). To play, inquire at the main tourist office in Praça dos Restauradores.

Spectator Sports

Bullfighting

For those not disturbed by bullfights, the events are held on Thursdays (and some Sundays) between Easter and September in the ornate Praça de Touros (bullring) at **Campo Pequeno** (☞ The Modern City *in* Exploring Lisbon, *above*). Some people defend the Portuguese bullfight as entertainment because the bull is not killed in the ring but is wrestled to the ground by a group of *forçados* (a team of eight men who fight the bull) dressed in traditional red-and-green costumes. Nonetheless, any bull injured during the contest is later killed. The first-class riding skills displayed by the *cavaleiro* (horseback fighter) during the fight are undeniable. After the cavaleiro performs, the forçados goad the bull into charging them, and one man throws himself across the horns (which have been padded) while the other men pull the bull down by grabbing hold of whatever bits they can, including the tail. ⊠ *Praça de Touros do Campo Pequeno, Avda. da República (metro: Campo Pequeno),* ☎ *01/793–2093.* ☜ *2,500$00–8,500$00, depending on seats.* ☉ *Performances start at 10 PM.*

Soccer

Soccer is Portugal's most popular sport, and Lisbon has three teams, which play at least weekly during the September–May season. The most famous team is **Benfica,** for whom the great Eusebio played in the 1960s, when he took his team to five European championship finals. Matches are held in the northwest part of the city, at the huge Estádio da Luz (⊠ Av. Gen. Norton Matos, ☎ 01/726–6129), one of Europe's biggest stadiums. A great rival of Benfica, the **Sporting Clube de Portugal,** plays at the Estádio José Alvalade (☎ 01/758–9021), near Campo Grande in the north of the city. Third best of the teams is Belém's **Belenenses,** which plays at Estadio do Rastelo (☎ 01/301–0461). You can buy tickets on the day of a game at the stadiums, but for most big matches (certainly when Benfica and Sporting play each other or when either play Porto's main team, FC Porto), you should purchase tickets in advance from the booth in Praça dos Restauradores. Plan to arrive at the stadium early, because there's usually a full program of entertainment first, including children's soccer, marching bands, and fireworks. (Note: Always be wary of pickpockets in the crowd.)

SHOPPING

Shopping in Lisbon can be a pleasant, even refreshing experience, not least because there are still many independent boutiques and few large stores. Handmade goods, such as leather handbags, shoes, gloves, embroidery, ceramics, and basketwork, are sold throughout the city at relatively reasonable prices. Most shops are open weekdays 9–1 and 3–7 and Saturday 9–1; shopping malls and supermarkets often remain open until at least 10, and some are also open on Sunday.

Shopping Districts

In 1988 a fire destroyed much of the Baixa's **Chiado** District, Lisbon's smartest shopping area, but there are still plenty of choice stores on and around the Chiado's Rua Garrett. The rest of the district, made up of the grid of streets from the Rossío to the Rio Tejo, remains a fine place to shop, with small stores given over mainly to fashion, jewelry, shoes, and delicatessen foods. Excellent shops continue to open in the residential districts in the north of the city, at **Praça de Londres** and **Avenida de Roma.**

Of the shopping centers, easily the best is the ★**Amoreiras** (⊠ Av. Eng. Duarte Pacheco; ⊙ Daily 9 AM–11 PM), west of Praça Marquês de Pombal, which contains a multitude of shops selling clothes, shoes, food, crystal, ceramics, and jewelry. It also has a hairdresser, restaurants, and 10 movie screens.

Markets

Lisbon has several markets and, although you are unlikely to find authentic antiques, you may find something traditional to take home. The best-known market is the **Feira da Ladra** (No metro; ⊠ Campo de Santa Clara in the Alfama), a flea market held on Tuesday morning (8 AM–1 PM) and all day Saturday. There is the occasional antique here waiting to be discovered, but the browser will find mainly junk, army clothing, and bric-a-brac. Still, this can be an amusing way to spend an hour or so. There's a market selling mostly clothes at **Praça de Espanha** (metro: Palhavã; ⊙ Mon.–Sat. 9–5). The best place for food, kitchenware, and general household items is the covered market at **Praça do Chile** (metro: Arroios; ⊙ Mon.–Sat. 9–5). There's also a general market, including produce, at the **Mercado 31 de Janeiro** (⊠ Avenida Fontes Pereira de Melo, metro: Picoas; ⊙ Mon.–Sat. 8–2), opposite the Sheraton Hotel. Most atmospheric of all is probably the fish-and-flower market opposite **Cais do Sodré** station (⊙ Mon.–Sat. 6 AM–2 PM), where the traders are an entertainment in themselves.

Specialty Stores

Antiques

Most of Lisbon's antiques shops are concentrated in the district of Rato and in the Bairro Alto along one long street, which changes its name four times as it runs southward from Largo do Rato: Rua Escola Politécnica, Rua Dom Pedro V, Rua da Misericórdia, and Rua do Alecrim. Also look on the nearby Rua de São Bento for more stores. One of Lisbon's best-known antiques shops is **Solar** (⊠ Rua Dom Pedro V 68–70).

Ceramics

Viuva Lamego (⊠ Largo Infante P. Manique 28; Rua do Sacramento 29) offers the largest selection of tiles and pottery in Lisbon—and at competitive prices. **Vista Alegre** (⊠ Largo do Chiado 18; Rua Ivens 52, Bairro Alto) founded its porcelain factory in 1824, and you can buy perfect reproductions of their original table services and ornaments. The **Fábrica Sant'Ana** (⊠ Rua do Alecrim 95), founded in the 1700s, sells wonderful hand-painted ceramics and tiles based on antique patterns; the pieces sold here may be the finest you'll find in the city. Also try **Aresta Viva** (⊠ Rua Antero de Quental 22), producers of handmade and hand-painted tiles, some based on 16th-century designs seen at the Museu do Azulejo. For handcrafted modern pottery, **Casa Ribeiro da Silva** (⊠ Trav. Fiéus de Deus 69) is worth a visit.

Clothing

Although Lisbon isn't on the cutting edge of fashion and design, there are young Portuguese clothing designers whose products are featured alongside the more established fashion names in a variety of stores. **Praça de Londres** and **Avenida de Roma**—both in the modern city—comprise the newest fashionable shopping district. For big international names under one roof, **Amoreiras** Shopping Center (☞ Shopping Districts, *above*) can't be beat. Designer-clothes stores are starting to creep into the Bairro Alto: **Manuel Alves** and **José Manuel Goncalves** have stores on Rua da Rosa at No. 39 (menswear) and at No. 85 (womens). For women's designer clothes, visit **Ana Salazar** (⊠ Rua do Carmo 87). **Eldorado** (⊠ Rua do Norte 23–25, Bairro Alto) sells antique clothing.

Food and Wine

There are some excellent delicatessens in the Baixa that sell fine foods, including delicious regional cheeses, and a wide selection of wines, especially varieties of port—one of Portugal's major exports. **Manuel Tavares** (⊠ Rua da Betesga 1a), just off the Rossío in the Baixa, has a particularly good selection of vintage ports and wines and also sells cheese and chocolate. At **Napoleão** (⊠ Rua dos Fanqueiros 70), in the Baixa, the helpful staff speaks English and can recommend vintages. The **Instituto do Vinho do Porto** (⊠ Rua de São Pedro de Alcântara 45) offers more than 100 varieties to sample and bottles to buy. Other places selling local wines are delicatessens, supermarkets, and—oddly—any shop that sells dried cod, which you'll see stacked outside on the sidewalk or hanging in the window. Rua do Arsenal has several such stores.

Other popular gourmet items are fresh chocolates, marzipan, dried and crystallized fruits, and pastries, on sale in most of the city's pastelarias. Try the **Pastelaria Suíça** (⊠ Rossío 96, eastern side), which has a particularly large selection of sweets.

Handicrafts

Rua da Conceição, one of the crossroads in the Baixa, is known for buttons, wools, cottons, and all sewing materials. For embroidered goods and baskets from the Azores, try **Casa Regional da Ilha Verde** (⊠ Rua Paiva de Andrade 4). Near the Castelo de São Jorge, you'll find **A Bilha** (⊠ Rua do Milagre de Santo António 10), which sells embroidery, lace, copper, gold, and silver. **Pessoa de Carvalho** (⊠ Costa do Castelo 4) is an old Alfama house selling candles, glassware, and jewelry, among other unique handicrafts. **Casa Quintão** (⊠ Rua Ivens 30) has a large selection of arraiolos (here you can also buy a kit for making your own rug). A showroom for traditional carpets is **Almoravida** (⊠ Rua da Senhora da Glória 130).

Jewelry

The Baixa is a good place to look for jewelry: Rua Aurea (formerly Rua do Ouro) was named for the goldsmiths' shops installed here under Pombal's 18th-century city plan—the trade has flourished here ever since. **Sarmento** (⊠ Rua Aurea 251) has a large display of characteristic Portuguese gold- and silver-filigree work. For antique silver and jewelry visit **António da Silva** (⊠ Praça Luis de Camões 40).

Leather Goods

Shoe shops can be found all over the city, but they may have limited selections of large sizes because the Portuguese tend to have small feet. However, all the better shops can make shoes to order. Gloves are sold or made to order in specialty shops in the Rua do Carmo and Rua Aurea.

Fine leather handbags and luggage are sold at **Galeão** (⊠ Rua Augusta 190). **Coelho** (⊠ Rua da Conceição 85) is excellent for leather belts and can also make leather-back fabric belts from your own material. Visit **Ulisses** (⊠ Rua do Carmo 87) for a good selection of leather gloves.

LISBON A TO Z

Arriving and Departing

By Bus

Most international buses and domestic express buses, including those to and from the Algarve, operate from within the **main bus terminal** (⊠ Av. Casal Ribeiro 18, ☎ 01/354–5439), which is very near Praça Duque de Saldanha. The Saldanha and Picoas metro stations are just a few minutes' walk away. Terminals at **Praça de Espanha** (Pavalha metro) and **Campo Pequeno** (Campo Pequeno metro) serve Setúbal and the northwest coast of Portugal respectively; the terminal at **Campo das Cebolas,** at the end of Rua dos Bacalheiros, east of Praça do Comércio, is for destinations in the Minho and Algarve; buses to and from Mafra operate from Largo Martim Moniz, northeast of Praca da Figueira.

For bus transportation schedules it's best to inquire in advance at the main tourist-information office, since routes and companies change frequently (particularly on the popular summer express runs to the Algarve). Most travel agents can sell you a bus ticket in advance; if you buy from the company ticket office at the main terminal, give yourself plenty of time to purchase before you depart. In summer it's wise to reserve a ticket at least a day in advance for destinations in the Algarve. There are four daily departures from Lisbon for the Algarve and Porto; towns closer to the capital receive more frequent service.

By Car

Lisbon sees some of the most reckless driving in all of Portugal. Add to this the notoriously difficult parking situation in the city center and in the cramped old-town quarters, and there's much to be said for not using a car in the capital. Nevertheless, most of the country's highways originate in Lisbon, including the fast roads west to Estoril, south to Setúbal, and north to Porto.

By Plane

International and domestic flights land at Lisbon's small, modern **Portela Airport** (☎ 01/840–2060, 01/840–2262 for arrival/departure information), north of the city. There is a tourist office here and an exchange bureau for changing money on your arrival. The airport is only about 20 minutes from the city center by car or taxi.

TAP (☎ 01/386–1020), the Portuguese national airline, flies to Lisbon from New York, Newark, Boston, Los Angeles, Montréal, and Toronto. TAP, **British Airways, Alitalia, Air France, KLM, TWA, Delta,** and **Air Canada** link Lisbon with London and other European capitals (☞ Air Travel *in* Important Contacts A to Z).

BETWEEN THE AIRPORT AND CENTER CITY

There are no trains or subways between the airport and the city, but getting downtown by bus or taxi is a simple matter and is relatively inexpensive.

By Bus. A special bus, the No. 91 Aerobus, runs every 20 minutes, 7 AM–9 PM, from outside the airport into the city center; tickets, bought from the driver, cost 420$00 or 880$00 and allow one or three days of travel respectively on all Lisbon's buses and trams. The journey takes 30 minutes, and the bus stops at several useful points, including Praça Marquês de Pombal, the Avenida da Liberdade, the Rossío, Praça do Comércio, and the Cais do Sodré train station.

City Buses 44 and 45, at 150$00 one-way, are cheaper than the airport bus. They depart every 15–30 minutes 5 AM–1:40 AM from the main road in front of the terminal building and pass through Praça dos Restauradores on the way to the Cais do Sodré train station (from there you can continue by rail to Estoril and Cascais).

By Car. Car-rental firms and the tourist-information office at the airport provide free maps of Lisbon and the Lisbon and its environs. The drive to the city center takes 20–30 minutes, depending on traffic conditions. Signs to the city center are posted along Avenida Marechal Craveiro Lopes, through Campo Grande, down Avenida da República, and to Praça Marquês de Pombal, and the main Avenida da Liberdade.

By Taxi. Taxis in Lisbon are so cheap and the airport is so close to the city center that many visitors make a beeline straight for a cab (lines form at the terminal). Expect to pay 1,500$00–2,000$00 to most destinations in the city center and around 6,000$00 if you're headed for Estoril or Sintra. If you put luggage in the trunk, add on another 300$00.

By Train

International trains from France and Spain and long-distance domestic service from Porto and the north arrive at and depart from the **Santa Apolónia station** (⌧ Av. Infante D. Henrique, ☏ 01/888–4142), on the riverfront to the east of Lisbon's center. One daily train runs to and from Paris; two daily trains to and from Madrid; and frequent daily trains to and from Porto from 7 AM to midnight. To reach the Rossío or Avenida da Liberdade from the station, take a taxi or Buses 9, 39, 46, or 90 from outside the station.

Local trains to Sintra and all destinations in Estremadura use the central **Rossío station** (☏ 01/346–5022), an unmistakably neo-Manueline building, which stands between Praça dos Restauradores and the Rossío itself. Trains to Sintra run daily every 15 minutes from 6 AM to 2:40 AM; three trains daily run to towns in Estremadura. The train-information office is on the street level, but for tickets and platforms take the escalators (through the shopping center in the station building) to the top floor.

Trains traveling along the coast to Estoril and Cascais arrive at and depart from the waterfront **Cais do Sodre station** (☏ 01/347–0181), a 10-minute walk west of the Praça do Comércio. Departures both ways are very regular—every 15–30 minutes, 5:30 AM–2:30 AM. Buses 44, 45, or 91 all run between Cais do Sodré and the central Lisbon squares; or there's a taxi stand outside the station.

Traveling by train to the Algarve and the south of the country is somewhat more complicated than train travel to other destinations. The **Barreiro station** (☏ 01/207–3028) is on the opposite side of the Rio Tejo but is linked to Lisbon by a ferry that docks at the **Terminal Fluvial** (also known as Sul e Sueste), adjacent to Praça do Comércio. The fare is included in the train-ticket price. There are seven daily trains to the Algarve, the first of which leaves at 6:40 AM and the last one—an overnight service—at about midnight.

For information about train service from any station in Lisbon (or the rest of the country), call 01/888–4025 daily 8 AM–11 PM.

Getting Around

The best way to see central Lisbon is on foot (in combination with various forms of public transport). It's a small city by any standard, and most of the points of interest are contained within the well-defined older quarters. A stroll through the Baixa—the gridded 18th-century down-town shopping area—can take less than a half hour; from there you can walk to the Bairro Alto to the west or the Alfama to the east. The latter two areas are the most interesting of the old-town quarters. A 30-minute walk north up the central Avenida da Liberdade takes you to the large Parque Eduardo VII; the Gulbenkian Foundation is about 15 minutes farther.

If you plan to walk the city, it's important to remember that Lisbon is hilly and has cobblestone sidewalks that can make walking tiring (especially in the hot summer), even when you wear comfortable shoes. At some point you'll probably want to use the public-transportation system, if only to sample the old trams and funicular railways and elevators that link sections of the city.

If you're staying in Lisbon for more than a few days, consider reducing transportation costs by buying one of the various transport passes. A **tourist pass** for unlimited rides on the tram or bus costs 420$00 for one day's travel, 880$00 for three days; four-day passes (1,500$00) and seven-day passes (2,120$00) are also valid on the metro and the elevador. Tourist passes can be purchased at the Cais do Sodré station, Restauradores metro station, and other terminals. Otherwise, you pay a flat fee of 150$00 to the driver every time you ride a bus, tram, or the elevador; it's cheaper to buy your ticket in advance from a kiosk (found at major squares and bus terminals), where it costs just 140$00 and is valid for two journeys. The metro has a different ticketing system (☞ *below*).

A note of warning: Avoid traveling on public transportation during rush hours, especially on the metro, which gets jammed. Also, be aware that pickpockets ply their trade on crowded trains, buses, and trams. Keep an eye on your possessions and carry bags and purses with the zipper side facing your body.

By Bus

Buses are generally quicker than trams. Each stop is posted with full details of routes, so it's simple to determine the correct bus to take. City buses operate 6:30 AM to midnight, and useful buses include 91, which links the airport with the main downtown areas, and 52 and 53, which make the spectacular journey across the Ponte 25 de Abril over the Rio Tejo. When you board, insert your ticket in the ticket-punch machine behind the driver and wait for the pinging noise. For information on bus routes, call 01/363–2044.

By Ferry

Ferries crossing the Rio Tejo leave from jetties at Praça do Comércio (Fluvial terminal), Cais do Sodré, and Belém and cost 95$00–275$00 one-way. The journey is worth making at least once for the spectacular view it affords of Lisbon from the water. For details of Lisbon-area destinations accessible by ferry, *see* Lisbon's Environs A to Z *in* Chapter 3.

By Funicular and Elevador

Small funicular-railway systems and an ingenious vertical lift (both are called the elevador) link some of the high and low parts of Lisbon. The lift, the Elevador de Santa Justa, whisks passengers from Rua de Santa Justa in the Baixa grid up to Largo do Carmo in the Bairro Alto. Of the funicular railways, the most useful are the Elevador da Glória, which runs from Calçada da Glória, just behind Praça dos Restauradores, to Rua de São Pedro de Alcântara in the Bairro Alto, and the Elevador da Bica, which runs from Rua do Loreto down to Rua Boavista, northwest of Cais do Sodré. Departures on all three services are every few minutes from 7 AM to 11 PM.

By Metro

The Metropolitano is modern and efficient but covers a limited route and is used mostly by local commuter traffic. However, you may find it convenient for transport to and from the Gulbenkian Foundation and to Praça de Espanha for the bus across the Ponte 25 de Abril to Setúbal; there are stops en route along Avenida da Liberdade and at the Parque Eduardo VII. The metro operates 6:30 AM to 1 AM, and individual tickets cost 70$00 or a 10-ticket strip, a *caderneta,* costs 500$00. There's also a one-day (200$00) or seven-day (600$00) Passe Metropolitano (Metro Pass), available at stations, for use just on the metro system. Insert your ticket in the ticket-punch machine at the barrier. For metro information, call 01/355–8547.

By Taxi

Taxis are plentiful and cheap, and if two to four people are traveling together, a cab is often the cheapest option. Drivers are generally reliable and use meters; small tips are appreciated. Rates start at 300$00, and most city journeys will run 600$00; supplementary charges are added at night, on weekends, for luggage, and for journeys outside the city limits. You may hail cruising vehicles, but it's sometimes difficult to get drivers' attention, especially late at night; there are taxi stands at most main squares. When you hail a cab, remember that when the green light is on, it means the cab is already occupied. To phone a cab, try **Radio Taxis** (☎ 01/815–5061), **Autocoope** (☎ 01/793–2756), or **Teletaxi** (☎ 01/815–2076).

By Tram

Taking an *elétrico* (tram) is one of the most amusing and enjoyable ways to get around Lisbon. The system, built by British engineers at the end of the last century, is one of the best in Europe and is easy to use. Stops are indicated by *paragem* (stop signs) on the sidewalks, and every stop has a route map for each tram that passes that way. The system operates 6:30 AM to midnight; insert your ticket in the ticket-punch machine by the driver. Useful routes and an inexpensive tour of the city include Trams 13, 24, 28, 29, and 30; Trams 15, 16, and 17 will take you to Belém; Tram 12 goes to the Alfama.

Contacts and Resources

Banks and Currency Exchange

Most major banks have offices in the **Baixa,** and there are currency-exchange facilities at the **airport** (open 24 hours) and at **Santa Apolónia train station** (daily 8:30–8:30). Large hotels and some travel agencies also offer exchange facilities, but the rates are usually relatively poor. Throughout the city you will find automatic currency-exchange machines (equivalent to ATMs in the United States), but they only take European money cards; Cirrus and Plus networks cannot be accessed in Lisbon or anywhere in Portugal.

Car Rental

Major car-rental companies have offices at the airport and at Santa Apolónia station. In central Lisbon you'll find: **Avis** (✉ Avda. Praia da Vitória 12c, ☎ 01/356–1176; airport, ☎ 01/849–9947); **Budget** (✉ Av. Fontes Pereira de Melo 62, ☎ 01/353–7717); **Europcar** (✉ Av. António Agusto de Aguiar 24, ☎ 01/353–6757; airport, ☎ 01/847–3181; Santa Apolónia station, ☎ 01/886–1573); and **Hertz** (✉ Av. 5 de Outubro 10, ☎ 01/353–2894; airport, ☎ 01/849–2722). Smaller local car-rental companies are also represented in Lisbon; the tourist office has full details.

Doctors

Ask the staff at your hotel or at the embassy to recommend a reliable local doctor. Many doctors who have trained abroad speak English. Also, you can contact the British Hospital (☞ *below*), whose switchboard staff speaks English.

Embassies

United States (⊠ Av. das Forças Armadas, ☎ 01/726–6600). **Canada** (⊠ Av. da Liberdade 144, ☎ 01/347–4892). **United Kingdom** (⊠ Rua S. Domingos â Lapa 37, ☎ 01/396–1191).

Emergencies

Police (☎ 01/346–6141). **Ambulance** (☎ 01/301–7777). **Fire** (☎ 01/606060). **SOS Emergencies** (☎ 115). For general problems or in case of theft, the **Tourism Police** (⊠ Rua Capelo 13, near Teatro de São Carlos, ☎ 01/346–6141) has an office open 24 hours. If you need to make a claim against your travel insurance, you must file a report here.

English-Language Bookstores

Many bookstores downtown carry at least a few English-language novels and guidebooks. **Livraria Bertrand** (⊠ Rua Garrett 73), **Livraria Britanica** (⊠ Rua Luis Fernandes 14), and **Livraria Bucholz** (⊠ Rua Duque de Palmela 4) have a broader selection than most. For American and European newspapers, go to one of the several small newsstands at the bottom of Praça dos Restauradores or on the Rossío, but expect periodicals to be a day or two out of date.

Guided Tours

ORIENTATION TOURS

Many companies organize half-day tours of Lisbon and its environs and full-day trips to more distant places of interest. Listed below are a handful of reliable sources. Reservations can be made through any travel agency or hotel; some tours will pick you up at your door. A half-day tour of Lisbon will cost about 6,000$00. A full-day trip north to Obidos, Nazaré, and Fatima will run about 13,500$00 (including lunch), as will a full day east on the "Roman Route" to Évora and Monsaraz. Contact any of the following companies: **Citirama** (⊠ Av. Praia da Vitória 12b, ☎ 01/355–8567). **Gray Line Tours** (⊠ Av. Fontes Pereira de Melo 14, ☎ 01/352–2594). **Top Tours** (⊠ Av. Duque de Loulé 108, ☎ 01/315–5877).

PERSONAL GUIDES

For names of personal guides, contact Lisbon's main tourist office (☞ Visitor Information, *below*) or the following organizations:

The **Syndicate of Guide Interpreters** (⊠ Rua do Telhal 4, ☎ 01/346–7170; ☺ Weekdays 9–1 and 2–5:30) can provide an English-speaking guide for half-day (11,000$00) or full-day (19,000$00) tours; the price remains the same for up to 20 people.

Walking Around Lisbon (☎ 01/340–4539) is run by Joseph Abdo, a Californian who fell in love with Portugal and has now been living in Lisbon for more than a decade. He gives tourism-related classes at a local school and, with his students, offers walking tours of a number of neighborhoods; the emphasis is on seeing both outstanding buildings and charming side streets. Tours last approximately three hours and cost 3,000$00.

Beware of unauthorized guides who approach you outside popular monuments and attractions: They are usually more concerned with "guiding" you to a particular shop or restaurant. This is not to suggest that persons offering you a tour of the interior of a church or museum should be ignored—knowledgeable people associated with the particular institution often volunteer their services for a tip of 200$00 or so.

Hospitals

British Hospital (⊠ Rua Saraiva de Carvalho 49, ☎ 01/395–5067 or 01/397–6329) has English-speaking doctors and nurses. Other hospitals include: **Hospital São José** (⊠ Rua José A. Serrano, ☎ 01/886–0131); **Hospital de São Francisco Xavier** (⊠ Est. Forte A. Duque, ☎ 01/301–7351); and **Hospital Santa Maria** (⊠ Av. Prof. Egas Moniz, ☎ 01/797–5171, emergency 01/793–2762).

Late-Night Pharmacies

Hours of operation and listings of druggists that stay open late are posted on most pharmacy doors. For information on the nearest drugstore open weekends or after hours, call **118.** Local newspapers also carry a current list of pharmacies that have extended hours.

Mail and Telephones

The **main post office** (⊠ Praça do Comércio) receives *poste restante* (general delivery) mail and is open weekdays 9–7. You'll need your passport to collect your mail.

The **post office** on the eastern side of Praça dos Restauradores, at No. 58, is open Monday–Friday 8 AM–10 PM, weekends 9 AM–6 PM. The **telephone office** here is the best place to make long-distance calls, but expect to take a numbered ticket and wait your turn in line. There's a second **telephone office,** on the northwestern corner of the Rossío, at No. 65, that's open daily 8 AM–10 PM. At both of these locations you can use your Visa card. You can also make direct-dialed long-distance calls from most city phone booths on the street, though it's easiest if you use a phone card (750$00 or 1,725$00), available from post offices.

If you have an AT&T, MCI, or Sprint calling card, you can dial the appropriate access number from your hotel phone (and some public phones) to be connected with an English-speaking operator to make an international call. For AT&T dial 05017–1–288; for Sprint dial 05017–1–877; for MCI dial 05017–1234. Be aware that you cannot get this service from all phones in the city.

Travel Agencies

You can save yourself a lot of time by purchasing train or bus tickets from one of Lisbon's many travel agencies. Major agencies include: **American Express** (c/o Top Tours, ⊠ Av. Duque de Loulé 108, ☎ FAX 01/315–5877); **Marcus & Harting** (⊠ Rossío 45–50, ☎ 01/346–9271); **Wagons-Lits** (⊠ Av. da Liberdade 103, ☎ 01/346–5344); and **Abreu** (⊠ Av. da Liberdade 158–160, ☎ 01/347–6441). All main branches generally have an employee who speaks English.

Visitor Information

Lisbon's main tourist office is in the **Palácio Foz** (⊠ Praça dos Restauradores, ☎ 01/346–3314), at the Baixa end of Avenida da Liberdade, open Monday–Saturday 9–8, Sunday 10–6. The staff speaks English, and there are plenty of free brochures and maps. You can also reserve a hotel room from here. There is a useful tourist office at the **airport** (☎ 01/849–3689; ☉ Daily 6 AM–2 AM). Both offices are closed December 25 and January 1.

3 Lisbon's Environs

Lisbon's backyard is rich in possibilities: Drive coastal roads that thread their way along breathtaking seaside cliffs, or laze about on a sandy beach, sipping a glass of the delicious local wine. At night, enjoy the active nightlife of the region's resort towns or retire to a room in a converted palace, castle, or country mansion.

By Jules Brown

SUCH FAMOUS DESTINATIONS as the Estoril Coast, Sintra, the palace at Queluz, even the city of Setúbal and its Manueline church, are all within an hour of Lisbon. You can see the greater part of Lisbon's environs by using the capital as a base. Since many visitors do indeed see these on day trips out of Lisbon, it's often difficult to get a true feel for the differences between the city and its environs, but be assured they exist. Within a 50-kilometer (31-mile) stretch north and south of the Rio Tejo (river Tagus) is found a succession of attractive coastal resorts and important towns. These are no mere dormitory suburbs of the city but are instead endowed with unique traditions and characteristics. Indeed, much of the region is, properly speaking, the most southerly part of the historic province of Estremadura (☞ Chapter 4), which reaches as far north as Alcobaça and borders on the province of Ribetejo to the east.

This was the first land taken back from the Moors in the 12th century under the Christian Reconquest, which had originated farther north in the region of the river Douro: Estremadura means "farthest from the river Douro," an indication of the early extent of the Christian advance against the Moors. Although the region encompasses glistening coastline, broad river estuaries, wooded valleys, and green mountains, its proximity to Lisbon means it tends to be heavily populated and geared toward the capital's needs: Beaches, restaurants, and rural hotels are filled with people escaping from the city, while coastal roads are often congested with slow-moving traffic.

Lisbon and Lisbon's environs are complementary: It's necessary to visit both the city and its surrounding towns to get a real sense of how they have served each other through history. Even the country's earliest rulers appreciated the importance of one to the other. It was the Moors who first built a castle northwest of the capital at Sintra as a defense against Christian forces under Dom Afonso Henriques, which moved steadily southward after the victory at Ourique in 1139. The castle at Sintra fell to the Christians in 1147, a few days after they defeated the Moors in Lisbon.

Once the Christian Reconquest had been consolidated in Estremadura, there was a less pressing need for defensive measures. The early Christian kings instead adopted the lush hills and valleys of Sintra as a summer retreat and designed estates and glorious palaces that survive today. Similarly, Lisbon's 18th- and 19th-century nobility desired a more leisurely life outside the city and so developed small resorts along the Estoril Coast; the amenities and ocean views are still greatly sought after (although the ocean itself is not as clean as it could be). For swimming, modern Lisboans look a little farther afield—across the Rio Tejo, where the beaches and resorts of the Costa da Caparica and the southern Setúbal Peninsula are becoming increasingly popular. In whichever direction you travel and whatever your interests, you should be delighted with all that Lisbon's environs have to offer.

Pleasures and Pastimes

Dining

City dwellers make a point of crossing the Tejo to the suburb of Cacilhas to eat platefuls of *arroz de marisco* (rice with seafood); *linguado* (sole) is especially popular, as are the mounds of shellfish displayed in restaurant windows. One of Caparica's summer delights is the smell of grilled sardines wafting from restaurants and beachside stalls. Seafood, naturally, is also the specialty along the Estoril coast, while even the inland villages here and on the Setúbal Peninsula are close enough to the sea to be assured a steady supply of quality fish.

In Sintra *queijadas* (sweet cheese tarts) are a local specialty, while in the Azeitão region of the Setúbal Peninsula, locals swear by the *queijo fresco,* a delicious white sheep's-milk cheese. Lisbon's environs also produce good wines, many of which are offered in local restaurants. From Colares comes a light, smooth red, a fine accompaniment to a hearty lunch; Palmela, the demarcated wine-growing district of Setúbal, produces distinctive amber-colored wines of recognized quality; in the Setúbal Peninsula, the Fonseca winery produces a splendid dessert wine called Moscatel de Setúbal.

Golf
The superb golf courses lying between Lisbon and Estoril attract players from far and wide. Most have been designed by renowned golfers, and the climate means that year-round play is possible. Many hotels offer golf privileges to guests—some even have their own courses.

Lodging
Many visitors are content to use Lisbon as a base from which to explore the environs. However, spending at least one night away from the capital—staying either at one of the popular resorts on the Estoril Coast or the Setúbal Peninsula or at the rural retreat of Sintra—may give you some perspective on the country. Regardless of where you stay, it's essential that you book a room in advance in the summer. If you do opt to spend a night or two outside Lisbon, you'll have an opportunity to experience two types of accommodations not available in the capital itself: *pousadas* and members of the *Turismo de Habatição* organization.

The pousadas often are in converted historic buildings, and they generally have superior facilities and restaurants. The two in this region are at Setúbal and Palmela and are reviewed under their respective accounts. Under the Turismo de Habitação (or Turismo no Espaço Rural) system, old manor houses and country estates offer rooms and sometimes meals. All lodgings listed with this association are in rural areas and provide comfortable accommodations. Some are reviewed below, but since they typically have few rooms, availability is limited; tourist offices can advise you about local vacancies.

Sailing
There are sailing clubs at Cascais, Sesimbra, and Setúbal, and local tourist offices can provide you with information on others. It's often possible to arrange a weeklong sail with some of the clubs in the coastal towns. Check with your local sailing organization to see if it has reciprocity with any Portuguese marinas.

Shopping
Throughout Lisbon's environs there are shopping opportunities galore, from clothes sold in smart Cascais and Estoril boutiques to the ceramics and woven and leather goods featured at roadside stalls and at weekly village markets. The area is also the site of several traditional country fairs and markets, where you'll be able to find a variety of local handicrafts and foods. Quality and prices vary greatly, so you'd do well to shop around before buying. Prices are fixed almost everywhere, although with a firm command of the Portuguese language you may be able to negotiate a small discount at some of the local markets and roadside stalls. Bargaining is not practiced in stores or boutiques.

Exploring Lisbon's Environs

The geography varies wildly once you're outside Lisbon's city limits. To the west, the Estoril Coast consists of a series of small beaches and rocky coves, at its most delightful around the towns of Estoril and Cascais; farther north, the Atlantic makes itself felt in the windswept beaches and capes beyond Guincho. Yet just a few miles inland, the Sintra hills are as charming a rural retreat as you could wish to find, crisscrossed by minor roads and dotted with old monastic buildings, country estates, gardens, and market villages.

To the south, across the Rio Tejo, the contrast couldn't be more pronounced. The beaches of the Costa da Caparica combine to form a 20-kilometer (12½-mile) sweep of sand, backed for the most part by the flat, wine-producing, market-garden country of the Setúbal Peninsula. The landscape changes in character only in the south, where the peaks of the Serra da Arrábida rise up above a rugged coastline sheltering small fishing villages and resorts. The only city of any size in the entire region, Setúbal, is just to the east of here, an obvious stop en route to Évora or the Algarve.

Great Itineraries

With a car it's possible to cover the main sights north and south of the Rio Tejo in two days, although this would give you very little time to linger. A week's touring would not be too long to spend, particularly if you intend to soak up the sun at one of the lively beach resorts or take a more in-depth look at Sintra, whose beautiful surroundings alone can occupy two or three days' leisurely exploring.

It's also worth bearing in mind that all of the main towns and most of the sights in the area are accessible by train, bus, or ferry from Lisbon. Consequently, it's possible to see the entire region in a series of day trips from the capital. This is particularly advisable for the seaside resorts of the Estoril Coast, west of Lisbon, and the beaches of the Costa da Caparica, south across the Rio Tejo: parking space and accommodations in both destinations are extremely limited in summer. You will probably also choose to see the palace at Queluz on a day trip, since it is only 20 minutes northwest of Lisbon by train, and many visitors take this in on the way to or from Sintra. Using Lisbon as your base, a realistic timescale for visiting the major sights is four days: one each for the Estoril Coast, Queluz and Sintra, Caparica, and Setúbal.

Numbers in the text correspond to numbers in the margin and on the Estoril Coast, Sintra, and Queluz map and the Setúbal Peninsula map.

IF YOU HAVE 2 DAYS

Start in Lisbon and drive to **Estoril** ①, where you can soak up the atmosphere in the gardens and on the seafront promenade. From here, it's only a short distance to ⚝ **Cascais** ②, where you can have a leisurely lunch at one of the outdoor restaurants. For the rest of the day, the little cove beaches are lovely, and the **Boca do Inferno** ③ is just a short walk way. The next day, it's under an hour's ride north to **Sintra** ⑤, where before lunch you'll have time to see Sintra Palace and perhaps climb to the **Castelo dos Mouros** ⑦. After lunch, head back to Lisbon, calling at the **Palácio Nacional de Queluz** ⑫ on the way. In the evening take the ferry from Lisbon to **Cacilhas** ⑬ for a seafood dinner.

You could, of course, reverse this itinerary and choose to spend the night in Sintra instead of Cascais. This is also an easy tour to undertake by public transportation; there are trains to Estoril and Cascais, buses from there to Sintra, and a regular train service back to Lisbon, via Queluz.

The Estoril Coast, Sintra, and Queluz

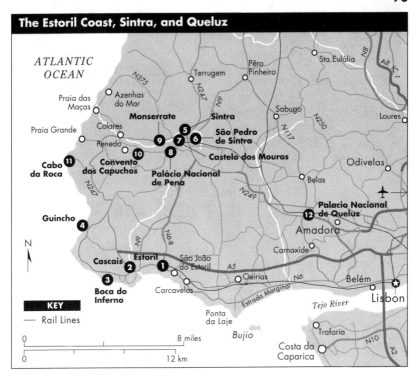

From Lisbon, head for the **Palácio Nacional de Queluz** ⑫ and have lunch in the old kitchen-restaurant. In the afternoon, it's a short drive on to ⌁ **Sintra** ⑤, where you can spend the rest of the day seeing the sights in and around the town. Consider taking dinner in the adjacent village of **São Pedro de Sintra** ⑥, where there are several recommended restaurants. The next day, head first to the extraordinary **Palácio Nacional de Pena** ⑧ before driving west to the intriguing **Convento dos Capuchos** ⑩. Beyond here, you reach the coast at the headland of **Cabo da Roca** ⑪—the westernmost point of mainland Europe—and then wind south to the wonderful beach at **Guincho** ④ in time for lunch. In the afternoon, stick to the coastal road as it heads east toward ⌁ **Cascais** ②, where you can spend the night.

On the third day, drive back into Lisbon via **Estoril** ① and cross the Rio Tejo by the mighty Ponte 25 de Abril, and then detour for lunch at either **Cacilhas** ⑬ or **Caparica** ⑭. It's then only an hour's drive to the region's two attractive pousadas, one at ⌁ **Palmela** ⑮, the other 10 kilometers (6 miles) down the road in ⌁ **Setúbal** ⑯. At either, you're perfectly poised to continue farther east or south into Portugal; if you're heading back to Lisbon, however, drive through the **Serra da Arrábida** ⑲ on your fourth morning and make time for lunch at an esplanade restaurant in **Sesimbra** ⑳. From there, you can return to Lisbon in around 90 minutes.

You will be able to spend considerably more time in the destinations outlined above. The main advantage will be the luxury of two nights in ⌁ **Sintra** ⑤, which will allow you to see all the surrounding sights

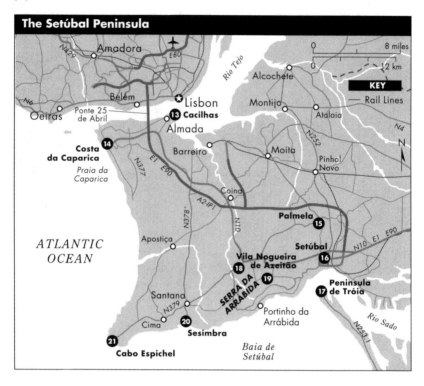

The Setúbal Peninsula

with ease. On the third day, you can then drive straight to **Cabo da Roca** ⑪ and then south to **Guincho** ④, if you fancy a half day at the beach before following the coast around to ⚄ **Cascais** ②. Two nights spent here allow you really to get to know the town and give sufficient time for a walk or train ride along the coast to **Estoril** ① and back.

When it's time to leave, drive back into Lisbon and aim for lunch at either **Cacilhas** ⑬ or **Caparica** ⑭, across the Rio Tejo. Your night is spent at one of the two pousadas, in ⚄ **Palmela** ⑮ or ⚄ **Setúbal** ⑯, leaving you with a stop for lunch in the region around **Vila Nogueira de Azeitão** ⑱ and a short, pleasant drive through the **Serra da Arrábida** ⑲ to occupy your final full day. If you spend the night in the attractive fishing port and resort town of ⚄ **Sesimbra** ⑳, you'll have time to visit the region's second windswept cape, **Cabo Espichel** ㉑, before driving back to Lisbon.

When to Tour Lisbon's Environs

If you're in the area in summer, particularly July and August, you *must* reserve accommodations in advance: Sintra, Estoril, Cascais, and Sesimbra are all very heavily booked at these times. If you can, consider traveling to the coastal areas in spring or early fall: The crowds are much reduced, and it's usually warm enough to swim in April and October.

Having said that, most of the region's distinctive festivals are held during summer, and you may want to have your trip here coincide with one of them. In São Pedro de Sintra, the annual Festa de São Pedro (St. Peter's Day) celebration is on June 29; there are summer music and arts festivals in Sintra, Cascais, and Queluz; September in Palmela sees the Festa das Vindimas (Grape Harvest Festival); while the Feira de Santiago takes place in Setúbal at the end of July. Year-round markets include the famous country fair in São Pedro de Sintra (second and fourth Sunday of every month) and a similar affair in Vila Nogueira de Azeitão (first Sunday of every month).

Finally, note that most museums and palaces in the region close for one day a week. If it's vital that you see a particular sight, always check the opening hours before you go.

THE ESTORIL COAST

Numbers in the margin correspond to points of interest on the Estoril Coast, Sintra, and Queluz map.

The Estoril Coast extends for 32 kilometers (20 miles) west of Lisbon, taking in the major towns of Estoril and Cascais, as well as some smaller settlements that are part city suburb, part beach town. It's a favored residential area, thanks to its proximity to the capital, while the charms of the rocky coastline and the good climate—the coast has milder winters than Lisbon—have conspired to make it one of the most popular resort areas in the country. Some, rather fancifully, know it as the Portuguese Riviera, and certainly the casino at Estoril and the rich villas and hotels dotted along the coast lend the region a social cachet, bolstered by the patronage over the years of wealthy expatriates and even exiled royalty.

Rich visitors aside, the Estoril Coast is where much of Lisbon comes to the beach, and you can count on sharing a visit in summer with great throngs of day-trippers and tourists. Not only are the towns and beaches crowded, but the ocean—sparkling from a distance—suffers from a long-standing local pollution problem, due to an inadequate sewage system. The quality of the water differs greatly from beach to beach, and although plans are underway to rectify the situation, you are strongly advised to avoid swimming in an area unless the water has been declared safe. Look for a blue Council of Europe flag, which signals a high standard of unpolluted water and beach; consult local tourist offices if you are unsure.

None of this is to suggest that the Estoril Coast should be avoided. Many of the beaches are still fine, the waterfront towns—especially Cascais—are attractive, and the train ride along the shore offers some of the most appealing views in the region. Sailboarding and surfing are popular sports along the coast, and many local beaches have rental outfits. The experts head for Guincho Beach, one of the venues of the World Windsurfing Championships.

Unless you intend to tour the wider region over several days, taking the train from Lisbon is an infinitely better option than joining the crowded roads (☞ Getting Around *in* Lisbon's Environs A to Z, *below*). This section has been arranged accordingly, with coverage of Estoril first, followed by Cascais, which marks the end of the train line; from there, it's an easy walk to the Boca do Inferno and a short bus ride from Cascais to the magnificent beach at Guincho. If you do choose to drive, leave Lisbon by car via the Estrada Marginal Road (follow signs for Cascais/Estoril) and take the curving coastal route to Estoril (the N6), or the parallel and faster Auto-Estrada da Oeste Highway (A5), which runs from the Praça Marquês de Pombal in Lisbon to Estoril.

Estoril

➊ *26 km (16 mi) west of Lisbon. The train runs directly to Estoril, or get off at the previous station, São João do Estoril, and walk 2 km (1¼ mi) along the seafront promenade path, a fine route with excellent views.*

Estoril perhaps makes too much of its erstwhile reputation as an exclusive resort. In the 19th century, its gardens and mansions were preferred by the European aristocracy, who wintered here in comfort and seclusion. These days, reminders of such days are few and far between: Straggling new residential and commercial developments stretch away on either side of town, and while Estoril still boasts plush hotels, restaurants, and sports facilities, there's little beyond these to delay visitors for long. The town presents its best face right in the center, where today's jet set descends on the town's casino, set at the top of the formal gardens of the **Parque do Estoril.** This overlooks the sea and is lined on both sides by several pleasant cafés, while down on the beachfront **Tamariz esplanade,** there are more alfresco restaurants. The best and longest local beach is at adjacent **Monte Estoril,** which adjoins Estoril's beach; here you'll find rest rooms and beach chairs for rent, as well as plenty of shops and snack bars.

Estoril Casino opened in the center of town in 1968, and besides the gambling salons, which have all the usual gaming tables and banks of American and European slot machines, there's a nightclub and restaurant. You can make an evening of dinner and the international floor show. In addition, the casino has regularly changing art exhibitions, a movie theater showing the latest films, and, every summer, musical concerts and ballets; call for details about performances and tickets or ask at Estoril's tourist office. Note that to enter the casino, all foreign visitors must show their passports to prove they are 21. ✉ *Parque do Estoril,* ☎ *01/468–4521.* 🎟 *Floor show 5,000$00, dinner with show from 8,500$00.* ☉ *Casino and restaurant 3 PM–3 AM, floor show nightly at 11. Reservations essential for restaurant and show. Jacket and tie required at all times. AE, DC, MC, V.*

Dining and Lodging

$$$ ✕ **A Choupana.** Just east of the town, in adjacent São João do Estoril, this long-established restaurant with beach views offers high-quality fresh fish, seafood, and local dishes in comfortable, plant-filled surroundings. The staff speaks English, which should help you to get the most out of the menu; be sure to ask about the daily specials. Live music accompanies dinner, and there's nightly dancing until 2. Parking is available, or you can get a taxi from the train station. ✉ *Estrada Marginal, São João do Estoril,* ☎ *01/468–3099. AE, DC, MC, V. Closed Mon.*

$$$ ✕ **The English Bar.** Despite the name and the mock-Tudor embellishments, this friendly restaurant (not bar) serves first-class Portuguese and international cuisine. Fish is always available, and the sole is a reliable choice; shellfish soup makes a fine starter. It's near Monte Estoril's Aparthotel Estoril Eden, only a few minutes' walk from the central beach (via the pedestrian underpass that starts behind Monte Estoril train station), and there are good views of the ocean from its windows. ✉ *Av. Sabóia, off Av. Marginal,* ☎ *01/468–0413. AE, DC, MC, V. Closed Sun.*

$–$$ ✕ **Frolic.** A bright, welcoming café-restaurant, set beside the Hotel Palácio, Frolic has a covered outdoor terrace overlooking the palm trees in the park opposite it. Portuguese specialties and even pizzas are served, but you could come for just a coffee or a snack—the cakes and pastries are all homemade—or stop in for late-night drinks until 2 AM. ⊠ *Av. Clotilde,* ☎ *01/468–1219. AE, DC, MC, V.*

$$$ ✕🏨 **Hotel Palácio.** During World War II, exiled European courts
★ waited out the war in this luxurious 1930s hotel. The hotel faces the town's central park and has pastel rooms decorated with Regency-style reproduction furniture and attractive and elegant public rooms. The bar and lounge are particularly comfortable, with views over the outdoor pool to the park beyond. The staff is deft and courteous, and reception can assist with anything from car rental to organizing tennis lessons. The Palácio also boasts one of Portugal's most famous restaurants—the Four Seasons Grill—which serves buffets around the garden pool in summer and adjusts its menus seasonally, using the freshest ingredients in its quest for perfection (reservations essential; jacket and tie). The hotel is a two-minute walk from the beach, and golfers can tee up on the championship golf course. ⊠ *Rua do Parque, Parque do Estoril, 2765 Estoril,* ☎ *01/468–0400,* ℻ *01/468–4867. 162 rooms. Restaurant, 2 bars, room service, pool, massage, sauna, golf privileges, tennis courts, exercise room, horseback riding, baby-sitting. AE, DC, MC, V.*

$$$ 🏨 **Estalagem Lennox Country Club.** Set on a hillside a few minutes' walk
★ above the casino, this extremely attractive hotel is a real favorite with golfers, who can take advantage of special packages. The 10 rooms in the main building are named after famous golf courses, and the Lennox even sponsors its own challenge cup every year. Nongolfers will feel equally at home here, sitting out on the balconies soaking up the sea views or relaxing by the poolside bar; there's also an indoor bar and a very cozy little lounge. Complimentary afternoon tea and cakes are served to all guests, and if you take meals here, house wines are included in the price. The most spacious rooms, on the top floor of the main building, have huge balconies and small separate lounges. Other rooms, including the 22 in the garden annex, are all comfortable and pleasingly decorated. ⊠ *Rua Eng. Álvaro Pedro de Sousa 5, 2765 Estoril,* ☎ *01/468–0424,* ℻ *01/467–0859. 32 rooms. Restaurant, bar, pool, golf privileges. AE, DC, MC, V.*

$$–$$$ 🏨 **Estoril Eden.** The comfortable, tastefully decorated rooms in this modern apartment hotel are reasonably sized and come with kitchenettes and satellite TVs, making it a good bet for families. Superb views of the sweeping Estoril Coast from the rooms' balconies, which are equipped with tables and chairs, are an added attraction, while children will enjoy the free summer-entertainment program and the good sports and leisure facilities. It's in a convenient beach location, just a few minutes' walk from the ocean via an underpass that starts behind Monte Estoril train station. ⊠ *Av. Sabóia, 2765 Estoril,* ☎ *01/467–0573,* ℻ *01/467–0848. 162 units. Restaurant, bar, outdoor café, kitchenettes, indoor pool, massage, sauna, golf privileges, exercise room, nightclub, baby-sitting, children's programs. AE, DC, MC, V.*

$$ 🏨 **Hotel Lido.** Set on a quiet street well away from the beach, overlooking the lush green hillside above Estoril, the Lido is justly popular for its good-value rooms and amenities, which include a pool, garden, and decent restaurant. All guest rooms have balconies, and there's a fifth-floor lounge bar. The hotel is signposted for drivers from the casino—it's less convenient for tourists without a car, since you're a steep 15-minute walk from the center of Estoril. ⊠ *Rua do Alentejo 12, 2765 Estoril,* ☎ *01/468–4123,* ℻ *01/468–3665. 62 rooms. Restaurant, bar, pool, billiards, baby-sitting. AE, DC, MC, V.*

Nightlife

Other than **Estoril Casino** (☞ *above*), the obvious evening attraction, nightlife in Estoril is based around several well-known bars and clubs, most of which are open 10 PM–3 AM. **Frolic** (✉ Parque do Estoril, ☎ 01/468–1219), in front of the casino next to the café-restaurant of the same name, is a mainstream disco attracting a sophisticated clientele. The young set head out to **Forte Velho** (✉ Av. Marginal, São João do Estoril, ☎ 01/468–1337), a medieval fort on the edge of town that has been converted into a lively dance club, open year-round.

Outdoor Activities and Sports

GOLF

Clube de Golfe do Estoril (✉ Av. da República, Estoril, ☎ 01/468–0176) has an immaculate 18-hole championship course, with special rates and privileges for guests staying at the Hotel Palácio. **Penha Longa** (✉ Lagoa Azul, ☎ 01/924–0320), 9 kilometers (5 miles) north of Estoril, features superb views, an 18-hole course, golf clinics, and putting greens. On the Estoril–Sintra road, 7 kilometers (4 miles) north of Estoril, the **Estoril Sol** (✉ Linhó, ☎ 01/923–2461) has a scenic nine-hole course on the fringes of the Serra de Sintra.

MOTOR RACING

The **Autódromo do Estoril** (Estoril Autodrome), on the Estoril–Sintra road, 5 kilometers (3 miles) north of Estoril, hosts Formula 1 car racing and can accommodate 40,000 spectators. The racetrack is also the start and finish point of the annual **Port Wine Rally,** an international car competition. Details about both events can be obtained from the Estoril tourist office.

TENNIS

Many of the larger hotels in Estoril have tennis courts, or contact the **Clube de Tenis do Estoril** (✉ Av. Amaral, Estoril, ☎ 01/468–1675).

Shopping

Each July and August Estoril holds the **Feira do Artesanato,** an open-air handicrafts fair, near the casino. Every evening, from 5 to midnight, stalls sell local arts and crafts and traditional Portuguese foods. The town of **Carcavelos,** 7 kilometers (4 miles) southeast of Estoril, has a busy Thursday market selling food, clothes, and local arts and crafts; you can get there by local train.

Cascais

★ ❷   *3 km (2 mi) west of Estoril; the train runs directly there, or you can walk along the seafront promenade.*

Once a mere fishing village, the pretty town of Cascais—with three small, sandy bays—is now a heavily developed tourist resort packed with shops, restaurants, and hotels. However, regardless of the masses of people, Cascais (unlike neighboring Estoril) has retained some of its erstwhile small-town character—most visible around the harbor, with its fishing boats and yachts, and in the old streets and squares off Largo 5 Outubro, behind the Hotel Baia, where you'll find lace shops, cafés, and restaurants galore. The beaches are very attractive, too, though you should remember that this part of the coast is polluted: Unless signs indicate otherwise, stay out of the sea.

The baroque **Igreja de Nossa Senhora da Assunção** (Church of Our Lady of the Assumption), with its plain white facade, is the most graceful of the churches in Cascais. Inside is an elegant golden altar and fine paintings by 17th-century Portuguese artist Josefa de Óbidos—a rare instance of a female artist of that day gaining an international reputation. ✉ *Largo da Assunção, no phone.* 🎫 *Free.* ⊙ *Daily 9–1 and 5–8.*

For an understanding of the rapid development in Cascais since the last century, visit the modern single-story building that houses the **Museu do Mar** (Museum of the Sea). Here, the town's former role as a fishing village is traced through model boats and fishing equipment, traditional costumes worn by 19th-century locals, an analysis of the fish caught in the waters off Cascais, and some splendid old photographs and paintings of the area. The museum is opposite the Pavilhão de Cascais (Cascais Pavilion), just a short walk west of the center. ✉ *Av. da República, no phone.* 🎫 *200$00, free Sun.* ⊙ *Tues.–Sun. 10–4:30.*

The most relaxing spot in Cascais, apart from the beach, is the municipal **Parque do Marechal Carmona** (⊙ Daily 9–6), where there is a shallow lake, a café, a small zoo, and tables and chairs set out under the trees for picnickers.

One of Cascais's elegant 19th-century town houses now serves as the **Museu Conde de Castro Guimarães**, a charming museum that displays 18th- and 19th-century paintings, ceramics, furniture, and some archaeological artifacts excavated nearby. It's set in the grounds of the Parque do Marechal Carmona. ✉ *Estrada da Boca do Inferno, no phone.* 🎫 *250$00, free Sun.* ⊙ *Tues.–Sun. 11–12:30 and 2–5.*

Dining and Lodging

$$$ ✗ **João Padeiro.** Not only does this basement restaurant serve excellently prepared sole, but it's also renowned for succulent lobsters accompanied by homemade mayonnaise. If you're a meat eater, you'll find a few choices on the menu, too, with pork the most reliable dish. The restaurant is housed in an odd building with roof slates at head height; walk down the narrow steps into the distinctive (if dim) wood-and-leather-paneled interior, which is enlivened by cheery decorations. Service is brisk and assured, and the location—along the main road next to the tourist office—couldn't be more convenient for visitors who are unfamiliar with the town. ✉ *Rua Visconde da Luz 12,* ☎ *01/483–0232. AE, DC, MC, V. Closed Sun.*

$$ ✗ **Beira Mar.** One of several well-established and unpretentious restaurants behind the fish market, the Beira Mar has a comfortable interior decorated with blue-and-white *azulejos* (glazed ceramic tiles). The menu includes a wide variety of fish and meat dishes, but the best seafood and shellfish are from the impressive central display of the day's catch; rice with clams or steaks cut from swordfish or tuna are always worth trying. ✉ *Rua das Flores 6,* ☎ *01/483–0152. AE, DC, MC, V. Closed Tues.*

$$ ✗ **Joshua's Shoarma Grill.** This popular local spot, in an old-town house close to the tourist office, specializes in tasty Middle Eastern food, including kebabs, pita bread, falafel, hummus, and the like. Main courses are served with rice and salad and are very filling—try the *combinado*, with two or three different kinds of barbecued meat. ✉ *Rua Visconde da Luz 19,* ☎ *01/284–3064. MC, V.*

$$ ✗ **O Pescador.** Fish and shellfish, picked fresh from the market, are the reliable items served in this folksy restaurant, where a cluttered ceiling and maritime-related artifacts distract the eye. The sole is a house specialty, and this is also a good place to try *bacalhau* (cod)—it's said that there are 365 ways of cooking this dish, one for every day of the year; the traditional bacalhau dish here is very tasty. ✉ *Rua das Flores 10,* ☎ *01/483–2054. AE, DC, MC.*

$ ✕ **Dom Manolo.** In this bustling Spanish-owned grill-restaurant, the waiters charge back and forth delivering excellent spit-roasted chicken to a largely local clientele. Accompany it with fries or salad, or both, and if you're still hungry, have a slab of the homemade crème caramel. These are not sophisticated surroundings: There are paper tablecloths, holiday posters tacked to the walls, and billowing smoke as the cooks battle with the huge spit-roast machinery at the front of the restaurant. But for inexpensive, down-to-earth food and company, it's hard to beat. ✉ *Av. Marginal 13,* ☎ *01/483–1126. No credit cards.*

$$$$ ✕⬚ **Hotel Albatroz.** On a rocky outcrop, this attractive old house—
★ once the summer residence of the dukes of Loulé—is the most luxurious of Cascais's hotels. Though the Albatroz has been expanded and modernized, its genteel character has been retained, particularly in the charming bedrooms and the pleasant terrace bar. Public areas are grand, while the traditionally decorated guest rooms combine elegance (flowers and floral drapes) with comfort (good beds); it's worth paying the extra money for a sea view. An outdoor pool and terrace overlook the ocean, and a bar is set up here in summer. Given its quality, this hotel is usually fully booked, so advance reservations are recommended, especially in summer. The hotel restaurant (also called the Albatroz), where fish dishes are the specialty, boasts superior views of the sea and the coast toward Lisbon (reservations essential; jacket and tie). ✉ *Rua Frederico Arouca 100, 2750 Cascais,* ☎ *01/483–2821,* ᶠᴬˣ *01/484–4827. 40 rooms. Restaurant, bar, room service, saltwater pool, golf privileges, baby-sitting. AE, DC, MC, V.*

$$ ⬚ **Casa da Pérgola.** This charming town house, which has been in the hands of the same family for over a century, provides an intimate lodging experience. The decor throughout is refined; the central location, excellent; and the style, thoroughly 19th century. A charming garden offsets the lovely painted-and-tiled facade, while the residents' lounge room sports period furniture, mirrors, and paintings. The house is part of the Turismo de Habitação scheme and has a limited number of rooms; you'll need to book well in advance. ✉ *Av. de Valbom 13, 2750 Cascais,* ☎ *01/484–0040. 6 rooms. Dining room. No credit cards. Closed Nov.–Feb.*

$$ ⬚ **Hotel Baia.** This modern stone hotel fronted with white balconies overlooks fishing boats on the quayside and the glistening blue waters of Cascais Bay. The Baia presents an air of efficiency, and the comfortable rooms are well-appointed, turned out in crisp colors, and have simple, attractive furnishings. Ask for one of the 66 that have balconies and sea views. There's a private esplanade along the ground floor, with a lounge, restaurant, grill, café, and bar. ✉ *Av. Marginal, 2750 Cascais,* ☎ *01/483–1033,* ᶠᴬˣ *01/483–1095. 114 rooms. Restaurant, bar, café, grill, pool. AE, DC, MC, V.*

$ ⬚ **Solar Dom Carlos.** This delightful inn tucked into quiet back streets is the most appealing budget bet in town. The handsome building dates from the 16th century and retains its original chapel—the house was formerly a nobleman's mansion—and beautiful gardens. There is attractive Portuguese tiling throughout, and although the rooms are not brimming with comforts, they are clean, comfortable, and reasonably spacious. Only breakfast is served, but you are just a short walk from the best of Cascais's restaurants. ✉ *Rua Latina Coelho 8, 2750 Cascais,* ☎ *01/486–8463. 12 rooms. Dining room. MC, V.*

Festival

The **Cascais music festival,** held every July and August, lures well-known orchestras and soloists to the town. Cascais holds a summer **jazz festival** each July.

Nightlife and the Arts

Cascais has plenty of bars and discos on and around the central, pedestrian Rua Frederico Arouca and in Largo Luiz de Camões. For drinks, try the English-style pub, the **John Bull** (⊠ Praça Costa Pinto 32, ☎ 01/483–3319), whose customers spill out into the square on hot summer nights. The trendy **Belbuerguer** (⊠ Trav. Visconde da Luz 20, ☎ 01/483–2312) serves burgers and fries to a rock-music accompaniment; it's busiest on Saturday nights. You can hear fado, the mournful Portuguese folk music, at **Forte D. Rodrigo** (⊠ Rua de Birre 961, ☎ 01/487–1373).

Outdoor Activities and Sports

FISHING

Contact the **Clube Naval de Cascais** (⊠ Esp. Príncipe Luís Filipe, in front of Hotel Baia, ☎ 01/483–0125), which organizes deep-sea fishing outings.

GOLF

Quinta da Marinha (⊠ 4 km/2½ mi west of Cascais, ☎ 01/468–9881) has an 18-hole course designed by Robert Trent Jones.

HORSEBACK RIDING

A particularly good equestrian center at **Quinta da Marinha** (⊠ 4 km/2½ mi west of Cascais, ☎ 01/486–9282) offers year-round riding.

WATER SPORTS

Surf rental equipment is available from **Equinócio** (⊠ Varandas de Cascais 3, ☎ 01/483–5354).

Shopping

Cascais is the best shopping area on the Estoril Coast, with pedestrian streets lined with shops and small market stalls. For smart fashions, gifts, and handmade jewelry, browse around **Rua Frederico Arouca.**

Markets are held north of town at Rua Mercado (⊠ Off Avenida 25 de Abril) on Wednesday and Saturday, selling fruit, vegetables, cheese, bread, and flowers. On the first and third Sunday of each month, a large market is held at the **Praça de Touros** (bullring) on Avenida Pedro Álvares, west of the center.

Boca do Inferno

❸ *2 km (1¼ mi) west of Cascais.*

The most visited attraction in the area around Cascais is the forbiddingly named **Boca do Inferno** (Mouth of Hell). Year-round the sea pounds this impressive natural grotto, one of several in the rugged local coastline. Walk along the fenced paths to the viewing platforms above the grotto and peer down into the abyss. It's a lively spot anytime, though it's best when the incoming tide thrusts waves high onto the surrounding cliffs. A path leads down to secluded spots on the rocks below, where fishermen cast their lines. Afterward, visit the daily roadside market of handicrafts, lace, and leather goods or one of the nearby cafés.

NEED A BREAK?

Walking along the coastal road west of Cascais, stop at the café-terrace **Esplanada Santa Marta** (⊠ Estrada da Boca do Inferno, ☎ 01/483–7779), which overlooks the tiny Santa Marta Beach and the adjacent lighthouse. This is a perfect spot for a cool drink on the way to or from the Boca do Inferno, a 20-minute walk beyond.

Guincho

❹ *9 km (5½ mi) north of Boca do Inferno.*

There's a superb wide beach at **Guincho,** where rollers from the Atlantic pound onto the sand even on the calmest of days, providing perfect conditions for windsurfing (the annual world championships are often held here during the summer). But beware: The undertow at Guincho beach is notoriously dangerous, and even the best swimmers should take heed. If you don't plan to take to the water, you should still drive out here to eat lunch at one of the several restaurants that overlook the beach. All have terraces and menus boasting absolutely fresh fish; if you don't want to drive—perhaps you would rather wash the meal down with wine and a glass of port?—then it's a simple matter to come by bus, which leaves from outside Cascais's train station every two hours (7:45 AM–5:45 PM, journey time 25 minutes).

Dining and Lodging

$$–$$$ ✕⊡ **Estalagem do Forte Muchaxo.** The lovely location of this restaurant and inn, nestled in the rocks over Guincho beach, may draw you here from Cascais (10 kilometers/6 miles away). Most of the comfortable rooms have splendid ocean views (though ones at the back overlook the nearby hills), and the pool and lounge room invite relaxation; the beach itself is just a step away. Despite the modern extensions, the theme inside the main part of the building is thoroughly rustic, with stone-flagged floors, wood paneling, and maritime bric-a-brac revealing the hotel's origins as a simple café where fishermen could go for drinks and coffee. Today, the inn contains one of the area's oldest and best-known restaurants, where fresh fish specialties (including *caldeirada,* Portuguese fish stew) are the order of the day. Meals are a little overpriced, and the service isn't always spot on, but what you're ultimately paying for is the unrivaled view of the beach through picture windows. ⊠ *Praia do Guincho, 2750 Cascais,* ☏ *01/487–0221,* FAX *01/487–0444. 24 rooms. Restaurant, bar, pool. AE, DC, MC, V.*

SINTRA AND ENVIRONS

Long considered one of the most beautiful places in Portugal, Sintra should not be missed. The district's lush woods and valleys on the northern slopes of the Serra de Sintra (Sintra Mountains) have been inhabited since prehistoric times, though the Moors were the first to build a castle on their peaks. Later Sintra became the summer residence of Portuguese kings and aristocrats, and its late medieval palace was the greatest expression of the royal wealth and power of the time. In the 18th and 19th centuries the area's charms were becoming widely known, as a succession of English travelers, poets, and writers—including an enthusiastic Lord Byron—were drawn by the region's beauty. The poet Robert Southey described Sintra as "the most blessed spot on the whole inhabitable globe."

Visitors tend to use the town as a base and travel out into the surrounding countryside during the day. Consequently, the various local attractions listed in this section—the market village of São Pedro de Sintra, Castelo dos Mouros, Pena Palace, Monserrate Gardens, Convento dos Capuchos, and Cabo da Roca—are arranged according to distance from Sintra, starting with the nearest attraction and ending at the coast. Driving is the easiest way to tour the sights, but there are local guided tours available (arranged through Sintra tourist office), or you can arrange to see the sights by taxi. The nearest attractions are within walking distance or accessible by horse-and-carriage ride.

Numbers in the margin correspond to points of interest on the Estoril Coast, Sintra, and Queluz map.

Sintra

❺ *30 km (18 mi) northwest of Lisbon, 13 km (8 mi) north of Estoril.*

There's no other word for it: The palaces, gardens, wooded paths, and viewpoints of Sintra are scintillating, while horse-drawn carriages and elegant old hotels in the vicinity add to its agreeable 19th-century air. If there's a drawback, it's the number of tour buses that sometimes clog the main square of the Vila Velha (Old Town). In front of Sintra Palace, cars and buses jostle for space, while hawkers wander the central area trying to interest tourists in toys and souvenirs. However, even in the height of summer, Sintra exudes charm, and with a little effort you can escape the crowds by taking one of several lovely rural walks through the surrounding countryside. Ask the Sintra tourist office for their guidebook to local walks.

★ The conical twin chimneys of the **Palácio Nacional de Sintra** (Sintra Palace), also called the Paço Real, are the town's most recognizable landmarks. There has probably been a palace here since Moorish times, although the present-day structure dates from the 14th century. The property was the summer residence of the House of Avis, Portugal's royal line, and it displays a combination of Moorish, Gothic, and Manueline architectural styles. To see the interior, you must join one of the guided tours, which is a pity since several of the rooms are exceptional and may demand more time than you're given. The **kitchen,** with its famous chimneys, is visited first, though this has little internal interest. Better is the **chapel,** decorated with some spectacular examples of mozarabic (Moorish-influenced) azulejos from the 15th and 16th centuries. The ceiling of the **Sala das Armas** is painted with the coats of arms of 72 noble families; another grand room has a ceiling of painted swans. One of the oldest rooms, the **Sala das Pegas,** figures in a well-known tale about an encounter between Dom João I (1385–1433), for whom the palace was largely rebuilt, and a lady-in-waiting whom he kissed. The king had the room painted with as many magpies as there were chattering court ladies, in order to stop their gossiping by satirizing them as loose-tongued birds. ⊠ *Largo Rainha D. Amelia,* ☎ *01/923–0085.* ◷ *400$00 June–Sept., 200$00 Oct.–May, free Sun. 10–12:30.* ⊙ *Thurs.–Tues. 10–1 and 2–5.*

NEED A
BREAK?

Well placed in Sintra's central square for fine views of Sintra Palace, the **Café Paris** (⊠ Largo Rainha D. Amelia, ☎ 01/923–2375) makes a pleasant stop for a drink or even a meal. Outside seating can be difficult to score; the lucky ones can soak up the bustling street scenes.

The **Museu Regional** (Regional Museum) not only displays a permanent collection of local archaeological, ethnological, and historical objects, but also hosts a variety of interesting temporary exhibitions. If the local scenery strikes you as particularly beautiful, be sure to take a look in the picture gallery, too, which specializes in works associated with Sintra. The museum is housed in the same building as the tourist-information office, close to the Paço Real. ⊠ *Praça da República 23, no phone.* ◷ *Free.* ⊙ *Picture gallery weekdays 9:30–noon and 2–6, weekends 2–6; museum Tues.–Fri. 9:30–noon and 2–6, weekends 2–6.*

Dining and Lodging

$$ ✕ **Alcobaça.** Up a tiny side street, the Alcobaça is one of the few restaurants in the center of town to offer a consistently good value. The friendly owner takes your order and then bustles around the small dining room to make sure everyone is happy. You will be—once you've tried the excellent grilled chicken or sampled the large, bubbling serving of arroz de marisco. The fresh clams *bulhão pato* (in parsley and garlic sauce) are also very tasty. These simple surroundings attract Portuguese tourists in search of honest home cooking, so trust their judgment and go right in. ✉ *Rua das Padarias 7–11,* ☎ *01/923–1651. MC, V.*

$$$$ ✕🏨 **Hotel Palácio de Seteais.** This luxurious 18th-century palace sits
★ on pristine grounds a kilometer or so (just over ½ mile) from the center of Sintra. Built by the Dutch Consul to Portugal, the palace's name, Seteais—meaning "seven sighs"—supposedly tells of the relief felt by the Portuguese after the signing of the 1807 Treaty of Sintra with the French. Today the sighs are more likely to be of admiration for the conservation of such a beautiful building and for the charming formal gardens. You'll enter under a superb, classical arch that joins the palace's two wings: Its public rooms are gloriously decorated with period and reproduction furnishings, delicate frescoes, and Arraiolos carpets; the guest rooms are individually styled, some with hand-painted wallpapers. If you're not planning an overnight stay, at least have yourself pampered in the splendid restaurant (reservations essential; jacket and tie), which serves a four-course set meal of impressively garnished Continental-style dishes. In summer, coffee or afternoon tea taken on the terrace is an added delight. ✉ *Rua Barbosa do Bocage 8, 2710 Sintra,* ☎ *01/923–3200,* FAX *01/923–4277. 30 rooms. Restaurant, bar, pool, tennis, horseback riding. AE, DC, MC, V.*

$$$ 🏨 **Quinta da Capela.** This long, low 16th-century manor house, built by the dukes of Cadaval, presents superb, spacious rooms adorned with rugs and period furniture. There is also a lovely garden, an old chapel on the grounds, and a pool, while the views stretch over to the Moorish Castle and Pena Palace. The manor house is just 3 kilometers (2 miles) west of Sintra, off the road to Colares. Breakfast is served, but as you'll probably want to take your other meals in town, a car is essential. ✉ *Estrada de Monserrate, 2710 Sintra,* ☎ *01/929–0170. 7 rooms, 6 with bath. Dining room, pool, sauna, exercise room. MC. Closed Nov.–Feb.*

$$–$$$ 🏨 **Quinta das Sequóias.** This lovely 19th-century manor house (for-
★ merly the Casa da Tapada) has been transformed into a lovely small hotel, superbly managed by owner Candida Gonzalez. The property is just 1 kilometer (about ½ mile) beyond the Palácio de Seteais, set in 40 acres of wooded grounds—look for the sign on the left-hand side of the road—and the half dozen rooms have charming furniture and modern bathrooms. One of the bathrooms has been cleverly built around monolithic boulders, while a tower contains a guest room as well as a flower-filled ground-floor sitting area; some rooms have distant views of the hills and coast. Antique touches proliferate: here an old parasol in a corner, there a period jewelry box or some rustic kitchen utensils. A fine buffet breakfast (and dinner if requested) is served in a large, galleried dining room that overlooks Pena Palace. The outdoor pool, Jacuzzi, and terrace form part of the landscaped gardens, and from the grounds you can walk to the gardens at Monserrate or the Capuchos Convent. ✉ *Quinta das Sequóias, Apartado 4, 2710 Sintra,* ☎ FAX *01/923–0342. 6 rooms. Bar, dining room, pool, hot tub, billiards. AE, DC, MC, V.*

$$–$$$ ⚏ **Tivoli Sintra.** The ultramodern Tivoli (a member of the chain of hotels in Lisbon by the same name) is right in the middle of town, very close to Sintra Palace. Comfortable chairs in the lounge and many of the smart rooms have excellent views of the local valley, and there's a welcoming restaurant, the Monserrate. Given the hotel's marvelous location, room rates are reasonable, especially in the winter, when they're reduced by at least 15%. Overall this is one of the region's best values. ⊠ *Praça da República, 2710 Sintra,* ☎ *01/923–3505,* FAX *01/923–1572. 75 rooms. Restaurant, bar. AE, DC, MC, V.*

$$ ⚏ **Hotel Central.** Dating from the turn of the century and exuding a certain faded charm, the Central appeals despite its lack of facilities. This was once *the* hotel in Sintra, and the interior reflects those bygone days: A smell of polished wood prevails, and Portuguese tiles and solid old furniture are everywhere. Its location opposite Sintra Palace is prime (although rooms that face the square can be noisy). Amenities include a large terrace with tables facing the palace and a simple Portuguese restaurant, whose wooden floors gleam and whose leaded picture windows look out over the back of town. Rooms here drop into the **$** range in winter. ⊠ *Praça da República 35, 2710 Sintra,* ☎ *01/923–0963. 14 rooms, 9 with bath. Restaurant, bar. AE, DC, MC, V.*

Festival

The excellent **Sintra Festival** runs from June through September every year and features piano recitals, operas, and ballet performances, which take place in the town's palaces, churches, and parks. Performances in the gardens of the Palácio de Seteais are especially popular. The **Sintra Tourist Board Cultural Department** (⊠ Praça da República 23, ☎ 01/923–5079) can provide more details and an events brochure.

Outdoor Activities and Sports

HORSEBACK RIDING

Sintra's pretty surroundings positively beg to be seen at a leisurely pace on horseback. Several local riding schools offer lessons; the local tourist office can provide addresses and phone numbers.

TENNIS

In Sintra, you can play tennis at the court in Parque Liberdade (☎ 01/924–1139) or at the Lourel municipal courts (⊠ Campo Raso, no phone).

Shopping

Sintra is a noted center for antiques, curios, arts, and crafts, although you'll need to choose carefully since the number of tourists not only keeps prices on the high side but also means a fair amount of poor-quality goods. **Almorábida** (⊠ Rua Visconde Monserrate 12–14), in front of Sintra Palace, is an outlet for genuine Arraiolos carpets, as well as lace, copper, and other artifacts. At **A Esquina** (⊠ Praça da República 20), the shop is stacked from floor to ceiling with hand-painted ceramics, many of them reproductions of 15th- to 18th-century designs, signed by the artists. For hand-embroidered linen tablecloths, bedspreads, towels, and sheets, visit **Violeta** (⊠ Rua das Padarias 19).

The small town of Pêro Pinheiro is known for its **marble,** with shops on both sides of the road selling stacks of cachepots, plaques, and other decorative garden objects. It's on the N9 road, 9 kilometers (5½ miles) northeast of Sintra.

São Pedro de Sintra

⑥ *2 km (1¼ mi) southeast of Sintra.*

São Pedro de Sintra is most famous for its **Feira da Sintra** (Sintra Fair), held every second and fourth Sunday of the month in the vast Praça Dom Fernando II (also called the Largo da Feira), where stalls are set up under the plane trees. Dating to the time of the Christian Reconquest, the fair is one of the best in the country, with livestock and agricultural displays, and local crafts, antiques, bric-a-brac, and food for sale. The village also host the large **Festa de Sã Pedro** (St. Peter's Day) each June 29, with all the riotous hullabaloo the Portuguese inject into their religious festivities. Even on nonfair days, it's worth coming to São Pedro to see the delightful village church in its own enclosed little square. There are also several good restaurants in São Pedro (☞ Dining, *below*), which makes it an attractive lunch stop.

The walk to São Pedro de Sintra along the main road from Sintra is not much fun, though you can cut out much of the distance by climbing up through the lush gardens of the **Parque Liberdade** (⊙ June–Sept., daily 9–8; Oct.–May, daily 9–6), which starts just east of Sintra. Otherwise, local buses leave from outside the Sintra train station (weekdays every 30–40 mins, reduced service on weekends), and you can catch one as it passes the tourist office; or take a taxi.

Dining

$$$ ✕ **Cantinho de São Pedro.** Imaginative Portuguese cuisine with a French influence is presented at this busy restaurant, at which locals consider the food well worth the wait for a table. Try the trout with almonds and cream or look for the fresh shellfish on the list of *pratos do dia* (dishes of the day). The restaurant is a rustic little plant-filled building in a small courtyard of artisans' workshops, just off the main square. ⊠ *Praça Dom Fernando II 18*, ☎ *01/923–0267. AE, DC, MC, V. Closed Mon.*

$$–$$$ ✕ **Solar de São Pedro.** Right on the square, the distinctive Solar de São Pedro has grandstand views of the bimonthly Sunday market—you'll have to book ahead for lunch if you want to eat then. There's a small menu of Portuguese specialties, but the São Pedro is best known for eclectic international food like its fresh fish and grilled steaks. It's all a good value, although meals that include fish tend to be more expensive. ⊠ *Praça Dom Fernando II 12*, ☎ *01/923–1860. AE, DC, MC, V. Closed Wed.*

$$–$$$ ✕ **Toca do Javali.** A few hundred feet past the market square in São Pedro, you climb down the steps into this highly attractive restaurant to be greeted by wild boar—that's what *javali* means—and in the cool, whitewashed, beamed interior, wild boar are either underfoot (a skin is spread under every table) or on your plate. A separate game menu suggests roast boar or boar ragout, as well as partridge and pheasant when in season; there are also regular dishes of both meat and fish. In summer you can eat in the delightful terraced garden; otherwise, go for a window table in the simple, traditional interior. At lunchtime, an extremely well-priced set meal consists of soup, main course, fruit, and wine for under 1,500$00. ⊠ *Rua 1 de Dezembro 18*, ☎ *01/923–3503. AE, MC, V. Closed Wed.*

Castelo dos Mouros

❼ *2 km (1¼ mi) south of Sintra.*

★ Only the battlemented ruins of the 8th-century Castelo dos Mouros (Moorish Castle) still stand today, but the extent of these give a fine impression of the solid fortress that finally fell from Moorish hands when it was conquered by Dom Afonso Henriques in 1147. It's visible from various points in Sintra itself—the steps of Sintra Palace is a favored vantage point—but for a closer look follow the steep, partially cobbled road that leads up to the ruins, a walk that will take around 40 minutes. Or rent one of the horse-drawn carriages outside Sintra Palace for a more romantic trip (8,000$00). Vast, panoramic views from the castle's serrated walls help explain why Moorish architects chose the site, while eagle-eyed visitors can also trace the remains of a mosque within the walls. ⊠ *Estrada da Pena, no phone.* ☎ *Free.* ☉ *June–Sept., daily 10–6; Oct.–May, daily 10–5.*

Palácio Nacional de Pena

❽   *4 km (2½ mi) south of Sintra.*

Of all the palaces in Sintra's environs, the most enjoyable is the draw-
★ bridged **Palácio Nacional de Pena** (Pena Palace), a glorious conglomeration of turrets, ramparts, and domes washed in an array of pastel shades. It's a long but very pleasant walk up here from the center of Sintra (about 1½ hours), although you can see the palace on one of the local tours or even come by horse and carriage, which costs 9,500$00. However, the walk from the Pena Palace back down to Sintra is delightful: You travel through shaded woods and have several opportunities to rest at viewpoints and take in the panoramic scenes.

Commissioned by King Consort Ferdinand of Saxe-Coburg in 1840, to be built where a 16th-century convent once stood, Pena Palace is a collection of clashing styles, from Arabian to Victorian. A splendid park surrounds the palace, filled with a lush variety of trees and flowers from every corner of the Portuguese empire. Perched atop a nearby crag, overlooking the grounds, is an enormous statue of Baron Eschwege (the building's German architect) cast as a medieval knight. The final kings of Portugal lived here, the last of whom—Dom Manuel II—went into exile in England in 1910 after a republican revolt. The pseudomedieval structure, with its ramparts, towers, and great halls, is decorated in late Victorian and Edwardian furnishings—a rich, sometimes vulgar, and often bizarre collection of furniture, ornaments, and paintings that makes the guided tour surprisingly interesting. ⊠ *Estrada da Pena,* ☎ *01/923–0227.* ☎ *Palace 400$00 June–Sept., 200$00 Oct.–May, free Sun. 10–2. Park 200$00, plus an extra charge for cars and carriages.* ☉ *Palace Tues.–Sun. 10–1 and 2–5; park June–Sept., daily 10–6, Oct.–May, daily 10–5.*

At the **Cruz Alta**, a 16th-century stone cross, you are 1,782 feet above sea level, at the highest point of the Sintra Mountains. A direct path leads here from Pena Palace, starting beyond the statue of Baron Eschwege. It's an arduous climb, especially in the summer sun, but the views from this altitude are stupendous.

Monserrate

❾   *4 km (2½ mi) west of Sintra.*

The gardens of **Monserrate** were laid out by Scottish gardeners in the mid-19th century at the behest of a wealthy Englishman, Sir Francis Cook. The ground's centerpiece—the architecturally extravagant, Moorish-style domed pavilion—is closed to visitors, but the gardens, with their streams, waterfalls, and imported Etruscan tombs, are worth a stop. In addition to the array of tree and plant species, you'll see one of the largest collections of ferns in the world (labels, unfortunately, are few and far between). The gardens are a popular picnic spot, and you'll easily be able to find your own glade as you follow the paths that wind their way through the grounds. ⊠ *Estrada da Monserrate,* ☎ *01/923–0137.* ⚏ *200$00.* ⊙ *June–Sept., daily 10–6; Oct.–May, daily 10–5.*

En Route   Past Monserrate the road leads west for 3 kilometers (2 miles) to the small village of **Colares,** associated with the locally produced red wine. The town, its winding streets alive with colorful flowers and trees, is also known for its parish church, which is adorned with ceramic tiles, and its main square, bordered by 18th-century houses. For terrific views of the sea and surrounding mountains, take the winding road that climbs up to the nearby village of **Penedo,** less than 2 kilometers (1½ miles) away.

Convento dos Capuchos

⑩   *9 km (5½ mi) west of Sintra, 4 km (2½ mi) west of Pena Palace.*

One of the most extraordinary religious foundations in Portugal is surely the tiny **Convento dos Capuchos** (Capuchos Convent), a friary built in 1560 by Franciscan monks. Sited on an isolated hillside, the 12 diminutive cells, the chapel, kitchen, and the refectory—all hacked out of solid rock—are insulated with cork panels, hence its popular nickname: the "Cork Convent." It can never have been very comfortable at the best of times, and as you're shown around the confined corridors and small rooms (some barely big enough to stand up in), the austerity of the monks' regime becomes awfully clear; in winter, it's particularly cold and damp here. The monastery was abandoned in the mid-19th century and has been neglected ever since, though the caretaker at the site does his best to show visitors the main points of interest and can even sell you some homemade honey—a luxury, you feel, the erstwhile monks would have been denied. ⊠ *Convento dos Capuchos,* ☎ *01/923–0137.* ⚏ *200$00.* ⊙ *June–Sept., daily 10–6; Oct.–May, daily 10–5.*

Cabo da Roca

⑪   *15 km (9 mi) west of Sintra, 20 km (12½ mi) northwest of Cascais.*

★   The windswept **Cabo da Roca** and its lighthouse marks continental Europe's westernmost point—which is the only reason that most people make the journey. As with many similar places, tourist stalls take advantage of its popularity and offer shell souvenirs and other gimmicks, while an information desk and gift shop sells a certificate that verifies your visit. They do a brisk trade for these every time a tour bus pulls into the parking lot. But even without the certificate, the memory of this desolate granite cape will linger; it's definitely worth spending some time strolling the headland, trying to avoid the crowds. The cliffs tumble down to a frothing sea below, while on the cape a simple cross bears an inscription by Portuguese poet Luis de Camões. The cape can also be reached from Cascais (30 minutes) or Sintra (40 minutes) by local bus, with regular departures from outside either town's train station.

OFF THE   **THE ATLANTIC COAST –** North of Cabo da Roca are the successive At-
BEATEN PATH   lantic-facing resort villages of **Praia Grande, Praia das Maças** and **Azen-has do Mar.** All three have good beaches (Praia Grande's is the longest), public swimming pools, and a selection of small restaurants. If you're visiting Praia das Maças between July and September, a 19th-century tram (the Elétrico de Sintra; ☎ 01/923–0662 for information) leaves hourly (eight times daily; closed Mon.) from **Banzão** (just outside Colares) and offers particularly engaging views as it approaches the beach.

QUELUZ

Halfway between Lisbon and Sintra (just off the N249) is the town of Queluz, dominated entirely by its magnificent palace. The drive from Lisbon takes about 20 minutes, making this a good half-day option or a fine stop on the way to or from Sintra. It's considerably easier to take the train: Get off at the Quelez-Belas stop, turn left outside the station, and follow the signs for the 1 kilometer (½ mile) walk to the palace.

Palácio Nacional de Queluz

⑫ *15 km (9 mi) east of Sintra, 15 km (9 mi) northwest of Lisbon.*

★ One of the most attractive of the royal residences near Lisbon, the **Palácio Nacional de Queluz** (Queluz Palace) was inspired, in part, by the palace at Versailles. Intended as a royal summer residence, the salmon-pink rococo edifice was ordered by Dom Pedro III in 1747 and took 40 years to complete. The building is surrounded by formal landscaping and waterways designed by a Frenchman, Jean-Baptiste Robillon. The ponds, canal, statues, fountains, hedges—and the palace—all fit a carefully executed baroque plan that implies harmony and wholeness. In 1934 a disastrous fire caused much damage, but the palace has been restored and is used today for formal banquets, music festivals, and as accommodations for visiting heads of state.

Visitors may tour the richly furnished interior and walk through the elegant state rooms: the frescoed Music Salon, the Hall of Ambassadors (where diplomats would present their credentials), the mirrored Throne Room with its crystal chandeliers and gilt trimmings, and so on. The room furnishings, gathered from all corners of the globe, including fine woods and precious metals from the old Portuguese colonies, are as ornate and spectacular as you might expect. ⊠ *Palácio Nacional de Queluz,* ☎ *01/435–0039.* 🎟 *400$00 June–Sept., 200$00 Oct.–May.* ⏱ *Mon. and Wed.–Sun. 10–1 and 2–5.*

Dining

$$$ ✕ **Restaurante de Cozinha Velha.** Formerly the great kitchen of the
★ Queluz Palace, this magnificent restaurant takes full advantage of its heritage: An imposing open fireplace and vast oak table catch the eye, old cooking utensils hang from the walls, and tables and chairs are fine reproduction antiques. The cooking hits the mark, with the Portuguese specialties occasionally tempered by a French touch; a spicy *cataplana* (stew) of salmon, monkfish, clams, and shrimp is just one superb main course. Certain dishes have been inspired by 18th-century recipes, notably some of the desserts, which are always a Portuguese obsession. Service is excellent, and the English-speaking staff can guide you through the impressive wine list. ⊠ *Palácio Nacional de Queluz,* ☎ *01/435–0232. Reservations essential. AE, DC, MC, V.*

Festival

For four weeks every summer the **Noites de Queluz** (Queluz Nights) festival is staged in the gardens of the Palácio Nacional de Queluz. Complete with costumed cast and orchestra, this event mimics the concerts, fireworks displays, and other activities held in the gardens to amuse Queen Maria I (wife of Dom Pedro III), who lived in the palace throughout her long reign (1777–1816) and whose eccentric behavior earned her the name "Mad" Queen Maria. For more information, contact the Sintra tourist office.

THE SETÚBAL PENINSULA

The extensive Setúbal Peninsula, south of the Rio Tejo, is visited mostly for its beaches on the Costa da Caparica, which provide the cleanest ocean swimming closest to Lisbon. Other attractions include the major port of Setúbal and the scenic mountain range—the Serra de Arrábida—that separates the port from the peninsula's southernmost beaches and fishing villages.

If you're intent on eating seafood at Cacilhas, spending the day at the beach or simply touring the town of Setúbal, traveling by public transportation from Lisbon is your easiest course of action. However, if you want to see most or all of the sites covered in this section—and particularly if you want to tour the southern coastal and mountainous region—renting a car will be your best move. Apart from the simple ferry ride to Cacilhas, all approaches to the Setúbal Peninsula from Lisbon involve first crossing the impressive Ponte 25 de Abril suspension bridge; car drivers will pay a toll of 150$00. From this route you're guaranteed stupendous views of the capital, though it pays to avoid crossing during rush hour and on Friday and Sunday evenings—the traffic can be horrendous.

Numbers in the margin correspond to points of interest on the Setúbal Peninsula map.

Cacilhas

⑬ *6 km (4 mi) south of Lisbon.*

Although a town in its own right, Cacilhas appears little more than a suburb of Lisbon, albeit one with the bonus of a group of reliable seafood restaurants lining its main street, Rua do Ginjal. It lies immediately across the Rio Tejo from the capital, and at night, and especially on weekends, Cacilhas is a popular destination for city dwellers who take the ferry across the river to dine. Waiters armed with menus linger outside their doors, ready to pounce on passersby who can't decide where to eat; once inside, you're tempted with the best of the day's catch. The ferries run every 10–15 minutes (7 AM–9 PM) from Fluvial terminal, adjacent to Praça do Comércio, or from Cais do Sodré (24-hour service). One-way tickets cost 95$00, and the journey takes about 15 minutes.

The **Cristo Rei**—a huge, white statue of Christ, built in 1959—was modeled on the famous statue of Christ the Redeemer in Rio de Janeiro. The figure stands proudly above Cacilhas, its outstretched arms seemingly embracing the city of Lisbon across the water; indeed, it's something of a waterfront landmark and can be seen easily from almost any high point in Lisbon. For a closer look, take the elevator to the top for remarkable panoramic views. Buses from the ferry station on the Cacilhas dockside can take you directly to the Cristo Rei statue every 20–30 minutes, daily 8 AM–9 PM; alternatively, from Lisbon, buses to Setúbal make a stop on the highway close to the turnoff for the statue; from there it's a 10-minute walk. Drivers should cross the Ponte 25 de Abril from Lisbon and, as they leave the bridge, follow the signs off the highway to the Cristo Rei. ⊠ *Cristo Rei, no phone.* ☜ *220$00.* ☉ *Daily 9–7.*

Costa da Caparica

★ **⑭** *8 km (5 mi) west of Cacilhas; take the minor N377, a slower, more scenic route than the main road. Also 14 km (8½ mi) southwest of Lisbon.*

When Lisbon's inhabitants want to go the beach, their preferred spot is the Costa da Caparica, a 20-kilometer (12-mile) stretch of sand on the northwestern coast of the Setúbal Peninsula. The coastal strip centers on the lively resort of **Caparica** itself, at the northern end of the beach, just an hour from the capital. Formerly a fishing village, it's now packed in summer with Portuguese tourists who come to enjoy the relatively unpolluted waters, eat grilled sardines in the seafood restaurants, and stroll the seafront promenade. You may be able to avoid the crowds if you keep heading south toward the less accessible, lonely dunes and coves at the end of the peninsula. From June to September, a small narrow-gauge train departs from Caparica and travels along an 8-kilometer (5-mile) stretch of coast, making stops en route; a one-way ticket to the end of the line costs 400$00. Each beach is unique: The areas nearest Caparica are family oriented, while the more southerly resorts tend to attract a younger crowd (among these beaches are some nudist spots as well).

Palmela

⑮ *38 km (24 mi) southeast of Lisbon.*

The small town of Palmela lies in the center of a prosperous wine-growing area. Every September the community holds a good-natured **Festa das Vindimas** (Grape Harvest Festival) that draws the inhabitants of Palmela's low, engaging, whitewashed houses into the town's cobbled streets. Besides a symbolic treading of the grapes and a blessing of the harvest, dancing, fireworks, wine tastings, processions, and religious services accompany the festival. Tourist offices in the region can provide exact dates.

The village is dominated year-round by the remains of a 12th-century castle that was captured from the Moors and enlarged by successive kings. In the 15th century the monastery and church of Sant'Iago were built within the castle walls. The buildings were damaged in the 1755 earthquake and lay abandoned for many years, until after extensive restoration, a pousada was opened in the monastic buildings. The views from this height are extensive: On a good day, Lisbon is visible in the distance.

Dining and Lodging

$$$ ✕⌂ **Pousada de Palmela.** Set on a hill at the eastern end of the Arrábida range, this historic building was originally a medieval fortress and later saw use as a monastery. In 1979 it was converted into a luxury pousada, and the designers made inspired use of the flagstone corridors and old cloister (now a lounge). Most of the pleasant rooms provide superb views of the valley and the sea; bathrooms are well equipped and the beds comfortable. There's little trace of monastic asceticism elsewhere, either: The monks' former refectory is now a dependable restaurant, serving traditional Portuguese food and a good range of wines. ⌂ *2950 Palmela,* ☎ *01/235–1226,* ℻ *01/233–0440. 28 rooms. Restaurant, bar. AE, DC, MC, V.*

Setúbal

⑯ *10 km (6 mi) south of Palmela, 50 km (31 mi) southeast of Lisbon.*

Sitting at the mouth of the Rio Sado, Setúbal is the country's third-largest port, and although it's one of Portugal's oldest cities, its character has become largely industrial. Nevertheless, the center remains an attractive blend of medieval and modern and boasts one of Portugal's most handsome churches, the Igreja de Jesus. This in itself is worth a stop in the city, though many travelers also use Setúbal as an overnight break before driving on to the Algarve, since the 16th-century Castelo de São Filipe has been converted into one of Portugal's finest pousadas. Even if you decide to go on, you may want to dine here or just pause to take in the views from the castle's privileged position over the city.

There's much to be said for spending half a day in the city, strolling the attractive, cobbled pedestrian streets around the cathedral, which open into pretty squares with cafés. Near the port, an agreeable clutter of fishing boats and warehouses is fronted by gardens, where you'll find a daily fish-and-produce market.

★ The major historic relic in Setúbal is the 15th-century **Igreja de Jesus** (Church of Jesus), perhaps Portugal's earliest example of Manueline architecture, built with local marble and later tiled internally with 17th-century azulejos. The architect was Diogo de Boitaca, and inside the church he built—which predates the Jerónimos Monastery at Belém in Lisbon—are twisted, ropelike pillars that support the vault. These details would soon become the very hallmark of Manueline style. Outside, you can still admire the original, though badly worn, main doorway and deplore the addition of a concrete expanse out front that makes the church square look like a roller-skating rink. ⊠ *Praça Miguel Bombarda,* ☎ *065/524772.* ⊡ *Free.* ☉ *Tues.–Sun. 9:30–1 and 2–5:30.*

The original monastic buildings and Gothic cloister of the Igreja de Jesus now house the **Museu de Setúbal,** a municipal museum that contains a fascinating collection of 15th- and 16th-century Portuguese paintings, several by the so-called Master of Setúbal. Other museum attractions include some lovely azulejos, local archaeological finds, and a coin collection. However, the museum is undergoing extensive renovation, and the only wing currently open is that devoted to 15th-century Portuguese art. ⊠ *Rua Balneário Paula Borba,* ☎ *065/524772.* ⊡ *Free.* ☉ *Tues.–Sat. 9–noon and 2–5.*

Dining and Lodging

$$ ✕ **O Baluarte do Sado.** There are several cafés and restaurants around the market, near the port, but this is the best, and the friendly owner speaks English. At the back of a parking lot, the simple dining room with a plain tiled floor and more elaborately tiled walls is the background for excellent grilled meals—the charcoal range out front is kept busy with orders for barbecued cuts of various fish, squid, and beef. Or you might order an arroz de marisco or caldeirada for two; accompaniments are mixed salads, new potatoes when in season, and fries. Sunday lunchtime is especially popular with local families. Everyone drinks the house wine—the white goes well with all fish meals. ⊠ *Praça da República 1,* ☎ *065/38780. No credit cards.*

$$ ✕ **Rio Azul.** Locals frequent this popular seafood restaurant—hidden on a side street off Rua L. Todi, on the way to the castle, west of the harbor. It's a little tricky to find but is signposted from the main road. As you'd expect at a *marisqueira,* the dishes to go for are the fresh fish grilled to perfection and the arroz de marisco, a house specialty. ⊠ *Rua Placido Stichini 1,* ☎ *065/522828. AE, DC, MC, V. Closed Wed.*

$$$ ✕▥ **Pousada de São Filipe.** Perched atop a hill where it overlooks the
★ town and the Rio Sado, this 16th-century castle turned into a picturebook pousada makes an exciting overnight stop and is given excellent reviews by most visitors. The approach to the main entrance from the parking lot is magnificent, up a tunneled flight of stairs and past a lovely 18th-century chapel decorated with azulejos depicting the life of São Filipe. Winter nights can be chilly, but the historic location, the splendid views from the rooms and ramparts, and the hotel's unique features compensate considerably for any fleeting moments of discomfort.

The interior is also awash with azulejo tiling, especially in the welcoming bar; a canopied terrace in front of the reception area affords fine views of town, the bay, and Troia. And the appealing restaurant, traditionally decorated, has a kitchen strong on Portuguese cuisine and especially good with fish. ⊠ *Castelo de São Filipe, 2900 Setúbal,* ☎ *065/523844,* 𝔽𝔸𝕏 *065/532538. 14 rooms. Restaurant, bar. AE, DC, MC, V.*

$$ ⊡ **Quinta do Patricio.** This manor house—a member of Turismo de Habitação—is close to the castle and provides a small-scale, pretty alternative to the grandness of the pousada. Furnishings throughout the property are homey, with open fires and bright-color rugs and paintings, and from the large private garden you'll get some nice views of the town. For those who fancy something a little different, there are two separate apartments for rent within the grounds, one with a kitchen, the other romantically converted from a former windmill. Breakfast is served, and other meals are available upon request; reservations made well in advance are essential. ⊠ *Estrada de São Filipe, 2900 Setúbal,* ☎ 𝔽𝔸𝕏 *065/33817. 3 rooms, 2 with shower, and 2 apartments. Bar, pool. No credit cards.*

Festival

The **Feira de Santiago** takes place in Setúbal at the end of July and includes various folkloric events, a fair with rides and food stalls, and other entertainment.

Peninsula de Tróia

⑰ *20 minutes from Setúbal by boat. Car and passenger ferries run every 30–60 minutes, 24 hours, from Setúbal's port; cost is 130$00 per person, cars 560$00.*

Across the estuary from Setúbal—reached by ferry from town—is the Peninsula de Tróia, a long spit of land blessed with fine beaches and clean water. To answer the demands of tourists, the peninsula has been much developed in recent years, and the large **Tróia Tourist Complex** here includes a golf course, tennis courts, and other amenities. The area has managed to retain a little of its history, though: The peninsula is the site of the Roman town of Cetobriga, destroyed by a tidal wave in the 5th century, and you can visit its scant ruins (opposite the marina).

Vila Nogueira de Azeitão

⑱ *14 km (9 mi) west of Setúbal.*

The region around the small town of Vila Nogueira de Azeitão, on the western side of the Serra da Arrábida (☞ *below*), retains a disproportionately large number of fine old manor houses and palaces. In earlier times, many of the country's foremost noblemen maintained country estates here, deep in the heart of a wealthy wine-making and market-garden region. Wines made here by the José Maria da Fonseca Company are some of the most popular in the country (and one of Portugal's major exports). If you're interested, ask the local tourist office about winery tours, where you can view all stages of the production process. Most people will settle for a taste of the product in one of the bars and restaurants; be sure to try the dessert wine called Moscatel de Setúbal.

Vila Nogueira de Azeitão's agricultural traditions are trumpeted on the first Sunday of every month, when a **country market** is held in the center of town. Apart from the locally produced wine, you can buy *queijo fresco* (sheep's milk cheese)—a good choice for a picnic lunch—as well as excellent fresh bread from one of the market's bakery stalls.

The grandest building in Vila Nogueira de Azeitão is the 16th-century **Tavora Palace,** once owned by the Duke of Aveiro. In the 18th century, the Marquês de Pombal accused the duke of collaborating in the assassination plot against the king, Dom José. Subsequently the duke was executed by the marquês, and the Tavora coat of arms was erased from the Sala das Armas in Sintra's National Palace. Unfortunately, the palace is not open for visits, but the fine Renaissance exterior is visible.

NEED A   The 16th-century **Quinta das Torres** (☎ 065/208–0001), at Vila Fresca
BREAK?   de Azeitão, 2 kilometers (1¼ miles) east of Vila Nogueira de Azeitão, is
              now an inn with a restaurant. Set in beautiful gardens, the fine old build-
              ing has been beautifully restored and features antique furniture and
              tapestries at every turn. The locally produced food served here is well
              prepared and moderately priced.

The main feature of the **Quinta da Bacalhoa,** a late-16th-century L-shaped mansion, is its box-hedged gardens, which sport striking azulejo-lined paths. You can't tour the villa which is a private house, but the gardens are open to the public. A pavilion with three pyramidal towers houses the oldest azulejo panel in the country: It depicts the story of Susannah and the Elders and dates from 1565. You'll find the mansion 4 kilometers (2½ miles) east of Vila Nogueira de Azeitão, along the N10 road to Setúbal. ⊠ *Quinta da Bacalhoa,* ✉ *Free; tips expected.* ☉ *Gardens Mon.–Sat. 1–5.*

Serra de Arrábida

⑲ *West of Setúbal, with access along the main N10 or minor N379; Port-inho da Arrábida is 14 km (9 mi) southwest of Setúbal.*

Dominating the entire southern coast of the Setúbal Peninsula is the Serra de Arrábida, a 5,000-foot-high mountain range whose wild crags fall steeply to the sea. There is profuse plant life at these heights, particularly in the spring, when the rocks are carpeted with wildflowers. The entire region is now a designated national park.

The main road through the park is the N10, which you can leave at Vila Nogueira de Azeitão to travel south toward the small fishing village of **Portinho da Arrábida,** at the foot of the mountain range. The village is a popular destination for Lisboans, who appreciate the good local beaches. In summer, when the number of visitors makes parking nearly impossible, leave your car above the village and take the steep walk down to the water, where you'll find several modest seafood restaurants that overlook the port.

From Portinho da Arrábida, the lower, coastal road hugs the shore nearly all the way to Setúbal; the upper road gives access to the ramshackle, white-walled **Convento de Arrábida,** an atmospheric 16th-century monastery built into the hills of the Serra de Arrábida. The views are glorious here, but you'll have to contact the tourist office in Setúbal in advance to arrange a visit to the monastery.

Sesimbra

★ ⑳ *30 km (18 mi) southwest of Setúbal, 40 km (24½ mi) south of Lisbon.*

Sesimbra, a lively fishing village surrounded by mountains and isolated bays and coves, owes its popularity to its proximity to the capital. However, despite high-rise apartments that now mar the approaches to the town, Sesimbra has some narrow central streets that are still thoroughly agreeable. Moreover, the long beach is lovely, if a little crowded in summer, and perfectly fine for swimming. The waterfront is guarded by a 17th-century fortress and overlooked by outdoor restaurants serving fresh-fish meals. A short walk along the coast to the west takes you to the main port, littered with nets, anchors, and coils of rope and packed with fishing boats—which unload their catches at an entertaining daily fish auction. More energetic visitors can make the 40-minute walk to the hilltop, northwest of town, where the remains of an old Moorish castle with five towers perches, overlooking the port.

Dining and Lodging

$–$$ ✕ **Café Felipe.** Set in a line of sidewalk restaurants overlooking the waterfront, the Felipe is one of the best in town, always busy with vacationers and locals digging into the terrific grilled fish—cooked outside on a charcoal grill—or arroz de marisco, the house specialty. There's no nicer spot on a summer's evening, but such is its popularity, you may have to wait in line for a table. It's worth it. ⊠ *Avda. 25 de Abril, no phone. MC, V.*

$$ ⌂ **Hotel do Mar.** This is typical of the comfortable family-oriented hotels that have sprung up in Sesimbra to cater to the influx of summer visitors. A low, stepped building tucked into the seaside cliffs, this property features reasonably sized, modern rooms with balconies that overlook either the sea or the private garden and pool area. Its many public rooms and amenities provide the mostly Portuguese guests with a complete vacation within the confines of the hotel. There's a garden grill in summer, and water sports and horseback riding can be arranged through the hotel. ⊠ *Rua General Humberto Delgado 10, 2970 Sesimbra,* ☎ *01/223–3326,* ℻ *01/223–3888. 160 rooms. Restaurant, bar, coffee shop, grill, indoor and outdoor pool, sauna, 2 tennis courts, babysitting, playground. AE, DC, MC, V.*

Festivals

Sesimbra celebrates saints' days and other religious holidays throughout the year, with particularly large festivals in June, July, and September. Some of the dates change every year, so contact the local tourist office for more information.

Outdoor Activities and Sports

Sesimbra, a deep-sea fishing center, is renowned for the huge swordfish that are landed in the area. Ask around the port for local people who rent boats or consult the tourist office.

Cabo Espichel

㉑ *12 km (7 mi) west of Sesimbra.*

The Setúbal Peninsula peters out at Cabo Espichel, a salt-encrusted headland on which 18th-century arcaded pilgrimage houses border a huge open space; at one end is a forsaken pilgrimage church. This is the southwestern point of the Setúbal Peninsula, a rugged and lonely place, where the cliffs rise hundreds of feet out of the stormy Atlantic. To the north, unsullied beaches extend as far as Caparica, with only local roads and foot paths connecting them. There are six buses a day here from Sesimbra.

LISBON'S ENVIRONS A TO Z

Arriving and Departing

Lisbon is the initial point of arrival for almost all the destinations covered here (☞ Lisbon A to Z *in* Chapter 2). It's also a highly convenient base, since from the city, it's easy to take public transportation or drive to all the surrounding towns. Visitors driving south from Peniche/Óbidos can take the N8, rather than the main highway, if they prefer to see Sintra before Lisbon. If you are traveling north from the Algarve, then you reach the city of Setúbal and its peninsula before arriving in Lisbon.

Getting Around

By Boat

Ferries cross the Rio Tejo from Lisbon to the suburb of Cacilhas every 10–15 minutes (7 AM–9 PM) from Fluvial terminal, adjacent to Praça do Comércio, or from Cais do Sodré (24-hour service). One-way tickets cost 95$00, and the journey takes about 15 minutes.

From Setúbal there's 24-hour ferry service for cars (560$00) and foot passengers (130$00) across to the Tróia Peninsula; the journey takes about 20 minutes. Departures are every 30–60 minutes.

By Bus

Although the best way to reach Sintra and most of the towns on the Estoril Coast is by train from Lisbon, there are some useful bus connections between towns. Tickets are cheap (under 500$00 for most journeys), and departures are generally every hour (though less frequent at weekends); local tourist offices have current timetables.

At **Cascais,** the bus terminal (☎ 01/483–6357) outside the train station operates regular summer services to Guincho (journey time is 15 minutes) and Sintra (one hour). From the bus terminal (☎ 01/923–0675) outside **Sintra** train station, there are half-hourly bus departures in summer to the resorts of Praia das Maçãs and Azenhas do Mar (30 minutes) in the west, and north to Mafra in Estremadura (one hour). There's also regular year-round service from Sintra to Cascais and Estoril (one hour).

Buses 52 and 53 to **Caparica** (45 minutes) depart from Praça de Espanha (metro: Palhavã) in Lisbon, traveling over the Ponte 25 de Abril. Regular buses to Caparica also leave from the quayside bus terminal at **Cacilhas** (⊠ Largo Alfredo Diniz, no phone), the suburb immediately across the Tejo from Lisbon, which you can reach by ferry from the Terminal Fluvial, adjacent to Praça do Comércio. Bus departures on both routes are as frequent as every 15 minutes in the summer, and services run from 7 AM until well after midnight, but can be very crowded.

Buses to **Setúbal** (one hour) leave regularly from Lisbon's Praça de Espanha (metro: Palhavã) and from Cacilhas. At Setúbal bus station (⊠ Avda. 5 de Outubro 44, ☎ 065/525051) you can connect with local services north to Palmela (20 minutes) and southwest to Sesimbra (30 minutes). Six buses daily run a 30-minute trip from **Sesimbra** bus station (⊠ Avda. da Liberdade, ☎ 01/223–3071) to the southwestern cape of Cabo Espichel.

By Car

Driving is certainly the most flexible way to see Lisbon's environs; fast highways connect Lisbon with Estoril and Setúbal, and the quality of other roads in the region is generally good. Take special care on hilly and coastal roads, though, and if possible, avoid driving (or at least driving to Lisbon) at the end of a weekend or during public holidays; the Ponte 25 de Abril is a notorious traffic bottleneck. Bear in mind, too, that parking can be problematic, especially in the summer along the Estoril Coast. When you do park, *never* leave anything visible in the car, and it's wise to clear the trunk as well.

By Taxi

If you don't have your own car, it may pay—at least in convenience—to take a taxi to some attractions in the area. Cabs can be relatively inexpensive, and you can usually agree on a fixed price that will include the round-trip to a specific attraction (the driver will wait for you to complete your tour). Tourist offices can give you an idea of what fares are reasonable for various local trips.

By Train

Electric commuter trains travel the entire Estoril Coast, with departures every 15–30 minutes from the waterfront Cais do Sodré station (☎ 01/347–0181) in Lisbon, just a 10-minute walk west from the Praça do Comércio. The scenic trip to Estoril, with splendid sea views, takes about 30 minutes, and four more stops along the seashore bring you to Cascais, at the end of the line. A one-way ticket to either costs 170$00; service operates daily 5:30 AM–2:30 AM. Trains from Lisbon's Rossío station (☎ 01/346–5022), situated between Praça dos Restauradores and the Rossío, run every 15 minutes to Queluz (a 20-minute trip) and on to Sintra (40 minutes total). The service operates 6 AM–2:40 AM, and one-way tickets cost 140$00 to Queluz, 170$00 to Sintra.

For current timetable information about all train services in Lisbon's environs, call ☎ 01/888–4025.

Although you can reach Setúbal by train and ferry, it's much easier to take the bus (☞ *above*). From June to September a narrow-gauge railway runs for 8 kilometers (5 miles) along the Costa da Caparica from the town of Caparica, on the Setúbal Peninsula. It makes 20 stops at beaches along the way, and a one-way ticket to the end of the line costs 400$00.

Contacts and Resources

Car Rental

There are better choices for car rentals in Lisbon (☞ Lison A to Z *in* Chapter 2), though the tourist offices in Cascais, Estoril, Sintra, and Setúbal can advise you of the local possibilities. Choices include **Avis** (⊠ Tamariz Esplanade, Estoril, ☎ 01/468–5728; ⊠ Avda. Luisa Todi 96, ☎ 065/526946), **Europcar** (⊠ Av. Marginal, Centro Comércial Cisne, Bloco B, Lojas 4 and 5, Cascais, ☎ 01/486–4438), and **Hertz** (⊠ Avda. Luisa Todi 277, ☎ 065/533786).

Emergencies

For all general emergencies dial **115.** For the **police,** in Sintra call (☎ 01/923–0761); in Cascais (☎ 01/483–0061); in Estoril (☎ 01/468–1396), or in Setúbal (☎ 065/522022). For local **medical** matters, contact the Sintra Health Center (⊠ Rua Visconde de Monserrate 2, ☎ 01/923–3400), Cascais Hospital (☎ 01/486–5891), or Setúbal Hospital (⊠ Rua Camilo Castelo Branco, ☎ 065/522133). In all the towns in Lisbon's environs, a notice on the door of every **farmácia** (drugstore) indicates the name and address of the nearest all-night pharmacy.

If you can afford to wait for attention, it's often easier to contact emergency and medical services in Lisbon (☞ Lisbon A to Z *in* Chapter 2).

Guided Tours

Most travel agents and large hotels in Lisbon or its environs can reserve you a place on a guided tour. **Citirama** (✉ Av. Praia de Vitória 12-B, ☎ 01/355–8567) has half-day trips to Queluz, to Sintra, and to Estoril and a tour of the area's royal palaces (each 7,300$00); nine-hour tours of Mafra, Sintra, and Cascais (12,500$00, including lunch); and even an evening visit to Estoril's famous casino (13,000$00, including dinner). **Gray Line Tours** (✉ Av. Fontes Pereira de Melo 14, ☎ 01/352–2594) offers half-day trips into the Arrábida Mountains and to local craft centers for around 8,000$00.

For guided tours of the Sintra area, it's best to ask first at the tourist-information center. In previous years, inclusive half-day tours have encompassed visits to all the principal sights and a wine tasting in Colares. The office has current schedules and prices and can sell tickets. **Sintratur** (✉ Rua João de Deus 82, Sintra, ☎ 01/923–3780) runs old-fashioned horse-and-carriage rides in the Sintra area. A short tour of Sintra costs 2,500$00; longer trips cost between 8,000$00 and 14,000$00 and take in attractions as diverse as the Moorish Castle and the nearby coastal resorts.

Mail

There are main post offices in **Cascais** (✉ Rua Manuel J. Avelar, ☎ 01/483–3175), **Sintra** (✉ Praça da República 26, ☎ 01/924–1590), and **Setúbal** (✉ Avda. 22 de Dezembro, ☎ 065/522778).

Visitor Information

Lisbon's main tourist office, in the Palácio Foz (✉ Praça dos Restauradores, ☎ 01/346–3314), can help with general inquiries concerning travel to the city's environs.

The local offices listed below are usually open June–September, daily 9–1 and 2–6, sometimes later in the tourist-resort areas. Hours are greatly reduced after peak season, and most offices are closed Sunday.

Cabo da Roca (✉ Azóia, ☎ 01/928–0081), **Caparica** (✉ Praça da Liberdade, ☎ 01/290–0071), **Cascais** (✉ Av. Marginal, ☎ 01/486–8204), **Estoril** (✉ Arcadas do Parque, ☎ 01/466–3813), **Palmela** (✉ Largo do Chafariz, ☎ 01/235–0089), **Sesimbra** (✉ Largo da Marinha, off Avda. dos Naufragios, ☎ 01/223–5743), **Setúbal** (✉ Trav. Frei Gaspar 10, ☎ 065/524284), **Sintra** (✉ Praça da Republica 23, ☎ 01/923–1157), and **Queluz** (✉ Palácio Nacional de Queluz, ☎ 01/436–3415).

4 The Estremadura and the Ribatejo

The populous Estremadura's rolling hills and glorious coastline contain some of the country's most famous towns and monuments. Across the Rio Tejo is the Ribatejo, a famous bullfight center and home to the shrine at Fátima, whose mainly flat lands fade into the vast plains of the southern Alentejo region.

By Dennis Jaffe

THE ESTREMADURA OCCUPIES a narrow stretch of land along the coast, extending north from Lisbon to include the onetime royal residence of Leiria, 119 kilometers (73 miles) from the capital city. Closely tied to the sea, which at no point in the province is more than a few miles away, the region is known for its fine beaches, coastal pine forests, and picturesque fishing villages. Some of these—such as Nazaré—have evolved, for better or worse, into popular international resorts. Fruits and vegetables grow in fertile coastal valleys, and livestock contentedly graze in rich pastures, but the Estremadura hasn't always been so peaceful. During the Wars of Reconquest, which raged from the 8th to the 13th centuries, it was the scene of a series of bloody encounters between Christians and Moors. In the aftermath of the wars Portuguese sovereignty was secured with the rout of the Spanish at Aljubarrota in 1385 and the turning back of Napoleon's forces in 1810 at Torres Vedras. The bloodshed left a positive legacy for today's traveler: Alcobaça and Batalha, masterpieces of religious architecture, were built to commemorate Portuguese victories.

The Ribatejo developed along both sides of the Tejo, and it is this waterway, born in the distant mountains of Spain, that has shaped and sustained the province that carries its name. In the north the inhabitants tend small groves of olive and fig trees, and the peaceful, sparsely populated landscape has changed little since the Romans settled.

Over the centuries Romans, Visigoths, Moors, and Christians built and rebuilt various castles and fortifications to protect the strategic Tejo. Some fine examples may be seen along the river at Belver, Abrantes, and Almourol. Tomar, spanning the banks of the Nabão (a tributary of the Tejo) is dominated by the hilltop Convent of Christ, an extraordinary example of medieval architecture, built in the 12th century by the Knights Templar. In the brush-covered hills at the western edge of the province lies Fátima, one of Christendom's most important pilgrimage sites. As it flows south approaching Lisbon, the Tejo expands, often overflowing its banks during the winter rains, and the landscape changes to one of rich meadows and pastures and broad, alluvial plains, where rice and other cereals grow in abundance.

The Ribatejans are said to be more reserved than their fellow Portuguese—that is, until they step into the arena to test their mettle against a ton or so of charging bull. The Ribatejo is bullfight country, the heartland of one of Portugal's richest and most colorful traditions. On the vast plains along the east bank of the Tejo, you'll encounter men on horseback carrying long wooden prods and often wearing the traditional waistcoats and stocking caps of their trade. These are *campinos,* the Portuguese "cowboys," who tend the herds of bulls and horses bred and trained for arenas throughout the country.

Pleasures and Pastimes

Beaches
Starting with Ericeira and extending north to São Pedro de Moel by Marinha Grande, there are a number of pleasant sandy beaches at convenient intervals along the coast. Some of the more popular beaches, where you will find the customary range of facilities, hotels, restaurants, and equipment, are in Nazaré, Peniche, Foz do Arelho, and Ericeira.

Dining

In Ribatejo and Estremadura restaurants, the culinary emphasis is on fish, including the ubiquitous *bacalhau* (codfish) and *caldeirada* (a hearty fish stew). The seaside resorts of Ericeira, Nazaré, and Peniche are famous for fresh lobster and other seafood. In Santarém and other spots along the Rio Tejo, a bread soup made with *savel*, a shadlike fish from the river, is popular, as are *enguias* (eels) prepared in a variety of ways. Roast lamb and kid are also widely enjoyed. Portuguese nuns have the reputation of making wonderful sweets, and the abundance of convents in the region has added many tasty and colorful-sounding dishes—such as *queijinhos do ceu* (little cheeses from heaven)—to local dessert menus. The straw-color white wines from the Ribatejo district of Bucelas rank with the country's finest.

Between mid-June and mid-September reservations are advised at upscale restaurants. However, most of the establishments we list are moderate or inexpensive, don't accept reservations, and have informal dining rooms where it's quite acceptable to share a table with other diners. Dress is casual at all but the most luxurious restaurants; any exceptions to the dress code or reservation policy are noted in the reviews.

Lodging

The Estremadura is well equipped with quality lodgings, especially along the coast. In summer, you will need reservations. Most establishments offer substantial off-season discounts. The Ribatejo is lacking in first-class hotels; the best accommodations in this region are the government-run inns called *pousadas*. The pousadas are small, some with as few as six rooms, so reserving well in advance is essential. There are also a number of high-quality, government-approved private guest houses in the region. Look for signs reading TURISMO RURAL or TURISMO DE HABITAÇÃO. Several of these are included in our listings.

Shopping

The regions around Alcobaça and Leiria are well known for their quality crystal and hand-blown glass. Traditional hand-painted ceramics are sold at shops and roadside stands throughout the Estremadura. Caldas da Rainha, a large ceramics-manufacturing center, produces characteristic cabbage-leaf and vegetable-shape ceramic pieces. Traditional cable-stitch Portuguese fishermen's sweaters are for sale in beach towns all along the coast.

Water Sports

The clear waters and bizarre rock formations along the Estremadura's coast make it a favorite with fishermen, snorkelers, and scuba divers. A wet suit is recommended for diving and snorkeling, as the chilly waters do not invite lingering, even in summer. The area's most commonly caught fish are sea bass, bream, and red mullet.

Exploring the Estremadura and the Ribatejo

The narrow province surrounding Lisbon and extending north along the coast for approximately 160 kilometers (100 miles) is known as the Estremadura, referring to the extreme southern border of the land the Portuguese reconquered from the Moors. This is primarily a rural region characterized by coastal fishing villages and small farming communities that mostly produce fruit and olives.

To the east of the Estremadura, straddling both banks of the Tejo, the Ribatejo is a placid, fertile region known for its vegetables and vine-

yards. As a consequence of its strategic location, the Ribatejo is home
to a number of imposing castles.

Great Itineraries

The Estremadura and Ribatejo region is relatively small. While it could
be covered in a day or two, this area deserves better, and those who
invest a few extra days will be well rewarded. Three days will give you
a feel for the region, five days will allow you to include a visit to the
shrine at Fátima and the Convent of Christ at Tomar, and a full week
will give you enough time to cover the major attractions as well as explore the countryside. With additional time you can easily extend your
itinerary to include Évora and the Alentejo (☞ Chapter 5) or you can
head north to include Coimbra and the Beiras (☞ Chapter 7). Unless
you have a great deal of time and patience, these regions are best explored by car. Trains do not serve many of the most interesting towns,
and bus travel is usually slow and tedious.

*Numbers in the text correspond to numbers in the margin and on the
Estremadura and the Ribatejo map.*

IF YOU HAVE 3 DAYS

Start with a visit to the imposing Monastery and Royal Palace at
Mafra ①, then head for the coast, with a stop at the popular seaside
resort and fishing village of **Ericeira** ②. Continue north along the coast
to **Peniche** ④, where an imposing fortress looms over the busy fishing
harbor. Head inland to spend the night in the enchanting walled city
of ⊡ **Óbidos** ⑥. The next morning continue north, stopping at the ceramic shops in **Caldas da Rainha** ⑦. En route to ⊡ **Nazeré** ⑧, tour the
church and cloisters at **Alcobaça** ⑨, one of Portugal's most impressive
religious monuments. On your third day head inland to visit the magnificent monastery church at **Batalha** ⑩. The soaring multispired structure contains the tomb of Prince Henry the Navigator. Return to
Lisbon along N1 with a stop in **Vila Franca de Xira** ⑫ to visit the Bullfight Museum.

IF YOU HAVE 5 DAYS

Follow the above itinerary to **Batalha** ⑩. From Batalha continue north
to **Leiria** ⑪, whose principal attraction is its hilltop castle. Take N356
east across the scrub-covered limestone hills of the Serra de Aire to ⊡
Fátima ⑲, one of Christendom's most renowned pilgrimage destinations. The next morning, continue east on N113 to **Tomar** ⑳, an attractive town dominated by the hilltop Convent of Christ, that was once
the headquarters of the Order of Knights Templar. After a few hours
exploring Tomar and the convent, take N358–2, a winding scenic road
that follows the Zêzere River to its union with the Tejo. Just west of
their confluence, perched on an island in the Tejo, is the castle of **Almourol** ㉒, one of Portugal's finest. From here, follow N118 southwest
along the Tejo, stopping in **Alpiarça** ⑯ to visit the Casa dos Patudos,
an expansive manor house, and in **Almeirim** ⑭ to see the winery at the
Quinta da Alorna. Spend the night in ⊡ **Santarém** ⑮, an important
farming and livestock center. The next day return to Lisbon with a drive
along the Tejo on N118 through the region of marshy plains known
as the **Lezíria** ⑬.

IF YOU HAVE 7 DAYS

Leave Lisbon and head north to **Mafra** ①, then visit **Ericeira** ②. From
there continue north along the coast, turning inland to **Torres Vedras** ③ to have a look at the castle and the fortifications erected by
Wellington during the Peninsular War. Continue on to **Peniche** ④. If
the weather is good, take the boat ride out to the **Berlenga Islands** ⑤.
From Peniche drive inland a few miles to ⊡ **Óbidos** ⑥. From Óbidos

The Estremadura and the Ribatejo

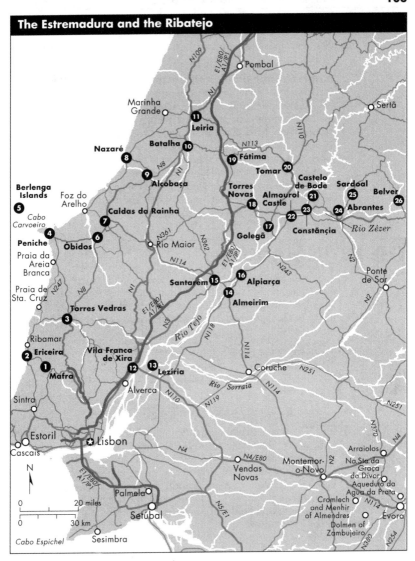

head north through **Caldas da Rainha** ⑦ and **Alcobaça** ⑨ to ⌂ **Naz-eré** ⑧. The next morning visit **Leiria** ⑪ and the glassworks at Marinha Grande. Make a stop in ⌂ **Fátima** ⑲ for two nights. There are several interesting caves to visit in the hills to the south and west of Fátima: São Mamede, Mira de Aire, Alvados, and Santo António. Fátima can also be used as a base for hiking and exploring the Parque Natural das Serras der Aire e Candeeiros. Leaving Fátima, head to **Tomar** ⑳ and then on to the lake at **Castelo de Bode** ㉑. To get a better feel for the countryside and visit a charming out-of-the-way village, take N244–3 from **Abrantes** ㉔ to **Sardoal** ㉕, an attractive back-country hamlet. From Sardoal, N244–3 traces a broad loop through a heavily forested region before returning to the Tejo and joining the main highway N118 at the hilltop castle of **Belver** ㉖. Return on N118 to spend the night in ⊞ **Abrantes** ㉔. In the morning visit the castle at **Almourol** ㉒ and continue to ⊞ **Santarém** ⑮ by way of **Alpiarça** ⑯ and **Almeirim** ⑭. The next morning return to Lisbon with a stop in **Vila Franca de Xira** ⑫.

When to Tour the Estremadura and the Ribatejo

To avoid the busloads of tourists who inundate these places during July and August, visit the major monuments and attractions such as Óbidos and Mafra in the early morning. This also helps to beat the oppressive summer heat, particularly in the inland regions. The best time of year for touring is in early spring and from mid-September until late October. The climate during this period is pleasant, and attractions and restaurants are not crowded. If crowds don't bother you, time your visit to Fátima to coincide with the pilgrimage that takes place every year on May 13, when between 500,000 and 1 million pilgrims overwhelm this otherwise sleepy country town. Less spectacular pilgrimages take place all year round.

THE ESTREMADURA

A tour through the Estremadura suggests visits to some of Portugal's most outstanding monuments and architectural treasures, including Mafra, Alcobaça, Óbidos, Tomar, and Batalha. The sites are discussed in the order that you would visit them as you travel north from Lisbon.

Numbers in the margin correspond to points of interest on the Estremadura and the Ribatejo map.

Mafra

❶ *28 km (18 mi) northwest of Lisbon.*

In 1711, after nearly three years of a childless union with his Hapsburg queen, Mariana, a despairing João V vowed that should the queen bear him an heir, he would build a Franciscan monastery dedicated to St. Anthony. In December of that same year, a girl—later to become queen of Spain—was born; João's eventual heir, José I, was born three years later. True to his word, the King built the enormous

★ **Mosteiro Palácio Nacional de Mafra** (Monastery and Royal Palace), which looms above the small farming community of Mafra. The original project—entrusted to the Italian-trained German architect Friedrich Ludwig—was to be a modest-size facility that could house 13 friars. What finally emerged after 18 years of construction was an immense, rectangular complex that contained a monastery large enough for 300 monks, an imposing basilica, and a grandiose royal palace, which has been compared to Spain's El Escorial outside Madrid. The numbers involved in the construction are mind-boggling: At times 50,000 workers toiled; there are 4,500 doors and windows, 300 cells, 880 halls and rooms, and 154 stairways. Perimeter walls that total some 19 kilometers (12 miles) surround the park. The story of the monastery is the subject of a bizarre but fascinating novel titled *Baltasar and Blimunda*, by the Portuguese author José Saramago.

There are many interesting details to note as you take the two-hour guided tour, but the highlight is the magnificent baroque library: The barrel-vaulted, two-tiered hall contains some 40,000 volumes of mostly 16th-, 17th-, and 18th-century works and a number of ancient maps. The Basilica, constructed entirely of limestone and containing 11 chapels, was patterned after St. Peter's Basilica in the Vatican. The balcony of the connecting corridor overlooks the high altar and was a favorite meeting place for Dom João and Mariana. This midway point between the "his" and "hers" royal bedrooms was considered neutral territory. When you're in the gilded throne room, pay attention to the life-size renditions of the seven virtues, as well as the impressive figure of Hercules, by Domingos Sequeira. On display in the game room is an early version of a pinball machine. Note the hard-planked beds in the monastery infirmary; the monks used no mattresses.

You'll be fortunate if you arrive on a Sunday afternoon between 4 and 5, when the sonorous tones of the 92-bell carillon ring out across the countryside. ☎ 300$00. ◷ *Wed.–Mon. 10–1 and 2–5.*

NEED A BREAK?	The **Pasteleria Dom João V,** directly across the street from the monastery, offers a welcome respite from the rigors of sightseeing. Homemade pastries and ice cream are specialties.

Ericeira

② *11 km (7 mi) northwest of Mafra.*

Ericeira, an old fishing village tucked into the rocky coast, is a popular seaside resort. The core of the village fans out from the sheer cliff, beneath which the fishing boats are hauled up onto a small, sheltered beach. Either end of the village has good sand for sunbathing, but the south end is preferred by surfers.

Dining and Lodging

$ ✕▥ **Hotel de Turismo.** Dramatically set at the edge of the breakers, this
★ sprawling, self-contained low-rise is a classic old Portuguese beach hotel. Public rooms are decorated with a delightful variety of colored tiles and accented with flowers and plants. Most of the spacious guest rooms have balconies with sea views. The large restaurant is lined with picture windows looking out on the water; you can opt to be served on the seaside terrace. The international menu emphasizes seafood, and the quality is good. ⊠ *Hotel de Turismo da Ericeira, 2655,* ☎ *061/864045,* ℻ *061/63146. 165 rooms. Restaurant, bar, 3 pools, tennis, beach, dance club. AE, DC, MC, V.*

$ ✕▥ **Pedro O Pescador.** If you prefer your hotels on a small scale, then you'll like this intimate, pastel blue, family-run hotel within walking distance of the beach. Cheerful rooms have planked floors and are decorated with flowered Alentejo furniture. The small, modern restaurant is frequented mostly by hotel guests. ⊠ *Rua Dr. Eduardo Burnay 22, 2655,* ☎ *061/62504,* ℻ *061/864302. 25 rooms. Restaurant, bar. AE, DC, MC, V.*

Torres Vedras

❸ *20 km (12 mi) northeast of Ericeira.*

Today a bustling commercial center crowned with the ruins of a medieval castle, Torres Vedras is best known for its extensive fortifications—a system of trenches and fortresses erected by Wellington in 1810 as part of a secret plan for the defense of Lisbon. It was here, at the Lines of Torres Vedras, that the surprised French army under Napoléon's Marshal Masséna was routed. Remnants of the fortifications can be seen throughout the region.

Dining and Lodging

$$$ ✕▥ **Golf Mar.** This hotel's idyllic location—on a rise overlooking a broad, sandy beach—is the main reason you'd choose to stay here: The high-rise's huge, concrete-block facade is hardly alluring, and the interior lacks inspiration. But if you're a golfer looking for a course, this is your only option in the region. The hotel is near the town of Lourinhã, 16 kilometers (10 miles) northwest of Torres Vedras. ⊠ *Praia do Porto Novo, 2560 Torres Vedras,* ☎ *061/984157,* 𝔽𝔸𝕏 *061/984261. 267 rooms, 9 suites. Restaurant, bar, indoor and outdoor pools, 9-hole golf course, tennis, horseback riding, billiards, dance club. AE, DC, MC, V.*

Outdoor Activities and Sports

GOLF

The one golf course in the region is at the beach at Praia de Porto Nova and is part of the Golf Mar hotel (☞ *above*). The par-67, nine-hole course, designed by Frank Pennink, is 5,259 yards long. Reserve greens in advance, even if you're a hotel guest.

En Route For the most scenic drive to Peniche, return to the coast and follow N247 north for 43 kilometers (25 miles) to Cape Carvoeiro. The jagged coast is interrupted by fine beaches at Santa Cruz, Ribamar, and Areia Branca.

Peniche

❹ *32 km (20 mi) northwest of Torres Vedras.*

Nestled in the lee of a rocky peninsula, Peniche is a major fishing-and-canning port, with a bustling harbor watched over by a sprawling 16th-century fortress. This popular summer resort is also known for its fine lace. The most interesting of the area's several churches is the 13th-century **Church of São Leonardo** in nearby Atouguia da Baleia.

For a good view of the fortress and the harbor, drive out to **Cape Carvoeiro.** The narrow road winds around the peninsula, along the rugged shore, and past the lighthouse and bizarre rock formations. Within the fortress walls there's a small museum. ▣ *Free.* ◷ *Tues.–Sun. 10–noon and 2–5.*

Dining and Lodging

$ ✕ **O Canhoto.** Unlike many of the expensive touristy restaurants along the harbor, O Canhoto puts less emphasis on the trappings and more on the simple but tasty food. This is a typical, no-frills Portuguese fish restaurant—set on a narrow side street—where you're almost always assured a good meal, especially if you ask for the *peixe do dia* (fish of the day). ⊠ *Rua Tenente Valadim 23,* ☎ *062/784512. No credit cards.*

$ ✕▥ **Estalagem Areia Branca.** This is a small, modern hotel with a favored cliff-top location, about 10 minutes by foot from a lovely sandy beach. The furnishings are not much more than serviceable, and the place could use an injection of charm (save for the fantastic views from some of the rooms). The restaurant looks out over the ocean and serves mostly seafood, including fresh shellfish taken from a large tank. ⊠ *Praia da Areia Branca, 2530, 12 km (8 mi) southeast of Peniche.* ☎ *061/412491,* 𝔽𝔸𝕏 *061/413143. 34 rooms. Restaurant, bar, pool. AE, DC, MC, V.*

$ ▥ **Praia Norte.** This modern three-story hotel on the outskirts of town offers reasonable rates. Most rooms are generous in size and overlook the hotel's large pool. Guest quarters are light and simply furnished but lack charm. The large water park adjacent to the hotel is a nice feature for families with children. ⊠ *Av. Monsenhor Basto, 2520,* ☎ *062/781166,* 𝔽𝔸𝕏 *062/781165. 97 rooms, 3 suites. Restaurant, bar, pool. AE, DC, MC, V.*

¢ **Areia Branca Youth Hostel.** This large, full-facility hostel on the beach provides 112 beds in multibedded single-sex rooms and two rooms for families, a lounge, bike rentals, and three meals a day. ✉ *Areia Branca beach, 12 km (8 mi) southeast of Peniche, 2530,* ☎ *061/422127.*

Outdoor Activities and Sports

WATER SPORTS

A great alternative to a day at the beach for kids and adults is **Peniche Sportagua,** a large water-park complex, with a separate slide area and adults' and children's swimming pools. The park also has a restaurant, cafeteria, and disco. ✉ *Av. Monsehnor M. Basto, R. Sonsa,* ☎ *062/789125.* *1,800$00 full day, 1,300$00 ½ day.*

Berlenga Islands

❺ *10 km (6 mi) northeast of Cabo Carvoeiro.*

The harbor at Peniche is the jumping-off point for excursions to the Berlenga Islands. The six small islands are a nature reserve and a favorite place for fishermen and divers. Berlenga, the largest of the the group, is the site of the **Forte de São João Baptista,** a 17th-century fortress built to defend the area from pirates. There's also a hostel on the island. For more information about accommodations, contact the Peniche tourist office (☞ Contacts and Resources *in* The Estremadura and the Ribatejo A to Z, *below*). *Boats leave Peniche for Berlenga July 15–Aug. at 9 AM, 11 AM, and 5 PM and return at 10 AM, 4 PM, and 6 PM; June–July 14 and Sept., boats leave at 10 AM and return at 4 PM. Trip takes approximately 1 hr.* *1,750$00.*

Outdoor Activities and Sports

DIVING

The clear waters and bizarre rock formations off the Berlenga Islands are popular with scuba divers and snorkelers. Spearfishing with scuba gear is prohibited. Boats may be rented at the harbor in Peniche. Fishermen like these waters, too. The most commonly caught fish are sea bass, bream, and red mullet. A fishing license is not required.

Óbidos

★ ❻ *20 km (12 mi) east of Peniche.*

Once a strategic seaport but now left high and dry 10 kilometers (6 miles) inland by the silting of its harbor, Óbidos is surrounded by fertile farmland. Cottages and cultivated fields abut the town walls where fishing boats and trading vessels once docked. As you approach Óbidos from the distance, you can see the bastions and crenellated walls standing as a hilltop sentinel guarding the now-peaceful valley of the Ria Arnoia. Enter the town through the massive, arched gates, and it may seem that you've been transported into medieval Portugal. The narrow Rua Direita, lined with boutiques and flower-bedecked white houses, runs the length of the town from the main gates to the foot of the castle: You may want to shop for ceramics and clothing on this street. The rest of the town is crisscrossed by a labyrinth of stone footpaths, tiny squares, and decaying stairways. Explore any route or all of them, for the town is small and you can't really get lost. Each nook and cranny will offer its own reward. Just be sure to include the **Castelo** (castle) in your explorations: Extensively restored after suffering severe damage in the 1755 earthquake, the multitowered complex—one of the finest medieval castles in Portugal—displays both Arabic and Manueline elements. Since 1952 parts of the castle have been a pousada.

Óbidos has a long association with women prominent in Portuguese history. So enchanted was the young Queen Isabel with Óbidos—which she visited with her husband, Dom Dinis, shortly after their marriage in 1282—that the king gave it to her as a gift, along with Abrantes and Porto de Móso; the town remained the property of the queens of Portugal until 1834. In the 14th century Inês de Castro sought refuge in this castle. Another queen associated with Óbidos was Leonor (the wife of João II), who came here in the 15th century to recuperate after the death of her young son; the town pillory bears Leonor's coat of arms. The 17th-century artist Josefa de Óbidos came to Óbidos as a small child and lived here until her death in 1684. Some of her work may be seen in the azulejo-lined **St. Mary's Church,** which dates to the 8th century.

Dining and Lodging

$$ ✕ **Alcaide.** From the upstairs dining room of this rustic tavern on the main street, patrons can enjoy a lovely view of the old town. The Alcaide is often jammed with hungry sightseers, especially from May through October; this is not a quiet, romantic hideaway. The food, however, is always carefully prepared, and the service is attentive. Try the *coelho a Alcaide* (grilled rabbit with potatoes). ⊠ *Rua Direita, between main gate and castle,* ☎ *062/959220. AE, DC, MC, V. Closed Mon.*

$$$ ✕🏠 **Pousada do Castelo.** If you've ever fantasized about living in lux-
★ ury within a medieval castle, this is a wonderful place to fulfill that wish. Pousada do Castelo occupies parts of the castle that King Dinis gave to his young bride, Isabel, in 1282. Except for the electric lights and the relatively modern plumbing, the style of the Middle Ages prevails throughout, from the guest rooms to the beautifully tiled lounge and dining room. Room 2, in one of the massive stone towers, is especially evocative of ancient times; other rooms are uniquely furnished with 16th- and 17th-century reproductions. The food and service are worthy of royalty, and there's a curtained alcove where you can dine in privacy and still enjoy a splendid view of the castle walls and valley below. Try the *cabrito assado* (roast kid). ⊠ *Pousada do Castelo, 2510,* ☎ *062/959105,* FAX *062/959148. 6 rooms, 3 suites. Restaurant, bar. AE, DC, MC, V.*

$ ✕🏠 **Albergaría Josefa d'Óbidos.** Built into the hillside at the main gate, this attractive, flower-bedecked country inn is the next best thing to the Pousada do Castelo. The rooms are outfitted with comfortable 18th-century reproductions, including massive wood furniture that enhances the old-country-inn feeling, even though the place was built in 1983. The Albergería has several reproductions of Josefa d'Óbidos's works hanging in the bar. A large, rustic restaurant with an open brick grill serves a variety of regional specialties: Try the *arroz de tamboril* (casserole with monkfish and rice) or one of the many varieties of *bacalhau* (codfish). The ambience of the otherwise-charming dining room is sometimes disturbed by the presence of large tour groups. ⊠ *Rua D. João de Ornelas, 2510,* ☎ *062/959228,* FAX *062/959533. 34 rooms, 2 suites. Restaurant, bar, dance club. AE, DC, MC, V.*

Caldas da Rainha

❼ *5 km (3 mi) north of Óbidos.*

Caldas da Rainha (the Queen's Baths) is the hub of a large farming area best known for its sulfur baths. In 1484 Queen Leonor, en route to Batalha, noticed some people bathing in a malodorous pool. Having heard of the healing properties of the sulfurous water, the queen interrupted her journey to soak in the pool and became convinced of its beneficial effects. She decided to build a hospital on the site and reputedly was so enthusiastic that she sold her jewels to help finance the project. There is a large bronze statue of Leonor in front of the hospital.

The expansive wooded park surrounding the spa contains the **Malhoa Museum,** primarily dedicated to the works of the local 19th- and 20th-century painter José Malhoa. 🎫 *300$00.* ☉ *Tues.–Sun. 10–noon and 2–5.*

Also in the park is the **Rafael Bordalo Pinheiro Ceramics Museum,** in the house of the noted 19th-century ceramist. 🎫 *300$00.* ☉ *Tues.–Sun. 10–noon and 2–5.*

Dining and Lodging

$ ✕ **Adega Típica do Coto.** This popular local restaurant on the main street in Coto, 2 kilometers (1¼ miles) north of Caldas, has a mainly Portuguese menu featuring many regional dishes. If it's in season, try the *javali* (wild boar). Another house specialty is the *arroz de tamboril* (casserole with monkfish and rice). The bread is baked fresh each day in a brick oven. ⊠ *Rua Principal,* ☎ *062/844898. AE, DC, MC, V.*

$ 🏨 **Hotel Malhoa.** Most business travelers to the area choose this modern eight-story hotel, conveniently placed near the town center. The rooms are comfortable, but there aren't many details to indicate you're in Portugal. ⊠ *Rua António Sergio 31, 2500,* ☎ *062/842180,* 🖷 *062/842621. 111 rooms, 2 suites. Restaurant, bar, pool, sauna, dance club. AE, DC, MC, V.*

$ 🏨 **Quinta da Foz.** This large two-story manor house dating from the
★ 16th century is beautifully situated amid lawns and trees at the edge of the Óbidos Lagoon, some 15 minutes' walk to the beach. This is a quiet base from which to explore Caldas da Rainha, only 9 kilometers (5½ miles) away, or other towns in the region. The bedrooms are large and comfortably furnished, with lots of flowers about. ⊠ *Foz do Arelho, 2500,* ☎ *062/979369. 5 rooms, 2 apartments. Tennis, horseback riding. No credit cards.*

Outdoor Activities and Sports

WINDSURFING
The Óbidos Lagoon at Foz do Arelho is popular with windsurfers. Equipment can be rented at the beach. The cost for just the rig is about 1,500$00 per hour; rental and lessons cost about 3,000$00 per hour.

Shopping
Caldas da Rainha is famous for its cabbage-leaf and vegetable-shape ceramic pieces. To visit a ceramics factory and showroom, contact **SECLA** (⊠ Rua S. João de Deus, ☎ 062/842151) and **Armando Baiana** (⊠ Rua Casais da Ribeira 37, ☎ 062/24355).

Nazaré

❽ *24 km (15 mi) northwest of Caldas da Rainha. For the most interesting route, head west from Caldas along the lagoon to the beach town of Foz do Arelho, then take the coast road 26 km (16 mi) north to Nazaré.*

Not so long ago tourists could mingle on the beach with the black-stocking-capped fishermen and even help as the oxen hauled the fishing boats in from the crashing surf. But Nazaré, one of the first quaint Portuguese fishing villages to feel the impact of tourism, is no longer a village and has long ceased to be quaint. The boats now motor comfortably into a safe, modern harbor, and the oxen have been put to pasture. But tourists still flock here, and in summer the broad, sandy beach is covered with a multicolor quilt of tents and awnings, and the beachfront boulevard is lined with the usual assortment of restaurants, bars, and souvenir shops. To find what's left of the Nazaré once hailed by many as "the most picturesque fishing village in Portugal," come in the winter, and either climb the precipitous trail or take the funicular to the **Sitio,** the 361-foot cliff overlooking the beach. Clustered at the cliff's edge is a small community of fishermen who live in tiny cottages and seem unaffected by all that's happening below.

Dining and Lodging

$$$ ✕ **Arte Xavega.** Set on a hill overlooking the town, this is by far Nazaré's classiest restaurant. Gardens and plants help to establish the comfortable blend of elegance and intimacy that owner Antonio Figueira has achieved for Arte Xavega. The international menu emphasizes local seafood specialties, including *arroz de marisco* (casserole of seafood and rice). ✉ *Ladeira Sitio-Meia Laranja,* ☎ *062/552136. AE, DC, MC, V.*

$ ✕⊞ **Ribamar.** This family-run restaurant and boardinghouse, on the main drag across from the beach, couldn't hope for a more convenient location, though sometimes in summer it's noisy. Bedrooms are small, but all are clean and well kept; ask for one that faces the sea. The restaurant, decorated like a country tavern, has large windows overlooking the beach; seafood is the main attraction, particularly the *caldeirada* (fish stew). ✉ *Rua Gomes Freire 9, 2450,* ☎ *062/551158. 23 rooms. Restaurant, bar. AE, DC, MC, V.*

$ ⊞ **Hotel Praia.** In spite of its popularity, Nazaré lacks a really first-rate hotel, but the 27-year-old, six-story Praia comes closest to filling the bill. The hotel is comfortable and clean and was remodeled in 1993. ✉ *Av. Vieira Guimaraes 39, 2450,* ☎ *062/561423,* 🖷 *062/561436. 40 rooms. AE, DC, MC, V.*

Shopping

The many shops and stands along the beachfront promenade have a particularly good selection of traditional fishermen's sweaters. You'll also find a wide array of wool plaid shirts and caps. The best are made of wool rather than acrylic blends. It pays to shop around, as prices vary widely and bargaining is the order of the day.

Alcobaça

❾ *10 km (6 mi) southeast of Nazeré, 20 km (12 mi) northeast of Caldas da Rainha.*

Alcobaça is the site of one of Portugal's most impressive religious
★ monuments, the **Mosteiro de Alcobaça.** Like the monastery at Mafra, the church and monastery of St. Mary of Alcobaça was built as the result of a kingly vow, this time in gratitude for a battle won. In 1147, faced with stiff Muslim resistance during the battle for Santarém, Portugal's first king, Afonso Henriques, promised to build a monastery dedicated to St. Bernard and the Cistercian Order. The Portuguese were victorious, Santarém was captured from the Moors, and shortly thereafter a site was selected. Construction on the monastery was begun in 1153 and concluded in 1178. The church, the largest in Portugal, is awe inspiring. The unadorned, 350-foot-long structure of massive granite blocks and cross-ribbed vaulting is a masterpiece of understatement: There's good use of clean, flowing lines, with none of the clutter found in the later rococo and Manueline architecture. At opposite ends of the transept, placed foot-to-foot some 30 paces apart, are the delicately carved tombs of King Pedro I and Inês de Castro, their serene faces looking upward. The story of Pedro and Inês, one of the most bizarre love stories in Portuguese history, was immortal-

ized by Camões in *Os Lusiads,* a renowned piece of Portuguese literature.

Pedro, son of King Afonso IV and heir to the throne, fell in love with the beautiful young Galician Inês de Castro, a lady-in-waiting to Pedro's Castilian wife, Constança. Fearful of any Spanish influence on his heir, the king banished Inês from the court. Upon the death of Constança, Pedro and Inês secretly married, and she lived in Coimbra, in a house later known as the Quinta das Lagrimas (the House of Tears); two sons were born of this union. King Afonso, ever wary of foreign influence on Pedro, had Inês murdered. Subsequently, Pedro took the throne and had Inês's murderers pursued: Two of the three were captured and executed, their hearts wrenched from their bodies. Pedro publicly proclaimed that he had been married to Inês and arranged an elaborate and macabre funeral for his wife. Before the procession, Inês's fleshless body, in royal garb, was enthroned beside him, and the courtiers were forced to kiss her lifeless hand. She was then placed in the tomb in Alcobaça that Pedro had designed, which lay, according to his wishes, opposite his own—so that on Judgment Day the lovers would ascend to heaven facing one another.

The graceful twin-tiered **cloister** at Alcobaça was added in the 14th and 16th centuries. The Kings Hall, just to the left of the main entrance, is lined with a series of 18th-century azulejos illustrating the construction of the monastery. ▨ *350$00.* ☉ *Daily 9–5.*

While you're in Alcobaça, you may want to visit the interesting **Wine Museum** to see wine-making implements and presses. The museum is in an old winery, on N8 heading north at the edge of town. ⊠ *Highway N8.* ▨ *150$00.* ☉ *Mon.–Sat. 9–12:30 and 2–5:30.*

Dining and Lodging

$ ✕ **Trindade.** An unpretentious, popular restaurant, Trindade is considered one of the town's best. The intimate dining room, lined with old photos of local scenes, reveals some of Alcobaça's history. Try the house specialty, *açorda de marisco* (bread porridge with shellfish), and for dessert the homemade pastry. ⊠ *Praça D. Afonso Henriques 22,* ☏ *062/42397. AE, MC, V. Closed Sat.*

$ 🏠 **Casa da Padeira.** In this family establishment Senhora Ventura
★ cooks and keeps house while son Miguel manages the place. Guests mingle freely with the hosts of this delightful country inn, 5 kilometers (3 miles) outside Alcobaça on N8, where comfortable living and sitting rooms are shared with the proprietors. The bedrooms are large, and each is furnished with period reproductions and covered with dainty, flowered wallpaper. Breakfast features just-out-of-the-oven homemade bread, and mom will cook you a wonderful dinner on request. ⊠ *Aljubarrota, 2460,* ☏ FAX *062/508272. 8 rooms, 2 apartments. Bar, pool, miniature golf, billiards. AE, MC, V.*

Shopping

Alcobaça is well known for its fine lead crystal. Casa Lisboa, across from the monastery, offers a good selection.

Batalha

🔟 *18 km (11 mi) northeast of Alcobaça.*

Batalha, which means "battle" in Portuguese, is the site of the monastery
★ church of **Santa Maria da Vitoria** (St. Mary of Victory), built to commemorate a decisive Portuguese victory over the Spanish on August 14, 1385, in the battle of Aljubarrota. In this battle the Portuguese king, John of Avis, who had been crowned only seven days earlier, took on

and routed a superior Spanish force. In so doing he maintained independence for Portugal, which was to last until 1580, when the crown finally passed into Spanish hands. The heroic statue of the mounted figure in the forecourt is that of Nuno Álvares Pereira, who, along with John of Avis, led the Portuguese army at Aljubarrota.

The monastery, a masterly combination of Gothic and Manueline styles, was built between 1388 and 1533. Some 15 architects were involved in the project, but the principal architect was Alfonso Domingues, whose portrait, carved in stone, graces the wall in the chapter house. In the great hall lie the remains of two unknown Portuguese soldiers who died in World War I: one in France, the other in Africa. Entombed in the center of the Founder's Chapel, beneath the star-shape, vaulted ceiling, is John of Avis, lying hand-in-hand with his English queen, Philippa of Lancaster. The tombs along the south and west walls are those of the couple's children, including Henry the Navigator. Perhaps the finest part of the entire project is the Unfinished Chapels, seven chapels radiating off an octagonal rotunda, started by Dom Duarte in 1435 and left roofless owing to lack of funds. Note the intricately filigreed detail of the main doorway. ✉ 400$00. ☉ Daily 9–5.

There is a small **battlefield museum** 5 kilometers (3 miles) south of the monastery on N8. ✉ 100$00. ☉ Tues.–Fri. 10–noon, weekends 10–noon and 2–5.

Dining and Lodging

$$$ ✕⛩ **Pousada do Mestre Afonso Domingues.** This pousada, named for
★   the architect who designed the famous Batalha Monastery, offers 20th-century comfort in a modern, two-story, white-stucco building, just steps from the historic monument. The good-size upstairs rooms with patterned wallpaper are furnished in 17th- and 18th-century style, and several look out on the monastery. The first-floor restaurant, with its polished *calçada* floor and wood ceiling, faces the monastery. The menu includes several types of *bacalhau* (codfish), and there's an extensive wine list. ⊠ *Largo Mestre Afonso Domingues 6, 2440,* ☏ *044/96260,* ℻ *044/96247. 20 rooms, 1 suite. Restaurant, bar. AE, DC, MC, V.*

$ ⛩ **Quinta do Fidalgo.** This historic two-story manor house adjacent to the monastery has a homey ambience: Guests gather and chat in the spacious living room or outside on the large terrace and in the pleasant garden. The rooms are comfortably and traditionally furnished. Reservations in summer are advised. ⊠ *Quinta do Fidalgo, 2440,* ☏ *044/96114,* ℻ *044/767401. 5 rooms. Bar. No credit cards.*

Shopping

South of Batalha (on N8) there are a number of roadside shops with good selections of hand-painted ceramics featuring classical patterns.

OFF THE
BEATEN PATH **PARQUE NATURAL DAS SERRAS DE AIRE E CANDEEIROS –** This sparsely populated rural region straddles the boundary between the Estremadura and the Ribatejo and is roughly midway between Lisbon and Coimbra. Within its 75,000 acres of scrublands and moors, you'll find small settlements, little changed in hundreds of years, where farmers barely eke out a living. In this rocky landscape, stones are the main building material for houses, windmills, and the miles of walls used to mark boundary lines. In the village of Minde, you can see women weaving the rough patchwork rugs for which this region is well known. The park is well suited for leisurely hiking or cycling. If you are driving, the N362, which runs for approximately 45 kilometers (28 miles) from Batalha in the north to Santarém in the south, is a good route for exploring the area.

Leiria

🔟 *11 km (7 mi) north of Batalha.*

Leiria is a pleasant, modern, industrial town at the confluence of the rios Liz and Lena. The region is known for its handicrafts, particularly the fine hand-blown glassware from Marinha Grande. Interesting highlights of Leiria are the hilltop castle and, beneath it, the old town quarter and the cathedral. The **castle,** built in 1135 by Prince Afonso Henriques (later Portugal's first king), was an important link in the chain of defenses along the southern border of what was at the time the Kingdom of Portugal. When the Moors were driven from the region, the castle lost its strategic significance and lay dormant until the early 14th century, when it was restored and modified and became the favorite residence of King Dinis and his queen, Isabel of Aragon. With these modifications the castle became more of a palace than a fortress and remains one of the loveliest structures of its kind in Portugal. Within the perimeter walls you'll encounter the ruins of a Gothic church, the castle keep, and—built into the section of the fortifications overlooking the town—the Royal Palace. Lined by eight arches, the balcony of the palace affords a lovely view of the town. ⊡ *150$00.* ◐ *Daily 9– 6:30.*

Dining and Lodging

$$ ✕ **O Casarão.** Five kilometers (3 miles) south of Leiria, in Azoia at the
★ Nazaré turnoff, O Casarão occupies a large rustic house surrounded by gardens. Chef José Rodrigues supervises the outstanding kitchen staff, while his wife, Clarissa, presides over the dining room. The service and presentation are flawless without being pretentious, and the extensive menu includes several ancient recipes from nearby monasteries. One of the best dishes is *bacalhau Tibarna* (thick cod fillets baked in a casserole with olive oil, corn bread, and potatoes). Be sure to leave room for the *bolo pinão* (pine-nut cake). The comprehensive wine list displays the labels of 120 different wines. ⊠ *Cruzamento de Azoia,* ☎ *044/871080. AE, DC, MC, V. Closed Mon.*

$ ✕▥ **Eurosol.** A pair of modern, "medium-rise" hotels, the Eurosol and Eurosol Jardim, occupy a hilltop that's about a 15-minute walk from the town center. These hotels are popular stops for businessmen; the lobbies and bedrooms are spacious and smartly furnished; and the eighth-floor restaurant is ringed with picture windows that give bird's-eye views of the town. ⊠ *Rua Dom JoséAlves Correia da Silva, 2400,* ☎ *044/812201,* ⑆ *044/811205. 128 rooms, 7 suites. Restaurant, bar, pool, fitness room. AE, DC, MC, V.*

¢ ▥ **Liz.** Conveniently situated in the town center across from the park, the Liz is a cozy old hotel with creaking floors and a lived-in feel. The large lounge with its fireplace can be particularly homey. Clean and comfortable bedrooms offer plain furnishings. ⊠ *Largo Alex, Herculano 10, 2400,* ☎ *044/814017,* ⑆ *0440/24310. 41 rooms. Bar. AE, DC, MC, V.*

Shopping

Marinha Grande, just west of Leiria, is the center for the production of fine-quality lead crystal. It is possible to visit several of the factories (opening times vary; call in advance). The most interesting are: **Santos Barrosa** (⊠ Zona da Estão–Cumeira, ☎ 044/569135; ⊡ 250$00) and **IVIMA** (⊠ Av. 1 de Maio, ☎ 044/568621; ⊡ Free).

THE RIBATEJO

Featured in this region are such diverse places as the bullfight centers of Vila Franca de Xira and Santarém, the shrine at Fátima, and the fishing port of Nazaré. The sites are discussed in the order you would visit them if starting out from Lisbon and traveling northeast.

Vila Franca de Xira

⑫ *30 km (18 mi) north of Lisbon via the A1 motorway.*

If you want to see a bullfight in Portugal, Vila Franca de Xira is the place to do it. The best time to visit Vila Franca de Xira is during the first week in July for the **Festa do Colete Encarnado** (Festival of the Red Waistcoat). Had Hemingway and his buddies taken a wrong train and wound up in Vila Franca de Xira some 60 years ago, perhaps Pamplona would have remained an unsung, grimy industrial town, and the world would have flocked instead to the Ribatejo each July for one of Portugal's greatest parties. The downtown streets are cordoned off, and the bulls are let loose as would-be bullfighters try their luck at dodging the charging beasts. At night the streets are alive with fado and flamenco dancing. The running of the bulls also takes place during the Autumn Fair held in early October. The bullring, one of Portugal's finest, contains a small museum with a collection of bullfighting memorabilia. Bullfights are held from Easter to October. For more information call the tourist office (☞ Contacts and Resources *in* The Estremadura and the Ribatejo A to Z, *below*). ✆ *200$00.* ☉ *Tues.–Sun. 10–12:30 and 2–6; closed holidays.*

The Portuguese bullfight—known as the *courada*—is quite different from any version of this ancient spectacle you might have seen in Mexico or Spain. In Portugal the bull's principal opponent is not a sword-carrying matador but a *cavaleiro*—a horseman elegantly attired as an 18th-century nobleman, with plumed hat and embroidered coat. Displaying finely tuned equestrian skills, he provokes the bull and, just inches away from the animal's padded horns, manages to deftly place a colorfully festooned *bandarilha* (dart) in a designated part of the bull's back. With each pass of an ever shorter bandarilha, the danger to horse and rider increases—in spite of the bull's blunted horns. At the proper moment, when the bull is sufficiently fatigued, the final dart is placed, and with a flourish the cavaleiro exits the arena. (Following a decree by the Marquis of Pombal in the 18th century, bulls are not killed in Portuguese rings.) The stage is now set for the *pega,* an audacious display of bravery with burlesque overtones. A file of eight men—the *forcados*—dressed in bright-crimson vests and green stocking caps parades into the arena and, hands on hips, confronts the tired but still-enraged bull. When the bull charges, the leader meets him head on with a running leap and literally seizes the bull by the horns. The other men rush in and by grabbing the bull's tail, try to force the animal to the ground. At times this can be quite an amusing sight, though there is the ever-present element of danger, and forcados have been killed during the pega. At the end of the spectacle, a few cows are led in to lure the bull from the ring. If he has shown exceptional bravery, the bull will be spared for stud purposes; otherwise, he will be slaughtered for the meat.

☾ Young aviation enthusiasts will enjoy seeing old planes at the **Museu do Ar** (Aviation Museum), in Alverca. ✉ *At the airport, 8 km (5 mi) south of Vila Franca de Xira,* ☎ *01/958–2782.* ✆ *150$00.* ☉ *Tues.–Sun. 10–8.*

Dining and Lodging

$$ ✕ **Redondel.** This restaurant inside the walls of the famous bullring
★ sees a lot of action and is considered Vila Franca's top eatery. There
are high-vaulted brick ceilings, and in keeping with the theme, the din-
ing room is adorned with bullfight posters and memorabilia. On the
menu are regional dishes including *açorda de saval* (bread porridge with
fish from the Rio Tejo). ✉ *Arcadas da Praça de Touros,* ☎ *063/22973.*
Reservations essential on bullfight and festival days. AE, DC, MC, V.
Closed Mon.

$ ✕ **Marisqueira Fartazana.** In this spotlessly clean local fish restaurant,
the accent is on good, simple food rather than decor, and the specialty
is shellfish of all kinds. Try the *arroz de marisco* (casserole of seafood
and rice), a good filling dish. ✉ *Rua Almirante Cândido Reis 131,* ☎
063/32943. No credit cards. Closed Mon.

¢ ✕🏨 **Flora.** For simple but well-maintained budget accommodations,
try this modern, four-story hotel conveniently located in the center of
town. The small, homey restaurant provides good food at reasonable
prices. ✉ *Rua Noel Perdigão 12, 2600,* ☎ *063/271272,* ℻ *63/26538.*
19 rooms. Restaurant, bar. MC, V.

$$$ 🏨 **Quinta do Alto.** Once you drive through the massive iron gates of
this hotel, you may have a hard time leaving. Situated on 50 choice
acres of orchards, gardens, and vineyards in the hills high above the
Rio Tejo, just 30 minutes from the Lisbon airport, the Quinta do
Alto—once the exclusive summer residence of a prominent Portuguese
family—has been opened for paying guests. Instead of feeling like a
lodger, you'll have the sense of visiting a wealthy friend or relative. Each
of the 10 large bedrooms is comfortably furnished and has a luxurious bathroom; half the units provide terraces and views of the countryside overlooking the Rio Tejo. Red brick adorns the vaulted ceilings,
and the tile floors are enhanced with Arraiolos carpets. The price includes use of all the facilities and transportation to and from the airport. ✉ *Quinta do Alta, 2600,* ☎ *063/26850,* ℻ *063/26027. 10*
rooms, 1 apartment. Bar, pool, sauna, 1 tennis court, exercise room,
squash, dance club, kennel. AE, DC, MC, V.

$ 🏨 **Lezíria Parque Hotel.** This four-story, modern hotel-and-apartment
★ complex offers the newest accommodations in Vila Franca de Xira. Conveniently situated off the main Lisbon–Porto road, the hotel provides
a comfortable base from which to explore the bull- and horse-breeding region across the Rio Tejo. The rooms are small and plainly furnished; there's a pleasant coffee shop on the ground floor. ✉ *Estrada*
Nacional 1, 2600 Povos, ☎ *063/26670,* ℻ *063/26990. 71 rooms. AE,*
DC, MC, V.

Lezíria

⓭ *Occupying the east bank of the Tagus River between Vila Franca de*
Xira and Santarém.

The Lezíria refers to a region of marshy plains and rich pasturelands
on the east bank of the Rio Tejo. This area contains many stud farms,
where the best bulls and horses in Portugal are bred. As you drive through
the town of Benavente and the surrounding countryside, look for
campinos (farmhands) in the fields working the bulls and horses.

Almeirim

⓮ *40 km (24 mi) northeast of Vila Franca de Xira, 4 km (2 mi) east of*
Santarém.

Almeirim is a pleasant village where you may visit a working stud farm and a winery at the **Quinta da Alorna.**

Santarém

⑮ *7 km (4 mi) northwest of Almeirim.*

Present-day Santarém, perched high above the Tejo, is an important farming and livestock center. Some historians believe that its beginnings date as early as 1200 BC and the age of Ulysses. Its strategic location led several kings to choose it as their residence, and the *Cortes* (parliament) frequently met here. To get the feel of the town, walk up to the **Portas do Sol,** a lovely park within the ancient walls. From this vantage point you can look down on a sweeping bend in the Rio Tejo and beyond to the rich farmlands stretching into the neighboring Alentejo.

Thanks to its royal connections, Santarém is more richly endowed with treasures and monuments than other towns of its size. The Portuguese refer to it as their "Gothic capital." Of particular interest are the 17th-century Seminary Church, built on the ruins of a royal palace, and the azulejo-bedecked Marvila Church. Inside the **Archaeological Museum** you'll find the finely sculpted tomb of Duarte de Meneses, which according to legend contains a single tooth, all that remained of the nobleman after his brutal murder by the Moors in Africa. The museum is on Rua Figueiredo Leal, directly across from the bell tower known as the Torre das Cabaças. ▨ *Free.* ◷ *Tues.–Sun. 9:30–1 and 2–3; closed holidays.*

Also in Santarém, on the Largo Pedro Alvares Cabral, is the **Graça Church,** which contains the gravestone of Pedro Cabral, the discoverer of Brazil. There is also a tomb of the explorer in Belmonte, the town of his birth, but no one is really sure just what is in which tomb. Of note in this 14th-century Gothic church is the delicate rose window whose setting was carved from a single slab of stone. ⊠ *Largo Pedro Alvares Cabral.*

The annual **Gastronomy Fair** takes place in Santarém in October and is a colorful exposition that brings together food producers and restaurateurs from all parts of the country, providing a wonderful opportunity to sample the best of Portuguese cuisine and wines. Check with the local tourist office for exact dates and details (☞ Contacts and Resources *in* The Estremadura and the Ribatejo A to Z, *below*).

Dining and Lodging

$$ ✕ **Portas do Sol.** A small restaurant in the town's most scenic location, the Portas do Sol is surrounded by flowers and trees in the gardens of the same name. This is a good place to combine a pleasant lunch on the brick-walled terrace with a walk around the gardens. Good regional dishes are offered here: Try the *bacalhau a bras* (cod slivers with scrambled eggs and onions). ⊠ *Jardim das Portas do Sol,* ☎ *043/29520. AE, DC, MC, V.*

$ ⌂ **Quinta de Vale de Lobos.** This is a delightful two-story, 19th-century farmhouse on N3, 6 kilometers (4 miles) from Santarém, among trees, ponds, and gardens. Guests enjoy lounging in the large comfortable living rooms and strolling in the adjacent woods; they also have access to a 600-acre hunting estate. The generously sized bedrooms and apartments are comfortably furnished. ⊠ *Azoia de Baixo, 2000,* ☎ *043/429264,* FAX *043/429313. 4 rooms, 2 apartments. Pool. No credit cards.*

$ ⊞ **Vitória.** On a quiet street in a residential apartment building, Vitória provides a relaxing stopover. The owner of this eponymous family-run lodging, Senhora Vitória, will make you feel right at home. The old section is a bit drab, so try for a room in the newer wing. ⊠ *Rua Visconde 2, 2000,* ☎ *043/22573,* 𝖥𝖠𝖷 *043/28202. 25 rooms. MC, V.*

¢ ⊞ **Alfageme.** This recently built, unpretentious establishment helps to fill out the otherwise sparse Santarém hotel scene. The rooms are comfortable but somewhat uninspiring in their decor. ⊠ *Ave. Bernardo Santareno 38, 2000,* ☎ *043/370870,* 𝖥𝖠𝖷 *043/370850. 67 rooms. Restaurant, bar. MC, V.*

Alpiarça

⑯ *10 km (6 mi) northeast of Santarém.*

Alpiarça is a pleasant little town where you'll have the chance to see how a wealthy country gentleman lived at the beginning of this century. The **Casa dos Patudos,** now a museum, was the estate of Jose Relvas, a diplomat and gentleman farmer. This unusual three-story manor house with its zebra-striped spire is surrounded by gardens and vineyards. An impressive assemblage of furnishings, including Portugal's foremost collection of Arraiolos carpets, is contained in the museum. ▨ *275$00.* ☉ *Wed.–Sun. and holidays 10–noon and 2–5; contact Alpiarça town hall at* ☎ *043/54354 for other opening hrs.*

Golegã

⑰ *25 km (16 mi) northeast of Santarém, 20 km (12 mi) northeast of Alpiarça.*

Golegã is one of Portugal's most notable horse-breeding centers. During the first two weeks of November, this is the site of the colorful **National Horse Fair,** the most important event of its kind in the country. The **parish church** has a large Manueline portal, with interesting twisted columns and rope ornaments.

Torres Novas

⑱ *10 km (6 mi) northwest of Golegã.*

Torres Novas is best known for the crenellated, 14th-century hilltop **castle** that encloses a delightful garden. At the foot of the castle stands a caricature statue of Dom Sancho I created by João Cutiliero, a prominent contemporary sculptor.

Dining and Lodging

$$ ✕ **A Tavolá.** This simple, friendly, family-run neighborhood restaurant,
★ presided over by Francisco and Isabel Vieira, emphasizes regional dishes, and their *cabrito assado no forno* (roast kid filled with bacon, sausage, and olives) garnered first prize at a regional gastronomic fair. Since it's only about a 10-minute walk from the castle, A Tavolá makes a good dining spot after seeing the sights. ⊠ *Av. Dr. Manuel de Figueiredo 12,* ☎ *049/23983. MC, V. Closed Sat.*

$ ✕⊞ **Hotel dos Cavaleiros.** Conveniently located facing the main square, this modern three-story hotel blends in well with the surrounding 18th-century buildings. Rooms are moderately sized and have plain, light-wood furnishings; ask for one on the third floor with a terrace. In spite of its sterile, coffee-shop appearance, the restaurant serves generous portions of well-prepared traditional dishes. Try the *espetada mista* (grilled pork, squid, and shrimp on a spit). ⊠ *Praça 5 de Outubro, 2350,* ☎ *049/812420,* 𝖥𝖠𝖷 *049/812052. 57 rooms, 3 suites. Restaurant, bar. AE, DC, MC, V.*

Fátima

 20 km (12 mi) northwest of Torres Vedras, 16 km (10 mi) southeast of Batalha, 20 km (12 mi) southeast of Leiria.

Surrounded by the scrub-covered limestone hills of the Serra de Aire lies Fátima, an important Roman Catholic pilgrimage site. (Ironically, this great Christian shrine is a village named after the daughter of Mohammed, the prophet of Islam!) If you visit this sleepy little Portuguese town in between pilgrimages, it will be difficult to imagine the thousands of faithful who come from all corners of the world to make this religious affirmation, cramming the roads, squares, parks, and virtually every square foot of space. Many of the pilgrims go the last miles on their knees.

When Pope John Paul II visited in 1991, it was estimated that more than 1 million people flocked to Fátima. Where there are so many people, there are bound to be opportunists, and Fátima is no exception— as shown by places like the "Virgin Mary Souvenir Shop" and the "Pope John Paul II Snack Bar."

It all began on May 13, 1917, when three young shepherds—Lúcia dos Santos and her cousins Francisco and Jacinta—reported seeing the Virgin Mary in a field at Cova de Iria, near the village. The Virgin promised to return on the 13th of each month for the next five months, and amid much controversy and skepticism, each time accompanied by increasingly larger crowds, the three children reported successive apparitions. This was during a period of anticlerical sentiment in Portugal, and after the sixth reputed apparition, in October, the children were arrested and interrogated. But they insisted the Virgin had spoken to them, revealing three secrets. Two of these, revealed by Lúcia in 1941, were interpreted to foretell the coming of World War II and the spread of communism and atheism. The third secret is still held by the Vatican. In a 1930 Pastoral Letter, the Bishop of Leiria declared the apparitions worthy of belief, thus approving the "Cult of Fátima." On the 13th of each month, and especially in May and October, the faithful flock here to witness the passing of the statue of the Virgin through the throngs, to participate in candlelight processions, and to take part in solemn masses.

At the head of the huge esplanade is a large, neoclassical **basilica** (built in the late 1920s), flanked on either side by a semicircular peristyle. Other pilgrimage sites include the cottages in the nearby hamlet of Aljustrel, where the children were born, and the **Chapel of Apparitions,** built on the spot where the appearances of the Virgin Mary are said to have taken place.

There is a **wax museum** in the center of town, with tableaux representing the story. 🎫 *600$00.* ☉ *Daily 9–5.*

The largest caverns in Portugal are found in the honeycombed limestone caves in the hills to the south and west of Fátima. Within about a 25-kilometer (15-mile) radius of Fátima, there are four sets of these chambers—the **São Mamede Caves, Mira de Aire Caves, Alvados Caves,** and **Santo António Caves**—equipped with artificial lighting and elevators; here visitors can see the subterranean world of limestone formations, underground rivers and lakes, and multicolor stalagmites and stalactites. The tourist office can assist you with further details. 🎫 *450$00.* ☉ *Oct.–Mar., daily 9–6; Apr.–June and Sept., daily 9–8; July–Aug., daily 9–9.*

Dining and Lodging

$$ ✕ **Tia Alice.** Considered the best restaurant in the area, Tia (Aunt) Alice
★ is concealed in an inconspicuous old house with French windows,
across from the parish church near the Sanctuary at Cova de Iria. A
flight of wooden stairs inside leads to a small, intimate dining area with
a wood-beam ceiling and stone walls. Try the *borrego assado* (roast
lamb). ⊠ *Rua do Adro,* ☎ *049/531737. MC, V. Closed Mon. and July.
No dinner Sun.*

$ ✕ **Retiro dos Caçadores.** A big brick fireplace, wood paneling, and stone
walls set the mood in this cozy hunter's lodge, where the food is sim-
ple, but portions are hearty and the quality good. This is the best place
in town for fresh game, especially *coelho con arroz* (rabbit with rice)
and *perdiz* (partridge). ⊠ *Lombo Egua,* ☎ *049/531323. MC, V. Closed
Thurs.*

$ 🏨 **Hotel de Fátima.** This modern four-story building—part of the Best
Western chain—is close to the Sanctuary. With its spacious lobby,
green-marble floors and wood-paneled walls, it is generally considered
to be Fátima's top hotel. ⊠ *Rua João Paulo II, 2496,* ☎ *049/533351,*
FAX *049/532691. 126 rooms, 7 suites. Restaurant, bar. AE, DC, MC,
V.*

¢ 🏨 **Casa Beato Nuno.** This large pink-stucco inn, in a quiet setting just
a few minutes' walk from the Sanctuary, is run by the Carmelites but
is open to visitors of all denominations. The austere rooms are clean
and comfortable. ⊠ *Av. Beato Nuno 51, 2496,* ☎ *049/533069,* FAX
049/532757. 136 rooms. Restaurant. MC, V.

Tomar

20 *24 km (15 mi) east of Fátima, 20 km (12 mi) northeast of Torres Ve-
dras.*

Tomar is an attractive town laid out on both sides of the Rio Nabão,
with the new and old parts linked by a graceful, arched stone bridge.
The river flows through a lovely park with weeping willows and an
old wooden waterwheel.

In the old town, walk along the narrow, flower-lined streets, particu-
larly Rua Dr. Joaquim Jacinto, where, in the heart of the old Jewish
Quarter, you'll find the **Sinogoga de Tomar** (Synagogue of Tomar),
housed in a modest building. Built in the mid-15th century, this is the
oldest Jewish house of worship in Portugal. Inside is a small museum
with exhibits chronicling the Jewish presence in the country. The once-
sizable Jewish population was considerably reduced in 1496 when Dom
Manuel issued an edict ordering the Jews either to leave the country
or convert to Christianity. Many, who became known as *Marranos,*
converted but secretly practiced their original religion. ⊠ *Rua Dr.
Joaquim Jacinto.* 🎫 *Free; donations accepted.* ☉ *Thurs.–Tues. 9:30–
12:30 and 2–5:30.*

★ Atop a hill rising from the old town is the **Convent of Christ,** a remarkable
architectural achievement. You can drive to the top of the hill or hike
for about 20 minutes along a path through the trees; at the top there
are wonderful views from the castle walls. You enter through a for-
mal garden lined with azulejo-covered benches. This was the headquarters
of the order of Knights Templar, from 1160 until the order was forced
to disband in 1314. Identified by their white tunics emblazoned with
a crimson cross, the Templars were at the forefront of the Christian
armies in the Crusades and during the years of struggle against the Moors.
King Dinis in 1334 resurrected the order in Portugal under the ban-
ner of the Knights of Christ and reestablished Tomar as its headquar-

ters. In the early 15th century, under the leadership of Prince Henry the Navigator (who for a time resided in the castle), the order flourished. The caravels of the era of discovery sailed under the order's crimson cross.

When they constructed the original fortifications in 1160, the Templars drew heavily on their experiences with the Moslems during the Crusades. The buildings within the battlements are made up of a series of cloisters formed around the **Templar's Rotunda**—the complex's showpiece. This two-story, octagonal church, constructed in the Byzantine style, is patterned after the Church of the Holy Sepulchre in Jerusalem and is part of the original 12th-century construction. The paintings and wooden statues are 16th-century Portuguese. To see what the Manueline style is all about, stroll through the nave with its many examples of the twisted ropes, seaweed, and nautical themes that typify the style and be sure to look at the **Chapter House Window**, probably the most photographed one in Europe. Its lichen-encrusted sculpture manifests the Manueline style and evokes the feeling and spirit of the great age of discovery. ✉ *300$00.* ☉ *Oct.–Mar., daily 9:15–12:30 and 2–5; Apr.–Sept., daily 9:15–6.*

Dining and Lodging

$$ ✕ **A Bela Vista.** The date on the polished *calçada* (pavement with
★ small black stones on a white background) reads "1922," which was when the Sousa family opened this attractive little restaurant next to the old arched bridge. For summer dining there's a small, rustic terrace with views of the river and the Convent of Christ. Carrying on the family tradition, son Eugenio Sousa presides over the kitchen, which turns out great quantities of hearty regional fare. Try one of the house specialties, such as *cabrito assado* (roast kid) or *dobrada com feijao* (tripe with beans), and wash it down with a robust local red wine. ✉ *Marquês de Pombal 68,* ☎ *049/312870. No credit cards. Closed Tues.*

$ ✕🏨 **Hotel dos Templários.** A large, modern hotel set in a tranquil
★ park along the Rio Nabão, the Templários offers many units with views of the Convent of Christ. The big, airy dining room has picture windows facing the park and serves interesting regional dishes. With its spacious grounds and several swimming pools, the hotel makes a good base from which to visit the area's many attractions. ✉ *Largo Candido dos Reis 1, 2300,* ☎ *049/321730,* 🖷 *049/322191. 170 rooms, 10 suites. Restaurant, bar, indoor and outdoor pools, barbershop, beauty salon, 1 tennis court. AE, DC, MC, V.*

Castelo de Bode

㉑ *10 km (6 mi) southeast of Tomar.*

The dam on the Rio Zêzere at Castelo de Bode has created a huge artificial lake that fans out north from the dam. This one of Portugal's most popular water-sports areas. For information regarding boat excursions on the lake, which include lunch on board, inquire at the Hotel dos Templários in Tomar or at the dock by the Pousada de São Pedro.

Dining and Lodging

$ ✕🏨 **Pousada de São Pedro.** Originally built in 1946 to house engi-
★ neers building the dam on the Rio Zezere, this pousada sits on a wooded hill and overlooks the man-made lake. It's location—18 kilometers (11 miles) from Tomar—makes it a good place from which to explore nearby villages. The restaurant, in a lovely setting, features high-quality regional fare. ✉ *Pousada de São Pedro, Castelo de Bode,*

2300, ☎ 049/381159, ℻ 049/381176. 25 rooms. Restaurant, lake. AE, DC, MC, V.

Almourol Castle

★ ㉒ 16 km (10 mi) south of Tomar, 16 km east of Torres Novas. For the most scenic route from Castelo de Bode, take the N358–2 south along the Zêzere to where it joins the Tejo, then continue west 4 km (2 mi) on N3 to the castle turnoff.

For a close look at Almourol Castle, a storybook edifice sitting on a craggy island downstream in the middle of the river, take the mile-long dirt road leading down to the water. The riverbank in this area is practically deserted, making it a wonderful picnic spot. (In summer you can take a boat to the island.) The setting could hardly be more romantic: an ancient castle with crenellated walls and a lofty tower sits on a greenery-covered rock in the middle of a gently flowing river. The stuff of poetry and legends, Almourol was the setting for Francisco de Morais's epic *Palmeirim of England.*

NEED A BREAK? On N3 just west of the castle is a good snack or lunch stop, **Restaurante Almourol,** in a lovely old house with gardens, orange trees, and a terrace overlooking the castle.

Constância

㉓ 4 km (2 mi) east of Almourol Castle.

The peaceful hamlet of Constância is set where the Zêzere joins the Rio Tejo. The town is best known as the place where Camões was exiled in 1548, the unfortunate result of his romantic involvement with Catarina de Ataide, the "Natercia" of his poems and a lady-in-waiting to Queen Catarina. There is a bronze statue of the bard in a reflective pose at the riverbank.

Dining and Lodging

$ ✕☷ **Quinta de Santa Barbara.** If you're looking for a place to immerse
★ yourself for a while in the peace and quiet of the Portuguese countryside, look no farther. The Quinta, about 3 kilometers (2 miles) east of Constância, has several sprawling buildings (a few of which date to the 16th century) and occupies some 45 acres of farmland and cork and olive groves overlooking the Rio Tejo. This country inn, opened in 1988, achieves a wonderful blend of old-world charm and modern convenience. Each of the eight spacious rooms in the main house is individually furnished with 18th-century Portuguese reproductions and has a modern tiled bathroom. The small restaurant, with a barrel-vault ceiling and stone walls, specializes in local dishes prepared from old recipes (many of the ingredients are from the Quinta's own organic gardens). ✉ *Quinta de Santa Barbara, 2250,* ☎ *049/99214,* ℻ *049/99373. 8 rooms. Restaurant, bar, pool, 1 tennis court, horseback riding. MC, V.*

Abrantes

㉔ 16 km (10 mi) east of Constância.

Strategically situated on a hilltop commanding the Rio Tejo, Abrantes flourished and became one of the country's most populous and prosperous towns during the 16th century, when the river was navigable all the way to the sea. With the coming of the railroad and the development of better roads, the town's commercial importance waned. The main attraction here is the castle (built in the 16th century). Walk up through the maze of narrow, flower-lined streets to the ruins of the ancient fortress. Much of the castle is in disrepair, but with a bit of imagination you can conjure visions of what an impressive structure this must have been. The attractive garden that's been planted between the twin fortifications makes a wonderful place to watch the sunset: The play of light on the river and the lengthening shadows along the olive groves provide an inspiring setting for an evening picnic.

Dining and Lodging

$ ✕ **Cristina.** In a town where good restaurants are scarce, this attractively decorated, rustic, family-run place on the N3, 5 kilometers (3 miles) west of Abrantes, is worth the drive. Ask the restaurant's namesake, Cristina Mota, to tell you the daily special and hope it's *bacalhau com natas* (dried cod baked in a casserole with cream and potatoes), one of her most popular creations. ⊠ *Rio de Moinhos,* ☎ *041/98177. MC, V. Closed Mon.*

$ ✕🏨 **Hotel Turismo.** This hotel is perched in such a spectacular location, on a hill high above the Rio Tejo, that it's a shame the architect didn't create a more pleasing exterior design than this nondescript pink-stucco eyesore. But inside is a different story, with an inviting, clubby lounge featuring a fireplace and comfy leather chairs. Guest rooms are on the small side but are comfortably furnished, and many of the newer rooms have terraces with wonderful vistas. The dining room—surrounded with picture windows—affords inspiring views and is an excellent place to sample the delicious *palha de Abrantes* (straw of Abrantes), a tasty local dessert specialty consisting of a thick egg and almond paste topped with yellow threadlike wisps made of eggs and sugar. ⊠ *Largo de Santo António, 2200,* ☎ *041/21261,* 🗚🗚 *041/25218. 41 rooms. Restaurant, bar, pool, 1 tennis court. AE, DC, MC, V.*

Sardoal

㉕ *12 km (7 mi) northeast of Abrantes, 20 km (12 mi) northeast of Constância.*

Sardoal, an island of white houses with red-tile roofs in a sea of wooded hills, is an enchanting place of narrow streets paved with pebbles from nearby streams, yellow-trimmed houses, and flowers everywhere—hanging from windows and from balconies and lining the winding streets and alleys. In such a spot you might expect art to flourish, and the 17th-century parish church *does* contain a collection of fine 16th-century paintings by the "Master of Sardoal," an unknown painter whose works have been found in other parts of the country and whose influence on other artists has been noted.

Belver

㉖ *30 km (18 mi) southeast of Sardoal. Follow N244–3 through the pine-covered hills to Chão de Codes, then take N244 south toward Gavião.*

A fairy-tale castle planted on top of a cone-shape hill (looking as if its top has been sliced off), the fortress of Belver was built in the last years of the 12th century by the Knights Hospitallers under the command of King Sancho I. The castle commands a superb view of the Rio Tejo. In 1194 this region was threatened by the Moorish forces who controlled the lands south of the river, except for Évora. The expected attack never took place, and the present structure is little changed from its original design. The walls of the keep, which stands in the center of the courtyard, are some 12 feet thick, and on the ground floor is a great cistern of unknown depth. According to local lore, an orange dropped into the well will later appear bobbing down the Rio Tejo.

THE ESTREMADURA AND THE RIBATEJO A TO Z

Arriving and Departing

The Estremadura and the Ribatejo are best served by Lisbon's international airport.

By Bus

Euroline has regular bus service between Lisbon and Spain's Costa del Sol, Seville, Madrid, and Barcelona. Euroline buses from France and northern Europe stop in Pombal, Leiria, Abrantes, and Santarém. For information and reservations in Lisbon, contact a travel agent or **Intercentro Eurolines** (✉ Rua Eng. Viera da Silva, 8-E, ☎ 01/547300).

By Car

The Estremadura and the Ribatejo can be reached easily from Lisbon, since both provinces begin as extensions of the city's northern suburbs. From Porto there is easy access via the A1 tollway.

By Plane

For flight information concerning Lisbon, *see* Chapter 2; for information about Faro's airport, *see* Chapter 6.

By Train

The region is served by the *Lusitania Express* and the *Lúis de Camões*, which run daily between Lisbon (Santa Apolónia Station) and Madrid. The *Lúis de Camões* leaves Lisbon's Santa Apolonia Station at 11:55 AM and arrives at Madrid's Atocha Station at 8:06 PM. The *Lusitania Express* departs Lisbon at 10:25 PM and arrives in Madrid's Chamartin Station at 8:40 the following morning. First-class seats cost 9,635$00. Second-class seats cost 7,225$00. Youth (under 26) seats cost 5,140$00. The *Sud Express,* linking Paris with Lisbon (Santa Apolónia Station)— via the Spanish cities of Burgos and Salamanca—stops at Pombal and Fátima. It leaves Lisbon daily at 5:05 PM and arrives at Paris's Austerlitz Station at 7 PM the following day. First-class costs 31,465$00; second-class costs 21,160$00. Those under 27 pay 18,410$00. Sleepers (couchettes) cost 2,574$00 extra. Although the schedule reads "Fátima," the actual station is some 25 kilometers (15 miles) away, but a bus— on a coordinated schedule—runs between the town and the station.

Getting Around

By Bus

There are few, if any, places in this region that are not served by at least one bus daily. Express coaches run by several regional bus lines travel regularly between Lisbon and the larger towns such as Santarém, Leiria, and Abrantes. If you have the time and patience, bus travel, which offers an opportunity to come in close contact with locals, can be a rewarding and inexpensive way to get around. The main bus terminal in Lisbon is on Avenida Casal Ribeira 18. For schedules call ☎ 01/545439.

By Car

A car is by far the most efficient way to tour this region, where bus service is often infrequent and train service nonexistent. Driving will give you access to many out-of-the-way beaches and villages. The roads are generally good, and traffic is light, except for weekend congestion along the coast. There are no confusing big cities in which to get lost, although parking can be a major problem in some of the towns. The best map for motorists, both in scale and ease of reading, is the Michelin map #440, Portugal–Madeira, available at bookshops throughout Portugal; in the United States go to any major bookstore or contact **Michelin Travel Publications** (✉ 1 Parkway S, Greenville, SC 29615, ☎ 803/458–6330). There are major car-rental agencies in Leiria and Nazaré.

By Train
Travel by train within central Portugal is not for people in a great hurry. Service to many of the more remote destinations is infrequent—and in some cases nonexistent. Even major tourist attractions such as Fátima, Nazaré, and Mafra have no direct rail links.

There is frequent service on the Lisbon–Porto line (Santa Apolónia Station) to Santarém. Torres Vedras, Caldas da Rainha, and Leiria, in the western part of the region, are served from Lisbon's Rossío Station.

Contacts and Resources

Emergencies
For emergencies in central Portugal, as well as throughout the country, dial **115.**

Guided Tours
Few regularly scheduled sightseeing tours originate within the region, but many of the major attractions are covered by a wide selection of one-day tours from Lisbon. For information contact **RN Tours** (✉ Av. Fontes Pereira de Melo 12–14, ☎ 01/356–0015) or **Cityrama** (✉ Av. Praia da Vitoria 12–B, ☎ 01/355–8567).

Boat trips on the São Cristovão, along the Rio Zêzere, depart daily in summer from the dam at Castelo de Bode and include lunch. The 4½-hour cruise costs 5,500$00. For reservations and information in Tomar, contact Hotel dos Templários (✉ Largo Candido dos Reis 1, 2300 Tomar, ☎ 049/312121) or the Estalagem Lago Azul (✉ Estrada Nacional 378, Castanheira, 2240 Ferreira do Zêzere, ☎ 049/361445).

Hospitals
The following cities have hospitals with emergency rooms, and their approaches are marked HOSPITAL; the emergency room is marked URGÊNCIAS: Caldas da Rainha (✉ Hospital Distrital, Parque Rainha Dona Leonor, ☎ 062/830300), Leiria (✉ Hospital Distrital, Largo D. Mel. Aguiar, ☎ 044/8107016), and Tomar (✉ Hospital Distrital, Av. Dr. Candido Madueira, ☎ 049/321100).

Late-Night Pharmacies
All sizable towns have at least one pharmacy open weekends, holidays, and after normal store hours. Local newspapers usually keep a schedule, and notices are posted on the door of every pharmacy.

Lodging
For information about *pousadas* (guest houses), contact **Promoções e Idéias Turisticas** (✉ Rua Fredrico Arouca 72, 2750 Cascais, ☎ 01/484–4207, FAX 01/484–2901).

Travel Agencies
Many travel agencies in the region are small, with limited services, and no English is spoken. In Leiria, **Viajes Melia** (✉ Av. Cidade Maringá 25, ☎ 044/33286) has English-speaking personnel and a full range of services.

Visitor Information

THE ESTREMADURA

In the Estremadura the principal tourist offices are in **Alcobaça** (✉ Praça 25 de Abril, ☎ 062/42377), **Batalha** (✉ Largo Paulo VI, ☎ 044/96180), **Caldas da Rainha** (✉ Rua Eng. Duarte Pacheco, ☎ 062/831003), **Ericeira** (✉ Rua Eduardo Burnay 33, ☎ 061/63122), **Leiria** (✉ Jardim Lúis de Camões, ☎ 044/823773), **Lourinhã** (✉ Praia da Areia Branca, ☎ 061/422167), **Mafra** (✉ Av. 25 de Abril, ☎ 061/812023), **Nazaré** (✉ Av. Vieira Guimarães, ☎ 062/561194), **Óbidos** (✉ Rua Direta, ☎ 062/959231), **Peniche** (✉ Rua Alex. Herculano, ☎ 062/789571), **Pombal** (✉ Largo da Cardal, ☎ 036/23230), **Torres Vedras** (✉ Rua 9 de Abril, ☎ 061/314094), and **Vila Franca de Xira** (✉ Rua Dr. Manuel de Arriagá 24, ☎ 063/26043).

THE RIBATEJO

In the Ribatejo you will find tourist offices in **Abrantes** (✉ Largo da Feira, ☎ 041/22555), **Constância** (✉ Câmera Municipal, ☎ 049/99205), **Fátima** (✉ Av. D. Correia da Silva, ☎ 049/531139), **Santerém** (✉ Rua Capelo e Ivens 63, ☎ 043/23140), **Tomar** (✉ Rua Serpa Pinto 1, ☎ 049/323113), and **Torres Novas** (✉ Largo do Paço, ☎ 049/812910).

5 Évora and the Alentejo

Known as the granary of Portugal, the Alentejo is a thinly populated, largely agricultural region of grain fields and cork and olive trees. The landscape ranges from the impressive west-coast beaches of the Lower Alentejo to the fortresses and rolling hills of the Upper Alentejo. The capital, Évora, is rich in architectural treasures.

THE **ALENTEJO,** which means "the land beyond the Rio Tejo (River Tagus)," in Portuguese, is a vast, sparsely populated region of heath and rolling hills

By Dennis Jaffe punctuated with stands of cork and olive trees. It is the country's largest province, stretching from the rugged west-coast beaches all the way east to Spain and from the Tejo in the north to the low mountains on the border of the Algarve, Portugal's southernmost province. Its capital, Évora, is a treasure chest of traditional Portuguese architecture. Over the centuries the pastoral countryside has been the scene of innumerable battles: between Romans and Visigoths, Moors and Christians, Portuguese and Spaniards, Portuguese and French, and finally (in the 1830s) between rival Portuguese factions in a civil war. Few hilltops in the region are without at least a trace of a castle or fortress.

One of the Alentejo's major industries is cork, of which Portugal is the world's largest producer. This is not, however, an industry for people in a hurry. It takes two decades before the trees can be harvested, and they may be carefully stripped only once every nine years. The numbers painted on the trees indicate the year of the last harvest. Exhibits at several regional museums chronicle this delicate process and display associated tools and handicrafts.

The undulating fields of wheat and barley surrounding Beja and Évora, the rice paddies of Alcácer do Sal, and the vineyards of Borba and Reguengos are representative of this rural province, Portugal's breadbasket. Traditions here are strong. Herdsmen tending flocks of sheep and goats wear the *pelico* (traditional sheepskin vest), and women in the fields wear broad-brim hats over kerchiefs and colorful, patterned dresses over trousers. Dwellings are dazzling white; more elegant houses have wrought-iron balconies and grillwork. The windows and doors of modest cottages and hilltop country *montes* (farmhouses) are trimmed with blue or yellow, and colorful flowers abound. The best time to visit the Alentejo is spring, when temperatures are pleasant and the fields are carpeted with wildflowers. Summer can be brutal, with the mercury frequently topping 100°F. As the Portuguese say, "In the Alentejo there is no shade but what comes from the sky."

Pleasures and Pastimes

Beaches

Some of Europe's finest and least crowded beaches are found along the rugged stretch of Portugal's west coast that extends from the southern extreme of the Alentejo at Odeceixe north to the tip of the Tróia Peninsula. Some beaches such as Praia do Carvalhal and Praia Grande at Almograve offer no facilities and are virtually deserted, even in July and August, when most of Europe's beaches are packed elbow to elbow. You can also find solitude by heading west on almost any of the unmarked tracks along the coast. The beaches at Vila Nova de Milfontes and at Porto Covo have restaurants and the usual beach facilities. Exercise great care when swimming on the west coast, as the surf is often high, and strong undertows and riptides are common.

Castles

As you drive through much of the Alentejo, you'll notice a castle or fortress crowning just about every hill. Some, such as the castles at Estremoz and Alvito, have been restored and converted into luxurious *pousadas*, while others, including the castles at Castelo de Vide and Viana do Alentejo, are open for you to clamber about the battlements.

Dining

In the Alentejo, a region known as the country's granary, bread is a major ingredient in the cuisine. It's the basis of a popular dish known as *açorda,* a thick, stick-to-the-ribs bread porridge to which various ingredients such as fish, meat, eggs, or shellfish are added. *Açorda de marisco,* a tasty combination of bread, eggs, seasonings, and a hearty portion of assorted shellfish, is one of the more popular varieties. Another version, *açorda da Alentejana,* is a clear broth with olive oil, slices of bread, garlic, and a poached egg floating on the surface. Pork from the Alentejo is the best in the country and often is combined with clams, onions, and tomatoes in the classic dish *carne de porco Alentejana.* The cheese is excellent, particularly the tangy sheep's cheese from the Serpa region. Elvas, near the Spanish border, is known for its tasty sugar plums. Alentejo wines—especially those from around Borba and Reguengos—are regular prizewinners at national tasting contests.

Between mid-June and mid-September reservations are advised at upscale restaurants. However, many of the establishments we list are moderate or inexpensive, most don't accept reservations, and they have informal dining rooms where it's quite acceptable to share a table with other diners. Dress at all but the most luxurious restaurants is casual throughout central Portugal; any exceptions to the dress code or reservation policy are noted in the reviews.

Horseback Riding

The sparse population and minimal automobile traffic make this region a delight for equestrian outings. Whether for a few hours or a few days, you will get a wonderfully different and authentic perspective of the Alentejo on horseback. Overnight tours are organized, with lodging at B&Bs and meals both on the trail and at local restaurants. Trails provide a variety of backdrops—including castles, villages, and prehistoric sites.

Lodging

The vast, primarily agricultural Alentejo is lacking in first-class hotels; the best accommodations in this region are the government-run inns called pousadas. Two of the finest in the country are in the Alentejo, one in the ancient convent in Évora and the other in the castle at Estremoz. The pousadas are small, some with as few as six rooms, so reserving well in advance is essential. There are also a number of high-quality, government-approved private guest houses in the region. Look for signs reading TURISMO RURAL or TURISMO DE HABITAÇÃO. Several of these are included in our listings.

Shopping

The brightly colored hand-painted plates, bowls, and figurines from the upper Alentejo are popular throughout Portugal. You'll find the best selection of this distinctive type of folk art in and around Estremoz, where the terra-cotta jugs and bowls are adorned with chips of marble from local quarries. Saturday morning the *rossío* (town square) is chock-full of vendors displaying their wares. Redondo and the village of San Pedro do Corval, near Reguengos, are also good sources of this type of pottery. The village of Arraiolos, near Évora, is famous for its hand-embroidered wool rugs.

Swimming

In addition to swimming in the ocean at the many beaches along the west coast, most larger towns and many smaller ones have modern municipal swimming pools—so even in the middle of the dry Alentejo, you'll never be very far from a refreshing dip.

Exploring Évora and the Alentejo

The Alentejo, Portugal's largest province, is a sprawling region that contains a wide variety of attractions—from the rugged west-coast beaches to the architectural treasures of Évora. The province is divided roughly into two parts: the more mountainous region north of Évora, and the flatter Lower Alentejo, in the southern part of the region, known as the country's granary.

Great Itineraries

Lisbon is a good base from which to explore the Alentejo. Whatever the length of your trip, you can make convenient loops starting and finishing in Lisbon, or you can extend your travels by continuing south to the Algarve from Beja or Santiago do Cacém. You should allow 10 days in order to get a feel for the region, exploring Évora and visiting some outlying attractions such as Monsaraz and Castelo de Vide. This will also allow time for a day or two of sunbathing on a west-coast beach. If you skip the beach, you can cover the most interesting attractions at a comfortable pace in seven days. Three days will give you time to explore Évora and its surroundings along with one or two additional highlights.

Numbers in the text correspond to numbers in the margin and on the Évora, the Upper Alentejo, and the Lower Alentejo maps.

IF YOU HAVE 3 DAYS

Be sure to include ⊡ **Évora** ①–⑳, one of Portugal's most beautiful cities. The following morning visit the rug-producing town of **Arraiolos** ㉔ and then continue on to **Estremoz** ㉛ and its imposing fortress, which doubles as a pousada. Head east past **Borba** ㉚ and its marble quarries to **Vila Viçosa** ㉙, site of the Ducal Palace. Then continue south to the whitewashed village of ⊡ **Terena** ㉘. In the morning visit the fortified hilltop town of **Monsaraz** ㉗ before returning to Lisbon.

IF YOU HAVE 7 DAYS

From Lisbon head for ⊡ **Évora** ①–⑳. The next day explore the **Aqueduto da Agua da Prata** ㉑ and the prehistoric sites just outside town, which include the **Cromlech and the Menhir of Almendres** ㉒ and the **Dolmen of Zambujeiro** ㉓. On the way to ⊡ **Estremoz** ㉛, stop at **Arraiolos** ㉔. From Estremoz head east to the fortified town of ⊡ **Elvas** ㉝, stopping en route at **Borba** ㉚ and the Ducal Palace at **Vila Viçosa** ㉙. The following day continue to ⊡ **Monsaraz** ㉗, with stops along the way at **Terena** ㉘ and the pottery shops in **São Pedro do Corval** ㉖. From Monsaraz head south to ⊡ **Beja** ㊶, inspecting the Roman ruins at **São Cucufate** ㊹ en route. The next day head west to ⊡ **Santiago do Cacém** ㊽ for more Roman ruins and a few hours at the beach. On your seventh day return to Lisbon, stopping along the way to see the castle at **Alcácer do Sal** ㊼.

IF YOU HAVE 10 DAYS

Spend two nights in ⊡ **Évora** ①–⑳ to visit the town and its **Aqueduto da Agua da Prata** ㉑, the nearby prehistoric sites of **Cromlech and the Menhir of Almendres** ㉒ and the **Domen of Zambujeiro** ㉓, and neighboring **Arraiolos** ㉔. Then head for ⊡ **Estremoz** ㉛, with a stop along the way to visit the castle and enjoy the spectacular view at **Évoramonte** ㉜. The next morning continue north to the **Coudelaria de Alter** ㊲ outside Alter do Chão. Then follow N245 north to **Castelo de Vide** ㊵, a friendly, whitewashed village known for its spa and healing waters. From there continue to ⊡ **Marvão** ㊳ (spend two nights), a fortified town perched atop a sheer cliff. The most scenic approach from Castelo de Vide is via the serpentine back roads rather than the main

The Upper Alentejo

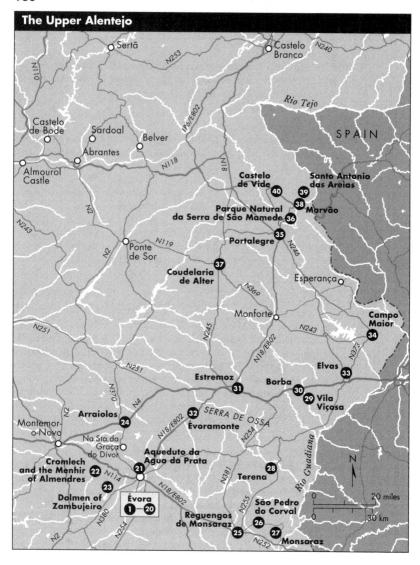

highway. Using either Castelo de Vide or Marvão as a base, you can explore the **Parque Natural da Serra de São Mamede** ㊱. Rich in wildlife, the park is ideally suited for walking and enjoying the peaceful countryside. At **Santo António das Areias** ㊴, a few kilometers north of Marvão, are some two dozen prehistoric dolmens scattered among the chestnut groves. From Marvão take N359, which winds its way across the low mountains of the Serra de São Mamede to **Portalegre** ㉟. Spend a few hours there and continue to ☒ **Elvas** ㉝, with its extensive fortifications and Manueline cathedral. Stop en route at **Campo Maior** ㉞, a pleasant town distinguished by its hilltop castle and tiny whitewashed houses with wrought-iron grilles and balconies. The next morning visit **Borba** ㉚, known for its fine wines and marble quarries, then tour the Ducal Palace at **Vila Viçosa** ㉙. Continue south by way

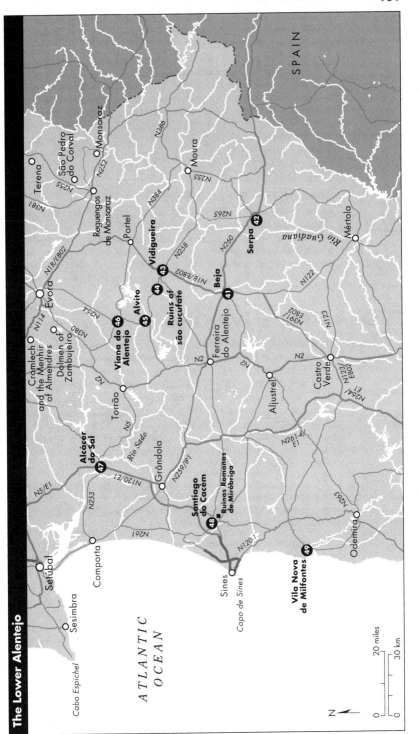

The Lower Alentejo

of **Terena** ㉘, **Reguengos de Monsaraz** ㉕, and **São Pedro do Corval** ㉖ to spend the night in ⊞ **Monsaraz** ㉗. The next day visit ⊞ **Beja** ㊶, a fortified town whose center still retains a Moorish character, stopping to see the Roman ruins at **São Cucufate** ㊹ en route. From Beja head west to ⊞ **Santiago do Cacém** ㊽ (spend two nights), where you can visit the Roman ruins and spend some time relaxing at the nearby beaches. From here you can either head south to the Algarve or return to Lisbon. The most scenic route to Lisbon is the N261, which runs along the coast to the tip of the Troia Peninsula; from there you can take the ferry across the Sado River estuary. You can also drive through the Sado River Nature Reserve by turning off at Comporta and following N253 to **Alcácer do Sal** ㊼. Visit the hilltop castle there and continue on to Lisbon via E1.

When to Tour Évora and the Alentejo

Spring comes early to this part of Portugal. Early April to mid-June is a wonderful time to tour, when the fields are full of colorful wildflowers. July and August in the Alentejo are brutally hot, with temperatures in places such as Beja often reaching 100°F or more. Air-conditioning is not widespread, and air-conditioned rental cars are rare. By mid-September things have cooled off sufficiently to make touring this region a delight.

ÉVORA AND ENVIRONS

Shepherds and farmers in traditional garb, with wizened faces bearing markings of a lifetime in the baking Alentejo sun, stand about Giraldo Square; a group of pretty, young college girls dressed in jeans and T-shirts chat animatedly at a sidewalk café; a local businessman in coat and tie purposefully hurries by; and clusters of tourists, ubiquitous cameras in hand, capture the historic monuments on film—all this is part of a typical summer's day in downtown Évora. The town is the flourishing capital of the rich agricultural Alentejo province, a university center, and one of the world's great architectural treasures (so classified by UNESCO in 1986).

Sitting atop a small hill in the heart of a vast cork-, olive-, and grain-producing region, Évora—with its astonishing variety of inspiring architecture—stands out from provincial farm towns the world over: The entire inner city is a monument.

Although the region was inhabited some 4,000 years ago—as attested to by the dolmens and phallic menhirs in the surrounding countryside—it was during the Roman epoch that the town called Liberalitas Julia in the province of Lusitania first achieved importance. A large part of present-day Évora is built on Roman foundations, of which the Temple of Diana, with its graceful Corinthian columns, is the most conspicuous reminder.

The Moors also made a great historical impact on the area. They arrived in 715 and remained more than 450 years. They were driven out in 1166, thanks in part to a clever ruse perpetrated by Geraldo Sem Pavor (Gerald the Fearless), the Portuguese counterpart to El Cid. Geraldo was able to trick Évora's Moorish ruler into leaving unguarded a strategic watchtower that protected one of the entrances to the town. With a small force, Geraldo took control of the tower, which prompted the main body of Moorish troops to leave its post at the principal entrance to the city, in an attempt to regain control of the watchtower. With the main entrance now undefended, the bulk of Geraldo's forces was able to storm the city unopposed.

Toward the end of the 12th century, Évora's fortunes increased, as the town became the favored location for the courts of the Burgundy and Avis dynasties; less than 164 kilometers (100 miles) from Lisbon, it attracted many of the great minds and creative talents of Renaissance Portugal. Gil Vicente, the founder of Portuguese theater; the sculptor Nicolas Chanterene; and Gregorio Lopes, the painter known for his renderings of court life, were some of the more prominent residents of the time. This concentration of royal wealth and Renaissance creativity superimposed upon the existing Moorish town was instrumental in the development of the delicate Manueline-Mudejar architectural style. You can see fine examples of this in the graceful lines of the Palace of Dom Manuel and the turreted São Bras Hermitage.

Évora is, above all, a town for walking. Wherever you glance as you stroll the maze of narrow streets and alleys of the old town, amid arches and whitewashed houses, you'll come face to face with reminders of the town's rich architectural and cultural heritage.

The area surrounding Évora is a rich agricultural region with scattered small villages and some of Portugal's earliest inhabited sites.

Numbers in the margin correspond to points of interest on the Évora and the Upper Alentejo maps.

Évora

164 km (100 mi) southeast of Lisbon.

★ ❶ The **Praça do Giraldo,** the bustling, arcade-lined square in the center of the old town is named after the city's liberator, Gerald the Fearless. During Caesar's time the square, marked by a large arch, was the Roman forum; in 1571 the arch was destroyed to make room for the fountain across from the entrance to the church. The graceful, flattened sphere made of white Estremoz marble was designed and executed by the Renaissance architect Afonso Alvares.

❷ Note the striking white Renaissance facade of the **Igreja de Santo Antão,** which stands at the top of the Praça do Giraldo. A medieval hermitage of the Templar Knights was razed in 1553 to make way for the present church, which, with its massive round pillars and soaring vaulted ceilings, is the finest example of the German style *Hallenkirche* to be found in the Alentejo. The marble altar in bas-relief is a holdover from the primitive hermitage.

NEED A BREAK?

The **Café Arcadia,** opposite the fountain on the Praça do Giraldo, is an Évora institution. The large hall, divided into snack bar and restaurant sections, is decorated with photos of the big bands that played here in the '40s. Outside tables set on the square are just the places from which to watch Évora on parade.

The narrow, cobblestoned **Rua 5 de Outubro,** a pedestrian thoroughfare lined with shops, hanging lanterns, and whitewashed houses with wrought-iron balconies, is one of the town's most attractive streets and connects the Praça do Giraldo and the cathedral. The massive twin tow-
★ ❸ ers and the battlement-ringed walls give the **Sé** (cathedral) a fortresslike appearance, a type of construction also seen in the Lisbon and Coimbra cathedrals. The Sé, one of Portugal's most striking architectural achievements, is a transitional Gothic-style building constructed in 1186 from huge granite blocks. It has been enhanced over the centuries with an octagonal, turreted dome above the transept, a blue-tiled spire atop the north tower, a number of fine Manueline windows, and several Gothic rose windows. At the entrance the Gothic arches are sup-

Évora

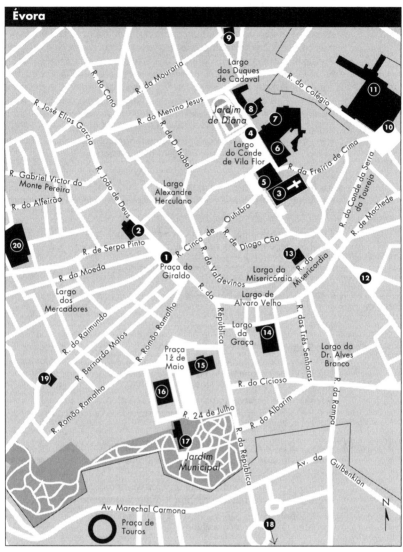

Biblioteca Pública, **6**
Ermida de São Bras, **18**
Igreja a Nossa Senhora da Graça, **14**
Igreja de Espirito Santo, **10**
Igreja de Misericórdia, **13**
Igreja de Santa Clara, **20**
Igreja de Santo Antão, **2**
Igreja de São Francisco, **15**
Igreja de São Mamede, **9**
Igreja e Convento dos Lóios, **7**
Largo da Porto de Moura, **12**
Municipal Market, **16**
Museu de Artes Decorativas, **19**
Museu Regional de Évora, **5**
Palácio de Dom Manuel, **17**
Palácio dos Duques de Cadaval, **8**
Praça do Giraldo, **1**
Sé, **3**
Templo Romano, **4**
Universidad de Évora, **11**

ported by marble columns bearing delicately sculpted 14th-century statues of the Apostles. With the exception of a fine baroque chapel, the
granite interior is somber. The cloister, a 14th-century Gothic addition
with Mudejar vestiges, is one of the finest of its genre in the country.
Statues of the Evangelists decorate the four corners. Housed in the towers and chapter room are the Treasury and Museum of Sacred Art. Of
particular interest is a 13th-century ivory triptych, the *Virgin of Paradise,* whose body opens up to show exquisitely carved scenes of her
life and whose head is a 16th-century wooden replacement, strangely
out of proportion. ▨ 250$00. ☉ *Tues.–Sun. 9–noon and 2–5.*

★ ❹ The well-preserved ruins of the **Templo Romano,** or Roman temple, dominate a large plaza. The edifice, considered one of the finest of its kind
on the Iberian Peninsula, makes use of the Corinthian style and was
built during the 2nd and 3rd centuries. Although it has been referred
to as the Temple of Diana, historians are uncertain as to which of the
many Roman deities it was actually dedicated. The temple, largely destroyed during the invasions of the barbarian tribes in the early 5th
century, has been used at various times as a fortification and was a municipal slaughterhouse in the 14th century. It was uncovered and restored to its present state just over 100 years ago.

❺ The **Museu Regional de Évora** (Museum of Évora) is housed in a stately
late-17th-century baroque building across from the Roman temple. The
structure, once a palace that accommodated bishops, contains a rich
collection of sculpture and paintings as well as a number of interesting archaeological and architectural artifacts. The first-floor galleries,
arranged around a pleasant garden, include several excellent carved
pillars and a fine Manueline doorway. Among the early Portuguese paintings on display in the upstairs gallery are works attributed to the 16th-
century Mestre of Sardoal. ✉ *Largo do Conde de Vila Flor, no phone.*
▨ 300$00. ☉ *Tues.–Sun. 10–noon and 2–5.*

❻ The **Biblioteca Pública** (Municipal Library) occupies the former town
hall and contains an outstanding collection of rare books and
manuscripts. ☉ *Mon.–Sat. 9–1 and 2–6.*

❼ The **Igreja e Convento dos Lóios** (Church and Convent of Lóios) is adjacent to the Pousada dos Lóios (☞ Dining and Lodging, *below*). To
enter the church go down several steps and through a portal framed
by a series of fan-shape arches in the flamboyant Gothic style. The sanctuary, dedicated to St. John the Evangelist, was founded in the 15th
century by the Venetian-based Lóios Order. Its interior walls are covered with 18th-century heroic *azulejo* panels created by Oliveira
Bernardes, the foremost master of this unique Portuguese art form. The
blue-and-white tiles depict scenes from the life of the church's founder,
Rodrigo de Melo, who, along with members of his family, is buried
here. The bas-relief marble tombstones at the foot of the high altar are
the only ones of their kind in Portugal. Note the two metal hatches on
either side of the main aisle: One covers an ancient cistern, which belonged to the Moorish castle that predated the church (an underground spring still supplies the cistern with potable water); and beneath
the other hatch lie the neatly stacked bones of hundreds of monks, which
have been collected over the centuries. This bizarre ossuary was uncovered in 1958 during restoration work. Enhanced by the 16th-cen-
tury Renaissance gallery, the cloister is now an integral part of the
Pousada dos Lóios. ✉ *Largo Conde de Vila Flor.* ▨ 400$00. ☉
Tues.–Sun. 10–12:30 and 2–5.

❽ The **Palacio dos Duques de Cadaval** is readily identified by two massive stone towers with pointed battlements. These towers, once part

of a medieval castle that protected the town, were later incorporated into the Palace of the Dukes of Cadaval, a former residence of Kings João I and João IV. A small ground-floor gallery contains historic documents, paintings, and the unusual Flemish-style bronze tomb of Rui de Sousa, a signatory of the Treaty of Tordesilhas. In 1494 the treaty divided the world into two spheres of influence: Spanish and Portuguese. Today the palace is being used by the city road department. ⊠ *Largo Conde de Vila Flor.* 🎫 *400$00.* ⊘ *Tues.–Sun. 10–12:30 and 2–5.*

NEED A BREAK? Opposite the Roman temple, the restful, tree-lined Jardim de Diana looks out over an aqueduct and the plains. From this park—in one sweeping glance that takes in the temple, the spires of the Gothic cathedral, the Church of Lóios, and the 20th-century pousada housed in the convent—you can take in nearly 2,000 years of Portuguese history. A snack bar at the corner of the park is a great spot to sit and reflect on the architectural marvels spread out before you.

---

❾ The small **Igreja de São Mamede** (Church of St. Mamede) contains a vaulted ceiling decorated with baroque frescoes. Note the fine azulejos that cover the wall of the nave. On the east wall is a marble bust of the Renaissance humanist Andre de Resende, created by João Cuteliero, a well-known contemporary Portuguese sculptor.

Facing the square known as the Largo de Colégio is the 16th-century **❿** **Igreja de Espirito Santo** (Espirito Santo Church). A squat structure with five arches in front, the building was originally a part of the ancient Évora University. The interior contains some fine azulejos and paintings, including artist Gregorio Lopes's painting of the *Last Supper*. As you explore the surrounding streets, you'll have a good view of the ancient town walls, and in some places, vestiges of the Roman foundations are visible.

From 1555 until its closure by the Marquis of Pombal in 1759, the **⓫** **Universidade de Évora** was a Jesuit college; in 1979, after a lapse of more than 200 years, Évora University resumed classes. Although the enrollment is small, the college's presence has given new life and vigor to this ancient city. The large courtyard is flanked on all sides by a series of graceful buildings with double-tier, white-limestone arched galleries in Italian Renaissance style. From the main entrance you'll see the imposing baroque facade of the gallery, known as the **Sala dos Actos** (Hall of Acts), which is crowned with allegorical figures and coats of arms carved in white marble that was quarried in the region. Lining the gallery's interior are azulejos representing historical, mythological, and biblical themes.

⓬ The **Largo da Porta de Moura**—perhaps Évora's most beautiful square—is characterized by paired stone towers that guard one of the principal entrances to the walled old town. Spires of the cathedral rise above the towers, and in the center of the square is an unusual Renaissance fountain. The large white-marble sphere, supported by a single column, bears a Latin inscription dated 1556. Overlooking the fountain is the **Cordovil Mansion** (closed to the public), on whose terrace are several particularly attractive arches decorated in the Manueline-Mudejar style. The square is in a lovely part of town with whitewashed houses and wrought-iron grillwork.

⓭ The interior of the 16th-century **Igreja de Misericórdia** (Misericordia Church) is lined with large azulejo panels depicting scenes from the life of Christ; the unsigned 18th-century tiles are thought to be the work of the renowned tile maker António de Oliveira de Bernardes.

⓮ The **Igreja a Nossa Senhora da Graça** (Church of Our Lady of Grace) is a splendid piece of classical Italian-style architecture. Note the impish figures perched above the portal: According to local legend, these four figures represent the first victims put to death in the Inquisition in Évora in 1543. The adjacent Largo de Alvaro Velho is an inviting square lined with metalsmith shops.

⓯ After the cathedral, the **Igreja de São Francisco** (Church of St. Francis) is the grandest of Évora's churches. Its construction in the early 16th century, on the site of a former Gothic chapel, involved the greatest talents of the day, including Nicolas Chanterene, Oliver of Ghent, and the Arruda brothers, Francisco and Diogo. The magnificent religious architecture notwithstanding, the bizarre **Casa dos Ossos** (House of the Bones) is the main attraction. The translation of the chilling inscription over the entrance reads: "We bones who are here are waiting for yours." The bones of some 5,000 skeletons dug up from cemeteries in the area line the ceilings and supporting columns. With a decorative flair worthy of Charles Addams, a 16th-century Franciscan monk placed skulls jaw-to-cranium so they form arches across the ceiling, and arm and leg bones are neatly stacked to shape the supporting columns. ▣ *50$00.* ☻ *Tues.–Sat. 9–12:30 and 2:30–5; Sun. 10–11:30 and 2:30–5.*

⓰ The **municipal market,** facing the spacious Praça 1 de Maio, is housed in a large, sprawling building. Wander around the stalls crammed with fresh fruits and vegetables and fish and meat to get a good idea of what the Alentejo produces and consumes. Mornings, except for Sunday, the pavement in front of the market overflows with displays of colorful pottery. Across from the market the extensive **Jardim Municipal** (Municipal Gardens) offer a pleasant respite from the rigors of sightseeing. They are landscaped with a variety of exotic plants and trees from all over the world.

⓱ At the entrance to the Jardim Municipal is the **Palácio de Dom Manuel** (Dom Manuel's Palace). Only a part of the former royal palace remains— restored after a fire in 1916. The existing wing displays a row of paired, gracefully curved Manueline windows, and on the south side of the building there's a notable arcade of redbrick Mudejar sawtooth arches. Currently used as an art gallery, the palace has witnessed a number of historic events since its construction in the late 15th century. It was here, for instance, in 1497, that Vasco da Gama received his commission to command the fleet that would discover the sea route to India.

NEED A
BREAK?

In the Municipal Gardens is a snack bar selling sandwiches and drinks. From a park bench or the Victorian gazebo, you'll have a lovely view of the Church of St. Francis.

⓲ The **Ermida de São Bras** (St. Blaise Chapel), a curious structure built in the late 15th century, was the first important building in the Alentejo to join Gothic and Moorish elements to form the Gothic-Mudejar style. The fortified church, a few hundred feet south of the city walls, is characterized by massive battlement-topped walls and a series of round towers crowned with steep spires.

⓳ The Igreja das Mercês is now the **Museu de Artes Decorativas** (Museum of Decorative Arts). Inside the late 17th-century building are several good examples of azulejos with scenes from the life of St. Augustine, the patron saint of the founding order of this church. There are also two unusual confessionals concealed behind tile panels. ✉ *Rua do Raimundo,* ☎ *066/22604.* ▣ *Free.* ☻ *Tues.–Sun. 10–12:30 and 2–5.*

⑳ Behind the baroque facade of the **Igreja de Santa Clara** (the Church of St. Clara) is an interior adorned with paintings, including a fine rendition on wood of the Procession of Santa Clara by the 16th-century Évora painter Francisco João.

Dining and Lodging

$$$ ✕ **Fialho.** Amor and Gabriel Fialho are the third generation of Fial-
★ hos to operate this popular, traditional restaurant, one of Évora's best. The beamed ceiling and painted plates on the walls lend a rustic ambience to what is quite a sophisticated kitchen. You might start with a selection of appetizers that includes an excellent *salada de polvo* (marinated octopus salad) and as a main course try *coelho de convent a cartuxa* (roast rabbit with potatoes and carrots, according to a recipe from a nearby monastery). A wide selection of Alentejo wines is offered. ✉ *Travessa das Mascarenhas 16,* ☎ *066/23079. AE, MC, V. Closed Mon.*

$$ ✕ **A Choupana.** Popular with the locals, this pleasant restaurant is just
★ off the main square. In one of its two rooms, there are a few tables and a counter with stools, and in the other there's a small, paneled dining area. Service is friendly, and the food is good. Try the *açorda de marisco* (bread porridge with shellfish). ✉ *Rua dos Mercadores 20,* ☎ *066/24427. AE, DC, MC, V. Closed Sun.*

$$$ ✕▥ **Pousada dos Lóios.** This pousada, in the historic 15th-century
★ monastery opposite the Roman Temple of Diana, rates among the most luxurious in the chain. Except for the small size of the rooms, which were formerly the monks' cells, and the need for anyone over 5 foot 2 to duck when entering, there's no trace of monastic austerity here. The opulent period furnishings compensate for the slightly cramped quarters, while the elegant lounges and public rooms deserve a visit even if you don't plan to spend the night. Superbly prepared Alentejo specialties are served in the restaurant in the former cloister, a marvel of Manueline ceilings and columns. ✉ *Largo Conde de Vila Flor, 7000,* ☎ *066/24051,* ℻ *066/27248. 31 rooms, 1 suite. Restaurant, bar, pool. AE, DC, MC, V.*

$ ✕▥ **Évora Hotel.** This pleasant, modern establishment opened in 1992 on the outskirts of town on the road toward Montemor-o-Novo, a welcome addition to Évora. The public areas are light and spacious as is the dining room, which presents a delicious buffet with regional specialties. Rooms are generous in size and all have small balconies. ✉ *Quinta do Cruzeiro. Estrada Nacional 114, 7001,* ☎ *066/734800,* ℻ *066/734806. 114 rooms. Restaurant, bar, pool, sauna, tennis, exercise room. AE, DC, MC, V.*

$ ▥ **Riviera.** This cozy, three-story old manor house is well situated between Giraldo Square and the Roman Temple. The small, cheerful entry is decorated with colorful azulejos, and the rooms are covered with flowered wallpaper. Furnishings are in the traditional, painted Alentejo style. ✉ *Rua 5 de Outubro 49, 7000,* ☎ *066/23304,* ℻ *066/20467. 22 rooms. Lounge. AE, DC, MC, V.*

$ ▥ **Solar de Monfalim.** In the heart of the old town, in a historic building with a delightful arched gallery, this comfortable, family-run guest house provides quiet, old-fashioned hospitality. The rooms, while small, are comfortably furnished, as is the TV lounge. ✉ *Largo da Misericórdia 1, 7000,* ☎ *066/22031,* ℻ *066/742367. 26 rooms, 1 suite. Bar. MC, V.*

Outdoor Activities and Sports

BALLOONING AND FOUR-WHEEL DRIVING

Hot-air balloon flights and four-wheel-drive excursions through the Alentejo are offered by **Turibalão Lda.** (✉ Ger2, 2E-F Escrivão Câmara, 7000 Évora, ☎ ℻ 066/26323).

🜲 **Kartó Dromo de Évora,** a go-cart track on the outskirts of Évora (take N114 in the direction of Montemor-o-Novo), provides an outlet for pent-up youthful energy. ⊠ *Quinta Lucena, EN 114, 7000 Évora,* ☎ *066/734990.* 🖆 *400$00–7,000$00, depending on vehicle and length of rental time.* ◎ *Tues.–Sun. 10–8.*

Cavalgada, in Montemor-o-Novo, 30 kilometers (18 miles) northwest of Évora, offers riding lessons as well as escorted rides lasting from one hour to 10 days. Theme rides include "Route of the Castles" and "White Villages." Reservations are advised. ⊠ *Apartado 68, 7050 Montemor-o-Novo,* ☎ *066/86680,* ⦀ *066/81227.* 🖆 *Hourly rates 1,500$00; ½-day ride 3,500$00; full-day ride 6,500$00; 2-day weekend ride, including 1 night's accommodation in a B&B, 18,000$00. Riding lessons cost 1,200$00 per ½ hr.*

Centro Hípico de Évora Picadeiro do Monte das Flores provides riding instruction. Hourly and day rides are available. ⊠ *Monte das Flores, 7000 Évora,* ☎ *066/21376.*

Aqueduto da Agua da Prata

㉑ *Extends 18 km (11 mi) north of Évora.*

The graceful arched Aqueduto da Agua da Prata (Silver Water Aqueduct), which once carried water 18 kilometers (11 miles) to Évora from the springs at Graça do Divor, is best seen along the road to Arraiolos. You can also see a section of it within Évora, along the Rua do Cano in the northwest corner of the city (walk east on Rua do Muro for about 200 yards from the entrance of N114–4, the Arraiolos road). Constructed in 1532 under the patronage of Dom João III, the aqueduct was designed by the famous architect Francisco de Arruda. Extensive parts of the system remain intact and can be seen from the road.

Cromlech and the Menhir of Almendres

㉒ *15 km (9 mi) west of Évora.*

A trip through the countryside surrounding Évora will take you to some of the earliest inhabited sites in Portugal, including the Cromlech and the Menhir of Almendres. In Guadalupe, the site of a 17th-century chapel, near the grain-storage bins of the Agricultural Cooperative, is the Menhir of Almendres, a massive 8-foot-tall Neolithic stone obelisk. Several hundred yards in the same direction is the Cromlech, some 95 granite monoliths arranged in an oval configuration in the middle of a large field.

Dolmen of Zambujeiro

㉓ *12 km (8 mi) southwest of Évora. From N380—the Évora–Alcáçovas road—take the turnoff to Valverde.*

The 20-foot-high Dolmen of Zambujeiro is the largest of its kind ever discovered on the Iberian Peninsula. This prehistoric monument is typical of those found throughout Neolithic Europe: Several great stone slabs stand upright, supporting a flat stone that serves as a roof. These structures were designed as burial chambers.

Arraiolos

㉔ *22 km (13 mi) northwest of Évora.*

Arraiolos, dominated by the ruins of a once-mighty fortress, is a typical hilltop Alentejo village of whitewashed houses and narrow streets. What distinguishes Arraiolos is its worldwide reputation as a carpet-producing center. In the 16th century, as Portuguese trade with the East grew, an interest developed in the intricate designs of the carpets from India and Persia, and these patterns served as models for the earliest hand-embroidered Arraiolos carpets. The colorful rugs are not mass-produced in factories but are handmade by locals in their homes and cottages. An authentic Arraiolos rug, made of locally produced wool, has some 44,000 ties per square meter. To discourage imitations, in 1992 the town council designed a special blue seal of authenticity to be affixed to each carpet. There is a permanent exhibition of carpets in the **town hall.** 🏛 *Free.* ☉ *Weekdays 9–12:30 and 2–5; weekend hrs vary; call the tourist office at Praça Lima Brito,* ☎ *066/42105, for information.*

Shopping
The main street of Arraiolos is lined with showrooms and workshops featuring the hand-embroidered wool rugs for which the town is so famous. Some of the best selections can be found at **Calantica** (✉ Rua Alexandre Herculano 20, ☎ 066/42356) and **Condestavel** (✉ Rua Bombeiros Voluntarios 7, ☎ 066/42219), a large shop with branches in Évora and Lisbon.

THE UPPER ALENTEJO

Occupying roughly the northern half of the province, the Upper Alentejo is a hilly, partly mountainous region that contains a number of interesting fortified towns. Some of Portugal's best wines are produced in the area between Borba and Reguengos. The towns are discussed in the order you would visit them if traveling north from Évora.

Numbers in the margin correspond to points of interest on the Upper Alentejo map.

Reguengos de Monsaraz

㉕ *35 km (31 mi) southeast of Évora.*

Reguengos de Monsaraz, a sleepy little Alentejo town, is arranged around a large square. Note the unusual pentagonal bell tower on the 19th-century Victorian church. The town, in the center of a large wine-producing region, is also known for its handwoven rugs.

São Pedro do Corval

㉖ *5 km (3 mi) northeast of Reguengos.*

The tiny hamlet of São Pedro do Corval, on the road to Monsaraz, is one of Portugal's major centers for inexpensive hand-painted pottery.

En Route   On the way to Monsaraz, just before the road begins to climb, you'll see an intriguing Moorish-style domed fountain across from the public laundry area, dated 1723 in Roman numerals. The road then snakes up the hill to a parking area outside the village walls; no cars except those of residents are permitted inside.

Monsaraz

★ ❷ *16 km (10 mi) east of Reguenos, 50 km (30 mi) southeast of Évora.*

The entire fortified hilltop town of Monsaraz is a living museum of narrow, stone-surfaced streets lined with ancient white houses. The town's 150 or so permanent residents (mostly older people) live mainly from tourism, and because they do so graciously and unobtrusively, Monsaraz has managed to retain its essential character.

Old women clad in black still sit in the doorways of their tiny cottages and chat with neighbors (as they have in villages all over the country for generations), their ever-present knitting in hand. At the southern end of the walls stand the well-preserved towers of a formidable castle. The view from atop the pentagonal tower sweeps across the Alentejo plain to the west and to the east over the Rio Guadiana to Spain. Within the castle perimeter is an unusual arena with makeshift slate benches at either end of an oval field. Bullfights are held here several times a year and always in the second week of September (during the festival of Senhora Jesus dos Passos, the village's patron saint).

The small **Monsaraz Museum,** next to the parish church, displays religious artifacts and the original town charter, signed by Dom Manuel in 1512. The former tribunal contains an interesting 15th-century fresco, which depicts Christ presiding over figures representing truth and deception. ☒ *150$00.* ☉ *Wed.–Mon. 10–noon and 2–5.*

The area around Monsaraz is dotted with megalithic monuments. The **Menhir of Outeiro,** 3 kilometers (2 miles) north of town, is one of the tallest ever discovered.

Dining and Lodging

$$ ✕ **Casa do Forno.** The labor of love of two ambitious women (Gloria
★ and Mariana), Casa do Forno is an upscale restaurant in a picturesque fortified village. At the entrance is a huge, rounded oven with an iron door, hence the name Forno—Portuguese for "oven." Picture windows line the dining room and offer a spectacular view over the rolling plains. The Alentejan menu appropriately features roasts, and one special dish worth trying is the *borrego Convento Orado* (roast lamb from an ancient recipe obtained at the nearby monastery). ☒ *Travessa da Sanabrosa,* ☎ *066/55190. MC, V. Closed Tues.*

$$$ ▦ **Horta da Moura.** This self-contained miniresort, 15 kilometers (9 miles) east of Reguengos de Monsaraz on a well-signed dirt road, is set on a working farm between the walled city and the Rio Guadiana. The main house, whose white-stucco facade is highlighted with blue trim and an arched portico, is typical of Alentejo-style architecture. Inside, vaulted brick ceilings with wood beams and traditional furnishings create a cozy atmosphere. The outlying buildings include stables, a riding school, a crafts room, a winery, and a recreation center with a large fireplace. The helpful staff eagerly arranges walking, horseback-riding, and cycling trips along the nearby Rio Guadiana, as well as four-wheel-drive and canoe excursions. Hunting and fishing trips can also be arranged. ☒ *Horta da Moura, Apt. 64, 7200 Reguengos de Monsaraz,* ☎ *066/55152,* 🖷 *066/55241. 6 rooms, 7 suites, 1 apartment. Pool, tennis, horseback riding, fishing, bicycles. AE, DC, MC, V.*

¢ ▦ **Estalagem Dom Nuno.** This small, rustic guest house occupies a restored old white house on the main street of the walled town. Clean rooms with modern furnishings offer fantastic views over the valley—the sunsets alone are worth the price of a room. Casa Nuno is a perfect little romantic hideaway in an ancient village. ☒ *Rua do Castelo 6, 7200,* ☎ *066/55146. 8 rooms. AE, DC, MC, V.*

Terena

28 *28 km (17 mi) north of Reguengos.*

A little jewel of a town, with a charter dating from 1262 and a castle on a hill, Terena is a place where tourists are still a pleasant curiosity. Drive—or better yet, stroll—along the narrow Rua Direita past the white houses, some with Gothic doorways, others with baroque or Renaissance ones. The small, well-preserved castle was one of several built in this area to defend the border with Spain, which lies across the Rio Guadiana, 11 kilometers (7 miles) east.

Dining and Lodging

$ ✕🏠 **Casa de Terena.** Several years ago Susanna Bianchi and her part-
★ ner, Arnaldo Aboim, gave up successful careers in Lisbon to buy and restore a dilapidated 18th-century town house in this out-of-the-way village. Now a charming inn, Casa de Terena offers six comfortably furnished bedrooms featuring period reproductions. In the morning guests dine in what was once the stable but is now a delightful breakfast room. Across the street the rustic Migas Restaurant—named after the family dog—serves simple but tasty traditional fare. ⊠ *Rua Direita 45, 7250 Alandroal,* ☎ *068/45132,* 🖷 *068/45155. 5 rooms, 1 suite. Restaurant, bar. MC, V.*

Vila Viçosa

29 *18 km (11 mi) north of Terena.*

A quiet town with a moated castle, Vila Viçosa occupies a gentle elevation in the heart of the fertile Borba plain. It has been closely linked with Portuguese royalty since the 15th century, but this association was not always a happy one: In 1483 King João II, seeking to strengthen his grip on the throne, moved to eliminate the second Duke of Bragança, his brother-in-law and most formidable rival, who from Vila Viçosa controlled more than 50 cities, castles, and towns. After much intrigue and counterintrigue, the unfortunate Duke was beheaded in the main square of Évora.

Court life in Vila Viçosa flourished in the late 16th and early 17th centuries, when the huge palace constructed by the fourth Duke of Bragança (Jaime) was the scene of great royal feasts, theater performances, and bullfights. This all came to an abrupt end in 1640, when King João IV, the eighth Duke of Bragança and the first Portuguese to occupy the throne after 60 years of Spanish domination, elected to move his court to Lisbon. Thereafter, Vila Viçosa slipped into relative oblivion. In more recent times Portugal's second-to-last king, Carlos I, and the young Prince Luís Filipe spent their last night in the palace. The following day, February 1, 1908, in response to a royal decree that mandated exile for "political" crimes, they were assassinated by members of a secret political society while they were crossing Lisbon's Terreiro do Paço in an open carriage.

The **Paço Ducal** (Ducal Palace), still in the hands of the Braganças, draws a great many visitors. Built of locally quarried marble, the main wing extends for some 360 feet and overlooks the expansive Palace Square and the bronze equestrian statue of Dom João IV. The interior of the palace was extensively restored in the 1950s and contains all you'd expect to find: azulejos, Arraiolos rugs, frescoed ceilings, priceless collections of silver and gold objects, Chinese vases, Gobelin tapestries, and a long dining hall adorned with antlers and other hunting trophies. The enormous kitchen is equipped with spits large enough to accommodate several oxen and enough gleaming copper to keep a small army of servants busy polishing. The apartments where the unfortunate Dom Carlos spent his last night have been maintained as they were. Carlos was quite an accomplished painter—some say a better painter than he was a king—and many of his works (along with private photos of Portugal's last royal family) line the walls of the apartments. ✉ 1,000$00. ⊙ Oct.–May, Tues.–Sun. 9:30–1 and 2–5; June–Sept., Tues.–Sun. 9:30–noon and 2–6.

Following the tour of the Ducal Palace you can visit the adjacent **Museu dos Coches** (Coach Museum), which features a collection of horse-drawn coaches and antique automobiles and is a pleasant postscript to your visit of the palace. However, if you've already seen the coach museum in Lisbon, you can skip this one. Vila Viçosa's is interesting but isn't in the same league. ✉ 200$00. ⊙ Oct.–May, Tues.–Sun. 9:30–1 and 2–5; June–Sept., Tues.–Sun. 9:30–noon and 2–6.

At the north end of the palace square is the **Knot Gate** with its massive stone ropes—an intriguing example of the Manueline style.

En Route Driving between Vila Viçosa and Borba you'll see mountainous dirt-and-rock piles strewn about the countryside. These tailings are evidence of the many local quarries and are the residue of centuries of extracting the high-quality marble. Marble is generously used throughout the region, even in the most modest of buildings.

Borba

③⓪ *4 km (2½ mi) northwest of Vila Viçosa.*

Borba is one of the Alentejo's major wine producers, and the town's vintners have won many national prizes. The village boasts a pleasant conglomeration of modest whitewashed houses, noble mansions, and small churches—all beautifully decorated with marble. Borba's most notable monument is the 18th-century **Fonte das Bicas,** a neoclassical white-marble fountain built to honor Queen Maria I, known as Maria the Pious, who reigned from 1777 to 1816.

Estremoz

③① *11 km (7 mi) west of Borba.*

Estremoz, which lies on the ancient road that connected Lisbon with Mérida, Spain, has been a site of strategic importance since Roman times, and the castle, which overlooks the town, was a crucial one of the Alentejo's many fortresses. Estremoz is most closely associated with Queen St. Isabel, though she spent only a short time here. Married to Dom Dinis—a Portuguese king—in 1282, she arrived in 1336 and after a brief stay became ill and died. The luxurious Pousada da Rainha Santa Isabel (☞ Dining and Lodging, *below*), which occupies the castle, was named for her. It was also in Estremoz in 1367 that the queen's grandson Pedro, the lover and secret husband of Inês de Castro, died. The Portuguese people loved Queen Saint Isabel and over the ages have handed down many tales and legends of her humility and charity. A statue in the castle square commemorates her. From atop the castle tower you'll have a magnificent view over the Alentejo plains.

The **Municipal Museum** is housed in a 16th-century almshouse across from the castle. Its displays chronicle the development of the region and range from Roman artifacts to contemporary pottery. ✉ 130$00. ⊙ Tues.–Sun. 9–11:45 and 2–6.

The lower town, a maze of narrow streets and white houses, radiates out from the **Rossío,** a huge, unpaved square. Stands lining it sell the colorful pottery for which Estremoz is so well known. In addition to the multicolored, hand-painted plates, pitchers, and dolls, note the earthenware jugs decorated with bits of local white marble.

NEED A
BREAK?

There are several refreshment stands and snack bars along the Rossío, but for more substantial fare try the **Café Alentejo.** From this popular 50-year-old café and restaurant, you can watch the goings-on in the square.

The tiny **Rural Museum,** on the opposite side of the Rossío from the Café Alentejo, is chock-full of handmade miniatures depicting various aspects of Alentejo country life. The museum was once a *Casa do Povo* (a sort of Portuguese senior citizens' center), where all the exhibits were originally made. Note that the finely carved bulls' horns are crafted in a fashion similar to that of the scrimshaw carvings of New England whalers. ☞ *100$00.* ☉ *Oct.–May, Tues.–Sun. 10–1 and 3–5; June–Sept., Tues–Sun. 10–1 and 2–6.*

Dining and Lodging

$ ✕ **Adega do Isaías.** Hidden away on a narrow side street a few min-
★ utes' walk from the town square, this is the best place in town for hearty, no-nonsense roasts and grilled meats. The front part of the former wine cellar is a rough-looking bar; walk through to the dining area—a sloping, cement-floored cave that's lined with huge terra-cotta wine jugs. During your meal you sit on benches at planked tables; expect the service to be casual, at best, but the food is great and the place—popular with the locals—is always jammed. ⊠ *Rua do Almeida 21,* ☎ *068/22318. No credit cards. Closed Sun.*

$$$$ ✕🏨 **Pousada da Rainha Santa Isabel.** Occupying a hilltop castle
★ steeped in history, this pousada is the most luxurious in the country. The sumptuous lobby and other public rooms display literally tons of gleaming Estremoz marble and are decorated with 15th-century tapestries, Arraioios rugs, and original paintings. The generous-size bedrooms are furnished with 17th- and 18th-century reproductions, and some of the rooms have elaborate four-poster beds. Just to sit in the baronial dining hall is a treat, and the food and service—in tune with the decor—are fit for a queen. ⊠ *Pousada da Rainha Santa Isabel, 7100,* ☎ *068/332075,* 🖷 *068/332079. 30 rooms, 3 suites. Restaurant, bar. AE, DC, MC, V.*

$ 🏨 **Monte Dos Pensamentos.** This comfortable old country manor
★ house surrounded by olive and orange trees is just 2 kilometers (1¼ miles) from Estremoz. The living room and large bedrooms are cluttered with enough painted plates, dolls, and antiques to stock a good-size museum. The mood is casual and relaxed, and guests typically sit around the fire and share the cozy sitting room. ⊠ *Estrada Estacão Ameixial, 7100,* ☎ *068/22375,* 🖷 *068/332709. 4 rooms. Bar, pool. No credit cards.*

Évoramonte

32 *17 km (10 mi) southwest of Estremoz, 42 km (26 mi) northeast of Évora.*

Évoramonte is a medieval town that sits along the western flank of the Serra da Ossa at an altitude of 1,550 feet. Drive up to the castle for a spectacular panoramic view that extends as far as the Serra da Estrela. The Évoramonte Castle, built in Italian Renaissance style, is distinguished by a massive round tower at each of its four corners. Also note the heavy Manueline ropes that run, like ribbons on a Christmas package, around the outside of the castle; they're joined together at the entrance with two tidy cement knots. (An interesting gastronomic aside: It was in Évoramonte that the famous *sopa Alentejana* is said to have originated. The convention held here in 1834 to end the civil war between the Liberals and the Miguelists took so long that by the end only stale bread was left to eat—and thus was born the popular Alentejo soup, made with stale bread, garlic, olive oil, coriander, and water.)

Elvas

33 *40 km (25 mi) east of Estremoz, 15 km (9 mi) west of the Spanish border town of Badajoz.*

Another of the white, fortified Alentejo towns, Elvas—because of its proximity to the Spanish town of Badajoz—was from its founding an important bastion in warding off attacks from the east. The extensive fortifications, 17th-century Portugal's most formidable, are characterized by a series of walls, moats, and reinforced towers. The enormity of the complex can be best appreciated by driving around the periphery of the town.

Another distinguishing landmark, the 8-kilometer (5-mile) **Amoreira Aqueduct**—which took more than a century to build—is still in use today. It was started in 1498 under the direction of one of the era's great architects, Francisco de Arruda—who also designed the Aqueduto da Agua da Prata (☞ *above*)—but not until 1622 did the first drops of water flow into the town fountain.

The former **Gothic cathedral,** within the town walls, is worth a visit if for no other reason than to see the 16th-century Manueline refurbishment designed by Francisco de Arruda. The blue-and-yellow azulejos lining the interior walls were added in the 17th century.

From the cathedral, which sits at the head of the Praça da República, walk up the hill past a pillory and two stone towers (spanned by a graceful Moorish loggia) to the **castle.** At the battlements you'll have a sweeping view of the town and its fortifications. ⊠ *Praça da República.* ☉ *Fri.–Wed. 9:30–12:30 and 2:30–5:30.*

Dining and Lodging

$$$$ ✕ 🏠 **Pousada de Santa Luzia.** Opened in 1942, this was Portugal's first
★ pousada, and its convenient location—just 12 kilometers (7 miles) from one of the major border crossings between Spain and Portugal—was no accident. The two-story, Moorish-style building has been remodeled several times, most recently in 1994. All bedrooms on the second floor are a good size and cheerfully decorated with hand-painted Alentejo furniture and bright floral fabrics. The modern tiled bathrooms are small but adequate. The large restaurant has arched windows overlooking an attractive garden and is a favorite with Elvas residents. One of the most popular dishes is *bacalhau dourado* (cod fish sautéed with eggs, potatoes, and onions). Reserve a room in advance of your visit. ⊠ *Pousada de Santa Luzia, 7350,* ☎ *068/622194,* 🏿𝖷 *068/622127. 24 rooms, 1 suite. Restaurant, bar, pool, tennis. AE, DC, MC, V.*

Campo Maior

34 *19 km (12 mi) northeast of Elvas.*

Campo Maior, surrounded by rows of gentle hills covered with the Alentejo's ubiquitous cork and olive trees, is a quiet, sparsely populated corner of the country where little has changed over the years. You may notice the smell of roasting coffee lingering in the air: It isn't coming from a nearby café but from the several coffee-roasting plants in the area. Campo Maior is the center of Portugal's coffee industry.

Try to make it to this town during the first week of September, when nearly 100 streets and squares are covered with a rainbow-colored mantle of paper flowers and decorations. The decorations for each neighborhood are a closely held secret for months, as the women nimbly assemble the paper flowers and the men construct the wooden framing. When the festival opens, all is revealed in a blaze of color and festivity. Check with the local or regional tourist office for exact dates.

At the top of the hill is a castle that was reconstructed after a disastrous explosion in 1732. As you walk around the fortifications, you'll notice some tiny whitewashed dwellings with laundry fluttering about like flags in the breeze. The little buildings are the old army barracks, the only part of the military complex still occupied. Before leaving Campo Maior, take time to stroll through the lower part of town, where the narrow streets are lined with many fine examples of wrought-iron grilles and balconies, giving the town a Spanish appearance.

Portalegre

 47 km (29 mi) northwest of Campo Maior.

Portalegre is the gateway to the Alentejo's most mountainous region, where the parched plains of the south give way to a greener, more inviting landscape. The town, which sits at the foot of the Serra de São Mamede, lacks the charm of the whitewashed hamlets in the south of the province but has long been noted for the quality of its tapestries.

Near the town center, on the second floor of an unmarked, dilapidated Jesuit monastery is a **tapestry factory** you can tour. Go up the stairs, turn left, and ring the bell. The workshop, Dickensian in appearance, is an ancient, wood-floored hall with two long rows of looms. World-famous tapestries—either copies of classical patterns or originals made to order—are handmade here. This is not a place for bargain hunters—it takes approximately two years to complete a piece, and the current price is about $6,000 per square meter. ⊠ *Rua Guilherme Gomes Fernandes 26,* ☎ *045/23283.* ▣ *Free.* ☉ *Weekdays 9:30–11 and 2:30–4:30.*

....

NEED A BREAK?   In the municipal park in the town center, the **O Tarro** restaurant and snack bar has a pleasant terrace, which overlooks a pond and the sprawling park.

....

To explore Portalegre, start at the park in the center of the lower town and walk uphill past a maze of shops and old houses to the twin-towered **cathedral.** The 18th-century facade of this, the town's most prominent landmark, is highlighted with marble columns and wrought-iron balconies. ☉ *Mon.–Sat. 8:30–11:30 and 3–6, Sun. 9–11:30.*

The **Municipal Museum,** in a former seminary next to the cathedral, contains a wealth of religious art, including a gilded, 16th-century Spanish pietà. ▣ *210$00.* ☉ *Wed.–Mon. 9:30–12:30 and 2–6.*

From the cathedral square, head east about 400 yards to the ruins of a once-formidable **castle,** whose tower walls afford a splendid view of the cathedral and its surroundings.

The **José Regio Museum,** just off the Avenida Poeta JoséRegio, roughly midway between the cathedral and the castle, was named for a local poet who died in 1969. He bequeathed his varied collection of religious and folk art to the museum, which is in his former home. ⊠ *Praça Município,* ☎ *045/23625.* 🖼 *210$00.* ⊙ *Tues.–Sun. 9:30–12:30 and 2–6.*

Dining and Lodging

$ ✕ **O Abrigo.** This small, very "local" restaurant is on a quiet street around the corner from the cathedral. The small, cork-lined dining room, presided over by owners Adriano and Pedro, is entered through a snack bar. One of the best dishes on the menu is the *açorda de marisco* (bread porridge with shellfish), served steaming hot in a terra-cotta bowl. ⊠ *Rua de Elvas 74,* ☎ *045/22778. MC, V. Closed Tues.*

$ ✕🖬 **Dom João III.** This modern multistoried hotel is across from the city park. Although the lobby and hallways are somewhat institutional, the rooms are more pleasant; many have balconies overlooking the park. The large top-floor restaurant, a favorite with local businessmen, is ringed with picture windows looking over the town. An international menu offers regional specialties. ⊠ *Av. da Liberdade, 7300,* ☎ *045/330192,* 🏛 *045/330444. 58 rooms, 2 suites. Restaurant, bar, pool. AE, DC, MC, V.*

Parque Natural da Serra de São Mamede

㊱ *5 km (3 mi) northeast of Portalegre.*

Rural in character, the sparsely inhabited 80,000-acre Parque Natural da Serra de São Mamede is made up of small family plots, and sheepherding is the major occupation. Portalegre is the principal gateway to this recently established national park, which extends north to the fortified town of Marvão and to the spa of Castelo de Vide and south to the little hamlet of Esperança, on the Spanish border. The region is rich in wildlife, including many rare species of birds, as well as wild boars, deer, and wildcats. This is not a spectacularly scenic park like Yellowstone or Yosemite but a quiet place for hiking, riding, or simply communing with nature. For information about activities, contact the park office. ⊠ *Praceta Herois da India 8, 7301 Portalegre,* ☎ *045/23631,* 🏛 *045/27501.*

Coudelaria de Alter

㊲ *22 km (14 mi) southwest of Portalegre. From Portalegre take N119 west for 21 km (13 mi), then turn south toward Alter do Chão. The farm is on a dusty track 3 km (2 mi) northwest of the town.*

If you're interested in horses, you must visit the Coudelaria Real (National Stud Farm), formerly the Royal Stud Farm, founded by Dom João V in 1748 to furnish royalty with high-quality mounts. The Coudelaria is the most important stud farm in Portugal. The town of Alter do Chão has an interesting castle opposite its main square. The road to the farm is marked COUDELARIA. If, at the farm, you try to speak Portuguese or you seem interested in horses, sympathetic employees may show you around. Otherwise, you can roam the farm yourself and look at the horses or maybe catch a training session. Of special interest is the annual horse auction held in late April. ⊙ *Daily 9:30–noon and 2–4:30.*

En Route For the most scenic approach to Marvão and the Serra de São Mamede from Portalegre, take N359 18 kilometers (11 miles) to Marvão. The narrow but well-surfaced serpentine N359 rises to an elevation of 2,800 feet, past stands of birch and chestnut trees and small vegetable gardens bordered by ancient stone walls. At Portagem take note of the well-preserved Roman bridge.

Marvão

★ ⏱️ *25 km (16 mi) northeast of Portalegre.*

The views of the mountains as you approach the fortress town of Marvão are spectacular, and the town's castle, perched atop a sheer rock cliff, commands a 360-degree panorama. Although it's possible to drive through the constricted streets of this medieval mountaintop village, Marvão is best appreciated on foot. First head for the castle and climb to the tower. From there you can trace the course of the massive Vauban-style stone walls (characterized by concentric lines of trenches and walls, a hallmark of the 17th-century French military engineer Vauban), adorned at intervals with bartizans, to enjoy breathtaking vistas from different angles. Given its strategic position, it's no surprise that Marvão has been a fortified settlement since Roman times or earlier. The present castle was built under Dom Dinis in the late 13th century and modified some four centuries later, during the reign of Dom João IV. At the foot of the path leading to the castle is the **Municipal Museum,** housed in the recently renovated 13th-century Church of Saint Mary. The small gallery contains a diverse collection of religious artifacts, azulejos, costumes, ancient maps, and weapons. 🎟️ *220$00.* ⏲️ *Daily 9–12:30 and 2–5:30.*

The village, with some 300 mostly older inhabitants, is laid out in several long rows of tidy, white stone dwellings terraced into the hill. The recently remodeled Pousada de Santa Maria (☞ Dining and Lodging, *below*) and the few guest houses and restaurants are well integrated into the village and do not detract from Marvão's pleasing traditional architecture.

Dining and Lodging

$$$$ ✕🏨 **Pousada de Santa Maria.** In 1976 several old houses within the
★ city walls were joined together to create the Pousada de Santa Maria. The rooms are decorated with traditional Alentejo furnishings, and the restaurant serves some of the best food in the village. Try some of the local favorites, such as *migas a Alentejana com carne de porco* (marinated pork with a bread-and-sausage stuffing). ⊠ *Rua 24 de Janiero 7, 7330,* ☎ *045/93201,* 🆇 *045/93440. 29 rooms. Restaurant, bar. AE, DC, MC, V.*

¢ 🏨 **Dom Dinis.** This comfortable country inn at the foot of the castle occupies a restored 200-year-old house with massive stone window and door frames. Bedrooms, which have fantastic cliffside views, are furnished with light pine furniture. ⊠ *Rua Dr. Matos Magalháes, 7330,* ☎ *045/93236,* 🆇 *045/93236. 9 rooms. Restaurant, bar. AE, DC, MC, V.*

Santo António das Areias

⏱️ *5 km (3 mi) northeast of Marvão. Head north from Marvão on the small country road and follow signs to Santo António das Areias.*

Scattered among the chestnut groves at Santo António das Areias are some two dozen prehistoric dolmens.

Castelo de Vide

⏱️ *8 km (5 mi) west of Marvão. An intriguing backcountry lane connects Marvão with Castelo de Vide. About halfway down the hill from Marvão, turn to the right toward Escusa and continue through the chestnut- and acacia-covered hills to Castelo de Vide.*

A quiet, hilltop spa town, Castelo de Vide is graced with flowers, which sprout from nearly every nook and cranny. When you encounter the local people, it will be clear that the beauty of Castelo de Vide has reached the hearts of its residents, who have kind and gentle natures. The large, baroque Praça Dom Pedro V is bordered by the Church of Santa Maria and the town hall. An alleyway to the right of the church leads to the village fountain, which taps one of the many springs in the area. (The waters are alleged to cure a wide variety of disorders ranging from diabetes to dermatitis.) The canopied, clam-shape marble fountain is the town symbol.

A cobblestone alley leads from the fountain up to the *Juderia* (Jewish Quarter). On the Rua da Juderia is a **medieval synagogue,** a modest, one-story building that was once the center of a thriving Jewish community. In medieval times, as the town prospered, many Jews and Marranos (Jews forced to convert to Christianity) settled here. ▨ *Free.* ⊙ *Oct.–May, daily 10–5:30; June–Sept., daily 10–8.*

As you walk along, notice the many houses with Gothic doorways and their various designs. (The tourist brochures proclaim that Castelo de Vide has the largest number of Gothic doorways of any town in Portugal.) From the Juderia it's a short climb to the ruins of the **castle.** Go up into the tower and inside the well-preserved keep to the large Gothic hall, which has a picture window looking down on the town square and the church. ▨ *Free.* ⊙ *Oct.–May, daily 10–5:30; June–Sept., daily 10–8.*

Dining and Lodging

$ ✕ **O Cantinho Particular.** This tiny place on a side street near the town square engages the help of all the family members—Mom cooks while Dad and Junior take care of the customers. The dining room is old but clean, and the basic Portuguese fare is simple and tasty. Your best bet is to ask Senhor Bernardo what he recommends. ⊠ *Rua Miguel Bombarda 9,* ☎ *045/91151. No credit cards.*

$ ✕▥ **Sol e Serra.** This modern, three-story, Mediterranean-style hotel sitting at the edge of town is just a five-minute walk to the castle and the Juderia. Large rooms have balconies looking over the park, and the bar with its spacious lounge, which overlooks the pool, is the town's most popular gathering place. The tastefully decorated restaurant with wooden beams is considered Castelo de Vide's best eatery and is one of the few places in Portugal that offers a kosher menu. ⊠ *Estrada de São Vincente, 7320,* ☎ *045/91301,* ℻ *045/91337. 51 rooms. Restaurant, bar, pool. AE, DC, MC, V.*

THE LOWER ALENTEJO

Extending south of Évora and from the rugged west-coast beaches east to the border with Spain, the Lower Alentejo, Portugal's principal grain-producing area, is a vast, mostly flat region of wheat fields, cork oaks, and olive trees. It rains very little here, and the summer months are particularly hot. The towns are discussed in the order you would visit them if traveling south from Évora.

Numbers in the margin correspond to points of interest on the Lower Alentejo map.

Beja

❹ *257 km (160) mi southeast of Lisbon, 128 km (80 mi) south of Évora.*

Spread across a small knoll midway between Spain and the sea is Beja, the Lower Alentejo's principal agricultural center. In the town's streets and squares, shepherds wearing broad-brimmed hats, and the traditional sheepskin vests mingle with the townspeople. In the fields at the edge of town, gypsies still set up camp, with makeshift tents, horse carts, and open campfires. These scenes from a rapidly disappearing way of life contrast sharply with the modern improvements taking place in the region, and much of the old part of Beja still retains a significantly Arabic flavor, the legacy of more than 400 years of Moorish occupation. Students of the Portuguese language even claim that the local dialect has Arabic characteristics.

Beja, founded by Julius Caesar and known as Pax Julia, was an important town in the Roman province of Lusitania during the first century. The name Pax Julia was chosen because it was here, after a long struggle, that peace was finally established between the Lusitanian chiefs and Julius Caesar. Roman artifacts can be seen at the Museu Regional on the second floor of the convent (☞ *below*) and at the excavations in nearby Pizões.

Facing a broad plaza in the center of the old town, the **Convento da Conceição,** once a Moorish *mesquita* (mosque), was founded in 1459 by the parents of King Manuel I. Favored by the royal family, the Franciscan convent thrived and became one of the richest of the period. The church and cloisters display some fine azulejos from the 16th and 17th centuries, including panels depicting scenes from the life of St. John the Baptist, and a section of multicolored Moorish tiles. Upstairs, at the far end of the second-floor gallery, is the famous "Mariana Window," named after a young Beja nun, Mariana Alcoforado. As the story goes, Mariana fell in love with a French count named Chamilly, who was in the Alentejo fighting the Spaniards. When he went back to France, the nun waited longingly and in vain at the window for him to return. The 1669 publication in France of five passionate love letters, known as the *Portuguese Letters,* written by Mariana to the count, documented the scandalous affair and brought a measure of lasting international literary fame to this provincial Alentejo town. ⊠ *Largo da Conceição.* 🎟 *150$00.* ⊙ *Tues.–Sun. 9:45–1:30 and 2–5:15.*

The **Visigoth Museum,** next door in the 6th-century Visigoth Church of Santo Amaro, houses an impressive collection of artifacts, such as tombstones, weapons, and pottery, which help document the Visigoth presence in the region. ⊠ *Largo da Conceição.* 🎟 *150$00.* ⊙ *Tues.–Sun. 9:45–1:30 and 2–5:15.*

The **Church of Santa Maria,** across the square from the convent, can be easily recognized by its massive round pillars, Mudejar arches, and its bell tower similar in design to that of the famed Giralda Tower in Seville.

NEED A
BREAK?

The **Café Pastelaria Santa Maria,** opposite the church, has outside tables looking out on the convent square and is a pleasant spot for cake and coffee or a light lunch.

Beja Castle is an extensive system of fortifications, whose crenellated walls and towers chronicle the history of the town from its Roman occupation through its 19th-century battles with the French. The castle keep houses a military museum where weapons dating to the 16th century are displayed. 🎟 *150$00.* ⊙ *Oct.–May, Tues.–Sun. 9–noon and 1–4; June–Sept., Tues.–Sun. 10–1 and 2–6.*

Dining and Lodging

$ ✕ **Gatus.** In a quiet alley close to the convent, the Gatus is a small, intimate establishment, with a marble floor and wood paneling, and is one of the best choices in this restaurant-poor town. The *ensopado de borrego* (lamb stew) and the *bife Gatus* (braised beef with mushrooms and cream) are recommended. ✉ *Rua João Conforte 16–18,* ☎ *084/25418. MC, V. Closed Mon.*

$$$$ ✕🔛 **Pousada do Convento de São Francisco.** This recently opened pousada fulfills a longstanding need for first-rate accommodations in the Beja region. Although little remains of the original 13th-century convent, the conversion has been accomplished in a tasteful manner, and the guest rooms are comfortably furnished. The pousada has an excellent restaurant and spacious gardens, and its ancient chapel has been largely preserved and incorporated into the complex. ✉ *Largo Dom Nuno Alvares Pereira, 7800,* ☎ *084/328441,* FAX *084/329143. 34 rooms, 1 suite. Restaurant, bar, pool, tennis, chapel. AE, DC, MC, V.*

¢ 🔛 **Cristina.** This comfortable pensão occupies a modern five-story building, conveniently located on one of the main shopping streets. Light and airy rooms are a bit sterile. ✉ *Rua de Mértola 71, 7800,* ☎ *084/323035,* FAX *084/329874. 28 rooms, 3 suites. Bar. AE, DC, MC, V.*

Outdoor Activities and Sports

AIR EXCURSIONS

To enjoy a thrilling bird's-eye view of Beja and its surroundings, take a sightseeing flight in a small plane or in a microlight aircraft. For details and reservations, contact **Aerobeja** (✉ Aeródromo Civil de Beja, ☎ 084/327003, FAX 084/328279).

Serpa

㊷ *29 km (18 mi) southeast of Beja.*

A sleepy agricultural town that seems to have missed the train of progress and development that's changed much of Portugal, Serpa is a place where men pass the time by gathering together in the compact Praça da República under the shadow of the ancient stone clock tower. Unemployment is high, and there is little else for many to do. In tiny cubbyholes along narrow, cobbled streets, carpenters, shoemakers, basket weavers, and other craftsmen work in much the same manner as their forefathers did generations earlier.

From the 13th-century castle walls, you can get a stunning view of the town. Note how an aqueduct forms an integral part of the walls. As for the huge ruined sections of wall tottering precariously above the entrance, they're the result of explosions ordered by the Duke of Ossuna during the 18th-century War of the Spanish Succession. Within the castle walls there's a small **municipal museum** with a particularly unusual exhibit—a life-size, bronze-color papier-mâché replica of the *Last Supper.* 🎫 *100$00.* ☉ *Tues.–Sun. 9–12:30 and 2–5:30.*

Dining and Lodging

$$$$ ✕🔛 **Pousada de São Gens.** Perched on a hill next to the Chapel of
★ Guadalupe and overlooking the white houses and fortifications of Serpa, this modern, white-domed, Moorish-style pousada offers a relaxed and informal lodging option. The Arabic influence continues as you walk through the green-tiled entrance to the lobby with its many arches and vaulted ceilings. Each of the rooms has a small terrace, and bright, cheery fabrics nicely offset the white walls and ceilings. The restaurant has a small, brick-floored dining room with an open fireplace, and in summer guests may dine on the terrace looking over the pool and

the plains. Tasty local specialties include *poejada de bacalhau* (dried cod fried with bread and seasoned with pennyroyal). ⊠ *Pousada de São Gens, 7830,* ☎ *084/53724,* 𝐅𝐀𝐗 *084/53337. 16 rooms, 2 suites. Restaurant, bar, pool. AE, DC, MC, V.*

Vidigueira

㊸ *32 km (20 mi) northwest of Serpa. For the most scenic route head north from Serpa on N265, a narrow road that parallels the Rio Guadiana as it runs through an isolated stretch of rolling hills and cork trees. At the intersection with N258, follow signs to Vidigueira.*

Vidigueira, a quiet farm town in the middle of the Alentejo plain, is best known as the onetime home of Vasco da Gama, the Portuguese explorer whose voyage in 1497 opened the sea route to India. A statue of him stands in the main square. At the edge of town, in a setting of gardens and ponds, is the Carmelite chapel where the explorer's body lay from the time it was returned from India in 1539 until it was moved in 1898 to Lisbon's Jeronimos Monastery.

Roman Ruins of São Cucufate

㊹ *5 km (3 mi) west of Vidigueira.*

Standing in an olive orchard are the 2,000-year-old ruins of a Roman villa. The two-story building, the Ruins of São Cucufate, was part of an extensive Roman settlement. (Coins and other artifacts that have turned up indicate a 1st-century Roman presence here.) It's believed that the ground floor was used as a barn, with the living quarters above it. Remnants of the original heating and drainage systems are visible. The building was later adapted and used in the 13th century as a convent; the frescoes were done in the late 15th and early 16th centuries and have not been restored. 🏷 *Free; donations accepted.* ☉ *Tues.–Fri. 10–noon and 2–5.*

Alvito

㊺ *11 km (7 mi) west of the Ruins of São Cucufate.*

Alvito is a typical, sleepy Alentejo town that occupies a low hill above the Rio Odivelas. Noted for its fortress-like 13th-century parish church, the town also boasts a rectangular, early 16th-century castle—recently converted into a pousada—with round towers at three of its corners and a number of fine Mudejar windows. In the village a surprising number of modest houses bear graceful Manueline doorways and windows.

Dining and Lodging

$$$$ ✗🏨 **Pousada do Castelo de Alvito.** This recently opened pousada is within the walls of a 15th-century fortress at the edge of the village. The essential architectural elements of a castle, including crenellated battlements and massive round towers, have been retained, and there is a large garden and courtyard. The cozy restaurant serves a variety of Alentejo specialties, including an excellent *caldeirada de bacalhau* (codfish stew). ⊠ *Castelo de Alvito, 7920,* ☎ *084/48343,* 𝐅𝐀𝐗 *084/48383. 20 rooms. Restaurant, bar, pool, chapel. AE, DC, MC, V.*

Viana do Alentejo

㊻ *10 km (6 mi) north of Alvito.*

The castle at Viana do Alentejo, with its rough stone walls, brick battlements, and round turrets, is one of the most attractive in the Alentejo. It was constructed in 1313 to the very specific orders of Dom Dinis, who decreed that the pentagonal walls be tall enough that a horseman with a lance measuring nine covados (an ancient unit of measure equal to 66 centimeters, or 26 inches) couldn't injure anyone on the battlements. The fortified parish church within the walls of the castle—designed by the famous Diogo de Arruda—has an eye-pleasing combination of battlements, spires, and ornate Manueline elements. Below the castle a delightful Renaissance fountain enhances the town square. Viana do Alentejo is also noted for a primitive-style pottery, sold in several of the small shops in town.

Alcácer do Sal

47 *46 km (29 mi) northwest of Alvito, 60 km (37 mi) southwest of Évora. For the most scenic route from Alvito, take N383 southwest and west to Torrão, then follow N5 west, close to the Rio Sado through a sparsely populated region of pine and olive trees, to Alcácer do Sal.*

Because of its favored location and its salt, Alcácer do Sal was one of the first inhabited sites in Portugal; parts of the castle foundations are around 5,000 years old. The Greeks were here, and, of course, the Romans, who established the town of Salatia Urbs Imperatoria—a key intersection in their system of Lusitanian roads. During the Moorish occupation, under the name of Alcácer de Salaria, this became one of the most important Muslim strongholds in all of Iberia. In the 16th century Alcácer prospered as a major producer of salt, and a brisk trade was conducted with the northern European countries, which used it to preserve herring. The hilltop castle is the town's most prominent attraction. A series of red-tile-roofed buildings descend from the castle in long, horizontal rows, reaching down the hill to the riverbank.

The marshlands and the estuary of the Sado River that extend to the west of Alcácer form the **Reserva Natural do Sado** (Sado River Nature Reserve). The riverbanks are lined with extensive salt pans and rice paddies, and the reserve gives shelter to wildlife such as dolphin, otter, white stork, and egret. From the beach town of Comporta, Route N261 runs south along the coast through a mostly deserted stretch of dunes and pine trees with some wonderful, undeveloped sandy beaches.

Dining and Lodging

$-$$ ✕ **O Brazão.** Don't be put off by the run-down exterior of this no-frills restaurant: It's the favorite eating place of local businesspeople. The open kitchen allows you to peek in and see for yourself what looks good. Sample the *ensopa da garoupa* (fish stew), a typical dish from this part of the country. ⊠ *Largo Prof. Francisco Gentil,* ☎ *065/62576. No credit cards. Closed Sun.*

$ ✕🛏 **Pousada do Vale do Gaio.** Twenty-seven kilometers (16 miles) east of Alcácer do Sal and 8 kilometers (5 miles) from Torrão in a secluded wooded area overlooking a man-made lake, this small, rustic lodge was built to house the engineers who constructed the nearby dam. In 1977 it was converted into a pousada and has become a favorite spot for hunters and fishermen. The rooms are utilitarian but comfortable and look out over the lake, and a surprising variety of excellent local dishes comes out of the tiny restaurant. This is a good place to get away from it all. At press time the Pousada was being remodeled and was scheduled to reopen in January 1997. ⊠ *Pousada do Vale do Gaio, 7595 Torrão,* ☎ *065/669610. 7 rooms. Restaurant, bar, fishing. AE, DC, MC, V.*

Santiago do Cacém

48 *40 km (24 mi) southwest of Alcácer do Sal, 64 km (40 mi) west of Beja.*

Santiago do Cacém, about 16 kilometers (10 miles) inland at the junction of N120 and N261, is a quiet regional market town. The castle, built by the Knights of the Order of Santiago (St. James) on the site of Moorish ruins, dominates the town and affords sweeping views to the sea, marred only by the oil refineries at Sines. Inside the parish church, which is surrounded by fortifications, you can see a sculpture of St. James battling the Moors. The old town, which occupies a maze of narrow streets just below the castle, has a number of well-preserved 17th- and 18th-century manor houses. The **regional museum,** housed in a former prison in the center of town, offers several well-organized exhibits portraying various aspects of Alentejo life, including one that shows the stages of and the implements used in cork production. ⌧ *120$00.* ☉ *Sun.–Thurs. 10–12:30 and 2–5:30.*

At the edge of town, just off of the road to Lisbon, you can explore the excavations of the Roman city of **Miróbriga.** Originally this site was settled by the Celts in the 4th century BC; later, in the 1st century, it became a Roman town. The ruins, although not nearly as extensive or well preserved as those at Conímbriga near Coimbra, contain the interesting sanctuaries of Venus and Esculapius (god of medicine). The excavations—some of which were done in the 1980s by a team from the University of Missouri—are not currently being worked. ⊠ *Rd. to Lisbon.* ⌧ *100$00.* ☉ *Oct.–May, Tues.–Sun. 9–noon and 1–5:30; June–Sept., Tues.–Sun. 9–1 and 2:45–6:45.*

Dining and Lodging

$$ ✕ **O Retiro.** The joint efforts of an Austrian and his Portuguese wife
★ have turned this Alentejo cottage in the heart of town into a cozy international restaurant. Farm implements adorning the walls help set a down-home tone in this friendly but professional restaurant, which also serves good solid Portuguese fare. ⊠ *Rua Machado dos Santos 8,* ☎ *069/22659. AE, MC, V. Closed Sun.*

$ ✕▥ **Pousada de Santiago.** Sitting atop a small rise at the end of town
★ is this rose-color, ivy-clad manor house surrounded by mature trees and gardens. One of the first pousadas created, the Santiago has had time to cultivate comfort. Over the years its guest and public rooms have been extensively remodeled so that visitors feel almost as if they're staying in a private house. Some rooms have views of the castle; all units are furnished with decorative Alentejan pieces. As for the restaurant, the intimate dining room has a wood-beamed ceiling and a tiled fireplace, and you'll be served good-quality local favorites such as *carne de porco Alentejana* (pork and clams). In summer the terrace opens up for meals under the stars. ⊠ *Pousada de Santiago, 7540,* ☎ 🅵🅰🆇 *069/22459. 8 rooms. Restaurant, bar, pool. AE, DC, MC, V.*

$ ✕▥ **Quinta da Ortiga.** This lovely old country estate, just 5 kilome-
★ ters (3 miles) from Santiago do Cacém, sits amid 10 acres of trees and farmland. Its interior decor—wood-panel ceilings and Arraiolos carpets—can best be described as "luxury rustic." The ambience is reminiscent of a comfortable rural villa, and the intimate restaurant, which serves the cuisine of the region, is more like an old-style family dining room than a commercial establishment. Try this inn—managed by Enatur, the government organization that also handles the pousadas—for a quiet, comfortable base from which to enjoy the Alentejo's beaches. ⊠ *Apartado 67, 7540,* ☎ *069/22871,* 🅵🅰🆇 *069/22073. 14 rooms. Restaurant, bar, pool, horseback riding, chapel. AE, DC, MC, V. 7-night stay with ½ board required July–Sept.*

Outdoor Activities and Sports

HORSEBACK RIDING

For instruction and for riding on the beach at nearby Sines, contact **Centro Equestre de Santo André** (⊠ Monte V. Cima, Santo André, ☎ 069/71235).

Vila Nova de Milfontes

🔞 *32 km (20 mi) southwest of Santiago do Cacém.*

Although the town itself is just another small beach resort without any special architectural merit, the location of Vila Nova de Milfontes at the broad mouth of the Rio Mira is delightful, and it has soft, sandy beaches on both sides of the river. Overlooking the sea is an ivy-covered fortress built on Moorish foundations in the late 16th century to protect Milfontes from the Algerian pirates who regularly terrorized the Portuguese coast. With the subsiding of the pirate threat, the fortress was abandoned and the ruins were sold at auction in 1906; in 1939 it was taken over by the present owner, who has converted it into a delightful inn called the Castelo de Milfontes (☞ Dining and Lodging, *below*).

Dining and Lodging

$ ✕ **O Quebra Mar.** If you're looking for fresh grilled fish and a fantastic view of the estuary and sand dunes, there's no better place in town than this simple beach bar-restaurant. ⊠ *End of Beach Rd at Praia da Franquia,* ☎ *083/99263. DC, MC, V.*

$ 🏨 **Castelo de Milfontes.** This 16th-century castle was built on ancient
★ foundations, for it was believed that the spirits there would ward off marauding Algerian pirates. In recent times owner and hostess Dona Margarida de Castro e Almeida has lovingly transformed this ivy-covered edifice into a comfortable guest house. Nearly everything you would expect a castle to have is still intact: battlements, a drawbridge, a moat, and a suit of armor. The rooms are comfortably furnished and offer inspiring views over the dunes and estuary. There is no public restaurant, but the hotel provides meals for guests in a lovely, intimate, family-style dining area lined with tiles. Full board is required. ⊠ *Castelo de Milfontes, 7645,* ☎ *083/96108. 7 rooms. Bar. No credit cards.*

ÉVORA AND THE ALENTEJO A TO Z

Arriving and Departing

By Bus

Euroline has regular bus service between Lisbon and Spain's Costa del Sol, Seville, Madrid, and Barcelona. Euroline coaches also stop in the Alentejo towns of Elvas and Estremoz. For information and reservations in Lisbon, contact a travel agent or **Intercentro Eurolines** (⊠ Rua Eng. Viera da Silva 8-E, ☎ 01/547300).

By Car

Three main roads connect the Alentejo with Spain: The N521 runs 105 kilometers (64 miles) from Caceres, Spain, to the Portuguese border near Portalegre; the N4 covers the 15 kilometers (9 miles) between Elvas and the Spanish city of Badajoz; and to the south the N433 runs from Seville, Spain, to Beja, 225 kilometers (136 miles) away. The Alentejo can also be easily reached from the Algarve, its southern neighbor. The fastest and smoothest of the main routes is the IP–1/N264, which extends north from Albufeira.

By Plane

Évora and the Alentejo can be conveniently reached either from Lisbon or Faro airports. Évora is 160 kilometers (100 miles) from Lisbon and 245 kilometers (147 miles) from Faro.

For flight information concerning Lisbon, *see* Chapter 2; for information about Faro's airport, *see* Chapter 6.

Getting Around

By Bus

There are few, if any places in this region that are not served by at least one bus daily. Express coaches run by several regional bus lines travel regularly between Lisbon and the larger towns such as Évora, Beja and Estremoz. If you have the time and patience, bus travel, which offers an opportunity to come in close contact with locals, can be a rewarding and inexpensive way to get around. The main bus terminal in Lisbon is at Avenida Casal Ribeira 18. For schedules call ☎ 01/545439.

By Car

A car is by far the most efficient way to tour the Alentejo, where distances are great and bus and train service infrequent. Driving will give you access to many out-of-the-way beaches and villages. The roads are generally good, and traffic is light. There are no confusing big cities in which to get lost, although parking can be a problem in some of the towns such as Évora. The best map for motorists, both in scale and ease of reading, is the Michelin map #440, Portugal–Madeira, available at bookstores throughout Portugal; in the United States go to any major bookstore or contact **Michelin Travel Publications** (✉ 1 Parkway S, Greenville, SC 29615, ☎ 803/458–6330).

By Train

Travel by train in the vast Alentejo is not for people in a great hurry. Service to many of the more remote destinations is infrequent—and in some cases nonexistent. The towns of Alcácer do Sal, Évora, and Beja are connected with Lisbon (Terreiro do Paço) by several trains daily.

Contacts and Resources

Car Rental

Major car-rental agencies include **Hertz** (✉ Donna Isabel 7/13, Évora, ☎ 066/21767) and **Europcar** (✉ Rua Angola 3–5, Beja, ☎ 084/328128).

Emergencies

For emergencies in central Portugal, as well as throughout the country, dial **115.**

Guided Tours

Few regularly scheduled sightseeing tours originate within the region, but many of the major attractions are covered by a wide selection of one-day tours from Lisbon. For information in Lisbon, contact **RN Tours** (✉ Av. Fontes Pereira de Melo 12–14, ☎ 01/356–0015) or **Cityrama** (✉ Av. Praia da Vitoria 12–B, ☎ 01/355–8567).

Walking tours of Évora and bus tours of the Alentejo are available from **Mendes and Murteira** (✉ Rua Corredoura 8, 7000 Évora, ☎ 066/23616).

Hospitals

The following cities have hospitals with emergency rooms, and their approaches are marked HOSPITAL; the emergency room is marked URGÊNCIAS: Beja (✉ Hospital Distrital, Rua Dr. António F C Lima, ☎

084/322133) and Évora (⊠ Hospital Distrital, Largo Sr. Pobreza, ☎ 066/22133).

Late-Night Pharmacies

All sizable towns have at least one pharmacy open weekends, holidays, and after normal store hours. Local newspapers usually keep a schedule, and notices are posted on the door of every pharmacy.

Lodging

For information about pousadas (guest houses), contact **Promoções e Idéias Turísticas** (⊠ Rua Fredrico Arouca 72, 2750 Cascais, ☎ 01/484–4207, FAX 01/484–2901).

Travel Agencies

Many travel agencies in the region are small, with limited services, and no English spoken. In Évora, **Touralentejo** (⊠ Rua Miguel Bombarda 7, ☎ 066/22717, FAX 066/29231) has English-speaking personnel and a full range of services.

Visitor Information

The regional tourist office for Évora is the **Região de Turismo de Évora** (⊠ Rua 24 de Julho 1, ☎ 066/742535).

LOWER ALENTEJO

In the Lower Alentejo there are tourist offices in **Beja** (⊠ Praça da Repúlica 12, ☎ 084/321369), **Moura** (⊠ Largo Santa Clara, ☎ 085/22301), **Odemira** (⊠ Trav. do Botequim 6, ☎ 083/22247), **Serpa** (⊠ Largo D. Jorge de Melo 2–3, ☎ 084/90335), and **Sines** (⊠ Jardim das Descobertas, ☎ 069/634472).

UPPER ALENTEJO

For the Upper Alentejo the regional office is the **Região de Turismo de São Mamede** (⊠ Estrada de Santana 25, 7300 Portalegre, ☎ 045/21815). There are local offices in **Alcácer do Sal** (⊠ Solar dos Salemas, ☎ 065/622603), **Alter do Chão** (⊠ Câmera Municipal, ☎ 045/62454), **Arronches** (⊠ Câmera Municipal, ☎ 045/52210), **Campo Maior** (⊠ Rua Mayor Talaya, ☎ 068/688936), **Castelo de Vide** (⊠ Rua Bartolomeu A. da Santa 81/3, ☎ 045/91361), **Elvas** (⊠ Praça da República, ☎ 068/622236), **Évora** (⊠ Praça do Giraldo 73, ☎ 066/22671), **Marvão** (⊠ Rua Dr. Matos Magalhães, ☎ 045/93226), **Monforte** (⊠ Praça da República, ☎ 045/53448), and **Portalegre** (⊠ Rua de Elvas, ☎ 045/21815).

6 The Algarve

Clean, sandy beaches and excellent sports facilities dot Portugal's southern coast, as do apartment complexes, hotels, discos, and bars, which sprout from every bay and cliff top. At the shore, interesting rock formations and grottoes make beaches more than sand and surf, while the inland countryside has a simple, rural atmosphere that seems a world away.

By Jules Brown

Updated by
Dennis Jaffe

PORTUGAL'S SOUTHERNMOST COASTAL REGION, the Algarve is the most favored destination of foreign visitors to the country. It's a well-known holiday center, with clean, sandy beaches and excellent sports facilities coupled with an equable climate and dining and lodging choices to suit all budgets. Many Europeans fly here directly and rarely stray more than a few miles from their resorts. Even for those visitors based in Lisbon, the Algarve is an easy 300-kilometer (186-mile) drive south, and it provides an interesting contrast to the rest of the country.

Along with the region's popularity has come progress, and during the past two decades, the Algarve has been heavily developed, with parts of the once pristine, 240-kilometer (149-mile) coastline now seriously overbuilt. In certain areas apartment complexes, hotels, discos, and bars sprout from every bay and cliff top.

Until the construction of the airport at Faro in the '60s, the Algarve was rarely visited by tourists, and for centuries before that it remained isolated from the rest of Europe. Phoenicians, Romans, and Visigoths established fishing and trading communities here, but it wasn't until the arrival of the Moors in the 8th century that the region became an important strategic settlement. It was the Moors who gave the province its name—El Gharb (the Land to the West)—and who established their capital at the inland town of Silves (then called Chelb). In those days it had direct access to the sea and at its peak was a grand city with a population of more than 30,000. Although Silves fell to the Christians in 1189, the Moors weren't completely out of the region until the middle of the 13th century, leaving many tangible reminders of their 500-year rule: Arabic place-names; the white, cubelike houses in the coastal fishing villages; the popular fruits and sweets of the region; and the physical features of many of the people.

In the 15th century Prince Henry the Navigator established a town and a pioneering navigation school near Sagres, where principles were developed that would enable Portuguese mariners of the 16th century to explore much of the world. After this flurry of activity, though, the Algarve once again settled into obscurity.

The region, a mere 40 kilometers (25 miles) long, is bordered on the north by the Serra de Monchique (Monchique Mountains) and the Serra de Caldeirão (Caldeirão Mountains) and on the east by the Rio Guadiana, a river that isolated the Algarve from contact with neighboring Spain. Over the centuries the region's geography has both enabled inhabitants to keep to themselves and provided many natural advantages. Its location in the south, protected by hills, makes the Algarve much warmer than any other place in the country. The vegetation is far more luxuriant; the land, originally irrigated by the Moors, supports a profusion of fruits, nuts, and vegetables; and the fishing industry has always flourished.

Despite development, the region still makes a fine coastal vacation spot. There are small fishing villages and secluded beaches, particularly in the west, that so far have escaped attention; an abundance of extraordinary rock formations and idyllic grottoes, also in the west; and to the east, a series of isolated sandbar islands and sweeping beaches that balance the crowded excesses of the middle. Even where tourist development is at its heaviest, new construction takes the form of landscaped villa and apartment complexes made of local materials, which not only fit in well with the surroundings but also keep money circulating within the community. However, to see the Algarve at its best, it's often necessary to abandon the popular beaches for a drive inland. Here, rural Portugal still survives in hill villages, market towns, and agricultural landscapes, which, though only a few miles from the coast, seem a world away in attitude.

One word of warning: The Algarve is one of Europe's most popular sites for vacation and retirement homes. If you didn't know that before you arrived, you'll soon get the picture in towns such as Albufeira and Praia da Rocha, where an entire industry exists to persuade visitors to tour apartment developments and proposed sites in the hopes that they'll sign on the dotted line. You may be approached by agents offering all sorts of inducements (such as free gifts, meals, and drinks) to encourage you to visit time-share properties and villa complexes. Even if you do agree to go on a tour, *never* sign anything, regardless of the promises made.

Pleasures and Pastimes

Beaches

The glory of the Algarve is its beaches, which are generally clear and impressive, some of the finest in the country. There are hundreds from which to choose on the long stretch of coast. Most beaches (especially those in the main resorts) have snack bars and showers, and many have water-sports equipment for rent. Remember that although it's possible to wade out for a swim from most Algarve beaches, you should heed local warnings about currents and steeply sloping seabeds.

The best cove beaches are at Lagos. Interesting beaches with enormous rock formations include those at Albufeira and Praia da Rocha. If you require more breathing space, particularly if traveling with young children, try the strands near Olhão and Tavira; these and the beaches near Sagres are less populated than those at major resorts.

Dining

Algarvian cooking is of very high quality, and menus usually feature local seafood whose quality is worthy of the cooking. Take, for example, that most unusual of regional appetizers: *espadarte fumada* (smoked swordfish), which is sliced thin, served with a salad, and best appreciated if accompanied by a dry white wine. Most restaurants serve their own version of *sopa de peixe* (fish soup) and a variety of succulent shellfish: *perceves* (barnacles), *santola* (crab), and *gambas* (shrimp). Main courses often depend on what has been landed that day, but there's generally a choice of *robalo* (sea bass), *pargo* (bream), *atum* (tuna), and espadarte. Perhaps the most famous Algarvian dish is *cataplana,* a stew of clams, pork, onions, tomatoes, and wine, which takes its name from the lidded utensil used to steam the dish. You will generally have to wait for cataplana to be specially prepared, but once you've tasted it, you won't mind waiting again and again.

In inland rural areas, game highlights most menus, with many meat dishes served *o forno* (oven roasted). Specialties include *cabrito* (kid), *leitão* (suckling pig), and *codorniz* (quail), as well as *ensopado de borrego* (lamb stew).

You don't need to dine in a proper restaurant to taste the Algarve's best. At simple beach cafés and harbor stalls the unmistakable smell of *sardinhas assadas* (charcoal-grilled sardines) permeates the air—they make a tempting lunch served with fresh bread and smooth red wine. Alfresco dining is possible all year, and in any season you're assured a wonderful array of fresh fruit and nuts—the Algarve is particularly known for its almonds, oranges, and figs.

For dessert there are rich egg, sugar, and almond custards that reflect the Moorish influence, including *doces de amendoa* (marzipan cakes in the shapes of animals and flowers), *bolos de Dom Rodrigo* (almond sweets with egg-and-sugar filling), *bolo Algarvio* (cake made of sugar, almonds, eggs, and cinnamon), and *morgado de figos do Algarve* (fig-and-almond paste).

Unless otherwise noted, casual dress is acceptable throughout the Algarve. Reservations are not needed off-season, but in summer, you'll need them at most of the better restaurants. In the larger resorts there are dozens of places serving good food of comparable price and quality.

Festivals

Most towns in the Algarve have annual festivals lasting several days, and locals and tourists alike join in the parades and celebrations. Nearly every town and village also features religious celebrations during Easter week and on St. John's Eve (June 23–24). The Algarve Regional Tourist Board produces a monthly calendar of events, available at local tourist offices and hotels, and provides information on the annual International Algarve Music Festival, a series of concerts and recitals throughout May and June, sponsored by the Gulbenkian Foundation.

Fishing

The best fishing grounds are considered to be the waters off Sagres and Carrapateira (on the west coast), and local fishermen recommend October through January as the most fruitful—or should we say fishful—months. You're likely to catch gray mullet, sea bass, moray eels, scabbard fish, and bluefish. Individuals and charter companies offer organized fishing trips from various ports along the coast. Check the boards on quaysides for prices and departure times or consult local tourist offices.

Golf

The Algarve has some of Europe's best golf courses, designed by the likes of Henry Cotton, Frank Pennink, and William Cotton. It's a year-round game here, and most courses have a clubhouse with bar and restaurant, practice grounds, and equipment rentals. Several courses are currently under construction (ask at local tourist offices for information and a copy of "Sportugal," a brochure that gives details on all Algarve courses). At the many hotels with golf facilities, greens fees are included in the room rate.

Horseback Riding

Equestrian centers at all the major resorts offer lessons and both ring and trail riding.

Lodging

The Algarve has some of Portugal's best hotels, whose leisure and sports facilities are second to none. There are busy beachside hotels in large resorts and secluded retreats in luxuriant country estates. In summer, advance reservations at most places are essential.

Apartment and villa complexes with luxurious amenities are popular in the Algarve. Some properties—built on the most beautiful parts of the coast—are fancy indeed. They may be a good distance from major towns, but most have bars, restaurants, shops, and other facilities.

Budget lodgings are also available. In most towns and resorts, travelers will be approached by people offering very reasonably priced *quartos* (rooms) in private houses, which are almost always clean and cheerful, if small and with shared bathrooms. You can expect to pay 5,000$00 for a double. Don't ever book a room without seeing it first, since it may be farther from the town center than you were led to believe.

Traveling off-peak is recommended, since the weather from October to April is still good, and most hotels reduce their rates by up to 50%. It's worthwhile to check in every instance whether a discount applies.

Markets and Country Fairs

Visitors will be charmed by the varied markets and fairs held around the Algarve. All the main towns and villages have regular food markets, usually open daily 8–2. Among the best are those in Olhão, Tavira, Lagos, and Silves. Larger weekly and monthly markets, where a wider variety of produce and goods is sold, are held in Albufeira, on the first and third Tuesdays of the month; in Loulé, every Saturday; in Lagos, on the first Saturday of the month; in Portimão, on the first Monday; in Quarteira, on the second Wednesday; in Sagres, on the first Friday; and in Silves, on the third Monday.

In addition, every town of any consequence holds an annual country fair, where alongside the market stalls you'll find crafts and entertainment. Dates vary from year to year. Ask tourist offices for up-to-the-minute details and directions on local happenings.

Nightlife

There are more bars, discos, and clubs in the Algarve than anywhere else in Portugal. In the major resorts, new places open and close with alarming speed or suddenly attract a different clientele, so it's not guaranteed that spots listed in this chapter will still be the trendiest when you visit. Still, they are representative of the range of nightlife available. If you prefer a quieter evening, the Algarve's open-air cafés are perfect for a drink and people-watching, and sometimes a traveling musician will stroll by. Many hotels also put on performances of fado and other traditional music.

To gamble, head for one of the Algarve's three casinos—at Alvor, Vilamoura, and Monte Gordo—and remember to take your passport.

Sailing

The coast is developing into a popular destination for mariners from all over the world, in particular those who come to escape the severe northern European winters. There are anchorage and harbor facilities at Faro, Lagos, Olhão, Portimão, Sagres, and Vila Real. Local tourist offices can provide details.

Shopping

Just about every town has centrally located shops as well as markets and country fairs, all with a selection of local crafts and souvenirs. Probably the best place to shop, however, is Portimão, where many visitors enjoy spending at least half a day. In summer, the main tourist resorts have a lot of casual roadside stalls (a good area is outside the fortress at Sagres), at which you can buy items such as jewelry, handicrafts, art, and clothes.

As for what's sold, reasonably priced hand-knit sweaters are available in stores all over the Algarve, and even better bargains are usually found at roadside stalls. For other clothing, you'd do best to visit Portimão's shopping streets, a shopping center like Modelo, or one of the regular markets.

Handmade copper items and other metal crafts can be found in Portimão, Lagos, and Loulé. Small woven sisal baskets make good souvenirs and are available nearly everywhere. You'll sometimes see women sitting in the doorways of their houses as they weave.

Tennis

Tennis can be played at every resort, and many hotels and villa complexes have their own courts.

Tours

In summer, various companies regularly run similarly priced guided tours from Faro, Quarteira, Vilamoura, Albufeira, Portimão, and Lagos. Ask for recommendations from your hotel reception staff or the local tourist office representatives.

Many companies and individual fishermen along the coast hire out boats for excursions. These range from one-hour tours of local grottoes and rock formations to full-day excursions that usually involve a stop at a beach for a barbecue lunch. Main centers for coastal excursions are Albufeira, Vilamoura, Portimão, Tavira, Lagos, Sagres, Vila Real, and Armação de Pêra. Consult the tourist offices in these towns for details or simply wander down to the local harbor, where the prices and times of the next cruise will be posted.

Water Sports

Snorkeling and scuba diving, possible at several places along the coast, are especially good in the western Algarve, where certified, experienced divers can explore the many caves and rock formations. Wind- and board surfing are popular at a number of spots as well. In fact, several of the more remote west-coast beaches have recently begun to attract surfers from all parts of Europe. Windsurfing equipment is available throughout the Algarve; you can rent from stands on the beaches at Meia Praia (Lagos), Quarteira, Vale do Lobo, Albufeira, Armação de Pêra, Ferragudo, and Burgau, and at the Luz Bay Club. Waterskiing is less widely practiced, though it can be arranged.

Exploring the Algarve

The Algarve may be the simplest region in Portugal to explore, since the main roads—N125 and the IP1 motorway—and the train line connect towns and villages along the entire coast. Towns are close together, and it's possible to see all of the Algarve in a week's time at a fairly relaxed pace. But even if you spend several days at one of the resorts, you should make an effort to see both the eastern and western ends of the province and an inland town or two, for each has a very distinct character.

For touring purposes, the province can conveniently be divided into four sections, starting with Faro—the Algarve's capital—and the nearby beaches and inland towns. The second section encompasses the region east to the border town of Vila Real de Santo António, from which you may cross into Spain. The most built-up part of the coast, bursting with attractions, is found from Faro west to Portimão, while the fourth area covers Lagos, the principal town of the western Algarve, and extends west to Sagres and Cabo São Vicente (Cape of St. Vincent).

Great Itineraries

Give yourself at least three days to really appreciate the important sights of the Algarve. In five days you can take in the most interesting sights, have a little time at the beach, linger over a delicious seafood lunch at one of the many excellent beachfront restaurants, and still have time to get away from the built-up coastal strip into some of the more remote inland villages, still relatively untouched by the tourist influx just a few miles away. A seven-day stay will allow you to spend a few days just relaxing on some of the many excellent beaches. After all, it was the discovery of these beaches by sun-starved northern Europeans that was responsible for transforming this sleepy province into one of Europe's most popular vacation destinations.

Numbers in the text correspond to numbers in the margin and on the Algarve map.

IF YOU HAVE 3 DAYS

Begin with a day exploring the provincial capital, ⊞ **Faro** ①–⑨, and its surroundings. The following morning, head west to see the lighthouse at **Cabo São Vicente** ㊺ and the fortress and museum at **Sagres** ㊹, where you can have lunch overlooking the fishing harbor. In the afternoon, head back to Faro, stopping along the way to visit **Lagos** ㉟– ㊴ and **Portimão** ㉙. On day three, drive east to **Vila Real de Santo António** ⑰, at the border with Spain. En route you can explore **Olhão** ⑩, with its Moorish-style architecture, and **Tavira** ⑭, one of the Algarve's most attractive towns.

IF YOU HAVE 5 DAYS

After a day in and around ⊞ **Faro** ①–⑨, drive west to visit **Portimão** ㉙ and the popular nearby beach resort of **Praia da Rocha** ㉛. Continue west to overnight in ⊞ **Lagos** ㉟–㊴, an attractive and historic city whose origins go back to Carthiginian times. After seeing the sights in Lagos, head out to **Cabo São Vicente** ㊺ for some spectacular views from the lighthouse and then to ⊞ **Sagres** ㊹, where you can walk out on the jetty and watch the fishermen unload their catch. The next morning, follow N268 along the west coast to Aljezur, where you take N267 through a remote part of the Algarve to the delightful mountain town of **Monchique** ㉞. Enjoy lunch at one of the several terrace restaurants that afford sweeping views across the countryside to the sea. After lunch, head down the mountain to the coastal road and swing east to **Olhão** ⑩ and ⊞ **Tavira** ⑭. On your last day, visit the castle at **Castro Marim** ⑱ and the border town of **Vila Real de Santo António** ⑰.

IF YOU HAVE 7 DAYS

With a week, you can see the attractions of the five-day itinerary at a leisurely pace and still have a few days left to just bask on one of the Algarve's fine beaches. Just pick a spot and spend an extra night nearby. If you like your beaches long and flat, then you will enjoy the sands of the Sotovento, the region extending east from Faro. The beaches at **Manta Rota** ⑮ and **Monte Gordo** ⑯ are two of the best. The Barlavento, west of Faro, has some of Europe's most spectacular beaches, with dramatic cliffs and bizarre rock formations as a backdrop. Although recently subject to much tourist development, **Praia da Rocha** ㉛, near Portimão, is still quite attractive. The farther west you go, the fewer tourist developments you will encounter. The beaches at **Lagos** ㉟–㊴ and nearby **Praia da Luz** ㊵ are well suited for stays of a day or longer.

When to Tour the Algarve

The Algarve's weather is welcoming year-round. Winters are mild, and spring is positively delightful. Summer is, of course, high season—with lodging at a premium, prices at their highest, and crowds at their thickest. But you'll also find warm seas, piercing blue skies, and golden sands at the foot of glowing ocher-red cliffs.

If you can, avoid the high season, which runs from early July to late August. Although not quite as congested as many other European seaside resorts, the Algarve's beaches are best appreciated in late spring and early fall, when the water is quite pleasant for swimming and finding a secluded spot to lay out your beach blanket is much less challenging. From a scenic perspective, the Algarvian spring, with its rolling carpets of beautifully colored wildflowers, is hard to beat. If you seek

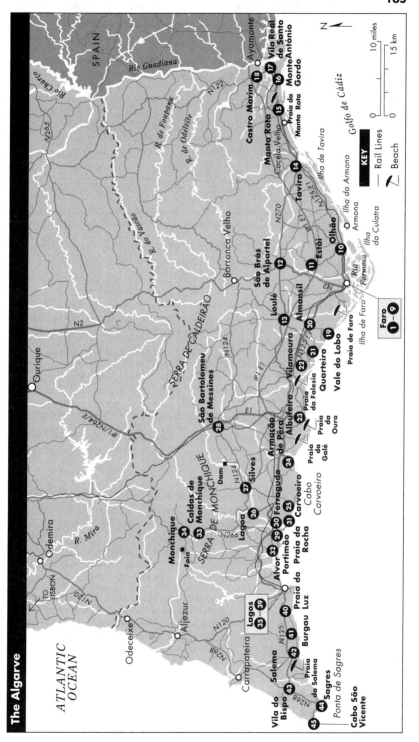

The Algarve

solitude and are willing to endure swimming in an ocean that is quite nippy, a winter visit can be very pleasant. There are many bargains to be had, particularly with respect to accommodations and car rentals.

FARO AND ENVIRONS

Many people fly in to Faro and pass straight through on their way to beaches east and west, which is unfortunate. The city's attractive harbor and Old Town are both worthy of a night's stay or more, and its many facilities make it a fine base for touring the region. The towns that ring Faro contain their own sights worth seeing, from beaches and markets to churches and ruins.

Numbers in the margin correspond to points of interest on the Algarve and Faro maps.

Faro

❶ *300 km (186 mi) southeast of Lisbon.*

The provincial capital of the Algarve is a prosperous city of around 30,000 residents. Founded by the Moors, it was taken by Afonso III in 1249, at the end of the Arab domination. Much of its architectural value was lost in the late 16th century, when it was sacked by the English under the Earl of Essex. It was further damaged by two 18th-century earthquakes, the latter of which, in 1755, also destroyed Lisbon.

Remnants of the medieval walls and some historic buildings can still be seen in the delightful **Cidade Velha** (Old Town). Here, quiet streets and squares, where balconies and tile work decorate even the most unappealing facade, are perfect for a stroll. Other than this, there's nothing to do in Old Town unless you can gain entry to one of the churches, many of which are locked.

❷ You enter Old Town through an 18th-century gate, the **Arco da Vila**, which stands in front of the central Jardim Manuel Bivar (Manuel Bivar Garden). Note the white-marble statue of St. Thomas Aquinas in a niche at the top.

❸ The squat, mostly Renaissance-style **Sé** (cathedral) faces the Largo da Sé, a grand square bordered by orange trees and whitewashed palace buildings. The cathedral retains a Gothic tower but is mostly of interest for its stunning interior of decorated 17th- and 18th-century *azulejos* (tiles). Another highlight, on one side of the nave, is the red Chinoiserie organ, dating from 1751. ⊠ *Largo da Sé.* 🎫 *Free.* ⊙ *Weekdays 10–noon, Sat. at 5 PM for services, Sun. 8 AM–1 PM for services.*

❹ The 16th-century Convento de Nossa Senhora da Assunção has been converted to house the **Museu Municipal** (Municipal Museum). The conversion makes fine use of the convent's beautiful two-story cloister. The best displays are the archaeological collections, including fascinating Roman remains from local settlements predating Moorish Faro as well as Roman statues from the excavations at Milreu. ⊠ *Praça Afonso III 14,* ☎ *089/822402.* 🎫 *120$00.* ⊙ *Weekdays 9–5.*

❺ The plain facade of the **Igreja de São Francisco** (Church of St. Francis) gives no hint of the richness of its baroque interior. Inside are glorious 18th-century blue-and-white azulejos and a chapel adorned with gilt work. ⊠ *Largo de São Francisco.* 🎫 *Free. Ask for key at tourist office.*

❻ The **porto**—flanked by Faro's main square, the Praça Dom Francisco Gomes, and the Manuel Bivar Gardens—is one of the prettiest places

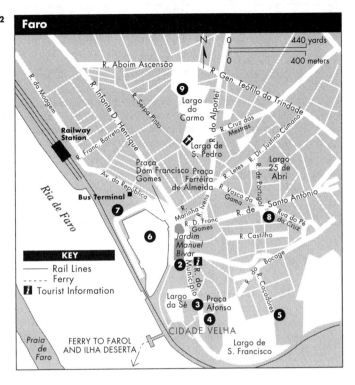

Faro

in town. You can sit at an outdoor café and watch the boats go about their business.

NEED A
BREAK?

The **Café Alianca** (⊠ Rua Francisco Gomes 7–11) is an old-style coffee-house situated halfway around the harbor, between Rua Francisco Gomes and Rua Marinha. Inside you'll find a timeworn ambience and outside a sidewalk café facing the water.

7 At the dockside **Museu Maritimo** (Maritime Museum), models of local fishing craft are displayed alongside real boats of war and exploration. ⊠ *Rua Comunidade Luisada,* ☎ *089/822001.* 🖼 *120$00.* ⏱ *Weekdays 9–12:30 and 3–5:30.*

East of the harbor, in the pedestrian shopping streets around **Rua de Santo António,** you'll find much of what makes Faro tick as a tourist town: dozens of bars, restaurants, shops, and sidewalk hawkers selling souvenirs and snacks.

8 Providing a bit of culture in an area otherwise dominated by stores and eateries, the **Museu Etnografico Regional** (Regional Ethnographic Museum) sheds light on the local fishing industry by way of various models and diagrams. Crafts and reconstructions of typical house interiors are displayed, too. ⊠ *Rua do Pé da Cruz,* ☎ *089/27610.* 🖼 *300$00.* ⏱ *Weekdays 9:30–6.*

9 Just northwest of the city center, the Baroque **Igreja do Carmo** (Carmo Church), looking very out of place amid the modern buildings surrounding it, is flanked by twin bell towers. The real interest, however, is inside. A door to the right of the altar leads to the Capela dos Ossos

(Chapel of the Bones), whose walls are covered in skulls and bones taken from nearby monks' graves—an eerie sight, to say the least! ⊠ *Largo do Carmo.* ▣ *50$00.* ⊙ *Mon.–Sat. 10–1 and 3–5.*

Beach

Though thick with crowds, the long, sandy beach on the Ilha de Faro (Faro Island), a sandbar 5 kilometers (3 miles) southwest of Faro, is the closest beach to town. Called the **Praia de Faro,** it can be reached via a ferry to Farol on Culatra Island or to Ilha Deserta or by a 25-minute ride on Bus 16. *Bus:* ⊠ *Stop opposite bus terminal.* ⊙ *Daily 8 AM–10 PM, buses leave hourly. Ferry:* ⊠ *Jetty below Cidade Velho.* ▣ *200$00 round-trip.* ⊙ *June–Sept., 3 ferries daily.*

Dining and Lodging

$$$ ✕ **Cidade Velha.** In an 18th-century house beside the cathedral and
★ within the walls of the Old Town, this small, intimate restaurant is easy to reach and serves excellent international cuisine. Many of the imaginative dishes utilize classic Portuguese ingredients. Try the pie made with *bacalhau* (dried codfish) or the rich house specialty: fillet of pork stuffed with dates and walnuts and cooked in port. ⊠ *Rua Domingos Guieiro 19,* ☎ *089/27145. AE, MC, V. Closed Sun. No lunch June–Sept. and Sat.*

$$ ✕ **Adega Nova.** This atmospheric *adega* (wine cellar) offers excellently prepared traditional Portuguese dishes in down-to-earth surroundings that foster the lively atmosphere. Drinks are served at the tile-covered bar, and you sit at long wooden tables and benches for dinner. The restaurant is close to the train station in an otherwise dreary area. ⊠ *Rua Francisco Barreto 24,* ☎ *089/813433. No credit cards.*

$$ ✕ **Dois Irmãos.** In business since 1925, this pretty and centrally located large restaurant (one of several on the square) specializes in cataplana, as evidenced by the utensils hanging from the wood-beamed ceiling. Almost any of the other seafood dishes are worth trying, too, but save room for the homemade *pudim caseiro* (crème caramel). Choose your wine from one of the hundreds of bottles that line the upper walls. ⊠ *Largo do Terreiro do Bispo 14–15,* ☎ *089/823337. AE, DC, MC, V.*

$$ ✕ **Sol e Jardim.** This restaurant offers dining with a difference—at outdoor tables in a covered "garden" setting. The decor consists of cooking utensils, farm equipment, flags, and other objects hanging from the ceiling, and the staff is good-natured. Among the traditional Portuguese dishes, the clams are good and so are the grilled meats and fish. The restaurant is next door to (and associated with) the Dois Irmãos, so it's guaranteed to be a good value. ⊠ *Praça Ferreira de Almeida 22–23,* ☎ *089/823337. MC, V.*

$$$–$$$$ ✕▥ **Hotel La Reserve.** Tucked in the hills at Santa Bárbara de Nexe,
★ a few miles inland from Faro, this intimate member of the Relais & Chateaux chain delivers luxury, seclusion, and comfort. The air-conditioned apartments (with a Moorish flavor) have private terraces or balconies, and lush plantings set off the low, white buildings. In a 6-acre park, the hotel's rural atmosphere is conducive to total relaxation, but you can work up an appetite at the tennis courts or pool and then satisfy it in the formal restaurant (closed Tues.; no lunch). Elegant cuisine with a French accent is the fare, with game dishes as specialties, and there's a complimentary Continental breakfast. Advance reservations are required for both the hotel and restaurant. ⊠ *Santa Bárbara de Nexe, 8000 Faro,* ☎ *089/90474,* ᴍ *089/90402; restaurant,* ☎ *089/90234. 12 studio apartments with kitchenette, 8 duplex apartments. Restaurant, bar, pool, tennis courts. No credit cards. Closed Nov.*

$$$ ▥ **Hotel Eva.** Featuring a new face-lift, this well-appointed hotel on
★ the main square has the best location in Faro, giving guests unique views of the yacht-filled harbor, the sea, and the Old Town. The public

rooms are comfortably furnished, there's a bar with evening entertainment, and the novel rooftop pool and top-floor restaurant add further ambience. Guest rooms are modern and comfortably furnished, though the best are enhanced by spacious balconies with vast views. There's also a courtesy bus to the town beach on nearby Faro Island. ⊠ *Av. da República 1, 8000,* ☎ *089/803354,* ℻ *089/802304. 150 rooms. Restaurant, bar, pool, dance club. AE, DC, MC, V.*

$ 🔝 **Casa de Lumena.** This graceful 150-year-old mansion has been
★ tastefully converted into a small hotel, and some rooms overlook the pretty square. Each guest room has a character of its own, and its unique furnishings reflect the care the English owners have taken in their restoration. The courtyard's Grapevine bar is an especially pleasant place for a drink. The hotel is near the central Rua de Santo António, just a five-minute walk from the harbor. ⊠ *Praça Alexandre Herculano 27, 8000,* ☎ *089/801990,* ℻ *089/804019. 12 rooms. Restaurant, bar. AE, DC, MC, V.*

$ 🔝 **Hotel Faro.** The functional but friendly Faro is decidedly second-best to the Eva, but as the only other harbor-front hotel in town, it's still a remarkably good value. The rooms are of reasonable size, if rather anonymous in character, and the ones in the front offer water views (but you must ask for them). Other amenities include a rooftop terrace and a dimly lit bar with picture windows. ⊠ *Praça D. Francisco Gomes 2, 8000,* ☎ *089/803276,* ℻ *089/803546. 52 rooms. Restaurant, bar. AE, DC, MC, V.*

Festivals

Mid-July sees the **Festa e Feira da Senhora do Carmo** (Festival and Fair of Our Lady of Carmen), a religious procession followed by an agricultural fair. In October, the **Feira de Santa Iria** (Fair of St. Iria) is another happy excuse for traditional celebrations held over several days.

Nightlife

Faro's central pedestrian streets are filled at night with throngs of café goers, and **Rua do Prior,** in particular, is known for its wide selection of late-closing, stylish bars. **Kingburger** (⊠ Rua do Prior 40) and **Bar Chaplin** (⊠ Rua do Prior 37) are current favorites. For a disco, visit either trendy **Megahertz** (⊠ Rua do Prior 38), which stays open until 4 AM, or the more mainstream **Sheherazade** (⊠ At the Hotel Eva, Av. da República 1). The **Hotel Eva** puts on traditional music and fado at least once a week in summer.

Olhão

⑩ *8 km (5 mi) east of Faro.*

During the Napoleonic Wars, the inhabitants of this small 18th-century port town on the Ria Formosa defied the French blockade on trade with Britain and profited greatly from smuggling. With the proceeds, they built North African–style, cube-shape whitewashed houses. In 1808, local fishermen reputedly sailed to Brazil to inform the exiled Dom João VI that the French had departed from Portugal—for which service, undertaken without navigational aids, Olhão was granted a town charter. Although modern construction has destroyed a great deal of its former charm, Olhão's fishing port is still colorful, and its intricate old-town quarter has retained some of its earlier attraction.

For a view over Olhão, visit the 17th-century **parish church,** from whose bell tower you can look down upon the narrow streets and cubical houses. ⊠ *South end of Av. da República.* ☉ *Tues.–Sun. 9–noon and 2–5.*

Beaches

Adding to the allure of the beaches here is the designation of this entire section of coastline, including islands and river inlets, as a nature reserve because a great number of migratory birds flock to the area on their way south for the winter. Of the nearby islands, **Armona** is the best. About 15 minutes east of Olhão, it possesses some fine, isolated stretches of sand, holiday villas, and café-bars. The sandy island of **Culatra,** 40 minutes east of Olhão, supports several ramshackle fishing communities; at the southern village of **Farol** (meaning lighthouse), you'll find agreeable beaches.

To get to the local beaches, take a **ferry.** If the kiosk is closed, you can buy tickets on board. ⊠ *Jetty east of town gardens.* 🎫 *Round-trip: 160$00 Armona, 200$00 Culatra.* ☉ *July–Aug., ferries run hourly; Sept.–June, 3 or 4 ferries daily. Schedule available at tourist office.*

Shopping

One of the Algarve's best food **markets** (☉ Mon.–Sat. 7–2) is held in the riverfront buildings in the town gardens. Feast your eyes on the shellfish for which Olhão is renowned; mussels, in particular, are a local specialty.

Estói

🕚 *8 km (5 mi) northeast of Faro.*

This village is the site of the 18th-century **Palácio do Visconde de Estói** (Palace of the Counts of Estói). Although the palace itself is closed to the public, visitors can stroll around the formal gardens. 🎫 *Free.* ☉ *Tues.–Sat. 10–12:30.*

<table>
<tr><td>OFF THE
BEATEN PATH</td><td>**MILREU –** These extensive Roman ruins, just ½ kilometer (⅓ mile) north-west of Estói, were first excavated in 1876. The settlement was once known as Roman Ossonoba, and the remains—including a temple (later converted into a Christian basilica) and mosaic fragments adorning some of the 3rd-century baths—date from the 2nd to the 6th centuries. Some of the more portable remains can be seen in the gardens of Estói's Palace of the Counts and in Faro's Municipal Museum. 🎫 *Free.* ☉ *Tues.–Sun. 10–12:30 and 2–5.*</td></tr>
</table>

São Brás de Alportel

🕛 *7 km (4 mi) north of Milreu.*

The town of São Brás is a regional center for the processing of cork from the surrounding countryside.

Dining and Lodging

$$$ ✗🏨 **Pousada de São Brás.** One of only two *pousadas* (inns) on the Algarve, this delightful 1940s hotel is set in low hills. The recently remodeled rooms are comfortably furnished, and there's a rustic restaurant serving good regional dishes and other Portuguese specialties. The major attractions are the peaceful surroundings and the splendid hill views from the terrace. ⊠ *Estrada de Lisboa, 8150,* ☎ *089/842305,* ℻ *089/841726. 23 rooms, 1 suite. Restaurant, bar, pool, tennis. AE, DC, MC, V.*

Loulé

⑬ *13 km (8 mi) west of São Brás de Alportel.*

This little market town is known for its crafts. The tiny, cobbled streets that run between the castle and the church—particularly Rua 9 de Abril—are lined with whitewashed houses and workshops (closed Sundays) where lace, leather, and copper goods are manufactured. It's fascinating to wander this area, watch the craftspeople at work, and explore the nooks and crannies of the old town. Note the many houses with sculpted plasterwork on their white chimneys, a typical Algarve sight. The rest of Loulé, which is more developed, is overwhelmed by the main boulevard and modern buildings, but there's a pleasant municipal park at the top of town.

Once a Moorish stronghold, Loulé has preserved the ruins of its medieval **castelo** (castle), which houses the historical museum and archives as well as the tourist office. ⊠ *Largo Dom Pedro I, no phone.* 🕾 *Free.* 🕙 *Daily 9–12:30 and 2:30–5.*

The restored 13th-century **Igreja Matriz** (Parish Church) is decorated with handsome tiles and wood carvings and has an unusual wrought-iron pulpit. ⊠ *Largo Pr. C. da Silva.* 🕙 *Mon.–Sat. 9–noon and 2–5:30.*

Festivals

A **street carnival**—held every February for Mardi Gras—is an enjoyable local affair, with a procession of floats, mask competitions, dancing, and more. On the second Sunday after Easter, Loulé hosts the **Romaria da Senhora da Piedade** (Festival of Our Lady of Mercy), a pilgrimage and procession to the local shrine of Monte da Piedade. Flower-decked celebrations enlivened by performances of traditional song and dance take place on **May 1.**

THE EASTERN ALGARVE

The eastern portion of the province, known as the Sotovento, is a region of flat, sandy beaches. Although there has been some development along the coast, this is primarily a quiet, low-key area. Its principal towns, like Tavira, are important fishing ports. Our tour of the area heads east toward Spain and then turns inland.

Numbers in the margin correspond to points of interest on the Algarve map.

Tavira

★ **⑭** *28 km (17 mi) east of Faro.*

Situated at the mouth of the Rio Gilão, Tavira is often called the prettiest town in the Algarve. With its riverfront gardens and its old streets and pastel-color houses strung along both sides of the quiet river, it is immediately endearing. Many of Tavira's white 18th-century houses retain their original doorways and coats-of-arms; others have peculiar four-sided roofs.

Since Tavira is a tuna-fishing port, you'll find plenty of fresh *atum* (tuna) as well as local color. Fresh tuna steaks, often grilled and served with onions, are on restaurant menus all over town at remarkably low prices. In the **harbor** area, you can sample no-frills dining at its best, alongside the local fishermen, at any of the little basic café-restaurants across from the picturesque tangle of fishing boats and nets. The vibrant covered **market** is lined with an array of fresh fish.

One of two, the low **bridge** adjacent to the arcaded Praça da República is of Roman origin, although it was rebuilt in the 17th century and again a few years ago after sustaining damage from floodwaters.

From the battlemented walls of the central **castelo** (castle), you can look down over Tavira's many church spires and across the river delta to the sea. ⊠ *Stepped street off Rua da Liberdade.* 🎟 *Free.* ⊙ *Weekdays 8–5:30, weekends 10–7.*

One of two major churches in Tavira, **Santa Maria do Castelo** (St. Mary of the Castle) was built on the site of a Moorish mosque in the 13th century. Although it was almost entirely destroyed by the 1755 earthquake, the church retains its original Gothic doorway.

The **Igreja da Misericórdia** (Misericórdia Church) is a beautiful Renaissance building with a portal dating from 1541. ⊠ *West of main square.* ⊙ *Daily 10–noon and 2–5.*

Beaches

Directly offshore and extending west for some 10 kilometers (6 miles) is the **Ilha de Tavira**, a long offshore sandbar with several good beaches. The island is served by regular ferry service, and in summer a bus (marked QUATRO ÁGUAS) shuttles from the center of town to the ferry's jetty. ⊠ *Jetty: 2 km (1¼ mi) east of Tavira.* 🎟 *130$00 round-trip.* ⊙ *May–June and Sept.–mid-Oct., ferries run hourly; July–Aug., ferries run every ½ hr.*

Dining and Lodging

$$ ✕ **Restaurante Imperial.** This restaurant behind the riverside gardens is the best on the riverfront. It's well known for its fish and shellfish, including clams, tuna, and a tasty mixed fried-fish plate, but desserts are not a strong point. In summer, there's seating on the sidewalk. Waiters are good at their job but a little aloof—after 40 years of service, the Imperial doesn't have to try hard to attract customers. ⊠ *Rua José Pires Padinha 22–24,* ☎ *081/22306. MC, V. Closed Wed. in winter.*

$ 🏨 **Residencial Princesa do Gilão.** Across the river from the main square, this small, gleaming white hotel stands on the quayside, offering fine views of the fishing harbor and castle walls. All the rooms are modern and compact and have tile floors; try for one that faces the front and has a balcony. The landings and reception areas sparkle with cool marble and Portuguese tiles. Continental breakfast is available. ⊠ *Rua Borda de Água de Aguiar 10–12, 8800,* ☎ *081/325171 or 081/22665. 22 rooms. No credit cards.*

Manta Rota

⑮ *12 km (7½ mi) east of Tavira.*

There isn't much of a town here aside from some nice stretches of beach, a campground, a few bars, restaurants, and hotels.

Beaches

This section of shore has several good beaches, but unfortunately, those long, unbroken beaches make ideal terrain for heavy touristic development. A particularly nice strand is the offshore sandbar at the tiny, undeveloped village of **Cacela Velha.** Where the sandbars merge with the shore is the excellent **Praia de Manta Rota** (Manta Rota Beach).

Monte Gordo

16 *6 km (4 mi) east of Manta Rota.*

Pine woods and orchards break up the flat landscape around this large resort, which lies just 4 kilometers (2½ miles) from the Spanish border. A town of brightly colored houses and extensive tourist facilities, Monte Gordo features plenty of hotels, restaurants, and nightspots.

Beach

The long, flat **Praia de Monte Gordo** (Monte Gordo Beach) is very popular, and visitors enjoy the highest average seawater temperature in the country. Be careful, though: The beach is steeply sloped, and swimmers can quickly find themselves in deep water.

Dining and Lodging

$ ✕ **Mota.** This large, lively, unpretentious restaurant, which has been around for more than 30 years, is on the sands of the Praia de Monte Gordo near the Vasco da Gama Hotel, a bit west of Vila Real de Santo António. During the day you can drop in for a snack or salad if you don't want a full meal. You sit on the large covered terrace facing the ocean, and in the evening you're served seafood, grills, and regional dishes, while live music accompanies your meal. ⊠ *Praia de Monte Gordo,* ☎ *081/42650. No credit cards.*

$$ ⊞ **Alcazar.** Its unusual exterior and interior design makes this hotel one of the most striking in Monte Gordo. White balconies contrast with the redbrick facade, while inside the sinuous arches and low, molded ceilings recall a cave's interior or an Arab tent. Guest rooms have their own terraces and window boxes. Alcazar has a pleasant atmosphere, a very accommodating staff, and a convenient location two blocks off the beach. ⊠ *Rua de Ceuta 9, 8900 Villa Real de Santo António,* ☎ *081/512184,* 📠 *081/512242. 95 rooms. Restaurant, bar, snack bar, pool, shops, dance club. AE, DC, MC, V.*

$$ ⊞ **Vasco da Gama.** This long, low-lying hotel, occupying one of the prime beach sites in town, has a red roof with two typical Algarvian chimneys. It's well equipped for water sports and has many other amenities. Families, especially, can make good use of the extensive stretch of sandy beach and the children's pool and play area, and everyone likes the capable and friendly staff. All the rooms have terraces, and the ones with a sea view are worth their extra cost. ⊠ *Av. Infante Dom Henrique, 8900,* ☎ *081/511321,* 📠 *081/511622. 200 rooms. Restaurant, bar, pool, miniature golf, tennis courts, bowling, billiards, dance club. AE, DC, MC, V.*

Nightlife

In addition to a wealth of nightclubs and discos, Monte Gordo has a **casino** (☎ 081/42224).

Vila Real de Santo António

17 *4 km (2½ mi) east of Monte Gordo, 10 km (6 mi) east of Manta Rota.*

This town, on the Rio Guadiana, is the last stop before Spain. The original town was destroyed by a tidal wave in the 17th century and was not rebuilt until the late 18th century, when the Marquês de Pombal constructed a new, gridded town. Consequently, Vila Real, which took only five months to complete, is a showpiece of 18th-century town planning. Like most border towns, it's a lively place, with plenty of bars and restaurants and some traffic-free central streets that encourage evening strolling. For all that, however, there's very little to see.

You might want to take an hour or so to visit the **Museu de Manuel Cabanas** (Manuel Cabanas Museum), which contains some paintings, engravings, and local ethnographical items. It's on the main square. ⊠ *Praça Marquês de Pombal, no phone.* ⊠ *Free.* ☉ *Tues.–Sun. 11–1 and 2–7.*

Although there's a suspension bridge a few miles to the north, a **ferry ride** to Spain is a pleasant option if you are not in a hurry (☞ Arriving and Departing *in* the Algarve A to Z, *below*). The trip yields attractive views of the border towns on both sides of the river.

Dining

$ ✕ **Caves do Guadiana.** In a large, old-fashioned building facing the fishing docks and the river estuary, this accommodating restaurant is popular for its well-prepared seafood and Portuguese specialties. Stop for lunch on the way to or from the Spanish border crossing. ⊠ *Av. da República 90,* ☎ *081/44498. DC, MC. Closed Thurs.*

Castro Marim

⑱ *5 km (3 mi) north of Vila Real de Santo António; take N122 north into the low hills, parallel to the course of the Rio Guadiana.*

The first headquarters of the monastic Order of Christ, founded in the 14th century after the dissolution of the Knights Templar, Castro Marim is an attractive village bathed in white and nestled in the low hills overlooking the Rio Guadiana. The town has the remains of what was once a massive castle, built by Afonso III, which was unfortunately laid to waste by the 1755 earthquake. The views from here are grand, and the surroundings have been turned into a nature reserve; there are paths through the nearby river marshes.

En Route For a side of the Algarve that most visitors never see, drive an inland route through beautiful, open countryside on your way back toward Faro. Take N122 north to N122–1 northeast to the border town of Alcoutim, a quiet little village with a ruined castle. Return to N122 and continue west along N124, a 65-kilometer (40-mile) route with especially fine views, until it joins N2, 14 kilometers (9 miles) north of São Brás de Alportel.

THE CENTRAL ALGARVE

The central Algarve, between Faro and Portimão, has the heaviest concentration of tourist resorts, some of which are household names in Europe. Nevertheless, in between built-up areas you can still discover quiet bays, amazing rock formations, and exclusive, secluded hotels and villas. With a car it's easy to travel the few miles inland that make all the difference: Minor roads lead into the hills, to towns that have resisted the changes wrought upon the developed coast. Towns in this section are covered basically from east to west, with side trips north to these inland jewels.

Numbers in the margin correspond to points of interest on the Algarve map.

Vale do Lobo

⑲ *10 km (6 mi) west of Faro.*

Like its neighbor Quinta do Lago, this luxury resort village—one of the Algarve's earliest—has superb facilities. Golf, tennis, and sailboarding are all popular.

Dining and Lodging

$$$$ ✕🏨 **Dona Filipa.** This is one of the most luxurious hotels in the Al-
★ garve, with a lavish and striking interior, superb service, and pleasant,
air-conditioned rooms with balconies (most of which overlook the sea).
It's on extensive, beautifully landscaped grounds near the beach west
of Faro. The hotel has its own tennis courts and is very close to the famous Roger Taylor Tennis Center. Also, guests have free use of the San
Lorenzo Golf Club, in Almansil, and receive a 20% discount at the
Vale do Lobo Golf Club. The hotel's chic restaurant offers an excellent international menu and an impressive wine list. ✉ *8135 Almansil,* ☎ *089/394141,* 🗟 *089/394288. 147 rooms. Restaurant, bar, grill,
pool, golf privileges, tennis courts, shops, dance club. AE, DC, MC,
V.*

Outdoor Activities and Sports

GOLF

The **Vale do Lobo Golf Club** (☎ 089/394444) has three nine-hole
courses.

TENNIS

The famous **Roger Taylor Tennis Center** (☎ 089/394311), one of Europe's best, has 12 all-weather courts, a clubhouse, sauna, pool, and
restaurant.

Almansil

⑳ *10 km (6 mi) northwest of Faro.*

Almansil is best known for its chapel of **São Lourenço** (St. Lawrence),
built in 1730. Notable are the chapel's blue-and-white azulejo panels
and its intricate gilt work.

Nightlife and the Arts

Some cottages next to the church of São Lourenço have been transformed into an **art gallery** (☎ 089/393281), which exhibits contemporary Portuguese works and holds occasional classical-music concerts.

Outdoor Activities and Sports

GOLF

The Portuguese Open Championship is held in October at the **Quinta
do Lago Golf Club** (☎ 089/396002 or 089/394529), which has a 36-
hole course on the superb Quinta do Lago estate. The **San Lorenzo Golf
Club** (☎ 089/396522) has 18 fine holes.

HORSEBACK RIDING

There are fully equipped riding centers at **Quinta dos Amigos** (✉ Es-
canxinas, ☎ 089/395269) and **Paradise Inn** (✉ Quinta do Lago Rd.,
☎ 089/396864).

Quarteira

㉑ *14 km (9 mi) northwest of Faro.*

When you see present-day Quarteira, now a bustling high-rise resort
with row upon row of concrete vacation silos, it is hard to imagine
that this was once a quiet fishing village. There was always an excellent beach, but now there are also golf courses and tennis courts.

Atlantic Park (✉ near Quarteira, ☎ 089/397–8282) is an aquatic
theme park filled with water-related rides.

Vilamoura

㉒ *3 km (2 mi) northwest of Quarteira.*

Once a prosperous Roman settlement, this highly developed upscale resort possesses an impressively large marina, several golf courses, a major tennis center, and other sports facilities, as well as luxury hotels and a casino. The excavations of the Roman ruins at **Cêrro da Villa** (⊠ Across from marina) have revealed an elaborate plumbing system as well as several mosaics.

Dining and Lodging

$$$$ ✕🏨 **Vilamoura Marinotel.** One of the Algarve's newest accommodations, the luxurious Marinotel overlooks Vilamoura's stupendous marina. The guest rooms come equipped with the most up-to-the-minute hardware, including VCRs, and the facilities are wide-ranging. Many people think the Marinotel is the best place to eat in town: The extrasmart grill overlooking the boats serves fish and has live music, while the restaurant that faces the hotel gardens specializes in Spanish and Portuguese food. ⊠ *8126,* ☎ *089/389988,* ℻ *089/389869. 385 rooms. Restaurant, bar, grill, pool, tennis, boating, shops. AE, DC, MC, V.*

$$$–$$$$ ✕🏨 **Sheraton Algarve.** This new luxury hotel, in a spectacular cliff-
★ top location overlooking the sea, has access to some of the Algarve's finest beaches. The architecture and decoration blend Moorish features with modern elements. For example, the spacious reception area incorporates arches and Eastern designs, whereas guest rooms mix traditional tiling with up-to-the-minute appointments. Service is superb. The hotel is 8 kilometers (5 miles) from town, and guests like to spend their time at the excellent private beach, to which they descend in a glass elevator and where there's a bar and a small restaurant. They can also use, without charge, the facilities of the associated Pine Cliffs Golf and Country Club. ⊠ *Praia da Falésia, 8200 Albufeira,* ☎ *089/501999,* ℻ *089/501950. 215 rooms. Restaurant, bar, indoor and outdoor pools, sauna, golf privileges, tennis, exercise room, beach. AE, DC, MC, V.*

$$$ ✕🏨 **Hotel Dom Pedro Golf.** Part of a highly successful vacation complex, the Dom Pedro is the best of the three hotels operated here by the Dom Pedro Hotel Group. It's close to the casino, not far from the splendid beach, and five minutes from the marina. Each bright room is attractively furnished and has its own balcony facing the sea. ⊠ *Vilamoura, 8125 Quarteira,* ☎ *089/389650,* ℻ *089/315482. 263 rooms. Restaurant, bar, 2 pools, golf, tennis courts, shops. AE, DC, MC, V.*

Nightlife

A big part of Vilamoura's nightlife scene is its **casino** (☎ 089/302996).

Outdoor Activities and Sports

GOLF

A recent addition to the local golf scene is the nine-hole **Pine Cliffs Golf and Country Club** (☎ 089/501787), a few miles west of Vilamoura. This Martin Hawtree course is magnificently situated, just back from some impressive, scenic cliffs. The **Vilamoura Golf Club** has three different courses, two with 18 holes and one with 27: Vilamoura I (☎ 089/313652), Vilamoura II (☎ 089/315562), and Vilamoura III (☎ 089/380722 or 089/380724).

HORSEBACK RIDING

Horses are available for lessons and for trail rides at the **Centro Hípico de Vilamoura** (☎ 089/313033).

SAILING

You can rent sailboats at the **Vilamoura Marina** (✉ 8125 Quarteira, ☎ 089/312023 or 089/302925; ☎ 089/313933 for sailboat rental), an enormous self-contained marina complex with apartments, shops, hotels, sporting and leisure facilities, and 1,000 berths.

If you'd like to relax and let someone else do the work, book a cruise on the **Condor de Vilamoura,** which sails toward Albufeira. ✉ *Vilamoura Marina, ☎ 089/314070. 🗺 4,000$00 for 3 hrs; 8,000$00 for 7 hrs, including lunch. ⊙ 2 cruises daily.*

TENNIS

The **Vilamoura Tennis Center** (☎ 089/380088) has four courts.

Albufeira

★ ㉓   *12 km (7½ mi) west of Vilamoura, 30 km (19 mi) northwest of Faro, 4 km (2½ mi) south of main highway.*

Brash Albufeira, a favorite with British holidaymakers, has mushroomed from an attractive fishing village into the Algarve's largest and busiest resort. The town beach attracts thousands of visitors daily, and the noisy center, around Largo Eng. Duarte Pacheco, is dominated by cafés, bars, restaurants, discos, and souvenir shops.

Despite the crowds, Albufeira has much to commend it, and a lunchtime stop at one of the cafés in the old town may be worth your while. One of the last Algarve towns to hold out against the Christian army in the 13th century, Albufeira still has a distinctly Moorish flavor, apparent in the steep, narrow streets and hundreds of whitewashed houses snuggled on the slopes of nearby hills. There are scant remains of a Moorish castle on the heights above town—under the Arabs the town was called Al-Buhera (Castle on the Sea)—and the bustling fish market and old harbor retain some interest, too.

🜊   **Zoo Marine** (✉ N125, Guia, ☎ 089/561104), 6 kilometers (4 miles) northwest of Albufeira, is a popular water park, with rides, swimming pools, gardens, a cinema, and dolphin and sea lion shows.

Beaches

On most summer days, the **town beach** (✉ Reached by tunnel from Rua 5 de Outubro) is so crowded that it may be hard to enjoy its interesting rock formations, caves, and grottoes, not to mention sand and sea. If you want more space, you'll have to move farther afield. Possibilities include the beautiful beaches of **São Rafael** and **Praia da Galé,** 4 kilometers (2½ miles) west on local roads, though there's been much recent development here, too. The coves and rocks are very attractive, but don't expect them to be deserted. **Praia da Falesia, Olhos d'Agua,** and **Praia da Oura** also fall within the ambit of Albufeira.

Dining and Lodging

$$$ ✕ **La Cigale.** This restaurant, 9 kilometers (5 miles) east of Albufeira, is renowned among locals and its many repeat customers for excellent French and Portuguese cooking. It's right on the beach, and the terrace is the most sought-after place to sit, though you'll have to reserve in advance. ✉ *Olhas d'Agua, ☎ 089/501637. DC, MC, V. Closed Dec.–Feb. No lunch Mar.–May.*

$$–$$$ ✕ **A Ruina.** This big, multilevel, rustic restaurant on the beach is the ★   place to go for charcoal-grilled seafood, especially the fresh sardines or tuna steak (the day's catch comes from the nearby fish market). Start with a shellfish salad and choose your main course from the display. You may sit outdoors, on the beach, or inside in one of two simple but attractively furnished dining rooms. There's a top-floor bar and a roof

terrace, too. ⊠ *Cais Herculano, Praia dos Pescadores,* ☎ *089/512094. No credit cards.*

$$–$$$ ✕ **Cabaz da Praia.** You'll have spectacular views of the beach from
★ the cliffside terrace of this long-established restaurant, named "beach
basket" in Portuguese, and converted from an old fisherman's cottage.
There's fine French-Portuguese cooking here—fish soup, grilled fish
served imaginatively, and chicken with seafood. Desserts are traditional
Algarvian sweets. Try the soufflé, perhaps the restaurant's most popular dish. ⊠ *Praça Miguel Bombarda 7,* ☎ *089/512137. AE, MC, V.
Closed Thurs. No lunch Sat.*

$$$$ ✕⌂ **Estalagem Vila Joya.** This is one of the most luxurious inns and
★ restaurants in the Algarve, situated above the Praia da Galé, just 4 kilometers (2½ miles) west of town. The 14 spacious, Moorish-style rooms
and three opulent suites, all with a sea view, are superbly appointed.
Internal arches create a delightful sense of space, and the exquisite bathrooms are adorned with rich mosaic tiling. The inn has direct access
to the beach, a heated pool, and excellent à la carte lunches. At night
you'll order from a mostly French menu and dine in a candlelit setting
(reservations essential; jacket and tie). ⊠ *Praia da Galé, 8200 Albufeira,* ☎ *089/591795,* ℻ *089/591201. 14 rooms, 3 suites. Restaurant, bar, pool, sauna, putting green. AE, DC. Closed Nov. 15–Feb.
15.*

$$$ ✕⌂ **Hotel Cerro Alagoa.** This modern hotel on the hill above town pro-
vides the most comfortable of Albufeira's central lodgings. The smart,
well-equipped guest rooms have private balconies; be sure to ask for
one with a sea view. The Cerro Alagoa is popular with Europeans, who
like to relax around the pleasant pool and garden. It's a 10-minute walk
to the center of town, which makes the hotel a good base for explor-
ing. A courtesy bus runs guests to nearby beaches. ⊠ *Via Rápida, Apt.
2155, 8200,* ☎ *089/580–2100,* ℻ *089/580–2199. 310 rooms. Restau-
rant, bar, indoor and outdoor pools, sauna, health club. AE, DC, MC,
V.*

$$$ ✕⌂ **Hotel Montechoro.** This modern development in the village of Mon-
techoro, 3½ kilometers (2 miles) north of town, is ideal for those who
like to be cocooned in the privacy of their own resort complex. Among
the health and fitness facilities are two pools, tennis and squash courts,
and a sauna. Guest rooms are furnished in up-to-date style and look
out over the surrounding countryside. Your every wish can be fulfilled
here, even if you never go off the property: There are four separate bars,
the Montechoro Restaurant, and the rooftop Amendoeiras Grill, from
which you can get stupendous views. ⊠ *Av. Dr. Francisco Sá Carneiro,
8200,* ☎ *089/589423,* ℻ *089/589947. 362 rooms. Restaurant, 4
bars, grill, 2 pools, sauna, tennis courts, exercise room, squash, shops,
billiards. AE, DC, MC, V.*

Nightlife

Albufeira tries hard to maintain its reputation as the Algarve's num-
ber-one nightspot. Many bars and discos here have promotional nights
that are enormously popular with the young, with free or reduced-price
drinks and admission, and Rua São Gonçalo de Lagos boasts several
places that guarantee a lively crowd. Of the discos, **Kiss** (⊠ Montechoro), **Silvia's** (⊠ Rua São Gonçalo de Lagos), and **Club 7½** (⊠ Rua
São Gonçalo de Lagos) are still hopping and stay open nightly until 4
AM. The **Classic Bar** (⊠ Rua São Gonçalo de Lagos 10) is a good late-
night haunt. For a less energetic evening, there's **Sir Harry's Bar** (⊠
Largo Eng. Duarte Pacheco), an English-style pub with an interesting
clientele of different nationalities. It's open daily 10 AM–3 AM.

Shopping

Albufeira boasts a **Modelo Shopping Center** (⊠ Bypass road above town), a complex of more than 60 shops open daily 10 AM–10 PM. For local handicrafts, ceramics, and leather goods, the best shopping area is in the pedestrian **Rua do Santo António** and the surrounding streets. **Infante Dom Henrique House** (⊠ Rua Cândido dos Reis 30) offers a wide selection of high-quality ceramics, including porcelain dishes and baskets and handmade Portuguese earthenware with 17th-century motifs. For fine shoes and leather bags, try the branch of the Parisian store **Charles Jourdan** (⊠ Edifício Tural, Av. de 25 Abril).

Armação de Pêra

㉔ *14 km (9 mi) west of Albufeira.*

At this bustling resort, local boats take sightseers on ✆ **cruises** to the caves and grottoes along the shore, past the Praia Nossa Senhora da Rocha (Beach of Our Lady of the Rocks) to the west, named after the Romanesque chapel above the beach.

Beach

Armação de Pêra has the largest beach in the Algarve: a wide, sandy stretch with a pretty promenade.

Dining and Lodging

$$ ✕ **A Santola.** This delightful restaurant, with windows that look out to the beach, is considered the best in town for everything it offers, but the seafood is especially good—the restaurant's name means "crab." Try the excellent cataplana, a real Algarve specialty chock-full of everything delicious. ⊠ *Largo da Fortaleza*, ☎ *082/312332. MC, V. Closed Sun.*

$$$ ✕⌂ **Hotel Garbe.** The bar, lounge, and restaurant—all with terraces that provide unhindered views of the sea—maximize the superb location of this squat, white hotel that looms over the western edge of the beach. It sits on top of a low cliff and is built on several levels, with a flight of steps to the beach below. Rooms are modern and smartly furnished, the public rooms are bright and attractive, and the bar has a fine sea view. ⊠ *Av. Marginal, 8365,* ☎ *082/315187,* 𝔽𝔸𝕏 *082/315087. 152 rooms. Restaurant, bar, coffee shop, pool. AE.*

$$$ ⌂ **Hotel Viking.** About 1 kilometer (½ mile) west of town, the Viking stands near the coast, not far from a good, sandy beach. Its swimming pools (one for children), tennis courts, and bars are situated between the main building and the cliff top. You may bargain with the town's fishermen for a sail around the impressive local grottoes. ⊠ *Praia Nossa Senhora da Rocha, 8365,* ☎ *082/314870,* 𝔽𝔸𝕏 *082/314852. 184 rooms. Restaurant, bar, 2 pools, tennis courts, boating, shops, dance club. AE, DC, MC, V.*

Carvoeiro

㉕ *20 km (12 mi) west of Albufeira, 5 km (3 mi) south of main highway.*

The picturesque harbor here merits a diversion, but like many small-scale fishing villages in the region, Carvoeiro is beginning to show the strain of recent development.

Tennis

The **Carvoeiro Tennis Club** (☎ 082/357847) has 10 courts.

Lagoa

 6 km (4 mi) north of Carvoeiro.

This market town is primarily known for its wine, *vinho Lagoa*; the red is particularly good. It's possible to tour the **winery** here, but you must ask the tourist office in Portimão to help you arrange for the visit.

The Algarve has several water parks, where you'll find huge water slides, rapids, surf pools, other water-based amusements, and restaurants and snack bars. One such park is **The Big One** (⌂ Alcantarilha, ☎ 082/322827), east of Lagoa.

Shopping

Along N125 in nearby **Porches,** you can stop at a variety of roadside shops that sell handmade pottery. **Artisans Village** (⌂ N125, between Porches and Alcantarilha) offers wine tastings and a variety of goods—from ceramics to candles and cork.

En Route   Driving in this area lets you see the rural side of the Algarve. It's not unusual to be stuck for miles behind tractors or donkey carts, and you may have to be bold when you pass. But while you're exercising your patience, note the surrounding fields planted with orange groves and nut—particularly almond—trees.

Silves

★ *7 km (4 mi) north of Lagoa, 11 km (7 mi) northeast of Carvoeiro.*

Once the Moorish capital of the Algarve, Silves is one of the region's most intriguing inland towns. Rich and prosperous in medieval times, it remained in Arab hands until 1249, though not without attempts by Christian forces to take it. In 1189, following a siege led by Sancho I, the city was sacked by Crusaders, who subsequently put thousands of Moors to the sword. Silves finally lost its importance after its almost complete destruction by the 1755 earthquake. Today it's an enjoyable excursion from the coast, as trains and buses make the 20-kilometer (12-mile) trip north from Portimão. The Rio Arade, once navigable from Silves to the sea, has been silted up for the past half century.

The Moors built an early **fortress** here, which survived untouched until the Christian sieges. The remains you see today of this 12th-century sandstone fortress with its impressive parapets were restored in 1835 and still dominate the upper part of town. You can walk around the walls for expansive views over Silves and the surrounding hills, but the rest of the castle is a mere shell, its interior a modern garden watched over by a statue of Sancho I. The fortress is a great favorite with kids, who love to clamber about its massive walls and crenellated battlements. Keep an eye open, as some places have no guardrails. ⌂ *Free.* ☉ *Daily 9–1 and 2:30–5:30.*

The 12th- to 13th-century **Santa Maria da Sé** (Cathedral of St. Mary), built on the site of a Moorish mosque, saw service as the Cathedral of the Algarve until the 16th century. The 1755 earthquake and indifferent restoration have left it rather plain inside, but its exterior gargoyles and tower still are interesting to see. ⌂ *Free; donations accepted.* ☉ *June–Sept., daily 8:30–1 and 2:30–6; Oct.–May, until 5:30.*

Although the labels are in Portuguese, the items on display at Silves's excellent **Museu Arqueologia** (Archaeological Museum) still give interesting insights into the history of the area. A primary attraction is an Arab water cistern, preserved in situ, with a 30-foot-deep well—which is among the best Arab remains in town. The museum is a few minutes' walk below the cathedral, off Rua da Sé. ⊠ *Rua das Portas de Loulé,* ☎ *082/444832.* ☜ *300$00.* ☺ *Mon.–Sat. 10–12:30 and 2–6.*

NEED A BREAK?	If you come in the morning when it's at its liveliest, snack on the edibles of the **produce market.** It's at the foot of town, close to the medieval bridge, and is open Monday through Saturday. If you arrive at lunchtime, you can have a delicious meal of spicy grilled chicken or fish from the outdoor barbecue at one of the simple restaurants facing the river.

OFF THE BEATEN PATH	**BARRAGEM DE ARADE –** For a pleasant excursion, take N124 northeast for 12 kilometers (7½ miles) to this scenic man-made dam, set in the hills. There's a restaurant, picnic area, and boat rentals.

Dining

$$ ✕ **Rui Marisqueira.** The food is the main event here, as the functional decor doesn't offer much in the way of atmosphere. The fish and shellfish are a remarkably good value, which is one reason the crowds from the coast come up into the hills to dine. Grilled sea bream and bass are usually offered, and there's locally caught game—wild boar, rabbit, and partridge—in season. ⊠ *South side of the river, at Albergaria Rui Marisqueira,* ☎ *082/443106. MC, V. Closed Tues.*

$ ✕ **Churrasqueira Valdemar.** At this inexpensive grill room on the riverfront behind the market, whole chickens are barbecued outside over charcoal. Eat under the stone arches and enjoy your *piri-piri* (spicy) chicken with salad, fries, and local wine. ⊠ *Facing the river, behind the market. No phone. No credit cards.*

Festival

In July, Silves hosts a thoroughly enjoyable **Beer Festival** on the castle grounds. Apart from being able to sample all the different kinds of Portuguese beer, you may watch folk dances and listen to traditional and orchestral music.

São Bartolomeu de Messines

28 *20 km (12 mi) northeast of Silves, 8 km (5 mi) northeast of Barragem de Arade.*

This attractive countryside village makes a nice place for a coffee break. The **parish church** dates from the late 14th century and has interior columns of spiraling, ropelike stonework.

Portimão

29 *52 km (32 mi) northwest of Faro.*

Portimão is the most important fishing port in the Algarve. Even before the Romans arrived, there was a settlement here, at the mouth of the Rio Arade. Devastated in the 1755 earthquake, the town was revived by the fish-canning industry in the 19th century. Though the colorful fishing boats now unload their catch at a modern terminal across the river, modern Portimão, sprawling with concrete high-rise buildings, remains a cheerful, busy place.

Rather than staying in Portimão, most visitors choose one of the excellent local beach resorts and visit Portimão as a day trip, especially to shop. If you prefer to stay in town, the local tourist office can help you find accommodation at one of the hotels or pensões, which are of reasonable quality.

Lunch outdoors at Portimão's **harborside** is a must. You sit at one of
many inexpensive eateries, eating the excellent charcoal-grilled sardines
(a local specialty), chewy fresh bread, a simple salad, and local red
wine, while around you the air is thick with barbecue smoke and the
tang of the sea.

The water park **Slide & Splash** (✉ Near Portimão, ☎ 082/341685) is
a refreshing stop on hot days.

Dining

$$ ✕ **A Vela.** A pleasant restaurant on one of Portimão's back streets, A
Vela has a serene, welcoming ambience. The cool, shaded dining area
is decorated in Moorish fashion with white-and-blue tiles, and the spa-
cious open kitchen produces a varied selection of tasty Portuguese and
international specialties. The accommodating staff adds to the enjoy-
ment of dining here. ✉ *Rua Dr. Manuel de Almeida 97,* ☎ *082/414016.*
AE, DC, MC, V. Closed Sun.

$ ✕ **Flor da Sardinha.** This is one of several open-air eateries next to the
bridge, by the fishing harbor. Fresh sardines are superbly grilled on stoves
at the quayside and served to the crowds sitting in informal rows at
plastic tables and chairs. A plateful of these delicious fish, with fries
and a bottle of the local red wine, is one of Portugal's best treats—at
giveaway prices. ✉ *Cais da Lota,* ☎ *082/24862. No credit cards.*

Festival

Every August, the town's **Sardine Festival** celebrates that most Portuguese
of fish and, of course, is an excuse to eat them at the open-air stalls
and cafés.

Shopping

Portimão's main shopping street is **Rua do Comércio. Rua de Santa Is-
abel** specializes in crafts, leather goods, ceramics, crystal, and fashion.
The enormous **Modelo Shopping Center** (✉ N124 at Av. Miguel Bom-
barda, toward Praia da Rocha), open daily 10 AM–10 PM, has 150 shops
and restaurants under one roof.

For handmade copper items and other metal crafts, visit **O Aquario II**
(✉ Rua Vasco da Gama 41). **O Aquario III** (✉ Rua Direita, Loja 10)
sells ceramics, porcelain, and crystal. There is a branch of the Parisian
shoe store **Charles Jourdan** (✉ Rua de Santa Isabel 26). For leather
goods, including bags and purses, stop in at **Gaby's** (✉ Rua Direita 5
and Praça Visconde Bívar 15), which sells high-quality items. A branch
of the well-known **Vista Alegre** (✉ Rua de Santa Isabel 21) has a show-
room displaying high-quality, hand-painted porcelain.

Ferragudo

 5 km (3 mi) east of Portimão.

Across the bridge from Portimão is the former fishing hamlet of Fer-
ragudo. Although it has not yet gone the tourist route of nearby Praia
da Rocha, its beach area is fast becoming developed. The town con-
tains the ruins of the 16th-century **Castelo de São João** (Castle of St.
John), built to defend Portimão from the marauding English, Dutch,
and Spanish.

Beach

Around Ferragudo's attractive beach, to the south, you can enjoy
restaurants and bars and rent sailboards.

Dining

$$ ✕ **A Lanterna.** This well-run restaurant, on the main road just over the bridge from Portimão, serves exceptional, rich fish soup and smoked swordfish, both genuine Algarvian treats. Other seafood specialties are worthy, too. ⊠ *Parchal,* ☎ *082/414429. MC, V. Closed Sun.*

Praia da Rocha

③① *3 km (2 mi) south of Portimão.*

Praia da Rocha was one of the first resorts in the Algarve to undergo a transformation for the mass market, and it's now dominated by high-rise apartments and hotels. Buses run throughout the day between the town and Portimão.

The 16th-century **Fortaleza de Santa Catarina** (Fortress of St. Catharine, ⊠ Av. Tomás Cabreira) is a defensive castle that has been partially restored and contains an open-air café.

Beach

Praia da Rocha's excellent beach is made all the more interesting by a series of huge colored rocks worn into strange shapes by the wind and sea.

Dining and Lodging

$$ ✕ **Fortaleza de Santa Catarina.** The 16th-century fortress, on the esplanade, has been converted into a bar, restaurant, and *salão de cha* (tearoom) complex. Come for a moderately priced full meal (the food is good, and there are picture windows that look out to the beach) or simply afternoon tea or a snack. Either way, the fort makes an atmospheric stop. ⊠ *Av. Tomás Cabreira,* ☎ *082/22066. No credit cards.*

$$ ✕ **Safari.** Set on a cliff above the beach, this lively Portuguese restaurant has a distinctly African flavor. Seafood and delicious Angolan recipes are the best choices: Try the chicken curry or one of the charcoal grills and enjoy your meal on the terrace. ⊠ *Rua António Feu,* ☎ *082/415540. AE, DC, MC, V.*

$$$–$$$$ ✕🖬 **Algarve.** This modern luxury hotel—the best in Praia da Rocha—is perched atop a cliff, with marvelous sea views, and even has a disco set into the rocks! Many of the public rooms are brightly decorated in Moorish style, and the spacious guest rooms have tile floors and balconies facing the water. Among the numerous facilities are two saltwater pools and a beach bar. The staff at all levels is most helpful, and there's 24-hour room service. ⊠ *Av. Tomás Cabreira,* ☎ *082/415001,* 𝔽𝔸𝕏 *082/415999. 220 rooms. Restaurant, bar, 2 pools, miniature golf, tennis courts, health club, boating, shops, dance club. AE, DC, MC, V.*

$$$ 🖬 **Bela Vista.** This small, tastefully decorated beachfront hotel was built
★ at the turn of the century as a private house in Moorish style. Magnificent azulejos, a wonderful staircase, and a large open fireplace are just some of the remarkable features that make this one of the most delightful accommodations in the Algarve. The guest rooms that face the sea are more expensive but worth the extra escudos. Early reservations are essential. ⊠ *Av. Tomás Cabreira,* ☎ *082/24055,* 𝔽𝔸𝕏 *082/415369. 14 rooms. Restaurant, bar. AE, DC, MC, V.*

Festival

In the first week of September, a **folklore festival** is held at various venues around the resort. Each evening, traditional song and dance are performed by special folkloric groups.

Alvor

③② *5 km (3 mi) west of Praia da Rocha.*

Characterized by a maze of streets, lanes, and blind alleys that intersect one another, the handsome old port of Alvor is one of the Algarve's best examples of an Arab village.

Beach

In the summer, many vacationers are attracted to Alvor's huge beach; while not one of the region's best, it does usually have space to spare.

Dining and Lodging

$$$–$$$$ ✕⊡ **Golfe da Penina.** This impressive golf hotel, on 360 well-main-
★ tained, secluded acres between Portimão and Lagos, has elegant public rooms and attentive service. It was one of the first luxury hotels in the Algarve and is now a member of the Forte Grand chain. Recent renovations are keeping up the hotel's high standards. Most of the smartly furnished guest rooms have balconies; those in back, with the best views, face the Serra de Monchique. The superlative golf course was designed by Henry Cotton, and hotel guests pay no greens fees. A bus shuttles you (in five minutes) to and from the hotel beach, which has a restaurant (reservations essential) and water-sports facilities. A supervised children's village has its own pool, zoo, and restaurant. The Grill Room serves excellent Portuguese dishes, and the Harlequin restaurant specializes in Italian fare. ⊠ *Montes de Alvor, Penina, 8502 Portimão,* ☎ *082/415415,* ℻ *082/415000. 192 rooms. 5 restaurants, bar, grill, 2 pools, sauna, 18-hole golf course and 2 9-hole courses, tennis courts, horseback riding, beach, windsurfing, boating, shops, children's programs (summer), private airstrip. AE, DC, MC, V.*

$$$ ✕⊡ **Hotel Alvor Praia.** This comfortable, split-level luxury hotel is set
★ on low cliffs overlooking the beach and the bay. The rooms in the rear face the Serra de Monchique, and those facing the sea have spacious balconies. The dining room has picture windows overlooking the coast, and there's a deck where you can enjoy alfresco lunches. An elevator (or an easy walk) will take you down to the pleasant sand beach below the hotel. Guests of this hotel get a 30% discount at nearby golf courses. [df]*Praia dos Tres Irmãos, 8500 Portimão,* ☎ *082/458900,* ℻ *082/458999. 241 rooms and suites. Restaurant, bar, pool, sauna, golf privileges, miniature golf, tennis courts, boating, shops. AE, DC, MC, V.*

$$ ✕⊡ **Aparthotel Torralta.** This large apartment complex near the beach is unappealing architecturally but has good-size rooms, fully equipped kitchens, a supermarket, and daily maid service—a very good value all around, particularly out of season. Some of the leisure facilities are appealing to children, making this an excellent choice for families. ⊠ *Praia de Alvor, 8500 Portimão,* ☎ *082/459211,* ℻ *082/459171. 655 units. Restaurant, bar, 2 pools, tennis courts, horseback riding, boating, billiards, dance club. AE, DC, MC, V.*

Nightlife

Action can be found at the **casino** (☎ 082/23141).

Caldas de Monchique

③③ *16 km (10 mi) north of Portimão; take N266.*

Tucked into the green hills of the fabulous Serra de Monchique, where the cool breezes will revive you after the summertime heat of the coast, is the spa of Caldas de Monchique, whose natural therapeutic waters have been in use since Roman times. A revival in popularity in the 19th

Your passport around the world.

- Worldwide access
- Operators who speak your language
- Monthly itemized billing

Calling Card

MCI

415 555 1234 2244
J.D. SMITH

Use your MCI Card® and these access numbers for an easy way to call when traveling worldwide.

Austria (CC)♦†	022-903-012
Belarus	
From Gomel and Mogilev regions	8-10-800-103
From all other localities	8-800-103
Belgium (CC)♦†	0800-10012
Bulgaria	00800-0001
Croatia (CC)★	99-385-0112
Czech Republic (CC)♦	00-42-000112
Denmark (CC)♦†	8001-0022
Finland (CC)♦†	9800-102-80
France (CC)♦†	0800-99-0019
Germany (CC)†	0130-0012
Greece (CC)♦†	00-800-1211
Hungary (CC)♦	00▼800-01411
Iceland (CC)♦†	800-9002
Ireland (CC)†	1-800-55-1001
Italy (CC)♦†	172-1022
Kazakhstan (CC)	1-800-131-4321
Liechtenstein (CC)♦	155-0222
Luxembourg†	0800-0112
Monaco (CC)♦	800-90-19

Netherlands (CC)♦†	06-022-91-22
Norway (CC)♦†	800-19912
Poland (CC)✠†	00-800-111-21-22
Portugal (CC)✠†	05-017-1234
Romania (CC)✠	01-800-1800
Russia (CC)✠♦	747-3322
For a Russian-speaking operator	747-3320
San Marino (CC)♦	172-1022
Slovak Republic (CC)	00-42-000112
Slovenia	080-8808
Spain (CC)†	900-99-0014
Sweden (CC)♦†	020-795-922
Switzerland (CC)♦†	155-0222
Turkey (CC)♦†	00-8001-1177
Ukraine (CC)✠	8▼10-013
United Kingdom (CC)†	
To call to the U.S. using BT■	0800-89-0222
To call to the U.S. using Mercury■	0500-89-0222
Vatican City (CC)†	172-1022

To sign up for the MCI Card, dial the access number of the country you are in and ask to speak with a customer service representative.

MCI

http://www.mci.com

It helps to be pushy in airports.

Introducing the revolutionary new TransPorter™ from American Tourister® It's the first suitcase you can push around without a fight. TransPorter's™ exclusive four-wheel design lets you push it in front of you with almost no effort–the wheels take the weight. Or pull it on two wheels if you choose. You can even stack on other bags and use it like a luggage cart.

Stable 4-wheel design.

TransPorter™ is designed like a dresser, with built-in shelves to organize your belongings. Or collapse the shelves and pack it like a traditional suitcase. Inside, there's a suiter feature to help keep suits and dresses from wrinkling. When push comes to shove, you can't beat a TransPorter™. For more information on how you can be this pushy, call 1-800-542-1300.

Shelves collapse on command.

Making travel less primitive®

©1996 American Tourister®

century left the town with an attractive set of period houses and municipal buildings, including a casino, which is now a handicrafts market. These somewhat make up for the unappealing modern spa buildings.

Dining and Lodging

$ ×🏠 **Albergaria do Lageado.** This charming little inn is right in the center of the spa town. Though guest rooms are rather small, they are attractively furnished and some overlook the lush gardens. There's no great wealth of facilities—in fact, just a cozy lounge and an outdoor pool—but the simplicity is in keeping with the quiet nature of the town. The tiled dining room serves good Portuguese cooking, and there's a terrace for summer dining. You can park in the little square just down the hill. ✉ *Caldas de Monchique, 8550 Monchique,* ☎ *082/92616. 19 rooms. Dining room, pool. No credit cards. Closed Nov.–Apr.*

Shopping

In a 19th-century former casino, the **handicrafts market** sells an excellent range of pottery, clothes, lace, jewelry, and silk. It's closed Sundays.

Monchique

34 *6 km (4 mi) north of Caldas de Monchique.*

This tiny market town, like its neighbor Caldas de Monchique, is known for its handicrafts, particularly carving and woodworking.

OFF THE   **FOIA –** A short drive west on N266-3 brings you to the highest point in
BEATEN PATH   the Serra de Monchique. At 2,959 feet, the peak offers a café and superb views over the western Algarve.

Dining and Lodging

$ × **Teresinha.** The interior decor of this modest restaurant is simple, but
★ real atmosphere can be found on the outdoor terrace, which overlooks a lovely valley and the coastline. Located just west of Monchique, Teresinha offers good country cooking: a particularly tasty local ham as well as chicken specials, such as chicken piri-piri, done on the outdoor grill. ✉ *Estrada da Foia,* ☎ *082/92392. MC, V.*

$-$$ ×🏠 **Estalagem Abrigo da Montanha.** This pleasant, rustic inn—in the heart of the Serra de Monchique—is noted for its magnolia trees, camellia-filled garden, and panoramic views. A leisurely lunch in the restaurant, where dependable regional dishes are prepared, always makes for an enjoyable afternoon. If you want to stay longer to take in the scenery, be sure to reserve in advance for one of the welcoming rooms (all with views). ✉ *Corto Pereiro, Estrada da Foia, 8550 Monchique,* ☎ *082/92131,* FAX *082/93660. 15 rooms. Restaurant, bar, pool. AE, DC, MC, V.*

Festival

The **Feira de Outubro** (October Fair), held at the end of the month, gathers together crafts, goods, and produce from villages throughout the Serra de Monchique. It's one of the best of the Algarve's annual fairs.

LAGOS AND THE WESTERN ALGARVE

From the bustling holiday town of Lagos, the rest of the western Algarve is easily accessible. This is the most unspoiled part of the region, with some genuinely isolated beaches and bays along an often windbuffeted route that reaches to the southwest and the magnificent Cabo São Vicente.

Numbers in the margin correspond to points of interest on the Algarve and Lagos maps.

Lagos

★ ㉟   *13 km (8 mi) west of Portimão.*

An attractive, busy fishing port with some beautiful cove beaches nearby, Lagos draws a mixed international crowd. Here, you feel, is a town whose inhabitants follow a way of life that goes beyond catering to tourists, although there is no shortage of attractions for visitors. The main pedestrian streets leading off the central Praça Gil Eanes are lined with shops, restaurants, cafés, and bars—all of which do a roaring business in summer.

The town has a venerable history, with sights to prove it. Lagos's deepwater harbor and wide bay have made it a natural choice for various groups of settlers, starting with the Carthaginians, who founded the town around 400 BC. Under the Moors, Lagos was a center for trade between Portugal and Africa. Even after the town fell to the Christians in 1241, trade continued and was greatly expanded under the rule of Prince Henry the Navigator, who used Lagos as his base. The town later became capital of the Algarve, a role it lost in 1756, after the great earthquake reduced much of the city to rubble. Nonetheless, some interesting buildings remain, as does the circuit of defensive walls, built between the 14th and 16th centuries over older, Moorish bastions. Some of the best-preserved parts of the walls can be seen from near the expansive Praça da República, at the southwest end of Avenida dos Descobrimentos.

㊱   In the 15th century, the first African slave market in Europe was held under the arches of the old **Casa da Alfandega** (Customs House, ⊠ Praça da República). The building now houses an art gallery.

It was from the Manueline window of the **Governor's Palace** (⊠ Praça da República) that the young king Dom Sebastião is said to have addressed his troops before setting off on his crusade of 1578. The crusade was a failure, and the king and his men died in Morocco at Alcácer-Quibir. (Dom Sebastião is further remembered by a much-maligned modernistic statue that stands in Praça Gil Eanes.)

★ ㊲   Lagos's most extraordinary building is the early 18th-century Baroque **Igreja de Santo António** (Church of St. Anthony), off Rua General Alberto Silveira. The decoration inside is a magnificent riot of gilt extravagance made possible by the import of gold from Brazil. Dozens of cherubs and angels clamber over the walls, among fancifully carved woodwork and azulejos. ⊠ *Rua Henriques Correira Silva,* ☎ *082/762301.* ☑ *200$00.* ⊙ *Tues.–Sat. 9:30–12:30 and 2–5.*

㊳   The **Museu Municipal** (Municipal Museum) houses an amusing jumble of exhibits, including mosaics, archaeological and ethnological items, and a town charter from 1504—all arranged haphazardly. ⊠ *Rua General Alberto Silveira.* ☑ *200$00.* ⊙ *Tues.–Sun. 9:30–noon and 2–5.*

㊴   The 17th-century fort **Pau da Bandeira** (Pole of the Flag) defended the entrance to the harbor in bygone days. From inside the fort you can look out onto sweeping ocean views. ⊠ *Av. dos Descobrimentos.* ☑ *200$00.* ⊙ *Tues.–Sat. 10–1 and 2–6, Sun. 10–1.*

For an interesting perspective on the rock formations and grottoes of the area's shoreline, take one of the **cruises** offered by fishing boats near the Ponta da Bandeira. Check for departure times at the boards on the quayside.

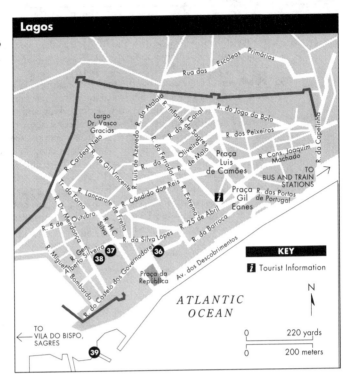

Beaches

The largest beach near town and one of the best centers for water sports
is the 4-kilometer (2½-mile) stretch of **Meia Praia,** to the northeast. Buses
leave for here from the riverfront Avenida dos Descobrimentos, and
in summer there's ferry service a few hundred yards from Ponta da Bandeira.

All the other good beaches are south of town and can be reached on
the main road (an extension of Avenida dos Descobrimentos). You can
drive to the prettiest one—**Praia de Dona Ana**—by following the signs
for the Hotel Golfinho or take an enjoyable 30-minute walk along the
cliff top. If you choose to hoof it, pass the fort, turn left at the fire station, and follow the footpaths, which go to the most southerly point,
Ponta da Piedade, and its lighthouse. Along the way are several delightful cove beaches with fascinating rock formations and some beach
cafés.

Dining and Lodging

$$$$ ✕ **No Patio.** This happy restaurant with an attractive inner patio is run
by a Danish couple, Bjarne and Gitte. The fare, some of the finest food
in Lagos, is best described as international with a Scandinavian accent.
Specialties include *matjes* herring, duck-liver mousse, and tenderloin
of pork with a Madeira and mushroom sauce. ⊠ *Rua Lançarote de
Freitas 46,* ☎ *082/763777. AE, MC, V.*

$$$ ✕ **Dom Sebastião.** Portuguese cooking, charcoal-grilled fish specials,
★ and unobtrusive service are the attractions at this cheerful restaurant
on Lagos's main pedestrian street. You can dine inside at elegant can-
dlelit tables set on a cobblestone floor or outside on the sidewalk ter-

race. While you ponder the menu, you'll be served an impressive array of appetizers (included in the cover charge). You may wish to start your meal with smoked swordfish and follow it with grilled tuna or the cataplana—all extremely good. ⊠ *Rua 25 de Abril 20,* ☎ *082/762795. AE, DC, MC, V. Closed Sun. Oct.–May.*

$$ ✗ Mirante. Perched on the cliff above the beautiful Praia de Dona Ana and just to the south of the town center, this restaurant shouts its fishermen's credentials loudly: A cork ceiling, ropes, and nets decorate the narrow interior. Mirante makes an excellent lunch stop or a place for an early dinner in summer, when the views over the sea are lovely. Try the splendid tuna steak stewed with onions and, for dessert, the filling homemade cream tart. The staff is very friendly and efficient. ⊠ *Praia de Dona Ana,* ☎ *082/762713. MC, V.*

$$ ✗ O Galeão. Tucked away on a back street, this restaurant is a popular local choice—so much so that you'll wait in line unless you've made a reservation. There's a bustling, informal atmosphere here, and the food is first-rate, particularly the steaks—for once, fish, though well cooked, isn't the main event. A reasonably priced wine list encourages you to sample some more unusual regional choices; ask for advice if you're unsure. ⊠ *Rua da Laranjeira 1,* ☎ *082/763909. AE, DC, MC, V.*

$ ✗ Piri-Piri. This small, low-key restaurant, done in understated pastel colors, is on one of the main tourist streets and offers an inexpensive but extensive menu. The long list of Portuguese dishes includes a variety of market-fresh fish, but the house specialties are the tasty piripiri pork and chicken that give the restaurant its name. ⊠ *Rua Afonso d'Almeida 10,* ☎ *082/763803. MC, V.*

$$$ ✗▥ Hotel de Lagos. This state-of-the-art hotel is attractively laid out
★ at the eastern edge of the Old Town, within easy walking distance of the center. The rooms are strung across several levels, and the uniquely designed building includes gardens, tasteful lounges, and patios. Guest rooms are large and elegantly appointed, with attractive tiling everywhere, even on lamps and tabletops. The rooms look out over a pool or across the river to the coast. A regularly scheduled courtesy bus shuttles guests to the Meia Praia beach, where the hotel has some outstanding club facilities. Guests also get reduced greens fees at nearby golf courses. ⊠ *Rua Nova da Aldeia, 8600,* ☎ *082/769967,* ℻ *082/769920. 317 rooms. Restaurant, bar, 2 pools, golf privileges, tennis courts, shops. AE, DC, MC, V.*

$$$ ✗▥ Hotel Golfinho. On the cliffs above a pretty cove beach, this hotel maximizes its location with balconies, which give lovely views of the sea and inland reaches. The Golfinho is large and modern, but its guest rooms are done in traditional Portuguese style, with attractive wood and leather furniture. It's geared toward tour groups, and the amenities tend to be practical—there's a ground-floor coffee shop and terrace, where many guests congregate. The hotel is just under a mile from the town center, and a courtesy bus shuttles people back and forth all day. Cliff-top paths lead from the Golfinho to beautiful cove beaches nearby. ⊠ *Praia de Dona Ana, 8600,* ☎ *082/769900,* ℻ *082/769999. 262 rooms. Restaurant, bar, coffee shop, pool, bowling, shops, dance club. AE, DC, MC, V.*

$ ▥ Pensão Mar Azul. Its choice central location makes this simple, budget-priced *pensão* (pension) a terrific value, although rooms that face the pedestrian thoroughfare can be noisy in high season. Nonetheless, the sparely furnished quarters—some with a terrace—are more than adequate, and there's a comfortable community lounge. ⊠ *Rua 25 de Abril 13–1, 8600,* ☎ *082/769749 or 082/769143,* ℻ *082/769960. 18 rooms. No credit cards.*

Nightlife

A good bar is **Mullens** (✉ Rua Cândido dos Reis 86), whose enthusiastic staff makes things swing until 2 AM; full meals are served, too. **Shots in the Dark** (✉ Rua 1 de Maio 16) is a raucous rock bar. Despite music that is brutally loud at times, the **Zanzibar** (✉ Rua 25 de Abril 93) is actually somewhat refined. For late-night dancing, **Phoenix** (✉ Rua 5 de Outubro 11) plays disco and pop until 4 AM.

Outdoor Activities and Sports

GOLF

The 18 holes of the **Palmares Golf Club** (✉ Monte Palmares, Meia Praia, ☎ 082/762953 or 082/762961) overlook Lagos Bay.

Shopping

Lagos has several good antiques shops. **Casa do Papagaio** (✉ Rua 25 de Abril 25) is more like a messy museum, with its dusty antiques and bric-a-brac piled high in every corner. It's great for browsing even if you don't buy.

Praia da Luz

40 *6 km (4 mi) west of Lagos.*

Until a few years ago, there was an active fishing fleet at this lovely spot, and one of visitors' favorite pastimes was to watch the boats being hauled onto the broad sandy beach. The boats are gone now, but despite the wave of development that has hit the village, this is still one of the Algarve's most attractive holiday destinations. At the western edge of town is a delightful little church facing an 18th-century fortress, which once guarded against pirates and has now been converted to an attractive restaurant. Many of the accommodations available in Luz are in private villas and apartments; the tourist office in Lagos can advise about them.

Dining and Lodging

$$$ ✕ **Fortaleza.** Housed in a fortress whose foundations date to Moor-
★   ish times, this pleasant seaside restaurant does an admirable job of preparing international and local specialties. Wednesday evenings there is traditional Portuguese folk music to accompany your meal, and on Friday nights (9 PM–2 AM) there is a fado show. ✉ *Rua da Igreja 3,* ☎ *082/789926. MC, V.*

$$$ ✕▣ **Bela Vista.** A new and welcome addition to the Luz accommo-
★   dation scene, this smart hilltop hotel is built in a horseshoe shape that provides every room with a magnificent sea view. Each of the generous rooms and suites has an ample terrace and is outfitted with all the modern conveniences, including a coffeemaker. The hotel is family owned and attentively managed. With its excellent restaurant, two swimming pools, and close proximity (500 yards) to a fine beach, this is an ideal spot for a brief or extended stay. ✉ *Praia da Luz, 8600 Lagos,* ☎ *082/788655,* FAX *082/788656. 39 rooms, 6 suites. Restaurant, bar, 2 pools, sauna, tennis, health club. AE, DC, MC, V.*

$$$ ✕▣ **Luz Ocean Club.** You may rent these well-appointed one-, two-, or three-bedroom self-service apartments (with daily maid service) for short or long stays, but you must reserve well in advance. One of the best complexes in the Algarve, the Luz Ocean Club blends well with the old village surroundings, yet still provides a high level of comfort in its carefully decorated units. They are all near the beach, where the water-sports facilities are excellent. The club is off the main road on the way from Lagos to Sagres, and there are several restaurants and bars nearby. Although there's plenty to do, you'll need a car to explore the area. ✉ *Rua Direita,* ☎ *082/789472,* FAX *082/789763. 210 apart-*

*ments with kitchen. 2 restaurants, 3 pools, 3 tennis courts, playground.
V.*

Outdoor Activities and Sports
SCUBA DIVING

Lessons by certified instructors, equipment sales and rentals, and boat outings are available at the **Sea Sports Center** (✉ Av. dos Pescadores, Loja 4, ☎ FAX 082/789538), which also arranges waterskiing.

TENNIS

The **Luz Ocean Club** (☎ 082/789472) has three courts.

WINDSURFING

The broad bay provides an excellent venue for this exciting sport. Instruction and equipment rental are available directly on the beach.

Burgau

❹❶ *4 km (2½ mi) west of Praia da Luz.*

Here again is an attractive fishing village that has succumbed to the wave of tourism that has swept over the Algarve in recent years. Luckily, its fine beach remains unchanged and the narrow, steep streets leading to it have held the masses back and helped to maintain the original character of the lower part of the village.

Outdoor Activities and Sports
The **Burgau Sports Centre** (☎ 082/69350), just off the Lagos–Sagres road, has tennis and squash courts, plus table tennis and a pool.

Salema

❹❷ *5 km (3 mi) west of Burgau.*

Salema is blessed with a lovely, 1,970-foot-long beach at the foot of surrounding green hills. New development is fast changing the face of this pretty place, until recently a simple fishing village, but it's still one of the most relaxed of local towns.

Outdoor Activities and Sports
GOLF

Sixteen kilometers (10 miles) west of Lagos you'll find the 18-hole course at **Parque da Floresta** (✉ Budens, ☎ 082/65333).

Vila do Bispo

❹❸ *6 km (4 mi) northwest of Salema, 22 km (14 mi) west of Lagos.*

At the western terminus of the N125 highway, this small inland town is a quiet place. The interior of its **church**—right in the center of town—is covered with 18th-century azulejos.

Sagres

❹❹ *10 km (6 mi) southwest of Vila do Bispo, 32 km (20 mi) southwest of Lagos.*

In the 19th century, this village, amid harsh, barren moorland, was rebuilt over earthquake ruins. Today there's little of note apart from a series of fine, sweeping beaches. It's mainly a young crowd that vacations here, staying the summer for the laid-back beach scene. Apartments and villas are growing steadily in number, and expansion threatens to overwhelm the little square and fishing harbor.

★ ☺ Views from the **Fortaleza de Sagres** (Sagres Fortress), an enormous run of defensive walls that sits high above the crashing ocean, are spectacular. Its massive walls and battlements make it popular with young visitors. (It's about a 15-minute walk from the village to the tunnel-like entrance.)

The fortress was rebuilt in the 17th century and contains buildings often claimed to be Prince Henry's house and famous navigation school, though it's more likely that Henry built his school at Cabo São Vicente. But this doesn't detract from the fort's powerful atmosphere. Certainly the **Venta da Rosa** (Wind Compass, or compass rose) dates from Prince Henry's period. Only uncovered this century, this large circular construction made of stone and packed earth is set in the courtyard just inside the fortress. Of the same age is the partially ruined and forlorn **Graça Chapel**.

A stark, modern building within the fortress walls houses a small **museum** with exhibits documenting the region's history. ✉ *Free.* ☉ *Tues.–Sun. 10–noon and 2–6.*

Dining and Lodging

$$$ ⨯🏠 **Pousada do Infante.** Beautifully poised on the cliffs across the bay
★ from the fortress, this modern pousada (1960) is a delightful two-story country house. There are relatively few facilities here, but the inn does have one attraction that really matters—the glorious view of the sea and the craggy rock cliffs. The public rooms have Moorish embellishments and are very comfortable, particularly the bar/terrace, a perfect place to watch the sun set. Guest rooms feel homey, and little touches around the property—such as the minarets and arches alongside the pool—make this place unique. The light, airy restaurant is a charming place for lunch or dinner, a well-respected spot that serves locally caught fish. The service is accomplished and the dessert selection particularly noteworthy—after-dinner coffee is served on the terrace. ✉ *8650,* ☎ *082/64222,* 𝕱𝕬𝕏 *082/64225. 39 rooms. Restaurant, bar, pool, tennis court. AE, DC, MC, V.*

$$–$$$ ⨯🏠 **Fortaleza do Belixe.** Two kilometers (1¼ miles) past Sagres on the
★ coastal road to Cabo São Vicente, the remnants of an isolated cliff-top fortress have been converted into the Fortaleza do Belixe. The restaurant and very small hotel are an annex of the Pousada do Infante. Although the lodgings are similar—the furnishings are smart and the rooms comfortable—the room rates here are a considerably better value. This is also an excellent spot for a meal, with good food served in the strikingly decorated dining room. ✉ *8650,* ☎ *082/64124,* 𝕱𝕬𝕏 *082/64225. 4 rooms. Restaurant, bar. AE, DC, MC, V.*

Nightlife

Since Sagres is a well-known haunt of young travelers, there are several music bars near the village square. **A Rosa dos Ventos,** in the square, and the **Last Chance Saloon,** on the road down to Praia da Mareta, are both loud, lively, and open late.

Outdoor Activities and Sports

FISHING
Turinfo (✉ Praça da República, ☎ 082/64520) can organize fishing trips around the Sagres Peninsula.

Cabo São Vicente

★ ㊺ *6 km (4 mi) west of Sagres.*

At the southwest tip of the European continent, where the landmass juts starkly into the rough waters of the Atlantic, is Cabo São Vicente, justly called *0 Fim do Mundo* (the end of the world). Legends attach themselves easily to this desolate place, which the Romans once considered sacred. It takes its modern name from the martyr St. Vincent, whose relics were brought here in the 8th century; it is said that they were transported to Lisbon 400 years later in a boat piloted by ravens.

Most historians agree it was here in the 15th century that Prince Henry built his house and the school of navigation where he trained his captains, including Vasco da Gama and Ferdinand Magellan, before they set out on their voyages of discovery. The ancient buildings were long ago destroyed by pirates and earthquakes.

The only remaining structure is a splendidly isolated **lighthouse,** the grounds of which are open to the public. The beacon is said to have the strongest reflectors in Europe—they cast a beam 96 kilometers (60 miles) out to sea—and the views are remarkable. Turquoise water whips across the base of the rust-color cliffs below, the fortress at Sagres is visible to the east, and in the distance lies the immense Atlantic.

THE ALGARVE A TO Z

Arriving and Departing

By Boat

A car/passenger ferry makes the 20-minute trip between Ayamonte in Spain and Vila Real de Santo António. ☒ *130$00 per person, 800$00 per car.* ☉ *Apr.–Oct., daily 8 AM–1 AM, ferries run every ½ hr; Nov.–Mar., daily 9–9, ferries run hourly.*

By Bus

Various companies run daily express buses between Lisbon and Lagos (5 hours 30 minutes), Portimão (4 hours 30 minutes), Faro (5 hours 30 minutes), Tavira (5 hours), and Vila Real de Santo António (5 hours 30 minutes). Generally this is more comfortable than traveling by train, and some of the luxury coaches have a toilet, TV, and food service. Any travel agency in Lisbon can reserve a seat for you; in summer, book at least 24 hours in advance.

Four buses a day run from the Spanish town of Ayamonte to Vila Real de Santo António. The 3:15 PM bus connects in Vila Real de Santo António with buses that go on to Faro and Lagos.

By Car

To reach the Algarve from Lisbon, cross the Rio Tejo bridge and take the toll road to Setúbal. Beyond here, the main IP1 highway runs via Alcácer do Sal, Grândola, and Ourique, eventually joining N125, the main east–west thoroughfare near Guia, north of Albufeira. To reach Portimão, Lagos, and the western Algarve, turn right; go straight to reach Albufeira; and turn left for Faro and the eastern Algarve. The drive from Lisbon to Faro, Lagos, or Albufeira takes about four hours, longer in the summer, on weekends, and on holidays.

Visitors driving from Spain can now cross a suspension bridge over the Rio Guadiana, from Ayamonte to Vila Real de Santo António. There are no longer any border controls between Spain and Portugal, a consequence of the European Union.

By Plane

International and domestic airlines use **Faro Airport** (☎ 089/818281; flight information, ☎ 089/818982), which is 6 kilometers (4 miles) west of town. The airport accommodates frequent flights from various European cities, and TAP has regular daily service from Lisbon and Porto. Flying time from Lisbon is 45 minutes; from Porto, 90 minutes.

It's easiest to take a taxi from the terminal building to the center of Faro. It should cost about 1,200$00, but ask the price in advance. Buses 14 and 16 make the same journey hourly, 8 AM–9 PM (until 11 PM July–mid-Sept.); buy tickets on board (✉ 140$00).

By Train
There are regular daily departures to the Algarve from Barreiro station, 10 kilometers (6 miles) south of Lisbon (☞ Lisbon A to Z *in* Chapter 2). The route runs through Setúbal to the rail junction of Tunes (3 hours from Barreiro) and continues on to Albufeira (another 10 minutes), Faro (another 40 minutes), and all stations east to Vila Real de Santo António (another 2 hours). For the western route to Silves (20 minutes) and Lagos (1 hour), you must change trains at Tunes.

Getting Around

Public transportation in general is fairly good, if sometimes infrequent on Sundays and holidays. Regardless, this region is one of the few in Portugal where having a car isn't essential (though, of course, it allows for more flexibility).

By Bus
The main form of public transportation in the Algarve is the bus, and every town and village has its own terminal. You may have to walk from the main road to the more isolated beaches, however. Tickets are relatively inexpensive, though a bus ride always costs more than the comparable train journey.

The major terminals are at **Lagos** (✉ Rossío São João, ☎ 082/762944), **Portimão** (✉ Largo do Dique, ☎ 082/23211), **Albufeira** (✉ Av. da Liberdade, ☎ 089/514301), **Faro** (✉ Av. da República, ☎ 089/803792), and **Vila Real de Santo António** (✉ Av. da República, ☎ 081/43195). Most ticket offices have someone who speaks at least a little English. The booklet *Guia Horário,* which costs 150$00 and is available at main terminals, lists every bus service, with timetables and information in English. Some local services are infrequent or don't run on Sunday.

By Car
The east–west N125 extends 165 kilometers (102½ miles) from the Spanish border to Vila do Bispo, in the far west of the Algarve. It runs parallel to the coast but slightly inland, with clearly marked turnoffs to the beach towns. New, faster stretches of highway are under construction everywhere, and roadwork and diversions add to the traffic that's normally to be expected near the busy resorts. A new high-speed motorway, IP1, extends from the Spanish border to Guia. In inland areas, minor country roads are not always well maintained; when driving at night in rural areas, look out for donkey carts and mopeds without lights.

By Train
The railroad connects Lagos in the west with Vila Real de Santo António in the east—running close to N125. Several trains a day run the entire scenic route, which takes three to four hours; tickets are very reasonably priced, and the trip is pleasant. Some of the faster trains don't stop at every station, and some of the stations are several miles from the towns they serve, though there is usually a connecting bus. The main train stations generally have someone who speaks some English, but it's easiest to get information at the tourist offices. At the Faro and Lagos offices, timetables are posted.

Contacts and Resources

Car Rental
Most of the major international firms have offices at Faro Airport, and many have branches elsewhere in the Algarve, too. Try **Auto Jardim** (Albufeira: ⊠ Av. da Liberdade, ☎ 089/589715; Faro: ⊠ Airport, ☎ 089/818433); **Avis** (Albufeira: ⊠ Rua da Igreja Nova 13, ☎ 089/52678; Faro: ⊠ Airport, ☎ 089/818538; Lagos: ⊠ Largo das Portas de Portugal 11, ☎ 082/63691; Praia da Rocha: ⊠ Hotel Algarve, Av. Tomás Cabreira, ☎ 082/415029; Quarteira: ⊠ Centro Comercial Abertura Mar, ☎ 089/314519), **Budget** (Albufeira: ⊠ Cerro Grande, ☎ 089/514997; Faro: ⊠ Airport, ☎ 089/818888, and ⊠ Hotel Eva, Av. da República 1, ☎ 089/803491; Praia da Rocha: ⊠ Av. Cabreira, ☎ 082/415370), **Europcar** (Albufeira: ⊠ Rua Dr. Diogo Leote 6, ☎ 089/512444; Faro: ⊠ Airport, ☎ 089/818777 or 089/818726, and ⊠ Av. da República 2, ☎ 089/823778; Monte Gordo: ⊠ Praça Luis de Camões, Loja D, ☎ 081/41747; Praia da Rocha: ⊠ Av. Tomás Cabreira, ☎ 082/415465), or **Hertz** (Faro: ⊠ Rua 1 de Maio, ☎ 089/824877).

Consulates
American and Canadian citizens must contact their consulates in Lisbon (☞ Lisbon A to Z *in* Chapter 2). However, Portimão does have a **British consular office** (⊠ Largo Francisco A. Mauricio 7, ☎ 082/417800).

Emergencies
The national emergency number is 115.

POLICE
Faro (⊠ Rua Serpa Pinto, ☎ 089/822022); **Lagos** (⊠ Rua General Alberto Silveira, ☎ 082/762930).

Guided Tours
Jeep "safaris" are a unique way to see fascinating inland villages on minor, rural roads. Lunch is usually included in the price. One safari operator is **Miltours** (⊠ Rua Veríssimo de Almeida 14, Faro, ☎ 089/802030).

Hospitals
Hospitals include those at **Faro** (⊠ Rua Leão Pinedo, ☎ 089/22011), **Lagos** (⊠ Rua do Castelo dos Governadores, ☎ 082/763034), and **Portimão** (☎ 082/803411). In addition, each Algarve region has a health center for primary medical (out-patient) treatment; local tourist offices will supply addresses and telephone numbers.

Late-Night Pharmacies
Each town in the Algarve has at least one pharmacy that stays open late; check with the local tourist office or consult the notice posted on every pharmacy's door for current schedules.

Travel Agencies
There are travel agencies on practically every corner in every town in the Algarve. Most of these can book guided sightseeing tours. Reliable ones include **Abreu** (⊠ Av. da República 124, Faro, ☎ 089/805335; ⊠ Rua Infante Dom Henrique 83, Portimão, ☎ 082/416151), one of the largest and oldest in the country; **Marcus & Harting** (⊠ Rua Conselheiro Bivar 69, Faro, ☎ 089/24034; ⊠ Rua Caetano Feu 2, Praia da Rocha, ☎ 082/416202; ⊠ Areias de São João, Albufeira, ☎ 089/512825); **Star** (⊠ Rua Conselheiro Bivar 36, Faro, ☎ 089/805525; ⊠ Rua J. Biker 26A, Portimão, ☎ 082/416063), agents for American Express; **Viagens Rawes** (⊠ Rua Conselheiro Bivar 72–78, Faro, ☎

089/803195; ✉ Rua da Hortinha 34C, Portimão, ☎ 082/23092); and **Wagon-Lits** (✉ Rua do Pé da Cruz 14, Faro, ☎ 089/805403).

Visitor Information

The provincial tourist office is the **Algarve Regional Tourist Board** (✉ Av. 5 de Outubro, 8000 Faro, ☎ 089/800400). There are also local tourist offices in **Albufeira** (✉ Rua 5 de Outubro, ☎ 089/512144), **Armação de Pêra** (✉ Av. Marginal, ☎ 082/312145), **Faro** (✉ Airport, ☎ 089/818582; ✉ Rua da Misericórdia 8–12, ☎ 089/803604), **Lagos** (✉ Largo Marquês de Pombal, ☎ 082/763031), **Loulé** (✉ Edifício do Castelo, ☎ 089/63900), **Monte Gordo** (✉ Av. Marginal, ☎ 081/44495), **Olhão** (✉ Largo da Lagoa, ☎ 089/713936), **Portimão** (✉ Largo 1 de Dezembro, ☎ 082/23695), **Praia da Rocha** (✉ Av. Tomás Cabreira, ☎ 082/22290), **Quarteira** (✉ Av. Infante de Sagres, ☎ 082/312217), **Sagres** (✉ Promontório de Sagres, ☎ 082/64125), **Silves** (✉ Rua 25 de Abril, ☎ 082/442255), **Tavira** (✉ Praça da República, ☎ 081/22511), and **Vila Real de Santo António** (✉ Praça Marquês de Pombal, ☎ 081/44495; ✉ Frontier Tourist Post, ☎ 081/43272).

7 Coimbra and the Beiras

From the dune-lined beaches and wide, shallow lagoon of the Atlantic coast to the soaring mountains and fortified towns near the Spanish frontier, the face of the Beiras is constantly changing. Lacing the province together is the Rio Mondego, the region's lifeblood and the most Portuguese of all rivers.

IT'S NOT FAR from one point in the Beiras to any other. In fact, you can drive from the Atlantic shore to the lonely fortified towns along the Spanish border—only 160 kilometers (100 miles)—in the time it takes many residents of Los Angeles or London to commute to work. But within this small area you will encounter tremendous diversity.

By Dennis Jaffe

To the east Portugal's highest mountains, the Serra da Estrela, rise to a height of nearly 6,600 feet and provide a playground of alpine meadows, wooded hills, and clear, rushing streams. High in the granite reaches of the Serra, a tiny trickle of an icy stream begins its tortuous journey to the sea. This is the Mondego, praised in song and poetry as the most Portuguese of all rivers. The longest river entirely within Portugal and the lifeblood of the Beiras, it provides vital irrigation to fruit orchards and farms as it flows through the heart of the province. Coimbra, the country's first capital and home to one of Europe's earliest universities, rises above its banks. Closer to the sea, under the imposing walls of Montemor Castle, the river widens to nurture rice fields before finally merging with the Atlantic at the popular beach resort of Figueira da Foz.

Historically, this region has played an important role in Portugal's development. The Romans built roads, established settlements, and in 27 BC incorporated into their vast empire the remote province known as Lusitania, which encompassed most of what is now central Portugal, including the Beiras. They left many traces of their presence in the region, including the well-known and well-preserved ruins at Conimbriga, near Coimbra.

Next came the Moors, who swept through the territory in the early 8th century and played a leading role for several hundred years. Many of the region's elaborate castles and extensive fortifications show a strong Moorish influence. The fortified towns stretching along the Spanish frontier have been the scene of many fierce battles, from the seesaw struggle against the Moors (known as the wars of Christian reconquest) to battles with the Spanish, as the fledgling Portuguese nation fought the invaders from neighboring Castile.

The Beiras also played a part in Portugal's golden age of discovery. In 1500 Pedro Álvares Cabral, a nobleman from the town of Belmonte on the eastern flank of the Serra da Estrela, led the first expedition to come upon what is now Brazil. Much of the wealth garnered during this period, when tiny Portugal controlled so much of the world's trade, financed the great architectural and artistic achievements of the Portuguese Renaissance. Throughout the region there are fine examples of the Manueline style, the uniquely Portuguese art form that reflects the nation's nautical heritage. The cathedrals at Guarda and Viseu, the Monastery of Santa Cruz at Coimbra, and the Convent of Jesus in Aveiro are especially noteworthy.

During the Peninsular War, between Napoleon's armies and Wellington's British and Portuguese forces in the early 19th century, a decisive battle was fought in the tranquil forest of Buçaco. Later in the same century, this area witnessed a much more peaceful invasion, as people from all corners of Europe came to take the waters at such well-known spas as Luso, Curia, and Caramulo. Around the turn of the century, when the now tourist-packed Algarve was merely a remote backwater, Figueira da Foz was coming into its own as an international beach resort.

Pleasures and Pastimes

Beaches

If you haven't already discovered that Portugal's beaches are some of the best in Europe, then you should during the course of exploring the western Beiras. There is a virtually continuous stretch of good sandy beach along the entire Beira Litoral—from Praia de Leirosa in the south to Praia de Espinho in the north. One word of caution: If your only exposure to Portuguese beaches has been the Algarve's southern coast, be careful here. West-coast beaches tend to have heavy surf and strong undertows and riptides. If you see a red or yellow flag, do not go swimming. The water temperature on the west coast is usually a few degrees cooler than it is on the south coast.

You can take your choice of beaches. There are fully equipped resorts, such as Figueira da Foz and Buarcos, or if you prefer sand dunes and solitude, you can lay your mat down at any one of the beaches farther north. Just point your car down one of the unmarked roads between Praia de Mira and Costa Nova and head west. The beaches at Figueira da Foz, Tocha, Mira, and Furadouro (Ovar) are particularly well suited to children; they all have lifeguards and have met the European Union standards for safety and hygiene.

Dining

The cuisine found in this region reflects the geographical diversity of the Beiras. Along the coast, as would be expected, the accent is on fresh fish. At almost any of the ubiquitous beach bar/restaurants, you can't go wrong by ordering the grilled *peixe do dia* (fish of the day). In most cases it will have been caught only hours before and will be prepared outside on a charcoal grill. You will usually be served the whole fish along with boiled potatoes and a simple salad. Wash it down with a chilled white Dão wine, and you have a tasty, healthy, and relatively inexpensive meal. In Figueira da Foz and also in the Aveiro region, *enguia* (eels), *lampreia* (lamprey), and *caldeirada,* a fish stew that is a distant cousin of the French bouillabaisse, are popular.

Moving inland, although fish is still readily available, the emphasis shifts to meat dishes. The Bairrada region, between Coimbra and Aveiro, and in particular the town of Mealhada are well known for *leitão assado* (roast suckling pig). In Coimbra the dish to try is *chanfana;* this is traditionally made with tender young kid braised in red wine and roasted in an earthenware casserole. In the mountains, fresh *truta* (trout) panfried with bacon and onions is often served, as is *javali* (wild boar). *Bacalhau* (salt cod) is found in one form or another on just about every menu in the region. Bacalhau *a brás* (slivers of cod fried in olive oil with eggs, onions, and sometimes potatoes) is one of many popular salt-cod dishes.

The Beiras contain two of Portugal's most notable wine districts: Bairrada and Dão. Particularly good years for these wines are 1983 and 1985; if you see a 1983 Porta dos Cavaleiros Reserva *tinto* (red) on a wine list, grab it. The full-bodied Dão will go wonderfully with your chanfana or leitão assado.

This region is also justly famous for its contribution to the country's dessert menus, although many of these pastry delights, such as the *arrufada* of Coimbra, are rarely found far from home. The tangy sheep's cheese of the Serra da Estrela is popular throughout the country.

With the exception of some luxury hotel dining rooms, restaurants are casual in dress and atmosphere, though a bit less casual than in the southern parts of the country. The emphasis is generally more on the food than on the trappings. Good restaurants are found throughout the region, and in many towns, hotel dining rooms are popular places to eat. Except for pizza, ethnic food is virtually nonexistent.

Festivals

In the Beiras, people are respectful of their traditions and folklore, and just about every town and village celebrates some sort of festival or fair. Dates often vary from year to year. Check with local tourist offices for details.

Fishing

There is excellent trout fishing in the Rio Vouga and in the rivers and lakes of the Serra da Estrela, particularly in the Rio Zêzere, which cuts through one of Europe's deepest glacial valleys, and in the Comprida and Loriga lakes. The coastal strip known as the Beira Litoral is full of beaches and rocky outcroppings, where you can try your luck with a variety of fish, including bass, bream, and sole. Check with the local tourist offices for information about obtaining permits. No permit is required for ocean fishing.

Lodging

Until recently, visitors to the Beiras in search of high-quality accommodations were almost solely dependent on the government-run chain of *pousadas* (inns) and a few venerable old luxury hotels, such as the Palace Hotel Buçaco. During the past few years, especially near the coast, a number of new hotels and inns have been built, and to keep up with the competition, many existing facilities have been refurbished. However, accommodations in the eastern portions of the Beiras are still limited. If you plan to travel during the busy summer months, study the maps and lodging recommendations and make advance reservations to avoid disappointment. There are seven pousadas within the Beiras, which can be used as bases to explore the entire region. (These pousadas are small; the one at Caramulo has just 12 rooms.) In addition, there are several government-approved private manor houses that take guests. Most establishments offer substantial off-season discounts. (High season varies by hotel but generally runs July 1–September 15.)

National Parks

Outdoorsy types find much to enjoy in the region's national parks. The most popular is the rugged Serra da Estrela. Portugal's largest national park, it's frequented by hikers, anglers, and those who just like to drink up its craggy alpine scenery. The newer, smaller, and less crowded Serra da Malcata was founded to help protect the Iberian lynx.

Nightlife and the Arts

With the exception of the casino at Figueira da Foz, this region is not known for its nightlife. In most of the larger towns, you can find theaters showing recent English-language films in their original version.

Shopping

The Beiras are rich in artisans' traditions, but surprisingly, even today much of what is made is only available within a limited geographic area. The region around Aveiro produces Portugal's finest china, including the well-known Vista Alegre brand, and in the Serra da Estrela, the famous Serra cheese and *presunto* (cured ham) are available in most towns, along with hand-carved wooden kitchen implements and wicker baskets.

Exploring Coimbra and the Beiras

The Beiras region encompasses the provinces of the Beira Litoral (Coastal Beira), the Beira Baixa (Lower Beira), and the Beira Alta

(Upper Beira), which together make up roughly one-quarter of continental Portugal's landmass. On the verge of being discovered, the Beiras contain some of the last remaining areas in Europe unscathed by mass tourism.

Portugal's first capital, the ancient university town of Coimbra, provides a good introduction to this part of the country. The western part of the region contains the seaside resort of Figueira da Foz and the canals and lagoons in and around Aveiro. Farther inland it includes Viseu, with its wonderful parks and historic old quarter. The mountain resort of Caramulo and the Belle Epoque towns of Luso and Curia are some of the country's most popular spas. The eastern portion of the region includes Portugal's highest mountains—the Serra da Estrela—and extends to the chain of ancient fortified towns along the Spanish border. Below we describe Coimbra and then the western and eastern Beiras, each in a separate section.

Great Itineraries

If you have 10 days, you will be able to explore the region's winding back roads and remote mountain hamlets at a comfortable pace and still have time to take in Coimbra and the beach resorts. A week is enough time to get the feel of Coimbra, visit a spa and the coast, and explore the Serra de Estrela. If you have just three days, you can visit Coimbra and the main towns and if you keep moving, include a stretch of the coast and the mountains. In any case, traveling by car is the best way to explore this part of Portugal and to capture its essence.

Numbers in the text correspond to numbers in the margin and on the Beiras map.

IF YOU HAVE 3 DAYS

Start your first day in ☷ **Coimbra** ①–㉔, with a stroll through the old town and the university. In the afternoon visit the Roman ruins at **Conimbriga** ㉕. The next day, follow the Rio Mondego to the fashionable beach resort of **Figueira da Foz** ㉗, head up the coast, and move inland to visit the china factory in **Vista Alegre** ㉙ and the Museum of the Sea at **Ilhavo** ㉚. Explore **Aveiro** ㉛, with its old town and famous Ria de Aveiro, and end the day by taking IP5 east to ☷ **Viseu** ㉞. On your third morning, visit Viseu's cathedral and Grão Vasco Museum and then continue east on IP5 to **Guarda** ㊼, before returning to Coimbra through the Serra de Estrela National Park.

IF YOU HAVE 7 DAYS

With a week, you'll be able to slow down the pace a bit and also include a few more places. Start in ☷ **Coimbra** ①–㉔ and **Conimbriga** ㉕, as above. The next day, explore the coast with visits to the beach resorts of ☷ **Figueira da Foz** ㉗ and **Buarcos** ㉘. While on the way to the former, visit the castle at **Montemor-o-Velho** ㉖ and in the evening drive out to Cape Mondego to enjoy the view and the sunset. Continue along the dune-lined coast on the third day, and after stops in **Vista Alegre** ㉙ and **Ilhavo** ㉚, explore the old-town section of ☷ **Aveiro** ㉛. The following morning, take the boat trip through the narrow waterways and marshlands that make up the Ria de Aveiro and after lunch continue on to ☷ **Viseu** ㉞ by way of **Ovar** ㉜ and the castle at **Santa Maria de Feira** ㉝. On your fifth day, continue east from Viseu and make a loop that includes visits to the fortified towns of **Celorico da Beira** ㊵, **Trancoso** ㊳, **Pinhel** ㊴, and **Almeida** ㊶—a pleasant drive through the sparsely settled countryside over little-traveled roads. Spend the night in the mountain bastion of ☷ **Guarda** ㊼. The next morning, after visiting the cathedral and museum, drive through the mountainous Serra de Estrela National Park, exiting at Seia. Continue by way of **Penacova** ㊶ to the forest of ▩ **Buçaco** ㊵, just north of Coimbra. Be sure to visit the opulent Palace Hotel and if it's within your budget, spend the night; more modest accommodations are found in the nearby spa town of ▩ **Luso** ㊴. On your last day, return to Coimbra.

IF YOU HAVE 10 DAYS

If you like castles and fortified towns, a little longer stay will allow you to view several interesting ones in the Beiras' eastern reaches. After exploring ▩ **Coimbra** ①—㉔ and **Conimbriga** ㉕, head for the coast, with a stop at **Montemor-o-Velho** ㉖. Spend two nights at ▩ **Figueira da Foz** ㉗ so you can enjoy a day relaxing on the beach there or at **Buarcos** ㉘. In the evening take in the casino's show and the next morning follow the coast north to ▩ **Aveiro** ㉛, detouring inland to pause at **Vista Alegre** ㉙ and **Ilhavo** ㉚. On the fifth day, after touring the Ria de Aveiro and stopping in **Ovar** ㉜ and **Santa Maria de Feira** ㉝, take the scenic route (N227) to ▩ **Viseu** ㉞. From there, drive a circuitous route that takes in **Celorico da Beira** ㋠, **Trancoso** ㋡, **Pinhel** ㋢, and **Almeida** ㋤ and ends at ▩ **Guarda** ㋥ for the night. Continue south from Guarda to visit the historic town of **Belmonte** ㊽ and the unusual Roman towers at Centum Celas. From Belmonte, trace an arc that includes the fortified mountain towns of **Sortelha** ㊼, **Sabugal** ㊻, and **Penamacor** ㊺, and overnight in the quiet provincial capital of ▩ **Castelo Branco** ㊷. In the morning, after seeing the gardens and exploring the town, head north through **Fundão** ㊹ to **Covilhã** ㊾, and spend a few hours exploring the Serra de Estrela National Park. Overnight at the pousada outside ▩ **Manteigas** or continue on for the 26 kilometers (16 miles) to ▩ **Gouveia** ㊿. Leave the park via N17 southwest to **Penacova** ㊶, and from there drive to the forest of ▩ **Buçaco** ㊵. You can spend the night there (at the Palace Hotel) or in nearby ▩ **Luso** ㊴ before returning to Coimbra on the 10th day.

When to Tour Coimbra and the Beiras

The Beiras, and their interior regions in particular, are some of the few attractive places in Europe where you can enjoy a July or August vacation in relative solitude. Although the Beiras' coastal beaches are quite popular during the summer months, the crowds are nothing like those you'd encounter on the Algarve. The water along this stretch of coast is not as warm as it is farther south, and as a consequence the season is considerably shorter. Plan your beach time here between early June and mid-September.

With the exception of the eastern regions, the interior is not subject to the blazing heat of the Alentejo or the interior of the Algarve and so is well suited for summertime touring. Aside from occasional showers, the weather is comfortable between early April and mid-November. Winters, especially in the eastern mountain towns, are harsh.

COIMBRA AND ENVIRONS

The exact origins of Coimbra lie deeply buried in prehistoric times. However, from its emergence as the Roman settlement of Aeminium to the present, this city on the banks of the Rio Mondego has played an influential and often crucial role in the country's development. In Roman times, it was an important way station, the midway point on the road connecting Lisbon with Braga to the north. Several of today's main thoroughfares are built on top of this ancient road. The open-air café on the Praça do Comércio is actually on the site of a Roman circus.

The year 711 marked the beginning of a centuries-long period of Moorish domination, which, except for one hiatus, lasted until the final

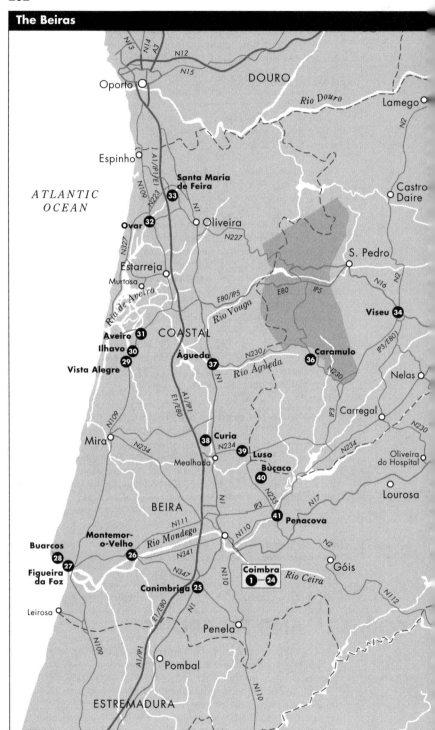

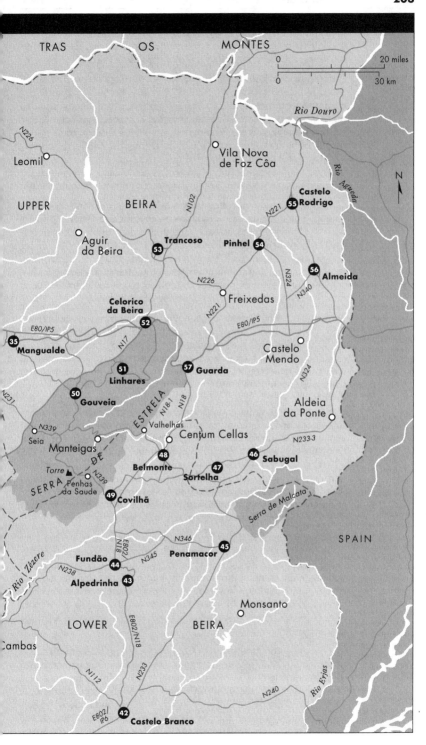

reconquest by Christian forces in 1064. At that time, Coimbra became the capital of a vast territory extending north to the Rio Douro and encompassing much of what are now the Beiras. By the 12th and 13th centuries, it had become the capital of the young Portuguese nation.

Coimbra is best known for its university. Although it was first established in Lisbon by King Dinis I in 1290 and subsequently transferred back and forth between Coimbra and Lisbon, it was finally installed on its present site in 1537. Since then the university has been one of Europe's major learning centers and has played an important role in the life of both the city and the nation. During the 1960s, the university was a focal point for much of the unrest preceding the 1974 revolution. Many current political leaders were educated there, as was Dr. António Salazar, who was the country's dictator from 1932 until 1968.

Coimbra, essentially a college town, is best visited when school is in session. The students, even in today's era of jeans and T-shirts, proudly wear the traditional black capes and adorn their briefcases with colored ribbons denoting which faculty they attend (for example: red for law, yellow for medicine). Their presence adds much color and life to the streets, bars, and restaurants of the city. After final exams in May, students, with great exuberance, burn their colored ribbons in a ceremony called *Queima das Fitas* (Burning of the Ribbons).

To devotees of fado, that uniquely Portuguese art of musical expression, Coimbra has a very special significance. It is here on the banks of the Mondego that the second great style of fado was born. With the exception of a few bars where it is performed mostly for tourists, you won't find fado "shows" in Coimbra; here it is more a form of personal expression than an entertainment medium. Wandering through the narrow, steep passageways of the old university quarter, you are likely to hear plaintive sounds drifting through the night air, perhaps from a student serenading his love. In contrast to the brasher Lisbon version, the Coimbra fado, performed only by men, is softer and gentler. Musical accompaniment is played on the traditional heart-shape, 12-string guitar, and tradition dictates that one does not applaud. During the Queima das Fitas, the square in front of the old cathedral is full of people listening in silence to fado. During the student demonstrations of the 1960s, this music was used as a form of protest in much the same manner as the folk song was in America.

Coimbra's romantic side is reserved for those willing to devote a bit more time than that required for quick hit-and-run visits to the obligatory sights. Sit in the cafés and student restaurants, watch young lovers walking hand in hand through parks, and stroll through the gardens of the Quinta das Lágrimas (House of Tears), where more than six centuries ago the ill-fated Inês de Castro was murdered. (To learn more about Inês de Castro's macabre story, check out the section on Alcobaça in Chapter 4.)

In a bucolic setting southwest of Coimbra, you'll find Conimbriga, one of the Iberian Peninsula's most important archaeological sites. It began as a small settlement in Celtic or possibly pre-Celtic times. In 27 BC, during his second Iberian visit, the emperor Augustus established the Roman province called Lusitania. It was in this period that, as the Portuguese historian Jorge Alarção wrote, "Conimbriga was transformed by the Romans from a village where people just existed into a city worth visiting." It still is.

Numbers in the margin correspond to points of interest on the Beiras and Coimbra maps.

Coimbra

❶ *165 km (102 mi) northeast of Lisbon.*

❷ The triangular plaza at the foot of the Ponte Santa Clara is the **Largo da Portagem.** The statue of Joaquim António de Aguiar, with pen in hand, represents the signing in 1833 of a decree banning religious orders throughout Portugal.

NEED A BREAK?
Why not succumb to the temptation of the pastry-filled windows of the inviting cafés along the Rua Ferreira Borges? The **Café Nicola** (⊠ Rua Ferreira Borges 35) is a good choice for sampling arrufada, Coimbra's most notable contribution to the great pastries of the world. This curved confection is said to represent the tortuous course of the Rio Mondego.

---

❸ Located on one of the city's principal shopping streets, the **Arco de Almedina** (Almedina Gate, ⊠ Rua Ferreira Borges) is a tall, graceful, arched opening in a massive stone wall. The 12th-century arch is one of the last vestiges of the medieval city walls and above it are a Renaissance carving of the Virgin and Child and an early Portuguese coat of arms. The adjacent **tower** houses the city's historical archives and the Sino de Correr (Warning Bell), used from medieval times until 1870 to signal the populace to return to the safety of the city walls. The tower is also used as an art gallery.

❹ **Rua Quebra Costas** (Street of the Broken Backs) is the main pedestrian link between the Baixa (lower town) and the Sé Velha (Old Cathedral). Try carrying a heavy load of groceries up this steep incline, and you will see where the name came from!

★ ❺ The imposing **Sé Velha** (Old Cathedral) was designed and constructed in the 12th century by the French master builders Robert and Bernard. Made of massive granite blocks and crowned by a ring of battlements, the cathedral looks more like a fortress than a house of worship. (Engaged in an ongoing struggle with the Moors, the Portuguese, who were building and reconstructing castles for defensive purposes throughout the country, often incorporated fortifications in their churches.) The harsh exterior is softened somewhat by graceful 16th-century Renaissance doorways. The somber interior has several interesting features, including a gilded wood altarpiece, a late-15th-century example of the Flamboyant Gothic style, created by the Flemish masters Olivier of Ghent and Jean d'Ypres. The walls of the Chapel of the Holy Sacrament are lined with the touching, lifelike sculptures of Jean de Rouen, whose life-size Christ figure is flanked by finely detailed representations of the apostles and evangelists. The cloisters, built in the 13th century, are distinguished by a well-executed series of transitional Gothic arches. ⊠ *Largo da Sé Velha,* ☎ *039/25273.* ⛶ *Cathedral free; cloisters 100$00.* ⊙ *Daily 10–12:30 and 2–6.*

NEED A BREAK?
The cathedral square is ringed with cafés and restaurants. **Café Sé Velha** (⊠ Rua da Joaquim António Aguiar 136), decorated with *azulejo* (tile) panels depicting local scenes, is one of the most inviting; you can sit outside in summer.

★ ❻ The **Museu Machado de Castro** (Machado de Castro Museum) contains one of Portugal's finest collections of sculpture, including works by Jean de Rouen and Master Pero and an intriguing little statue of a mounted medieval knight. The Bishop's Chapel, adorned with 18th-century azulejos and silks, is a highlight of the upstairs galleries, which also contain a diverse selection of Portuguese paintings and furniture.

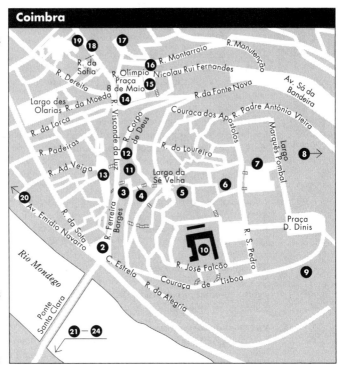

The building, itself a work of art, was constructed in the 12th century to house the prelates of Coimbra; it was extensively modified 400 years later and was converted to a museum in 1912. Be sure to take in the view from the terrace of the Renaissance loggia. As you exit the museum, note the large 18th-century azulejo panel depicting Jeronimo translating the bible. ⊠ *Largo Dr. José Rodrigues,* ☎ *039/23727.* ☞ *500$00, Sun. morning free.* ☉ *Tues.–Sun. 10–5.*

❼ The 17th-century Jesuit **Sé Nova** (New Cathedral) was patterned after the baroque church of Il Gesù in Rome, as were many such churches of the day. ⊠ *Largo da Sé Nova.* ☞ *Free.* ☉ *Daily 9:30–12:30 and 2–5:30.*

❽ **Parque de Santa Cruz** (Santa Cruz Park, ⊠ Praça da República), east of the old city, offers a pleasant mixture of luxuriant vegetation, ornate fountains, and meandering walking paths.

❾ Relief from Coimbra's oppressive summer heat can be found in the shade and greenery of the **Jardim Botânico** (Botanical Gardens, ⊠ Alameda Dr. Julio Henriques), not far from the university.

Built in 1634 as a triumphal arch, the **Porta Férrea** is adorned with the figures of the kings Dinis and João III. It marks the entrance to the principal university courtyard. ⊠ *Praça Porta Férrea.* ☉ *Daily 9:30–12:30 and 2–5.*

★ ❿ The **Velha Universidade** (Old University) is steeped in centuries-old tradition. Although there are modern dormitories and apartments available, many of the 20,000 students, some because of tradition and some for economic reasons, choose to live in one of approximately 30 old, ramshackle *repúblicas* (student republics) scattered around the university quarter. Groups of students live together (coed since the revolution) in these old houses, with the bare minimum in creature comforts, sharing costs and chores; the one indulgence they allow themselves is a cook. Traditionally to the left on the political spectrum, the repúblicas were a hotbed of anti-Salazar activity during the years of the dictatorship. The **República Bota-Abaixo** (⊠ Rua São Salvador 6), near the Machado de Castro Museum, is a typical example of this Portuguese-style cooperative. The repúblicas are not really tourist attractions, nor are they open to the public, but if you can get an invitation, don't pass up the opportunity for a glimpse of Portuguese student life.

The statue in the center of the **university courtyard** is of Dom João III; it was during his reign that the university moved permanently to Coimbra. Walk to the far end of the courtyard for a view of the Mondego and across it to the Convento de Santa Clara-a-Nova. The double stairway rising from the courtyard leads to the graceful colonnade framing the **Via Latina** (Latin Way), the scene of colorful student processions at graduation time. Amid much pomp and ceremony, doctoral degrees are presented in the **Sala dos Capelos** (Ceremonial Hall, 🎟 250$00, ⏲ Daily 10–noon and 2–5), which is capped with a fine paneled ceiling and lined with a series of portraits of the kings of Portugal.

The 18th-century **clock-and-bell tower,** rising above the courtyard, is one of Coimbra's most famous landmarks. The bell, which summons students to class and in centuries past signaled a dusk-to-dawn curfew, is derisively called the *cabra* (goat). In the southwestern corner of the courtyard is a building with four huge columns framing a set of massive wooden doors. It contains one of the world's most beautiful libraries, the **Biblioteca Joanina** (🎟 250$00, ⏲ Mon.–Sat. 10–noon and 2–5). Constructed in the early 18th century, the library contains three dazzling book-lined halls and has one of the loveliest baroque interiors in the country. The large painting in the center is of Dom João V, the monarch responsible for the library's construction.

⓫ The **Palácio de Sobre Ribas** (Palace above the Riverbanks, ⊠ Rua Sobre Ribas) occupies a tower in the ancient walls in the lower part of the old town. Converted into a private residence in the 16th century, the exterior of the building is graced by several Manueline doorways and windows.

⓬ Now containing a regional handicrafts center, the converted **Torre de Anto** (Tower of Anto) was named for the nickname of Portuguese poet Antònio Nobre, who lived in it during the 19th century. ⊠ *Rua Sobre Ribas.* ⏲ *Handicrafts center weekdays 9–12:30 and 2–5:30.*

⓭ One of the lower town's most attractive and active plazas, the **Praça do Comércio** is ringed with a variety of fashionable shops in 17th- and 18th-century town houses, while in its corners, street vendors sell everything from combs to carpets. In Roman times this was the site of the circus. The **Rua Eduardo Coelho,** which fans out from the square, is lined on both sides with shoe shops and was once known as the Street of the Shoemakers. Currently closed to the public, the **Church of Sant'Iago,** in the northeast corner, is a small, late-13th-century stone structure with finely carved Romanesque columns. At the opposite corner is the **Church of São Bartolomeu.** Dating to 957, it is one of the oldest churches in the city. Destroyed several times, it was rebuilt in its present form in 1756. The interior is of no special interest.

⓮ The **Igreja e Mosteiro de Santa Cruz** (Church and Monastery of Santa Cruz) is one of the country's richest in history and culture. The stark

12th-century stone facade is greatly enhanced by the Renaissance entrance, added as part of an extensive renovation in 1507. Unfortunately, much of the fine detail has been damaged by corrosion. Inside you will see the delicate features of the Renaissance altar carved in 1521 by Nicolas Chanterene. The high altar is flanked on either side by the intricately detailed tombs of the first two kings of Portugal, Dom Afonso Henriques and his·son, Dom Sancho I. In the sacristy are several notable examples of 16th-century Portuguese painting. The lower portions of the interior walls are lined with azulejos depicting various religious motifs. From the sacristry, a door opens to the Casa do Capitulo (Silent Cloister); this double-tier Manueline cloister contains scenes from the *Passion of Christ*, attributed to Nicolas Chanterene. ⊠ *Praça 8 de Maio*, ☎ *039/22941*. ⌺ *Church free; cloister 200$00.* ⊙ *Daily 9−noon and 2−6.*

NEED A BREAK?   Even if you aren't hungry or thirsty, take the time to stop at the **Café Santa Cruz** (⊠ Praça 8 de Maio), one of the most popular and unusual watering holes north of Lisbon. Until its conversion to more pedestrian uses in 1927, this was an auxiliary chapel for the Santa Cruz Monastery. Now its high-vaulted Manueline ceiling, stained-glass windows, and wood paneling provide a wonderful setting in which to indulge a favorite Portuguese pastime: sitting in a café with a strong, murky *bica* (Portugal's answer to espresso) and a brandy, reading the day's newspaper. In summer there are tables outside. Be forewarned: It's closed Sundays.

---

⑮ A small park with an odd assortment of domed, rose-color turrets grouped around a fountain, the **Jardim de Manga** (Manga Garden, ⊠ Rua Olímpio Fernandes) was designed by Jean de Rouen in the 16th century and once belonged to the cloisters of the Santa Cruz Monastery. The fountain symbolizes the fountain of life, and the eight pools radiating from it represent the rivers of paradise.

⑯ The impressive **Fonte dos Judeus** (Jewish Fountain, ⊠ Rua Olímpio Fernandes), dating to 1725, marks one of the boundaries of the old Jewish quarter. It's across from the Manga Garden.

⑰ A small alley leads into the notorious **Patio da Inquisição** (Patio of the Inquisition, ⊠ Rua Pedro da Rocha). This once-feared site is now home to the local Red Cross.

⑱ The broad, busy, one-way **Rua da Sofia** is one of the city's main thoroughfares. Developed in the 16th century, the road is famous for its many fine religious monuments, including the Carmo, Graça, São Pedro, and Santa Justa churches. To preserve the architectural integrity of the neighborhood, the entire street has been classified as a national monument.

⑲ The **Palácio da Justiça** (Hall of Justice) occupies a stately 16th-century building that was once the College of St. Thomas. To the left of the main entrance is a large azulejo panel depicting the goddess of justice watched over by a Knight Templar. The three panels in front read WORK, JUSTICE, and ORDER. Gracing the interior is a two-tier cloister, decorated with azulejo panels depicting historical themes associated with Coimbra. ⊠ *Rua da Sofia.* ⌺ *Free.* ⊙ *Weekdays 9−12:30 and 2−5:30.*

⑳ **O Choupal,** near the railroad bridge, is a lovely wooded area along the river at the west end of the city.

㉑ Across the river from the Largo da Portagem, the **Convento de Santa Clara-a-Velha** (Old Santa Clara Convent, ⊠ Rua de Baixo) is a stark Gothic structure with a single pointed tower. Although the convent is steeped in history, there isn't much left to see of the original 13th-century building, since the periodic flooding of the Mondego has taken its toll. At one time both Inês de Castro and Queen Isabel, the patron saint of Coimbra, were interred here.

☾ ㉒ At Coimbra's **Portugal dos Pequenitos** (Portugal of the Little Ones), children will have great fun poking around the models of Portugal's most important buildings, built to the scale of a five-year-old child. Then they can compare them with what they have seen firsthand. ⊠ *Rossio de Santa Clara,* ☎ *039/441225.* ☜ *400$00.* ☾ *Daily 9–5:30, until 7 in summer; closed Easter, Nov. 1, Dec. 25.*

㉓ Dom Pedro and Inês de Castro lived with their children in the **Quinta das Lágrimas** (House of Tears), and as the legend goes, it was here on a black January night in 1355 that Inês was killed by agents of Dom Pedro's father, Afonso IV. The 19th-century manor house on the grounds is closed to the public, but you can wander around the gardens and pause at the celebrated Fonte dos Amores (Fountain of the Lovers). ⊠ *Rua António Augusto Gonçalves.* ☜ *Free.* ☾ *Daily 9–7.*

㉔ The **Convento de Santa Clara-a-Nova** (New Santa Clara Convent) stands on a hill overlooking the city, about a 20-minute climb after crossing the river. The term "new" is relative; it was built nearly 300 years ago to escape the periodic flooding that beset the old convent, which was abandoned in 1677. The new building was consecrated in 1696, and the body of Queen Isabel was relocated there. The original painted stone tomb may be seen at the end of the lower chancel, and the 17th-century tomb, a fine example of the silver craftsmanship of the time, is in the main chancel. The church also contains an impressive statue of Isabel in nun's garb, carved from a single 10-foot-high block of limestone. During the Peninsular War, the French general Massena used the convent as a hospital for 300 troops wounded during the battle of Buçaco. The carefully hidden convent treasures escaped the desecration inflicted on so many Portuguese monuments during this period. Don't leave Santa Clara without a relaxing stroll through the enormous cloisters. ⊠ *Rua Santa Isabel.* ☜ *50$00.* ☾ *Daily 9–12:30 and 2– 5:30.*

Dining and Lodging

$$ ✕ **Dom Pedro.** The entrance, next to a car dealer, is hardly impressive,
★ but inside it's a different story. A tasteful blend of arches, tile, and wood creates just the right atmosphere in which to enjoy some of Coimbra's best food, including excellent chanfana and *açorda de mariscos* (a sort of bread porridge mixed with eggs and mounds of fresh shellfish). There is an extensive list of Portuguese wines, and service is efficient without being stuffy. The restaurant is just a few steps along the riverfront from the tourist office. ⊠ *Av. Emidio Navarro 58,* ☎ *039/29108. DC, MC, V.*

$ ✕ **Democratia.** The best that can be said about the decor is that it's functional, although the rustic *adega* (like a wine cellar) adds a touch of old Portugal. The students and locals who frequent this popular old establishment are here for the food, however, not the atmosphere. The fare is simple and inexpensive. A tasty *caldo verde* (potato soup with shredded cabbage and sausage) and some fresh grilled fish make a typical meal. ⊠ *Traves da Rua Nova 7,* ☎ *039/23784. MC, V. Closed Sun.*

$ ✕ **Kanimambo.** This pleasant, small, no-frills restaurant on a side street off the Praça Comércio offers pleasant service and occasional live music. Try their special dessert: *doce da casa* (a layered vanilla and chocolate pudding with cream). ⊠ *Rua das Azeiteiras 65–69,* ☎ *039/27115. No credit cards.*

$ ✕ **Zé Manel.** It's just a hole-in-the-wall in a back alley. The open
★   kitchen is a jumble of pots and pans, walls are plastered with an odd
assortment of yellowing paper announcements, and simple wooden tables and chairs constitute the decor, but the food is great and cheap.
If you can get in, don't pass this one up. It's a favorite with students
and hasn't yet succumbed to the tourist trade. For such a small place,
there is an amazing choice of dishes, including a wonderful *sopa da
pedra* (a rich vegetable soup served with hot stones in the pot to keep
it warm). ⌖ *Beco do Forno 10/2,* ☎ *039/23790. Reservations not accepted. No credit cards.*

$ ✕⌂ **Astoria.** Occupying a prominent downtown location facing the
★   Mondego, the domed, triangular Astoria (owned by the people who
own the Buçaco Palace) has been a Coimbra landmark since its construction in 1927. In spite of a recent face-lift, the 1920s ambience has
been largely maintained, although the aluminum windows around the
balconies seem out of step. If you like your hotels with old-world
charm and tradition and almost state-of-the-art comforts, then you will
like this veteran. Ask for a room facing the river. The wood-paneled
L'Amphitryon Restaurant is one of the city's finest in both ambience
and quality, and Buçaco wines are served here. ⌖ *Av. Emidio Navarro
21, 3000,* ☎ *039/22055,* ⅏ *039/22057. 64 rooms. Restaurant, bar.
AE, DC, MC, V.*

$ ✕⌂ **Tivoli.** This four-star addition to the Coimbra hotel scene, opened
★   in 1990, is currently the best address in town. It's sleek, efficient, well
located, and outfitted with all the latest gadgets. The only thing lacking is that certain sense of place that the other great hotels in the Tivoli
chain have achieved: Once in your comfortable room, you could be
anywhere. The Porta Férrea restaurant serves excellent food, both international and regional, in a subdued setting. ⌖ *Rua João Machado
4–5, 3000,* ☎ *039/26934. 90 rooms, 10 suites. Restaurant, bar, pool,
health club. AE, DC, MC, V.*

$ ⌂ **Dona Inês.** This modern glass-and-marble hotel, conveniently located
★   on the banks of the Mondego, is just a few minutes' walk from Coimbra's main commercial district. Although simply furnished, the rooms
are light and airy. ⌖ *Rua Abel Dias Urbano 12, 3000,* ☎ *039/25791,*
⅏ *039/25611. 72 rooms, 12 suites. Restaurant, bar, tennis court. AE,
DC, MC, V.*

¢ ⌂ **Larbelo.** A quiet, family-run *residencial* (inn that was once a private residence) in an old, green-tiled building, it has a good, central
location facing the Largo da Portagem, adjacent to the tourist office.
The 17 upstairs rooms have high, ornate ceilings, and some have views
to the river. Room 209 has the best view. Only breakfast is served. ⌖
Largo da Portagem 33, 3000, ☎ *039/29092. 17 rooms (9 with bath
and toilet, 8 with shower). No credit cards.*

Festivals

The **Quiema das Fitas,** the burning of the ribbons by the university students, is quite a party. Held during even years in early July, the **Festas
da Rainha Santa** (Festival of the Queen Saint) is marked by colorful
processions and fireworks along the Mondego.

Outdoor Activities and Sports

HORSEBACK RIDING

Riding by the hour and excursions are available at the **Centre Hippique
de Coimbra** (⌖ Mata do Choupal, ☎ 039/37695).

TENNIS

There are courts available at the university stadium and at the **Club
Tennis de Coimbra** (⌖ Av. Urbano Duarte, Quinta da Estrela, ☎
039/403469).

Shopping

The ceramics produced in and around Coimbra, mostly blue-and-white reproductions of delicate 17th- and 18th-century patterns, are among the loveliest in the country. A good selection may be found at **Bazar de Louças** (⌧ Rua das Padeiras 44), across from the Hotel Oslo.

Conimbriga

★ ㉕ *16 km (10 mi) southwest of Coimbra.*

You enter this important archaeological site via a brick reception pavilion with pools and gardens surrounding a **museum**. Exhibits chronicle the development of the site from its Iron Age origins, through its heyday as a prosperous Roman town, to its decline following the 5th-century barbarian conquests. The museum is best appreciated after visiting the excavations.

At the site's entrance is a portion of the original **Roman road** that connected Olissipo (as Lisbon was then known) and the northern town of Braga. If you look closely, you can make out ridges worn into the stone by cart wheels. The uncovered area represents just a small portion of the Roman city, but within this area are some wonderful mosaic floors. The 3rd-century **House of the Fountains** has a large, macabre mosaic depicting Perseus offering the head of Medusa to a monster from the deep, an example of the amazing Roman craftsmanship of the period.

Across the way is the **Casa do Cantaber** (House of Cantaber), named for a nobleman whose family was captured by invading barbarians in 465. A tour of the house reveals the comfortable lifestyle of Roman nobility at the time. Private baths included a *tepidarium* (hot pool) and *frigidarium* (cold pool). Remnants of the underfloor central heating system are also visible. Fresh water was carried 3 kilometers (2 miles) by aqueduct from Alcabideque; parts of the original aqueduct can still be seen. There is daily bus service between Conimbriga and Coimbra. ⌧ *Condeixa-a-Velha,* ☎ *039/941177.* 🎟 *Ruins and museum June–Sept. 400$00, Oct.–May 300$00; ruins only 150$00.* ☉ *Ruins daily 9–1 and 2–6, until 8 in summer; museum Tues.–Sun. 10–12:30 and 2–5, until 6 in summer. Closed holidays.*

Dining and Lodging

$ ✕🏨 **Pousada de Santa Cristina.** This pousada in the delightful town ★ of Condeixa-a-Nova makes an ideal base for visiting the Roman ruins at Conimbriga, a kilometer (½ mile) away, and Coimbra, 15 kilometers (9 miles) to the north. The pousada occupies a converted palace and contains spacious, comfortably furnished bedrooms and one of the area's best traditional restaurants. ⌧ *Condeixa-a-Nova 3150,* ☎ *039/941286,* 🖷 *039/943097. 45 rooms. Restaurant, bar, pool, tennis. AE, DC, MC, V.*

THE WESTERN BEIRAS

Almost as diverse as the Beiras as a whole, the western Beiras encompass shore and mountain, fishing villages and country towns, wine country and serene forest. And within this varied landscape, you'll find an equally diverse selection of activities to pursue. Sights to see range from castles to cathedrals, monasteries to museums. For those more interested in R&R, you can lie in the sun by the Atlantic or sample the restorative powers of the air and water in any of a cluster of inland towns.

We start on the gentle-faced coast. Long, sandy beaches and sunbaked dunes—some of the most inviting you will find in all of Europe—stretch from Figueira da Foz north toward the great lagoon at Aveiro, with its colorful kelp boats. A bit farther inland are the vineyards of the Dão region, the Serra do Caramulo mountains, the lush forests of Buçaco, and the sedate spa resorts of Curia and Luso, not far from Coimbra.

Numbers in the margin correspond to points of interest on the Beiras map.

Montemor-o-Velho

 20 km (12 mi) west of Coimbra, 16 km (10 mi) northwest of Conimbriga; the most scenic route, N341, runs from Coimbra along the south bank of the Rio Mondego.

Occupying a strategic hilltop position overlooking the fertile Mondego basin between Coimbra and Figueira da Foz, Montemor-o-Velho figures prominently in the history and legends of the region. One popular story tells how the castle's besieged defenders cut the throats of their own families to spare them a cruel death at the hands of the Moorish invaders; many died before the attackers were repulsed. The following day the escaping Moors were pursued and thoroughly defeated. Legend has it that all those slaughtered at Montemor were resurrected but forever carried a red mark on their necks as a reminder of the battle.

The castle walls and tower, which command the hill and fertile plains below, are largely intact, although little remains inside the impressive ramparts that suggests this was a noble family's home that once garrisoned 5,000 troops. Archaeological evidence indicates the hill has been fortified for more than 2,000 years. Although **Montemor Castle** played an important role in the longstanding conflict between the Christians and Moors, changing hands many times, the structure seen today is primarily of 14th-century origin. The two churches on the hill are also part of the castle complex. The **Church of Santa Maria de Alcaçova** dates back to the 11th century and contains some well-preserved Manueline additions.

Here again are threads of the story of Inês de Castro, for in January 1355 Dom Afonso IV, meeting in the castle with his advisers, made the decision to murder her. In 1811 during the Napoleonic invasions, the castle was badly damaged. ⌂ *Free.* ⊙ *Tues.–Sun. 10–12:30 and 2–5.*

Figueira da Foz

 14 km (9 mi) west of Montemor-o-Velho.

There are various theories as to the origin of the name Figueira da Foz. The consensus around the fishing harbor at this popular seaside resort favors the literal translation: the fig tree at the mouth of the river. The belief is that when this was just a small settlement, oceangoing fishermen and traders from up the river would arrange to meet at the big fig tree to conduct their business. Although today there are no fig trees to be seen at this busy fishing port, the name has stuck.

Shortly before the turn of the century, with the improvement of road and rail access, Figueira, with its long, sandy beach and mild climate, developed into a popular seaside resort. Today, although the beach is little changed, a broad four-lane divided boulevard runs along its length. The town side is lined with the usual melange of apartments, hotels, and restaurants, but, fortunately, the beachfront has been spared from development.

⏱ An interesting activity, here or in any Portuguese fishing town, is to go down to the **docks** early in the morning to watch the *lota* (the auctioning of the day's catch). Although this colorful spectacle is closed to the public, if you are lucky perhaps the customs police will look the other way. Watching the unloading of the big ships can also be fun for the whole family.

One of the town's more curious sights is the 18th-century **Casa do Paço,** the interior of which is decorated with about 7,000 Delft tiles. These traditional Dutch tiles were salvaged from a shipwreck at the mouth of the harbor. ⊠ *Largo Prof. Vitor Guerra 4, around corner from main post office.* 🎫 *Free.* ⊙ *Weekdays 9:30–12:30 and 2–5.*

The triangular 17th-century **Fortaleza da Santa Catarina** (Santa Catarina Fortress, ⊠ Adjacent to beachfront tennis courts) was occupied by the French during the early days of the Peninsular War.

NEED A
BREAK?

There are a number of brightly painted wooden-shack restaurants sitting directly on the beach. These are wonderful places for fresh grilled fish or just a cold drink. **A Platforma** is one of the best.

Palácio Sotto Mayor, a luxurious, elegantly furnished, French-style manor house, was constructed as part of the wave of development in the late 19th and early 20th centuries that made Figueira da Foz a world-class resort. Long in the hands of one of Portugal's leading families, the palace now belongs to the owners of the casino, and local gossip has it that it was "donated" as payment for gambling debts. Its collection includes paintings and fine furnishings. ⊠ *Rua Joaquím Sotto Mayor,* ☎ *033/22121.* 🎫 *100$00.* ⊙ *Weekends 2–6.*

Dining and Lodging

$$ ✕ **Covil do Caçador.** An open kitchen and a dining room with a vaulted, beamed ceiling cluttered with hanging strings of corn, garlic, and other herbs and vegetables give this restaurant a comfortable country feeling. It's across the river from downtown at the foot of the bridge and looks out over the bay. Chef José Olivio does a fine job with a varied menu. Try the *arroz de tamboril* (cubes of monkfish mixed with rice and seasonings). ⊠ *Morraceira,* ☎ *033/31507. AE, DC, MC, V.*

$ ✕ **O Peleiro.** In the quiet village of Paião, 10 kilometers (6 miles) from
★ Figueira, is this popular restaurant that was once a tannery, and that's what the name means. Owner Henrique has achieved a tranquil ambience through the use of wood and tile. Heavy on regional specialties, the menu includes *sopa da pedra* (stone soup), a thick vegetable soup with sausage, beans, and potatoes, served in a tureen with hot stones—a must. Grilled pork or veal on a spit is excellent, and there's a good wine selection. ⊠ *Largo Alvideiro, Paião,* ☎ *033/940159. MC, V. Closed May 1–15, Sept. 1–15, and Sun.*

$$ ✕🏨 **Grande.** This five-story, 1950s-vintage hotel, popular with tour groups, enjoys a favored location overlooking the broad, sandy beach. Public and guest rooms are spacious and airy, and seafront rooms have a small balcony. A large swimming pool has a view of the beach. The restaurant is a large, rather sterile room with picture windows, and the menu is international with regional specialties. Although this dowager of a hotel is beginning to show her age, she is still the top choice directly in town. ⊠ *Av. 25 de Abril, 3080,* ☎ *033/2146,* 🖷 *033/22420. 102 rooms. Restaurant, piano bar, pool. AE, DC, MC, V.*

$ 🏨 **Aparthotel Atlantico.** In this high-rise tower at the beach, the accommodations—apartments with kitchenettes—are small but adequate, with plain, functional furnishings. Some apartments have a wonderful sea view. ⊠ *Av. 25 de Abril, 3080,* ☎ *033/24045,* FAX *033/22420. 70 apartments. Bar, pool. AE, DC, MC, V.*

$ ⊡ **International.** A comfortable, small hotel on a quiet street just a five-
★ minute walk from the beach, this classic stone building was built in 1914 and completely remodeled in 1989, retaining the original ambi-ence. ⊠ *Rua da Liberdade 32, 3080,* ☎ *033/22051,* FAX *033/22420. 50 rooms. Bar, breakfast room, pool. AE, DC, MC, V.*

$ ⊡ **Pensão Esplanada.** This turn-of-the-century corner house is across from the beach. The floors creak and the rooms have seen better days, but it's clean and well-maintained and the price is right. Ask for a room with a sea view. ⊠ *Rua Engenheiro Silva 86, 3080,* ☎ *033/22115. 19 rooms, 10 with bath. No credit cards.*

Festival

Every year during the last week in June, the **Festas de São João** (Festival of St. John) features dancing around huge bonfires until dawn. The exhausted dancers then plunge into the sea for the ancient ritual of the "holy bath."

Nightlife

The casino is part of an entertainment complex that, although small by Las Vegas standards, is pretty big stuff for this part of the world. Built in 1886, the gambling room, with its frescoed ceilings and chandeliers, provides a subdued atmosphere in which to try your luck at a variety of games, including blackjack, American and Continental roulette, and an old European game played with three dice, known simply as the French table. Within the same building, there is also a large belle-epoque showroom featuring a Vegas-type revue. Although dress is casual, jeans and T-shirts are not permitted. ⊠ *Av. Bernado Lopes,* ☎ *033/22041. Gambling room:* ▤ *1,500$00; minimum age 18 (bring your passport);* ☉ *Daily 3 PM–3 AM. Show room:* ▤ *1,500$00 minimum;* ☉ *Shows 11 PM and 1 AM. Reservations advised July–Sept.*

Outdoor Activities and Sports

BIKING

You can rent bikes and mopeds by the day and week at the **AFGA Travel Agency** (⊠ Av. Miguel Bombarda 79). Bicycles can be rented from **Gabriel Grácio** (⊠ Rua Dr. Calado 24).

FISHING

There is good fishing for sea bream, bass, and mullet at Costa de Lavos and Gala beaches, just south of town.

TENNIS

There are good hard-surface courts at the **Figueira da Foz Tennis Club** (⊠ Av. 25 de Abril, ☎ 033/22287).

WINDSURFING

Windsurfers can be rented at most of the popular beach resorts.

Buarcos

⓴ *2 km (1 mi) north of Figueira da Foz.*

This town, with its fine sandy beach, has managed to retain some of the character of a Portuguese fishing village in spite of a heavy influx of tourists. Here colorfully painted boats are still pulled up onto the beach, and fishermen sit around mending nets.

CAPE MONDEGO LIGHTHOUSE – Take a trip out to the cape for a wonderful, uncluttered view of the coastline. The road traces a loop and returns to Buarcos.

Dining and Lodging

$$ ✕ **Teimoso.** This seaside restaurant with large picture windows has become a local institution. Although the menu choices are varied, seafood is what put this place on the map. Shellfish comes fresh from the restaurant's huge saltwater tanks. ⊠ *Estrada do Cabo Mondego,* ☎ *033/32785. MC, V. Closed Wed.*

$ 🏨 **Clube Vale de Leão.** This self-contained cluster of Mediterranean-style, semidetached villas is unobtrusively nestled in the hills high above Buarcos. Rooms and apartments are small but comfortable, and the views over the bay are magnificent. The restaurant, a bit garish in decor, does a good job with both international and regional dishes. ⊠ *Vais-Buarcos, 3080,* ☎ *033/33057,* 𝔽𝔸𝕏 *033/32571. 6 rooms, 17 studios, 1 apartment. Restaurant, piano bar, tea shop, pool, massage, sauna, tennis, exercise room, squash. AE, DC, MC, V.*

Outdoor Activities and Sports

FISHING
Cape Mondego has good fishing for sea bream, bass, and mullet. Carp and barbel are caught in the Quiaios Lakes, northeast of town.

TENNIS
The **Vale de Leão Tennis & Squash Club** (⊠ Vais, ☎ 033/23057), in the Boa Viagem hills northwest of Buarcos, has good hard-surface courts.

WATER SPORTS
The bay here is a popular **windsurfing** location, as are the Quiaios Lakes. **Board surfers** often find 10- to 12-foot waves at Quiaios Beach (just north of Cape Mondego).

En Route The most scenic route north from Buarcos is a winding road that climbs through a wooded area to the little village of Boa Viagem (Good Journey). From here you can trace the course of the Rio Mondego as it flows into the sea and then head north, following a narrow road that runs along the sand dunes to Aveiro or turn inland to Vagos and pick up N109 to Vista Alegre.

Vista Alegre

➋➒ *50 km (31 mi) northeast of Buarcos.*

Portugal's finest china is produced here by a business that was started in 1824 as a sort of commune. Housing was furnished for workers from all parts of the country, training was provided by French master craftsmen, and the clay came from the nearby town of Ovar. Today the settlement's large, tree-filled square is bordered by the factory, a china museum and gift shop, and a small 17th-century chapel with the delicately carved tomb of the chapel's founder. Through its collection of hundreds of magnificent pieces, the **china museum** traces the history of the development of chinaware. ⊠ *Fabrica Vista Alegre,* ☎ *034/322365.* 🎫 *Free.* ☉ *Museum and gift shop Tues.–Sun. 9–12:30 and 2–4:30.*

Ilhavo

➌➋ *2 km (1 mi) northeast of Vista Alegre.*

This small town of attractive, tiled manor houses is best known for the **Museu do Mar** (Museum of the Sea). In a drab concrete building next to a fish-processing plant, the museum documents the region's close relationship with the sea and has a collection of local pottery and Vista Alegre china. ⊠ *Rua Vasco da Gama,* ☎ *034/321797.* ☞ *200$00.* ☉ *Wed.–Sat. 9–12:30 and 2–5:30, Sun. and Tues. 2–5:30.*

Aveiro

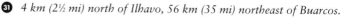

31 *4 km (2½ mi) north of Ilhavo, 56 km (35 mi) northeast of Buarcos.*

To refer to Aveiro as the Venice of Portugal, as is sometimes done, does not make for a good comparison. Yes, there are a few canals running through its center, and the swan-necked *moliceiros* (kelp boats) do remotely resemble Venetian gondolas, but that's the extent of the similarity. Aveiro's mood is not the drama and splendor of Venice but rather a quiet confidence and dignity.

Like Venice, though, Aveiro is first and foremost a water city. Its traditions are closely tied to the sea and to the **Ria de Aveiro,** the vast, shallow lagoon that fans out to the north and west of the city. This 45-kilometer (28-mile) hydralike delta of the Rio Vouga was formed in 1575, when a violent storm caused shifting sand to block the river's flow into the ocean. The unique combination of fresh and salt water, narrow waterways, and tiny islands is bordered by salt marshes and lush pine forests, and the ocean side is lined with lovely sandy beaches. The tranquil ria is the realm of the moliceiros, the graceful, colorfully painted craft that glide along the shallow waterways harvesting seaweed.

If you have a car, a drive through the ria's back roads is recommended, but a boat trip through the ria is a must. From mid-June to mid-September, **excursion boats** (☞ 2,000$00, ☉ Boats leave daily at 10 AM, return at 5 PM) depart from the main canal just in front of the tourist office. There's a small bar on board, and a stop is made along the way for lunch. For additional information contact the tourist office.

With the loss of its seaport, Aveiro, once a major center for boats working the Newfoundland codfish banks, suffered a prolonged decline. It was only in 1808, when a breakwater was built of stones from the old city fortifications, that a passage to the sea was reestablished and the town once again flourished. Deep-sea fishing was reinstituted, new industries were established, and the city took on the prosperous air it maintains today.

Aveiro is great for walking because most of the industry and the new university are on the periphery, and places of interest in the old town are easily accessible on foot. In many parts of town, the sidewalks and squares are paved with *calçada* (traditional Portuguese hand-laid pavement) in intricate nautical patterns.

Aveiro's most attractive buildings date back to the latter half of the 15th century. In 1472 Princess Joana, daughter of King Afonso V, retired against her father's wishes, to the **Convento de Jesus** (Convent of Jesus)—established by papal bull in 1461—where she spent the last 18 years of her life. This royal presence gave impetus to the city's economic and cultural development. The late-18th-century facade is not particularly interesting, but the interior of the church, completed in the early 18th century, is a masterpiece of baroque art. The elaborately gilded wood carvings and ornate ceiling, done by António Gomes and José Correia from Porto, are among the finest in Portugal. Scenes depicting the life of Joana, who was canonized in 1693, can be seen on azulejo panels, and Joana's tomb is in the lower choir. The multicolor inlaid-marble sarcophagus is supported at each corner by delicately carved

In case you want to be welcomed there.

We're here to see that you're always welcomed at establishments everywhere. That's why millions of people carry the American Express® Card — for peace of mind, confidence, and security, around the world or just around the corner.

do more

Cards

In case you're running low.

We're here to help with more than 118,000 Express Cash locations around the world. In order to enroll, just call American Express before you start your vacation.

do more

Express Cash

And just in case.

We're here with American Express® Travelers Cheques and Cheques *for Two*.® They're the safest way to carry money on your vacation and the surest way to get a refund, practically anywhere, anytime.

Another way we help you...

do more ®

Travelers Cheques

angels. Also within the convent, the **Museu de Aveiro** (Aveiro Museum) contains an assortment of sculpture, coaches and carriages, artifacts, and paintings, including a particularly fine 15th-century portrait of Joana by Nuno Gonçalves. ⊠ *Rua Santa Joana Princesa.* ▣ *Museum 300$00.* ⊙ *Tues.–Sun. 10–12:30 and 2–5.*

The austere stone structure across from the Convent of Jesus is the Aveiro Cathedral, more commonly known as the **Church of São Domingos** (⊠ Rua Santa Joana Princesa). The interior of the church has no definitive architectural style but does contain some fine azulejos.

NEED A BREAK?	Overlooking the central canal, the **Sonatura** (⊠ Praça Humberto Delgada, Rua Clube dos Galitos 6) offers a rare opportunity to have a vegetarian snack or meal in Portugal. Service is cafeteria style inside a health-food store. To your right as you leave the restaurant, which is closed Sundays, note the modern tile relief showing kelp gatherers at work.

The graceful three-story **town hall** (⊠ Praça da República) has a pointed bell tower. On the same plaza as the town hall, the 18th-century **Misericórdia Church** (⊠ Praça da República) has an imposing baroque portal set against a background of blue-and-white azulejos.

Also of interest in Aveiro is the **headquarters of the port captain,** an attractive two-story building perched on arches in the middle of the central canal. The best place for viewing the brightly decorated fishing boats is along the **Canal de São Roque.** To the west are huge, glistening mounds of white salt, recovered by evaporation from the lagoon. At the northeast edge of the city, the **train station** (⊠ Rua João de Moura) displays some lovely azulejo panels depicting traditions and customs of the region.

For restless youngsters, the large **city park** (⊠ Av. Artur Ravara), with its well-equipped playground, offers a welcome respite from the rigors of sightseeing with the family.

Dining and Lodging

$$ ✕ **A Nossa Casa.** On a quiet street a few blocks from the town center, this small, unassuming, family-operated restaurant produces some ★ of the best meals in town. The dining room is lined with wine bottles, and the tables are separated by wooden dividers. The favorite dish of proprietor Manuel Facteira is *parrilhada de peixes e mariscos no churrasco* (a generous assortment of grilled fish and shellfish served on a large platter around a special sauce made from ground shellfish). ⊠ *Rua do Gravito 10,* ☎ *034/29236. DC, MC, V. Closed weekends.*

$$ ✕ **O Mercantel.** This restaurant is the brainchild of Sr. Costa da Lota, who, after 13 years of working at the nearby fish market, decided to try his hand at the other side of the business. He has done quite well. In 1990 O Mercantel took first prize in the national gastronomic fair in Santarem. Specialties include fresh fish, fish stew, and *arroz de marisco* (shellfish with rice). ⊠ *Rua António dos Santos Le 16,* ☎ *034/28057. AE, DC, MC, V. Closed Mon.*

$$$ ✕▥ **Pousada da Ria.** Built on the edge of the lagoon, this light and ★ airy two-story inn is filled with and surrounded by plants and flowers. The entry is a tasteful blend of wood and tile, with a loft sitting area. Ten of the 19 cheerfully furnished rooms have large picture windows and look out over the water; you can stand on your balcony and watch the colorfully painted moliceiros glide by. Midway down the narrow, pine-covered peninsula separating the lagoon from the sea, this pousada is in a great location for exploring. It's about 30 minutes by car to Aveiro. The restaurant has an open, spacious feeling and a lovely view. There is also a terrace for outside dining during the summer. The tasty *ensopada de cabrito* (kid stew) is recommended. ⊠ *3870 Murtosa,* ☎ *034/48332,* ℻ *034/48333. 18 rooms, 1 suite. Restaurant, bar, pool, tennis court. AE, DC, MC, V.*

$ ✕⌷ **Imperial.** If you like an efficient, business-oriented, modern hotel in the heart of a city, then the Imperial is for you. Rooms are comfortable but lack charm, though some on the upper floors have small balconies and nice views. The restaurant is luxurious without being ostentatious and is popular with the business community. Specials include *enguias fritas* (fried eels) and *bacalhau com natas* (cod with cream). The breakfast buffet is the best in town. ⊠ *Rua Dr. Nascimento Leitão, 3800,* ☎ *034/22141,* ℻ *034/24148. 100 rooms, 8 suites. Restaurant, 2 bars. AE, DC, MC, V.*

$ ⌷ **Arcada.** A comfortable, family-owned Portuguese classic more than
★ 50 years old, this arched, four-story building with a red-tile roof is well kept up, and its location at the foot of the bridge over the central canal couldn't be more convenient. Room size is adequate, and the furnishings vary from blond 1950s to traditional Portuguese. The lounge and bar are reminiscent of a gentleman's club slightly past its prime. ⊠ *Rua Viana do Castelo 4, 3800,* ☎ *034/23001,* ℻ *034/21886. 49 rooms, 1 suite. Bar, breakfast room. AE, DC, MC, V.*

Festival

The large, colorful, regional **Feira do Marco,** held in March, has been celebrated for more than 500 years. It features folk music and dancing on weekends.

Outdoor Activities and Sports

BIKING

A bike is great for exploring the practically traffic-free back roads between Aveiro and Ovar. In summer, bicycles can be rented in front of the tourist office.

HORSEBACK RIDING

Escola Equestre de Aveiro (Equestrian School of Aveiro, ⊠ Quinta Chãs Agra, Vilarinho, ☎ 034/912108), about 6 kilometers (4 miles) north of Aveiro on N109, offers riding classes at all levels and trekking rides to explore the wetlands around Aveiro. Reservations are necessary for trekking.

Shopping

The **Armazéms de Aveiro** (⊠ Rua Conselheiro Luís de Magalhães 1) carries leading Portuguese brands of high-quality ceramics and chinaware, including Vista Alegre, Quinta Nova, and Artebus. They will also ship your purchases.

Ovar

❸❷ *24 km (15 mi) north of Aveiro; head north on N109 from Aveiro to Estarreja, then turn west and follow N109–5 through quiet farmlands, and after crossing the bridge over the ria, continue north on N327 to Ovar.*

At the northern end of the ria, Ovar provides a convenient jumping-off point for visiting the string of beaches and sand dunes to the north. This small town, with its many tiled houses, is a veritable showcase of azulejos. The **courthouse,** built in the 1960s, is adorned with some unusually beautiful multicolor tile panels. The exterior of the late-17th-century **parish church** is completely covered with blue-and-white azulejos.

The small **Museu Regional de Ovar,** in an old house in the town center, exhibits many tiles and local handicrafts. ⊠ *Rua Heliodoro Slagado,* ☎ *056/52822.* 🖃 *200$00.* ☉ *Daily, 10–noon and 2–6; closed holidays.*

Santa Maria de Feira

㉝ *8 km (5 mi) northeast of Ovar.*

Your reward here is the lovely fairy-tale **Castle of Vila da Feira.** The four square towers are crowned with a series of cone-shape turrets in a display of Gothic architecture more common in Germany or Austria than in Portugal. Although the original walls date back to the 11th century, the present structure is the result of modifications made 400 years later. From atop the tower you can make out the sprawling outlines of the Ria de Aveiro. 🖃 *300$00.* ☉ *Tues.–Sun. 9–12:30 and 2–6.*

Viseu

㉞ *70 km (43½ mi) southeast of Santa Maria da Feira, 60 km (37 mi) east of Aveiro; you can take the scenic but twisting and bone-jarring N227 across the Serra da Gralheira or the smoother, faster, but much less interesting IP1 and IP5.*

A thriving provincial capital in one of Portugal's prime wine-growing districts, the Dão region, Viseu has managed to preserve the ambience of a country town in spite of its obvious prosperity. The newer part of town is comfortably laid out. Parks and wide boulevards radiate from a central traffic circle, but, unlike many Portuguese towns, through traffic does not have to go into its center.

A good place to start a visit is the tree-lined **Praça da República,** also known as the Rossío. This pleasant square is framed at one end by a massive **azulejo mural** depicting scenes of country life. The heroic figure in bronze, standing sword in hand, is Prince Henry the Navigator, the first duke of Viseu. The stately building across from the tile mural is the **Câmara Municipal** (town hall). Walk inside to admire the colorful Aveiro tiles and fine woodwork, and be sure to see the courtyard. Just to the south of the square, a graceful stairway leads to the 18th-century, baroque **A Igreja dos Terceiros de São Francisco** (Church of the Terceiros de São Francisco). Behind the church is a large, wooded park with paths and ponds, offering an ideal respite from the summer heat.

Almeida Moreira, the first director of the Grão Vasco Museum, bequeathed his house, a Moorish-style mansion on a hill, and a diverse collection of paintings, furniture, and ceramics to the city. Today it's the **A Casa-Museu de Almeida Moreira** (Almeida Moreira Museum). The house alone is worth the admission price. ⊠ *Rua Soar Cima,* ☎ *032/23769.* 🖃 *250$00.* ☉ *Tues.–Sun. 10–12:30 and 2–5 except holidays.*

★ One of the most impressive squares in Portugal, the **Largo da Sé,** in the old town, is bounded by three imposing edifices—the cathedral, the palace housing the Grão Vasco Museum, and the Misericórdia Church.

★ The **Sé** (cathedral), a massive stone structure with twin bell towers, lends a solemn air to the large plaza that it faces. Construction was started in the 13th century and continued off and on until the 18th century, resulting in an interior marked by a mixture of Gothic and Manueline elements. Massive Gothic pillars support a network of twisted, knotted forms that reach across the high, vaulted roof, while a dazzling, gilded, baroque high altar contrasts with the otherwise somber stone interior. The harsh lines of the upper level (added in the 18th century) appear awkward when compared to the graceful Italianate arches of the lower level, built in the 16th century in the style of the Italian Renaissance. The walls of the lower level are adorned with a series of excellent azulejo panels depicting various religious motifs. To the right of the Mannerist main portal is a double-tiered cloister. A well-preserved, transitional, Gothic-style doorway connects the cloister with the cathedral. ⊠ *Largo da Sé.* ☎ *Free.* ☉ *Daily 9:30–12:30 and 2–5:30.*

The second-floor galleries of the **Museu de Grão Vasco,** once the 16th-century Bishop's Palace, are devoted to the works of the great 16th-century Portuguese painter Vasco Fernandes (Grão Vasco) and his Viseu school. The museum is directly adjacent to the cathedral. ⊠ *Adro de Sé,* ☎ *032/26249.* ☎ *300$00, weekends free.* ☉ *Tues.–Sun. 10–12:30 and 2–5 except holidays.*

The white, rococo **Misericórdia Church** has soft, graceful lines that contrast sharply with the harsh, gray lines of the cathedral, which stands directly opposite. ⊠ *Largo da Sé.* ☎ *Free.* ☉ *Daily 9:30–12:30 and 2–5:30.*

★ The **Praça de Dom Duarte** is one of those rare places where just the right combination of rough stone pavement, splendid old houses, wrought-iron balconies, and views of an ancient cathedral (it's just below the cathedral square) come together to produce a magical effect. Try to be here at night, when the romance of the setting is further enhanced by the soft glow of the streetlights.

A statue of a warrior stands on a rock at the edge of town. It's a **monument to Viriáto** (⊠ Road to Aveiro), the leader of the Lusitanian resistance to the Roman invasion in the 2nd century BC. Some historians believe this was the site of his encampment.

Dining and Lodging

$$ ✕ **A Veranda da Sé.** After 37 years of running a restaurant in Rio de
★ Janeiro, João Correira became homesick for his native Portugal. Now back in the town of his birth, he is doing what he does best: running a restaurant. In an ancient stone building that was once a warehouse, he has created a cozy Portuguese bistro. There is a small loft for dining, and the original stone walls and floor remain. The menu is Portuguese, with an accent on grilled meats. Saluting his days in Brazil, João serves *feijoada do Brasil* (a tasty stewlike dish of beans, sausage, and meat) on Sundays. ⊠ *Rua Augusto Hilario 55,* ☎ *032/421135. AE, DC, MC, V. Closed Tues.*

$ ✕ **O Fontelo.** This is a storefront grill restaurant specializing in chicken that tastes as good as it looks in the window. ⊠ *Av. Alfonso da Melo 45,* ☎ *032/424221. No credit cards. Closed Sat.*

$ ✕🏠 **Grão Vasco.** For many years the Grão Vasco has been Viseu's lead-
★ ing hotel. Its location in a wooded park just a few steps from the main square is ideal, offering the convenience of the city and the quiet of the countryside. Many of the rooms have balconies looking out on the oval pool. The restaurant, which serves a wide variety of principally Portuguese dishes, is one of the best in town. If it's in season, try the *javali.* ⊠ *Rua Gaspar Barreiros, 3500,* ☎ *032/423511,* 🖷 *032/426444. 110 rooms. Restaurant, bar, pool. AE, DC, MC, V.*

$ ✕🏠 **Onix.** This cozy hotel on the outskirts of Viseu offers just the right
★ combination of tasteful decor and modern comfort to make it one of the best of its kind in the region. Ask for a room on the third floor

with a balcony facing the Serra da Estrela. The restaurant provides surprisingly good food and service. If you've acquired a taste for bacalhau, try their version of the tasty *bacalhau a Zé do Pipo* (a wonderful combination of baked, breaded cod with mayonnaise, pimentos, onions, and potatoes). ⊠ *N16, Via Caçador, 3500,* ☎ *032/479243,* ℻ *032/478744. 73 rooms. Restaurant, bar, pool. AE, DC, MC, V.*

$ ⊞ **Monte Belo.** This modern hotel, built in a quiet residential neighborhood just a few minutes' walk from the center of town, is a welcome addition to the hotel scene. ⊠ *Urbanização Quinta do Bosque,* ☎ *032/415444,* ℻ *032/415400. 100 rooms, 16 suites. Restaurant, bar, pool, tennis, health club. AE, DC, MC, V.*

¢ ⊞ **Bela Vista.** This comfortable residencial on a quiet street about a mile from the center of town has rooms that are small but comfortable. ⊠ *Rua Alexandre Herculano 510, 3500,* ☎ *032/422026,* ℻ *032/428472. 44 rooms. No credit cards.*

Festival

Held from mid-August through mid-September, the **Feira de São Mateus** (St. Matthew's Fair) is like a giant county fair. Agricultural products and handicrafts are exhibited, and there is folk music and dancing.

Shopping

A walk along the **Rua Direita,** in the old town, can be rewarding. The narrow street is lined with shops displaying locally made wood carvings, pottery, and wrought iron.

Mangualde

③⑤ *13 km (8 mi) southeast of Viseu.*

★ The principal attraction in this market town is the **Palácio des Condes de Anadia** (Palace of the Counts of Anadia). The two-story, 17th-century, rococo manor house is one of the best in the region from this era. The walls are decorated with 18th-century Coimbra azulejos, and the interior contains period furniture and paintings from the 17th to the 19th centuries. ▤ *400$00.* ⊙ *Oct.–Aug., Tues.–Sun. 9–noon and 2–6. Note: At press time there were tentative plans to close the palace to the public. For the latest information check with the regional tourist office in Viseu.*

Dining and Lodging

$$ ✕ **Quinta Magarenha.** This large, attractive, French-style manor house has been a great success for owner José Oliveira. There is a comfortable lounge with plush sofas and tiled walls. The single, large dining room has an attractive wooden ceiling and tile floors. The atmosphere is gregarious, with rows of long tables, and the food is Portuguese with an emphasis on fish. The *lombino de pescada* (fillets of whiting with a sauce made from ground shellfish) is recommended. ⊠ *Exit Viseu-leste from IP5, Caçador 18,* ☎ *032/479106. MC, V. Closed Mon.*

$ ✕⊞ **Senhora do Castelo.** A large four-story complex that shares a hilltop park with the church of the same name, the recently remodeled hotel is conveniently located adjacent to the IP5 highway but far enough away to avoid the noise. The buildings are pseudo-Mediterranean. Many of the rooms have small balconies; those facing south have the best view. The restaurant and public rooms, while spacious and cheerful, lack character, but the views, especially from the terrace restaurant, are spectacular. Of the two indoor restaurants, the Grill Restaurant has a warmer atmosphere. Try the *bacalhau espiritual* (literally "spiritual codfish"); what you get is a tasty plate of dried, salted cod baked with potatoes, onions, and tomatoes. ⊠ *Monte Senhora do Castelo 4, 3531,* ☎ *032/611608,* ℻ *032/623877. 85 rooms, 3 suites.*

3 restaurants, bar, indoor and outdoor pools, sauna, 2 tennis courts. AE, DC, MC, V.

En Route   Driving to Caramulo from Mangualde or Viseu takes you through the heart of the **Dão region.** Here you will see many vineyards, some carefully terraced. The wines pressed from these grapes are some of Portugal's finest.

Caramulo

 35 km (22 mi) southwest of Mangualde, 24 km (15 mi) southwest of Viseu.

In the early part of this century when tuberculosis was rife, people came here for the beneficial effects of the fresh mountain air. Though tuberculosis is no longer the problem it once was, Caramulo has not lost its appeal. People still come to enjoy the heather-clad wooded slopes and to walk through the lovely parks and gardens. Mineral water bottled at the nearby spring is popular throughout the country.

The **Museu de Arte do Caramulo and Museu do Automóvel** form an unlikely but interesting pair. The unusual **Museu de Arte do Caramulo** (Caramulo Art Museum) was founded and supported by Abel Lacerda, a local doctor. Its varied collections, all from donations, include jewels, ceramics, and a fine assortment of paintings, representing such diverse artists as Salvador Dali, Picasso, and Grão Vasco. Next door is the **Museu do Automóvel,** whose collection of perfectly restored antique cars includes such rare items as a 1902 Darracq. Also on exhibit are vintage bicycles and motorcycles. *Both museums: ☎ 032/86270; 🎟 600$00; ⏱ Tues.–Sun. 10–12:30 and 2–6.*

OFF THE BEATEN PATH   **CARAMULINHO** – From the trailhead on N230–3, it's about a 30-minute climb to Caramulinho, at an elevation of 3,500 feet. Here at the tip of the Serra do Caramulo, you can look out across a vast panorama taking in the coastal plain to the west and the Serra da Estrela to the southeast.

CABEÇA DA NEVE – Like Caramulinho, this observation point west of town offers spectacular vistas, but this one yields a bird's-eye view of the Mondego basin.

Dining and Lodging

$ ✕🏨 **Pousada de São Jeronimo.** One of the smallest pousadas, with
★   just 12 rooms, this one is in the Serra do Caramulo, between Viseu and Coimbra. Reminiscent of an Alpine chalet, it sits alone on a hill 1 kilometer (⅔ mile) from the spa resort of Caramulo. The reception area has lovely Arraiolos carpets hung on a knotty-pine wall. Rooms are small but adequate, each with a modern marble bathroom and a small balcony with a table and chairs. Views are spectacular. The lounge, restaurant, and bar are divided by a see-through wood partition, and there is an inviting open fireplace. The cozy dining room's picture windows frame a mountain panorama extending to the Serra da Estrela. The fare is country style, with *chanfana de borrego* (roast lamb with red wine) one of the favorites. The pool, cabana bar, and a badminton court are in a private wooded park across from the main building. ✉ N230, 3475, ☎ 032/861291, ℻ 032/861640. *12 rooms. Restaurant, bar, pool, badminton. AE, DC, MC, V.*

Águeda

 25 km (15½ mi) west of Caramulo, 18 km (11 mi) southeast of Aveiro.

This industrial town is a center for the production of paper products and boasts an attractive parish church and several well-preserved manor houses. Although Águeda itself is not particularly appealing, the peaceful greenery of the surrounding countryside makes a visit to this area worthwhile.

🕲 **The Portuguese Railway Museum** contains exhibits that include four steam locomotives dating from 1886. ⊠ *At the train station,* ☎ *034/521123.* 🖅 *100$00.* ⊙ *Weekdays 9–noon and 2–5.*

Dining and Lodging

$$$ 🛏 **Palácio.** A favorite with the Lisbon film-and-TV set, this converted
★ early 17th-century manor house, just off the N1 toward Coimbra, was completely rebuilt to the highest standards and opened as a hotel in 1990. It has that rare blend of Old World charm and elegance with modern convenience. Generous-size bedrooms are furnished with excellent 15th- and 16th-century French reproductions, and the reception area, lounges, and reading room tastefully combine elements ranging from baroque to Italian Romantic. In addition, there are 5 acres of ponds and gardens—a delight for strolling—and even a private chapel. The intimate restaurant overlooking the gardens puts a strong emphasis on regional dishes, such as leitão assado; the house specialty is *bacalhau a palácio* (cod fillets baked with cheese, onions, mayonnaise, and potatoes). ⊠ *Quinta da Borralha, 3750,* ☎ *034/601977,* 🖷 *034/601976. 41 rooms, 7 suites. Restaurant, bar, pool, tennis court, chapel. AE, DC, MC, V.*

$$$ 🛏 **Pousada de Santo António.** Conveniently located outside Águeda in Serem, near the junction of the IP1 and IP5 highways, this comfortable, three-story, pink-stucco country house is based on a concept of Raul Lino, one of the country's foremost architects. A tranquil retreat with good access to the region's attractions, it is 48 kilometers (30 miles) from Coimbra and 19 kilometers (12 miles) from Aveiro. The pousada sits atop a knoll surrounded by trees and looks over the Rio Vouga Valley. Although it was built in 1942 and was one of the first in the pousada chain, it has been remodeled, and the 12 wood-floor bedrooms are comfortably furnished in traditional style. The circular dining room has large windows facing the valley, and the walls are trimmed with azulejos. There is a small terrace for outside dining and a bar with a brick fireplace. The restaurant does well with regional dishes. One tasty specialty that you probably won't find at your favorite restaurant back home is *ensopada da enguias* (a delicate stew made with eels from the Ria Aveiro). ⊠ *Serem, 3750 Águeda,* ☎ *034/523230,* 🖷 *034/523192. 12 rooms. Restaurant, bar, pool, tennis court. AE, DC, MC, V.*

Curia

㊳ *16 km (10 mi) south of Águeda, 20 km (12 mi) north of Coimbra.*

This small but popular spa is in the heart of the Bairrada region, an area noted for its fine wines and roast suckling pig. The waters of the spa, with their high calcium and magnesium-sulphate content, are said to help in the treatment of kidney disorders. Curia offers a quiet retreat of shaded parks, a small lake, and grand belle-epoque hotels just a half hour's drive from the clamor of the summer beach scene. In fact, any of the three resorts in this area—Curia, Luso, and Buçaco—makes a good, quiet base for visiting the beaches and other attractions of the region. Coimbra, Aveiro, Figueira da Foz, the Serra do Caramulo, and Viseu are all within an hour's drive.

Dining and Lodging

$$ ✕ **Pedro dos Leitões.** Of the several restaurants specializing in suck-
★ ling pig, clustered on the N1 from Coimbra to Porto, "Suckling Pig
Pete" is the most popular. A meal here is one of those traditional
things you do when you visit Portugal. You eat sardines by the old bridge
in Portimão, and you have suckling pig at Pedro's in Mealhada. The
size of the parking lot is a dead giveaway that this is no intimate little
bistro. In the busy summer season, Pete's spitted pigs pop out of the
huge ovens at an amazing rate. In spite of the volume, quality is main-
tained. ⊠ *N1, Sernadelo, Mealheada,* ☎ *031/22062. MC, V. Closed
Mon.*

$$$ ✕🏨 **Curia Palace.** The approach down a long tree-lined drive past for-
★ mal gardens is like the beginning of an old movie. In fact, parts of the
Buster Keaton Story were filmed here. Enter the spacious, polished,
marble-floored reception area, and you will be transported back to the
Europe of the 1920s. The four-story hotel is the centerpiece of 15 acres
of gardens, vineyards, a deer park, an aviary, orchards, and a duck pond,
all of which support the hotel kitchen. A meticulously restored 18th-
century water mill grinds wheat and corn for the bakery. There are also
a winery, a distillery, and a chapel on the premises. The swimming pool
is 60 feet by 107 feet, one of the largest in Portugal, and for car buffs
there is a small collection of antique autos. These facilities make this
a wonderful place to stay with children. Bedrooms are large, with high
ceilings and modern bathrooms, and the spacious corridors all have
names (the Avenue of the Roses, for example). Room 255 is one of the
larger rooms and has a fine view of the gardens. The dining room is
light and airy—the enormous height of the ceiling broken somewhat
by an encircling mezzanine—and the cuisine, prepared from garden-
fresh ingredients, is excellent. ⊠ *3780 Anadia,* ☎ *031/512131,* 𝔽𝔸𝕏
*031/515531. 114 rooms. Restaurant, bar, pool, miniature golf, 2 ten-
nis courts, horseback riding, billiards, playground, kennel. AE, DC,
MC, V. Closed Nov.–Mar.*

$$$ ✕🏨 **Grande Hotel de Curia.** The task of taking a grand old 1890s spa
★ hotel and bringing it up to 1990s standards is not an easy one, but the
Belver Hotel Group did just that. And it was not merely a cosmetic
face-lift. New polished-marble floors, mahogany furniture and panel-
ing, elegant bathroom fixtures, and fine carpets and draperies are
some of the more visible changes. The hotel also has its own fully
equipped, state-of-the-art health center, with a full-time medical staff.
Various exercise and diet programs are available. The restaurant, with
wood-plank floors and soft draperies, exudes a subdued elegance. The
menu is primarily international, with a few regional specialties. ⊠ *3780
Anadia,* ☎ *031/515720,* 𝔽𝔸𝕏 *031/515317. 78 rooms, 6 suites. Restau-
rant, bar, indoor and outdoor pools, hot tub, massage, sauna, Turk-
ish bath, tennis, exercise room, library. AE, DC, MC, V.*

$ 🏨 **Quinta de São Lourenço.** This delightful 18th-century country manor
house surrounded by vineyards and pine groves is in the tiny village
of São Lourenço do Bairro, 3 kilometers (2 miles) from Curia. The house
has six comfortable-size bedrooms with wood floors, period furniture,
and modern bathrooms. There is also a small apartment. Meals can
be arranged upon request. ⊠ *São Lourenço do Bairro, 3780 Anadia,*
☎ *031/528168,* 𝔽𝔸𝕏 *031/528594. 6 rooms, 1 apartment. Bar, billiards,
recreation room, library. No credit cards.*

Luso

🏁 *8 km (5 mi) southeast of Curia, 18 km (11 mi) northeast of Coimbra.*

This charming town, built around "the taking of the waters," is on
the main Lisbon–Paris train line. It sits in a little valley at the foot of

the Buçaco Forest and attracts visitors from all over the world. Like Curia, it has an attractive park with a lake, elegant hotels, and medicinal waters. The water emerges at a warm 27°C (81°F) from the Fonte de São João, a fountain in the center of town. Slightly radioactive and with a low-sodium and high-silica content, the water is said to be effective in the treatment of a wide range of kidney and rheumatic disorders.

Dining and Lodging

$ ✕ O Cesteiro. At the western edge of town just past the Luso bottling plant, this popular local restaurant serves simple fare that includes several types of cod, roast kid, and fresh fish. ⊠ *Rua Dr. Lucio Abranches,* ☎ *031/939360. MC, V.*

$$ ✕⌂ Grande Hotel das Termas. This hotel is a large, yellow-stucco complex in a park at the center of town. The buildings, constructed in 1945, are an architectural zero, but the interior is attractive. Rooms are large and airy, with modern tiled bathrooms; some bedrooms have terraces overlooking the Olympic-size pool. The hotel is adjacent to the renowned Luso Spa, which offers a wide range of therapeutic programs. If you are looking for a hotel where you can settle in and really make use of the facilities, either this or the Palace in nearby Curia is ideal. The restaurant offers a good selection of international and regional foods in a pleasant environment overlooking the pool. ⊠ *Luso 3050, Mealhada,* ☎ *031/930450,* 𝖥𝖠𝖷 *031/930350. 173 rooms. Restaurant, bar, indoor and outdoor pools, sauna, miniature golf, tennis, dance club. AE, DC, MC, V.*

$ ⌂ Vila Duparchy. As you pass through the old gate and go up the long,
★ curved, tree-lined driveway, you'll soon realize this is no ordinary hotel. The two-story stucco house was built in the late 19th century. In 1988 Maria and Oscar Santos, the current resident owners, opened it as a guest house. Upstairs there are just six rooms; each has a fireplace, modern bath, and individually selected period furnishings. On the ground floor are three comfortable sitting rooms, which guests share with the Santoses. The spacious grounds are full of trees and flowers, and there is a small swimming pool. Breakfast is included, and other meals, far superior to the local restaurant fare, are prepared on request. ⊠ *Luso 3050, Mealhada,* ☎ *031/939120,* 𝖥𝖠𝖷 *031/930307. 6 rooms. Pool. AE, MC, V.*

¢ ⌂ Pensão Alegre. On a hill overlooking the park, this 19th-century
★ manor house has been receiving guests since 1931. The present owner, Manuel Alegre, took over the pension from his father. Filled with colorful tiles and rich wood, it exudes charm. If you're after Old World ambience and hospitality at bargain prices, look no farther. There are 20 rooms, all with high ceilings and plank floors. Ask for Number 103; it has a large terrace. Home-cooked meals are available on request. ⊠ *3050,* ☎ *031/930256. 20 rooms. Pool. MC, V.*

Buçaco

㊵ *3 km (2 mi) southeast of Luso, 16 km (10 mi) northeast of Coimbra.*

In the early 17th century, the head of the Order of Barefoot Carmelites, searching for a suitable location on which to found a **monastery,** came upon an area of dense virgin forest. Having rejected an offer to settle in Sintra because there were too many distractions, he chose instead the tranquil forest of Buçaco. A site for the monastery was selected halfway up the hill on the greenest slope, and by 1630 the simple stone structure was occupied. To preserve their world of isolation and silence, the monks built a wall enclosing the forest. Their only link with the outside world was through one door facing toward Coimbra, which one of them watched over. The **Coimbra Gate,** still in use today, is the most decorative of the eight gates constructed since that time.

So concerned were the Carmelites for the well-being of their forest that they obtained a papal bull in 1643 calling for the excommunication of anyone caught cutting down even a single tree. They planted many trees, including a number of exotic varieties, and the forest flourished. Attracted by the calm and tranquility of the forest, individual monks would leave the monastery to be alone with God and nature. They built simple **hermitages,** where they would stay, without human companionship, for several months at a time. You can still see vestiges of these hermitages as you walk through the forest.

In 1810 this serenity was shattered by a fierce battle in which the Napoleonic armies under Massena were repulsed by Wellington's British and Portuguese troops. An **obelisk** marks the site of the Battle of Buçaco, a turning point in the French invasion of the Iberian peninsula.

The small **Museu da Guerra Peninsular** (Peninsular War Museum) houses uniforms, weapons, and various memorabilia from the Battle of Buçaco. 🖼 *150$00.* ⊗ *June 15–Sept. 15, Tues.–Sun. 9–5:30; Sept. 16–June 14, Tues.–Sun. 10–4.*

A decree in 1834 banned religious orders throughout Portugal, and the monks were forced to leave the monastery. In the early years of this century, much of the original structure was torn down to construct what was to be a royal hunting lodge. The commission was given to the Italian architect Luigi Manini, and the project grew and grew. The opulent, multiturreted, pseudo-Manueline extravaganza that is now the

★ **Palace Hotel Buçaco** was the result. With the exception of one brief vacation and a dubious romantic fling involving the 20-year-old Manuel II, Portugal's last king, this "simple hunting lodge" was never used by the royal family. The hotel prospered, and in the years between the two world wars it became one of Europe's most fashionable vacation addresses. Tales told in the local villages have it that during World War II, when neutral Portugal was a hotbed of espionage activity, Nazi agents ensconced in the hotel's tower rooms beamed radio signals to submarines off the coast. Today the hotel is still going strong, somewhat of a dinosaur among the sleek new breed of glass-and-steel hostelries. Many come to Buçaco just to view this unusual structure, to stroll the shaded paths that wind through the forest, and to climb the hill past the Stations of the Cross to the Alta Cruz (High Cross), their efforts rewarded by the spectacular view extending all the way to the sea.

Dining and Lodging

$$$ ✕🖼 **Palace Hotel Buçaco.** They just don't make them like this anymore.
★ This is one of the few remaining great old hotels in the world. Staying at the Palace, even if just for one night, is an experience to be remembered. Yes, there is an elevator, but who can resist the temptation to walk up the grand, red-carpeted stairway, its walls lined with heroic azulejo panels, and past the suit of armor with the electric lights for eyes—a refreshing bit of kitsch in the midst of so much splendor? A former royal hunting lodge set in a historic 250-acre forest, the hotel is a hodgepodge of architectural styles, ranging from Gothic to neo-Manueline to early Walt Disney. It's worth ordering a meal in the dining room just to sit at the finely laid table and take in the ornate, carved-wood ceiling, inlaid hardwood floors, and massive, arched Manueline windows. In keeping with the decor, Chef Manuel Lorenço

turns out some masterpieces of his own. The hotel also has its own winery: The fine Buçaco wines laid down in the cellars, which contain some 200,000 bottles, are only available here. ⊠ *3050 Mealhada,* ☎ *031/930101,* FAX *031/930509. 53 rooms, 6 suites. Restaurant, bar. AE, DC, MC, V.*

Penacova

④ *12 km (7½ mi) southeast of Buçaco, 12 km (7½ mi) northeast of Coimbra; from Buçaco, the most scenic route is N235, through wooded countryside along the foot of the Serra do Buçaco; from Coimbra, take N110 along the Rio Mondego.*

A delightful little town perched on a hill at the junction of three low mountain ranges, Penacova affords panoramic views wherever you look and wonderful opportunities for hiking. The attractive **parish church** (⊠ Town square) was built in 1620.

OFF THE
BEATEN PATH

MONASTERY IN LORVÃO – In a delightful setting among the hills above the Mondego, this structure is patterned after the massive baroque edifice at Mafra. Archaeological evidence places the existence of a monastery here as far back as the 6th century, but the present church is principally an 18th-century construction. It has a fine carved choir and the intricate silver tombs of Teresa and Sancha, daughters of Dom Sancho I. A large part of the original monastery has been taken over by a psychiatric hospital, but it is possible to visit the church, choir, and sacristry. There is also a small museum next door. ⊠ *Turnoff on N110, 2 km (1 mi) south of Penacova.* ✆ *Free.* ⊙ *Daily 10–5.*

Dining

$ ✕ **O Panorâmico.** This small family-run restaurant is an ideal spot to stop for lunch while driving through this lovely countryside. It's easy to see where the name came from: There is a wonderful panoramic view looking down on the Rio Mondego as it snakes its way along to Coimbra. Maria da Graça, the proprietor, suggests the house specialty, *lampreia a mode de Penacova* (lampreys cooked with rice). ⊠ *Largo Alberto Leitão,* ☎ *039/477333. MC, V.*

Outdoor Activities and Sports

HIKING

Several paths lead over the hills to the Monastery of Lorvão or through the vineyards and fields down to the Mondego.

KAYAKING

Between April 1 and October 15, there are kayak trips down the Mondego from Penacova to Coimbra. Information can be obtained from **Pioneiro do Mondego** (⊠ Cheira, ☎ 039/478385) or from the local tourist office.

Shopping

The intricate, hand-carved willow toothpicks sold here are rarely found outside this little town on the Mondego.

THE EASTERN BEIRAS

In the mountains and along the frontier with Spain, life is difficult. Winters are cold and harsh, and summers are broiling hot. The rugged mountains of the Serra da Estrela and the sparse vegetation of the stone-strewn high plateau present a sharp contrast to the sandy beaches, lush valleys, and densely forested mountains along the coast. As you drive east, the red-tile roofs and brightly trimmed white-stucco houses are replaced by stone-and-slate construction, reflecting the more somber environment.

This harsh, rocky country is a tough place to make a living, as crops do not flourish. Traditionally, many inhabitants supplemented their meager farming incomes by smuggling contraband across the Spanish border. Between 1950 and 1970, many of the villages lost their ablest workers to the factories of northern Europe; a half-million Portuguese went to France alone. As a consequence, many towns are populated primarily by senior citizens.

Still, it's worth visiting this region to stand atop a centuries-old castle wall and look out on the rugged beauty of the landscape. And in this part of the country, where tourists are still somewhat of a curiosity, you will find perhaps the warmest welcome.

Destinations are listed roughly from south to north, with some loops along the way. In between discussions of towns—some modern but many still dominated by what remains of their fortifications—is a visit to the Serra da Estrela National Park.

Numbers in the margin correspond to points of interest on the Beiras map.

Castelo Branco

㊷ *90 km (56 mi) southeast of Coimbra.*

The provincial capital of Beira Baixa is a modern town of wide boulevards, parks, and gardens. Lying at the confluence of three major roads—the N112 from Coimbra; the N118, which runs along the Tejo; and the N18, which connects Guarda in the North with the Alentejo—it is easily accessible from all parts of the country.

Of course there is an old town, and there you'll find the **Praça Luis de Camões,** the town's best-preserved medieval square. The building with the arched stone stairway is the 16th-century **town hall.** At the top of the town's hill are the ruins of the 12th-century **Templar's Castle.** Not much remains of the series of walls and towers that once surrounded the town. Adjoining the castle is the flower-covered **Miradouro de São Gens** (Terrace of São Gens), which provides a fine view of the town and surrounding countryside.

A small regional museum, the **Tavares Proença National Museum,** is housed in the old Episcopal Palace. In addition to the usual Roman artifacts and odd pieces of furniture, the collection contains some fine examples of *bordado,* the embroidery for which Castelo Branco is well known. Adjacent to the museum is a workshop where embroidered bedspreads in the traditional patterns are made and sold. ⊠ *Rua Bartolomeu da Costa,* ☎ *072/24277.* ☐ *250$00, Sun. free.* ☉ *Daily 10–12:30 and 2–5:30; closed holidays.*

★ Take a stroll through the **Jardim do Antigo Paço Episcopal** (Gardens of the Old Episcopal Palace). These 18th-century gardens are planted with rows of hedges cut in all sorts of bizarre shapes and contain a most unusual assemblage of sculpture. Bordering one of the park's five small lakes are a path and stairway lined on both sides with granite statues of the Apostles, the Evangelists, and the kings of Portugal. The longstanding Portuguese disdain for the Spanish is graphically demonstrated here; the kings who ruled when Portugal was under Spanish domination are carved to a noticeably smaller scale than the "true" Portuguese rulers. Unfortunately, many statues were damaged by

Napoléon's troops when the city was ransacked in 1807. ⊠ *Rua Bartolomeu da Costa.* 🎫 *150$00.* ☉ *Daily 9–6.*

NEED A
BREAK? For a refreshing pause, drop into the **Cervejeria Bohemia** (⊠ Av. 1 de Maio, near the tourist office), an inviting snack bar–restaurant with a long marble-top bar.

Dining and Lodging

$$ ✕ **Praça Velha.** Set in a historic stone building on a lovely square (the
★ plaque outside reads 1685), this is by far the best restaurant in town. Of the two dining rooms, the older section with the beamed ceiling and stone floors is preferred. One intriguing specialty is *bife na pedra* (grilled beefsteak served on a hot slab of marble). ⊠ *Largo Luis Camões 17,* ☎ *072/328640. AE, DC, MC, V.*

$ 🏨 **Rainha Dona Amelia.** Castelo Branco's first new hotel to be opened in decades, the Dona Amelia is housed in a graceful, modern five-story building conveniently placed in the center of the city. The no-frills rooms are pleasant, functional, and airy. ⊠ *Rua de Santiago 15, 6000,* ☎ *072/326315,* ⊠ *072/326390. 64 rooms. Restaurant, bar. AE, MC, V.*

¢ 🏨 **Arraina.** Although this modern residencial is conveniently located and offers small but clean rooms, it is strictly a one-nighter. ⊠ *Av. 1 de Maio 16, 6000,* ☎ *072/21634,* ⊠ *072/331884. 31 rooms. Bar. MC, V.*

Shopping

Tradition in Castelo Branco dictates that a new bride make an embroidered bedspread for her wedding night. This custom is still followed, and these delicately patterned, hand-embroidered linen-and-silk spreads are among the finest examples of Portuguese handicrafts. There is a display-and-sales room next to the Tavares Proença National Museum.

En Route As you travel north from Castelo Branco on N18, you cross broad plains dotted with olive trees. From here you can see the Serra da Estrela in the distance.

Alpedrinha

43 *30 km (19 mi) north of Castelo Branco.*

This village known for its fine fountains also has well-preserved remnants of the Roman road that connected this fertile agricultural region with the Spanish town of Merida.

Fundão

44 *5 km (3 mi) north of Alpedrinha, 36 km (22 mi) north of Castelo Branco, 16 km (10 mi) south of Covilhã.*

The pears and cherries grown in this region are the best in Portugal, and Fundão is the principal market town for the area's many orchards. It's also a convenient gateway to the fortified towns along the Spanish border. The 18th-century **parish church** is noted for its azulejos and decorative ceiling.

Dining and Lodging

$ ✕ **O Casarão.** This quiet neighborhood restaurant's three small dining areas have beamed ceilings and are divided by brick pillars. Owner José Pereira proudly proclaims that he serves the best food in Fundão, and in this restaurant-poor town he is probably right. Try the Porto-style tripe. ⊠ *Rua José Germano da Cunha 2/4,* ☎ *075/52844. No credit cards.*

¢ ✕▦ **Estalagem da Neve.** A small, cozy, Victorian-style inn on the road from Castelo Branco, it has small but comfortably furnished rooms. The restaurant, with its beamed ceiling and tiled walls, provides an inviting setting in which to enjoy a fine Portuguese meal. Try the trout or roast kid. ⊠ *Calçada de São Sebastião, 6230,* ☎ FAX *075/52215. 22 rooms, 6 with bath. Restaurant, bar, pool. MC, V.*

Penamacor

⑮ *28 km (17 mi) east of Fundão, 28 km (17 mi) southeast of Covilhã.*

Like many of the towns in this region, Penamacor is a mix of old and new. Dominated by the ruins of an ancient castle, it was a key link in the chain of strategically placed fortified towns. On its outskirts are newer stucco houses, many built by Portuguese emigrants with money earned working in France and Germany.

Up on the hill, the **castle** once guarded the northern approaches to the Rio Tejo. In the wake of the 11th- and 12th-century campaigns to reconquer this region from the Moors, Penamacor lay in ruins. In 1180 Dom Sancho I ordered the reconstruction of the fortifications. Although you can still find traces from that period, much of what you now see, including the solitary watchtower, dates from the early 16th century. The tower, which has no entrance, was used as an observation post and has a direct line of sight with the fortifications at Monsanto to the south and Sortelha to the north. *If castle is closed, ask for the key at tourist office.*

The 16th-century **Misericórdia Church** is distinguished by a fine Manueline entrance. A rare **octagonal pillory** in front of the old town hall is also worth a look.

A small but interesting **regional museum** is housed in a building that was a political prison until the 1974 revolution. One of the original cells has been kept intact, and among the other exhibits is the only complete Roman crematorium on the Iberian Peninsula. ▣ *Free.* ☉ *Daily 10–noon and 2:30–5:30.*

Dining and Lodging

¢ ✕▦ **Vila Rica.** If you like to "collect" quaint country inns, this is a place
★ to add to your collection. The 19th-century converted farmhouse is surrounded by trees and gardens and is adjacent to a popular hunting area. Not coincidentally, the excellent restaurant serves many game dishes, including rabbit, quail, and wild boar. The 10 large bedrooms are simply but comfortably furnished. ⊠ *N233, 6090,* ☎ *077/94311,* FAX *077/94321. 10 rooms. Restaurant, bar, chapel. No credit cards.*

Sabugal

⑯ *20 km (12 mi) northeast of Penamacor, 36 km (22 mi) northeast of Covilhã; from Penamacor, follow N233 north across the high plateau.*

The main attraction here is the 13th-century **Sabugal Castle,** which sits majestically atop a grassy knoll and is noted for its unusual pentagonal tower. Some historians maintain that the five sides represent the five shields of the Portuguese national coat of arms. Climb the stone stairs in the courtyard and walk around the battlements. The castle overlooks the Rio Côa, an important tributary of the Douro. ▣ *Free.* ☉ *Mon.–Sat. 10–5. If castle is closed, ask for key at tourist office.*

OFF THE
BEATEN PATH

SERRA DA MALCATA NATIONAL PARK – One of Portugal's newest national parks, the Serra da Malcata is virtually unknown to foreign tourists. The

50,000-acre area along the Spanish border between Penamacor and Sabugal was created primarily to protect the natural habitat of the Iberian lynx, which was threatened with extinction. Although this is not a place of rugged beauty and spectacular vistas, such as you would find in Yosemite or even in the Serra da Estrela, it is nevertheless an attractive, quiet region of heavily wooded, low mountains with few traces of human habitation. In addition to the lynxes, the park shelters wildcats, wild boars, wolves, and foxes.

Sortelha

★ **❹⓻** *10 km (6 mi) southwest of Sabugal, 26 km (16 mi) east of Covilhã.*

If you only have time to visit one fortified town, then this should be it. From the moment you walk through its massive ancient stone walls, you feel like you are experiencing a time warp. Except for a few TV antennas, there is little to evoke the 20th century. The streets are not littered with souvenir stands, nor is there a fast-food outlet in sight. Stone houses are built into the rocky terrain and arranged within the walls roughly in the shape of an amphitheater.

NEED A BREAK?
The **Bar Dom Sancho I** (⊠ Main square) occupies the lower level of a carefully restored stone house. A "hobby project" of a local mining engineer, it is a pleasant place to pause for drinks and snacks. Upstairs you can purchase locally made handicrafts.

☾ Perched above the village are the ruins of a small but imposing **castle.** The present configuration dates back mainly to a late-12th-century reconstruction, done on Moorish foundations; additional alterations were made in the 16th century. Note the Manueline coat of arms at the entrance. Wear sturdy shoes so that you can walk along the walls (it's possible to circle the entire village this way). Children of all ages can let their fantasies run wild while taking in views of Spain to the east and the Serra da Estrela to the west. The three holes in the balcony projecting over the main entrance were used to pour boiling oil on intruders. Just to the right of the north gate are two linear indentations in the stone wall. One is exactly a meter in length, and the shorter of the two is a *covada* (66 centimeters). In medieval times, traveling cloth merchants used these markings to ensure an honest measure.

Dining and Lodging

$ ★ ✕ **Alboroque.** This is the sort of place that interior designers are always trying to re-create with imitation wood beams and plastic rocks. The town's only real restaurant, it occupies an ancient stone building. You walk up some rickety wood stairs to a cozy, stone-walled dining area with massive wood beams overhead. Owner Raul Clara has done more than create an inviting atmosphere; he also manages to turn out some wonderful food. Specialties include wild boar and venison in season as well as a first-rate *caldeirada de borrego* (lamb stew). ⊠ *Rua da Mesquita,* ☎ *071/68129. No credit cards. Closed Mon.*

Although this medieval town has no hotels or pensions, several ancient stone houses have been converted into tourist accommodations. These are comfortable but not luxurious. They do have running water and bathrooms and offer an unusual opportunity to actually live in a medieval Portuguese village.

¢ ⌂ **Casa Arabe.** ⊠ *Rua dá Mesquita, Sortelha, 6320 Sabugal,* ☎ *071/68129. 1 apartment, sleeps 4. No credit cards.*

¢ ⌂ **Casa do Vento que Soa.** ⊠ *Sortelha, 6320 Sabugal,* ☎ *071/68182. 2 rooms. No credit cards.*

Belmonte

❹❽ *14 km (9 mi) northwest of Sortelha, 20 km (12 mi) southwest of Guarda.*

As you approach Belmonte, three distinct objects that say a lot about the town catch your eye. The first two, the ancient castle and the church, represent its historic past, while the third structure, an ugly water tower, symbolizes the new industry of the town, now a major clothing-manufacturing center. Historically, Belmonte's importance can be traced back to Roman times, when it was an important outpost on the road between Merida, the Lusitanian capital, and Guarda. Elements of this road may still be seen.

Ask a Portuguese, or better yet any Brazilian, what Belmonte is best known for, and the answer will undoubtedly be Pedro Álvares Cabral. In 1500 this native son "discovered" Brazil and in doing so contributed to making Portugal one of the richest and most powerful nations of that era. The **monument to Cabral** (⊠ Town center) is an important stop for Brazilians visiting Portugal.

🕙 Of the mighty complex of fortifications and dwellings that once made up the **castle,** only the tower and battlements remain intact. As you enter, note the scale-model replica of the caravel that carried Cabral to Brazil. On one of the side walls is a coat of arms with two goats, the emblem of the Cabral family. ("Cabra" means goat in Portuguese.) The graceful Manueline window incorporated into the heavy fortifications seems misplaced. ▣ *Free.* ◷ *Mon.–Sat. 10–12:30 and 2– 5:30.*

A cluster of old houses makes up the **juderia** (old Jewish Quarter, ⊠ Adjacent to castle). Belmonte had (and, in fact, still has) one of the largest Jewish communities in Portugal. Many present-day residents are descendants of the Morranos, the Jews who were forced to convert to Christianity during the Inquisition.

The 12th-century stone **Igreja de São Tiago** (Church of St. James) contains fragments of original 12th-century frescoes and a fine pietà carved from a single block of granite. The tomb of Pedro Cabral is also in this church. Actually there are two Pedro Cabral tombs in Portugal, the result of a bizarre dispute with Santarem, where Cabral died. Both towns claim ownership of the explorer's mortal remains, and no one seems to know just who or what is in either tomb. ⊠ *Adjacent to castle.* ▣ *Free.* ◷ *Daily 10–6. If closed, ask at tourist office.*

OFF THE
BEATEN PATH
CENTUM CELLAS – A couple of miles outside Belmonte, on a dirt track leading off N18, is a strange archaeological find. This massive, solitary tower constructed of granite blocks is thought to be of Roman origin, and some archaeologists believe it's part of a much larger complex. Excavations of the surrounding area are planned.

Dining and Lodging

¢ ✕⌂ **Belsol.** Pleasant and modest, the hotel is conveniently situated in a quiet spot off N18. Rooms are large, and a number have balconies with views of the Zêzere. Owner João Pinheiro is representative of a new breed of enterprising young Portuguese businesspeople looking to provide quality and service. The downstairs restaurant, although simple in decor, offers excellent food and is a favorite with local businesspeople. Try the fresh trout from the local rivers. ⊠ *Quinta do Rio, 6250,* ☎ *075/912206,* FAX *075/912315. 55 rooms. Restaurant, bar, pool, playground. DC, MC, V.*

Covilhã

🔑 *16 km (10 mi) southwest of Belmonte, 48 km (30 mi) north of Castelo Branco.*

Although its origins go back to Roman times, there is little in present-day Covilhã of historic significance. Built into the foothills of the Serra da Estrela, the mostly modern town is closely linked to sheep raising. Its tangy *queijo da Serra,* a ewe's-milk cheese, is popular throughout the country, and the town is Portugal's most important wool-producing center. However, most visitors come to Covilhã because it is a convenient gateway to the Serra da Estrela.

Dining and Lodging

$ ✕🛏 **Hotel Turismo.** This attractive, modern hotel, conveniently situated at the eastern edge of town, is the first new hotel to be built in Covilhã in several decades. The decor is simple but pleasant and functional. Among the local specialties served in the panoramic rooftop restaurant is fresh trout from nearby mountain streams. ⊠ *Acesso a Variante, Quinta da Olivosa, 6200,* ☎ *075/324545,* FAX *075/324630. 60 rooms. Restaurant, bar, sauna, health club, squash, dance club. AE, DC, MC, V.*

¢ 🛏 **Solneve.** In the town center, Solneve had been the prime hotel in Covilhã since its opening some 50 years ago. It's now starting to fray a bit around the edges and has been eclipsed by the Hotel Turismo. The restaurant, in spite of a decor reminiscent of a high-school cafeteria, offers a nice variety of tasty regional dishes, including *truta a solneve* (fresh trout grilled with cured ham and onions). ⊠ *Rua Visconde da Coriscada 126, 6200,* ☎ *075/323001,* FAX *075/315497. 32 rooms, 6 suites. Restaurant, bar. MC, V.*

Serra da Estrela National Park

Until the end of the 19th century, this mountainous region was little known except by shepherds and local hunters. The first scientific expedition to the Serra was in 1881. Since that time it has developed into one of the country's most popular recreation areas. In summer the high, craggy peaks, alpine meadows, and rushing streams become the domain of hikers, climbers, and trout fishermen. The lower and middle elevations are heavily wooded with large stands of deciduous oak, sweet chestnut, and pine. Above the tree line, at about 4,900 feet, is a rocky, subalpine world of scrub vegetation and boggy meadows, which in late spring is transformed into a vivid, multicolored carpet of wildflowers. The Serra da Estrela is home to many species of animals, the largest of which include wild boar, badger, and, in the more remote areas, the occasional wolf.

If you prefer to take in the scenery from the comfort of your car, the roads through the Serra da Estrela, although hair-raising at times, are well maintained and offer many inspiring vistas. The drive between Covilhã and Seia on N339, the highest road in the country, affords a breathtaking view of the Zêzere Valley. Along the way you will pass a small fountain marking the source of the Rio Mondego.

Dining and Lodging

For additional hotels and restaurants in and around the park, *see* listings under individual towns.

$ ✕ **Cabana do Pastor.** A cozy mountain restaurant with a fireplace and ★ panoramic views, this is a good place to partake of the locally made cheese—queijo da Serra—and presunto. It's 12 kilometers (7½ miles) southwest of Gouveia. ✉ *Behind souvenir shop on N339,* ☎ *038/23879. AE, DC, MC, V.*

$$$ ✕⊡ **Pousada de São Lourenço.** At an elevation of 4,231 feet, this pou- ★ sada is in the heart of the Serra da Estrela, 13 kilometers (8 miles) from Manteigas, a pleasant spa town at the foot of the Zêzere Valley. The remodeled granite mountain lodge is a favorite stopover for Portuguese and foreign visitors. Ample use of wood and brick in the rooms and a cozy fireplace in the lounge contribute to the high-country ambience. Ask for Room 207; it has a loft for sleeping and one of the best views. If you are just driving through, stop for lunch at the restaurant and try the unusual but delicious *bacalhau a lagareiro* (baked cod with corn bread, olive oil, and potatoes). ✉ *6260 Manteigas,* ☎ *075/982450,* FAX *075/982453. 21 rooms, 1 suite. Restaurant, bar. AE, DC, MC, V.*

$$ ✕⊡ **Pousada de Santa Barbara.** In the pines high on the western ★ flank of the Serra da Estrela, 20 kilometers (12 miles) southwest of Gou- veia, this mountainside pousada offers a restful and cool respite from the summer heat. Many of the rooms have balconies supported by mas- sive stone columns. The restaurant features a variety of tasty local dishes. ✉ *N17, Povoa das Quartas, 3400 Oliveira do Hospital,* ☎ *038/59551,* FAX *038/59645. 16 rooms. Restaurant, bar, pool, tennis court. AE, DC, MC, V.*

$ ✕⊡ **Hotel Serra da Estrela.** Originally built in the early part of this century as a tuberculosis sanitorium, this hotel 12 kilometers (7½ miles) from Covilhã has been completely renovated. Rooms are large, and those in the front have good views looking down into the valley. At an elevation of 3,936 feet, the hotel provides an excellent base for a few days in the mountains. The restaurant is light and spacious, with lots of glass and wood. ✉ *Penhas da Saude, 6203 Covilhã,* ☎ *075/313809,* FAX *075/323789. 38 rooms. Restaurant, bar, snack bar, tennis courts. AE, DC, MC, V.*

¢ ⊡ **Albergaria Senhora do Espinheiro.** This recently built mountain inn ★ is next to the Cabana do Pastor restaurant, 12 kilometers (7½ miles) from Gouveia. Both are the labors of love of Antonio Mora, a big, gen- tle bear of a man who will enhance your stay or meal. The use of wood and tile throughout gives the inn a warm feeling. Rooms are small and furnished in pine. Ask for one at the back, where the views are best. ✉ *N339, 6270 Seia,* ☎ *038/22073. 24 rooms. Bar. AE, DC, MC, V.*

Outdoor Activities and Sports

CAMPING

There are several official campsites within the park, but if you are dis- creet about it, you can pitch a small tent just about anywhere without being bothered.

HIKING

This is a hiker's paradise, amply supplied with well-marked trails. A comprehensive trail guide is available at tourist offices in the region, and, although it's in Portuguese, the maps, elevation charts, and pic- tures are useful.

SKIING

With the coming of winter and the first snows, the area becomes a win- ter playground, offering many Portuguese their only exposure to win- ter sports. Although there are two ski lifts at **Torre**—the highest point in continental Portugal, with an elevation of 6,539 feet—the conditions and facilities are not on a par with ski resorts in the rest of Europe.

Gouveia

 28 km (17 mi) northwest of Covilhã, 20 km (12 mi) southeast of Mangualde.

Nestled into the western side of the Mondego Valley, this quiet town of parks and gardens is a popular base from which to explore the Serra da Estrela.

The exterior of the baroque **parish church** is covered with blue-and-white tiles, while a series of well-executed azulejos depicting the Stations of the Cross lines the inside walls of the small, dimly lit **chapel** across the street.

The **Museu Abel Manta,** in an 18th-century manor house, displays the paintings of this local 20th-century artist. ▣ *Free.* ⊙ *Tues.–Sun. 10–noon and 2–5.*

OFF THE BEATEN PATH | **MONTES HERMINIOS KENNELS –** Gouveia is the principal center for the famous Serra da Estrela dogs, beautiful sheepdogs known for their loyalty and courage. In earlier days, when marauding wolf packs were an ever-present menace, the dogs wore metal collars with long spikes to protect their throats. To learn more about the dogs, you can visit these kennels, one of the major breeding kennels in the Vale do Rossim. ▣ *N232 between Gouveia and Manteigas, Solar do Cão da Serra, Estrada da Serra,* ☎ *038/42426.* ⊙ *Visits by appointment.*

Dining and Lodging

$ ✕ **O Foral.** On the ground floor of the Hotel Gouvia, this comfortable restaurant is the eatery of choice among the town's civic and business community. Service is attentive, and the kitchen is noted for its roast kid. ▣ *Av. 1 de Maio,* ☎ *038/491010. AE, DC, MC, V.*

$ ✕ **O Julio.** Thanks to the talents of chef and owner Julio, this simple, ★ unassuming restaurant was chosen to represent the Serra da Estrela region at the 1992 tourist fair in Lisbon. Julio recommends the *vitela estufada na maneira antiga* (veal stew). ▣ *Travessa do Loureiro 1,* ☎ *038/42142. MC, V. Closed Tues.*

¢ ⊞ **Hotel Gouveia.** This small, modern hotel on one of the main approaches to the Serra da Estrela offers comfortable rooms furnished in traditional style. Several have small balconies. ▣ *Av. 1 de Maio, 6290,* ☎ *038/491010,* ℻ *038/41370. 27 rooms, 4 suites. Restaurant, bar, pool, tennis. AE, DC, MC, V.*

Festival

The **Festa do Senhor do Calvario** (Festival of Our Lord of Calvary), during the first week in August, starts on a Sunday with a colorful procession. Other events include a handicrafts fair, games, and a sheepdog competition.

Linhares

 16 km (10 mi) northeast of Gouveia.

Perching atop a rocky outcrop on the northeastern shoulder of the Serra da Estrela at an elevation of 2,625 feet, this fortified hamlet is a good place for a lookout. This small, quiet village of stone houses, a church, and a few shops is encircled by walls, much of which remain intact, as do two square, crenellated towers from the time of King Dinis. There's a 16th-century **pillory** in front of the church.

Celorico da Beira

❷ *14 km (9 mi) northeast of Linhares, 16 km (10 mi) northwest of Guarda.*

Celorico da Beira is a major producer of Serra cheese and the site of one of Europe's largest cheese markets, held every other Friday. The cheese is made from the best-quality ewe's milk, using traditional methods. Cheese production takes place between December and March.

Celorico also has the requisite **fortress,** and a large portion of the castle walls and an impressive tower have remained intact. *Key to castle can be obtained at town hall.* ⊙ *Mon.–Sat. 10–12:30 and 2–5.*

Dining and Lodging

$ ✕▣ **Mira Serra.** This modern four-story hotel is conveniently located just off IP5. Owner Fernando Batista was the manager of a five-star luxury hotel in the Algarve before striking out on his own. The rooms are comfortable and furnished in traditional style; some have a small balcony. The restaurant serves the best food in the area. Try the *bacalhau a brás* (slivers of dried cod fried with eggs and onions). ✉ *6360,* ☎ *071/72604,* ▣ *071/741382. 42 rooms. Restaurant, bar. AE, DC, MC, V.*

Trancoso

❸ *18 km (11 mi) northeast of Celorico da Beira, 26 km (16 mi) northwest of Guarda.*

This town reached its pinnacle in 1282, when King Dinis chose it as the site for his marriage to Isabel of Aragon. Portions of the town's well-preserved castle walls and towers date to the 9th century. Above one of the gates, the **Porta do Carvalho,** you can make out the figure of a knight. This was a local lad who, during one of the many battles with the Spanish, left the safety of the castle walls to capture the Spanish flag. He was caught, but before being spirited away, he was able to defiantly hurl the flag over the wall.

Pinhel

❹ *38 km (24 mi) east of Trancoso; the best route is the scenic but tortuous N226.*

Sitting atop a hill in the Marofa range, this town was a key bastion during the wars of restoration. Pinhel's most striking remnants of the 17th century are two solitary **towers** that rise above town. On one of the towers, below the balcony facing the town, you can make out the graceful form of a Manueline window.

En Route Taking N221 north, you'll cross the Serra da Marofa and a desolate, rocky moonscape. Before some recent improvements, this stretch was known as the Accursed Road, because of its many bends.

Castelo Rodrigo

❺ *12 km (7½ mi) northeast of Pinhel.*

This old fortified town is now mostly deserted, many of its former residents having emigrated to France and Germany. The ruins of the **fortress** afford a panoramic view of the surrounding countryside. In neighboring Figueira de Castelo Rodrigo, the 18th-century **parish church** contains several attractive gilded wooden altars.

Almeida

🐚 **56** *18 km (11 mi) southeast of Castelo Rodrigo.*

Enclosed within a star-shaped perimeter of massive stone walls, moats, and earthen bulwarks lies the quiet little town of Almeida. Less than 10 kilometers (6 miles) from the Spanish border, it's been the scene of much fighting over the centuries. This is a place for walking, for clambering along the walls and bulwarks, and for giving your imagination free rein, perhaps to conjure up ghosts of battles past.

Dining and Lodging

$$$ ✕🏨 **Pousada Senhora das Neves.** Portuguese architect Cristiano Mor-
★ eira has mastered the difficult task of integrating this modern hotel into historic fortress walls. The bedrooms as well as the public rooms are spacious and light, and there are large terraces that look out across the high tablelands into Spain. You can sip your afternoon glass of chilled white port and imagine Wellington's troops facing Napoléon's armies on this very spot. The restaurant, divided into two inviting plank-floor dining rooms, serves a wide variety of regional dishes, including *sopa de peixe do rio Côa* (a rich tomato-based soup made with fish from the nearby Rio Côa). The extensive wine list offers more than 60 selections. ✉ *6350,* ☎ *071/54283,* 🆕 *071/54320. 20 rooms, 1 suite. Restaurant, bar. AE, DC, MC, V.*

¢ 🏨 **A Muralha.** This modern residencial, just outside the fortifications, is the creation of two ex-schoolteachers, Manuel and Eliza Dias. He has traded teaching English for running the 24-room residencial, and Eliza gave up her geography courses to oversee the small restaurant. The rooms are clean and simply furnished. Cork floors in the bedrooms and cork paneling in the hallways contribute to a homey atmosphere. The restaurant's specialties include roast suckling pig and curried shrimp. ✉ *Bairro de São Pedro, 6350,* ☎ *071/54357. 24 rooms. Restaurant, bar. MC, V.*

Guarda

57 *38 km (24 mi) southwest of Almeida, 36 km (22 mi) northeast of Covilhã, 60 km (37 mi) east of Viseu.*

At an elevation of about 3,300 feet, Guarda is Portugal's highest city and is aptly referred to by the four Fs: *forte, feia, fria, e farta* (strong, ugly, cold, and wealthy). A somber conglomeration of austere granite buildings set in a harsh, uncompromising environment, Guarda is no charming mountain hamlet. The winters are cold and gloomy, often cutting into the short springtime.

From pre-Roman times, Guarda has been a strategic bastion on the northeastern flank of the Serra da Estrela, protecting the approaches from Castile. The town is thought to have been a military base for Julius Caesar. Following the fall of the Roman Empire, the Visigoths and later the Moors gained control. Guarda was liberated in the late 12th century by Christian forces and, along with a number of towns in the region, enlarged and fortified by Dom Sancho I.

The castle tower, perched on a small knoll above the cathedral, and a few segments of wall are all that remain of Guarda's extensive **fortifications.** From atop the ruins there is an impressive view across the rock-strewn countryside toward the Castilian plains.

Construction on the fortresslike **Sé** (cathedral) started in 1390 but was not completed until 1540. As a consequence, the imposing Gothic building also shows Renaissance and Manueline influences. Although built on a smaller and less majestic scale, the cathedral shows similarities to the great monastery at Batalha. Inside, a magnificent four-tier relief contains more than 100 carved figures. The work is attributed to the 16th-century sculptor Jean de Rouen.

In the **Praça Luis de Camões,** a square lined with some fine 16th- and 18th-century houses, stands a statue of Dom Sancho I.

The **Regional Museum,** in a stately early 17th-century palace adjacent to the 18th-century Misericórdia Church, is worth a visit. ⊠ *Rua Alves Rocadas,* ☎ *071/23460.* ▣ *300$00, Sun. free.* ☉ *Tues.–Sun. 10–12:30 and 2–5:30.*

Dining and Lodging

$ ✕ **Belo Horizonte.** Guarda is not noted for its good restaurants, but this modest establishment in the old quarter is one of the few exceptions. It features hardy regional fare and a different type of bacalhau daily. ⊠ *Largo de São Vicente 2,* ☎ *071/211454. AE, MC, V. Closed Sat.*

$ ✕▥ **Filipe.** Across the street from the Misericórdia Church, this redecorated, family-run residencial offers plain but comfortable rooms and a personal touch not found at the more-formal Hotel Turismo. Owner Americo Alexis has traveled the world and will be happy to pass the time of day in just about any language. The upstairs restaurant (closed Nov.–Jan.), the domain of Senhora Alexis, is a good place to enjoy *camarões piri-piri* (giant prawns with hot-pepper sauce). ⊠ *Rua Vasco da Gama 9, 6300,* ☎ *071/223659,* FAX *071/221402. 41 rooms. Restaurant, bar. AE, DC, MC, V.*

$ ✕▥ **Hotel Turismo.** Since it opened in 1940 in a stately, country-style
★ manor house, the Turismo has been Guarda's leading hotel. Extensively remodeled in 1988, it has maintained its position, albeit in a town with little competition. The, extensive use of wood and leather in the bar and lounges lends a comfortable, clubby atmosphere to the place. Bedrooms are adequate in size and furnished in traditional style. The restaurant serves the best food in town in a quiet, refined atmosphere. ⊠ *Av. Cor. Orlindo de Calvalho, 6300,* ☎ *071/223366,* FAX *071/223399. 100 rooms, 2 suites. Restaurant, bar, pool. AE, DC, MC, V.*

COIMBRA AND THE BEIRAS A TO Z

Arriving and Departing

By Bus

The **Rodoviária Nacional** (RN) provides comfortable motor-coach service between Lisbon, Porto, and Coimbra. RN stations in Coimbra (⊠ Av. Fernão de Magalhães, ☎ 039/27081), Castelo Branco (⊠ Rodrigo Rebelo 3, ☎ 072/323301), and Covilhã (⊠ Largo das Forcas Armadas, ☎ 075/24914) all have international as well as domestic service. International **Euroline** motor coaches link Coimbra with London, Paris, Amsterdam, and Frankfurt. For information call Euroline in Lisbon (☎ 01/547300) or contact a travel agent.

By Car

Although you can zip from Lisbon to Coimbra on the A1 *auto-estrada* (tollway) in less than two hours or drive from Porto to Coimbra in under an hour, smaller roads provide a much richer and more varied travel experience. The eastern part of the Beiras is readily accessible from Spain. It's 90 kilometers (56 miles) on N620 from Salamanca and 320 kilometers (199 miles) from Madrid to the border crossing at Vilar Formoso.

By Plane

There are some international flights into Porto (to the north); however, Lisbon is the preferred choice for the international air traveler. It's 160 kilometers (99 miles) northeast from the Lisbon airport to Coimbra via the A1 motorway.

By Train

Coimbra, Luso, Guarda, Mangualde, Ovar, and Aveiro are on the main Lisbon/Porto–Paris line. Two trains arrive from Paris and two depart daily. There is also regular train service linking the principal cities in the Beiras with Madrid, Lisbon, and Porto. In summer a daily car-train operates between Paris and Lisbon. There are two train stations in Coimbra: **Coimbra A** (Estação Nova), along the Rio Mondego, a five-minute walk from the center of town (for domestic routes), and **Coimbra B** (Estação Velha), 5 kilometers (3 miles) west (for international trains). There are frequent bus and rail links between stations. For information call ☎ 039/34998. Schedules for all trains are posted at both stations.

Getting Around

By Bus

For those who choose not to drive, an extensive bus network provides the next best way of getting around. Vehicles of various vintages can take you to almost any destination, and unlike train stations, which are often some distance from the town center, bus depots are centrally located. Rural buses, often packed with people going to and from regional markets, provide a wonderful microcosm of Portuguese life. Regional and local bus schedules are posted at the terminals. Information may also be obtained at local tourist offices. Although this a great way to travel and get close to the local people, it does require a great deal of time and patience.

By Car

The Beiras, with their many remote villages, are particularly suited to exploration by car. Distances between major points are short; there are no intimidating major cities to negotiate; and except for the coastal strip in July and August, traffic is light. Roads in general are quite good and destinations well marked; however, parking is a problem in the larger towns.

Although it is possible to whiz through the region in a few hours on the Lisbon–Porto highway or the IP5 that links Aveiro with Vilar Formoso at the Spanish frontier, resist the temptation. The heart and soul of the Beiras are to be found along the many miles of those squiggly yellow-and-white lines lacing the road map of Portugal. The best map for motorists, both for scale and ease of reading, is Michelin map #440 (Portugal-Madeira), available at bookstores throughout Portugal and in the United States from **Michelin Travel Publications** (✉ 1 Parkway S, Greenville, SC 29615, ☎ 803/458–6330).

By Train

Although the major destinations in this chapter are linked by rail, service to most towns, with the exception of Coimbra, is infrequent. The equipment on the Beira line, which connects Lisbon with Guarda and the Serra da Estrela, has been upgraded.

Using Coimbra as a hub, there are three main rail lines serving the Beiras. Line 110 goes northeast to Luso, Viseu, Mangualde, Celorico da Beira, and Guarda. Line 100 extends south through the Ribatejo to intersect with Line 130, which runs from Lisbon northeast through the Beira

Baixa towns of Castelo Branco and Fundão to Covilhã, the gateway to the Serra da Estrela. Going north from Coimbra, Line 100 services Curia, Aveiro, and Ovar and continues north to Porto and Braga. Schedules are posted at all train stations.

Contacts and Resources

Car Rental
If you don't get a car from one of the numerous agencies in Lisbon, you can rent in Coimbra or Viseu: **Hertz** (⊠ Rua João Ruão 16, Coimbra, ☎ 039/37491; ⊠ Rua da Paz 21, Viseu, ☎ 032/421846) and **Avis** (⊠ Coimbra A, Largo das Ameias, Coimbra, ☎ 039/34786; ⊠ Hotel Grão Vasco, Rua Gaspar Barreiros, Viseu, ☎ 032/25750).

Emergencies
The national emergency number is **115.**

Guided Tours
There are very few regularly scheduled guided tours originating in the Beiras. **RN Tours** (⊠ Rua da Sofia 102, 3000 Coimbra, ☎ 039/22849) offers a half-day tour of Coimbra on Wednesday and Sunday during summer. **Mivitur** (⊠ Av. do Ramalhão, 3220 Miranda do Corvo, ☎ 039/52304) has an all-day tour of the Rio Mondego region on Tuesday and Thursday, mid-June–mid-September. There are also one- to seven-day tours that leave from Lisbon and Porto and cover the Beiras. For further information contact a travel agency or, in Lisbon, **RN Tours** (⊠ Av. Fontes Pereira de Melo 14–12, ☎ 01/353–8846) or **Tip Tours** (⊠ Av. Costa Pinto 91–A, Cascais, ☎ 01/486–5159).

Hospitals
Hospitals with *urgências* (emergency rooms) are in **Castelo Branco** (Hospital Distrital de Castelo Branco, ⊠ Av. Pedro A. Cabral, ☎ 072/322133), **Coimbra** (Hospital da Universidade Coimbra, ⊠ Praça Prof. Mota Pinto, ☎ 039/400400), **Figueira da Foz** (Hospital Distrital da Figueira da Foz, ⊠ Gala, ☎ 033/31033), and **Guarda** (⊠ Rua Dr. Francisco Prazeres, ☎ 071/222133).

Late-Night Pharmacies
Pharmacies in all sizable towns operate on a rotating system for staying open after normal closing hours, including weekends and holidays. Consult a local newspaper or the notice posted on the door of every pharmacy.

Mail
The central post office in Coimbra, **CTT Estação Central** (⊠ Av. Fernão de Magalhães 223), is adjacent to the train station and is the center for *poste restante* (general delivery). Most other towns have just one central post office, where poste restante is received.

Travel Agency
In Coimbra, a useful agency is **Abreu** (⊠ Rua da Sota 2, ☎ 039/27011).

Visitor Information
The regional tourist offices for **Coimbra** and the surrounding area are the **Região de Turismo do Centro** (⊠ Largo da Portagem, 3000 Coimbra, ☎ 039/33028; ⊠ Edificio Marisol, Av. 25 de Abril, 3080 Figueira da Foz, ☎ 033/22610). Within this region there are local tourist offices in **Arganil** (⊠ Praça Simões Dias, ☎ 035/22859), **Buarcos** (⊠ Largo Tomas de Aquino, ☎ 033/25019), **Condeixa** (⊠ Edificio da Câmara, ☎ 039/941114), **Curia** (⊠ Praça Dr. Luís Navega, ☎ 031/512248), **Figueiro dos Vinhos** (⊠ Av. Padre Diogo Vasconcelos, ☎ 036/52178), **Lousa** (⊠ Edificio da Câmara, ☎ 039/991502), **Luso/Buçaco** (⊠ Rua Emidio Navarro, Luso, ☎ 031/93133), **Mira** (⊠ Edificio da Câmara,

☎ 031/451506), **Montemor-O-Velho** (✉ Praça da República, ☎ 039/68187), and **Penacova** (✉ Miradouro do Terreiro, ☎ 039/477114 or 477115).

For information about **Aveiro** and the **Rota da Luz** region, consult the **Região de Turismo da Rota da Luz** (✉ Rua Joâo Mendonça 8, 3800 Aveiro, ☎ 034/20760). The principal local tourist offices in this region are in: **Águeda** (✉ Estrada Nacional 1, ☎ 034/601412), **Costa Nova** (✉ Praia da Costa Nova, at the beach, ☎ 034/369560, ☺ June–Sept.), **Ilhavo** (✉ Av. Mario Sacramento, ☎ 034/325911), **Ovar** (✉ Edificio da Câmara, Praça da República, ☎ 056/572215), and **Torreira** (✉ Av. Hintze Ribeiro, ☎ 034/48250).

The regional tourist office for the **Dão-Lafões** area is the **Região de Turismo de Dão-Lafões** (✉ Av. Gulbenkian, 3500 Viseu, ☎ 032/422014). Local tourist offices are in: **Caramulo** (✉ Estrada Principal do Caramulo, ☎ 032/861437), **Nelas** (✉ Largo Prof. Veiga Simão, ☎ 032/944384), and **São Pedro do Sul** (✉ Largo dos Correios, ☎ 032/711320).

The **Serra da Estrela** district is represented by the **Região de Turismo da Serra da Estrela** (✉ Praça do Município 1, 6200 Covilhã, ☎ 075/322170). There are local tourist offices in: **Belmonte** (✉ Praça Pedro Álvares Cabral, ☎ 075/911488), **Castelo Branco** (✉ Alameda da Liberdade, ☎ 072/21002), **Fundão** (✉ Av. da Liberdade, ☎ 075/52770), **Gouveia** (✉ Av. 1 de Maio, ☎ 038/42185), **Guarda** (✉ Praça Luis Camões, ☎ 071/222251), **Manteigas** (✉ Rua Dr. Gaspar de Carvalho, ☎ 075/981129), **Oliveira do Hospital** (✉ Praça do Município, ☎ 038/52522), **Penamacor** (✉ Praça 25 de Abril, ☎ 077/314316), **Sabugal** (✉ Praça da República, ☎ 071/63316), and **Seia** (✉ Praça do Mercado, ☎ 038/922272).

8 Porto and the North

The vibrant, cosmopolitan, baroque-flavored city of Porto is famous for the wine that bears its name, but the rest of the north is undiscovered country for most visitors. The Minho region combines beaches and fishing villages along its Atlantic coast, the Costa Verde, with a lush inland landscape dotted with ancient towns and country markets. The isolated northeastern province of Trás-os-Montes was until recently largely inaccessible, but new roads have penetrated the region's forests and moors, and visitors can now marvel at a dramatic landscape rich in wildlife and populated by castles, fortresses, and medieval villages where it's easy to imagine time has stood still.

By Jules Brown

Updated by
Mary Ellen
Schultz

THE REMOTE CORNERS OF NORTHERN PORTUGAL seem far away in Porto, a trading center since pre-Roman times and still a vibrant, cosmopolitan city that makes a fine contrast to Lisbon. The Moors never had the same strong foothold here that they did farther south, and the city remained largely unaffected by the great earthquake of 1755; as a result, Porto shows off a baroque finery lacking in the capital. Its grandiose granite buildings were financed by the trade that made the city wealthy: Wine from the upper valley of the Rio Douro (River of Gold) was transported to Porto, from where it was then exported. Visitors may follow that trail today by boat or by the beautiful Douro Line train route along the river.

Though it's not immediately apparent, northern Portugal *is* a popular holiday destination—with the Portuguese. The north can be beautiful, as it is in the valley of the Rio Douro and the deep, rural heartland of the Minho, the coastal province north of Porto; it can also be hostile, as in the Terra Fria (Cold Land), the remote, rugged uplands of the northern Trás-os-Montes (Beyond the Mountains). From here come the mysterious, prehistoric *porcas* (stone pigs), reminders of early tribes who scratched a living from the cold earth. Some towns, like Chaves (Keys), bear curious names and complicated histories. Festivals such as the Holy Week parade at Braga (complete with a torchlit procession through dark old-town streets) evoke an earlier time.

The Minho, which takes its name from the river forming Portugal's northern border with Spain, is bounded by the Atlantic in the west and cut by the long, peaceful Lima and Cávado rivers. The Minho coast is advertised as the Costa Verde (Green Coast), a sweeping stretch of beaches and fishing villages named for its lush, green landscape. Some locations have been appropriated as resorts by the Portuguese, but there are still plenty of places where you can find solitary dunes or splash in the brisk Atlantic away from crowds. Inland you can lose yourself in ancient villages with country markets and fairs that have hardly changed for hundreds of years. You'll also see that little of the green countryside is wasted. Vines are trained on poles and in trees high above cultivated fields, forming a natural canopy, for this is *vinho verde* country. This refreshing "green wine"—so called because it is drunk young and has a slightly greenish cast—is a true taste of the north, one to which you'll quickly become accustomed as you sit, glass in hand, by a river or the coast and reflect upon the day's events.

To the northeast there's adventure at hand, in the winding mountain roads and remote towns and villages of the Trás-os-Montes region. After centuries of isolation, the area is being accessed by new roads, but there's still great excitement in the rattling trans-mountain train ride from Porto to Bragança, in the far northeastern corner of the country. The imposing, medieval castle towers and fortress walls of this frontier region are a great attraction, but—unusual in such a small country—it's often the journey itself that's the greatest prize: traveling past voluminous man-made lakes, through forested valleys rich in wildlife, across bare crags and moorlands, and finally down to coarse, stone villages where TV aerials sit oddly in almost medieval surroundings.

Pleasures and Pastimes

Beaches
Swimming in the Atlantic can be very cold, even at the height of summer, and beaches along the Costa Verde are notoriously windswept. More pleasant is river swimming in the small towns along the Lima

and Minho rivers, though you should take local advice about currents and pollution before plunging in. Ponte de Lima has a particularly nice wide, sandy beach.

Espinho, south of Porto, and the main resorts to the north (Póvoa de Varzim and Ofir) are the best places for water-sports enthusiasts. Equipment rental is usually available at the beaches, or inquire at local tourist offices.

Castles
There are towers, castles, and forts galore to explore in this part of the country, some of them so complete they provide a virtual medieval playground. The best include those at Guimarães, Monção, Bragança, and Chaves. Don't miss the region's two vast ornamental staircases, good for clambering up, at the pilgrimage sights of Lamego and Bom Jesus do Monte.

Dining
The cooking in Porto is rich and heavy. It is typified by the city's favorite dish, *tripas á moda do Porto* (Porto tripe), a heavy concoction made with beans, chicken, sausage, vegetables, and spices. So fond are the locals of tripe that elsewhere in Portugal they're known as *tripeiros* (tripe eaters)—a nickname earned when the city was under siege during the Napoleonic Wars, and tripe was the only meat available. However, tripe doesn't dominate the menu in Porto, and dishes tend to resemble those served in the Minho region. *Caldo verde* (literally "green soup") is ubiquitous; it's made of potato and shredded kale (cabbage) in a broth and is usually served with a slice or two of *chouriço* sausage. Fresh fish is found all the way up the coast, and every town has a local recipe for *bacalhau* (dried cod); in the Minho it's often cooked with potatoes, onions, and eggs. *Lampreias* (lampreys)—oily, eel-like fish—are found in Minho rivers from February to April and are a particular specialty of Viana do Castelo and Monção. Pork is the meat most often seen on menus, appearing in inventive stews and sausages. For adventurous palates a typically *Minhoto* dish is *papas de sarrabulho*, a hearty stew of shredded pork in a flour-thickened, cumin-scented pigs-blood soup. Roast *cabrito* (kid) is very popular, too.

In the mountains there is little fish and shellfish to offer, except for the wonderful *truta* (trout), available at any town or village close to a river. Trás-os-Montes menus are enlivened by hearty meat stews, which usually include parts of the pig you may wish had been left out (turning up an ear or a trotter is common). Sausages are a better bet, particularly *alheira* (a legacy of the Sephardic Jews, who devised this mock sausage of chicken and spices to fool religious authorities) or chouriço, the spicy, smoked variety. The other smoked specialty of the region is *presunto de Chaves*, a delicious smoked ham from Chaves. Most dishes will be served with *batatas* (potatoes) or *arroz* (rice), both fine examples of staples being raised to an art form. Spuds here, whether roasted, boiled, or fried, have an irresistibly nutty and sweet flavor. Rice is lightly sautéed with chopped garlic in olive oil before adding water, resulting in a side dish that could easily be devoured as a main course.

The wine available throughout the north is of very high quality. The Minho region is home to *vinho verde*, a light, slightly sparkling red or white wine referred to as "green" because it's drunk at a young age. The taste is refreshing, both fruity and acid. Both reds and whites are served chilled (most people prefer the white), and vinho verde goes exceptionally well with fish and shellfish. Vinho verde from Ponte de Lima is prized throughout the country. Port enjoys the most renown of the local wines (ask for *vinho do Porto*). Try a chilled white port as an aperitif. Other good regions for wine include the area around Chaves, particularly at Valpaços, which produces some excellent, full-bodied, and almost creamy reds.

On the whole, restaurants in Porto and the north offer extremely good value, although they often do not accept credit cards. Dress throughout the region is informal, and reservations are usually unnecessary.

Lodging

Most of the lodgings in the Minho and Trás-os-Montes are very reasonably priced compared to their counterparts elsewhere in the country—perhaps a reflection of the previous lack of attention paid by tourists to these regions. The government-run group of *pousadas* offers a variety of settings in the north, from a 12th-century monastery in Guimarães to more rustic, hunting-lodge digs high on a hill in Bragança. In Porto, however, matters are much the same as in Lisbon, and, if at all possible, you should reserve a room well in advance to avoid disappointment. The north also hosts some of the country's most famous festivals and markets, at which times available lodging quickly dries up; book well in advance if your visit coincides with a festival, many of which are discussed throughout this chapter (*see also* Festivals and Seasonal Events *in* Chapter 1).

The **Turismo de Habitação** (Manor House Tourism) system allows visitors to spend time at a variety of private historic manor houses and country farms scattered throughout the Minho. Most of these converted 17th- and 18th-century buildings are found in the lovely rural areas around Ponte de Lima (☞ *below*), where the organization has its headquarters and reservations office, with others near Barcelos, Braga, Caminha, Guimarães, Mesão Frio, Monção, and Viana do Castelo.

Shopping

The north is an excellent region in which to shop for souvenirs, with a wide range of folk art and crafts available in many towns and villages. Porto, of course, has the best selection of shops, but don't miss the smaller towns of the Minho, which often specialize in particular handicrafts; Vila do Conde, for example, is known for its lace. The region's weekly and monthly markets are also famous throughout Portugal for having the best local crafts at very reasonable prices.

Exploring Porto and the North

The north of Portugal can be divided into three basic regions—Porto and its immediate environs (the nearby coastal resorts and the Douro Valley), the evergreen Minho and Costa Verde to the north, and the somewhat remote and untamed Trás-os-Montes area to the east, a region still slightly short on tourist amenities yet long on spectacular scenery and superb country cooking. Porto and each of the other regions is described in its own section, below.

Great Itineraries

Remember that Portugal is a small country. If you had to, you could drive from top to bottom in less than a day, sunrise to sunset. Porto is just 3½ hours north of Lisbon by highway or express train, so even a short trip to Portugal can include a night or two here. From Porto, it's but another two hours through the Minho and along the Costa Verde coastline up to the Spanish border, or another three–four hours east to the less visited Trá-os-Montes and the eastern border with its Iberian neighbor, Spain. Size should not be equated with sights to see, however—the north has enough to keep you intrigued for days or even months. Traveling by car allows you the freedom to stop and start as mood and inspiration strike, although trains also have a compelling charm, and certain scenic routes are described below.

It takes only a day or two to experience the more urban pleasures of Porto and its wine lodges and the nearby coastal resorts. Several more days would permit a visit to the history-rich towns of Braga or Guimarães or a trip through the lovely scenery of the Douro Valley. A full week would allow you to cover all of this and the peaceful inland towns and villages along the rivers Lima and Minho, or you could set off for the remote northeastern Trás-os-Montes and its fascinating towns of Bragança and Chaves. Two weeks would give you the opportunity to do the complete circuit and return sated on the riches of the north.

Numbers in the text correspond to numbers in the margin and on the North: Douro, Minho, and Trás-os-Montes map and the Porto map.

IF YOU HAVE 3 DAYS

Devote the morning of your first day to taking in the sights of ⊞ **Porto** ①–⑬, followed by an afternoon tour of the port-wine lodges in Vila Nova de Gaia, right across the Douro River. Before turning in, spend some time enjoying the city's lively riverside cafés and restaurants. In the morning, drive north through the sandy coastal towns of **Vila do Conde** ⑭, **Póvoa de Varzim** ⑮, and **Ofir and Esposende** ⑯. After the bracing air, shopping to the sound of the waves and a seafood lunch, head inland to the ancient Visigothic city of ⊞ **Braga** ㉒, sometimes referred to as the religious capital of the country, with its profusion of churches and reputation for the most sumptuous Easter celebrations around. Overnight there or in the delightfully medieval ⊞ **Guimarães** ㉔, which you should explore on day three. Worth a side trip from either town is the nearby, fascinating hilltop **Citânia de Briteiros** ㉓, site of an ancient Celtic settlement.

Alternatively, you could spend your second two days savoring the pastoral pleasures of the Douro Valley. Follow the winding N108 road east from Porto along the north bank of the river. Don't miss the view at Entre-os-Rios, where the Douro and Tàmega rivers converge. Head back up toward **Penafiel** ⑱, admiring the sculptural beauty of the terraced hillside vineyards; this region is known for its vinho verde and Romanesque churches, a legacy of the wine-making Benedictine monks. Stop here for some religion and respite from the road and then move on to ⊞ **Amarante** ⑲, one of the north's most picturesque towns, its two halves joined by a narrow 18th-century bridge. It's worth overnighting here. On day three, wind your way back along N101, passing through Mesão Frio, to the Douro, where you can follow the river east to **Peso da Regua** ⑳, heart of the port-wine country, and tour a wine cellar or two. Across the river and a bit farther south is **Lamego** ㉑; don't miss the town's most famous monument, the impressively baroque 18th-century pilgrimage shrine of Nossa Senhora dos Remedios. From either of these towns, it's not far to **Vila Real** ㉝, gateway to the remote and beautiful region of Trás-os-Montes. You could spend the night there and head east the next day, or return to Porto.

IF YOU HAVE 5 DAYS

More time means you can see more towns and more in those you visit. Spend a day and night in ⊞ **Porto** ①–⑬, then head inland and north. Take two days to explore ⊞ **Braga** ㉒, **Citânia de Briteiros** ㉓, and ⊞ **Guimarães** ㉔. On day four go west to **Barcelos** ㉕, folk-art center of the country; try to arrive on a Thursday, when Portugal's largest weekly market is filled with purveyors of everything from live pigs to colorful, hand-painted pottery. Continue north to graceful **Viana do Castelo** ㉖, along the banks of the Lima River. Wander its narrow stone

The North: Douro, Minho, and Trás-os-Montel

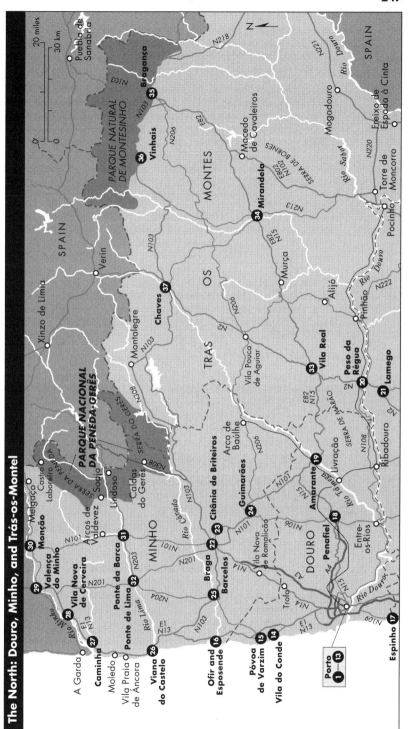

streets (with a stop at the Municipal Museum—a must for lovers of ceramics) and stay the night in the luxurious art-deco pousada on a hill overlooking town or drive up along the Costa Verde to **Caminha** ㉗ or one of the other partially walled castle towns along the Spanish border: **Vila Nova de Cerveira** ㉘, **Valença do Minho** ㉙, and **Monção** ㉚.

On day five, head back south to quaint Arcos de Valdevez and rent a rowboat for a couple of leisurely hours on the river, then continue on to two nearby towns with beautiful bridges, **Ponte da Barca** ㉛, with its 15th-century arched passageway, and **Ponte de Lima** ㉜, graced with a long, low Roman footbridge. If you're in Ponte de Lima on the second Monday of the month, you'll be able to visit the oldest market in the country. From here, set your sails back to Porto or Lisbon, or on to Trás-os-Montes.

IF YOU HAVE 7 DAYS

Porto ①–⑬ is the ideal first day and night for your exploration of the region. On day two, head inland for **Penafiel** ⑱ (stop to admire the architecture of its solid, granite mansions and to sample some of the local vinho verde) and ☷ **Amarante** ⑲, where you can have dinner in the romantic, old part of town and spend the night. Next day, onward to ☷ **Vila Real** ㉝, the capital and first sizable town in the Trás-os-Montes region. Rosé-wine lovers might want to visit the nearby Solar de Mateus, a baroque mansion open to the public; the building's facade adorns the widely exported Mateus wine label. Overnight in Vila Real. On day four, head northeast to Murça and admire the town's Iron Age granite *porca* (stone pig), the largest of what are believed to be many ancient fertility symbols dotting the region. Farther north is the attractive town of **Mirandela** ㉞; visit the 17th-century Palacio dos Tavoras, today used as the town hall. Stay on the E82 and head into the Serra de Nogueira (Nogueira Mountains) toward the northeastern corner of the country. Eventually you'll see the great castle at ☷ **Bragança** ㉟ rising in the distance; plan on spending two nights here. Rest up overnight and on day five, visit the sites of the city, which dates to about 600 BC. Next day, head west along the N103, one of the most spectacular drives in the country. You'll pass through **Vinhais** ㊱ on the way to **Chaves** ㊲, originally settled as a Roman military base and still popular today for its thermal springs. From Chaves, you could head back toward Vila Real and on to a final night in Porto.

Another alternative would be to stay on the N103 and continue west until reaching the lake and hydroelectric dam system along the Rio Cavado. The winding road allows for marvelous views and has several access points into the **Peneda-Gerês National Park,** where you could quite understandably choose to stay overnight (the São Bento Pousada overlooks the Caniçada dam) for a bit of hiking in the woods and howling at the moon, or you could continue down the road to **Braga** ㉒, spend the night, and then onward back to Porto.

When to Tour Porto and the North

It's best to visit the north in summer, when Porto and the Costa Verde have a generally warm climate, but be prepared for drizzling rain at any time. Temperatures in the north are a good few degrees cooler than in the south. Inland, and especially in the northeastern mountains, traveling in winter can be cold, hard going.

PORTO

321 km (199 mi) north of Lisbon, 255 km (158 mi) southwest of Bragança, 71 km (44 mi) south of Viana do Castelo.

Industrious Porto—Portugal's second city, with a population of half a million—considers itself the capital of the north and, more contentiously, the economic center of the country. Locals support this claim by quoting a typically down-to-earth maxim: "Coimbra sings, Braga prays, Lisbon shows off, and Porto works." Certainly wherever you look, there's evidence of a city in robust financial health. Massive new business developments on the outskirts give way to a fashionable commercial area in the heart of town; shops and restaurants bustle with high-spending locals; and the city's buildings, churches, and monuments—both old and new—impress with their solid construction. There's poverty here, of course, primarily down by the river in the ragged old-town areas, parts of which are positively medieval. But in the shopping centers, the stately Stock Exchange building, and the affluent port-wine industry, Porto oozes confidence. Hard work, one feels, is the city's biggest asset.

This emphasis on worth rather than beauty means that Porto is not a graceful city. Significant sights are few, and aesthetically pleasing monuments are rare. Visitors may find their first impression disappointing, although the city's glorious location—on a steep hillside above the Rio Douro—does much to compensate.

The river has influenced the city's development since pre-Roman times, when the town of Cale on the left bank prospered sufficiently to support a trading port, called Portus, on the site of today's city. Under the Romans this twin town of Portus-Cale became a thriving commercial center, and it continued to be successful despite the later ravages of Moorish occupation and Christian reconquest. Given the outward-looking nature of its inhabitants, it's fitting that Henry the Navigator—the great explorer king—was born here at the end of the 14th century.

The importance of the river trade to the city is reflected in its current name, whose use began in early medieval times. Porto means simply "the port," and over the centuries the city has traded widely in fish, salt, and wine. As the result of an agreement with England in 1703, the region's most notable product—wine, made from the grapes of the Douro's vineyards—found a new market and was shipped out of the city in ever-increasing quantities. The port-wine trade is still big business, based just over the river from the city, in the suburb of Vila Nova de Gaia (site of the Roman town of Cale).

Exploring Porto

Numbers in margin correspond to points of interest on the Porto map.

Having reached the city center (often a slow business because of the traffic), you'll do best to tour Porto on foot, taking buses or taxis to
❶ the few outlying attractions. The **Avenida dos Aliados** is an imposing, sloping boulevard that lies at the commercial heart of the city and points toward the river. Providing some welcome open space in Porto's busy center, it is planted with bright flower beds and lined with grand buildings, including the broad **câmara municipal** (town hall), which stands at the top of the avenue. A tall bell tower sprouts from the roof of this palacelike, early 20th-century building, inside of which an impressive Portuguese wall tapestry is displayed. At the other end of the avenue, **Praça da Liberdade** is the hub from which downtown Porto radiates. Two statues adorn the square: a cast of Dom Pedro IV sitting on a horse and an unusual, modern statue of the great 19th-century Portuguese poet and novelist Almeida Garrett.

Porto

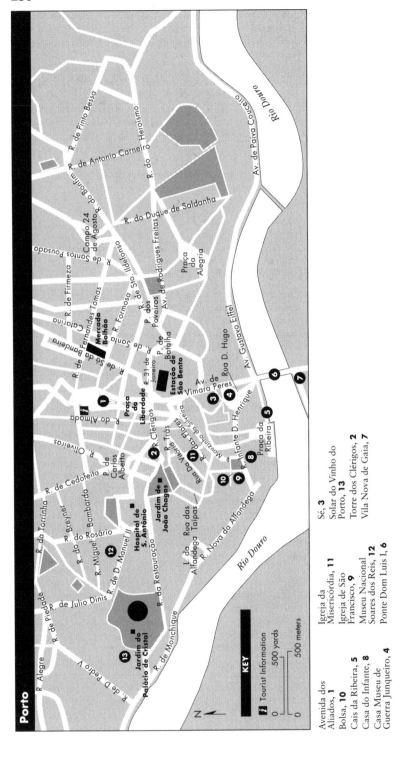

R. de Pinto Bessa
R. de Antonio Carneiro
R. do Bonfim
R. do Heroismo
Av. de Paiva Couceiro
Rio Douro
Campo 24 de Agosto
R. do Duque de Saldanha
R. de Santos Pousada
R. de Firmeza
R. de Fernandes Tomás
Mercado Bolhão
R. de Sta. Catarina
R. Formosa
R. de Sto. Ildefonso
R. de Rodrigues Freitas
Praça da Alegria
P. dos Poveiros
P. de Sta.
Estação de São Bento
P. de Batalha
R. 31 de Janeiro
Av. de Rodrigues Freitas
Rua D. Hugo
Av. de Gustavo Eiffel
R. de Sá da Bandeira
R. do Almada
Praça da Liberdade
R. Clérigos
R. de Cedofeita
P. de Carlos Alberto
R. Oliveiras
R. Trás
R. das Flores
R. de Mouzinho de Silveira
Av. de Vimara Peres
Infante D. Henrique
Praça da Ribeira
Sé
R. da Torrinha
R. de Breyner
R. de Miguel Bombarda
R. do Rosário
Jardim de João Chagas
Hospital de S. António
Jardim de S. António
Rua da Vitória
R. das Alfandega Taipas
R. Nova da Alfandega
R. de D. Manuel II
R. da Restauração
R. Alegre
R. de Piedade
R. de Julio Dinis
Jardim do Palácio de Cristal
Av. de D. Dinis
R. de Monchique
Rio Douro

KEY

ⓘ Tourist Information

0 — 500 yards
0 — 500 meters

N

Avenida dos
Aliados, **1**

Bolsa, **10**

Cais da Ribeira, **5**

Casa do Infante, **8**

Casa Museu de
Guerra Junqueiro, **4**

Igreja da
Misericórdia, **11**

Igreja de São
Francisco, **9**

Museu Nacional
Soares dos Reis, **12**

Ponte Dom Luis I, **6**

Sé, **3**

Solar do Vinho do
Porto, **13**

Torre dos Clérigos, **2**

Vila Nova de Gaia, **7**

NEED A
BREAK?

The Avenida dos Aliados area has several fine old-style coffeehouses, which, like those in Lisbon, feature turn-of-the-century decor. The large **Café Imperial,** on the eastern side of Praça da Liberdade, is a good place to sit and sip a *cimbalino* (espresso) while watching the busy traffic and shoppers; there are tables inside and out. Around the corner, the similarly decorated **A Brasileira** (⊠ Rua Sá da Bandeira 61) has brisker service. For just a drink or snack, pay first at the cash desk and present your receipt at the busy bar.

The odd, oval-shape **Igreja dos Clérigos** (Clérigos Church) is visible from Praça da Liberdade if you can peer down Rua dos Clérigos. The ★ ☾ ❷ **Torre dos Clérigos,** the Tower of Clérigos Church, is an immediately recognizable finger on the Porto skyline. Designed by Italian architect Nicolau Nasoni and begun in 1754, the tower consists of six stories that leap to a height of 249 feet, making it one of the tallest towers in the country. There are 225 steep stone steps to the belfry at the top, and the very considerable effort required to climb them is rewarded by stunning views of the old town, the river, and beyond to the mouth of the Douro. The church itself, also built by Nasoni, predates the tower and is an elaborate example of Italianate baroque architecture. ⊠ *Rua dos Clérigos,* ☎ *02/200–1721.* ☎ *Tower 125$00; church free.* ☾ *Tower Thurs.–Tues. 10–noon and 2–5, Sun. 10–noon and 2–5:30; church Mon.–Sat. 7:30–9, 10–noon, 2–5, and 6–7:30; Sun. 10–1.*

Use the pedestrian underpass from the Praça da Liberdade to cross to the **Estação de São Bento,** Porto's central railroad station; the main hall is decorated with enormous azulejos depicting the history of Portuguese transportation. From the steps of the train station, you can look across to the city's cathedral.

❸ Originally constructed in the 12th century by the parents of Afonso Henriques (the first king of Portugal), Porto's granite **Sé** (cathedral) has been rebuilt twice: first in the late 13th century and again in the 18th century, when the architect of the Torre dos Clérigos, Nasoni, was among those commissioned to work on its expansion. Despite these renovations, it remains a severe, fortresslike structure, perched on a sweeping terrace over the old town, which is a few minutes' walk to the south. It is an uncompromising testament to the city's medieval wealth and power. Sheer size apart, the cathedral's interior is unusually disappointing, and only when you enter the two-story 14th-century **cloister** does the building come to life. Decorated with gleaming azulejos, a staircase added by Nasoni leads to the second level and into a magnificent, richly furnished chapter house, from which there are fine views of the old town through narrow windows. Nasoni also designed the **Archbishop's Palace,** behind the cathedral, although since it was converted to public offices, visitors can see no farther than the impressive 197-foot-long facade. ⊠ *Terreiro da Sé,* ☎ *02/314837.* ☎ *Cathedral free; cloister 200$00.* ☾ *Daily 9–noon and 3–5:30.*

❹ **Casa Museu de Guerra Junqueiro** (Guerra Junqueiro House and Museum), another 18th-century building attributed to Porto's favorite architect, Nasoni, lies on Rua de Dom Hugo, a narrow street that curves around the eastern side of the cathedral. This white mansion was home to the poet Guerra Junqueiro (1850–1923) and is a quiet retreat. However, the short tour of the elegant interior and enviable collection of furniture, sculpture, paintings, and silver is less than enlightening if you don't speak Portuguese. ⊠ *Rua de Dom Hugo 32,* ☎ *02/313644.* ☎ *150$00.* ☾ *Tues.–Sat. 11–12:30 and 2:30–6.*

Rua de Dom Hugo leads you by way of steep steps that cut through surviving sections of the medieval city walls into a web of tangled alleys, leaning buildings, and down-at-the-heel street markets. This decaying neighborhood has missed out on the city's economic progress, however colorful the timeworn buildings with their long rows of balconies may appear. The stepped alleys all eventually emerge at the riverfront quayside of the Ribeira District. Along the **Cais da Ribeira,** there's a small daily market and a string of excellent fish restaurants and *tascas* (taverns) built into the street-level arcade of the old buildings (☞ Dining, *below*). In the Praça da Ribeira, people sit and chat around the odd, modern, cubelike sculpture, while farther on, steps lead up to a raised walkway, backed by tall houses, that runs above the river. The quay also provides the easiest access to the lower level of the middle bridge across the Douro.

⑥ The two-tier **Ponte Dom Luis I** (Dom Luis Bridge) was built in 1886 and leads directly to the suburb of Vila Nova de Gaia. Its real glory, however, is not its practical calling but the nearly magical view it affords of downtown Porto. A jumble of red-tile roofs on pastel-color buildings mixes with gray-and-white Gothic and baroque church towers, and all is reflected in the majestic Douro; if the sun is shining just right, everything appers to be washed in gold.

★ ⑦ **Vila Nova de Gaia,** across the Rio Douro from central Porto, has been the headquarters of the port-wine trade since the late 17th century, when import bans on French wine led British merchants to look for alternative sources. By the 18th century, the British had established companies and a regulatory association at Porto to control the quality of the wine they were importing from Portugal. The wine was transported from vineyards on the upper Rio Douro to port-wine "lodges" (warehouses) at Vila Nova de Gaia, where it was allowed to mature before being shipped out of the country. Very little has changed in the relationship between Porto and the Douro since those days, as wine is still transported to the city, matured in the warehouses, and bottled. However, instead of traveling down the river on traditional *barcos rabelos* (flat-bottomed boats), the wine is now carried by truck. A couple of the boats are moored at the quayside on the Vila Nova de Gaia side as a reminder of bygone days.

There are more than 25 companies with **port-wine lodges** in Vila Nova de Gaia (many still foreign-owned), from such well-known names as Sandeman, Croft, and Cockburn to lesser-known Portuguese firms, such as Ramos Pinto and Borges. All are signposted within a few minutes' walk of each other, and their names are displayed in huge white letters across their roofs. Each company offers free guided tours of its facility and the fascinating process of port-wine making and bottling—tours that always end with a tasting of one or two wines and an opportunity to buy bottles from the company store. Children are usually welcome and are often fascinated by the huge warehouses and all sorts of interesting machinery. The major lodges are open weekdays 9–12:30 and 2–7, Saturday 9–12:30, from June though September; the rest of the year, tours end at 5 and are conducted only on weekdays. Tours begin regularly, usually when enough visitors are assembled. The tourist office at Vila Nova de Gaia (☞ Contacts and Resources *in* Porto and the North A to Z, *below*) offers a small map of the main port-wine lodges and can advise you on hours of the smaller operations.

Vila Nova de Gaia isn't solely devoted to the port-wine trade. Combine a tour of the wine lodges with a visit to the **Casa Museu de Teixeira Lopes,** the home of the sculptor António Teixeira Lopes (1866–1942), who was born here. It contains some excellent sculpture as well as a varied collection of paintings by Teixeira Lopes's contemporaries. A selection of books, coins, and ceramics is also interesting. ⊠ *Rua Teixeira Lopes 32,* ☎ *02/301224.* ⊠ *Free.* ⊙ *Oct.–May, Tues.–Sat. 9:30–12:30 and 2–5:30; June–Sept., Tues.–Sat. 9:30–12:30 and 2–5:30, Sun. 1–7.*

From Vila Nova de Gaia you can cross back to the city, using the narrow footway on the upper level of the Ponte Dom Luis I, which puts you on Avenida de Vimara Peres, close to the cathedral. But at 200 feet above the river and with traffic thundering past, this is not a crossing for the faint of heart or for those who have tasted of the port "not wisely but too well." To continue the city tour, retrace your path to the Cais da Ribeira.

Away from the water, Rua do Infante Dom Henrique, which used to be known as Rua dos Ingleses (English Street), contains shipping offices and warehouses. Where it meets Rua de São João stands the granite **Feitoria Inglesa** (Factory House of the British Association), built at the end of the 18th century as the headquarters of the Port Wine Shippers' Association.

❽ The **Casa do Infante** earned its name (House of the Prince) as the reputed birthplace of Porto's most famous son, Prince Henry the Navigator (born in 1394). The foursquare restored mansion now holds part of the city archives and is open to the public for temporary exhibitions. ⊠ *Rua do Infante,* ☎ *02/316025.* ⊠ *Free.* ⊙ *Weekdays 9–noon and 2–5.*

A statue of Prince Henry stands in the nearby Praça do Infante Dom Henrique, which also holds a remarkable church. The late-14th-century **Igreja de São Francisco** (Church of St. Francis) may be an undistinguished Gothic building on the outside, but it reveals an astounding interior to inquisitive visitors. The profusion of gilded carving was added in the mid-18th century and swarms over every inch of the building—up the pillars, over the altar, and across the ceiling. An adjacent museum houses valuable furnishings from the Franciscan monastery that once stood here. ⊠ *Rua do Infante Dom Henrique,* ☎ *02/200–6493.* ⊠ *500$00.* ⊙ *Sept.–June, Tues.–Sat. 9–noon and 2–5; July–Aug., daily 9–5.*

❿ The **Bolsa,** Porto's 19th-century, neoclassical stock exchange, is behind the Igreja de São Francisco and takes up much of the site of the old Franciscan monastery. Guided tours (the only way to see the interior) stroll around the huge, showy edifice, much of it in questionable taste. The Arab-style ballroom, in particular, has critics as numerous as the glowing adjectives with which the guides describe it. ⊠ *Rua Ferreira Borges,* ☎ *02/200–4497.* ⊠ *Guided tours 500$00.* ⊙ *May–Sept., weekdays 10–5:30, weekends 10–noon and 2–5; Oct.–Apr., weekdays 9–noon and 2–5.*

North of the stock exchange, at Largo de São Domingos, Rua das Flores—a street known for its silversmiths and striking wrought-iron balconies—leads toward São Bento station. Although it dates from the 16th ⓫ century, the **Igreja da Misericórdia** (Church of the Misericórdia) was largely remodeled two centuries later by Nicolau Nasoni. Call at the adjacent offices, and you will be shown the *Fons Vitae* (Fountain of Life), considered one of the country's finest paintings. It is an anonymous Renaissance work of brilliant colors, showing the founder of the church, Dom Manuel I, his queen, and their eight children kneeling before a crucified Christ. ⊠ *Rua das Flores,* ☎ *02/200–0941.* ⊠ *Free.* ⊙ *Weekdays 8–noon and 3–5.*

Rua das Taipas will lead you to the Jardim João Chagas (João Chagas Gardens), where the Palácio da Justiça (Palace of Justice) towers on your left. Facing the corner of the gardens is the large, 18th-century **Hospital de Santo António.**

A former royal palace west of the Hospital de Santo António is now the **Museu Nacional Soares dos Reis,** named for the 19th-century Portuguese sculptor whose works are contained within. The large art collection includes several Portuguese primitive works of the 16th century as well as superb collections of silver, ceramics, glassware, and costumes. Repairs closed the museum for a time in 1996; check at the tourist for any change in open hours. ⊠ *Rua de Dom Manuel II,* ☎ *02/200–7110.* ☑ *250$00, free Sun.* ☉ *Tues.–Sun. 10–noon and 2–5.*

Follow Rua de Dom Manuel II to the **Jardim do Palacio de Cristal** (Crystal Palace Gardens), named for a 19th-century palace that once stood here—it was replaced in the 1950s by an enormous domed pavilion used for sports and exhibitions.

On the far side of the Crystal Palace Gardens, the **Quinta da Macierinha** is a charming 19th-century country house containing the **Museu Romântico** (Romantic Museum), featuring period furniture and decoration. ⊠ *Rua de Entre Quintas 220,* ☎ *02/691131.* ☑ *200$00.* ☉ *Tues.–Sat. 10–12:30 and 1:30–5.*

The ground floor of the Quinta da Macierinha is of special interest; for here the **Solar do Vinho do Porto** (Port Wine Institute) offers relaxed tastings of Porto's famous wine in much the same fashion as its counterpart in Lisbon. However, Porto's Solar has a much friendlier reputation, and in addition, the wine has only had to travel across the river before being served! Tasting prices vary but start at 100$00 per glass. ⊠ *Rua de Entre Quintas 220,* ☎ *02/694749.* ☉ *Weekdays 11–11, Sat. 5–11:30.*

This is a fine place to end your tour of the city, and when it's time to return downtown, either catch Bus 78 (which runs along Rua de Dom Manuel II, past the Soares dos Reis Museum, to Praça da Liberdade) or jump into a taxi.

OFF THE   **MUSEU NACIONAL DE ARTE MODERNA –** The Museu Nacional de Arte
BEATEN PATH   Moderna (National Museum of Modern Art), run by the Gulbenkian
                 Foundation, which administers a similar collection in Lisbon, is in western Porto, beyond the range of any walking tour. The museum occupies the Serralves Mansion, set on impressive grounds, and displays the work of a representative selection of modern Portuguese painters, sculptors, and designers. Exhibitions change constantly, and the museum closes for two weeks at a time for rehanging. Check with the tourist office for the latest information. You can take either a taxi or Bus 78, which takes 30 minutes from the town center and passes the Palácio de Cristal. ⊠ *Rua de Serralves 977,* ☎ *02/680057.* ☑ *250$00.* ☉ *Tues.–Sun. 2–8.*

Dining

$$$ ✕ **O Escondidinho.** High-quality food from the Douro region and a range of French-influenced dishes are served here. Steak is prepared no less than six ways (try the woodsy-smoky version with truffles), and the sole is always deliciously fresh. The ubiquitous *pudim flan* (egg custard) is outstanding. The surroundings are engaging; the restaurant's on a central shopping street, and a tiled entrance announces its coun-

try-house decor. ⊠ *Rua dos Passos Manuel 144,* ☎ *02/2001079. Reservations essential. AE, DC, MC, V. Closed Sun.*

$$$ ✕ **Portucale.** On the top of the modern building that houses the hotel
★ Albergaria Miradouro, the Portucale is known equally for the excellence of its food and the citywide views from its windows. Dishes are rich, making imaginative use of local ingredients, such as tripe and game, and mountain-style roast cabrito is sometimes served. If dessert is too much to contemplate, sip some port from the impressive selection. ⊠ *Rua da Alegria 598,* ☎ *02/570717. Reservations essential. AE, DC, MC, V.*

$$ ✕ **Casa Filha da Mãe Preta.** One of the best choices at the riverside
★ Cais da Ribeira, this restaurant is part of the parade of tall buildings facing the water. The lovely first-floor dining room is decorated with charmingly animated azulejos. Reserve ahead or arrive early enough, and you can eat by the arched windows and look across to the port-wine suburb of Vila Nova de Gaia. There's a reasonable tourist menu, and—as at every restaurant down here—any of the fish specialties are worth trying. Many dishes, including *sardinhas grelhadas* (grilled sardines), come with an ample serving of rice and beans. ⊠ *Cais da Ribeira 39–40,* ☎ *02/315515. Reservations essential for window tables. AE, DC, MC, V. Closed Sun.*

$$ ✕ **Taverna do Bebobos.** A stone tavern in business since 1876, the gloomily authentic Bebobos has survived the century's floods (water levels are marked on the wall outside) to offer modern-day diners the atmosphere of a crumbling, rustic interior. There's a very pleasant upstairs dining room with views of the river. Specialties are mostly fish—the *bacalhau gomes de Sa* (flakes of codfish sautéed with onions, eggs, and black olives) is a veritable symphony in the mouth—though there are some meat dishes on the menu, too. Accompany your meal with some of the local wine from a cask balanced on the bar. ⊠ *Cais da Ribeira 24–25,* ☎ *02/313565. Reservations essential. No credit cards. Closed Sun.*

$$ ✕ **Tripeiro.** This is just the place to try tripe, which is nearly always on the menu in one form or another. In case you don't appreciate Porto's favorite food, the spacious restaurant is also good for most meat dishes, and there are several bacalhau specialties, too. Along with the typically Portuguese food comes typically Portuguese decor: wooden ceiling beams, whitewashed walls, and potted plants throughout. ⊠ *Rua de Passos Manuel 195,* ☎ *02/200–5886. AE, DC, MC, V. Closed Sun.*

$ ✕ **Majestic Café.** One of Porto's grand old coffeehouses, the art-deco Majestic doubles as a reasonably priced grill-restaurant. Sit amid the sculpted wood, carved nymphs, and mirrors and choose from a fair list of steaks, burgers, and omelets, or just take coffee and cake. Service is brisk (and occasionally brusque), but you'll have plenty of opportunity to observe the bustling local crowd, both inside and outside on the busy pedestrian shopping street. ⊠ *Rua de Santa Catarina 112,* ☎ *02/23887. No credit cards. Closed Sun.*

$ ✕ **O Castiço da Sé.** Above a bar on a steep old-town street close to the cathedral, this tiny upstairs dining room does a roaring lunchtime trade. Make a stab at the indecipherable handwritten menu, and you'll be rewarded with huge portions of grilled and stewed meat and fish, which come with salad and vegetables. The clientele is mostly local business people, who know a bargain when they see one. The stone walls, beams, and lanterns provide atmosphere, while the fine food is dispensed with little ceremony. Be prepared to wait in line at lunchtime. ⊠ *Rua da Bainharia 18, no phone. No credit cards.*

$ ✕ **Pedro dos Frangos.** In an area full of budget restaurants, the popular Pedro dos Frangos stands out for the quality of its barbecued chicken, which grills temptingly in the window. If you're in a hurry, sit at the bar, though it's more comfortable upstairs in the plain dining room, where ordering a *meia frango* gets you a sublime half chicken and fries. Order a side of *esparregado* (greens, usually spinach or turnip tops, sautéed with olive oil and garlic, then puréed), a delicious dish that can sometimes resemble library paste, and you'll have plenty of energy to go out and see the rest of the city. ✉ *Rua do Bonjardim 219–223,* ☎ *02/200–8522. No credit cards. Closed Tues.*

Lodging

$$$$ ☎ **Infante de Sagres.** This, Porto's first luxury hotel built after World ★ War II, is named after the city's most famous son, Prince Henry the Navigator, and does indeed provide formal, princely service. Visiting royalty have been happy to stay here for years, and you'll be pleased by its very central location, close to Avenida dos Aliados. Public rooms are very impressively turned out, in a style closer to the 1890s than the 1990s, with a lot of intricately carved wood. Guest rooms have a more 20th-century character; though all are supremely comfortable and have good marble bathrooms. ✉ *Praça D. Filipa de Lencastre 62, 4000,* ☎ *02/200–8101,* ℻ *02/314937. 83 rooms. Restaurant, bar. AE, DC, MC, V.*

$$$ ☎ **Dom Henrique.** The Dom Henrique attracts business travelers who want a central base; its elegant rooms and amenities are spread throughout the 22 floors of an octagonal downtown tower. The spacious guest rooms are extremely well appointed, and many have superb city views—as do the main restaurant and bar. While perhaps not the place for a leisurely vacation, the hotel is ideal if you require more than just the basic comforts. ✉ *Rua Guedesa Azevedo 179, 4000,* ☎ *02/200– 5755,* ℻ *02/201–9451. 112 rooms. Restaurant, bar, grill. AE, DC, MC, V.*

$$$ ☎ **Tivoli Porto Atlântico.** This small hotel lies west of the city center, ★ off Avenida da Boavista, in a residential suburb near the Museum of Modern Art. Part of the Lisbon-based Tivoli group, it's a quiet, relaxed base from which to tour the city and the surrounding area. The comfortable interior is unobtrusively modern. Guest rooms share a terrace and provide every little service, down to a shoe-shine kit; bathrooms are marble-clad and luxurious. Other facilities are good, including two pools. A fine buffet breakfast is the only meal served, but there's an excellent French-style restaurant, the Foco, associated with and adjacent to the hotel. ✉ *Rua Afonso Lopes Vieira 66, 4100,* ☎ *02/694941,* ℻ *02/667452. 58 rooms. Restaurant, bar, indoor and outdoor pools. AE, DC, MC, V.*

$$ ☎ **Grande Hotel do Porto.** Once Porto's finest hotel, the Grande offers a touch of old-fashioned style at reasonable prices. It's on the city's best shopping street, and visitors are immediately impressed with its turn-of-the-century public rooms and restaurant and its efficient staff. Guest rooms are furnished with such modern touches as air-conditioning and satellite TV, but the hotel's genteel ambience has been preserved. ✉ *Rua de Santa Catarina 197, 4000,* ☎ *02/200–8176,* ℻ *02/311061. 100 rooms. Restaurant, bar. AE, DC, MC, V.*

$ ☎ **Hotel Peninsular.** Centrally located between São Bento Station and Praça da Liberdade, this popular small hotel has a grand tiled entrance hall, spick-and-span rooms with TVs, and a modern—if slightly cheerless—bar. ✉ *Rua Sá da Bandeira 21, 4000,* ☎ *02/200–3012,* ℻ *02/384984. 57 rooms. Bar. AE, MC, V.*

$ ☏ **Pensão Estoril.** The Estoril offers compact but smart rooms at rea-
sonable rates. It's in a quiet location near the city center and has a terrace and small garden, a bar, and parking nearby. Ask for a room with
a balcony. ✉ *Rua de Cedofeita 193, 4000,* ☎ *02/200–2751,* 🖷
02/208–2468. 18 rooms. Bar. No credit cards.

Festivals

Porto's major celebration is the **Festas de São João** held June 23–24
every year. The whole city erupts with bonfires and barbecues, and people gather to eat the traditional roast kid, washing it down with vinho
verde. The local population roams the streets all night, hitting passersby
on the head with, among other things, leeks and plastic hammers.

Nightlife and the Arts

For concerts and recitals consult the tourist office, whose staff will advise you of events worth attending. Noted as a center for modern art,
Porto enjoys regular exhibitions at the Museum of Modern Art, as well
as at a variety of galleries, some of which are on the main street,
Avenida da Boavista. Films in Porto are shown in their original language; check local newspapers for current listings.

Bars

The nicest places for an evening drink are the old-style cafés; try the
Brasileira (✉ Rua Sá da Bandeira 61, ☎ 02/200–7146), the **Majestic**
(✉ Rua de Santa Catarina 112, ☎ 02/200–3838), or the **Imperial** (✉
Praça da Liberdade, no phone), all of which are open daily until around
10 PM. For a restful glass of port, the best place is the **Solar do Vinho
do Porto** (✉ Rua de Entre Quintas 220, ☎ 02/694749), which is open
11 every day except Sunday. **Postigo do Carvão** (✉ Rua Fonte Tau-
rina 26, ☎ 02/245339), a former warehouse in the Ribeira District,
has been converted into a fashionable bar.

Casinos

For a more sophisticated—or just riskier—evening's entertainment, there
are two casinos within reach of Porto (☞ Espinho *and* Póvoa de
Varzim *in* Porto's Environs: The Coast and the Douro, *below*). Both
are open daily throughout the year 3 PM–3 AM and feature dining, dancing, and cabaret in addition to the gaming tables. Foreign visitors
must take their passports.

Dancing and Music

Porto has a number of fashionable discos west of the city center in the
new commercial developments; these clubs are open until 4 AM. In the
Centro Comercial Brasília, try **Griffon's** (✉ Rua Júlio Dinis, ☎
02/666091) and **Don Giovanni** (✉ Rua Júlio Dinis, ☎ 02/693256). A
very funky, very hip crowd shows up late at **Industria** (✉ Av. do Brasil
843, ☎ 02/617–6806), in the Centro Comercial da Foz. **Swing** (✉
Praçeta Eng. Amaro da Costa 766, ☎ 02/690019) is said to have an
excellent disc jockey.

The **Mal Cozinhado** (✉ Rua do Outeirinho 13, ☎ 02/381319) is a lively
restaurant hosting traditional music and dancing, including the plaintive sounds of fado, Monday–Saturday during the summer.

Outdoor Activities and Sports

Golf

There are two golf clubs at resorts south of Porto (☞ Espinho *in*
Porto's Environs: The Coast and the Douro, *below*).

Soccer

The main sporting obsession in Porto is soccer, and the city has one of the country's best teams, **FC Oporto,** which rivals Lisbon's Benfica for domestic fame and fortune. Matches are played September through May at the Antas Stadium (⊠ Av. de Fernão de Magalhães, ☎ 02/410–5844) in the east of the city; Buses 6, 78, and 88 run past it. The other regional team is **Guimarães,** a small soccer club that has enjoyed unexpected success in recent years.

Shopping

Excellent shopping can be found in the downtown streets off the central Praça da Liberdade—particularly on Rua 31 de Janeiro, Rua dos Clérigos, Rua de Santa Catarina, Rua Sá da Bandeira, and Rua das Flores. You'll see port on sale throughout the city. But first taste the wine at either the Solar do Vinho do Porto or the lodges at Vila Nova de Gaia (☞ Exploring Porto, *above*). You may want to buy a bottle of the more unusual white port, drunk chilled as an aperitif, as it's not commonly sold in North America or Britain.

Crafts

Traditionally, Rua das Flores has been the street for silversmiths. **Pedro A. Baptista** (⊠ Rua das Flores 23) deals in antique and modern silver. Gold-plated filigree is also a regional specialty, and examples are numerous along the same street and along Rua de Santa Catarina. Rua 31 de Janeiro and nearby streets are the center of the shoe trade, and many shops make made-to-measure shoes upon request.

For a general handicrafts emporium, try **Artesanato dos Clérigos** (⊠ Rua da Assunção 33, next to Clérigos Tower). The **Artesanato Centro Regional de Artes Tradicionais** (Center for Traditional Arts; ⊠ Rua da Reboleira 37), in the Cais da Ribeira District, sells an excellent selection of regional arts and crafts.

Markets

For a good general market, visit the **Mercado Bolhão,** held Monday–Saturday at Rua Formosa and Rua Sá da Bandeira (then stop at the Confeitaria do Bolhão, a delicious-smelling pastry and candy shop at Rua Formosa 339, for your choice of exquisite cakes). There's a daily **flea market** in the streets below the cathedral, particularly lively on Calçada Vandoma.

Shopping Malls

New shopping centers are a feature of Porto's burgeoning commercial life. One of the best, with lots of shops on several floors, is the **Centro Comercial de Brasileira** (⊠ Av. da Boavista), in the city's northwest, or try **Centro Comercial Dallas** (⊠ Av. da Boavista 1588).

PORTO'S ENVIRONS: THE COAST AND THE DOURO

Both north and south of Porto are relaxing resort towns much favored by locals. To the north there are beaches in nearby Foz do Douro and Matosinhos, but they are unattractive places, much influenced by the industrial port of Leixoes. Espinho, south of Porto, and the main resorts to the north (Vila do Conde, Póvoa de Varzim, Ofir, and Esposende) are the best places for water-sports enthusiasts. Equipment rental is usually available at the beaches, or inquire at local tourist offices.

Inland, the beautiful Douro Valley awaits, with its carefully terraced vineyards dotted with farmhouses stepping down to the river's edge.

Drives along the river lead to romantic ancient towns where you may want to stop for awhile, rent a rowboat, and do some paddling. If all that rowing works up a powerful thirst, this is the heart of prizewinning wine country, and every town has charming bars where you can pull out a chair, order a bottle and a plate of *petiscos* (mixed appetizers), and watch small-town life unfold.

Vila do Conde

⓮ *27 km (17 mi) north of Porto.*

Vila do Conde has a long sweep of fine sand and an interesting fishing port, shipbuilding industry, and medieval quarter. Try to time your visit to coincide with the **Festas de São João,** held June 23–24 every year. As in Porto, locals gather for feasting and boisterous street celebrations; many end up on the beach, building bonfires and waiting for the first sunbeams of St. John's Day.

The town is further distinguished by the huge **Convento de Santa Clara** (Convent of St. Clara), overwhelming the north bank of the Rio Ave, on which the town is situated. The convent was founded in the 14th century by Dom Afonso Sanches and his wife, Dona Teresa Martins, and it retains its original cloister and the beautiful tombs of its founders. The convent is open Monday–Saturday 9–noon and 2–5. The 16th-century **Igreja Matriz** (parish church), in the center of town near the market, is worth seeing for its superb Gothic portal.

Shopping
Vila do Conde is known for its lace and has supported a lace-making school since the end of the century. Today it is the center of a flourishing lace industry. If you're looking for souvenirs, the tourist office will direct you to a lace-making school in the town center that welcomes visitors. Local artisans also produce excellent hand-knit and embroidered sweaters, which are on sale in shops and at numerous roadside stands along the road in and out of town. An international handicrafts exhibition takes place here every year, usually at the end of July.

Póvoa de Varzim

⓯ *4 km (2½ mi) north of Vila do Conde, 31 km (20 mi) north of Porto.*

Póvoa de Varzim has a long beach, but the town has little of Vila do Conde's charm (except for the many shops and roadside stalls selling similarly beautiful and reasonably priced handknit sweaters). It is, instead, a major resort, with high-rise hotels used mostly by vacationing Portuguese. The casino (⊙ Daily 3 PM–3 AM) on the waterfront attracts much attention. Entertainment includes nightly floor shows; to gamble, take along your passport.

Ofir and Esposende

⓰ *46 km (29 mi) north of Porto.*

Ofir, on the south bank of the Rio Cávado estuary, has a lovely beach with sweeping white sands, dunes, pinewoods, and water sports, a combination that's made it a popular resort in recent years. On the opposite bank of the river, Esposende, which also has a beach, retains elements of the small fishing village it once was. Mid-August is the time for celebrating the **Festas do São Bartolomeu do Mar** (Festival of St. Bartholomew of the Sea), when occasionally rowdy revelries can be enjoyed at the water's edge. You'll have to drive there to appreciate these twin towns: The train line runs inland at this point, passing through Barcelos.

Espinho

 18 km (11 mi) south of Porto, 45 km (27 mi) south of Vila do Conde.

South of Porto, frequent trains and Route N109 run past a string of quiet family beaches to Espinho. Built on a grid pattern, this has become an increasingly fashionable resort over the years, with a full range of leisure facilities and good shopping. A casino, open daily throughout the year 3 PM–3 AM, has dining, dancing, and cabaret in addition to gaming tables; foreign visitors must present their passports. The long, sandy beach is very popular in summer, but you can find some space by walking through the pinewoods to less developed areas to the south.

Outdoor Activities and Sports
The 18-hole **Oporto Golf Club** (⊠ Pedreira Silvalde, ☎ 01/722008), founded in 1890 by members of the Port Wine Shippers' Association, is just 2 kilometers (1¼ miles) south of Espinho. The **Miramar Golf Club** (⊠ Praia de Miramar, ☎ 02/762–2067) has nine holes and is a few miles north of Espinho.

OFF THE   **THE DOURO TRAIN LINE –** Even if you are traveling by car, it's worth con-
BEATEN PATH   sidering at least a day trip using the Douro Line train. The main route
                 runs 40 kilometers (25 miles) inland from Porto, past Penafiel, then
                 swings south to join the Rio Douro and follow the north bank of the river
                 to Peso da Régua, a 2½-hour journey. From Peso da Régua the train con-
                 tinues east to the end of the line at Pocinho, providing a glorious 70-kilo-
                 meter (43½-mile) ride that hugs the river all the way. Between Penafiel
                 and the Douro, at Livração, the Tâmega Line branches off the main line
                 and runs northeast up the Rio Tâmega tributary to Arco de Baulhe, past
                 Amarante. Service on both routes has been under review for the past
                 couple of years, with an eye to discontinuing most service since it's used
                 less and less by locals, who prefer the fast inland roads gradually ex-
                 tending from Porto.

Penafiel

 40 km (25 mi) east of Porto, 33 km (20 mi) west of Amarante.

The valleys surrounding Penafiel are terraced with vineyards, not of the heavy port variety but of the slightly sparkling vinho verde (green wine). Other than some fading mansions, there's little in the town itself to see, but do stop for a glass of the always-refreshing local wine.

Amarante

★ *73 km (45 mi) northeast of Porto, 33 km (20 mi) east of Penafiel, 35 km (21 mi) northwest of Peso da Régua.*

Small, agreeable Amarante is charming, if ever a town deserved the adjective, and it's the one place in Porto's environs that really demands an overnight stop. Straddling the Rio Tâmega, its halves are joined by a narrow 18th-century bridge that stretches above the river's tree-shaded banks. Although the river is polluted (which precludes swimming), it's beautiful to look at. Rowboats and pedal boats are for hire at several points along the riverside paths.

NEED A
BREAK? Along Rua 31 de Janeiro, the narrow main road leading to the bridge, several small cafés and restaurants have terraces overlooking the river. Enjoy a drink, a snack, or a meal as you soak up the views.

On the north side of the Tâmega River, across the bridge from the main part of town, is the imposing, 16th-century **Convento de São Gonçalo** (Convent of St. Gonçalo). The effigy of the saint, on the left of the altar, is reputed to guarantee marriage to anyone who touches it. Not surprisingly, his features have almost been worn away over the years, as desperate suitors try one last time for success. ⊠ *Praça da República.* 🎫 *Free.* ☉ *Daily 9−noon and 2−5.*

Adjacent to Amarante's church are the cloisters and associated buildings of the convent, now housing the tourist office and the **Museu Municipal Amadeo de Sousa,** a small but intelligent collection of modern art revolving around the largely abstract paintings of Cardoso, who was born in the area. In 1906 Cardoso moved to Paris and shared a studio with Modigliani, but he returned to Portugal in 1914 and died four years later, at the early age of 31. The museum also hosts exhibitions of other artists' work, and there's some intriguing modern sculpture displayed in the attractive courtyard. ⊠ *Alameda Teixeira de Pascoais,* ☎ *055/432663.* 🎫 *Free.* ☉ *Tues.−Sun. 10−12:30 and 2− 5:30.*

The riverside beyond the municipal museum is the site of the local **market,** held every Wednesday, which is perhaps the best day to be in Amarante. Until lunchtime this entire area is alive with activity, and the usually peaceful town is disturbed by manic traffic racing along the main street and over the bridge.

On the first weekend in June, Amarante hosts the **Festa de São Gonçalo** (Festival of St. Gonçalo), when the saint is commemorated by the baking of phallus-shape cakes, which are exchanged between unmarried men and women. Other celebrations include a fair, folk dancing, and traditional singing.

Dining and Lodging

$$$ ✕ **Zé da Calçada.** On the town's narrow main street, this restaurant specializes in regional food, including a traditional baked bacalhau dish that takes the restaurant's name. Sweets and wines are local, too. A very elegant reception area leads into a comfortable dining room decorated in homey fashion; there's also a fireplace and a terrace that provides admirable riverside views. If you're taken with the decor, there are a few similarly turned-out, inexpensive rooms available. ⊠ *Rua 31 de Janeiro,* ☎ *055/422023. Reservations essential. MC, V.*

$ ✕ **Restaurante Estoril.** This simple, family-run restaurant makes a good lunch stop. It features river views from its windows and summer terrace and serves up plenty of good-value standard Portuguese dishes. Their *canja* (chicken-and-rice soup, seasoned with mint and lemon) is rumored locally to cure just about whatever ails you. There's a short local wine list, and service is cheerful and friendly. The English-speaking owner also has some inexpensive rooms available on the other side of the river. ⊠ *Rua 31 de Janeiro 49,* ☎ *055/431291. No credit cards.*

¢ ✕🕎 **Pousada de São Gonçalo.** The small, modern São Gonçalo pousada lies 16 kilometers (10 miles) east of Amarante on the road to Vila Real. In the Serra do Marão at an altitude of nearly 3,000 feet, it offers wonderful views. The rugged terrain outside is matched by rustic decor within, and the pousada has lovely wood furniture, a large fireplace, and tile floors. Having worked up an appetite in the hills, you can count on the restaurant to satisfy you with good, hearty regional cooking. *Costaletas de porco com feijão branco de tomatada* (pork chops served with white beans cooked with tomatoes), a bottle of red wine from the pousada's carefully chosen list, and creamy cinnamon-scented *arroz doce* (rice pudding) will make you feel that all's right with the world, or at least in the north of Portugal. ✉ *Curva do Lancete, Ansiães, 4600 Amarante,* ☎ *055/461113,* FAX *055/461353. 15 rooms. Restaurant, bar. AE, DC, MC, V.*

¢ **Hotel Navarras.** The Navarras is part of a modern shopping complex in the center of Amarante, a five-minute walk from the river. Decor throughout is smart and up-to-date, though unexceptional, and service is competent. Given the local river pollution, which prevents swimming, perhaps the greatest attraction is the hotel's covered pool. ✉ *Rua António Carneiro, 4600,* ☎ *055/431036,* FAX *055/432991. 61 rooms. Restaurant, bar, pool, shops. AE, MC, V.*

¢ **Hotel Silva.** This modest, friendly hotel lies on the road past the convent. Rooms in the back have French windows opening on to a long balcony with splendid views of the river and adjacent gardens; there's also a pretty terrace for calm contemplation of the river. The interior has seen better days, though the simply furnished rooms remain comfortable, and bathrooms are functional. Breakfast is the only meal served, taken outside on the terrace in summer. ✉ *Rua Cândido dos Reis 53, 4600,* ☎ *055/423110. 21 rooms, 7 with bath. No credit cards.*

Festival

Every Saturday night from July through September, the gardens of the **Casa da Calçada,** near the bridge in town, host a festival with traditional music and dancing. It starts at 8 PM, and the entrance price includes as much barbecued and buffet food as you can eat.

Peso da Régua

20 *108 km (67 mi) east of Porto, 35 km (21 mi) southeast of Amrante, 25 km (15 mi) south of Vila Real.*

This small river port is in the heart of port-wine country, and through it passes all the wine from the vineyards of the Upper Douro Valley on its way to Porto. Local wine lodges offer tours of their cellars, which make a nice contrast to the large-scale operations in Vila Nova de Gaia.

Lamego

21 *121 km (75 mi) southeast of Porto, 13 km (8 mi) south of Peso da Régua, 38 km (23 mi) south of Vila Real.*

A prosperous wine-producing town, Lamego is rich in baroque churches and mansions, though none is so impressive as the town's most famous monument—the 18th-century pilgrimage church and shrine of **Nossa Senhora dos Remedios** (Our Lady of Cures). It stands on a hill to the west of the town center, and a marvelous granite staircase leads up the hillside to the church. The steps and terraces are decorated with azulejos, small chapels, and statues; at the top, rest under the chestnut trees and enjoy the view over the town to the distant mountains. During the **Festas de Nossa Senhora dos Remedios,** the annual pilgrimage to the shrine, many penitents climb the steps on their knees, just as they do at the shrine of Bom Jesus, near Braga. The main procession is September 8, but the festivities start at the end of August and include concerts, dancing, parades, a fair, and torchlit processions.

THE MINHO AND THE COSTA VERDE

The coastline of Minho Province, north of Porto, is known as the Costa Verde (Green Coast), a largely unspoiled stretch of small towns and sandy beaches that runs all the way to the border with Spain. Most coastal towns are easily accessible by train from Porto, and regular buses connect with the most interesting inland destinations. By car, a leisurely tour of the major points of interest could occupy three or four days.

The weather in this region of Portugal is more inclement than elsewhere, a fact hinted at in its name: The Costa Verde is green because it sees a disproportionate amount of rain. It is a land of emerald valleys, endless pine-scented forests, and secluded beaches that are beautiful but not for fainthearted swimmers. Summers can be cool, and swimming in the Atlantic is bracing at best. "These are real beaches for real people," is the reply when visitors complain about the water temperature.

Days spent at the coast can be alternated with trips inland to medieval towns along the lush Ria Lima or through the historic border settlements along the Rio Minho. Everywhere are remains of ancient civilizations; you'll come across dolmens, Iron Age dwellings, Celtic and Roman towns. Old traditions are carefully incorporated into modern-day hustle and bustle. Up here, you'll see more than the occasional oxcart loaded with some sort of crop, being led by a long-skirted, wooden-shoed woman on both highway and country lane.

Numbers in the margin correspond to points of interest on the North: Douro, Minho, and Trás-os-Montes map.

Braga

㉒ *53 km (33 mi) northeast of Porto, 7 km (4 mi) northwest of Citânia de Briteiros, 22 km (14 mi) northwest of Guimarães.*

Braga is one of the outstanding surprises of northern Portugal. Its attractive city center is a delight to negotiate, featuring many fine buildings whose baroque facades front on small squares and pedestrian streets. A city of ancient origin, Braga prospered under the 6th-century Visigoths, when it became an important bishopric, marking the start of the religious authority it maintains today. Braga's later archbishops often wielded greater power than the Portuguese kings themselves. During the city's golden age, in the 16th century, Braga was beautified with churches, palaces, and fountains, many of which were subsequently altered (some say ruined) in the 18th century.

The city feels like the religious capital it is. Shops selling religious artifacts, from candles to lovely hand-carved angels, line the pedestrian streets around the cathedral, and the city hosts the most impressive of Portugal's *Semana Santa* (Holy Week) festivities—including eerie torch-lit processions of hooded participants—which reach their climax on Good Friday. Braga also has a conservative reputation, since it was here that the military coup began that brought Salazar to power. However, the city seems increasingly dynamic, both in its local economy and artistic life, and the population of 65,000 is growing fast. The preserved city center is now surrounded by noisy streets and apartment blocks, and traffic congestion is assuming legendary proportions.

The center of the old town is marked by the huge **Sé** (cathedral), originally Romanesque in character but now an impressive blend of styles. The delicate Renaissance stone tracery on the roof is particularly eye-catching. Enter from the main Rua do Souto through the 18th-century cloister; the cathedral interior is on your left, and there are various interesting chapels. Steps by the entrance to the cathedral lead to the **Museu de Arte Sacra** (Museum of Religious Art), which has a fascinating collection of religious art and artifacts, including a 14th-century crystal cross set in bronze. From the magnificent *coro alto* (upper choir), which you cross as part of the treasury tour, there are views of the great baroque double organ. Across the cloister, you'll see the **Capela dos Reis** (Kings' Chapel), a 14th-century chapel containing the tombs of Afonso Henriques's parents, Henry of Burgundy and his wife, Teresa. ☎ 053/23317. ☜ *Cathedral free; treasury 300$00.* ☼ *Daily 8:30–12:30 and 2:30–6:30.*

Across narrow Rua do Souto from the Sé is Largo do Paço, a park flanked by the impressive, well-proportioned **Paço dos Arcebispos** (Archbishop's Palace), which overlooks an attractive, castellated fountain. Parts of the building date from the 14th century. Today it's occupied by faculties from the city's university and functions as the public library, one of the most impressive in the country, with more than 300,000 volumes.

The pedestrian Rua Diogo de Sousa leads down from the cathedral and Archbishop's Palace to one of the city's former gateways, the 18th-century **Arco do Porta Nova.** Past the Arco do Porta Nova and to the right is the **Palácio dos Biscainhos** (Biscainhos Palace), a baroque mansion typical of many in the city. The elegant rooms are furnished in 18th-century style and display silver and porcelain collections. Interestingly, the ground floor of the palace is stone flagged, which allowed carriages to run through the interior to the stables beyond. At the back of the palace is a formal garden with decorative tiles. ⊠ *Rua dos Biscainhos,* ☎ *053/27645.* ☜ *300$00.* ☼ *Tues.–Sun. 10–noon and 2–5:30.*

Past the garden gateway of the Biscainhos Palace, in the area beyond the **Igreja de São Sebastião** (Church of St. Sebastian), you'll find the **Zona Arqueologica** (Archaeological Zone), which contains the excavations of an old Roman city known as Bracara Augusta. (The site isn't usually open to the public.) To the east, the Roman city stretched as far as the large Largo de São Tiago. An imposing building at Largo de São Tiago contains the **Museu Pio XII e Medina** (Pio XII Museum), which displays two collections, one of religious works and the other of paintings and sculpture. Perhaps the most interesting elements of the museum, however, are the few architectural and archaeological fragments gathered from local sites and churches. ⊠ *Largo de São Tiago,* ☎ *053/23370.* ☜ *300$00.* ☼ *Tues.–Sun. 10–12:30 and 3–6.*

The city center is found at the **Praça da República,** the square at the head of Braga's elongated central gardens. The west side of the square is arcaded, while behind it stands the dominating 14th-century tower, the **Torre de Menagem,** which is being restored.

NEED A BREAK?	There are two inexpensive cafés in the arcade at Praça da República, either of which makes a pleasant stop. **Café Astoria** is the most elegant, with mahogany-paneled walls, mirrors, marble tables, and a molded ceiling. **Café Vianna** has been in business since 1871 and serves a wider variety of snacks. It's also a good place for breakfast and offers views of the fountain and gardens. ☼ *Both, 8 AM–11 PM.*

Dining and Lodging

$$ ✕ **A Ceia.** One of the city's best finds, A Ceia is a truly local haunt,
★ with crowds of regulars digging into vast helpings of authentic Portuguese food. As the restaurant fills up, service becomes frenetic, but it's always friendly and lively. Try the spit-roasted chicken platter and

save room for one of the homemade desserts; the almond cake is good. There's a short list of reasonably priced local wines. If you haven't reserved a table and don't want to wait in line, it's possible to eat diner style at the long bar. ⊠ *Rua do Raio,* ☎ *053/23932. Reservations essential after 8 PM Fri. and Sat. No credit cards. Closed Mon.*

$$ ✕ **Restaurante Inácio.** Just outside the 18th-century town gate, the Arco da Porta Nova, this appealing restaurant emphasizes locally inspired dishes. Bacalhau is a favorite, and there's usually roasted kid, too. The house wine is just fine, or try one of the other local wines that appear on the decent wine list. Service in the stone-clad interior is brisk and efficient. ⊠ *Campo das Hortas 4,* ☎ *053/513235. Reservations essential. AE, DC, MC, V. Closed Mon.*

$ 🏨 **Hotel de Turismo.** Braga is not well endowed with hotels, and the Turismo is among the best of a rather poor selection. It's a smart, rather boxy-looking white high-rise on a main road, just a few minutes away from the old town. Everything is uncompromisingly modern, from the soaring lobby to the spacious rooms, whose balconies provide views of the downtown traffic. There's a comfortable bar, a good restaurant, and the bonus of a rooftop pool. ⊠ *Praceta João XXI, Av. da Liberdade, 4700,* ☎ *053/612200,* FAX *053/612211. 134 rooms. Restaurant, bar, pool. AE, DC, MC, V.*

¢ 🏨 **Residencial Inácio Filho.** This central, old-town guest house, a two-minute walk from the cathedral, is a wonderful bargain. A friendly private home, the well-cared-for building is decorated with antiques and bric-a-brac: Bellows, old typewriters, and what looks like Grandma's cherished porcelain lie side by side on the polished wooden floors and staircase. The few, simple rooms are spotless, if rather bare. There are no facilities, but many cafés and restaurants are within easy walking distance. Be sure to reserve in advance for a summer visit. ⊠ *Rua Francisco Sanches 42–2, 4700,* ☎ *053/23849. 8 rooms, 6 with bath. No credit cards.*

Nightlife

Braga has a surprisingly active nightlife for such a conservative, religious city. Its central café-bars, such as **Café Vianna** and **Café Astoria,** both in the arcaded Praça da República, are good places for a drink and are lively at any time of the day or night. **O Nosso Café** (⊠ Av. da Liberdade) is a popular bar with a late-night disco. Along the same avenue, Braga's youth also converge on the notorious disco under the **Hotel Turismo** (⊠ Praceta João XXI). Others frequent the less trendy but enjoyable **Salsa** (⊠ Rua de Diu), a little farther down the avenue. Bands from Brazil have been known to show up from time to time to set the place on fire (musically speaking) with sensuous samba music.

Outdoors Activities and Sports

There's canoeing on the Rio Cávado near Braga. Contact the **Clube Nautico de Prado** (☎ 053/921101) in the nearby hamlet of Prado.

Bom Jesus do Monte

★ 🕒 *5 km (3 mi) east of Braga.*

Many people visit Braga specifically to see the pilgrimage center of Bom Jesus do Monte, a 1,312-foot-high, densely wooded hill east of the city. Here, a stone staircase, started in 1723, climbs up to an 18th-century sanctuary-church, whose terrace commands wonderful views. But it's the stairway itself—a marvel of baroque art—that is the most extraordinary attraction. Many pilgrims climb up on their knees. Fountains placed at various resting places represent the five senses and the virtues, and small chapels display a series of tableaux, with life-size figures illustrating the Stations of the Cross. If you don't want to climb up the staircase (which would be a pity!), you can take the funicular (🚠 50$00) or drive up the winding road. There are restaurants, refreshment stands, and even a couple of hotels beside the sanctuary at the top. On weekends the area is popular with local families, who come here to picnic. Buses run every half hour from the center of Braga.

Citânia de Briteiros

㉓ *7 km (4 mi) southeast of Braga, 15 km (9 mi) northwest of Guimarães. From Guimarães, go north toward Braga on N101 and after 8 km (5 mi), turn right at Caldas das Taipas (Caldelas on some maps).*

These fascinating remains of a Celtic *citânia* (hill settlement) date from around 300 BC and were probably not abandoned until AD 300, making them one of the last Celtic strongholds against the Romans in Portugal. The walls and foundations of 150 huts and a meeting house have been excavated (two of the huts have been reconstructed to show their original size), and paths are clearly marked between them. Parts of a channeled water system also survive. The site was excavated in the late 19th century by Dr. Martins Sarmento, who gave his name to the museum in Guimarães (☞ *below*), where most of the finds from Briteiros were transferred. If you intend to visit the site, don't miss the museum. 🎫 *200$00.* ☉ *Daily 9–6.*

Guimarães

★ ㉔ *22 km (14 mi) southeast of Braga, 51 km (32 mi) northeast of Porto.*

Afonso Henriques was born in 1110 in Guimarães, and Portuguese schoolchildren are taught that "*aqui nasceu* Portugal (Portugal was born here)" with him. Within 20 years he was being referred to as king of *Portucale* (the united Portuguese lands between the Minho and Douro rivers) and had made Guimarães the seat of his power. From this first "Portuguese" capital, Afonso Henriques drove south, taking Lisbon back from the Moors in 1147. Today Guimarães is a provincial town proud of its past, and this is evident in a series of delightful medieval buildings and streets. In the narrow, cobbled thoroughfares of the old town, small bars open onto the sidewalk; balconied, pastel-color houses overhang little squares; and flowers brighten every windowsill.

Traditional festivals still bring celebration to Guimarães's streets. The first week in July marks the **Festas de São Torcato,** when there's a fair and procession to the nearby village of São Torcato. The biggest celebration is the following month: The first Sunday in August sees the **Festas Gualterianas** (Festival of St. Walter), a boisterous festival and fair that dates to the 15th century. Music bands and folk dance groups liven up the festivities. On the second Sunday in August, drivers (of cars and trucks, not horses) celebrating the **Festa de São Cristovão** (Festival of St. Christopher) converge on the church in nearby Penha to commemorate their patron saint.

☺ The best place to start exploring the city is at the **Castelo** (castle) at the top of the town. It was built (or at least reconstructed from earlier remains) by Henry of Burgundy; his son, Afonso Henriques, was born within its great battlements and flanking towers. Standing high on a solid rock base above the town, the castle has been superbly preserved. A path leads down from the castle walls to the tiny Romanesque **Igreja de São Miguel de Castelo,** the plain chapel where it's believed that Afonso Henriques was baptized. ✉ *Rua D. Teresa de Noronha, no phone.* ☉ *Castle Tues.–Sun. 9:30–12:30 and 2–5; church has irregular hrs.*

The **Paço dos Duques** (Palace of the Dukes), below the castle, is a much-maligned, renovated 15th-century palace belonging to the dukes of Bragança. Critics claim that the restoration during the Salazar regime, which turned the building into an official state residence, damaged it irrevocably. Certainly the palace's brick chimneys and turrets bear little relation to the original structure, which was an atmospheric ruin for many years, but you can judge for yourself on a guided tour of the interior. The collections inside contain much of interest, from tapestries and furniture to porcelain and paintings. Guided tours can be booked at the main desk. ☎ *053/412273.* 🎫 *400$00 June–Sept.; 250$00 Oct.–May.* ⊙ *Daily 10–12:30 and 2–5.*

Walk down Rua de Santa Maria into the peaceful old town, and the centuries roll away with every step. You'll see granite archways, wooden balconies, iron grilles, and paving stones underfoot. In Largo da Oliveira, a delightful square enclosed by buildings, stands the Romanesque **Colegiada de Nossa Senhora da Oliveira** (Church of Our Lady of the Olive Branch). It was founded in the 10th century to commemorate one of Guimarães's most enduring legends. Wamba, elected king of the Visigoths in the 7th century, refused the honor and thrust his olive-branch stick into the earth, declaring that only if his stick were to blossom would he accept the crown—whereupon the stick promptly sprouted foliage. In the square in front of the church, an odd 14th-century Gothic canopy sheltering a cross marks the alleged spot.

The convent buildings surrounding the Colegiada de Nossa Senhora da Oliveira house the **Museu Alberto Sampaio,** a beautifully displayed collection of religious art. The cloister itself holds medieval statuary, sarcophagi, and various coats of arms, but the interior rooms provide the highlight: a 14th-century silver triptych of the Nativity, full of animation and power. This is said to have been captured from the King of Castile at the crucial Battle of Aljubarrota and presented to the victorious Dom João I, whose tunic, worn at the battle, is preserved in a glass case nearby. ⊠ *Largo da Oliveira,* ☎ *053/412465.* 🎫 *250$00.* ⊙ *Tues.–Sun. 10–12:30 and 2–5.*

NEED A BREAK? An inexpensive café in Largo da Oliveira, **A Medieval,** has seats outside in the square. Relax over coffee and a cake every day but Sunday.

The old-town streets peter out at the Almeida da Liberdade, a swath of gardens at the southern end of Guimarães, whose benches and cafés are often full. Here the **Igreja de São Francisco** (Church of St. Francis) is worth seeing. Its chancel is decorated with 18th-century azulejos depicting the life of the saint. The church also boasts a fine Renaissance cloister. ⊠ *Largo de São Francisco,* ☎ *053/412228.* ⊙ *Daily 9–noon and 3–6.*

At the top of the Largo do Toural is the excellent **Museu Martins Sarmento.** Like the Museu Alberto Sampaio, Guimarães's other museum, it too is contained within the cloister and buildings of a church, the **Igreja de São Domingos.** The museum has rich finds from the Celtic settlement of Citânia de Briteiros (☞ *above*), as well as Lusitanian and Roman stone sarcophagi, a strange miniature bronze chariot, various weapons, and elaborate ornaments. Two finds stand out: the decorative, carved stone slabs known as the *Pedras Formosas* (beautiful stones), one of which was found at a funerary monument at Briteiros, and the huge, prehistoric, granite *Colossus of Pedralva*, a figure of brutal power, thought to have been used in ancient fertility rites. ⊠ *Rua de Paio Galvão,* ☎ *053/415969.* 🎫 *400$00.* ⊙ *Tues.–Sun. 10–noon and 2–5.*

Dining and Lodging

$$$ ✗▥ **Pousada de Santa Marinha.** Guimarães has two pousadas: This
★   one, overlooking the town from the Penha National Park to the north-
west, is one of the finest in the country. It occupies a beautifully con-
verted 12th-century monastery, which was originally founded by the
wife of Dom Afonso Henriques to honor the patron saint of pregnant
women. The history contained within the building is almost tangible:
Some of the attractive guest rooms used to be monks' cells; antiques
from Lisbon's Ajuda Palace brighten the public rooms (already knock-
outs with extraordinarily lovely azulejo panels gracing the walls); and
the great stone dining room (serving regional and Continental dishes)
was once the monastery kitchen. *Rojões á Minhota* (pieces of browned
pork, reddened with paprika and then simmered until meltingly ten-
der, served with mixed pickled vegetables) is delicious here, especially
when you sop up the sauce with chunks of *broa* (a dense, chewy corn
bread). A fitting dessert is *toucinho do Céu* (bacon from heaven), an
exceedingly rich egg-and-almond pudding cake. ✉ *Estrada de Penha,
4800,* ☎ *053/514453,* 𝔽𝔸𝕏 *053/514459. 51 rooms. Restaurant, bar. AE,
DC, MC, V.*

$ ✗▥ **Pousada da Nossa Senhora da Oliveira.** An elegant mansion, this
pousada was fashioned when various adjacent 16th- and 17th-century
town houses in the center of Guimarães were remodeled. Antique re-
productions throughout provide old-style atmosphere, and the service,
too, is straight from the old school—courteous and efficient. Guest rooms
are elegantly cheerful, if not particularly large, but there's compensa-
tion at hand in the superb restaurant (reservations essential), whose
windows overlook the lovely Largo da Oliveira. A large fireplace
catches the eye, and the menu features a wide range of regional Minho
dishes; try *coelho á fundador* (a fragrant fricassee of rabbit scented with
fennel and red wine). A local favorite for dessert is the *bolo de amên-
doa* (a dense almond cake made with flour and mashed potatoes). Even
if you don't stay here, this would make a fine place for lunch while
sightseeing. ✉ *Rua de Santa Maria, 4800,* ☎ *053/514157,* 𝔽𝔸𝕏
053/514204. 16 rooms. Restaurant, bar. AE, DC, MC, V.

Shopping

Guimarães is a center for the local linen industry. The linen is hand-
spun and hand-woven, then embroidered, all to impressive effect; it is
available in local shops. Here the weekly market is on Friday.

Barcelos

㉕   *12 km (7 mi) west of Braga, 60 km (35 mi) northeast of Porto, 45 km
(27 mi) southeast of Viana do Castelo.*

Easily reachable by car or train and attractively situated on the banks
of the Rio Cávado, Barcelos is the center of a flourishing handicrafts
industry, particularly ceramics and wooden toys and models. It pays
to come here if you plan to carry home a host of souvenirs. Unques-
tionably, the best time to visit is during the famous weekly market. The
★ ☾   **Feira de Barcelos** (Barcelos Market) is a vast affair—the largest in the
country—held every Thursday in the central Campo da República
starting very early in the morning. Stalls appear overnight, and on mar-
ket day the square resembles a small city, with rows of covered stalls
selling almost anything else you can think of. At times, when the early
mist rises off the ground, the cries of the vendors ring the air, and the
smell of roasting chestnuts wafts across the square, it seems almost me-
dieval. Parking is available, although you may have to maneuver
around a pig or cow for a spot.

NEED A
BREAK? There are any number of attractive cafés in the center of town. From the market in the Campo da Republica, head for the **Avenida da Liberdade** and to the front of the Turismo building on the **Largo Dr. José Novais** for clean, well-lighted places to sit, have a cup of coffee and piece of pastry, and think about heading back to the market to get an extra suitcase for all the great stuff you just bought.

From the Campo da República, Rua Dom António Barroso leads down through the old town toward the river. On the left, the former medieval town tower now houses the tourist office and the excellent **Centro Artesanato** (Artisans' Center), which brings together some of the best local handicrafts at very reasonable prices. Ceramic dishes and bowls, often signed with the artist's name, are a good buy. Figurines, too, are popular, though none approach the individuality of those made by the late Rosa Ramalho and Mistério, local potters whose work first made famous the ceramics of Barcelos. ⊠ *Torre de Menagem, Largo de Porta Nova,* ☎ *053/811882.* ⊘ *Mon.–Sat. 9–noon and 1:30– 5:30.*

The Cávado River, crossed by a medieval bridge, is the most attractive part of town, shaded by overhanging trees and bordered by municipal gardens. High above the river stands the ruin of the medieval Paço dos Condes (Palace of the Counts), whose grounds constitute the **Museu Arqueologico** (Archaeological Museum). Among the empty sarcophagi and stone crosses is the 14th-century crucifix known as the *Cruzeiro do Senhor do Galo* (Cross of the Rooster Man). According to local legend, after sentencing an innocent man to death, a judge prepared to dine on a roast fowl. When the condemned man said, "I'll be hanged if that cock doesn't crow," the rooster flew from the table and the man's life was spared. The Barcelos cock is on sale in pottery form throughout the town; indeed, it's become almost a national symbol. ⊠ *Paço dos Condes.* ⊴ *Free.* ⊘ *Daily 10–noon and 2–6.*

Ceramic buffs can indulge in their passion for pottery in the **Museu de Olaria** (Pottery Museum), a five-minute walk from the town's medieval bridge. The collection of over 6,000 pieces—including selections from current and now-extinct Portuguese workshops, private donations, and excavation finds from both Portugal and all over the world—resides in a spacious and well-lighted ocher-color building. ⊠ *Rua Cónego Joaquim Gaiolas,* ☎ *053/824741,* ⊴ *200$00.* ⊘ *Tues.–Sun. 10– 12:30 and 2–8, Thurs. 10–6.*

Legend has it that back in the early 16th century, a local peasant, who insisted on working on the Day of the Holy Cross, saw a perfumed, luminous cross appear on the ground he was digging. Ever since, Barcelos hosts the colorful **Festas das Cruzes** (Festival of the Cross) in the first week of May, when the whole town is lit up by bright lights and the river illuminated by a grand fireworks display.

Dining and Lodging

¢ ✕▯ **Pensão Bagoeira.** The Bagoeira is a genuine and friendly old inn
★ on the edge of the main square, perfect for a night's rest before an early visit to the Thursday market. The few large, bright rooms are individually furnished with some nice old pieces, and there's a spotless bathroom down the hall. Downstairs, the excellent country restaurant does a fast and furious business on market day, as the vendors call in for a bowl of warming soup. Dishes are prepared in full view on a huge range, with all the spluttering flames and hisses that entails. Decor is rustic to the point of parody, with a wood ceiling, great metal chandeliers, and fresh flowers at every turn. Specialties include broa, good vegetable

soup, and any number of meat and fish grills, including tasty cod steaks; *arroz de frango* (chicken with rice) and *arroz de sarrabulho* (stewed meats with pork blood and rice) are very popular with the neighborhood crowd. Because of the large number of visitors who come for the market, restaurant reservations are essential for Thursday lunch, and room reservations are essential Wednesday night. ⊠ *Av. Dr. Sidonio Pais 495, 4750,* ☎ *053/811236. 6 rooms share bath. Restaurant, bar. No credit cards.*

Shopping

The great Thursday market, **Feira de Barcelos,** is the place to buy traditional Barcelos ceramics (brown pottery with yellow-and-white decoration) as well as more workaday earthenware, baskets, rugs, glazed figurines (including the famous Barcelos cock), decorative copper lanterns, ox yokes and cartwheels, and wooden toys. Plus there are mounds of vegetables, fruits, cheese, fresh bread and cakes, clothes, shoes, leather, and kitchen equipment. There's also the **Centro Artesanato** (☞ *above*), a handicrafts center in the old-town tower.

Viana do Castelo

★ *45 km (27 mi) northwest of Barcelos, 71 km (43 mi) north of Porto, 67 km (40 mi) northwest of Braga.*

An enjoyable resort at the mouth of the Ria Lima, Viana do Castelo has been a prosperous trading center since it received its town charter in 1258. While you shouldn't miss the excellent local beach, Praia do Cabedelo (reached by ferry from the riverside at the end of the main street), there's plenty in town to occupy an inveterate stroller. Ask at the tourist office for their English-language brochure, which includes a walking tour of the town.

Many of Viana's finest buildings date from the 16th and 17th centuries, the period of its greatest prosperity, and the town's best face is presented in the old streets and squares that radiate from the charming Praça da República. The most striking building here is the **Misericórdia,** a 16th-century almshouse, whose two upper stories are supported, unusually, by tall caryatids (carved, draped female figures). The stone fountain, also Renaissance in style, harmonizes perfectly with the surrounding buildings, which include the restored town hall and its lofty arcades.

NEED A BREAK?
Natário, a small café right off the main drag, is a perfect place to soak up the Minho atmosphere. The owner makes his own pastries, cakes, and croquettes. It's been rumored that the Brazilian writer, Jorge Amado, comes here for coffee when he's in town. ⊠ *Rua Manuel Espregueira 37, no phone.* ☺ *Daily 8 AM–10 PM.*

A 10-minute walk west across the town's main avenue, the **Avenida dos Combatentes da Grande Guerra,** takes you to the **Museu Municipal** (Municipal Museum), housed in one of Viana's most impressive mansions. The early 18th-century interior has been carefully preserved, and the collection of 17th-century ceramics and ornate period furniture shows how wealthy many of Viana's merchants were.

A little way beyond the municipal museum are the great ramparts of the **Castelo de São Tiago da Barra,** the 16th-century fortification that added the words "do Castelo" to the town's name and protected Viana against attack from pirates eager to share in its wealth. Outside the walls Viana holds a large market every Friday. ⊠ *Museum: Largo de*

São Domingos, ☎ *058/24223.* ✆ *250$00.* ☉ *Tues.–Sun. 10–noon and 2–5.*

An *elevador* (funicular railway) behind the train station climbs to the modern basilica of **Santa Luzia,** a white, domed building overlooking the town from its wooded heights. The views from the steps of the basilica are magnificent, and a staircase to the side (marked ZIMBÓRIO) allows access to the very top of the dome for some extraordinary coastal views. Be warned that this steep climb, up a very narrow staircase to a little viewing platform, is for the agile only. ✉ *Estrada de Santa Luzia.* ✆ *Funicular 75$00, dome 50$00.* ☉ *Funicular operates 10–7, every 30 mins; basilica 10–noon and 2–6.*

The most spectacular Minho festival is the **Romaria de Nossa Senhora da Agonia** (Procession and Fair of Our Lady of Sorrows), held in Viana do Castelo in August (over the weekend closest to the 20th) and attracting thousands of pilgrims. Although it is in honor of Our Lady of Sorrows, the three-day festival features the tragic Virgin carried over carpets of flowers to her chapel, a parade of fishermen heading down to the sea to be blessed by the town bishop, a parade of local beauties in colorful hand-embroidered costumes and weighed down with what looks like 20 pounds of gold jewelry, and ends with a huge fireworks display down near the river.

Dining and Lodging

$$ ✕ **Os Tres Arcos.** This locally renowned seafood restaurant, facing the town gardens and river, is always a good bet. Sole, trout, and eel are especially recommended, and while the selection of shellfish changes according to the season, what there is sits temptingly in the window. You can eat in the arched interior (the restaurant's name means "the three arches") or choose from a less expensive menu at the bar. ✉ *Largo João Tomás da Costa 25,* ☎ *058/24014. MC, V. Closed Mon.*

$$ ✕ **Os Tres Potes.** The cellarlike dining room, converted from a 16th-century bakery, gets very busy in summer as people crowd in to eat to the accompaniment of the weekend folksinging and dancing sessions. Sitting at tables under stone arches or on the open-air terrace, you can choose from a fine range of regional dishes: Start with a bowl of caldo verde or the *aperitivos regionais* (a selection of ham, spicy sausage, cheese, and olives); move on to the house-style baked bacalhau and potatoes or try the exceedingly tender *polvo grelhado* (grilled octopus). There's a good wine list, too. For dessert, have the house specialty: hazelnut cake. ✉ *Beco dos Fornos 7, off Praça da República,* ☎ *058/23432. Reservations essential. MC, V.*

$ ✕▥ **Pousada Santa Luzia do Monte.** Majestically situated on a wooded, ★ rocky outcrop behind the basilica, this large, white country mansion overlooks the town and coast. The pousada was renovated in 1996 and restored to its original sumptuous 1920s style. The grand public rooms are a delight (especially in winter, when the newly added fireplaces add crackling, romantic warmth to the sometimes chilly lounges), as are the private gardens and terrace. There's an outdoor pool, too. Guest rooms are spacious and equipped with glamorous marble bathrooms; some have a beautiful view of the sea. The restaurant serves regional and continental cuisine in an enchanting setting, with sweeping views of both the countryside and the nearby Atlantic Ocean. For location and solitude, the Santa Luzia can't be beat, but note that it's 4 kilometers (2½ miles) from the center of Viana. Archaeology buffs will be pleased to know that directly in front of the hotel are the recently excavated remains of an Iron Age citânia. ✉ *Monte de Santa Luzia, 4900,* ☎ *058/828889 or 058/828890,* ℻ *058/828892. 53 rooms. Restaurant, bar, pool, tennis courts. AE, DC, MC, V.*

Nightlife

The center of Viana do Castelo is lively in the summer, and several bars and cafés cater to the mostly Portuguese tourists. The young crowd hangs out at the **Ministerio** (✉ Rua do Tourinho 41), a fun bar with loud music. On the town beach, Praia da Cabedelo, **Petra** and the **Luzia-mar** bar and disco are popular.

Shopping

Viana is regarded as the folk capital of the region and specializes in producing traditional embroidered costumes, which are worn at the most important festivals. These make colorful souvenirs, though the town also sells less elaborate crafts, including ceramics, lace, and jewelry. The large Friday market is a good place to shop, and the tourist office also displays a nice selection.

En Route Leaving Viana, both the train and the N13 continue north, following the coast, and pass a succession of small villages with delightful beaches. There are good stretches of sand at the local resorts of **Vila Praia de Âncora** and **Moledo,** and if you keep your eyes open, you'll find some side roads that lead to fairly isolated beaches.

Caminha

㉗ *25 km (16 mi) north of Viana do Castelo, 97 km (60 mi) north of Porto.*

At Caminha you reach the Rio Minho, which forms the border with Spain. The fortified town hall on the main square once was part of Caminhas' defenses; its loggia, supported by graceful pillars, is very pleasing to the eye. There's a 16th-century clock tower in the square, too, while the nearby **Igreja Matriz** (parish church) resembles a Gothic fortress and was built a century earlier, when Caminha was an important trading port. The rich interior of the church and the surviving mansions in the surrounding streets are reminders of the town's former wealth, but by the 17th century Caminha had lost much of its business to flourishing Viana do Castelo.

Vila Nova de Cerveira

㉘ *12 km (7½ mi) northeast of Caminha.*

With granite hills on one side and the Minho River on the other, Vila Nova de Cerveira is another border town with history dating from the 13th century, when it was fortified to ward off any marauding Spaniards. Nowadays, the Spanish who do come ashore on the minor ferry that connects Vila Nova to the Spanish town of Goian, come in cars (not on horseback) for day trips and good shopping. The most visited building in town is a medieval castle that has been converted into the luxurious, government-run Pousada de Dom Dinis (☞ Dining and Lodging, *below*).

Dining and Lodging

$ ✗🏠 **Pousada de Dom Dinis.** Open since 1982, this pousada was built inside the town's 14th-century fortified castle walls, which face the Rio Minho. Ancient, mottled buildings within the ramparts now house the guest rooms, which have been enhanced by lovely reproductions of traditional Minho furniture. Some rooms have private patios. The modern restaurant features local Minho dishes, including the popular river fish. In season, lamprey is a particular favorite. Enjoy *robalo grelhado com molho manteiga* (grilled bass with butter sauce) or *coelho estufado com ervilhas* (stewed rabbit with peas). For dessert, try the pears poached in red wine. ✉ *Praça da Liberdade, 4920,* ☎ *051/795601,* FAX *051/795604. 29 rooms. Restaurant, bar. AE, DC, MC, V.*

Valença do Minho

29 *15 km (9 mi) northeast of Caminha, 53 km (33 mi) northeast of Viana do Castelo, 123 km (76 mi) northeast of Porto.*

Valença do Minho is the major border crossing point in this area, with road-and-rail service to Spain. The old town of Valença is enclosed by perfectly preserved walls, which face the similarly defended Spanish town of Tuy. Strolling along the river and ramparts is very pleasant—even more so in the evening, when the day-trippers from Spain have retreated to their own side of the river. As at Vila Nova de Cerveira, Valença's fortifications contain a pousada, from which there are fine river views.

Monção

30 *18 km (11 mi) northeast from Valença do Minho, 144 km (89 mi) northeast of Porto.*

The riverside town of Monção is another fortified border settlement with a long history of skirmishes with the Spanish. In town there are the remains of a 14th-century castle, which withstood a desperate siege in 1368; when the Portuguese supplies ran low, a local woman baked some small cakes with the last of the flour and sent them to the Spaniards with the message that there was plenty more where that came from. The bluff worked, the Spanish retreated, and the little cakes are still on sale in town in honor of the event. There is a spa to the east of Monção, which attracts some tourists, but the town is generally peaceful. If you stop, try a glass of the local vinho verde, a noteworthy wine available in several bars.

In mid-June, Monção celebrates the **Festa do Corpo de Deus** (Festival of Corpus Christi), which includes a symbolic battle between good and evil.

En Route South of Monção the N101 traverses glorious rural countryside before descending to the valley of the Rio Vez, a tributary of the Lima. **Arcos de Valdevez,** 35 kilometers (22 miles) south of Monção, makes a nice stop. It is a typically serene little river town, where you can rent rowboats for a closer look at the surroundings. Five kilometers (3 miles) farther south you arrive at the Rio Lima itself, one of the most beautiful rivers in the country. It was known to the Romans as the River of Oblivion, because its blissful beauty was said to make travelers forget their home.

Ponte da Barca

31 *5 km (2 mi) south of Arcos de Valdevez on N101, 39 km south of Monção.*

At the old town of Ponte da Barca, the *ponte* in question is a beautiful, 10-arched bridge, built in the 15th century. At the junction of four main roads, the small town has been an important market center for centuries, and the Tuesday market here is well worth catching. On other days you can spend time quite happily walking along the riverbank.

Ponte de Lima

★ **32** *18 km (11 mi) west of Ponte da Barca on N203, 57 km (35 mi) southwest of Monção, 23 km (14 mi) east of Viana do Castelo, 38 km (24 mi) south of Valença do Minho, 33 km (20½ mi) north of Braga.*

Ponte de Lima is as delightful a town as you're likely to come across in the region. The graceful bridge here is of Roman origin, long and low and open only to foot traffic; drivers cross a concrete bridge at the edge of town. The square tower near the old bridge still stands guard over the town, while beyond, in the narrow streets, there are several fine 16th-century mansions and a busy market. Walking around town, you'll return again and again to the river, which is the real highlight of a visit. A wide beach usually displays lines of drying laundry, and a riverside avenue lined with plane trees leads down to the Renaissance Church of São António. The twice-monthly Monday market, held on the riverbank, is the oldest in Portugal, dating from 1125. On market days and during the mid-September **Feiras Novas** (New Fairs)—an enjoyable festival, also held since the 12th century, which includes a fair, a religious procession, fireworks, music, and various traditional entertainments—you'll see the town at its effervescent best.

NEED A BREAK?   The main square by the old bridge in Ponte de Lima has a central fountain and benches and is ringed by little cafés. It's a perfect place to stop for a leisurely drink.

Dining and Lodging

$$ ✕ Restaurante Encanada. Close to the old town and market, the Encanada is adjacent to the tree-lined avenue along the riverfront. A terrace provides river views. The menu is limited, but you can count on good local cooking, with dishes that depend on what's available at the market. Homemade fish cakes, with rice and salad, make a tasty, light lunch. ⊠ *Praça Municipal,* ☎ *058/941189. MC, V. Closed Thurs.*

¢–$ ✕⌂ Turismo de Habitação. ★ The Ponte de Lima region is well known for its Manor House Tourism program; the organizing body, Turihab, has its central reservations office in Ponte de Lima. Bookings are for a minimum stay of three nights at each house. The cost includes bed and breakfast, although some manor houses will also arrange other meals on request. There are 26 properties in the area, mostly concentrated on the north bank of the Rio Lima, no more then several miles from town. Facilities are usually minimal; houses may have a communal lounge or bar, a pool or access to local swimming facilities, fishing, and gardens. Ask about the early 18th-century **Paço de Calheiros,** which has lovely gardens; the 17th-century **Casa de Pomarchão** (closed Dec.–Jan.); the **Moinho de Estorãos,** a converted water mill by an old Roman bridge (open May–Sept.); and the 18th-century manor house **Casa do Outeiro.** ⊠ *Praça da República, 4990 Ponte de Lima,* ☎ *058/943327 or 058/942729,* ℻ *058/941864. No credit cards.*

Parque Nacional da Peneda-Gerês

Lindoso, in the park's center section, is 30 km (19 mi) east of Ponte da Barca.

The 172,900-acre Parque Nacional da Peneda-Gerês (Peneda-Gerês National Park), bordered to the north by the frontier with Spain, was created in 1970 to preserve the diverse flora and fauna that exist in the region. Even a short trip to the main towns and villages contained within the park shows you wild stretches of land framed by mountains, great woods and lakes, and the peaceful beauty of a region allowed to live a traditional, unmolested life. Access is free, and general information is available at tourist offices in Porto, Braga, and Caldas do Gerês. There's also a park information center at Caldas do Gerês, which can provide a walking map and more specific hints and help.

Accommodations are concentrated mostly in the attractive spa town of **Caldas do Gerês,** in the southern section around the Serra do Gerês (Gerês Mountains). It's a two-hour drive from Braga; turn off the N103 just after Cerdeirinhas, along the N304; there is bus service, too. The central region of the park is accessible from Ponte da Barca, from which the N203 leads to **Lindoso,** or from Arcos de Valdevez, from which the minor N202 leads to the little village of **Soajo.** Both offer basic accommodations and superb hiking. To see the northern part of the park, encompassing the Serra da Peneda (Peneda Mountains), it's best to come from Melgaço, a small town on the Rio Minho, 25 kilometers (15½ miles) east of Monção. From Melgaço, it's 27 kilometers (17 miles) on the N202 to the village of **Castro Laboreiro,** at the northernmost point of the park. There's just one small hotel—and lots of fine long-distance hiking.

TRÁS-OS-MONTES

The remote and beautiful region of Trás-os-Montes, in Portugal's extreme northeast, attracts very few foreign visitors. The name means "Beyond the Mountains," and though new roads have made it easier to reach in recent years, exploring the region still requires a certain sense of adventure. Great distances separate the fascinating towns, and twisting roads can drive you to the point of distraction. Medieval villages exist in a landscape that alternates between splendor and harshness, and the population, thinned by emigration, retains rural customs that have all but disappeared elsewhere. Many still believe in the evil eye, witches, wolfmen, golden-haired spirits living down wells, and even the cult of the dead.

Having a car is obviously the easiest way to tour the region, but making the trip solely by car would mean missing out on some of the finest train journeys in the country. The trip from Porto to Bragança provides an excellent opportunity to see the changing landscape, but it is slow going. Trains stop at every village, and the entire journey, a distance of 280 kilometers (174 miles), takes eight to nine hours.

Vila Real

㉝ *116 km (72 mi) northeast of Porto, 89 km (53 mi) southwest of Chaves, 140 km (87 mi) southwest of Brangança. By train from Porto, change at Peso da Régua (☞ above) to the Corgo line.*

The capital of Trás-os-Montes boasts the only significant industry in the northeast and has modern suburbs and a traffic-choked center to match. Still, Vila Real is superbly situated between two mountain ranges, and much of the city retains a pleasant small-town air. Although there's no great wealth of sights, it's worth stopping here to stroll down the attractive central avenue, which ends at a rocky promontory poking out over the gushing Rio Corgo below. A path around the church at the head of the promontory provides views of stepped terraces and green slopes. At the southern end of the avenue, a few narrow streets are filled with 17th- and 18th-century houses, their entrances decorated with coats of arms.

The finest baroque work in Vila Real is the **Capel dos Clérigos,** also called the Capela Nova (New Chapel), a curious fan-shape building set between two heavy columns. ⊠ *Between Rua 31 de Janeiro and Rua Direita.* 🎟 *Free.* ⊙ *Daily 10–noon and 2–6.*

★ An exceptional baroque mansion built in the mid-18th century, the **Solar de Mateus** is 4 kilometers (2½ miles) east of Vila Real. Its U-shape facade, with high, decorated finials at each corner, is recognized worldwide as the building pictured on the Mateus Rosé wine label. The building is believed to have been designed by Nasoni (architect of Porto's Clérigos Tower), and typically, the huge portal is approached by a double staircase. Set back to one side is the chapel, with an even more extravagant facade. The elegant interior is open to the public, as are the formal gardens, which are enhanced by a cypress tunnel, with trees trained to shade the path. ⊠ *N322, Sabrosa Road, Mateus,* ☎ *059/323121.* 🎟 *500$00.* ⊘ *Guided tours daily 9–1 and 2–6.*

The **Sogrape** winery, just before the Mateus mansion, offers tours of its premises. At the end of the tour, you'll have an opportunity to taste the wine and perhaps purchase a bottle. ⊠ *Circuito Internacional,* ☎ *059/323074.* 🎟 *Free.* ⊘ *Weekdays 10–noon and 2–5.*

Dining and Lodging

$ ✕ **O Aldeão.** A popular local restaurant, the Aldeão piles its plates high with Portuguese specialties, which include a full range of meat grills. The steak comes garnished with a bit of everything and satisfies even the largest of appetites. A regional favorite, *feijoada branca á transmontana* (a hearty white bean-and-charcuterie stew), is prepared to perfection here. Service is friendly, the surroundings straightforward, and the prices unbeatable for this quality and quantity of food. ⊠ *Rua Dom Pedro de Castro 70,* ☎ *059/24794. MC, V.*

$ ✕🏨 **Pousada do Barrao de Forrester.** This member of the pousada group of lodgings is named for the Baron of Forrester, a 19th-century Scotsman whose family opened the Douro River to navigation and were very successful port vintners. A nice alternative if you don't feel like staying in Vila Real, it's in Alijó, some 30 kilometers (18 miles) southeast. Time fades away as you sit reading by the fire in the lounge, glass of port at your side. The restaurant has two terraces for sunlit lunches and star-filled suppers. Try the Douro River mackerel in marinade, *meia desfeita de bacalhau* (cod cut into fine strips and served raw in an olive-oil marinade), or the *alheira* sausage (highly seasoned chicken-and-flour sausage). For dessert, pears poached in muscatel go down easy. ⊠ *5070 Alijó,* ☎ *059/959215,* 🟥 *059/959304. 20 rooms. Restaurant, bar, pool, tennis court, fishing. AE, MC, V.*

$ 🏨 **Miracorgo.** This hotel is a rather unattractive modern block in the center of town, but its exterior can be forgiven once you've secured a room that faces the valley, with views of the dramatic stepped terraces of the Rio Corgo below. The handsome reception area, bright guest rooms, and good service add to the hotel's attractions. ⊠ *Av. 1 de Maio 76–78, 5000,* ☎ *059/25001. 76 rooms. Bar, indoor pool, health club, shops. AE, DC, MC, V.*

Shopping

Vila Real is the place to purchase some world-famous, slightly sparkling wine direct from the source: the winery close to the Solar de Mateus. The **Sogrape** winery, just before the mansion, offers tours of its premises and has bottles (or cases) for sale. ⊠ *Circuito Internacional,* ☎ *059/323074.* 🎟 *Free.* ⊘ *Weekdays 10–noon and 2–5.*

En Route   The main road northeast of Vila Real (the N15) has recently been straightened for much of its length. You'll drive through exceptionally fine, high countryside; rolling, arable land continues as far as **Murça,** 40 kilometers (25 miles) away. Here you'll see the most famous of the ancient zoomorphic images, and the largest of the Iron Age porcas, which are found all over the region. This particular granite boar stands on a plinth in the town's central square and is presumed to be a fertility symbol.

Mirandela

③④ *72 km (44 mi) from Vila Real, 68 km (42 mi) from Bragança. Train service, via Tua from Peso da Régua, runs through pastures and barley fields, following the course of the Rio Tua, a tributary of the Douro.*

Mirandela, an attractive town midway between Vila Real and Bragança, has a medieval castle and a Roman bridge with 20 arches of uneven sizes, but its grandest monument is the 17th-century **Palácio dos Tavoras** (Tavora Palace), right in the center of town. Its great facade has elaborate pediments and baroque ornaments. Once the residence of the prominent Tavora family, it's now used as the town hall. The **Festa de São Tiago** (Festival of St. James), held at the end of July, includes traditional dancing, games, and fireworks over the river.

Bragança

③⑤ *255 km (168 mi) northeast of Porto, 137 km (85 mi) northeast of Vila Real, 60 km (37 mi) northeast of Mirandela.*

This ancient town in the very northeastern corner of Portugal has been inhabited since Celtic times (from about 600 BC). The town lent its name to the noble family of Bragança (or Braganza), whose most famous member, Catherine, married Charles II of England; the New York City borough of Queens is named for her. Descendants of the family ruled Portugal until 1910; their tombs are contained within the church of São Vicente de Fora in Lisbon (☞ Chapter 2). Unfortunately, since improved roads have encouraged development, the approaches to Bragança have been spoiled by many ugly new buildings.

★ ⟳ Above the modern town rises the magnificent 12th-century **Castelo** (castle), found within the ring of battlemented walls that surround the **Cidadela** (citadel), the best-preserved medieval village in the country and one of the most thrilling sights in Trás-os-Montes and, indeed, all of Portugal. This fortified town developed as the medieval community drew close to its castle for protection. Within the walls you'll find the **Domus Municipalis** (city hall), a rare Romanesque civic building dating from the 12th century. If it's closed, the key can be obtained from one of the local cottages, as can the key to the 18th-century **Igreja de Santa Maria** (Church of St. Mary), which has a superb painted ceiling. Another prehistoric granite boar stands below the castle tower, this one with a tall medieval stone pillory sprouting from its back. The tower itself, the **Torre de Menagem,** now contains a military museum that's well worth visiting. ☎ 073/22378. ◻ *Museum 200$00.* ☼ *Castle and walls always open; tower and museum daily 10–noon and 2–5.*

As you leave the castle walls on your way back down to town along this route, you'll pass the Renaissance **Igreja de São Bento,** with a fine Mudejar (Moorish-style) vaulted ceiling and a gilded retable. The church may or may not be open.

The exhibits at the excellent **Museu do Abade de Baçal,** housed in Bragança's former bishop's palace, were collected by a local priest with eclectic tastes. The Abade de Baçal, who died in 1947, acquired more prehistoric pigs, ancient tombstones, some nice furniture, local costumes, fine silver, coins, and paintings—anything that caught his eye. ⊠ *Museum: Rua do Consilheiro Abílio Beca 27,* ☎ *073/23242.* ◻ *200$00.* ☼ *Tues.–Sun. 10–12:30 and 2–5.*

Once you've seen the castle and nearby buildings, you've seen almost everything Bragança has to offer. The central cathedral is unusually small and disappointing, but the modern town center is attractive in its way, with a wide central avenue and several cafés that open onto the sidewalk in summer. You'll easily exhaust all the local sights in under a day, but it's worth staying overnight for the views of the castle from the pousada on the outskirts of town (☞ Dining and Lodging, *below*).

Dining and Lodging

$$–$$$ ✕ **La Em Casa.** This low-key but attractive town-center restaurant lies between the castle and the cathedral. It serves regional Portuguese food with—unusual this far inland—a decent menu of fish and shellfish. These are expensive, though. You can get a more moderately priced meal by choosing from the extensive selection of meat dishes, and there's a particularly reasonable tourist menu available, too. If you're lucky, you might catch one of the occasional evening fado performances. ⊠ *Rua Marquês de Pombal,* ☎ *073/22111. Reservations essential. AE, DC, MC, V. Closed Mon.*

¢ ✕🏨 **Pousada de São Bartolomeu.** Bragança's pousada is on a hill just
★ to the west of the town center and offers terrific views of the citadel. It's a modern building, though very comfortable; its bar and lounge feature an open fireplace and wooden furnishings. Guest rooms are rustically decorated and have scenic balconies. The pousada is a few miles from the town and its restaurants, but it doesn't matter, since the formal dining room is the best in Bragança. It serves fine regional mountain cooking, including good stews and game. ⊠ *Estrada do Turismo, 5300,* ☎ *073/331493,* 𝐅𝐀𝐗 *073/23453. 16 rooms. Restaurant, bar, tennis court. AE, DC, MC, V.*

Shopping

Bragança has locally made ceramics, and there's also a good crafts shop within the walls of the citadel. Baskets, copper objects, pottery, woven fabrics, and leather goods are all well made and a change of pace from the traditional gift of a key ring.

OFF THE
BEATEN PATH
SOUTH OF BRAGANÇA – Trás-os-Montes is remote to begin with, and the minor roads south of Bragança are even more isolated; a number of attractive small towns are the reward of a wandering drive through the area. The N218 leads southeast through high, cultivated country to **Mirando do Douro,** a winding 84-kilometer (52-mile) journey to the Spanish border that takes the better part of two hours. A small town with a Renaissance cathedral and cobbled streets, Miranda do Douro has an excellent pousada, where you can stop before crossing into Spain; Zamora is due east. Back in Portugal the N221 shadows the frontier for the 50-kilometer (31-mile) drive southwest to **Mogadouro,** formerly a border stronghold and now a market town with a 13th-century tower. Continue south for 46 kilometers (29 miles), and you'll reach the oddly named **Freixo de Espada à Cinta** (Ash Tree of the Girded Sword), which retains a tall defensive tower and a fine parish church. Or turn off the N221 14 kilometers (9 miles) before Freixo and take the N220 to **Torre de Moncorvo,** which surrounds an enormous church with a high, solid tower. Just to the north you can pick up the main N102, which eventually joins the N15, running between Vila Real and Bragança.

Vinhais

㊱ *31 km (19 mi) west of Bragança.*

Vinhais provides a welcome break from the beautiful though rather desolate scenery along the N103—bleak uplands with the mountains of Spain to the north and the distant mass of the Serra da Estrela (Estrela Mountains) to the south. Most probably a pre-Roman *castro* (settlement), the present town was founded in the 13th century by King Sancho II. Its most notable sight is the structure housing the former **Convento de São Francisco** (Convent of St. Francis), whose great baroque facade incorporates two churches. The church has a beautiful painted ceiling.

En Route   Shortly before reaching Chaves, you'll see the ruins of the 13th-century **Castelo do Monforte** (Monforte Castle), built upon the site of an earlier Roman fort, a remote outpost of the great empire.

Chaves

★ ㉗ *96 km (60 mi) west of Bragança, 62 km (38 mi) northeast of Vila Real.*

Chaves was known to the Romans as Aquae Flaviae (Flavian's Waters), in honor of the emperor Flavian. They established a military base here and popularized the town's thermal springs, which are still in use today. The impressive 16-arch Roman bridge across the Rio Tâmega, at the southern end of town, dates from the 1st century AD and displays two original Roman milestones. Today Chaves is characterized most by a series of fortifications built during late-medieval times, when the city was prone to attack from all quarters. The town lies only 12 kilometers (7½ miles) from the Spanish border. Its name means "keys"—whoever controlled Chaves held the keys to the north of the country.

Of the town's three surviving defensive structures, the most obvious landmark is the great, blunt fortress overlooking the river, the 14th-century **Torre de Menagem.** As at Bragança, this now houses a military museum, and its grounds offer grand views of the town. The tower is surrounded by narrow, winding streets filled with elegant houses, most of which have lovely ironwork balconies on their top floors. ⊠ *Largo da Câmara Municipal de Chaves,* ☏ *076/21965.* 🎫 *200$00.* ☉ *Daily 9–noon and 2–5.*

In Praça de Camões, the main square below the Torre de Menagem, the late 17th-century **Igreja da Misericórdia** is lined with huge panels of blue-and-white azulejos that depict scenes from the New Testament. The **Museu da Região Flaviense,** adjacent to Igreja da Misericórdia, is thoroughly recommended for its indiscriminate hodgepodge of local archaeological finds and relics that tell the town's history; it's open Tuesday–Friday 9:30–12:30 and 2–5, weekends 2–4:30.

The spa buildings are contained within the **Parque Termal** (Thermal Park), below the tower and close to the river. Local legend has it that the hot water here was cast up from the entrails of the underworld, which is exactly what a mouthful tastes like, so be warned. ⊠ *Largo das Termas,* ☏ *076/21446.* 🎫 *Free.* ☉ *Apr.–Oct., daily 9–5.*

Chaves hosts the **Feira dos Santos** at the beginning of November, a winter fair that emphasizes the region's rural character and attracts people from miles around. You can buy anything from livestock and farm equipment to wonderfully warm wool capes, the regional black pottery, rugs, baskets, and gold filigree jewelry.

Dining and Lodging

$ ✕ **O Pote.** A little way out of town on the Bragança road, this family-run restaurant has no pretensions. It serves tasty Portuguese food to an enthusiastic local clientele. Ask about the daily specials or order what everybody else is eating. You can't go wrong if you choose the *posta á mirandesa* (grilled steak seasoned with olive oil and garlic). To reach the restaurant, cross the bridge from the town center and drive for 1 kilometer (⅔ mile). The restaurant is on the right, and parking is available. ✉ *Estrada da Fronteira,* ☎ *076/21226. No credit cards. Closed Mon.*

¢ ✕🏨 **Trajano.** The basement restaurant of the Hotel Trajano is a good place to try the presunto and chouriço for which the town is famous. *Truta á Transmontana* (river trout wrapped in paper-thin slices of smoky presunto) is another good choice, served with boiled potatoes and salad. There's a reasonably priced selection of local wines to accompany your meal, which is served promptly on elegantly rustic monogrammed plates. Such touches, and the very attentive service, more than make up for the rather subdued basement surroundings. The good service continues upstairs, where the hotel's pleasant guest rooms are cheerily decorated in Portuguese country style. ✉ *Travessa Cândido dos Reis, 5400,* ☎ *076/332415,* FAX *076/25722. 40 rooms. Restaurant, bar. MC, V.*

$ 🏨 **Hotel Aquae Flaviae.** Although it bears the ancient Roman name for Chaves, this is a gleaming modern hotel, adjacent to the Parque Termal and a cannon shot away from the town's fortified tower. It's well equipped, and rooms are spacious and attractively decorated. The facade has an art-deco touch—it looks more like an enormous movie house than a hotel—and the interior impresses with its smooth lines and polished surfaces. ✉ *Praça do Brasil, 5400,* ☎ *076/26711,* FAX *076/26497. 170 rooms. Restaurant, bar, piano bar, pool, shops. AE, DC, MC, V.*

En Route If you continue west along the N103, after 35 kilometers (22 miles) you'll come to an enormous system of lakes and hydroelectric dams along the Rio Cávado. At this point it's possible to make a short side trip to see the ruined castle at **Montalegre,** which is visible from miles around. Take a right turn onto the N308 and drive for 12 kilometers (7½ miles). The views are worth the detour. Back on the N103, you'll follow along the edge of the great lake system, skirting drowned valleys in an endless series of long loops. Allow plenty of time, because you're sure to want to stop often to take in the incredible views. To the north is the Peneda-Gerês National Park (☞ *above*); there are occasional access points along the road. Finally, after passing the village of Cerdeirinhas, the road runs for 30 kilometers (19 miles) through rocky heights and down tree-clad slopes to reach Braga, where you are firmly in the center of the Minho province again.

PORTO AND THE NORTH A TO Z

Arriving and Departing

By Plane
Porto's Sá Carneiro Airport (☎ 02/941–3141) is 13 kilometers (8 miles) north of the city and is the gateway to all of northern Portugal. There is direct service from European and South American cities but not from the United States. TAP runs regular flights from Lisbon. The airport has car-rental agencies and money-exchange facilities. In addition, there are regional airports handling domestic flights in Bragança (☎ 073/22075) and Chaves (☎ 076/21995). For regional service, contact the airline LAR Transregional at the Porto airport.

BETWEEN THE AIRPORT AND CENTER CITY
Buses 56 and 87 run from the airport to downtown Porto and cost 150$00. It takes up to an hour, depending on the traffic, to reach the stop at Cordoaria, the area behind the Clérigos Tower. Taxis are available, too, outside the terminal; fare will run 1,500$00–2,000$00.

By Train

Most trains into Porto (including those from Lisbon) arrive at **Estação de Campanhã** (✉ Campanhã, ☎ 02/565645), just east of the city center. From here, you take a five-minute connecting ride to the central **Estação de São Bento** (✉ Praça Almeida Garrett, ☎ 02/200–1054 or 02/200–1055); connecting trains run regularly. When leaving Porto, be sure to leave plenty of time from São Bento Station to make your connection. For the express service to and from Lisbon, it's necessary to reserve your seat at least a day in advance.

A few trains, those from Guimarães and from the coast immediately north of the city, use the **Estação da Trindade** (✉ Rua Alferes Malheiro, ☎ 02/200–5224), which is a few minutes' walk from downtown Porto, behind the town hall at the top of Avenida dos Aliados.

From Spain, the Vigo–Porto through-train uses the Tuy/Valença border crossing and runs south down the Costa Verde to Porto via Viana do Castelo. These trains usually stop at the Campanhã and São Bento stations, but some only stop at Campanhã, and you'll have to change for São Bento.

Getting Around

By Boat

Cruises on the Rio Douro are offered by various companies based in Porto. These range from short trips taking in Porto's bridges and the local fishing villages to one- and two-day cruises that include meals and accommodations. Expect to pay around 1,500$00 for one- to two-hour cruises, most of which depart several times daily from the Cais da Ribeira, at the foot of Porto's old town. The longer cruises usually depart weekly and often involve taking a train from São Bento Station that connects with a boat farther down the Douro. The cost for these is 12,000$00–35,000$00 per person.

The cruise company with the best reputation is **Endouro** (✉ Rua da Reboleira 49, Porto, ☎ 02/324236, ⒻⒶⓍ 02/317260). **Turisdouro** (✉ Rua Machado dos Santos 824, ☎ 02/306389) specializes in rides on the typical *Rabelo* sailboats traditionally used to transport port wine downriver. More information can be obtained from the tourist office in Porto.

By Bus and Tram

Porto has a decent public transportation system, consisting of *carris* (buses) and *elétricos* (trams). The tourist office provides a city map with all the main routes and numbers. Main stops are at Praça da Liberdade, Praça de Dom João I, and Cordoaria, behind the Clérigos Tower. A useful bus route is No. 78, which runs from Praça da Liberdade, past the Soares dos Reis Museum and the Palácio de Cristal gardens, along the main Avenida da Boavista, to the Museum of Modern Art. The tram system is of less use to visitors, though Trams 1 and 18 make a pleasant run along the river to the beach at Foz.

Ticket prices vary according to the distance traveled, but most trips through the downtown area cost between 100$00 and 150$00. The driver will tell you how much to pay when you get on. If you're going to make considerable use of public transportation, purchase a block of 20 tickets (1,500$00) or a four-day (1,500$00) or seven-day (1,900$00) *Passe Turístico*. All are available at kiosks at the main bus stops.

Outside the city system there's a confusion of bus companies in the north, with several providing service between the same destinations. Generally, however, companies use one central station in each town. Major terminals are found at Porto, Braga, Guimarães, Vila Real, and Chaves. The best source of information about departures is the local tourist office, since bus station personnel invariably speak no English. However, most bus stations do offer timetables for main routes, which you should be able to decipher with the aid of a dictionary.

The main company operating in Trás-os-Montes is **Cabanelas,** whose terminal in Porto is at Rua da Alegria (☎ 02/200–2870). Bus trips in this region are slow and, on some of the minor routes, uncomfortable. One useful tip is to take the bus rather than the train between the neighboring towns of Guimarães and Braga. It's only 22 kilometers (14 miles) on the road, but the circuitous train ride involves two changes.

By Car
Outside Porto a car is the most convenient way to get around, but be prepared for lengthy journeys, particularly in the northeast, where roads can be tortuous. Many roads have been improved in recent years—the fast N15 highway between Porto and Bragança has been completed, and there are quick routes from Porto to towns both north and south, as well as to Braga in the northeast—but, given the nature of Portuguese terrain, some journeys will never be anything but slow. Examples are the routes Bragança–Chaves–Braga (N103), Vila Real–Chaves (N2), and Bragança–Mirando do Douro (N218). It's best simply to accept the roads' limitations, slow down, and appreciate the scenery.

Off the beaten track, particularly in the northeast, always check with local tourist offices to make sure that the routes you wish to follow are navigable. Road work and winter landslides can cause detours and delays. In isolated regions, take special care at night, because many roads are unlit and unpaved.

On Foot
You'll be able to walk around most of central Porto, although be prepared for the hills, which can prove tiring in the summer heat. The city is very congested, so leave your car at your hotel while sightseeing in the city. Central parking is difficult to find, and much of the downtown area (in particular, the riverside and the winding streets of the old town below the cathedral) is not accessible to cars.

By Taxi
In Porto there is a taxi stand in Praça da Liberdade, or you may phone for a cab (☎ 02/528061, 02/482691, or 02/676093). Make sure that the driver switches on the meter. Note that taxis add a surcharge for crossing the Ponte Dom Luis I to Vila Nova de Gaia, the suburb known for its port wine.

By Train
All the region's train routes originate in Porto; from here some of the finest lines in the country stretch out into the river valleys and mountain ranges of the northeast. Even if you've rented a car, try to take a day trip on at least one of the beautiful lines that traverse the region, because the countryside is often best seen from a rattling train window.

The **Douro Line** runs from Porto's São Bento Station east to Pocinho via Livração, Peso da Régua, and Tua (a four-hour journey). Three narrow-gauge lines branch off from it: the **Tâmega Line,** linking Livração with beautiful Amarante (25 minutes); the **Corgo Line,** from Peso da Régua to Vila Real (one hour); and the **Tua Line,** from Tua to Mirandela/Bragança (two hours/four hours). The trains on these lines generally have just one class of car and stop at every station. Journeys are slow but rewarding. (Tickets are reasonably priced.) Recently there have been service cuts on the minor lines, and some route sections have been closed altogether. The lines mentioned above should still be operational, but for reservations and current schedules contact São Bento Station (☎ 02/2002722) or the tourist office in Porto.

Trains on the main route north along the Costa Verde depart approximately hourly from both São Bento and Campanhãstations and run through Barcelos and Viana do Castelo, as far as Valença do Minho. Branch lines connect with Braga and Guimarães.

Contacts and Resources

Car Rental

All the major companies are represented at Porto's airport, and some have offices at the larger hotels. Other addresses include: **Avis** (⊠ Rua Guedes de Azevedo 125, Porto, ☎ 02/315947; ⊠ Braga train station, Rua Gabriel P. Castro 28, ☎ 053/72520; ⊠ Rua do Gontim 35, Viana do Castelo, ☎ 058/823994), **Europcar** (⊠ Rua de Santa Catarina 1158, Porto, ☎ 02/318398; ⊠ Campanhã Station, Porto, ☎ 02/580723), **Hertz** (⊠ Rua de Santa Catarina 899, Porto, ☎ 02/312387; ⊠ Rua Gabrial P. Castro 28, Braga, ☎ 053/616744; ⊠ Av. Conde da Carreira, Viana do Castelo, ☎ 058/822250). In other towns consult the tourist office for the best deals with local companies.

Consulates

In Porto: **United Kingdom** (⊠ Av. da Boavista 3072, ☎ 02/6184789). There isn't a U.S. or Canadian consulate in the north.

Emergencies

The general emergency number is 115. In Porto specific services include: the **Red Cross** (☎ 02/6006353), **hospitals** (Hospital de Santa Maria, ⊠ Rua de Camões, ☎ 02/550–4844; Hospital Geral de Santo António, ⊠ Largo Professor Abel Salazar, ☎ 02/200–5241; Hospital de São João, ⊠ Alameda Professor Hernâni Monteiro, ☎ 02/527151), **Police** (⊠ Rua Augusto Rosa, ☎ 02/200–6821), **Fire** (☎ 02/524121).

Fishing

Inland, especially in the northeast, fishing is a traditional leisure activity. The best freshwater fishing is in the Lima and Minho rivers, where trout can be caught. Local tourist offices can assist with fishing licenses, or contact Direção Geral dos Desportos (☎ 02/666227) in Porto.

Guided Tours

BY BICYCLE

For something different, consider seeing the region on two wheels. **Cycling through the Centuries** (⊠ Rua Dra. Iracy Doyle 9–3E, 2750 Cascais, ☎ 01/486–2044; or in the U.S. through ExperiencePlus!, ⊠ 1925 Wallenberg Dr., Fort Collins, CO 80526, ☎ 303/484–8489 or 800/685–4565) offers 11-day biking tours through the valleys and vineyards of the Minho wine country.

BY BUS

In Porto, consult a tourist office or travel agency (☞ Visitor Information, *below*) for the latest information on bus tours of the city. Usually these last half a day and take in all the principal sights, including a visit to the port-wine lodges (where the vintage is stored) at Vila Nova de Gaia. Short river cruises from Porto are also a pleasant way to orient yourself (☞ By Boat *in* Getting Around, *above*).

For tours farther afield, **RN Tours** (⊠ Rua Sá da Bandeira 629, Porto, ☎ 02/2001109) and **SGV Viagens e Turismo** (⊠ Rua Damião de Góis 425, ☎ 02/550–8760) operate half- and full-day coach tours throughout the region to destinations as diverse as the Douro Valley, the Costa Verde, and Peneda-Gerês National Park. Consider, too, the longer cruises operated by Endouro (☞ By Boat *in* Getting Around, *above*), which cover the towns of the Douro Valley.

Late-Night Pharmacies

Pharmacies take turns staying open late. Schedules and addresses are posted on the door of each pharmacy, and listings of late-night services are carried in the local press.

Mail and Telephones

The main post office in Porto is in Praça General Humberto Delgado (☎ 02/208–0251). It is open weekdays 8 AM–10 PM, Saturday 8–8. General-delivery mail (mark it POSTE RESTANTE) is received here, and telephones are available for international calls.

Travel Agencies

Travel agencies are the best places to obtain tickets and travel information without difficulty. In Porto, many are found around the central Avenida dos Aliados. Reliable ones include: **Abreu** (⊠ Av. dos Aliados 207, ☎ 02/323524); **Star**, agents for American Express (⊠ Av. dos Aliados 202, Porto, ☎ 02/200–3637; ⊠ Av. Dom Afonso Henriques 638, Guimarães, ☎ 053/515750); **Viagens Rawes** (⊠ Largo Ferreira Lapa 34, Porto, ☎ 02/666148); and **Wasteels-Expresso** (⊠ Rua Pinto Bessa 29, Porto, ☎ 02/570589).

Visitor Information

There are two tourist offices in **Porto:** one just east of Avenida dos Aliados (⊠ Praça Dom João I 43, ☎ 02/317514) and one to the west of the town hall, at the top of Avenida dos Aliados (⊠ Rua Clube dos Fenianos 25, ☎ 02/312740). Both will provide maps of the city, information about tours, and help in finding accommodations. There is also a tourist office at the airport (☎ 02/941–2534).

There are local tourist offices providing similar services in the following towns: **Amarante** (⊠ Rua Cândido dos Reis, 4600, ☎ 055/432259), **Arcos de Valdevez** (⊠ Av. da Marginal, 4970, ☎ 058/66001), **Barcelos** (⊠ Torre de Menagem, Largo da Porta Nova, 4750, ☎ 053/811882), **Braga** (⊠ Av. da Liberdade 1, 4700, ☎ 053/22550), **Bragança** (⊠ Av. Cidade de Zamora, 5300, ☎ 073/331078), **Caminha** (⊠ Rua Ricardo Joaquim Sousa, 4910, ☎ 058/921952), **Chaves** (⊠ Rua de Santo António 213, 5400, ☎ 076/21029), **Espinho** (⊠ Angulo das Ruas 6 e 23, ☎ 02/720911), **Esposende** (⊠ Rua 1 de Dezembro, 4740, ☎ 053/961354), **Gerês** (⊠ Av. Manuel Ferreira da Costa, 4700, ☎ 053/391133), **Guimarães** (⊠ Av. Resistentes ao Fascismo 83, 4800, ☎ 053/412450), **Lamego** (⊠ Av. Visconde Guedes Teixeira, 5100, ☎ 054/62865), **Monção** (⊠ Largo do Loreto, 4950, ☎ 051/652757), **Ponte da Barca** (⊠ Largo da Misericórdia, 4980, ☎ 058/42899), **Ponte de Lima** (⊠ Praça da República, 4990, ☎ 058/942335), **Póvoa de Varzim** (⊠ Av. Mouzinho de Albuquerque 166, ☎ 052/614609), **Valença do Minho** (⊠ Av. de Espanha, 4930, ☎ 051/23374), **Viana do Castelo** (⊠ Rua do Hospital Velho, 4900, ☎ 058/822620), **Vila do Conde** (⊠ Rua 25 de Abril, 4480, ☎ 052/642700), **Vila Nova de Cerveira** (⊠ Rua Dr. A. Duro, 4920, ☎ 051/795787), **Vila Nova de Gaia** (⊠ Rua General Torres, 1141, 4400, ☎ 02/303653), **Vila Praia de Âncora** (⊠ Av. Ramos Pereira, 4915, ☎ 058/911384), and **Vila Real** (⊠ Av. Carvalho Araújo 94, 5000, ☎ 059/322819).

9 Madeira

Madeira is a veritable floating garden. The balmy air is filled with the smell of flowers: calla lilies and birds of paradise grow wild; pink and purple fuschia weave lacy patterns up pastel walls; and jacaranda trees provide perfumed, shady canopies across city and country roads. The natural beauty on this island is like no other. Here, mountain summits pierce the sky, terraced ravines are lush and green, and the colors of the sea and sky are ever changing.

By Deborah
Luhrman

Updated by
Mary Ellen
Schultz

MADEIRA IS A MOUNTAINOUS, subtropical island blanketed with colorful flowers and overflowing with waterfalls. It's warmed by Atlantic currents in winter (making swimming possible on sunny days) and cooled by trade winds in summer. Madeira, which is 900 kilometers (560 miles) southwest of Lisbon, has roughly the same latitude as Casablanca. In the middle of the island is a backbone of high, rocky peaks and the crater of a now-extinct volcano. Steep-sided green ravines fan out from the center like the spokes of a wheel. Although Madeira is only 57 kilometers (35 miles) long and 22 kilometers (13 miles) wide, the distances seem much greater, as the roads climb and descend precipitously from one ravine to the next. Grouped with Madeira are: tiny Porto Santo, about 50 kilometers (30 miles) northeast, which has a popular sandy beach and only 5,000 inhabitants; the Ilhas Desertas, a chain of waterless and unpopulated islands 20 kilometers (12 miles) southeast of Madeira; and the also-uninhabited Ilhas Selvagens, much farther south, near the Canary Islands.

Madeira was discovered and claimed for Portugal in 1419 by explorer João Gonçalves Zarco, whose statue you can see at the main intersection in Funchal, the capital. Because the uninhabited island was at that time covered with a nearly impenetrable forest, Zarco named it Madeira, which means "wood" in Portuguese. The colony gradually became populated and in the 15th and 16th centuries grew rich from sugar plantations. After alternative sources of sugar were developed in the New World, Madeira's wine industry sustained the island's growth, and later, banana plantations prospered. More recently, tourism—which now accounts for 20% of the economy—has become big business.

Madeira displays an unmistakable air of British colonialism, which dates to the 1650s and the marriage of Portuguese princess Catherine of Bragança to England's King Charles II. Charles gave Madeira an exclusive franchise to sell wine to England and all its colonies, and he granted Madeirans the same free-trade rights as English captains. The wine sales created a business boom on the island, and that prosperity lured many British families to live in Funchal.

Today the British still flock to Madeira, although nowadays most visitors arrive with large tour groups; it's also a popular holiday destination for Germans and Scandinavians. Although the island has lots of sports and entertainment, it's best loved by a reserved crowd that enjoys wandering through gardens and sipping afternoon tea. Young people seeking an action-packed vacation may be unfulfilled by Madeira. Traditionally Madeira has been a winter resort, but that has begun to change—even though some still believe the best (and most crowded) time to visit is still during Christmas week, when every tree in Funchal is decorated with lights, and the main boulevard becomes an open-air folk "museum." Traditional pastimes, from making bread and pressing sugarcane to weaving and basketry, are demonstrated throughout the week. On New Year's Eve, cruise ships from all over the world pull into the harbor for an incomparable fireworks display from the hilltops surrounding Funchal. In April, the Flower Festival capitalizes on Madeira's best natural resource; and in September there's the Festa da Nossa Senhora do Monte (Festival of Our Lady of the Mountains), which commemorates the patron saint of the island.

Since Madeira has only rock beaches, and sea access is somewhat limited, Madeirans head to the nearby island of Porto Santo when they want a sandy beach. This idyllic, undeveloped strand of soft, golden sand is 9 kilometers (5½ miles) long. Although the beaches near Vila Baleira, Porto Santo's only town, may get crowded in summer, you can always find empty stretches and quiet sand dunes. The warm ocean currents make swimming possible here year-round.

Pleasures and Pastimes

Dining

There are a number of restaurants on Madeira that specialize in island cuisine, and most typical meals revolve around a deep-sea fish known as *espada* (in Madeira this is a soft whitefish that's like scabbard or cutlass fish; on mainland Portugal it means "swordfish"). This eel-like fish is served everywhere and prepared dozens of ways, from poached à la Provençal to fried with bananas. You can see freshly caught espada, which are really quite ugly (although very delicious), at the Mercado dos Lavradores (Workers' Market) in Funchal. There are only two places in the world where espada is fished for extensively—in Madeira and in Japan. Seafood fans will also want to try the Portuguese version of bouillabaisse, called *caldeirada de peixes variados,* a slowly simmered combination of fish, shellfish, potatoes, tomatoes, onions, and olive oil. The other popular fish plate is *bife de atum,* a hearty tuna steak. Those with more adventurous tastes should search out *polvo com vinagre*—a tangy octopus salad.

A favorite meal of tourists and locals alike is *espetada,* a beef shish kebab seasoned with bay leaves and butter. Traditionally it was a party dish prepared in the country over open fires, and the meat was skewered on laurel branches. Nowadays, the delicacy is served on iron skewers and is hung vertically from special stands placed in the center of each table so the kebabs are shared by all diners. Another island specialty is *carne de vinhos e alhos* (pork marinated in wine, oil, garlic, and spices, then gently boiled and quickly browned over a high flame). Also worth trying are *milho frito* (fried cubes of savory corn pudding), a side dish native to Madeira, and *bolo de caco,* a round, flat bread made with sweet potatoes traditionally cooked on a hot stone.

Typical dessert menus include bananas (small, sweet, silvery ones, which are not exported), mango, *paw paw* (papaya), *anonas* (custard apples), and *maracujá* (passion fruit). Don't leave without trying the *bolo de mel,* a spicy Christmas cake (sold year-round) made with molasses and traditionally served with a glass of Madeira, the unique wine that has become synonymous with the island.

Most restaurants serve Madeira wine. Actually, many offer diners a complimentary glass. In restaurants, you should look for *vinho da casa,* a local table wine that's not exported. It's much cheaper than imported ones and generally of high quality. Another local wine is *vinho verde* (green wine)—a refreshing sparkling wine that's served chilled. Coral, a light lager, is the local *cerveja* (beer). For a tasty nonalcoholic drink, try *brisa maracujá,* a sparkling passion-fruit soda.

Funchal has a variety of dining places and two restaurant rows: One is in the old town on Largo do Corpo Santo, and the other is between the Carlton and Casino Park hotels, on Rua Imperatriz Dona Amelia. Eating out in Funchal is a fairly formal activity, especially in hotel restaurants, where men are expected to wear suits, and reservations are always required. Village restaurants in other parts of the island are informal and generally serve huge plates of fish and vegetables at bargain prices.

Fishing

Madeira and Porto Santo are meccas for those hoping to reel in huge blue marlin, yellowfin tuna, albacore, swordfish, and dorado. The European marlin weight record—1,212 pounds—was set here. In fact, the list of gilled gentry inhabiting the surrounding waters also includes bigeye tuna, barracuda, dolphin, wahoo, and blue, hammerhead, and mako shark.

Folkloric Traditions

Madeira proudly makes the most of its folkloric traditions. No matter when you visit, there's a good chance you'll see folk dances performed at a restaurant or hotel or in one of the towns celebrating a local holiday. Costumed dancers whirl to the music of a small guitar-like instrument called a *machête,* the forerunner of the ukelele. Musicians also shake a colorful pole decorated with tiny folk-dancer dolls that jangle like a tambourine.

Hiking

Walking is without a doubt one of the most popular and enjoyable outdoor activities in Madeira. The island is covered with fabulous footpaths that run among the mountain peaks and alongside the irrigation system formed by canals called *levadas.* This network of irrigation canals crisscrosses the island and often flows through tunnels, bringing valuable water from the mountains to the tiny terraced farms. You can follow the thin cement or dirt paths that run alongside the irrigation canals for hundreds of miles. The footpaths were made so the *levadeiro,* the person tending the *levadas,* could clear any matter that blocked the flow of water through the canals. Although most were built in the 20th century, some date back as far as the 15th century.

Because of the island's many microclimates, you'll encounter powerful jagged mountains; dry, desertlike valleys; waterfalls; dense forest; and luxuriant, green, junglelike hillsides. It seems every view you take in is better than the last. One of the most breathtaking is from Madeira's highest peak, Pico Ruivo. On a clear day you can nearly see from one end of the island to the other. The tourist office sells a book called *Landscapes of Madeira,* listing 45 hikes of varying length and difficulty.

Lodging

Nearly all visitors to Madeira stay in Funchal for at least a day or two, if not for the entire time. Here you'll find a range of accommodations, from majestic old hotels to small, quiet *pensãos* (pensions). However, if you do venture out to explore the island (which you really should do), you may want to stay in a *pousada* (which means resting place, not to be confused with mainland Portugal's government-owned *pousadas*). You'll find these three small, quiet inns in the heart of Madeira's mountains. At the Pousada do Pico do Arieiro, which is at an altitude of 6,107 feet, you'll feel as if you're above the clouds because sometimes you actually are! There are also several low-key hotels and bed-and-breakfasts scattered around the island.

Madeiran hotels cater to package-tour operators, who offer better prices and reserve huge blocks of rooms during peak holiday-travel periods. This may be one place where do-it-yourself travelers are better off going through an agency.

Wine Tasting

Madeira's wines have been enjoyed for more than 500 years, and they graced the tables of Napoléon, the Russian czars, and even George Washington. In fact, the glasses raised to toast the signing of America's Declaration of Independence were filled with this island's delicious elixir.

It is a fortified wine served as an aperitif or with dessert, depending on its sweetness. Unlike other wines, Madeira is heated to produce its distinctive mellow flavor—a process that supposedly developed after thirsty sailors sampled the Madeira that had been shipped through equatorial heat and discovered its improved taste. There are four varieties of Madeira. From driest to sweetest, they are: *sercial, verdelho, boal,* and *malmsey.*

There are many famous brands of Madeira, including Blandy's, Leacock's, and Cossart Godorn, to name a few. Although all of the aforementioned wines are now produced by the Madeira Wine Company, each brand is blended to maintain the individual characteristics unique to each firm. If you'd like to learn the history of these wines, see how they're made, and sample a few, you can visit the São Francisco Wine Lodge in Funchal or the Henriques & Henriques Vinhos (Winery) in Câmara de Lobos.

Exploring Madeira

Geographically, Madeira can be divided into five regions: the capital city of Funchal; its environs; the eastern side of Madeira; the central peaks, gorges, and plateaus of the interior; and the powerful cliffs of the rocky northwest coast. Additionally, there are the neighboring islands of Porto Santo and Ilhas Desertas. We describe each region in its own section below.

Great Itineraries

Most any tour of Madeira would begin in the capital city of Funchal. The town is small, though, and often overrun with tour groups. Nearly 80% of visitors never leave Funchal. But to get a true feel for the island, you should get out and explore it. Discover Madeira's greatest asset: nature. The rocky mountains and green hillsides are astounding and are accessible by bus or taxi. However, a rental car does provide the most freedom. Take a hike or two along a levada in the central part of the island. Spend a night on the north coast. This is how you'll discover Madeira's true tranquility. Consider giving this floating garden at least a few days to work its magic and perfume your psyche with its lush, subtropical carpet of flowers. And don't wait until the last day to leave Funchal and see the rest of the island. You'll only leave disappointed that you didn't give the island more time. Perhaps begin with half-day trips from the city to orient yourself, as full-day tours can involve many hours of sitting on a bus.

Three days would give you enough time to get to know Funchal and its environs, along with some of the interior or the western coast; five days would allow for a less hurried and more complete exploration of the island including the northeast; a full week would permit enough time to both circumnavigate the "big" island and loll about the golden sands of nearby Porto Santo, as the Madeirans do when they want to get away.

Be sure to allow plenty of time when driving around the island. Destinations often appear close on the map but take a long time to reach, due to winding mountain roads and slow-moving trucks. Likewise, bear in mind that the distances between towns given below may sound short, but can actually take hours.

Numbers in the text correspond to numbers in the margin and on the Madeira and Funchal maps.

For many visitors, a three-day jaunt to Madeira is the perfect way to end (or begin) a visit to mainland Portugal. Devote your first day to the flower-bedecked capital city of **Funchal** ①–⑫. On day two, get up early and head for the hills just outside the city. In the morning, visit the nearby **Jardim Botânico,** planted on the grounds of an aristocratic plantation. Also in the vicinity is the mountain village of **Monte** ⑬, home of the unusual snowless sled ride. Next, go west from Funchal toward **Pico de Barcelos,** whose view of the city provides an excellent photo opportunity. Use up a roll of film, then head for the coast and the charming fishing village of **Câmara de Lobos** ⑯, where you can have a late lunch. Afterward, continue to **Cabo Girão** ⑰, with its spectacular views across the island. The terrain changes to forests as you continue along the coast to **Ribeira Brava** ⑱, another lovely seaside village. Turn inland through a rugged canyon and into a vivid green forest, all the while being serenaded by waterfalls cascading down the canyon walls. You'll soon come to the magical, mystical, cloud-shrouded peaks of the ▣ **Serra de Agua** ⑲. Overnight here at the charming pousada. On your last day, wake up very early and take a short hike in the mountains. Keep an eye on the time, though, as it can be a three- to four-hour drive back to Funchal, where you can spend another night or get a late flight back to Lisbon.

Spend your first day and night getting into the island rhythm by exploring ▣ **Funchal** ①–⑫. During the morning of your second day, explore the city's environs and visit the **Jardim Botânico** and **Quinta da Palheiro** (Blandy's Gardens), where you'll swoon over the amazing array of flowers. Next, head toward the village of **Monte** ⑬ for a quick look around. Afterward, using a good road map, follow the road to Poiso. Here, turn left and follow the signs to ▣ **Pico de Ariero** ㉕. You'll be driving above the tree line into what looks like a moonscape leading to the island's third-highest mountain. Overnight in the charming pousada here, and early the next day, head out the front door for an exhilarating hike. If you're up to the challenge, try to reach Pico Ruivo, the highest point on the island. Spend the day hiking and spend one more night here. The next morning, backtrack to Poiso and head north to **Ribeiro Frio** ㉖. You may want to stop here for a quick walk along a levada or maybe just a snack at Victor's Bar, near the village's trout hatchery. Notice the dramatic change in landscape from brown-and-gold tones to rich greens and blues as you drive north over the island. Next head directly for **Santana** ㉗ to see the thatched-roof houses for which the village is famous. From Santana, head west along the coast road toward ▣ **São Vincente** ㉑. Be sure to have a roll or two of film on hand, as the views are staggering. You can either overnight in São Vincente or push on to ▣ **Porto Moniz** ㉒, where you can also spend the night. The same coastal road takes you to this small town in the northwest corner of the island. Watch for the many roadside waterfalls, some of which may cascade right over your car!

From Porto Moniz, head along the coast toward Santa and turn inland toward **Rabaçal** ㉓, long a favorite summertime picnic area of Madeirans and full of waterfalls and quiet pools. Follow the road to **Paúl da Serra** ㉔, the closest thing to flatland on the island, where you'll see sheep grazing across the moors. Next, follow the signs to the pretty, flower-filled town of Canhas and on to the coastal road that leads straight back into Funchal. Spend your fourth night among the bright lights of the capital and the next day see any of the sights you missed, then bid the island a fond *até a prossima* (until the next time) and head for the airport to catch your flight home.

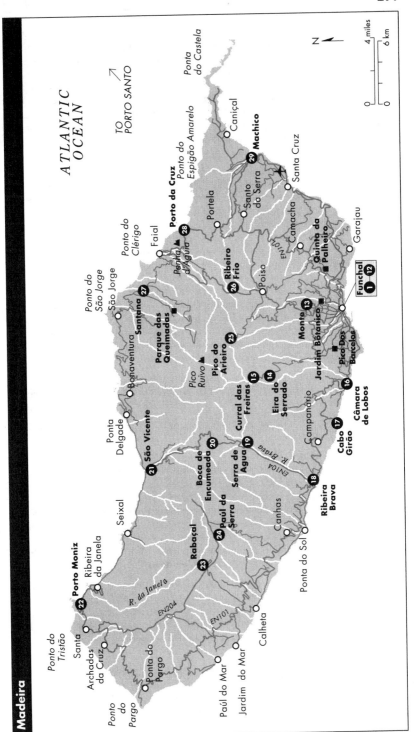

Madeira

ATLANTIC OCEAN

TO PORTO SANTO

N

4 miles
6 km

Ponta do Castela

Caniçal

Machico **29**

Santa Cruz

Porto da Cruz **23**

Ponta do Espigão Amarelo

Portela

Santo da Serra

Camacha

Garajau

Faial

Ponta do Clérigo

Penha d'Águia ▲

Ribeiro Frio **26**

Poiso

Quinta da Palheiro ■

Funchal **1** **12**

Ponta do São Jorge

São Jorge

Santana **27**

Parque das Queimadas ■

Pico do Arieiro **25**

Monte **13**

Jardim Botânico ■

Pico Dos Barcelos ■

Bonaventura

Pico Ruivo

Curral das Freiras

Eira do Serrado **14** **15**

Câmara de Lobos **16**

Ponta Delgada

São Vicente

Boca de Encumeada **20**

Serra de Agua **19**

Campanário

Cabo Girão **17**

Seixal

Paúl da Serra

Canhas

Ribeira Brava **18**

Rabaçal **23** **24**

R. da Janela

EN204

EN101

Ponta do Sol

Porto Moniz **22**

Ribeira da Janela

Santa

Archadas da Cruz **21**

Ponta do Tristão

Ponta do Pargo

Paúl do Mar

Jardim do Mar

Calheta

If you're lucky enough to have a full week's time to explore the island, you may want to consider combining the suggested five-day itineraries described above with an overnight stay on **Porto Santo,** the tiny island 50 kilometers (30 miles) northeast of Madeira. A quiet resort island, it provides sun-and-beach lovers with a long, sandy stretch along its shores. There are also some scenic walks or drives if you get bored (or burned!) by the sun; don't miss the **Casa de Cristóvão Colombo** (Columbus Museum and Home), actually the first governor's house, who also happened to be the explorer's father-in-law.

When to Tour Madeira

This is truly an island blessed by constant soft, warm breezes, sun-kissed skies, and lush, subtropical vegetation that perfumes the air with a fresh, green scent year-round. Everyday seems like spring. The Christmas and New Year's holiday period is the busiest season to visit Madeira, and reservations must be made far in advance. Summer can also be crowded, especially during August, when the Portuguese take vacations.

FUNCHAL

When the first colonists arrived in Madeira in July 1419, the valley they were about to settle was a mass of bright yellow fennel, or *funchal* in Portuguese. Today the bucolic fields are gone, and the city of Funchal is the bustling business-and-political center of the island.

Exploring Funchal

Although a number of historic buildings can be toured, the best way to get to know Funchal is to observe the activities at the waterfront, market, and city squares, all of which are daily haunts of the islanders.

Numbers in the text correspond to numbers in the margin and on the Funchal map.

A Good Walk

A good place to start exploring the city is at **Parque Santa Catarina** ①, which overlooks the harbor and Avenida Arriaga, the main street of Funchal. In spring, the street is ablaze with the bright purple blossoms of the jacaranda trees lining both sides. From Avenida sa Carneiro, descend to the **doca** ② and take in the fresh sea air. Across the street from the yacht harbor you'll pass **Palácio de São Lourenço** ③. One block east of the palace is **parlamento** (parliament), which is housed in the restored 16th-century **Antigua Alfândega** ④.

At the traffic circle head up Rua Profetas to the **Mercado dos Lavradores** ⑤, where pyramids of tropical fruits and stalks of bananas, as well as flowers and fish are sold. If you're interested in learning more about the flowers you saw in the market, this is a good spot to head out of town for a jaunt to the **Jardim Botânico** (Botanical Garden). The gardens are reputed to be some of the most outstanding in all of Iberia.

Return to Rua Dr. Fernão Ornelas, the main commercial street of Funchal. It changes into Rua do Aljube and then to Avenida Arriaga at the 15th-century **Sé** ⑥. From the square in front of the cathedral, go north on Rua João Tavira and turn right at Rua do Bispo to the **Museu de Arte Sacra** ⑦, in the old bishop's house.

When strolling on Avenida Arriaga, be sure to stop in at the **São Francisco Adega du Vinho** ⑧, if not for a tour, at least to try some Madeira. Next, head uphill and north three blocks on Rua São Francisco and Calçada Santa Clara for the **Museu Municipal** ⑨. Afterward, climb

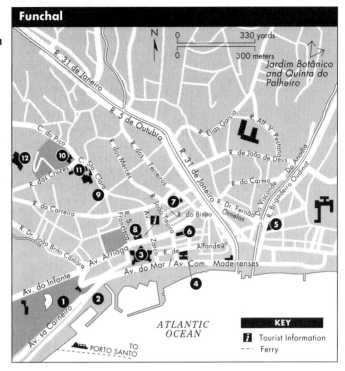

Calçada Santa Clara to **Museu da Quinta das Cruzes** ⑩, a museum housed in a gracious mansion that was once the home of Zarco. The big pink building near the top of Calçada Santa Clara is **Convento de Santa Clara** ⑪, where Zarco is buried. Near the Santa Clara Convent, you can't miss the old walls of the **Fortaleza do Pico** ⑫, which dominates the upper part of the city. From here, you may want to end your day with a trip outside the city to **Quinta do Palheiro,** also known as the Blandy Gardens, where the heady scent of the blooms will relax you for the rest of your evening in Funchal.

Sights to See

❹ **Antigua Alfândega** (Old Customs House). This stately building houses Madeira's parliament. Its original 16th-century Manueline style was amended with baroque renovations following the devastating 18th-century earthquake that almost leveled far away Lisbon. From this building deputies govern the island, which is part of Portugal but enjoys greater autonomy than other mainland provinces. The building is open to visitors. ⊠ *Av. do Mar and Av. das Comunidades Madeirenses.*

⓫ **Convento de Santa Clara** (Santa Clara Convent). Inside, the painted wood walls and ceiling are lined with ceramic tiles, giving the sanctuary an Arabic look. ⊠ *Calçada de Santa Clara,* ☎ *91/742602.* ☉ *Daily 10–noon and 3–5.*

❷ **Doca** (dock). This is where luxury cruise ships moor for day visits to the island and big container ships—mostly from northern Europe—unload. Walk east on Avenida Comunidades Madeirenses (commonly known as Avenida do Mar), the seafront boulevard, and enjoy the ocean view.

⑫ Fortaleza do Pico (Fort of the Peak). The fort was built in the late 1500s to protect the settlement against pirate attacks. One of the worst raids on Funchal was made in the 16th century by the pirating nobleman Bertrand de Montluc, who sacked the churches and stole barrels of Madeira. He resold the wine to his noble friends and unwittingly helped spread the reputation of the island's drink. Today the fort is home to *Pico Radio,* a local radio station; unfortunately it's not open to visitors. ⊠ *Calçada do Pico.*

OFF THE
BEATEN PATH
QUINTA DO PALHEIRO – Also known as the Blandy Gardens, here you can stroll the 30-acre estate owned by the Blandy wine family. Garden enthusiasts come here for the famous collection of camellia trees that bloom between December and April and for the formal gardens with flowering perennials. Unfortunately, visitors are not invited to tour the big, white house in which the family lives. The gardens are 5 kilometers (3 miles) northeast of Funchal. Head out of Funchal on EN101, the road to the airport. At the fork make a left on to EN102 and follow signs toward Camacha. Also, the Bus 36 departs weekday mornings at 9:45 from the stop at the intersection of Avenida do Mar and Avenida das Comunidades Madeirenses (next to the marina, in front of the Palácio de São Lourenço). It returns to Funchal at 1 PM. ⊠ *Follow signs to Camacha.* 🚻 *450$00.* ⊗ *Weekdays 9:30–12:30.*

★ ❺ Mercado dos Lavradores (Workers' Market). Riotous displays of orchids, bird-of-paradise flowers, anthuriums, and other, less exotic blooms are sold in the center patio of this market by women who dress in Madeira's native costume—a full, homespun skirt with yellow, red, and black vertical stripes and an embroidered white blouse. Downstairs the seafood market features rows of fierce-looking espada; those huge, bulging eyes are caused by the change in pressure between their deepwater habitat and the sea level. ⊠ *Av. Zarco and Hospital Velho,* ⊗ *Sat.–Thurs. 7–2, Fri. 7 AM–8 PM.*

OFF THE
BEATEN PATH
JARDIM BOTÂNICO (Botanical Garden) – These impressive gardens, with wonderful views of the town, were opened by the government in 1960 on the grounds of the old plantation Quinta do Bom Sucesso and include well-labeled subtropical plants from Asia, Africa, South America, and Australia; anthurium, bird-of-paradise plants, and a large cactus collection are just some examples. Be sure not to miss the petrified trunk of an ancient heather tree that was found near Curral das Freiras: It's been dated 10 million years old. A house on the grounds serves as a simple natural-history museum. The gardens are 3 kilometers (2½ miles) northeast of Funchal. You can reach them by taking Bus 30, which stops across the street from the market in front of the big building housing the Empresa de Electricidade da Madeira (Madeira Electric Company). You can also walk: Turn uphill on Rua da Rochina from Avenida Arriaga to Caminho do Meio and follow it for at least 45 minutes. ⊠ *Caminho do Meio,* ☎ *91/200200.* 🚻 *300$00.* ⊗ *Daily 10–6.*

❼ Museu de Arte Sacra (Museum of Sacred Art). Here you'll find Flemish paintings, polychrome wood statues, and other religious treasures gathered from the island's churches. Most of the paintings were commissioned by the first merchants of Madeira, many of whom came from Brugge, Belgium. For example, the *Adoration of the Magi* was painted in 1518 for a rich merchant from Machico and paid for, not in gold, but in sugar. You can tell how important sugar was to the island by examining the coat of arms of Funchal, which depicts five loaves of sugar in the shape of a cross. ⊠ *Rua do Bispo 21,* ☎ *91/228900.* 🚻 *250$00.* ⊗ *Tues.–Sat. 10–1:30 and 2:30–6:00, Sun. 10–1.*

A good place to stop for a light lunch or afternoon tea is **O Patio** (✉ Rua da Carreira 43, ☎ 91/224490), which entirely lives up to its name—it's a tiled open-air patio. At the same address you can find **Livraria Inglesa,** Funchal's only English-language bookstore, where magazines, novels, and books about Portugal are sold.

⑨ Museu Municipal (City Museum). Animals found on Madeira and in its seas—including a ferocious-looking collection of stuffed sharks—are on display here. Attached is a small aquarium, where you may watch the graceful movements of an octopus and view a family of sea turtles. ✉ *Rua Mouraria 31,* ☎ *91/229761.* 🎟 *75$00.* ⊙ *Tues.–Fri. 10–6, weekends noon–6.*

⑩ Museu da Quinta das Cruzes. The building itself is impressive, as is this museum's collection of antique furniture. Of special interest are the *palanquins*—lounge chairs that were once used to carry the grand ladies of colonial Madeira around town. Outside the Quinta is a botanical garden filled with stone columns and tombstones. ✉ *Calçada do Pico 1,* ☎ *91/741388.* 🎟 *100$00.* ⊙ *Tues.–Sun. 10–12:30.*

① Parque Santa Catarina. At the top of this park, where flowers bloom year-round, is a pink mansion called **Quinta Vigia,** the residence of the president of Madeira. In the center of the park rests the tiny **Capela de Santa Catarina** (St. Catherine's Chapel), built by Zarco in 1425 and one of the oldest buildings on the island. ✉ *Between Av. do Infante and Av. Sa Carneiro, overlooking the harbor.*

A classic spot to sit back and smell the jacaranda is the **Casa Minas Gerais** (✉ Av. do Infante 2, at the corner of Rua João Brito Câmara, ☎ 91/223381). Pick out your pastry from the central bar, and a waiter will bring it to your table with a pot of tea or coffee.

③ Palácio de São Lourenço (St. Lawrence Palace). Built in the 17th century as Madeira's first fortress, this palace is still used as a military headquarters. You can walk the grounds, but the building is not open to visitors. ✉ *Av. Zarco and Av. Arriaga.*

★ **⑧ São Francisco Adega du Vinho** (wine lodge). Don't miss this opportunity to see a demonstration of how the barrels are made, visit cellars where the wine is stored, and hear tales about Madeira wine. The wineries, however, are outside town and are closed to visitors. One legend has it that when the bloodthirsty duke of Clarence was sentenced to death in 1478 for plotting against his brother, King Edward IV, he was given his choice of execution methods. He decided to be drowned in a "butt of malmsey," a barrel of the drink! There is plenty of time for tasting at the end of the visit. ✉ *Av. Arriaga 28,* ☎ *91/223065.* 🎟 *500$00.* ⊙ *Tours weekdays at 10:30 and 3:30, Sat. at 11; wine shop weekdays 9–7.*

⑥ Sé (cathedral). Renowned for its mozarabic ceiling with intricate geometric designs of inlaid ivory, this cathedral reveals an Arabic influence throughout. Be sure to have a look at the carved choir stalls in the side entrance and in the chancel, which depict the prophets and the apostles, and the antique tilework at the side entrance and in the belfry. ✉ *Av. Arriaga, no phone.* ⊙ *Daily 9–1 and 3–6.*

Dining

$$$$ ✕ **Les Faunes.** Named for the series of Picasso lithographs that adorns
★   the walls, Les Faunes is the crown jewel of Reid's Hotel. The interior is done in a sophisticated blue-gray with tables placed on two tiers so

all diners can enjoy the stunning view of Funchal at night. A pianist plays romantic background music during your meal. The nouvelle menu changes daily, but expect to find such dishes as artichoke custard with sweet red-pepper sauce, avocado mousse with shrimp, salmon crepes with grilled fresh vegetables, carpaccio of sea bass with caviar, duck breast baked with peaches, and hot passion-fruit souffle. ⊠ *Reid's Hotel, Estrada Monumental 139,* ☎ *91/763001. Reservations essential. Jacket and tie. AE, DC, MC, V. No lunch.*

$$$ ✕ **Casa Dos Reis.** A favorite with regular visitors to Madeira, the Casa dos Reis serves high-quality international food in a dining room reminiscent of Grandma's house. Lobster crepes, sole in lemon-mustard sauce and medallions of veal sautéed in Armagnac are all among the accomplished chef's repertoire. For dessert, try the pears poached in wine. ⊠ *Rua Penha de França 6,* ☎ *91/225182. AE, DC, MC, V.*

$$$ ✕ **Casa Madeirense.** Wedged into a restored house next to Reid's Hotel, this restaurant has been lavishly decorated with Portuguese tile, hand-painted murals, and a bar that resembles one of the thatch-roof houses of Santana. The menu leans heavily toward fresh seafood and regional dishes (including traditional espetada), which the chef likes to dress up with tropical fruits and flambé presentations. ⊠ *Estrada Monumental 153,* ☎ *91/766700. AE, DC, MC, V. Closed Mon.*

$$–$$$ ✕ **Casa Velha.** This restored 19th-century house has been converted into an inviting eatery that appeals to the eyes as well as the stomach. Ceiling fans, exuberant floral displays, tiled walls, white-lace curtains, and green tablecloths hint at the care paid to the menu offerings. Start with salmon fillets with shrimp or seafood cream soup. For your main course try the seafood fricassee or *frango assado* (grilled chicken). Dessert might be a pear poached in red wine or mango au gratin. The coffee is good and strong here. ⊠ *Rua Imperatriz Dona Amelia 69,* ☎ *91/225674. AE, MC, V.*

$$–$$$ ✕ **O Celeiro.** The farmhouse decor provides a dignified atmosphere for
★ the traditional Portuguese home cooking served at O Celeiro. A favorite for business lunches, the dining room fills up at night with a mix of tourists and local families celebrating special occasions. Among the most popular items on the menu are the Algarve-style *cataplanas*, seafood stews served in special copper-lidded pots. *Pudim,* a flanlike pudding, makes a soothing dessert. ⊠ *Rua dos Aranhas 22,* ☎ *91/230622. MC, V.*

$$–$$$ ✕ **Quinta Palmeira.** This lovely private estate, built in 1735, has been converted into a restaurant and funky bar. You can dine in the airy, pastel dining room or out on the large terrace. You'll find both traditional island specialties and international dishes served here with creative flair. Try *espetada com bananas e molho de maracujá* (the ubiquitous local fish served with a rich banana and passion-fruit sauce) or *filete de carneiro com molho de menta* (grilled lamb fillet with a fresh mint sauce). For dessert, try the *cassata de abacate com natas frescas* (homemade avacado ice cream topped with whipped cream) or perhaps *tarta de requeijão* (a traditional fresh cheesecake). ⊠ *Av. do Infante 5,* ☎ *91/221814. AE, DC, MC, V.*

$$–$$$ ✕ **Solar do F.** Nothing but the most delectable Portuguese dishes are
★ served here, and the atmosphere is stunning. Choose your dining area: a stone chamber that looks like a wine cellar or an elegant French-provincial dining room. The restaurant, one block uphill from the Madeira Carlton Hotel, is perched at the edge of an overgrown ravine, and in good weather tables are placed outside in the garden. The outdoor patio is a great place to sip an aperitif before your meal. Try the avocados stuffed with shrimp or the espada served Madeiran style, with mushrooms in a spicy tomato sauce. Baked bananas with chocolate sauce

occasionally appear as a dessert temptation. ⊠ *Av. Luís Camões 19,* ☎ *91/220212. AE, DC, MC, V.*

$$ ✕ **A Seta.** It's not fancy, and the parking area is crammed with tour
★ buses, but this hilltop restaurant high above Funchal serves some of the best espetada on the island. You'll share long narrow tables with other diners, while high-energy waiters dodge in and out among folk dancers and fado singers. The meat is cooked over a charcoal fire in the dining-room fireplace, then the skewers are suspended from ingenious wrought-iron hooks at each table. Bolo de caco is the perfect tool to sop up the gravy from the meat. It may be a messy meal, but it's lots of fun. ⊠ *Estrada do Livramento 80,* ☎ *91/743643. AE, DC, MC, V. Closed Wed.*

$$ ✕ **Carochinha.** Amber Victorian lamps, candlelight, and lace tablecloths create the romantic atmosphere of this English-style restaurant beside the municipal gardens in the center of town. Salads are available at lunch, as well as traditional British fare such as roast beef and Yorkshire pudding. Evening diners usually go for specialties with French accents, such as duck in orange sauce and *coq au vin* (chicken in wine sauce). Afternoon tea is served weekdays 3:30–5:30, with "veddy" English scones and jam. ⊠ *Rua São Francisco 2A,* ☎ *91/223695. AE, DC, MC, V. Closed Sun.*

$$ ✕ **Gavina's.** Beyond the Lido swimming complex, at the edge of the sea, is this unadorned seafood house with a long tradition of providing Funchal with the freshest fish and shellfish. The plain and somewhat gloomy concrete exterior may be off-putting, but once inside you can choose your dinner from the seafood tank and then settle down in front of the long picture windows that look out over the waves. Free transportation to and from most hotels is provided on request. ⊠ *Rua do Gorgulho (Praia),* ☎ *91/62918. Reservations not accepted. AE, DC, MC, V.*

$$ ✕ **Golfinho.** Owner Virgilio Gavina, a former championship swimmer and water-skier, has a passion for the sea, and it shows in his old-town restaurant. Resembling the inside of a submarine but with a beautifully polished wood interior, the dining area displays an eclectic collection of old scuba gear and brass ship fittings. Gavina owns a fleet of three fishing boats and goes fishing whenever possible to bring his customers a wide selection of fresh seafood. In addition to the ubiquitous espada, there are usually three or four varieties of fish on the menu, often *dourada* (sea bass), red mullet, and turbot. Meat dishes are also served, including a tasty espetada. Don't miss the house special, *espadarte* (an appetizer of smoked swordfish), garnished with sweet roasted red-pepper salad. ⊠ *Largo do Corpo Santo 21,* ☎ *91/226774. Reservations not accepted. AE, DC, MC, V. Closed Sun.*

$ ✕ **Combatentes.** This large plain dining room behind the municipal gardens is where Funchal's businesspeople go for inexpensive daily lunch specials. You can get big portions of simple Madeiran cooking, such as espada, tuna, chicken, and grilled pork chops, usually served with *milho frito* (fried cornmeal). If you want something lighter, try the *sopa de tomate e cebola com ovo* (tomato and onion soup, garnished with a poached egg). ⊠ *Rua Ivens 1,* ☎ *91/221388. Reservations not accepted. MC, V.*

$ ✕ **Xaramba.** When young Madeirans want a break from seafood, they usually head for this lively pizza place tucked behind the church in the old section of town. Individual-size pies are prepared behind a long bar as hungry customers watch. The ovens stay hot until 3 AM, and the tiny restaurant fills up late at night, so come early or be prepared to wait for a table. ⊠ *Rua Portão São Tiago 11,* ☎ *91/229785. Reservations not accepted. No credit cards. No lunch.*

Lodging

$$$$ ⊞ **Cliff Bay Resort.** Down the coast from Reid's (☞ *below*) on the out-skirts of town, this elegant resort sits on a spectacular promontory, over-looking the Atlantic Ocean and the Bay of Funchal. Cheerful rooms have sweeping views of the bay, the ocean, or the inviting gardens. Mar-ble bathrooms come complete with twin sinks. This resort is part of the Inter-Continental group. ⊠ *Estrada Monumental 147,* ☎ *91/761818,* ℻ *91/762525. 201 rooms. 4 restaurants, 3 bars, pool, 2 saltwater pools, massage, sauna, golf privileges, health club. AE, DC, MC, V.*

$$$$ ⊞ **Reid's.** This is a marvelously old-fashioned and decadently luxuri-
★ ous hotel with corridors that smell of furniture wax, bathwater that comes out tinted blue (from water softeners), and a bellhop who plays a chime to announce dinner each evening. For more than 100 years Reid's has been an exclusive British resort, where aristocrats and busi-ness tycoons get away from it all—in fact, it is often considered one of the best and most gracious hotels in the world. A 15-minute walk from the center of town, the hotel, prominently set on a rocky point, is surrounded by 10 acres of flowering gardens with hibiscus, salvia, and jasmine that scents the air—the feel here is definitely that of a coun-try estate. The large rooms are extremely comfortable, with wain-scoting and pastel bedspreads (and fresh linen sheets daily); all have wide balconies with sea views. Baths include towel warmers and Molton Brown toiletries. ⊠ *Estrada Monumental 139, 9000,* ☎ *91/763001,* ℻ *91/764499. 169 rooms. 5 restaurants, 3 bars, 2 salt-water pools, massage, sauna, golf privileges, 2 tennis courts, waterskiing, billiards. AE, MC, V.*

$$$ ⊞ **Madeira Carlton.** This 18-story beachfront high-rise is 10 minutes on foot from central Funchal. Many of the guests are repeat visitors who have come here every season since the hotel opened in 1971 and are still attracted by the friendly service and a range of sports facili-ties. The Carlton has a bustling lobby furnished in a passé '70s-mod-ern style and large bedrooms with terraces that provide sweeping views of the ocean or mountains. Ask for one of the rooms with large tiled terraces, which are on the first four floors. All rooms have coordinated drapes and bedspreads in airy pastel colors and baths with—what else?—Portuguese tile. ⊠ *Largo António Nobre, 9000,* ☎ *91/231031,* ℻ *91/223377. 377 rooms. 4 restaurants, 3 bars, 2 saltwater pools, minia-ture golf, tennis court, windsurfing, scuba-diving school, dance club. AE, DC, MC, V.*

$$$ ⊞ **Quinta do Bela Vista.** Formerly the mansion of Dr. Roberto Mon-
★ teiro, this elegant hotel provides a hospitality that makes you feel you're visiting a well-to-do family friend. The Quinta, which opened in 1991, is in the hills above Funchal and offers only four guest rooms in the original house; the downstairs has been converted into a so-phisticated restaurant. The other rooms are arranged in two buildings, constructed in the same gracious colonial style as the main house. All guest quarters have French doors that open onto the gardens and are classically decorated with mahogany furniture, four-poster beds, and beautifully framed pastoral prints. ⊠ *Caminho do Avista Navios 4, 9000,* ☎ *91/764144,* ℻ *91/765090. 72 rooms. Restaurant, bar, pool, hot tub, sauna, tennis court, exercise room. AE, DC, MC, V.*

$$–$$$ ⊞ **Casino Park.** Part of the casino complex designed by Oscar Niemeyer, the architect of Brasília (capital of Brazil), this hotel is a rather drab gray-concrete building that sits next to what looks like a nuclear re-actor but is actually the casino. Inside, the public rooms, though be-decked with lots of glass and mirrors, are much more pleasant and are flooded with natural light from floor-to-ceiling windows that overlook the gardens and sea. An orange, blue, and beige color scheme pervades the bright and airy guest rooms. The restaurant is popular for its buffet dinner and folklore performances. ⊠ *Quinta da Vigia, 9000,* ☎ *91/233111,* FAX *91/232076. 381 rooms. 2 restaurants, 2 bars, coffee shop, saltwater pool, hot tub, sauna, tennis court, fitness center, convention center. AE, DC, MC, V.*

$$–$$$ 🏨 **Eden Mar.** This seven-story inn up the street from the Lido swimming complex is one of the newest hotels to capitalize on the package-tour trade. It's a favorite with families, who settle in for long stays and appreciate the kitchenettes in each unit. The lobby is white marble, but the rest of the hotel has a homey floral-print decor and cheerful tiled bathrooms. All rooms have sea views. ⊠ *Rua do Gorgulho 2, 9000,* ☎ *91/762221,* FAX *91/761966. 70 2-room suites and 37 studios, all with kitchenettes. Restaurant, bar, coffee shop, saltwater pool, sauna, exercise room, squash. AE, MC, V.*

$$ 🏨 **Quinta da Penha França.** In an unbeatable area—just above Funchal Harbor—this is the place for those who prefer their resorts casual rather than glitzy. The homey, four-story white Portuguese manor house with green shutters is surrounded by gardens and a sunny pool. Every room is slightly different, and the furnishings border on the antique. A new seaside wing, which is about a five-minute walk from the main house, opened in 1995. Although newer, with large terraces overlooking the sea, the rooms here are motel style and much less charming than the older ones. When making reservations, be sure to specify where you'd like to stay. ⊠ *Rua da Penha França 2, 9000,* ☎ *91/229087,* FAX *91/229261. 73 rooms. 2 restaurants, bar, 2 saltwater pools, billiards. AE, MC, V.*

$ 🏨 **Estrelicia.** Named for Madeira's exotic bird-of-paradise flower, the Estrelicia is the topmost of three high-rise towers built uphill from the hotel strip. Perhaps because of its somewhat inconvenient location, the hotel is an especially good value. This Best Western accommodation has a lively waterfall in its lobby and gold bedspreads and brown-leather chairs in its large, carpeted guest rooms. ⊠ *Caminho Velho da Ajuda, 9000,* ☎ *91/765131,* FAX *91/761044. 145 rooms. Restaurant, 2 bars, saltwater pool, tennis court, dance club. AE, MC, V.*

$ 🏨 **Hotel Madeira.** This hotel on a quiet street in central Funchal has a pleasant marble lobby and tiny rooftop pool. Rooms are basic but carpeted, and the beds are comfortable. Each room has a balcony—some overlook the municipal gardens. ⊠ *Rua Ivens 21, 9009,* ☎ *91/230071. 53 rooms. Restaurant, bar, pool. AE, MC, V.*

Nightlife and the Arts

Evening entertainment in Funchal is sedate and centers around the big hotels, which offer Las Vegas–style floor shows and bands for cheek-to-cheek dancing.

Nightlife

BARS

If you're looking to meet someone or simply to have a quiet chat against a backdrop of live jazz, an "in" spot is the terrace-bar **Salsa Latina** (⊠ Rua Imperatriz D. Amélia 101, ☎ 91/225182). For a more unusual evening's entertainment, try the Japanese-style **Karaokki Bar** (⊠ Hotel do Mar, Estrada Monumental, ☎ 91/761001), where would-be singing stars from the audience have a chance to show their stuff. A fairly recent addition to the nighttime scene is **Formula One** (⊠ Rua do Favila 5, just north of the Carlton Hotel, ☎ 91/65755), a combination pub and disco where you can have an intimate chat in a cozy alcove or dance the night away under flashing strobe lights.

CABARET

Young entertainers perform nightly dinner shows at the **Madeira Carlton Hotel** (✉ Largo António Nobre, ☎ 91/231031) and the **Casino Park Hotel** (✉ Quinta da Vigia, ☎ 91/233111).

CASINO

Gamblers will want to try their luck in the **Casino da Madeira** (✉ Av. do Infante, ☎ 91/231121), which opens nightly at 8 and is housed in a modern building that resembles a roulette wheel.

DISCOS

Funchal's elegant younger set gravitates to **Baccará** (✉ Av. do Infante, ☎ 91/231121), a postmodern disco beneath the casino, or **Vespas** (✉ Av. Sá Carneiro 7, ☎ 91/234800), a warehouse-style disco next to the docks. The over-30 crowd sometimes prefers the huge **O Farol** (✉ Largo António Nobre, ☎ 91/231031) at the Madeira Carlton Hotel, where hits from the '70s and '80s are mixed in with contemporary disco tunes. Another hot spot is **Formula One** (☞ *above*). Note that these joints are usually jumping until 4 AM.

FADO

A steady stream of tourists fills the tables of the Funchal fado club **Marcelino Pão y Vinho** (✉ Travessa da Torre 22–A, ☎ 91/230834). In the center of the old town, the club attracts aficionados as well as the just plain curious, who come to hear Portugal's soulful national music played each night from 9:30 until about 2 AM. Also in the neighborhood is **Arsenios** (✉ Rua de Santa Maria 169, ☎ 91/224007), which is open for lunch and dinner, with both fado (if you need a fado fix during the day) and Brazilian music.

The Arts

THEATER

The **Teatro Municipal Baltazar Diaz** (✉ Av. Arriaga, ☎ 91/220416), in Funchal, offers occasional concerts and plays. The local newspaper carries listings, but the easiest way to find out the schedule is to check posters outside the theater. Tickets can be purchased at the box office.

Shopping

Not many visitors to Madeira escape without purchasing some local products. In addition to wine, island merchants specialize in embroidered table linens, needlepoint, basketry, and tropical flowers.

Two of the oldest and most well-known shops on the island are the **Casa Regional** (✉ Av. Zarco 15, ☎ 91/224943), across from the post office, and **Casa do Turista** (✉ José S. Ribeiro 2, ☎ 91/24907), near the Funchal marina.

Basketry

The wickerwork industry of Madeira is centered in the village of Camacha, about 10 kilometers (6 miles) northeast of Funchal, where there's a large cooperative shop on the main square that sells every imaginable type of basket as well as some wicker furniture. Most of the work is done at home, and on many rural roads it's common to see men carrying large bundles of willow branches to be used for basketry. Baskets and other wicker items are found all over Funchal.

Sousa & Gonçalves (✉ Rua do Castanheiro, ☎ 91/223626) is one of the largest manufacturers and exporters of handmade wicker furniture and basketwork.

Embroidery

Thousands of local women spend their days stitching intricate flow-ered patterns on organdy, Irish linen, cambric, and French silks. Their handiwork decorates tablecloths, place mats, and napkins, all of which are expensive and highly prized by northern Europeans. When buying embroidery, make sure it has a lead seal attached, certifying it was made on the island and not imported. One of the most popular shops is **Patri-cio & Gouveia** (⊠ Rua do Visconde de Anadia 33, ☎ 91/22928), where you can visit the upstairs factory and see the white-uniformed employees stencil patterns and check production; the actual embroi-dery is done by an army of women in their homes. Some of the most beautiful work can be found at the **Casa do Turista** (⊠ José S. Ribeiro 2, ☎ 91/24907), near the Funchal marina. Another shop with exquisitely finished work is **Bordados de Madeira** (⊠ Rua Visconde de Anadia 44, ☎ 91/223241).

Flowers

Tropical flowers, such as orchids and birds of paradise, are available boxed from any florist for shipping home. It's legal to bring flowers into the United States from Madeira as long as they are inspected at the U.S. airport upon arrival. Flower stands in the market and behind the church in Funchal also sell bouquets wrapped to withstand an air-plane ride home. The **Quinta Boa Visita** (⊠ Rua L.F. Albuquerque, ☎ 91/220468) grows orchids and will pack them for shipping Mon-day–Saturday 9–5:30.

Needlepoint

Needlepoint and tapestry making were introduced to Madeira in the early part of this century by a German family. You can visit their fac-tory, **Kiekeben Tapestries** (⊠ Rua da Carreira 194, ☎ 91/22073), and buy pieces at their shop, **Bazar Maria Kiekeben** (⊠ Av. do Infante 2, ☎ 91/27857), which also has a branch in Tampa, Florida.

SIDE TRIPS FROM FUNCHAL

Numbers in the margin correspond to points of interest on the Madeira map.

Monte

★   *6 km (4 mi) northeast of Funchal, from which you can take Bus 20 or 21 or hire a taxi.*

From Funchal, turn up Rua 31 de Janeiro to get to the village of Monte, home of one of Madeira's oddest attractions: the snowless sled ride. Although the toboggans may seem a bit touristy, you really should check them out. You'll recognize the sled drivers because they'll be lined up on the street where the church is and adorned in white pants, a white shirt, and goatskin boots soled with rubber tires. The sleds look like big wicker baskets on wood runners and have flowered cushions for passengers to sit on. Running alongside the sleds are two drivers, who control the vehicle with ropes as it careens over the slippery cobble-stones for the 20-minute ride back to Funchal. The sled's runners are greased with lard, but if the basket starts going too fast, the drivers jump on the back to slow it down; if it stalls, they push and pull until it gets going again. The life span of the sleds is only about two years, since they were first created to carry only supplies from Monte to Fun-chal; later, passenger sleighs were developed that could haul as many as 10 people at a time and required six drivers. Nowadays people gen-erally take the bus or a taxi to Monte, and the sled ride back down is purely a joyride. Don't worry about your safety on the ride down; it's very safe—and exhilarating fun.

Before taking the plunge, stop at the white-stucco church **Nossa Senhora do Monte** (Our Lady of the Mountain). The tiny statue above the altar was found by a shepherdess in the nearby town of Terreira da Luta in the 15th century and has become the patron saint of Madeira. The small church also contains the tomb of Emperor Charles I of Austria, the last Habsburg monarch, who died here from tuberculosis in 1922 after being sent to the beneficial climate of Madeira.

NEED A BREAK?

If you need refreshment before you take part in the traditional sled ride back to Funchal, stop at the **Bar Catanha,** just uphill from the church. While sipping your beer, notice the old photos of sleds and drivers. Not much has changed over the years.

Eira do Serrado

⑭ *16 km (9½ mi) northwest of Funchal. Head west out of Funchal on Rua Dr. João Brito Câmara, which turns into the new highway, and go to the* miradouro *(lookout) at Pico dos Barcelos; this is a fine spot from which to take pictures of the city. From Pico dos Barcelos, continue on EN105 and then EN107 and follow signs to the village of Curral das Freiras, which is north of Eira do Serrado.*

There is a viewpoint at Eira do Serrado that looks over the Grande Curral—the crater of a long-extinct volcano in the center of the island, sometimes referred to as the bellybutton of Madeira. From here, Pico Riuvo and the craggy summits of central Madeira look like a granite city shimmering in the sunlight or shrouded in mist. Island legend says the peaks are the castle fortress of a virgin princess, who can be seen sleeping peacefully in the *rocha da cara* (rock face). It's said that she wanted to live in the sky like the clouds and the moon and was so unhappy at being earthbound that her father—the volcano god—caused an earthquake that pushed the rocky cliffs high into the sky so she could live near the heavens.

Curral das Freiras

⑮ *6 km (4 mi) north of Eira do Serrado.*

If you drive from Eira do Serrado, you'll pass through a series of switchbacks and two tunnels leading down to the village of Curral das Freiras (Nuns' Shelter). The sisters of the Convent of Santa Clara took refuge here from bands of lonely, marauding pirates. Nearly the geographic center of Madeira, the valley sits in the middle of a circle of extinct volcanoes that long ago pushed the island up from the bottom of the sea.

WESTERN MADEIRA

The western part of Madeira includes the greenest and lushest part of the island: In some places you can see a dozen waterfalls spilling into a cool pine forest. On the dramatic north coast, a narrow highway clings to the cliff face and passes under and through several more waterfalls. You can't avoid getting your car wet as you drive through the cascades.

Numbers in the margin correspond to points of interest on the Madeira map.

Câmara de Lobos

🔞 *20 km (12 mi) west of Funchal. Take EN101 west along the coast from Funchal.*

From Funchal, you'll pass many banana plantations en route to Câmara de Lobos. This impoverished fishing village was made famous by Winston Churchill, who painted pictures of the multicolor boats and the fishermen's tiny homes during a visit here in the 1950s. The boats are still here, pulled up onto the rocky beach during the day. You will also see women doing the wash in public fountains and bare-bellied children running riot in the narrow streets. A crumbling promenade, which protrudes from the main plaza, offers views west to Cabo Girão.

If you're interested in sampling some Madeira wine, visit the **Henriques & Henriques Vinhos** (winery), in the center of town. You'll be made to feel right at home during a tour of a state-of-the-art facility that combines high technology with down-home hospitality. And yes, the bottles are for sale. ⊠ *Sitio de Belém, 9300,* ☏ *91/941551.* 🎫 *Free.* ☉ *Weekdays 9–1 and 2–5:30.*

Dining

$$ ✗ **Santo António.** To try Madeira's most authentic and delicious espetada, seek out this unassuming restaurant in the hills above Câmara de Lobos in the hamlet of Estreito near the Funchal–Ribeira Brava Highway. The big dining room is plain, with a linoleum floor and paper tablecloths, but it is cheered by the sunlight flooding through the windows and the sight and smell of rows of espetadas being grilled over an open hearth. The small menu also features the typical bolo do caco bread with garlic butter. For dessert, try the mango fruit shake with a dash of Cointreau. ⊠ *Estreito,* ☏ *91/945439. MC, V.*

$ ✗ **Coral Bar.** Ignore the pleasant tables on the plaza and head upstairs to the simple rooftop terrace, where you can look out over Madeira's most famous fishing village and beyond to the spectacular cliffs of Cabo Girão. The day's catch is unloaded about a block away and served here in big earthenware bowls. Try the *peixe mista* (mixed seafood) in spicy tomato-and-mushroom sauce or the espada with fried bananas. ⊠ *Largo República 2,* ☏ *91/942469. AE, DC, MC, V.*

Cabo Girão

🔞 *12 km (7½ mi) west of Câmara de Lobos, 32 km (20 mi) west of Funchal.*

At 1,900 feet, Cabo Girão is on one of the highest sea cliffs in the world. From here you can see ribbons of terraces carved out of even the steepest slopes and farmers daringly cultivating grapes or garden vegetables. Neither machines nor animals are used on Madeiran farms because the plots are so small and difficult to reach. Not long ago, farmers blew into conch shells as a means of communication with neighbors across the deep ravines.

En Route The road skirts eucalyptus and pine forests as you travel toward the town of Ribeira Brava from Cabo Girão.

Ribeira Brava

🔞 *14 km (9 mi) west of Cabo Girão, 46 km (29 mi) west of Funchal.*

This pleasant village, with a pebbly beach and bustling seafront fruit market, was founded in 1440 at the mouth of the Ribeira Brava (wide river); hence the name. This village is one of the sunniest spots on the island. Visit the ruins of the 17th-century **Forte de São Bento,** built to protect the townspeople from marauding pirates.

Dining

$$ ✕ **Agua Mar.** This restaurant, with sun umbrellas and bright blue tablecloths, has a popular beachfront setting and is frequented on the weekend by large families who drive out from Funchal to lunch here. Just about all the classic Portuguese specialties are served; the house favorites are the fresh fish and *peixe com arroz* (seafood with rice), and if caldeirada de peixe is on the menu, you'll have a hard time deciding. ☎ 91/951148. MC, V.

En Route From Ribeira Brava, turn right on EN104, where the road snakes through a sheer-sided canyon. In every direction you can see high waterfalls tumbling down canyon walls and into a pine forest.

Serra de Agua

⑲ *7 km (4 mi) north of Ribeira Brava.*

This is an ideal starting spot for a good hike in Madeira's interior. For that matter, it's also a great place to end your hiking tour. In fact, you may want to spend the night here at the stone pousada, surrounded by moss-green rocks, ferns, and more waterfalls.

Dining and Lodging

$$ ✕🏠 **Pousada dos Vinháticos.** This tiny stone lodge perched on the edge of a pine forest provides accommodations for nature lovers, most of whom swear this is the most beautiful part of Madeira. The guest rooms are invitingly cheerful in shades of blue, green, and orange. Madeira specialties, such as espetada and *carne vinho e alho,* a braised meat that has been marinated in wine with fennel, laurel, and garlic, are featured in the restaurant. ✉ *Hwy. EN104 between Brava and Encumeada Pass, 9350,* ☎ *91/952344 or 91/765658,* 🖷 *91/952148. 15 rooms. Restaurant. AE, MC, V.*

Boca de Encumeada

⑳ *41 km (25½ mi) northeast of Funchal, 15 km (10 mi) northeast of Ribeira Brava, 6 km (4 mi) north of Serra de Agua.*

The road from Funchal climbs northeast until it reaches Boca de Encumeada (Mouth of the Heights), where there are good views of both the north and south coasts of Madeira. Many hiking trails begin here.

São Vicente

㉑ *15 km (9½ mi) northwest of Encumeada, 56 km (35 mi) northwest of Funchal.*

At the town of São Vicente, the road joins the one-lane north-coast highway that is chiseled out of the cliff face and is said to be one of the most expensive road projects, per mile, ever undertaken. At the beginning of the century, workers in baskets were suspended by rope so they could carve out ledges and tunnels along the planned route. Proceed with caution and make sure to sound your horn when going around blind curves. Large tour buses constantly use this narrow road; if you happen to meet a coach, you may be forced to back up to a turnout.

Dining and Lodging

$–$$ ✕📷 **Estalagem do Mar.** All the rooms in this inn have ocean views. Bedrooms are seagreen and white with floral curtains and bedspreads. The sparkling white-tiled bathrooms are a comfortable place to freshen up after a day of exploring the area. ✉ *Fajã da Areia,* ☎ *91/842615. 83 rooms. Restaurant, indoor and outdoor pools. MC, V.*

En Route As you wind west along the coast, there are a number of waterfalls ahead: At one point the road passes behind a falls, and there's another delightful falls cascading right onto the road, so you have to drive through it. Stop at one of the viewpoints and notice the windbreaks, made of thick mats of purple heather, which protect the terraced vineyards. You'll pass through Seixal, the site of many of the island's most respected vineyards.

Porto Moniz

㉒ *16 km (10 mi) west of Sao Vicente.*

Porto Moniz, with its natural pools formed by ancient lava, is the destination of nearly all visitors taking full day-trips in Madeira. Although it's a popular day-trip destination, there's not much to do here except splash around the pools (no changing facilities), eat, and sunbathe: It's getting here that's fun.

Porto Moniz is the northernmost town on the island, and back in the 19th century, it was a fairly busy whaling station. The lovely old, bougainvillea-draped houses and twisting cobblestone streets make this town absolutely picturesque (as if every other spot on Madeira wasn't). Its serenity also makes it a good place to spend the night.

Dining and Lodging

$ ✕📷 **Residencial Orca.** The tidy, simple rooms here are as pleasant as can be for a low-budget hotel. However, if you want to make your stay here unforgettable, be sure to specify a seaside room. It's these that turn this place into a dream. Large, tiled terraces overlook the lava-walled pool and past that, the blue-green sea. The Orca Restaurant, with equally good views, serves espada prepared in every way imaginable. Try it fried with orange, banana, kiwi, or passion fruit. ✉ *By rocks at end of rd.,* ☎ *91/853359. 16 rooms. Restaurant, saltwater pool. AE, MC, V.*

En Route As you drive along the winding uphill road to the viewpoint at **Santa,** be sure to look back and see the patterns made by the heather windbreaks in the village of Porto Moniz. At the fork, turn left on EN204, a road that crosses through Madeira's widest valley and provides a unique perspective of both sides of the island.

Rabaçal

㉓ *22 km (14 mi) from Porto Moniz.*

If you have time, be sure to sop in Rabaçal, a true water wonderland. Madeirans love to come here in summer to picnic alongside the cascades and quiet pools. It's also a good spot to begin a walk along a levada; this irrigation system was built over 250 years ago without cement and still serves as a water source for much of the island.

Paúl da Serra

㉔ *5 km (2 mi) southeast of Rabaçal.*

Past Rabaçal, the road heads into a moorland called Paúl da Serra (Desert Plain), where sheep and cattle graze and seagulls spiral above the marshes. This is the closest thing to flatland in Madeira, and it looks strangely out of place. The landscape is scrubby and is very reminiscent of the high-altitude plateaus of Norway or Scotland.

En Route   From Paúl da Serra, you can turn right on EN208 and follow signs to the town of **Canhas.** The twisting road passes more terraced farms and houses outshone by their bright flowering gardens and in 20 kilometers (12 miles) joins the southern coastal road EN101, which returns you to Funchal.

CENTRAL PEAKS AND THE VILLAGE OF SANTANA

The barren high peaks of central Madeira offer spectacular views of the island and ample opportunity for hiking. This part of the island includes the much-photographed village of Santana, with its thatch-roof A-frame houses.

Numbers in the margin correspond to points of interest on the Madeira map.

Pico do Ariero

★ ㉕   *12 km (7½ mi) northwest of Poiso, 30 km (19 mi) northeast of Funchal. Head out of Funchal on Rua 31 da Janeiro, which turns into EN103 as it passes the village of Monte. At the pass of Poiso (10 km/6 mi north of Monte), turn left and follow signs to Pico do Arieiro. This stretch travels over a barren plain above the tree line: Watch for errant sheep and goats wandering across the pavement on their way to graze stubbly gorse and bilberry.*

This is a must for any visitor to Madeira. Pico do Arieiro, at 5,963 feet, is Madeira's third-highest mountain; stop in the parking lot of the pousada and make the short climb to the lookout, where you can scan the rocky central peaks. There are views of the clouds below and to the southeast is the Curral das Freiras crater. Look in the other direction and try to spot the huge **Penha d'Aguia** (Eagle Rock), which stretches up like a monolith on the north coast. The trail from the lookout that crosses the narrow ridge leads to **Pico Ruivo** (6,104 feet), the highest point on the island. Winter days can be chilly at these heights, so there is usually an inviting fire blazing in the bar of the strategically placed pousada here.

Lodging

$$ 🏠 **Pousada do Arieiro.** Designed for visitors who would rather hike than sunbathe, this inn is high above the tree line in Madeira's rocky peaks. The exterior of the white-stucco building is bleak, but inside you'll find cozy rooms with chintz curtains and bedspreads. The dining room has spectacular views of the mountains and serves traditional island cooking, including delicious soups, good for warming when you come in from the bracing mountain air. ⊠ *Mailing address: Apart. 478, 9006 Funchal,* ☎ *91/230131 or 91/229267,* 📠 *91/228611. 22 rooms. Restaurant. AE, MC, V.*

Ribeiro Frio

★ ㉖   *11 km (7 mi) north of Poiso.*

The landscape grows more lush on the northern side of the island, and the road is full of waterfalls that splash the passing cars. At Ribeiro Frio, there's a trout hatchery, the starting point for an interesting 40-

minute levada walk to the lookout of Balcões. This is one of the easiest and prettiest walks on the island, ideal for those who are not even slightly passionate hikers. At Balcões the jagged peaks of central Madeira tower behind you, and there are views of villages along the north coast.

Dining

$$ ✕ **Victor's Bar.** If you need some refreshment after your hike, stop here for a beer or afternoon tea and the best *bolo de mel* (spice cake) on the island. More substantial meals, including trout prepared many ways, are served here too. Inside the rustic wood-and-glass building is a welcoming fireplace. ⊠ *Rua do Ribeirinho,* ☏ *91/782898. No credit cards.*

En Route   Continue north from Ribeiro Frio on EN103 and follow signs to **Faial**; expect the road to descend in a series of switchbacks into a deep ravine. The tiny A-frame huts that dot the terraces along the steep sides are used as barns for cows, which are never allowed to graze freely on Madeira. The prohibition was made both because there is not enough land for the animals to graze and because the animals could easily fall off a ledge.

Santana

㉗ *6 km (4 mi) northwest of Ribeiro Frio, 39 km (24 mi) north of Funchal.*

Santana is a village famous for its A-frame, thatch-roof cottages (*palheiros*) painted in bright colors. Most of these are upscale versions of traditional Madeiran homes. Sadly, this style has been replaced elsewhere on the island by nondescript concrete-block houses.

OFF THE   **PARQUE DAS QUEIMADAS –** From Santana, you can follow a road that
BEATEN PATH   leads southwest to this spot, where you can stop to picnic or pick up a hiking trail that approaches Pico Ruivo.

Dining

$$–$$$ ✕ **Quinta do Ferão.** Set amid a newly planted vineyard with sweeping views of the sea, this restaurant is a premier draw on the north coast—Funchal residents are helicoptered here for Sunday lunches. A 40-room hotel is planned for 1998. Food is a cut above the typical island fare, featuring such dishes as steak in pastry with Roquefort sauce, lamb chops in thyme and honey, and prawns on a spit with avocado sauce. Local north-coast wines are served. ⊠ *Achado do Gramacho,* ☏ *91/572132. AE, DC, MC, V.*

Porto da Cruz

㉘ *20 km (12 mi) from Santana.*

The road from Santana to Porto da Cruz skirts the back of the landmark **Penha D'Aguia Rock,** whose sheer cliffs tower over the village. Positioned in a fertile valley filled with tiny farms and gardens, the town is as pretty as any on Madeira. It's also where you can find the island's last working sugar mill, used during March and April to make *aguardente* (fire water, a sugarcane brandy).

En Route   Start your climb again on EN101 and continue to **Portela,** where the view looks south over the gentler valley of Machico. From here it's an easy drive through banana plantations and sugarcane fields and into the village of Machico.

Machico

 15 km (9 mi) southeast of Porto da Cruz, 26 km (16 mi) northeast of Funchal.

Local folklore says the bay of Machico was discovered in 1346 by two English lovers, Robert Machin and Anne d'Arfet, who set sail from Bristol for France to escape Anne's disapproving parents. The couple's boat was thrown off course by a storm and was wrecked in this bay. Anne died a few days after becoming ill, and Robert then died of a broken heart. But their crew, according to legend, escaped on a raft, and news of the island made its way back to the court of the Portuguese king, who sent Zarco to investigate. When the explorer arrived, he found a wood cross with the lovers' sad story, and he named the place in memory of Machin.

Explore the village church and wander through the fishermen's quarter. From the seafront you can capture clear views of the **Ponta São Lourenço Peninsula,** which sticks out into the ocean to the east.

OFF THE   **CANIÇAL –** Multicolored boats bob in water that has been witness to this
BEATEN PATH   village's long history as a whaling station, which it remained until the not-so-distant year of 1981. In 1985, 5 acres of the sea surrounding the town was designated a national park for marine life. Caniçal is 10 kilometers (6 miles) northeast of Machico.

PORTO SANTO

Beachcombers will love Porto Santo, some 50 kilometers (30 miles) northeast of Madeira. This tiny island is very dry, and its wide, sandy beach runs along the entire south coast—perfect for long walks in the surf. The rest of the island has little to offer and remains refreshingly underdeveloped. It once supported many farms, but a severe drought in the 1970s killed the vineyards and drove most farmers out of business. Fields now lie barren, and residents have either moved away or switched to tourism-related jobs. However, if you drive between the airport and Vila Baleira, notice flourishing trees and shrubs. They are part of a government conservation plan to prevent erosion.

Exploring Porto Santo

Porto Santo's main village, **Vila Baleira,** is a sleepy town with cobblestone streets and whitewashed buildings. A flower-filled park extends from the center to a fishing pier that is flanked on both sides by endless beach. The park contains an idealized statue of Christopher Columbus, the most important personage in Porto Santo's history. Columbus married Isabela Moniz, daughter of Bartolomeu Perestrelo, the first governor of the island. This was before Columbus was famous, when he sailed for Portuguese merchants and simply dreamed of a shortcut to the Indies. The young couple never lived on the island, but they spent some time in Funchal.

The **Casa de Cristóvão Colombo** (Columbus Museum and Home) is in the old governor's house. Inside, lithographs illustrate the life of Columbus, and there are copies of 15 portraits of the discoverer, which prove nobody really knows what he looked like. Ask to see the restored kitchen and bedroom in the upper part of the house. ⊠ *Rua Cristóvão Colombo 12,* ☏ *91/938405,* 🎟 *Free.* ☉ *Weekdays 10–noon and 2–5:30, Sat. 10–noon.*

One of your first stops on the island should be at the scenic **Portela** viewpoint, which overlooks the harbor, the town, and the long ribbon of beach. Move on to **Serra de Foca,** where a dirt track passes old salt flats before winding down to a rocky beach popular with divers. As you continue around the island, you may have to dodge goats grazing along the edges of the road.

Pico do Castelo is a favorite picnic spot, named in memory of the castle that once stood here to protect the town from pirates. All that remains, however, is one of the castle's four cannons. The young pine trees covering the slopes were planted by the government to help retain moisture; they're a special variety that will never grow taller than 9 feet so the view will not be obstructed. From here it's an easy walk to **Pico do Facho** (1,552 feet), the highest point on the island.

Fonte da Areia (Spring in the Sand) is a spring that flows out of a sandstone cliff. Women came here to do their washing before water began to be piped into town. As you head to the southern tip of the island, you'll pass several windmills in disrepair that were once used for grinding wheat.

Pico dos Flores—another lookout—is worth a trip down the bumpy dirt roads. From here you can enjoy long-distance views of Madeira and the rocky, uninhabited islet south of Porto Santo called Ilhéu de Baixo. Back on the road that runs along the beach, encroaching development becomes apparent: You'll see a handful of high-rise apartment blocks. Since there is no longer any agriculture, islanders seem anxious to sell their property. But it could be that Porto Santo's remote location will help protect it from uncontrolled growth.

Dining and Lodging

$$ ✕ **Gazela.** Not far from the Campo de Cima Airport, this large, modern dinner house is where islanders go for Sunday lunch or to celebrate special occasions. The menu is basic Madeiran—espada, espetada, and a delicious seafood soup. ⊠ *Campo de Cima,* ☎ *91/984425. MC, V.*

$ ✕ **Arsénios.** Red-and-white-check tablecloths are your clue that this is the place for pizza, spaghetti, and lasagna. Portuguese specialties are also served in the rustic, comfortable dining room. ⊠ *Av. Dr. Manuel Pestana Jr.,* ☎ *91/982348. AE, MC, V.*

$ ✕ **Baiana.** A covered patio serves as a combination sidewalk café and town meeting place, as just about everybody in town seems to wander by in the morning for a cup of coffee. Baiana also serves sandwiches, *feijoada* (bean stew), and *carne com vinho e alho* (pork marinated in wine and garlic). ⊠ *Rua Dr. Nuno S. Teixeira,* ☎ *91/984649. No credit cards. No dinner.*

$ ✕ **Pôr do Sol.** At the far end of the beach, near Ponta da Calheta, an island housewife makes sandwiches and fries burgers and fresh seafood in a primitive kitchen. The dining room is gleaming white and spotless, and there's a wide terrace at the beach's edge. This place has tables on the terrace, which make you feel like you're picnicking on the beach. ⊠ *Ponta da Calheta,* ☎ *91/984380. Reservations not accepted. No credit cards.*

$ ✕ **Teodorico.** In this farmhouse restaurant, authentic espetada is the one and only dish available. It can be accompanied by carafes of the dry red wine that's produced on the island and served here, along with *pao de caco,* a local bread. In warm weather you can eat outdoors at tables and chairs made from tree stumps; indoors you'll sit in a tiny tiled dining room with four tables and a wood-burning oven at one end. ⊠ *Sera de Fora,* ☎ *91/982257. No credit cards. No lunch.*

$$–$$$ ⚇ **Hotel Porto Santo.** On the beach about a 15-minute walk from town,
★ this hotel—a member of the Forte chain—is a beachcomber's dream come true. Aside from the seemingly endless stretches of golden sand, there's a country-club atmosphere, numerous sports activities, and a library-lounge that resembles a comfortable living room. Rooms overlook the countryside instead of the beach and are heavily booked throughout August, but during spring and fall you may have the place to yourself. ⊠ *Campo de Baixo, Porto Santo, 9400,* ☎ *91/982381,* ℻ *91/982611. 94 rooms. Restaurant, bar, saltwater pool, miniature golf, tennis court, Ping-Pong, bicycles. AE, MC, V.*

$$ ⚇ **Torre Praia Suite Hotel.** Right on the beach, a five-minute walk from the center of town, this simple two-story hotel was built around an old watch tower that now houses the restaurant. All rooms come with kitchenettes, and the hotel has all the amenities you really need for a relaxing holiday in the sun. ⊠ *Rua Goulart Medeires, 9400,* ☎ *91/985292,* ℻ *91/982487. 65 suites. Restaurant, bar, coffee shop, pool, dance club.*

$ ⚇ **Praia Dourada.** This comfortable white-stucco hotel in the middle of the village is a five-minute walk from the beach and is popular with budget-minded German and Portuguese travelers. Inside, the corridors are dark, but the carpeted rooms are bright, and there's a small pool with a sundeck. ⊠ *Rua D. Estevão D'Alencastre, 9400,* ☎ *91/982315,* ℻ *91/982468. 182 rooms. Saltwater pool. AE, MC, V.*

Porto Santo A to Z

Arriving and Departing

BY BOAT

The *Independência,* a sleek 244-passenger catamaran, plies between Funchal and Porto Santo twice daily June through September and once a day (except Tues.) October through May, weather permitting. The boat sails from Funchal Harbor at 8 AM for the 1½-hour voyage and heads back from Porto Santo at 5, making this a popular day trip. A round-trip ticket costs 8,700$00. Tickets may be purchased in advance at the Funchal marina (☎ 91/230195), which is open weekdays 9–12:30 and 2–5:30 and Saturday 9–12:30, or at the dock before the boat departs. For sailings on summer weekends, it's a good idea to buy tickets in advance.

BY PLANE

The interisland flight to Porto Santo from Madeira provides spectacular low-altitude views of Machico and São Lorenço peninsula. **TAP Air Portugal** runs a shuttle, using an 18-sheet turboprop for a 15-minute flight between the islands four times daily, six times during the summer months. Tickets cost 13,600$00. Reservations should be made in advance, especially for July and August.

Getting Around

Porto Santo roads are easy to handle by car, but the 10-kilometer-long (6-mile-long) island is so small that most visitors get around on foot or by taxi.

Contacts and Resources

CAMPING

On Madeira there are really no organized campgrounds, but on Porto Santo there is Parque Porto, a stretch of beach set up for campers, just waiting for you to unroll your sleeping bag and pitch a tent. Contact the Porto Santo Tourist Office (☎ 91/983111).

CAR RENTAL
Call **Moinho** (⌧ Hotel Praia Dourada, Rua Estevádo D'Alencastre, ☎ 91/982403 or 91/982780).

OUTDOOR ACTIVITIES AND SPORTS
Fishing: For organized fishing trips from Porto Santo, contact the **Dive Center** (⌧ Rua J.G. Zarco 5, ☎ 91/982162) or **Anguilla** (☎ 91/983573).

Horseback Riding: For horse rentals, call **Quinta dos Profetas** (☎ 91/983165).

Scuba Diving: For underwater excursions and boat trips in Porto Santo contact **The Dive Center** (⌧ Rua J. G. Zarco 5, ☎ 91/982162).

Visitor Information
On the island of Porto Santo, a tiny tourist office (⌧ Av. Henrique Vieira de Castro, Vila Baleira, ☎ 91/982361) with a helpful staff attends to visitors weekdays 9–5:30 and weekends and holidays 10–12:30.

MADEIRA A TO Z

For information on transportation to and resources in Porto Santo, *see* Porto Santo A to Z, *above.*

Arriving and Departing
By Plane
There is no longer any regularly scheduled passenger-boat service to Madeira, so visitors must arrive by plane at the **Aeroporto Santa Catarina** (St. Catharine's Airport; ☎ 91/524941 or 91/524972), east of Funchal in Santa Cruz and about 35 minutes away by car. The island is served by **TAP Air Portugal** (⌧ Av. Comunidades Madeirenses 8–10, Funchal, ☎ 91/239290; ⌧ Aeroporto Santa Catarina, ☎ 91/524362; in the U.S., 800/221–7370), which makes six flights daily from Lisbon (1¾ hours) and at least four trips daily from London (4 hours). **British Airways** (⌧ Rua São Francisco 8, ☎ 91/524864 or 91/524362; in the U.S., 800/247–9297) has nonstop service between London and Funchal several times a week. **TAP Air Portugal** and a Canadian charter operator, **Lawson Tours** (⌧ 2 Carlton St., Suite 620, Toronto, Ontario M5B 1J2, ☎ 416/977–3000; in Canada, 800/268–9126; ℻ 416/977–7782) offer several flights a week along the Toronto–Montréal–Lisbon–Funchal route. There are no direct flights from the United States to Madeira. Numerous charter flights link Funchal with most northern European capitals.

Getting Around
By Bus
Madeira has two extensive bus systems frequently used by visitors and islanders. Yellow buses serve Funchal and its surrounding neighborhoods: Buses 1 and 3 run west from the city and make stops along Estrada Monumental, where most of the hotels are; beige-and-red buses fan out to other points on the island. Both systems leave from an outdoor terminal at the end of Avenida do Mar, near the old town. Generally several buses a day travel to each village on the island, but schedules change constantly, so inquire at your hotel or the tourist office for departure times.

By Car
The best way to explore Madeira is by car. Although it's a small island, the terrain is steep, so bear in mind that driving can be torturously slow. For example, the drive from Funchal to Porto Moniz on

the western end is only 156 kilometers (93 miles) round-trip but takes all day, as the roads twist and turn up the mountains and along terraced ravines.

When driving in Madeira, beware: There are few road signs, and it's easy to get lost. However, the island is so small, you won't be lost for long. Get a good road map, and if you still get lost, think of it as a detour and enjoy the scenery.

Contacts and Resources

Car Rental
Most major agencies have rental offices at the Madeira Airport and in Funchal, including **Hertz** (⊠ R. Ivens 12, ☎ 91/226026), **Avis** (⊠ Largo António Nobre 164, ☎ 91/763495 or 91/764546), **Atlas** (⊠ Rua da Alegria 23, ☎ 91/223100), **Budget** (⊠ Hotel Duas Torres, Estrada Monumental, ☎ 91/765619), and **Europcar** (⊠ Aeroporto Santa Catarina, ☎ 91/524633).

Consulates
United States (⊠ Av. Luís Camões, Block D, Apt. B, Funchal, ☎ 91/743808), **Great Britain** (⊠ Av. Zarco 2, 4th floor, Funchal, ☎ 91/221221).

Emergencies
In the event of an emergency in Madeira you can dial the nationwide number **115.** In Funchal call the **police** (☎ 91/222022), **fire department** (☎ 91/222122), or for **medical emergencies,** the **Red Cross** (☎ 91/220008).

Outdoor Activites and Sports

FISHING
Fishing excursions can be arranged at the Funchal Harbor through **Turipesca** (☎ 91/231063 or 91/742468).

GOLF
Golf enthusiasts have managed to carve two courses from Madeira's hillsides. The oldest club is the 27-hole **Campo de Golfe da Madeira** (⊠ Hwy. EN102, ☎ 91/552345 or 91/552356), near the airport in Santo da Serra. Somewhat closer to Funchal is the 18-hole **Palheiro Golf** (⊠ São Gonçalo, ☎ 91/792116), at the edge of Blandy Gardens and operated by a consortium of five-star hotels.

HIKING
Viva Travel (☎ 91/922661 or 91/221751) offers a different hiking tour through the mountains every day. Levels of difficulty vary, and each excursion includes something extra, such as a peek at local weavers or a wine tasting in a hidden cave.

HORSEBACK RIDING
Horse rentals are available through the **Riding Club of Choupana** (reservations at Hotel Estrelicia, ☎ 91/792582).

SCUBA DIVING
Madeira is too far north for colorful tropical fish, but divers enjoy the clear, still seas of summer and report lots of interesting marine life and coral formations. A diving center at the **Carlton Hotel** (⊠ Largo António Nobre, ☎ 91/934611) rents scuba gear, as does **Scorpio Divers** (⊠ Rua Gorgulho, ☎ 91/762023) at the Lido Swimming Complex.

SWIMMING
There's no doubt that Madeirans head for Porto Santo. Although Madeira has no sandy beaches, sea swimming is possible from access

points at three hotels: the **Carlton**, the **Savoy**, and **Reid's**. Also available are two public swimming pools and sea access, slightly west of Funchal, at the **Lido Swimming Complex** (⊠ Rua Gorgulho, ☎ 170$00; ⊙ Summer, daily 9–7, winter, daily 9–6) and **Quinta Magnolia** (⊠ Rua Dr. Pita, ☎ 91/764598; ☎ 135$00; ⊙ Daily 9–4), which has beautiful views of Funchal. The onetime British Country Club, now a public park, includes acres of gardens and lawns, as well as a jogging-and-fitness course and tennis courts available by reservation.

In **Porto Moniz** cement pools have been built around the rocky coastline for delightful summer wading. When Madeirans want a sandy beach, they head for nearby **Porto Santo**.

Guided Tours

BOAT TOURS
Boat excursions near Funchal's coast take place year-round. Choose from a 2½-hour sortie to Cabo Girão and back, costing 3,000$00 per person, or a full day (7½-hour) sail to the Ilhas Desertas, including lunch on board and plenty of time for swimming and tanning, for 7,500$$00 per person. Tickets are available in advance; ask at the tourist office for schedules or contact **Costa do Sol, Lda.** (⊠ Marina do Funchal, ☎ 91/238538 or 91/224390, FAX 91/235735).

ISLAND TOURS
Travel agencies specializing in island tours abound in Funchal. Visits usually include multilingual motor-coach tours to Cabo Girâdo, the inland peaks, Porto Moniz, the village of Santana, as well as meals or snacks in typical island restaurants. Some of the best operators are **InterVisa** (⊠ Av. Arriaga 30, 3rd floor, ☎ 91/22-83-44 or 91/25642), **Madeira Express** (⊠ Av. Arriaga 38–40A, ☎ 91/225250 or 91/221817), and **Orion** (⊠ Rua de João Gago, 2–A, ☎ 91/228576).

WINE-TASTING TOURS
Blandy's (reservations at: ⊠ Adegas de São Francisco, Av. Arriaga 28, ☎ 91/220121) runs full-day excursions for wine lovers on Friday, visiting vineyards on the north side of the island, as well as the village of Santana. Visit the Madeira Wine Lodge for extensive tastings.

Late-Night Pharmacies
Pharmacies are open at night and on Sunday according to a rotating schedule. Dial **166** for information.

Telephones

INFORMATION
The general information number on Madeira is **118.**

INTERNATIONAL CALLS
Dial the international access code, 00, then the country code, and the number. For operator-assisted calls dial 098. To reach U.S. operators, dial the following access numbers: AT&T ☎ 05017288; Sprint ☎ 050171877; MCI ☎ 050171234.

Visitor Information
The busy tourist office of **Madeira** (⊠ Av. Arriaga 18, Funchal, ☎ 91/229057 or 91/225658) is open weekdays 9–8 and weekends 9–6. It dispenses maps, brochures, and up-to-date information on the constantly changing bus schedules. There are also tourist offices in **Machico** (⊠ Forte do Amparo, Praça José António Almada, ☎ 91/962289), open weekdays 9–12:30 and 2–5 and weekends and holidays 10–12:30, and **Ribeira Brava** (⊠ Forts de São Bento, Vila de Ribeira Brava, ☎ 91/951675), same hours as Machico.

PORTUGUESE VOCABULARY

If you have reading knowledge of Spanish and/or French, you will find Portuguese easy to read. Portuguese pronunciation, however, can be somewhat tricky. Despite obvious similarities in Spanish and Portuguese spelling and syntax, the Portuguese sounds are a far cry—almost literally so—from their ostensible Spanish equivalents. Some of the main peculiarities of Portuguese phonetics are the following.

Nasalized vowels: If you have some idea of French pronunciation, these shouldn't give you too much trouble. The closest approach is that of the French *accent du Midi*, as spoken by people in Marseille and Provence, or perhaps an American Midwest twang will help. Try pronouncing *"an," "am," "en," "em," "in," "om," "un,"* etc., with a sustained *"ng"* sound (e.g. *"bom"-"bong,"* etc.).

Another aspect of Portuguese phonetics is the vowels and diphthongs written with the tilde: *ã, ão, ães*. The Portuguese word for *"wool," "lã,"* sounds roughly like the French word *"lin,"* with the *"-in"* resembling the *"an"* in the English word *"any,"* but nasalized. The suffix *"-tion"* on such English words as "information" becomes in Portuguese spelling *"ção,"* pronounced *"-sa-on,"* with the *"-on"* nasalized: *"Informação,"* for example. These words form their plurals by changing the suffix to *ções*, which sounds like *"-son-ech"* (the *"ch"* here resembling a cross between the English *"sh"* and the German *"ch"*: hence *"informações"*).

The cedilla occurring under the *"c"* serves exactly the same purpose as in French: It transforms the *"c"* into an *"ss"* sound in front of the three so-called "hard" vowels (*"a," "o,"* and *"u"*): e.g., *graça, Açores, açúcar*. The letter "c" occurring without a cedilla in front of these three vowels automatically has the sound of "k": *pico, mercado, curto*. The letter "c" followed by "e" or "i" is always "ss," and hence needs no cedilla: *nacional, Graciosa, Terceira*.

The letter "j" sounds like the "s" in the English word "pleasure." So does "g" except when the latter is followed by one of the "hard" vowels: hence, *generoso, gigantesco, Jerónimo, azulejos, Jorge*, etc.

The spelling *"nh"* is rendered like the *"ny"* in *"canyon"*: cf. *"senhora."*

The spelling *"lh"* is somewhere in between the *"l"* and the *"y"* sounds in *"million"*: cf. *"Batalha."*

In the matter of syllabic stress, Portuguese obeys the two basic Spanish principles: (1) in words ending in a vowel, or in "n" or "s," the tonic accent falls on the next-to-the-last syllable: *fado, mercado, azulejos*; (2) in words ending in consonants other than "n" or "s," the stress falls on the last syllable: *favor, nacional*. Words in which the syllabic stress does not conform to the two above rules must be written with an acute accent to indicate the proper pronunciation: *sábado, república, politécnico*.

Numbers

1	um, uma
2	dois, duas
3	três
4	quatro
5	cinco
6	seis
7	sete
8	oito

9	nove
10	dez
11	onze
12	doze
13	treze
14	catorze
15	quinze
16	dezaseis
17	dezasete
18	dezoito
19	dezanove
20	vinte
21	vinte e um
22	vinte e dois
30	trinta
40	quarenta
50	cinquenta
60	sessenta
70	setenta
80	oitenta
90	noventa
100	cem
110	cento e dez
200	duzentos
1,000	mil
1,500	mil e quinhentos

Days of the Week

Monday	Segunda-feira
Tuesday	Terça-feira
Wednesday	Quarta-feira
Thursday	Quinta-feira
Friday	Sexta-feira
Saturday	Sábado
Sunday	Domingo

Months

January	Janeiro
February	Fevereiro
March	Março
April	Abril
May	Maio
June	Junho
July	Julho
August	Agosto
September	Setembro
October	Outubro
November	Novembro
December	Dezembro

Useful Phrases

Do you speak English?	Fala Inglês?
Yes	Sim

No	Não
Please	Por favor
Thank you	Obrigado
Thank you very much	Muito obrigado
Excuse me, sorry	Com licença, desculpe
I'm sorry	Desculpe-me
Good morning or good day	Bom dia
Good afternoon	Boa tarde
Good evening or good night	Boa noite
Goodbye	Adeus
How are you?	Como está?
How do you say in Portuguese?	Como se diz em Português?
Tourist Office	Turismo
Fine	Optimo
Very good	Muito bem (muito bom)
It's all right	Está bem
Good luck	Felicidades (boa sorte)
Hello	Olá
Come back soon	Até breve
Where is the hotel?	Onde é o hotel?
How much does this cost?	Quanto custa?
How do you feel?	Como se sente?
How goes it?	Que tal?
Pleased to meet you	Muito prazer em o (a) conhecer
The pleasure is mine	O prazer é meu
I have the pleasure of introducing Mr., Miss, Mrs., or Ms. . . .	Tenho o prazer de lhe apresentar o senhor, a senhora . . .
I like it very much	Gosto muito
I don't like it	Não gosto
Don't mention it	De nada
Pardon me	Desculpe-me (Perdão)
Are you ready?	Está pronto?
I am ready	Estou pronto
Welcome	Seja benvindo
I am very sorry	Desculpe (Lastimo muito)
What time is it?	Que horas são?
I am glad to see you	Muito prazer em o (a) ver
I don't understand	Não entendo
Please speak slowly	Fale lentamente por favor
I understand (or) It is clear	Compreendo (or) Está claro
Whenever you please	Quando quizer
Please wait	Faça favor de esperar
Toilet	Casa de banho
I will be a little late	Chegarei um pouco atrasado

I don't know	Não sei
Is this seat free?	Está vago este lugar?
Would you please direct me to . . . ?	Por favor indique-me . . . ?
Where is the station, museum . . . ?	Onde é a estação, museu . . . ?
I am American, British	Eu sou Americano, Inglês
It's very kind of you	É muito amavel
Please sit down	Por favor sente-se

Sundries

cigar, cigarette	charuto, cigarro
matches	fosforos
dictionary	dicionário
key	chave
razor blades	laminas de barbear
shaving cream	creme de barbear
soap	sobonete
map	mapa
tampons	tampões
sanitary pads	pensos higiénicos
newspaper	jornal
magazine	revista
telephone	telefone
envelopes	envelopes
writing paper	papel de carta
airmail writing paper	papel de carta de avião
postcard	postal
stamps	selos

Merchants

bakery	padaria
bookshop	livraria
butcher's	talho
delicatessen	charutaria
dry cleaner's	limpeza a seco
grocery	mercearia
hairdresser, barber	cabeleireiro, barbeiro
laundry	lavandaria
shoemaker	sapateiro
supermarket	supermercado

Emergencies/Medical

ill, sick	doente
I am ill	Estou doente
I have a fever	Tenho febre
My wife/husband/child is ill	Minha mulher/marido/criança está doente
doctor	doutor/médico
nurse	enfermeira/o

prescription	receita
pharmacist/ chemist	farmacia
Please fetch/call a doctor	Por favor, chame o doutor/medico
accident	acidente
road accident	acidente na estrada
Where is the nearest hospital?	Onde é o hospital mais proximo?
Where is the American/British Hospital?	Onde é o hospital Americano/Britanico?
dentist	dentista
X-ray	Raios-X
aspirin	aspirina
painkiller	analgésico
bandage	ligadura
ointment for bites/stings	pomada para picadas
cough mixture	xarope para a tosse
laxative	laxativo
thermometer	termómetro

On the Move

plane	avião
train	comboio
boat	barco
taxi	taxi
car	carro/automovel
bus	autocarro
seat	assento/lugar
reservation	reserva
smoking/ no-smoking compartment	compartimento para fumadores/não fumadores
rail station	estação caminho de ferro
subway station	estação do Metropolitano
airport	aeroporto
harbor	estação mártima
town terminal	estação/terminal
shuttle bus/train	autocarro/comboio com ligação constante
sleeper	cama
couchette	beliche
porter	bagageiro
baggage/luggage	bagagem
baggage trolley	carrinho de bagagem
single ticket	bilhete de ida
return ticket	bilhete de ida e volta
first class	primeira classe
second class	segunda classe
When does the train leave?	A que horas sai o comboio?
What time does the train arrive at . . . ?	A que horas chega o comboio a . . . ?

INDEX

X = *restaurant,* 🏠 = *hotel*

NOTES

NOTES

WHEREVER YOU TRAVEL, *H*ELP IS NEVER FAR AWAY.

From planning your trip to providing travel assistance along the way, American Express® Travel Service Offices are always there to help.

Portugal

Top Tours (R)
Rua Brigadeiro Couceiro
Funchal, Portugal
91/742-611

Top Tours (R)
Estrada Da Rocha
Portimao, Portugal
82/417-552

Top Tours (R)
Av. Duque De Loule 108
Lisbon, Portugal
1/315-5885

Top Tours (R)
Rua Alfères Malheiro 96
Porto, Portugal
2/208-2785

Top Tours (R)
Av. Infante De Sagres 73
Quarteira, Portugal
89/302-726

Travel

http://www.americanexpress.com/travel